Patent Office Great Britain.

Patents for Inventions

Patent Office Great Britain.

Patents for Inventions

ISBN/EAN: 9783744692618

Printed in Europe, USA, Canada, Australia, Japan

Cover: Foto ©ninafisch / pixelio.de

More available books at **www.hansebooks.com**

PATENTS FOR INVENTIONS.

ABRIDGMENTS

OF

Specifications

RELATING TO THE

PREPARATION OF INDIA-RUBBER AND GUTTA PERCHA.

A.D. 1791–1866.

PRINTED BY ORDER OF THE COMMISSIONERS OF PATENTS.

SECOND EDITION.

LONDON:
PRINTED BY GEORGE E. EYRE AND WILLIAM SPOTTISWOODE,
PRINTERS TO THE QUEEN'S MOST EXCELLENT MAJESTY.
PUBLISHED AT THE
OFFICE OF THE COMMISSIONERS OF PATENTS FOR INVENTIONS,
25, SOUTHAMPTON BUILDINGS, HOLBORN.

1875.

PREFACE.

The Indexes to Patents are now so numerous and costly as to render their purchase inconvenient to a large number of inventors and others, to whom they have become indispensable.

To obviate this difficulty, short abstracts or abridgments of the Specifications of Patents under each head of Invention have been prepared for publication separately, and so arranged as to form at once a Chronological, Alphabetical, Subject-matter, and Reference Index to the class to which they relate. As these publications do not supersede the necessity for consulting the Specifications, the prices at which the printed copies of the latter are sold have been added.

The number of Specifications from the earliest period to the end of the year 1866 amounts to 59,222. A large proportion of the Specifications enrolled under the old law, previous to 1852, embrace several distinct inventions, and many of those filed under the new law of 1852 indicate various applications of the single invention to which the Patent is limited. Considering, therefore, the large number of inventions and applications of inventions to be separately dealt with, it cannot be doubted that several properly belonging to the group which forms the subject of this volume have been overlooked. In the progress of the whole work such omissions will, from time to time, become apparent, and be supplied in future editions.

This volume contains Abridgments of Specifications to the end of the year 1866. From that date the Abridgments will be found in chronological order in the "Chronological and "Descriptive Index" see (List of Works at the end of this book). It is intended, however, to publish these Abridgments in classes as soon as the Abridgments of all the Specifications from the earliest period to the end of 18██████ appeared in a classified form. Until that takes place ████ler (by the aid of the Subject-matter Index for each ██████ continue his examination of the Abridgments rela████ ████bject of his search in the Chronological and De████

PREFACE

This series comprises inventions relating to machines or apparatus for preparing, cleansing, cutting, masticating, vulcanizing, hardening, and moulding or otherwise treating india-rubber or gutta percha or compounds thereof; it also contains the processes, mechanical and chemical, for preparing, cleansing, bleaching, vulcanizing, hardening, deodorizing, devulcanizing, recovering, or otherwise treating the same, and likewise methods of producing the materials used in some of the above processes; and it further includes the preparation and recovery of some of the solvents employed in the treatment or manipulation of the foregoing substances.

The first edition contained, besides the method of treating india-rubber and gutta percha, the application of these materials to a great variety of uses. In the present volume however it has been considered advisable to exclude such applications as well as inventions for the manufacture of india-rubber, gutta percha, or their compounds into articles of any description, unless there appears to be an improvement in the mode of vulcanizing or treating the manufactured articles.

The subject of waterproofing, which was included in the first edition of this book, has been transferred to a volume which will shortly be published entitled "Artificial Leather, " Floor Cloth, and Waterproof Fabrics."

B. WOODCROFT.

November, 1875.

INDEX OF NAMES.

[The names printed in *Italic* are those of the persons by whom the inventions have been communicated to the Applicants for Letters Patent.

	Page
Abel, F. A.	247
Agostini, P. A.	202
Alsop, W.	22
Anthoine, J. J.	222
Archerau, H. A.	88
Arthur, R.	92
Assanti, D.	86
Audemars, G.	99
Baggs, I.	198
Baker, S. W.	161
Baldamus, A.	211, 214
Barlow, W. H.	40
Barrett, B.	72
Barwick, J.	174
Bastida, De la, E.	207
Bateman, D.	235
Baudouin, A.	237
Belling, B. M.	147
Bethell, J.	12
Beuchot, L. X.	141
Bewley, H.	25
Bielefield, C. F.	105
Bingham, R. J.	148
Blizzard, W.	126, 131
Boniere, M., the younger	120
Bonneville, H. A.	223
Boulet, L.	183
Bourn —	177, 178
Bourne, S.	254
Bousfield, G. T.	113, 120, 157, 217, 225, 230, 232, 256
Bowra, E.	200
Bradbury, H.	137
Brant, J. C.	205
Briansky, D.	223
Bridges, W.	172
Briggs, T. J.	225
Briou, De, H. E. F.	236, 251
Brockedon, W.	22, 30
Brookes, W.	74
Brooman, R. A.	22, 23, 75, 96, 99, 185, 190, 211, 222
Brossette, F. E. H.	222
Brown, —	177, 178
Buchholz, G. A.	48
Buckingham, J.	253
Buff, H. L.	195
Burke, W. H.	20, 44
——, W. H., the elder	183
——, W. H., the younger	183
Butcher, M.	107
Candelot, L. F.	127
Cantelo, W. J.	155
Cartwright, M.	204, 210, 216
Cattell, T.	145
Chaffee, —	177, 178
Chamberlain, A. P.	124, 159
Chapa. J.	184, 195
Chapman, G.	113
Chartier & Com., Société	209
Chatterton, J.	159, 166, 171, 186
Chaudet, H.	98
Cheever, J. H.	168, 171, 178, 179, 181
Childs, J.	144, 153, 162
Christopher, W.	74, 112
Clark, J.	2, 24, 147, 229, 235
——, W.	183, 237, 245
Clarkson, T. C.	228

INDEX OF NAMES.

Clippèle, C. de............125
Codet-Negrier, J. L..........122
Cohen, A..................207
Coles, G...................235
Collins, B..................244
Cooke, B. F................95
Cooley, A. J...............61
Cornides, L................102
Cowper, C............138, 148
Crosby, J. B..............107
Crossley, F................261
Crump, C...................258
Cumenge, L. P. B. E.........83
Cuppers, G................138

Daft, T. B.........160, 164, 208
Dalton, J..................45
Danne, L. J. A.............122
Darlow, W.................260
Davenport, H..............115
Day, A. G............135, 153
———, *A. S*................106
Day, H. H..............122, 123
H. H. Day................164
Debons, F.................201
De Briou, H. E. F......236, 251
De Clippèle, C.............125
Defever, C. L...............75
De Fontainemoreau, P. A. le
  comte..............240, 243
De la Bastida, E............207
De Normandy, A. R. le Mire
 67
Denny, T..................201
Deplanque, L. E............119
Deseille, L. F. A..........77
De Varroc, E................78
Devlan, P. S...............209
Dodge, N. S....110, 133, 141,
 154
Duhousset, J. D...........185
Dumeste, J. F. M............5
Duncan, C. S...............212
———, J. W......50, 71, 143
———, T....................113
Dundonald, Admiral, the Earl
  of....................65, 69

Dunlop, J. M...94, 187, 255, 261
Duthoit, A. M...............51
Duvivier, H. J..............98

Eatin, A. K...............163
Ellis, T...................118
Elmer, W..................206
Emerson, F. W..............204
Engelhard, G. A...........164

Fajole, J. J. H............202
Fanshawe, H. R..............98
———, J. A...15, 98, 142,
  148, 150, 152, 235
Felt, J. G................252
Felt, N. H.................252
Flanders, J. F.............197
Fleetwood, C. B..............3
Fonrobert, C. F. J.........116
Fontainemoreau, P. A. le
  Comte de...........240, 243
Ford, A.....108, 110, 112, 115,
  197, 198, 220
Forster, T....19, 22, 36, 37, 40,
  44, 199, 258
Forty, A. E.................87
Freeman, W.................14
Fry, J.....................82
Fuller, J..................211

Gabriel, A.................204
———, M...................204
Galpin, T.........148, 150, 152
G. E. M. Gérard....47, 66, 214,
  236
Gérard, G. E. M...........223
Ghislm, T. G...............234
Gidley, G..........74, 81, 112
Gilbee, H..................219
Gilpin, W. L................63
Gisborne, F. N.............160
Gobert, C. L. C. C.........190
Godefroy, P. A...105, 133, 192,
  193
Gooderham, J...............128

INDEX OF NAMES.

Goodyear, C?...49, 52, 53, 54, 55, 56, 57, 58, 59
Goodyear, C...72, 76, 77, 78, 79, 84, 101, 105, 106, 114
———, C., junior..........100
Granier, E.....................245
Gras, Le, L. N................63
Green, J. H...................157
Griffin, H..............188, 212
Guibal, C. E. F.................83

Hall, H. L......................154
Hall, H. L......................242
Hamy, L.........................183
Hancock, C...16, 20, 25, 29, 33, 36, 40, 41, 167, 213, 241
———, J...................13, 15
———, T....4, 10, 11, 17, 27, 30, 38
———, W..........10, 17, 142
Harby, J. B....................203
Harrison, C. W..........61, 182
———, J. J......................61
Hartley, J. G....................7
Harton, G......................244
Havemann, R. F. H.....165, 184
Hay, W. J......................188
Haynes, W......................87
Hayward, D....................217
Henry, M...............145, 209
Henson, H. H...131, 142, 216, 235
Hill, H. C......................101
Hodgskin, J...................219
Holl, L..........................226
Hooper, W...149, 170, 175, 218
Hope, L.........................137
Hughes, E. J..................117
———, E. T....................219
Hull, L..........................215
Humfrey, C.............230, 231
Hunt, E.........................257
———, J. R....................192

Innocent, L. D................243

Jacques, J. A....142, 148, 150, 152, 235
James, H. B...................254
Jennings, J. G....221, 228, 233
Jeune, F. C..............112, 118
———, W. R...................194
Job, A. M......................107
Johnson, H.......................1
———, J. H...61, 66, 77, 81, 83, 100, 103, 104, 106, 109, 111, 119, 120, 135, 153, 155
———, R.........................91
———, W......68, 90, 93, 94, 104, 110, 116

Keene, C...................14, 24
Kemp, F. J....................239
———, H........................239
Kidd, J. H.....................205
King, J.........................124
Kirrage, W..............140, 222
Kleist, F. W...................174

La Bastida, Ede..............207
Lacaze, ——....................184
———, E........................195
Lainé, A........................231
Lake, W. R....................250
Latta, A........................109
Lavater, M. L. J...221, 228, 233, 238
Lawrence, F. L...............158
Lecocq, J. F. J...............173
Lees, W. L.....................241
Lefevre, J.......................81
Le Gras, L. N..................63
Lemaistre, H., and Company 240
Lemettais, P. E...............120
Lemoine, F. H................172
Lerenard, A. A.........207, 249
Ley, G. W.......................64
Loewenberg, H................245
Lorimer, A..........41, 116, 117
Luis, J...................134, 173

INDEX OF NAMES.

McBurney, C. 256
Macintosh, C. 2
———, J...56, 60, 126, 127, 130, 136, 161, 176, 252
Macmillan, W. J. C. 250
McKay, M. 195
Magen, H. 96
Magnus, L. S. 160, 167
Manifold, J. T. 233
Marland, J. 121
Marquard, F. 250
Martin, A. J. 203
———, J. 6
Mason, J. 250
Mathevon, J. 219
Mayall, T. 230
———, T. F. 245, 246
Mayall, T. J. 156
Meeus, P. J. 86
Mennons, M. A. F. 201, 223
Merrian, M. H. 107
Metcalf, J. 114
Miller, J. W. M. 248
———, T. 191
Moissant & Co. 145
Morey, A. C. 119
———, C. 100
———, C., *widow of* 119
Moseley, C. 255, 260
———, D. 131, 144, 149
———, J. 258
Moulton, S. 32, 50, 185
Mulet, L. A. 224
Mulholland, F. G. 224, 227, 248
Murphy, J. 157
Muschamp, J. B. 81
Myers, E. 202
———, T. 202

Newey, T. H. 107
Newton, A. V....24, 48, 49, 68, 91, 104, 115, 130, 156, 164, 178, 179, 181
———, W. E...19, 47, 89, 90, 118, 120, 121, 125, 157, 161, 165, 168, 171, 184, 206

Nickels, C. 8, 13, 43, 70, 72
———, E. 70
Ninck, J. 119
Noirot, J. B. J. 177
Normandy, A. R. le Mire de...67
Norris, L. H. 226

Ogg, A. 92

Palmer, C. R. N. 112
Parker, B. 125, 128
Parkes, A....16, 27, 108, 240, 247
———, J. T. 199
Parmelee, S. T. 129
Patrick, H. W. 146, 155
Payne, E. J. 45
Peal, S. 1
Penney, H. 100
Perroncel, F. 75, 243
Phillips, R. 38
Pickersgill, J. 8
Pidding, W. 69
Pitman, J. T. 163, 177, 178
Pontifex, S. R. 253
Poole, M. 52, 53, 54, 55, 56, 57, 58, 59
Putnam, C. S. 132

Quinet, *A. M.* 237

Rémière, H. A. 211
Ricardo, J. L. 42
Richard, A. C. 173
Richards, T. 46
Richardson, B. 123
Rider, E. 51, 80, 116
Rigg, R. 220
Rimmel, E. 96
Ritchie, G. 114
———, J. H. junior 238
Ross, G. 95
Rostaing, C. S. 167
Ryder, J. 87
———, W. 87

Sarazin, *A.* 183
Sautelet, E. C. F. 106

INDEX OF NAMES.

Name	Page
Scarborough, J. V.	250
Schiele, C.	174
Scoutetten, H. J.	73
Seager, R.	162
Seymour, P. W.	260
Shephard, W. A.	200
Siemens, C. W.	218
——, E. W.	46
Sievier, R. W.	6
Silver, H. A.	174, 188
——, S. W.	213, 233, 241
Simpson, E. L.	220, 259
——, G.	44
Sinnock, W.	150, 167
Smith, H. F.	249
——, W.	135, 166, 171
Snell, W.	223
Société Chartier et Companie.	209
Sorel, S. T. M.	85, 122
Spill, D.	225
——, G.	124, 225
Spilsbury, F. G.	204
Stansbury, C. F.	92, 107
Steinlen, C. V.	111
Stevens, B. F.	242
——, C.	184, 195
Stevens, S.	242
Stoneham, J. T.	93
Story, R.	240
Tayler, C.	121
Taylor, A.	225, 232
Taylor, W.	46
Thomas, P. E.	185
Tomlinson, E.	107
Tooth, W. H.	193
Truman, E. T.	182, 187, 190
Trumble, P.	86
Turner, A.	186, 235
——, J. A.	163
——, W. A.	111
Twilley, F. H.	231
Tyler, J. T.	60
Vaillant, C.	207
Varroc, De, E.	78
Vasserot, C. F.	141
Vaughan, E. P. H.	253
Wacrenier, H. V.	109
Waithman, R. W.	84
Walton, F.	156
Warden, G. C.	214
Warne, W.	136, 142, 148, 150, 152
Warren, P.	60
West, C.	139, 197
Westhead, J. P.	5, 38
White, D. B.	85
Whitehead, J. H.	252
Wiese, J.	223
Wilkinson, W.	65
Williams, J. F.	196
Willis, E. C.	89
Wiese, W. P.	3
Woodcock, A. B.	176
Wray, L.	137, 140
Wright, W.	18
Wylde, J., the younger	46
Yeadon, S.	113

PREPARATION OF INDIA RUBBER AND GUTTA PERCHA.

A.D. 1791, May 2.—N° 1801.

PEAL, SAMUEL.—"An improved method of making and ren-
"dering perfectly waterproof all kinds of leather, cotton, linnen,
"and woollen cloths, silks, stuffs, paper, wood, and other manu-
"factures and substances, for the purpose of being worked up
"into shoes, boots, and other wearing apparel, and to be used on
"all occasions where dryness or a power of repelling wet or
"moisture may be required." This consists, in reference to this
subject, as follows:—"Take caoutchouc or (what is called in this
"country) elastic gum or india rubber; dissolve the same by
"distillation, or by infusion in a small quantity of spirits of
"turpentine, over a brisk fire; it may also be dissolved by in-
"fusion in other spirits, and in most kinds of oils; or the gum
"may be used with equal advantage in its native fluid state."

[Printed, 4d. No Drawings.]

A.D. 1797, July 26.—N° 2183.

JOHNSON, HENRY.—"A certain waterproof compound, and a
"vegetable liquid, which liquid is for the purpose of bleaching,
"whitening, and cleansing woolens, linens, cottons, and other
"articles;" "and also for preparing stuffs or cloths made of
"woolen, linen, cotton, or silk, in order, by the application of the
"aforesaid waterproof compound to render them impenetrable to
"wet, and more elastic and durable when made into garments,
"&c. for wear, and which stuffs or cloths I call hydrolaines."
This consists, in reference to this subject, as follows:—" Dissolve
"caoutchouc or india rubber in spirits of turpentine (the smell of

" which is taken off by oil of wormwood) and spirits of wine in
" equal quantities."

[Printed, 4d. No Drawings. See Repertory of Arts, vol. 9, p. 310.]

A.D. 1813, July 14.—N° 3718.

CLARK, JOHN.—"A method for making or constructing beds,
" pillows, hammocks, cushions, and other articles of the like
" kind, &c." This invention consists, first, in rendering "the
" case of the bed, pillow, bolster, hammock, cushion, or pad
" impervious to air;" secondly, in strengthening the said case
" by enclosing it in another [but smaller] case, which said
" external case need not be impervious to air;" thirdly, in filling
" the internal case with common atmospheric air instead of down
" or feathers or other materials hitherto used."

This consists, in reference to this subject, as follows:—" To one
" ounce of caoutchouc (usually called elastic gum or india rubber),
" cut in small pieces, add eight ounces of spirit of turpentine;
" let it stand inclosed in a glass vessel for two or three days, or
" until the caoutchouc be considerably distended, and almost in a
" state of solution; then throw the whole into an open or un-
" covered furnace or vessel containing seventy ounces of linseed
" oil, and boil it slowly for several hours, stirring it frequently
" until the composition becomes of a thick, glutinous consistency;
" then let it cool, and filter it through a fine cloth."

[Printed, 4d. No Drawings. See Repertory of Arts, vol. 24 (*second series*),
p. 157; Rolls Chapel Reports, 8th Report, p. 97.]

A.D. 1823, June 17.—N° 4804.

MACINTOSH, CHARLES.—"A process and manufacture where-
" by the texture of hemp, flax, wool, cotton, and silk, and also
" leather, paper, and other substances may be rendered imper-
" vious to water and air." These are in reference to this subject,
preparing a solution by dissolving thin shreds or parings of
caoutchouc in " the substance which is produced in making coal
" gas, commonly called coal oil," the relative proportion employed
depending on the quality of each article. " But when the caout-
" chouc is of the best quality, and the oil pure, from ten to twelve
" ounces of the former to a wine gallon of the latter will be found
" to answer. This infusion I submit to a gentle heat obtained
" from a water or steam bath, and I employ constant trituration

" until such time as the ingredients are reduced to a thin pulpy
" mass, when, to render the whole as homogenious as possible I
" pass it through a very fine wire or silk sieve, or searce; and if
" this part of the process has been duly followed out the varnish
" will then be without any granular particles, and will in ap-
" pearance resemble thin transparent honey."

" Now whereas caoutchouc in a state of solution and dissolved
" in manner herein-before described is well known to chemists and
" others and not new therefore, I do not claim any right, title, or
" privilege in respect of the same."

[Printed, 4d. No Drawings. See Repertory of Arts, vol. 46 (*second series*), p. 199; also vol. 6 (*new series*), pp. 317 and 365; London Journal (*Newton's*), vol. 8, p. 305; Mechanics' Magazine, vol. 9. p. 108; vol. 2, p. 291; and vol. 24, pp. 460, 469, 489, 508, and 529; Register of Arts and Sciences, vol. 2, p. 131; Engineers' and Mechanics' Encyclopædia, vol. 1, p. 315; Webster's Reports, vol. 1, p. 739; Webster's Patent Law, p. 9; also p. 137, case 161; Carpmael's Reports, on Patent Cases, vol. 2, pp. 186 and 188; and Hindmarch on Patents, p. 563.]

A.D. 1824, February 28.—N° 4915.

FLEETWOOD, CHARLES BAGENALL.—" A liquid and compo-
" sition for making leather and other articles waterproof." These
are, in reference to this subject, as follows :—" I dissolve 10 lbs. of
" caoutchouc or india rubber in twenty gallons of pure spirits of
" turpentine," by putting them both into a tin vessel capable of
" holding at least 35 gallons, 40 perhaps would be as well. The
" caoutchouc should be cut into pieces or slices of about $\frac{1}{16}$th
" part of an ounce weight to hasten the solution, I then immerse
" the vessel into a boiler previously filled with cold water, and
" apply the fire so as to produce the boiling of the water, occasion-
" ally supplying the waste caused by evaporation. In this
" situation it remains until a perfect solution of the caoutchouc
" in the spirits of turpentine is effected."

[Printed, 4d. No Drawings. See Repertory of Arts, vol. 4 (*third series*), p. 129; London Journal (*Newton's*), vol. 8, p. 183; and Register of Arts and Sciences, vol. 2, p. 67.]

A.D. 1824, October 14.—N° 5018.

WEISE, WILLIAM PHILIP.—" Improvements in the preparing
" of and making waterproof cloth and other materials for the
" manufacturing hats, bonnets, and caps, and wearing apparel,
" and in manufacturing the same therefrom." These are, in

reference to this subject :—" Mix and unite together equal parts
" of shellac, caoutchouc or india rubber, gum mastic, gum anime,
" and gum sandaric; the caoutchouc to be cut into very small
" pieces, and the shellac and gums to be ground very fine, and
" the whole dissolved in spirits of wine or turpentine, or any
" other spirit, to the consistence of water."

[Printed, 4d. No Drawings. See Repertory of Arts, vol. 1 (*third series*), p. 468; and London Journal (*Newton's*), vol. 11, p. 21.]

A.D. 1824, November 29.—N° 5045.

HANCOCK, THOMAS.—" A method of making or manufactur-
" ing an article which may be, in many instances, substituted for
" leather, and be applied to various other useful purposes."

This consists, in reference to this subject, in the use of " the
" juice obtained from certain trees which grow in several parts
" of South America, the East Indies, and other places abroad.
" The tree called the 'Hevaea' is said to produce this liquid.
" When this liquid becomes inspisated or dried, it forms a sub-
" stance which the patentee believes to be identical with 'caout-
" chouc' or india-rubber." The liquid may be deprived of
color when desired, by shaking or washing it in water contained
in a suitable vessel, and this operation is repeated as often as is
found necessary.

[Printed, 4d. No Drawings. See Repertory of Arts, vol. 2 (*third series*), p. 281; London Journal (*Newton's*), vol. 10, p. 22; and Engineers' and Mechanics' Encyclopædia, vol. 2, p. 76.]

A.D. 1825, March 15.—N° 5120.

HANCOCK, THOMAS.—" A new or improved manufacture,
" which may, in many instances, be used as a substitute for
" leather and otherwise."

This is, in reference to this subject, the use of caoutchouc dissolved in equal parts of oil of turpentine and highly rectified coal tar oil along with other things for saturating tissues.

[Printed, 4d. No Drawings. See Register of Arts and Sciences, vol. 4, p. 292.]

A.D. 1825, March 15.—N° 5121.

HANCOCK, THOMAS.—" Improvement or improvements in the
" making or rendering ships' bottoms, vessels, and utensils of

" different descriptions and various manufactures, and porous or
" fibrous substances, impervious to air and water, and for coating
" and protecting the surfaces of different metallic and other
" bodies."

No Specification of this Patent was enrolled, but Mr. Hancock forwarded the following description of the invention to the Great Seal Patent Office, on the 4th of January, 1859 :—

"The Specification was intended to embrace the compounding
" the liquid or original juice of caoutchouc, as mentioned in my
" Patent of the 29th November, 1824, with vegetable or Stock-
" holm tar, and some other vegetable matters, but Stockholm
" tar principally, with the view of rendering the tar entirely or
" less missible in water. This compound was to be used in
" cementing fibrous substances into sheets for the purposes
" mentioned in the title, and to render the other matters and
" things therein comprised more or less impermeable to air or
" water."

[No Specification enrolled.]

A.D. 1832, December 7.—N° 6342.

DUMESTE, JULIEN FREDERIC MAILLARD.—"A machine to reduce caoutchouc or india rubber into elastic thread, calibered of different sizes.

[No Specification enrolled.]

A.D. 1836, February 16.—N° 7004.

WESTHEAD, JOSHUA PROCTER.—" An improved method of
" cutting caoutchouc or india rubber, leather, hides, and similar
" substances, so as to render them applicable to various useful
" purposes." The patentee claims as his invention " a machine,
" or any modification of machine, by which my improved
" method of cutting caoutchouc or india rubber, hides, and similar
" substances into a band, tape, or fillet, by means of a revolving
" or other cutter acting on the exterior edge of such materials,
" and regularly cutting the same in a spiral or helical direction
" towards the centre, can or may be effected," the mode adopted in preference, and described by the patentee, and shewn in the Drawings, consists in causing the mass of caoutchouc or other substance to advance against the edge of a revolving knife with a

slow combined forward and circular motion. The knife is caused to revolve at a high speed, and meeting the caoutchouc cuts it into the required ribbon. The cautchouc advances towards the knife, and rotates till the mass is entirely cut away into a long ribbon, down to its centre. Various modes may be adopted to cause the caoutchouc to advance to the knife; and a longitudinal knife, to which a rapid reciprocating motion may be given, may be employed instead of the revolving knife.

[Printed, 10d. Drawing. See Repertory of Arts, vol. 6 (*new series*), p. 203; also vol. 12 (*new series*), p. 107; London Journal (*Newton's*), vol. 13 (*conjoined series*), p. 280; Webster's Patent Law, pp. 28 and 107 (also p. 139, cases 140 and 145); Carpmael's Reports on Patent Cases, vol. 2, pp. 425 and 434; Law Journal (Chancery), p. 89; and Beavan's Reports, vol. 1, p. 309.]

A.D. 1836, February 27.—N° 7015.

SIEVIER, ROBERT WILLIAM.—" An improvement in the means
" of dissolving and preparing caoutchouc or india rubber for
" various purposes. For this purpose I take caoutchouc or india
" ruber, cut into small pieces, and put them into any convenient
" vessel that may be closed at the mouth; I then fill the vessel
" with liquor ammonia, so as to entirely cover the india rubber;
" in a few months it will be dissolved, or its particles separated.
" I then put the solution so made into a still or large retort, and
" by the application of heat nearly the whole of the ammonia will
" be distilled over in a gaseous form, and is to be taken up in the
" usual way by cold water; in that state it again becomes liquor
" ammonia. In this operation of distillation I prefer using a
" water bath, as the india rubber by that means cannot be sub-
" jected to a heat of more than 212° of Fahrenheit; the ammonia
" assumes a gaseous form at 130°.

[Printed, 4d. No Drawings. See London Journal (*Newton's*), vol. 11 (*conjoined series*), p. 83; Mechanics' Magazine, vol. 26, pp. 282, 397, and 510; and Rolls Chapel Reports, 7th Report, p. 171.]

A.D. 1836, February 27.—N° 7016.

MARTIN, JAMES.—(*A communication.*)—" An improvement in
" dissolving and preparing caoutchouc and india rubber, to render
" it applicable to various useful purposes." This invention consists in the production of "an olefiant or etherial essence for the
" purpose of dissolving caoutchouc." The " olefiant or etherial
" essence " may be produced by causing steam to pass through a

suitable vessel, in which is contained "fifty gallons of water," "fifteen or more pounds of the concentrated sulphuric acid of commerce," and "three hundred gallons of rough or brown volatile oil or spirit, whether vegetable, mineral, or animal." "The volatile or etheral parts of the rough oil or spirit" are distilled over, condensed in a worm, and collected in a receiver. The olefiant or etherial essence so produced is "eminently valuable" for the purpose of dissolving caoutchouc, "permitting it to return to its natural and original state in a more perfect manner than hitherto, and without leaving behind it any trace of the aroma, odour, or smell of the menstruum used."

[Printed, 6d. Drawing. See London Journal (*Newton's*), vol. 9 (*conjoined series*), p. 331; and Rolls Chapel Reports, 7th Report, p. 171.]

A.D. 1836, March 8.—N° 7020.

HARTLEY, JOHN GALLEY.—"Improvements in preparing or manufacturing caoutchouc or india rubber for various useful purposes. The first object of this invention "is the preparation or manufacture of threads or strands from that description of caoutchouc or india rubber which is imported into this country in thick sheets or masses, and is commonly called black caoutchouc or india rubber, in contradistinction to that usually called 'bottles,'" from which threads or strands may be obtained of any required degree of fineness, and nearly white. For this purpose the patentee uses the ordinary revolving knife, kept wet by revolving in a trough of water; he places the block of caoutchouc on a pin or centre, and having cut a slit into the caoutchouc, passes this slit or slip between the edge of the knife and the periphery of a regulating roller, which can be adjusted further from or nearer to the edge of the knife, as desired. The slit or slip of caoutchouc is then pulled forward by the operation between the regulating roller and the knife edge, and is thereby cut in a continuous manner into strips of the required thickness. The strips so cut are again cut by a similar apparatus into smaller strips, the breadth of which shall be equal to their thickness. These small strips are then "soaked in the usual liquor," and drawn out between the fingers into threads and reeled, after the manner heretofore practised with threads made from "bottles." The patentee applies his mode of cutting also to the cutting of "bottles." The "bottle" is first cut or divided nearly into two equal parts, leaving just a slip of continuity. This slip is passed between the regulating roller and the knife edge, and drawn forward till the one half of the bottle is entirely cut into a long ribbon. The other half of the bottle is then cut in a similar manner.

[Printed, 1s. 6d. Drawings.]

A.D. 1836, September 1.—N° 7178.

PICKERSGILL, JOHN.—(*A communication.*)—" Improvements " in preparing and applying india rubber (caoutchouc) to fabrics."

The invention in reference to this subject is as follows: "The " preparing india rubber by pressing or rolling it into thin sheets, " and applying them to the surfaces of fabrics, that the same may " be rendered air and water proof, without the aid of solvents, and " without the necessity of bringing the india rubber into a state " or fluidity." To effect the preparation of the india rubber, the patentee proposes, first, to cut it into small pieces, and then to pass these pieces several times between heated rollers and under rubbing bars, till the whole becomes so "intimately blended" that it will readily allow of being rolled into sheets.

[Printed, 2s. 4d. Drawings. See Repertory of Arts, vol. 7 (*new series*), p. 291.]

A.D. 1836, October 24.—N° 7213.

NICKELS, CHRISTOPHER.—(*Partly a communication.*)—" Im- " provements in preparing and manufacturing caoutchouc, ap- " plicable to various useful purposes." These are, in reference to this subject, first, treating "any cuttings or small pieces of " caoutchouc" so "as to become suitable for making thread," by well washing in hot water, then keeping them warm (about 200° F.) in a vessel heated by steam, or otherwise, while they are being continually shaken up; they are then passed through a pair of pressing rollers, which are about one-sixteenth of an inch apart. The caoutchouc is then placed in a mill, consisting of a hollow cylinder in which revolves "a roller, with projecting surfaces or " strong spikes cast or formed thereon" where it is worked for about two hours. "From the mill the ground caoutchouc is next " to be placed into a mould" and pressed by gradual hydraulic pressure up to "seventy tons." In preference, the moulds are round. The caoutchouc when cold is removed at once from the mould, or gradually pressed out of it by a screw, so "that thin "layers of the proper thickness of the intended thread may be "cut off by a suitable knife" supplied with a "continuous small "stream of water." Or a "hollow cylinder may be obtained by "having a suitable core placed in the inside" of the mould and having a hollow piston or plunger. This cylinder may "be cut "spirally into a tube, as heretofore practised in cutting bottle "caoutchouc for making thread." "Another mode of obtaining "like cylinders of such ground caoutchouc is by means of a pair "of pressing rollers having equal and smooth surfaces," and a continous thin sheet passing through them is wound upon "a "wooden roller (suitable for it to be cut on)." The tapes or thin sheets may then "be cut into thread by any known means," although other modes described are preferred. Second, "the "combining of a series of circular knives on an axis with "a suitable roller on which they may act, and whereby the "knives may revolve at a greater speed than the roller," also, the "application of a series of discs" "for the purpose of dividing "tapes or narrow sheets of caoutchouc into thread." Third, "the "cutting of thread from a series of circular discs of 'caoutchouc' "kept together in the form of a cylindrical block, each circular "disc being of the thickness of the intended thread."

By a "Disclaimer" dated 18th June, 1838, the patentee disclaims those parts of the preceding invention included under the third head; and by a "second disclaimer," dated "30th April, "1846," the patentee disclaims also the second head of the invention, and at the same time alters and reduces in extent the title of the invention, as follows:—"Improvements in preparing and "manufacturing caoutchouc thread, applicable to various useful "purposes." The invention so circumscribed consists in converting into threads "cuttings produced in the former modes of "making thread from the better classes of caoutchouc, or any "cuttings or small pieces of caoutchouc, or from cuttings of "caoutchouc, which are at present considered inferior, in conse- "quence of their porous condition, or want of equality or close- "ness." The patentee does not claim any mode for grinding the coautchouc, not for preparing the same. It may be stated generally, that the cuttings or porous caoutchouc are to be heated, and passed repeatedly through pressing rollers, then ground in a mill till the mass becomes equal; the mass is then placed in a mould, of a cylindrical form in preference, and there brought to a proper degree of density by means of pressure. India rubber so compressed may be cut into sheet or ribbons, and again into threads, then drawn out and spun in like manner to what has been heretofore practised in making thread from other caoutchouc.

[Printed, 2s. 10d. Drawings. See Repertory of Arts, vol. 3 (*new series*), p. 193; and London Journal (*Newton's*), vol. 12 (*conjoined series*), p. 222.]

A.D. 1836, December 7.—N° 7247.

HANCOCK, WILLIAM. — "Improvements in bookbinding." This invention consists, in reference to this subject, "in the " employment of a solution of caoutchouc in bookbinding" obtained by dissolving sheet caoutchouc in pure spirits of turpentine, in the proportion of a pound of the former to a gallon of the latter, or thereabouts.

[Printed, 4d. No Drawings. See Repertory of Arts, vol. 9 (*new series*), p. 162; and London Journal (*Newton's*), vol. 11 (*conjoined series*), p. 10.]

A.D. 1837, April 18.—N° 7344.

HANCOCK, THOMAS.—"An improvement or improvements in " the process of rendering cloth and other fabrics partially or " entirely impervious to air and water, by means of caoutchouc " or india-rubber. This consists, in reference to this subject, as follows :—

The india rubber, cut in small pieces, is cleaned, dried, and passed through rollers two or three times. This forms it into a sheet, and warms it. It is then put into a masticator, which may be described as a hollow cylinder with closed ends, having a grooved shaft passing through it, and filling a considerable part of the cylinder; this shaft revolves, and kneads the india rubber into a compact roll. This roll is cut into proper pieces, and these are warmed in a stove to a given heat, passed through heated rollers, also of a given temperature, to reduce them into sheets; these are moistened by any suitable means; with "coal, " oil, or other solvent of india rubber, and, if it is required, coloring matter may be sifted in now or afterwards. They are left in a covered vessel for several hours, and blended together in the masticator. The mass will be "rather more firm than dough " or putty."

[Printed, 10d. Drawings.]

A.D. 1838, January 23.—N° 7549.

HANCOCK, THOMAS. — "Improvements in the method of " manufacturing or preparing caoutchouc, either alone or in " combination with other substances," and these consist as follows:—The caoutchouc having been prepared as described in No. 7344, Old Law is spread by the machine, "a hollow box of " metal brought down at the bottom nearly to an edge, not quite " sharp, but rounded," with arrangements to fix it at any particular distance from the machine over which the fabric passes, upon " linen, silk, cotton, or other suitable cloth," which has been previously saturated so as to "fill the texture with common glue, " size, gum, paste, or any other similar substance easily remove- " able by water," and dried. "If one coating is not sufficient " the coating operation is repeated, "and when the coating is dry " the whole is immersed "in moderately warm water," and kept there "until the gum or size is sufficiently softened to allow the " caoutchouc to be separated from the cloth." If "sheets are " required of greater thickness than can be conveniently made by " successive coatings upon one cloth," the caoutchouc is spread upon two cloths, and the two coated sides are united together before they are quite dry, and the cloth stripped off from one side. A third coating, which has been spread upon prepared cloth as before described, may be added to it, "and continue to add fresh " coatings in the same manner until the required thickness is " obtained." Instead of filling the cloth with gum, &c., one side " may be covered with paper pasted on and caoutchouc spread " upon it," &c. "Sheets to be used as tablets for writing or " drawing on with crayons, French chalk, &c." are formed "by " adding pumice powder, fine emery, or other similar gritty sub- " stances," either in the manner described in No. 7344, Old Law, with reference to coloring matters, " or by coatings of these sub- " stance smixed with a thin solution of caoutchouc after the sheets " are made as before described." Sheets are formed "from the " originaly native and liquid caoutchouc, as imported from South " America, by preparing the cloth with gum or size, as before " stated." "A convenient mode of doing this is by attaching " two of the gummed cloths together by means of paste or gum, " and then immersing the cloth in the liquid caoutchouc, and " allowing the superfluous liquid to run off." The cloth is hung up, and when dry again immersed "in the contrary direction," and again dried; and this is repeated until "the sheet has " acquired the desired thickness." The cloth is separated by immersion in water, as before. Small sheets, or sheets of particular shapes, may be made by pouring the liquid caoutchouc on moulds of plaster of Paris. If considerable thickness is required, a thin coating is poured on first, and allowed to dry; and this is repeated "until the desired thickness is obtained." "A raised " edge of wood," &c. may be employed " to regulate the required " thickness of the sheet, and to prevent the caoutchouc from " spreading too far." "A coating of native liquid caoutchouc " improves the sheets formed of manufactured caoutchouc first " described." This is applied in a certain manner.

Long uniform slips or threads are manufactured as follows by immersing a cylinder, which has a spiral groove cut into it of the width or depth of the required slip or thread, in liquid caoutchouc, clearing the liquid by a straight piece of wood or metal "from " the projecting parts, and when dry" immersing, &c. again, " and continue so to do until the groove is filled," when the cylinder is immersed in moderately warm water; and the thread drawn off, it will be "the length and size of the spiral groove." A plain cylinder may be coated with the liquid uniformly, and of the required thickness, and the cylinder "put into a machine " attached to a screw motion, and the slips or threads cut with a " circular knife to the required size." "The machine is well " known to persons conversant with this manufacture."

[Printed, 4d. No Drawings. See Repertory of Arts, vol. 10 (*new series*), p. 168; and Mechanics' Magazine, vol. 28, p. 101.]

A.D. 1838, July 11.—N° 7731.

BETHELL, JOHN.—"Improvements in rendering wood, cork, " leather, woven and felted fabrics, ropes, and cordage, stone " and plasters or compositions, either more durable, less pervious " to water, or less inflamable, as may be required for various " useful purposes."

These are in reference to this subject, the caoutchouc used is dissolved in coal tar thinned with from one third to one half of its quantity with the essential oil or spirit obtained by the distillation of coal tar and the common spirit left, after the naptha is obtained, called dead oil by heat or the well-known caoutchouc paste or varnish is thus treated, and the solution is used.

[Printed, 6d. No Drawings. See Repertory of Arts, vol. 16 (*new series*), p. 356; London Journal (*Newton's*), vol. 20 (*conjoined series*), p. 111; and Mechanics' Magazine, vol. 31, p. 309.]

A.D. 1839, August 1.—N° 8171.

NICKELS, CHRISTOPHER.—" Improvements in cutting india-
" rubber," and these are said to be as follows :—

First. " The mode of cutting sheets of india-rubber from the
" internal towards the external surface." To effect this, a grand
" hood or ring of metal and caoutchouc " is moved by a worm
at a very slow speed towards a reciprocating knife, having a constant supply of water at its edges, and " the sheet or veneer of
" caoutchouc cut off " is wound up upon a roller. The caoutchouc may be in its native state or prepared, but preference is given to that prepared according to process in No. 7213, Old Law.

Second. " The mode of dividing flat surfaces of india-rubber
" by means of rotatory cutters on flat tables." And this is effected by causing " slabs of india-rubber (which have been pre-
" viously cut or prepared by any of the well-known means to the
" right thickness) upon " a bed, to pass through a set of rotatory cutters, and then through another " set of cutters which divides
" it into squares."

Third. " The mode of employing india-rubber as a surface on
" which other india-rubber is cut, by which the knife will be
" preserved longer and the cutting performed more advanta-
" geously," and this is performed as follows :—The india-rubber to be cut is stretched upon an india-rubber cylinder fixed upon a screw shaft, which is placed in a square socket in a hollow cylinder, and also in a screw nut. " The water is turned on and the
" machine set in motion, when, after the first revolution or more," the end of the ribbon cut is laid over a drawing roller, which gradually draws the ribbon from the cylinder as fast as it is cut, and the india-rubber falls into " a water tank below.

[Printed, 1s. 6d. Drawings. See Inventors' Advocate, vol. 2, p. 134.]

A.D. 1840, February 8.—N° 8382.

HANCOCK, JAMES.—" A method of forming a fabric or fabrics,
" applicable to various uses, by combining caoutchouc, or certain

" compounds thereof, with wood, whalebone, or other fibrous
" materials, vegetable or animal, manufactured or prepared for
" that purpose, or with metallic substances manufactured or
" prepared."

This consists, in reference to this subject, as follows :—

" Take any quantity of caoutchouc and steep it in coal tar oil,
" or oil of turpentine, or a mixture of both, sufficient to dissolve
" it coal tar oil is much cheaper than oil of turpentine, but it
" has an offensive smell, which makes it desirable to use a pro-
" portion of oil of turpentine or oil of turps altogether, for all
" purposes where the smell of coal tar oil would be objectionable),
" when dissolved it must be passed through an iron strainer."

[Printed, 4d. No Drawings. See London Journal (*Newton's*), vol. 23 (*conjoined series*), p. 170; and Inventors' Advocate, vol. 3, p. 99.]

A.D. 1840, March 23.—N° 8441.

KEENE, CHARLES.—(*A communication.*)—" Improvements in
" producing surfaces on leather and fabrics."

These are, in reference to this subject,—

India-rubber, cut in small pieces, is saturated with a certain
amount of "'turpentine, or any of the known solvents for caout-
" chouc, allowed to stand for a given time, and passed through
" rollers, while lampblack, or other coloring matter, is being added
" to it, to give it the required hue." When it is of the consistency
" of stout dough or putty it is ready for use, and may be kept in
" a reservoir of water."

[Printed, 4d. No Drawings. See Repertory of Arts, vol. 14 (*new series*), p. 233; London Journal (*Newton's*), vol. 23 (*conjoined series*), p. 357; and Mechanics' Magazine, vol. 33, p. 397.]

A.D. 1840, September 7.—N° 8617.

FREEMAN, WILLIAM.—(*A communication.*)—" Improvements
" in paving or covering roads and other ways or surfaces."

These are, in reference to this subject,—

The india-rubber, in small pieces, is ground in an iron cylinder with a strong axis, and teeth projecting until the rubber becomes reduced to a strong pasty state.

[Printed, 4d. No Drawings. See Repertory of Arts, vol. 16 (*new series*), p. 118, and vol. 5 (*enlarged series*), p. 55; London Journal (*Newton's*), vol. 20 (*conjoined series*), p. 429; Mechanics' Magazine, vol. 34, p. 223; and Inventors' Advocate, vol. 4, p. 164.]

A.D. 1840, October 15.—N° 8662.

HANCOCK, JAMES.—" An improved method of raising water " and other fluids." This consists, in reference to this subject, as follows :—

To bands for the above purpose employing the compound solution referred to, known under the name of india rubber varnish, described under No. 8382, Old Law. Or ",the following " is the mode in which I am usually in the habit of preparing " the said solution :—I take any quantity of caoutchouc and steep " it in coal tar or oil of turpentine, or a mixture of both sufficient " to dissolve it, when dissolved I pass it through an iron strainer, " and it is then fit for use."

[Printed, 4d. No Drawings. See Inventors' Advocate, vol. 4, p. 262.]

A.D. 1841, December 16.—N° 9189.

FANSHAWE, JOHN AMERICUS.—" An improved manufacture " of waterproof fabric, applicable to the purposes of covering " and packing bodies, buildings, and goods exposed to water and " damp."

This consists, in reference to this subject, of a masticator consisting of a cylindrical vessel surrounded with a jacket, intended to contain steam or hot air. In the centre of this cylindrical vessel is a strong iron roller mounted, its axle turning in plummer boxes bearing upon brackets affixed to the outer sides of the steam box. This roller is furnished with a great number of pins 'or teeth, and it revolves "by means of a pulley and band or winch " affixed to the outer part of its axle." The upper portion of the cylindrical vessel is made to open upon a hinge, to allow the caoutchouc cut into small pieces to be introduced, and when this is done it is shut down and confined by a lever clamp made fast by hand screws ; steam or hot air is admitted by a pipe into the jacket, any condensed steam is drawn off by a pipe with a tap below. Rotary motion is now given to the rollers, " by the action " of which, aided by the heat, the caoutchouc will soon become " soft and plastic."

[Printed, 8d. Drawings. See Repertory of Arts, vol. 5 (*enlarged series*), p. 55 ; and London Journal (*Newton's*), vol. 22 (*conjoined series*), p. 110 ; Patent Journal, vol. 4, p. 205.]

A.D. 1843, January 31.—N° 9622.

HANCOCK, CHARLES.—"An improved means of dyeing or
" staining cotton, woollen, silk, and other fabrics, and rendering
" them repellent of water and moisture." This consists, in reference to this subject, " to three pounds of linseed oil I add
" one pound of caoutchouc and two ounces of raw or burnt umber,
" and boil them together till the caoutchouc has thoroughly com-
" bined with the oil. The caoutchouc which I prefer is what is
" called sheet india-rubber and sometimes stationers india-rubber;"
also " I make a solution of caoutchouc in oil of turpentine or any
" other suitable solvent, to which I sometimes add acetate of
" alum or other metallic salts and colouring matters."

[Printed, 4d. No Drawings.]

A.D. 1843, June 27.—N° 9807.

PARKES, ALEXANDER.—"Improvements in preparing solutions
" of certain vegetable and animal matters applicable to preserving
" wood and other substances, and for other uses;" and these are,
in reference to this subject, taking either eupion or bisulphuret of
carbon, the latter preferred, in the proportion of "two pounds of
" the solvent to half a pound of caoutchouc; but these propor-
" tions may be varied, according to the viscidity required in the
" solution," and straining the solution through a linen or other
strainer to remove impurities. This preparation is kept "in closed
" vessels or under water to prevent its drying." "For some
" purposes I use a quarter of a pound of bisulphuret of carbon
" and three pounds of best turpentine, or three pounds of naptha
" to one pound of caoutchouc, which will cheapen the solution;
" the volatilizing power of the bisulphuret of carbon being re-
" tarded by such addition." When a solid mass of caoutchouc
of any given form or size is required, " I take the gum in scrap"
or otherwise and " add to every ten pounds weight thereof about
" seven pounds of the bisulphuret of carbon;" after remaining
in a covered vessel for two hours the gum will generally be found
penetrated, and may be kneaded by hand or machinery into cakes
of any size and dried in the open air, but preferably in moulds in
a close stove with a condenser and refrigerator and the solvent
collected. "These blocks may be afterwards cut up for threads
" or strands of the sizes required."

[Printed, 4d. No Drawings. See London Journal (*Newton's*), vol. 24 (*conjoined series*), p. 251; and Repertory of Arts, vol. 6 (*enlarged series*), p. 247.]

A.D. 1843, November 9.—N° 9935.

HANCOCK, WALTER. — " Improvements in manufacturing
" caoutchouc, and caoutchouc in combination with other sub-
" stances, and in machinery or apparatus for preparing caout-
" chouc and other materials." This consists, in reference to this
subject as follows, first, the cutting machine, consisting of a pair
of rollers the peripheries of which are toothed and work nearly
up to each other. A steel bar with teeth passes upwards, and
the teeth of the rollers work between the teeth of the bar. The
india rubber is fed in by a hopper above the rollers, and pressed
down upon them by a weight, and after passing through the cutting rollers falls into a cistern or vessel.

Second. The apparatus for dissolving the india rubber is a
cylindrical iron vessel, capable of bearing pressure, and contains
the india rubber; the lid is fixed by bolts, nuts, &c. The vapour
of the solvent is passed by a pipe into this vessel from another
vessel attached to it, or stopped from it by a cock. The cylindrical vessel has a means of being heated, and a tube by which
it may be exhausted before " the admission of the vapourized
" solvent."

[Printed, 10d. Drawing. See Repertory of Arts, vol. 4 (*enlarged series*), p. 20.]

A.D. 1843, November 21.—N° 9952.

HANCOCK, THOMAS.— " An improvement or improvements
" in the preparation or manufacture of caoutchouc in combina-
" tion with other substances, which preparation or manufacture
" is suitable for rendering leather, cloth, and other fabrics water-
" proof, and to various other purposes for which caoutchouc is
" employed;" and these improvements are said to be, combining
" caoutchouc with silicate of magnesia, whereby manufactured
" caoutchouc is rendered free from that clammy and adhesive
" character which it usually possesses;" the india-rubber is passed
through rolls till formed into a sheet, and the silicate is then
added and mixed with it; fuller's earth may also be added; "the
" modes of combining asphalt with caoutchouc," by powdering
it and treating it in the same manner as the silicate, plumbago
may also be added; treating " caoutchouc (either alone or in com-
" bination with other substances) with sulphur when acted on by
" heat, and thus changing the character of caoutchouc " by im-

mersing the caoutchouc in melted sulphur or mixing it in sulphur in any way whatever, and submitting it to high temperatures, and thus changing the nature of the rubber completely. The heating is by oven or by water or steam under pressure. The result may be stated to be no longer effected by temperatures or by the usual solvents for ordinary india rubber. Other things may be blended in the caoutchouc with the sulphur and the " change " effected by heat. The temperature from 200° to 400° varies with the nature, quality and size of the material to be changed ; at first, the rubber is elastic, but by higher temperatures, or by longer keeping in high temperatures, the caoutchouc gradually changes until it ultimately becomes black, "and has something the appearance " of horn, and may be pared with a knife similarly to that " substance."

By a Memorandum of Alteration, inrolled 14th October 1845, it is said "that having described the methods by which I blend " sulphur with caoutchouc, and the manner in which I apply the " same to various purposes, I would here observe that the com- " bination is still as soluble as before," "I add the words," " except when I use a solvent that has been saturated at a high " temperature, as in the case of oil of turpentine."

[Printed, 6d. No Drawings. See Repertory of Arts, vol. 5 (*enlarged series*), p. 154; London Journal (*Newton's*), vol. 26 (*conjoined series*), p. 178; and vol. 39 (*conjoined series*), p. 158; Exchequer Reports, vol. 9, p. 388 ; Law Journal (Exchequer), vol. 23, p. 110; and Patent Journal, vol. 11, p. 152.]

A.D. 1844, January 11.—N° 10,006.

WRIGHT, WILLIAM. — "Certain improvements in rendering " leather skins or hides impervious to wet, more flexible and " more durable." Three compositions are described which contain caoutchouc; one consists of 25 gallons linseed, rape, or neats-foot oil reduced by boiling to 20 gallons, 40 lbs. of fat of bullock, sheep, or deer strained, boiled in water and dried between cloths, and 40 lbs. fresh bees'-wax melted together at about 150° F. by a sand bath. Take 2½ lbs. of caoutchouc in small pieces and dissolve them by heat 115° F. in 15 pints rectified oil of turpentine. Take 12½ lbs. of Burgundy pitch and dissolve them by heat of 200° F. in 20 pints rectified turpentine, allow these mixtures to cool to 150° F. and add both to the oil, fat, and bees'-wax, and stir the whole until it is cold. Another composition consists of from 15 to 20 lbs. of caoutchouc sliced in small pieces, dissolved by heating at from 200° to 250° F. in 20 gallons purified cod or highly purified spermacetti whale oil. A third composition is made by submerging 15 or 20 lbs. caoutchouc in small pieces in rectified oil of turpentine, simmer it at 250° F. until dissolved, add 20 gallons purified cod or highly purified spermacetti whale oil, either of the latter being at 200° F., and continue this temperature until all is " a fluid smooth mass;" the temperature is then lowered to 150° F. when 10 lbs. fresh bees-wax is added, and the whole stirred up until it is cold.

[Printed, 4d. No Drawings. See Repertory of Arts, vol. 4 (*enlarged series*), p. 101; London Journal (*Newton's*), vol. 25 (*conjoined series*), p. 118, and Mechanics' Magazine, vol. 41, pp. 189 and 200.]

A.D. 1844, January 30.—N° 10,027.

NEWTON, WILLIAM EDWARD.—(*A communication.*)—" Im-
" provements in the preparation of caoutchouc or india rubber,
" and in manufacturing various fabrics, of which caoutchouc
" forms a competent part;" and these are in reference to this
" subject, first, combining india rubber with sulphur and with
" white lead, so as to form a triple compound;" the salts or oxides
of lead may be substituted for the carbonate; second, "exposing
" the india-rubber fabric to the action of a high degree of heat,"
" by means of which this improved compound is effectually
" changed in its properties, so as to protect it from decomposition
" or deterioration by the action of those agents which have here-
" tofore been found to produce that effect upon india-rubber
" goods."

[Printed, 8d. Drawing. See Repertory of Arts, vol. 4 (*enlarged series*), p. 271; and London Journal (*Newton's*), vol. 5 (*conjoined series*), p. 252.]

A.D. 1844, March 6.—N° 10,092.

FORSTER, THOMAS.—" Improvements in preparing composi-
" tions of india rubber and other matters for forming articles
" therefrom, and for the coating of surfaces of leather and woven
" and other fabrics; and these are in reference to this subject,
first, " combining such a quantity of shell lac or other gum, with
" or without arseniate of potash, with india rubber, as to produce
" a composition which may be moulded into various forms, and
" retain the desired figure;" second, blocks are also made which
may be cut into sheets, making "sheets of the composition"
" by spreading the same on a previously prepared surface;"

" third, grinding and mixing the materials in a machine com-
" posed of two angular rollers placed in a heated vessel."

The materials mentioned are mixed in certain proportions according to what is to be done with the mixture. They are also mixed in a certain manner. When moulded, the mixture is put into the moulds hot, and pressed till it is cold. This composition submitted to the "rays or light of the sun for a few hours loses " its sticking character, and will not be injured by any heat " which it may be afterwards exposed to, by being in the sun," &c. Cloth, &c. coated with it is submitted to the rays of the sun afterwards.

[Printed, 8d. Drawing. See Repertory of Arts, vol. 5 (*enlarged series*), p. 238; and London Journal (*Newton's*), vol. 27 (*conjoined series*), p. 188.]

A.D. 1844, March 19.—N° 10,110.

BURKE, WILLIAM HENRY.—" Certain improved machinery for " cutting india rubber, and other elastic substances, into balls " and other solid figures ;" and two machines are described, one of which cuts out of a block a solid cylindrical piece, with a hole through the centre for attaching it to the second machine.

The first machine is a wooden bench supporting an iron arched frame, through which works, by a screw, a vertical spindle, the point of which is inserted into a block of india rubber, &c., made fast to the wooden bench ; near to the bottom of the spindle is an arm affixed to it, to which is attached an adjustable cutting blade, rotary motion being given to the spindle by a winch ; the spindle gradually descends, and along with it the cutter, until a solid cylindrical piece is cut out, and with its spindle is introduced into the second machine into a frame ; the frame is raised so as to bring the india rubber into contact with a gouge cutter. The crank shaft revolves, and communicates oscillatory movements to a shaft which carries the gouge cutter, causing it to pare the surface of the india rubber, whilst by other arrangements the lump of india rubber is brought " up to the edge of the cutter, " and its surface is pared away until the cylinder is reduced in " form to the spherical figure."

[Printed, 1s. 2d. Drawings.]

A.D. 1844, May 15.—N° 10,185.

HANCOCK, CHARLES.— " *Certain improvements in corks and other stoppers, and* a new composition or substance which may be " used as a substitute for, and in preference to, cork ; and a

" method or methods of manufacturing the said new composition
" or substance into bungs, stoppers, and other useful articles;"
and these were said to be, first, the new composition or substance "gutta percha," "gutta tuban," "in any of the states,
" and according to any of the methods" described "in the
" manufacture of cork and other stoppers and useful articles, but
" confining always" the "claim as regards caoutchouc to the use
" of the same in combination with gutta percha, *or when combined by itself with ground cork or wood sawdust,* for the purpose
" of being manufactured into cork and other stoppers."

Second, "the employment of gutta percha in any of the states,
" or according to any other methods before described in the
" manufacture of cork and other stoppers and useful articles;
" and"

Third, "*the making of corks and other stoppers and useful articles
" of common cork, cased or coated in manner*" described "*with
" the said new composition, or with a mixture of ground cork, and
" any suitable oil or varnish, or with caoutchouc alone, or gutta
" percha alone, or with a mixture of caoutchouc and gutta percha,
" excepting always stoppers made of fibrous materials, in so far as
" respects the application of caoutchouc alone.*"

By a Memorandum and Disclaimer enrolled June 10, 1851, the parts printed in italic above were struck out of the Specification, and all parts relating to the same were struck out; and likewise the part describing "the use of treacle and glue in the manufacture
" of corks and other stoppers and useful articles," is struck out.

The new composition is made by rasping or grinding the cork to powder, or sawdust may be used; the gutta percha by itself, or with caoutchouc, is either dissolved by a solvent, such as is used for dissolving caoutchouc, and is mixed with cork or sawdust; or it may be put into a masticating machine in the solid state with the other substances, and, after mastication, put into square moulds, afterwards to be cut into corks; or it is moulded at once into corks or stoppers, or useful articles, into which the same is intended to be formed, &c. Gutta percha alone or combined with caoutchouc, is manufactured by similar processes as in manufacturing caoutchouc by itself, and is applied to similar useful purposes.

[Printed, 6d. No Drawings. See Repertory of Arts, vol. 9 (*enlarged series*), p. 54, and vol. 18 (*enlarged series*), p. 50, for Disclaimer; London Journal (*Newton's*), vol. 26 (*conjoined series*), p. 81, and vol. 40 (*conjoined series*), p. 237.]

A.D. 1844, July 24.—N° 10,270.

BROCKEDON, WILLIAM.—"Improvements in covering the
" roofs of buildings, in covering the valves used when propelling
" by atmospheric pressure, in covering the sleepers of railways,
" and in covering parts of stringed and keyed musical instru-
" ments." These are, in reference to this subject,' employing
for these purposes caoutchouc mixed with about 10 per cent.
sulphur and about its own weight of calamine or other substances
by passing through rollers, and made into sheets by rolling.
These sheets are subjected to a high degree of temperature; "such
" process of treating india rubber having already been made the
" subject of a patent to Mr. Thomas Hancock" No 9952, Old
Law. It is understood that this "invention consists of certain
" new mechanical adaptations."

[Printed, 4d. No Drawings. See Repertory of Arts, vol. 5 (*enlarged series*),
p. 241; and London Journal (*Newton's*), vol. 26 (*conjoined series*), p. 183;
and Engineers' and Architects' Journal, vol. 8, p. 159.]

A.D. 1844, November 25.—N° 10,407.

ALSOP, WILLIAM, and FORSTER, THOMAS. — " Improve-
" ments in the manufacture of elastic fabrics, and in making
" articles from elastic fabrics, and for weaving fabrics for the
" driving bands of machinery, and other uses. This consists, in
reference to this subject, in cutting india-rubber sheets, or a
composition thereof as described in No. 10,092, Old Law, into
threads by a circular knife cutting against a cylinder or drum.

[Printed, 6d. Drawing. See Repertory of Arts, vol. 6 (*enlarged series*),
p. 77.]

A.D. 1845, March 11.—N° 10,550.

BROOMAN, RICHARD ARCHIBALD. — (*A communication.*)—
" Certain improvements in the preparation and application of
" artificial fuels, mastic, and cements;" and these are said to be
employing in the manufacture of such substances "the natural
" resin, resin-like substance, or mastic called gutta percha, some-
" times gutta tuban."

In reference to this subject, the gutta percha is purified by
soaking, and passing several times through a cleansing machine
consisting of a tank with water and steam and rollers described.

When clear it may be applied as above, or in a granular or pulverized state, or in a state of solution, either alone or combined with other substances.

After cleansing as above, the gutta percha is subjected to the operation of a kneading machine much resembling the masticator for caoutchouc; and if certain properties are required, it is mixed with certain things and in certain proportions, as caoutchouc, sulphur, pigments, and colours. Pulverized French or Turkey chalk, &c., improves its smoothness, and emery roughens it. Alone or mixed it may be manufactured by moulding, stamping, embossing, casting, &c. into various articles. In the plastic state, or in solution, it may be used for all the purposes to which caoutchouc has been applied, and applied by much the same machines.

Granular Applications.—Taking casts and busts and impressions in relief from flat surfaces engraved or perforated as described.

" The following are good average proportions :—About 3
" parts of caoutchouc for every 6 parts of gutta percha, or 1
" part of sulphur for every 8 parts of gutta percha, or 2 parts of
" caoutchouc and 1 part of sulphur for every 8 parts of gutta
" percha, or 2 parts of caoutchouc and 1 part of sulphur for
" every 6 parts of gutta percha." When caoutchouc is employed to increase the elasticity of the gutta percha they are amalgamated at a temperature of not less than 150° F. Gutta percha may be dissolved in most essential oils and by the application of gentle heat, using in preference rectified naptha or oil of turpentine. It may be used in this state either by itself or mixed with sulphur, caoutchouc, colours, French chalk, or any other of the substances before used with it in the plastic state. In this state it may be made into sheets by floating it on glass or polished slabs of slate, &c., and leaving them to cool or dry.

[Printed, 1s. Drawing. See Repertory of Arts, vol. 7 (*enlarged series*), p. 215; London Journal (*Newton's*), vol. 28 (*conjoined series*), p. 215; and Mechanics' Magazine, vol. 44, p. 22.]

A.D. 1845, March 27.—N° 10,582.

BROOMAN, RICHARD ARCHIBALD.—(*A communication.*)—" A
" thread made from a substance not hitherto applied to that
" purpose, and also the application of it to the manufacture of

" piece goods, ribbons, paper, and other articles." The substance is " the resinous or resin-like substance called gutta percha."

In reference to this subject, the gutta percha, if necessary, is purified and prepared with sulphur, &c., &c. as described in No. 10,550, Old Law, and threads are cut from it in the sheet "by " means of revolving circular knives, according to the well-known " modes followed in the cutting of bottle or sheet caoutchouc " into threads." These are rounded by twisting, &c., or round threads may be obtained by employing a machine as follows :— A roll of prepared gutta percha is put into a cylinder with a die box; a piston is placed over the gutta percha, and pressed upon it, presses it against the die box which is hot, the gutta percha is pressed out in threads, which fall into a tank with water below, and are cooled.

[Printed, 8d. Drawing. See Repertory of Arts, vol. 8 (*enlarged series*), p. 363; London Journal (*Newton's*), vol. 27 (*conjoined series*), p. 33; and Mechanics' Magazine, vol. 44, p. 238.]

A.D. 1845, May 22.—N° 10,682.

CLARK, JAMES.—"Certain improvements in the manufacture of " fabrics from fibrous materials."

These are, in reference to this subject, gutta percha steeped in boiling water is kneaded by the hand into a mass twelve inches long and two inches broad, and made into a web by passing between heated rollers.

[Printed, 6d. Drawing. See Repertory of Arts, vol. 7 (*enlarged series*), p. 29.]

A.D. 1845, May 29.—N° 10,692.

KEENE, CHARLES.—"Improvements in boots, shoes, gaiters, " overalls, and other like articles of apparel." These are, in reference to this subject, "sulphurizing the said boots, &c., when made of unsulphurized caoutchouc or gutta percha," by exposing them to the fumes of sulphur from half an hour to an hour in close vessel, or immersing them in a bath of melted sulphur.

[Printed, 4d. No Drawings. See Repertory of Arts, vol. 9 (*enlarged series*), p. 170; London Journal (*Newton's*), vol. 28 (*conjoined series*), p. 432; Mechanics' Magazine, vol. 44, p. 209.]

A.D. 1845, August 28.—N° 10,820.

NEWTON, ALFRED VINCENT.—(*A communication.*)—"Improve- " ments in machinery for manufacturing india-rubber fabrics."

These are, in reference to this subject, employing "a series of
" knives or cutters in combination with a small grooved roller,
" upon which the india rubber to be cut is pressed in a smooth and
" even state," by which arrangement the sheet may be divided
into threads suitable for being worked up into india-rubber
fabrics.

. [Printed, 10d. Drawing. London Journal (*Newton's*), vol. 29 (*conjoined
series*), p. 325.]

A.D. 1845, September 4.—N° 10,825.

BEWLEY, HENRY.—" Certain improvements in flexible syringes
" tubes, bottles, hose, and other like vehicles and vessels."

In reference to this subject, gutta percha is employed "either in
" its natural liquid state, or in an artificial state of solution, or in
" a plastic state, or in a sheet state, or in a granular state, or in
" a state of combination with other substances, one, two, or more."
It is brought into these states by the means directed to be used
for the purpose in the Specifications of Patents, No. 10,550, Old
Law, and No. 10,582, Old Law.

[Printed, 6d. Drawing. Repertory of Arts, vol. 9 (*enlarged series*), p. 295;
London Journal (*Newton's*), vol. 31 (*conjoined series*), p. 214; and Mechanics' Magazine, vol. 44, p. 319.]

A.D. 1846, January 12.—N° 11,032.

HANCOCK, CHARLES.—" Certain improvements in the manu-
" facture of gutta percha, and its applications alone and in
" combination with other substances." These are, in reference
to this subject, first preparing "gutta percha for manufacturing
" purposes;" and this is effected as follows:—If the gutta percha
requires cleansing, it is submitted to the process described in No.
10,550, Old Law; if otherwise it is placed "in a plastic state
" in a cylinder screw press, kept hot by a " steam jacket, and
" having a bottom perforated with numerous holes." Upon this
perforated bottom are placed one, two, three, or more strainers,
and it is squeezed through them "either once or twice, or as
" much oftener as may seem expedient;" or the gutta percha,
as imported, may be dissolved in a solvent, and filtered, while
warm, through flannel, felt, or fine wire gauze, after which distil
off the solvent, &c.

Second, combining gutta percha with jintawan and caoutchouc, or jintawan alone. This is done, in the usual way, by means of a masticator.

Third, combining orpiment and other sulphurets, or sulphur, with gutta percha and the above substances. The mixture is made in the ordinary masticating machine. When heated to a high temperature for some time, either "by high-pressure steam, " or of water heated under pressure, or of hot air," a substance is obtained much more lasting than when the heating is dispensed with.

Fourth, manufacturing gutta percha and its compounds into "porous or spongy substances." This is effected by mixing the article intended to be made spongy with a quantity "of alum, " carbonate of ammonia, or some readily volatilizable substance, " either in the" masticator or by other means. Putting into moulds of the shape required, and heating in an oven, it swells up, and becomes spongy.

Fifth, "manufacturing gutta percha and its compounds into " hard substances," by confining the mass in moulds, and keeping these moulds in a chamber raised to a high temperature for some days.

Sixth, "rendering gutta percha and its compounds softer and " more pliable by treating it with an acid," by exposing them to sulphurous-acid gas, or steeping in a solution of sulphurous acid, or covering with a paste of sulphuric acid and some charcoal, "and placing in a steam-heated chamber or vessel."

Seventh, "rendering gutta percha and its compounds softer " and more pliable by the addition of wax, tallow," &c.

Eighth, two varnishes and the mode of forming them: for these purposes, gutta percha or its compounds are to be dissolved by heating under pressure to a temperature of from 300° to 380° Fahrenheit; or gutta percha and its compounds, animal or vegetable wax, or animal and vegetable fatty matter, are dissolved in turpentine and evaporated.

Twelfth, "combining gutta percha and its compounds with " resinous and bituminous matters," by mixing with it in the masticating machine shell-lac, resin, asphalte, &c.

[Printed, 8d. Drawing. See Repertory of Arts, vol. 8 (*enlarged series*), p. 164; Mechanics' Magazine, vol. 45, p. 138; and Patent Journal, vol. 1, p. 164.]

A.D. 1846, March 18.—N° 11,135.

HANCOCK, Thomas.—"Improvements in the manufacturing
" and treating of articles made of caoutchouc, either alone or
" in combination with other substances, and in the means
" used or employed in their manufacture;" and these are,
first, " making, forming, or shaping articles from the combination
" of caoutchouc with other substances, in or upon moulds, plates,
" or forms, and retaining such articles in or upon such moulds
" or forms during the process of vulcanizing, whereby the form
" of such articles is rendered permanent."

Second, " the making, forming, or shaping articles of caout-
" chouc, in or upon engraved or otherwise ornamented plates or
" moulds, and, after forcing the caoutchouc into such moulds by
" pressure and heat, submitting the whole, by means of a water
" or steam bath, or any other suitable mode, to a high tempera-
" ture, whereby the articles are sufficiently set to be removable
" from the moulds, and which may be afterwards, if desired,
" subjected to the vulcanizing process."

Third, " the manufacturing articles by combining caoutchouc
" with vegetable pitch, resin, wood and cork dust, and fibrous
" substances, and subjecting them to the process of vulcanizing."

In all the compounds, and most of the articles named, sulphur
and heat are employed, which process is now termed vulcanizing,
described in No. 9,952, Old Law. To prevent adhesion to the
mould, silicate of magnesia is employed, dusting it on, or otherwise.

[Printed, 4d. No Drawings. See Repertory of Arts, vol. 10 (*enlarged series*),
p. 28; and Mechanics' Magazine, vol. 45, p. 400.]

A.D. 1846, March 25.—N° 11,147.

PARKES, Alexander.—" Improvements in the preparation of
" certain vegetable and animal substances, and in certain com-
" binations of the same substances alone, or with other sub-
" stances." These are, the mode of obtaining " the change
" upon caoutchouc, gutta percha, and their compounds, by
" employing agents in a state of solution capable of producing
" such change." Chloride or hypochloride of sulphur is dissolved in certain quantities in bisulphuret or sulphuret of carbon,
coal naphtha, or turpentine, &c., and the articles immersed in the
same for a few minutes, the change is produced. Mixtures of

other matters with the " solvents may be employed to effect the
" change, such as the chlorides, nitrites, nitrates, fluorides, brom-
" ides, iodides, sulphurets, phosphurets of the earths and metals,
" preferring those of sulphur, of antimony, of arsenic, and
" carbon." Caoutchouc in a dry state, if kneaded with a certain
amount of dry chloride of sulphur; the change gradually takes
place, and while the mass is hot it is pressed into moulds, &c.

A new solvent for caoutchouc, gutta percha, &c. is prepared by
passing sulphurous acid gas over granulated camphor, until a
liquid is produced; this is used alone, or with the substances
which produce " the change" for dissolving caoutchouc, &c.

Caoutchouc and its compounds may be submitted to gases.
The gases are, " sulphurous acid, chlorine, nitrous acid, fluorine or
" the vapours of bromine or iodine." These gases, are employed
in some cases alone, in others, two together, are passed into a
chamber, in which the article is suspended in a vapour of a solvent
for caoutchouc, &c.

Caoutchouc and its compounds, previously to producing the
change, are combined with wool, flax, cotton, &c., also wood and
cork dust, earths, and oxides of metals, and metallic bronzes;"
also resins and resinous gums, also " cowree gums," or " cowtree
" gum," and "wood tree gum," from Van Dieman's Land.
These articles are ornamented by painting and printing, by means
of engraved rollers or otherwise, any pattern or device, first
giving them a coloured ground, by certain salts, or by mixing the
compounds with colours, after which they are changed.

Caoutchouc and gutta percha, and compounds of these substances which have undergone " the change," cannot be wrought
advantageously by any of the usual means, being very partially
soluble in the usual solvents for india rubber, and may be considered as waste; to recover this waste, it is boiled in a solution of
muriate of lime in certain proportions, until by pressure the pieces
can be readily united, when it is washed in alkaline water hot,
and afterwards in clean hot water.

Purifying gutta percha by dissolving it in turpentine, naphtha,
&c., keeping the solution at a temperature of 100° to 150° F. for an
hour or more; on the colouring matter, &c. subsiding, the solution is decanted and the solvent evaporated, "and the purified
" gutta percha may have 'the change' produced thereto."

By a Disclaimer, enrolled 25th September 1846, the patentee
states that since obtaining his Letters Patent "he has not had

" time to mature that part of the invention which was intended
" to have been described under that part of the title which is
" contained in the following words, 'and animal.'"

[Printed, 6d. No Drawings. See Repertory of Arts, vol. 9 (*enlarged series*), p. 40; Mechanics' Magazine, vol. 45, p. 400; and Patent Journal, vol. 1, p. 342.]

A.D. 1846, May 15.—N° 11,208.

HANCOCK, CHARLES.—" Certain improvements in the manu-
" facture of gutta percha, and its applications alone and in
" combination with other substances." These are in reference
to this subject " preparing gutta percha, for manufacturing
" purposes;" this " consists in taking gutta percha as imported,
and which is said to be acid, and to have a fœtid or unpleasant
smell, and cutting it into small pieces, and steeping it "in an
" alkaline solution, or in a solution of chloride of some alkali or
" earth," where it is to remain until the acid or fœtid impurities
are removed. Common soda or potash are preferred for forming
the solution, which is to be of a given strength. " If it is desired
" further to diminish the acidity or smell of the gutta percha
" it may be first subjected to an alkaline solution, and then to
" a solution of chloride of lime." " Gutta percha thus prepared
" may then be subjected to the process" given in No. 10,550,
Old Law.

Giving "shape and configuration to articles to be made of
" gutta percha, or any of its compounds, by casting, moulding,
" pressing, stamping, and otherwise," as described. " The com-
" pounds of gutta percha most applicable for this purpose are
" produced by mixing gutta percha with caoutchouc and jinta-
" wan, or either of them, and thoroughly blending the several
" materials in the manner described" in the Specification of
Patent, No. 11,032, Old Law, " or by adding to the mixtures or
" compounds bronze or other metallic powders, plaster of Paris,
" or other earthy powders, pigments, fibrous materials cut up
" short, paper pulp, or dust, &c." The shape is given " by
" means of moulds, patterns, or dies, &c., which may be of
" metal, glass, wood, or earthenware," to the gutta percha and
compounds in a plastic state; or solutions of gutta percha, &c.,
may be applied to the moulds, &c., and several layers may be
dried upon such moulds, &c. In forming articles of several
sheets, " the sutures or joints may be" joined by heat and pres-

sure, or solutions of gutta percha, &c., that in bisulphuret of carbon is preferred, or in the plastic state. "Excellent moulds, "&c. may be made of gutta percha," &c., and applied to "give "form or shapes, &c." "to articles to be made of gutta percha," &c., "or of such other substances as can be moulded at a low "temperature." "Although pieces of gutta percha, &c., in a "warm and soft or plastic state unite together, yet a piece of "gutta percha, &c. will not adhere to any other piece of gutta "percha, &c. which is in a cold and rigid state." "Forms of "types, woodcuts, printers' blocks, &c., to be used in printing, "are made by placing the pattern in a shallow box or frame "clamped together, and a sufficient thickness of gutta percha "&c. is pressed by a screw or other means upon it," &c. "Blacklead or French chalk may be used as a facing, to secure "a perfect delivery from the mould."

Sheets of gutta percha may be punched or cut through and through according to any pattern required, and cemented upon blocks or other sheets of gutta percha.

Preparing a solution of gutta percha or a combination of gutta percha, caoutchouc, and jintawan, or either of them, by dissolving the same in bisulphuret of carbon.

[Printed, 6*d*. No Drawings. See Mechanics' Magazine, vol. 46, pp. 280 and 295; and Patent Journal, vol. 2, p. 447.]

A.D. 1846, November 19.—N° 11,455.

BROCKEDON, WILLIAM, and HANCOCK, THOMAS.—" Im-"provements in the manufacture of articles where india-rubber "or gutta percha is used." These are the peculiar means of applying india-rubber or gutta percha to a variety of purposes to which they have not heretofore been so applied by means of the processes described in the Specification of a Patent granted to Mr. Alexander Parkes, No. 11,147, Old Law. "The processes "enumerated in this Patent produce certain changes in the "qualities of caoutchouc and gutta percha, similar to those pro-"duced by sulphur and heat in the process now termed vul-"canizing."

"In calling those substances by the names of caoutchouc and "gutta percha, it is to be understood that they" "comprehend "all those peculiar hydrocarbon substances known to botanists "as a vegetable constituent under those names." "Some of

" these are named from the country they are obtained, some are
" native names, as saikwah, jintawan, gutta tuban, gutta percha,
" dolla, &c." These substances, under whatever name they may
be called, are all liquified by the same solvents, by distilling give
caoutchoucine and manipulate in the same way by rollers, masticating, spreading, cutting, &c., colouring, embossing, printing,
moulding, &c. &c., as is well known, and has been described in
the Specifications of other Patents. Amongst others are those of
Mr. Thomas Hancock, Nos. 7344, 7549, 9952, 11,135, Old Law,
as well as in the first-named Patent of Mr. Parkes. " Leather,
" cloth, linen, silk, and other fabrics are rendered partially or
" entirely waterproof by coating their surfaces, or uniting two
" or more of them together with caoutchouc, gutta percha, or a
" compound of these matters in a state of solution or otherwise,
" as described in the Patents of Thomas Hancock " referred to,
and " the coated surfaces either plain, colored, embossed, printed
or otherwise ornamented, are then" changed " by immersion "
in Mr. Parkes' solution. Printed or dyed fabrics, coated on
one side only, the selvedges and ends are joined and made waterproof, and in this bag-like shape immersed in the liquid. Fibrous
and other substances liable to be injured by the changing solvents are coated with glue size, which is afterwards removed by
water; when lac is used, it is removed by any suitable alkaline
solution.

In this way the effect of the changing liquid is stopped out in
" any part of an article formed of caoutchouc, gutta percha, or
" a compound thereof." These manufactures are introduced
into a great variety of articles, such as cloaks, capes, coats, overalls, fishing stockings, collars, stocks, hats, caps, bonnets, hat
linings, hatbands, aprons, and other articles of dress or to be
worn about the person; also table cloths, wrappers, carriage roofs,
seats, and linings, portable baths, driving dresses, life preservers,
beds, cushions, pads, and other pneumatic articles, printers'
blankets, sieve cloths, card backs, &c., &c., &c.

When these articles require seams, &c. the waterproof substance
employed to such parts will require to be afterwards changed by
applying the converting solvent with a brush, &c. Garments, or
other article of dress, either of leather, cloth, &c. are made up,
and dipped or otherwise covered with a solution of caoutchouc,
&c., and afterwards immersed to obtain the change. An interior
lining is changed by pouring in the changing liquid. Caoutchouc,

gutta percha, or a compound thereof, with or without gritty or colouring matters and fibrous substances, is formed into sheets of any thickness, by means similar to those in Thomas Hancock's Specifications, and these are made up into articles or not before the " change " is effected. From these sheets, whether combined with fabrics and fibrous and other substances or not, a great number of articles are made. These are enumerated at great length, and a great number of applications are detailed. Caoutchouc, gutta percha, and the compounds thereof are moulded into various forms, engraved by plates, &c., &c. as described in Thomas Hancock's Specification, and afterwards immersed. Gutta percha, and compounds thereof, are made into numerous articles by the means directed in Nos. 7344, and 7549, Old Law, and changed by immersion. Sometimes these articles are coated with a solution of caoutchouc before submitting them to the change. A great number of articles made of cloth, paper, metal, cast plaister, cord, string, are dipped in the solutions of caoutchouc, &c. and dried, are immersed to produce "the change."

Woollen or worsted yarn, of a size proportionate to the strength of the required hose or tubing, is saturated with a solution of the compound, and when dry it is braided upon a core and pressed with heat, and changed by immersion. A flock is produced by giving the article to be flocked a coating of caoutchouc varnish, dusting on the flock or powder, and when dry immersing it in the changing liquid. Articles are coated with coloured caoutchouc varnishes, and changed by immersion. By repeated immersion and drying, the compounds "become as hard or harder than " ivory, and may be filed or wrought with tools and highly " polished."

[Printed, 6d. No Drawings. See Repertory of Arts, vol. 10 (*enlarged series*), p. 103; and Mechanics' Magazine, vol. 46, p. 504.]

A.D. 1847, February 8.—N° 11,567.

MOULTON, STEPHEN.—"Improvements in treating caoutchouc " with other materials to produce elastic and impermeable com- " pounds." These are, "treating caoutchouc, by combining " therewith calcined and carbonate of magnesia, and hyposulphite " of lead, and the artificial sulphuret of lead, and subjecting it " to high degrees of temperature." If the goods "are intended " to be elastic, the caoutchouc is mixed" with variable quantities

" of hyposulphite of lead, and the artificial sulphuret of lead,
" both or either." If the goods "are intended to be hard, of
" greater tenacity, and less elasticity," the caoutchouc is mixed
with variable quantities of "calcined or carbonate of magnesia,"
" and then add both the hypo-sulphite and sulphuret of lead, or
" either." These mixtures are made by passing the materials
through sets of heated rollers, and they are spread upon cloth by
means of three heated rollers. "The compound is placed between
" the upper rollers, and passes to the lower one, on which the
" cloth for its reception passes round, and thus receives on its
" surface the different coatings of the compound." If sheets of
rubber are required, the cloth is dispensed with, "and the sheet
" taken from the lower roller." The goods are then heated by
steam or dry heat, the former preferred, of from 220° to 280°, or
300°. "Some heats may require three hours, and some five
" hours, or thereabouts."

[Printed, 4d. No Drawings. See Repertory of Arts, vol. 10 (*enlarged series*),
p. 178; London Journal (*Newton's*), vol. 31 (*conjoined series*), p. 123;
Engineers' and Architects' Journal, vol. 10, p. 320.]

A.D. 1847, February 10.—N° 11,575.

HANCOCK, CHARLES.—" Certain improvements in the prepa-
" ration of gutta percha, and in the application thereof, alone and
" in combination with other materials, to manufacturing purposes
" which improvements are also applicable to other substances."

These are, in reference to this subject, first, preparing "gutta
" percha for manufacturing purposes, by means of the machines
" or machinery represented," "that is to say," "as regards the
" peculiar adaptation and order of sequence of the parts," and "the
" general arrangement and combination thereof," without claim-
ing any of the parts singly and separately considered. The
machinery may be described as follows:—A slicing machine,
consisting of a circular iron plate having three slots, in which are
inserted three radial knives; this plate is made to revolve, and
" the lumps of crude gutta percha " fall down an inclined shoot
against the knives, "by which they are cut into slices of a thick-
" ness corresponding to the degree of projection given to the
" knives." A vertical cutter with a rising and falling motion
may be employed, instead of a revolving one as described. The
slices are collected, and put into hot water till they are soft, after
which they are fed in by a pair of fluted rollers against a breaker

or roller with serrated blades inserted in it, revolving over a tank filled with cold water, to which may be added a solution of caustic soda or chloride of lime. At the opposite end of the tank to the roller is an inclined endless web revolving and dipping at its lower end into the water, while at its upper end it comes opposite to the feeding rollers of a breaker over a tank a little lower than the first, also filled with water; and a similar arrangement is made by which the gutta percha is brought into a third tank still lower than the second tank. In this tank, but revolving partly in the water, is a "mincing cylinder," with an arrangement of edge plates " so fixed that the blades of the cylinder shall in revolving " come into such close parallelism with them as to produce by " their approximate conjunction a scissor-like sort of action." The gutta percha is fed from the tank into this cylinder, &c. by an endless web, and after passing through the mincing cylinder it is agitated by a rotary agitator wholly immersed in the tank after which it is carried by a revolving endless web through a series of rollers mounted over the after part of the tank, " so that " the under rollers revolve under the water and the upper just free " of it." From the last pair of these rollers it is taken by an endless web and passed "to a pair of metal pressing and finishing " rollers " set to the size required, and passing over the topmost of these rollers and over a wooden drum "it is wound upon a " taking-up roller."

Second, " the new combination of materials for sulphuretting or " metallo-thionising gutta percha." In Specification of Patent, No. 11,208, Old Law, it is stated " that though a portion of sulphur " may be used in place of an equal portion of sulphuret," yet the use of sulphur was considered "altogether objectionable, because " of its offensive smell and tendency to efflorescence," but this is not the case, "& a better result is obtained from a combination of " the two than from either substance alone," "if a very minute " portion of the sulphur be used with the sulphuret." The proportions "best are forty-eight parts gutta percha, six parts of " sulphuret of antimony or hydrosulphuret of lime, or some " other analogous sulphuret, and one part of sulphur." The compound is boiled under pressure. Caoutchouc and jintawan are treated similarly.

Third, " the several methods of combining sulphur and sul- " phurets." Instead of mixing these substances in the masticator with the gutta percha, &c., the gutta percha, or caoutchouc or

jintawan "are submitted to the combined action of steam of a
"high temperature, and the vapours of orpiment (or other vola-
"tile sulphuret) and sulphur mixed in the proportions" given
above. Or caoutchouc, &c. are rubbed in a dry state with the
combination, and submitted to steam heat, or water heated under
pressure; or, after dry rubbing, they are submitted to steam at a high
temperature and the vapours of the compound; or a paste is made
of the sulphuret and sulphur with a solution of caoutchouc or
gutta percha, and brushed over the articles, which are afterwards
submitted "to one or other of the three processes."

Fourth, "employing binoxide of nitrogen and chloride of zinc,
"for the purpose of improving the quality of gutta percha."
Gutta percha, caoutchouc, and jintawan, sulphuretted or unsul-
phuretted, may be either exposed for a minute or two to binoxide
of nitrogen gas, or by putting them with the materials used in
making the gas, or immersing them in a boiling concentrated
solution of zinc for a few minutes.

Fifth, applying the binoxide and chloride as above to the improvement of ordinary sulphurized or vulcanized caoutchouc.

Sixth, "compounds of gutta percha, caoutchouc, and jintawan,"
produced by mixing each of these substances with a certain
amount of chloride of zinc. They may be afterwards sulphuretted.

Seventh, "combination of materials for producing spongy or
"porous gutta percha fit for stuffing or forming the seats of chairs,
"cushions," &c., &c. The combination consists of gutta percha,
caoutchouc, or jintawan, softened with a solvent, and mixed with
hydrosulphuret of lime, &c., carbonate of ammonia or carbonate of
lime, or other substance that is either volatile or capable of yielding a volatile product, and sulphur; and this is submitted to a
certain heat.

Eighth, "applying the various processes described under the
"third and fourth heads to the improvement of articles of gutta
"percha in a manufactured state."

Ninth, "giving to sulphuretted or metallo-thionized gutta
"percha a japan like lustre," whether before or after making up
for use. "Gutta percha, caoutchouc, or jintawan" sulphuretted
in any way "is brushed over with a solution of resin in boiling
"oil" and placed in a heated chamber from 75° to 100° F. for
some hours; it is afterwards polished. In some instances, colours
are mixed with the japanning materials; and these materials are
applied "by blocks, cylinders, or rollers, in the usual way of
"floorcloth printing."

Tenth, "machine or apparatus for cutting gutta percha into
" strips or ribbands, and manufacturing it into thread." This
consists of a pair of grooved rollers of steel or iron, mounted in
suitable framework. The grooves of each roller are semi-
circular, so that they form together a series of circular holes.
The projecting divisions between the grooves are made with
knife edges, so as to divide readily any sheet or mass of gutta
percha presented to them. Thin sheets are cut into ribbands or
strips, when the material is passed through it cold. To make
round thread, either a sheet of a thickness equal to the diameter
of the holes is passed through at a temperature of about 200° F.,
and received in a tank of cold water, or the plastic gutta percha is
passed towards the machine under a gauge. Other forms of cords
are produced by altering the grooves of the rollers.

Applying all these "improvements to caoutchouc and jintawan
" (in so far as such application has not been already claimed)."

[Printed, 1s. 10d. Drawings. See Repertory of Arts, vol. 10 (*enlarged
series*), p. 203; London Journal (*Newton's*), vol. 34 (*conjoined series*),
p. 96, and Mechanics' Magazine, vol. 47, p. 157.]

A.D. 1847, September 2.—N° 11,850.

FORSTER, THOMAS.—" Improvements in machinery for cutting
" india rubber, in rendering fabrics waterproof, and in making
" articles therefrom, and in dissolving india rubber and other
" gums;" These are, in reference to this subject, first, " coating
" metal cylinders with india rubber or gutta percha, or combina-
" tion thereof. for cutting india rubber and its compounds;"
and the means used to regulate the sizes of thread cut, "in place
" of having a different screw for each size " of thread. This last
is effected by " using only one screw, which is caused to move at
" different speeds by changing certain of the drums according to
" the size of the thread required."

Sixth, using " alcohol and coal oil combined as solvents for
" gums," &c., and " their combination with india rubber and
" gutta percha;" also " the use of alcohol when combining india
" rubber with shellac."

[Printed, 1s. Drawings. See Repertory of Arts, vol. 11 (*enlarged series*),
p. 209; and Patent Journal, vol. 4, p. 430.]

A.D. 1847, September 24.—N° 11,874.

HANCOCK, CHARLES.—"Improvements in the preparation of
" gutta percha, and in the application thereof, alone, and in com-

" bination with other materials, to various manufacturing pur-
" poses;" and these are, first, "the mode of preparing or treating
" gutta percha alone, and in combination with other materials, by
" means of baths." For temperatures a little above boiling water,
a bath is made of a solution saturated, or nearly so, of some alkaline salt or earth, or any other soluble substance. Carbonates of
potash or soda, or muriate of lime, or any salt which will not act
prejudicially upon the material, may be employed. For higher
temperatures, fixed oils or fats, &c., are used. If the temperature
of the bath is too high, or if the substance of which it is composed would act injuriously upon the gutta percha, &c., the gutta
percha, &c., should be enveloped in cloth, plaster of Paris, clay,
&c. A bath which will produce a chemical change upon the
gutta percha, &c., is sometimes selected, such as of a caustic alkali,
or sulphuret of an alkali.

Second, "the method of manufacturing gutta percha, or any
of its compounds, into vessels and hollow wares," "by blowing or
" forcing air or some other fluid into a bag or piece of caoutchouc
" placed within the material of which any vessel or article is
" intended to be made, and at the same time (if necessary) sub-
" jecting the exterior parts of the material to pressure" of
moulds, to give it the form required. In some cases it may be
necessary to protect the outside of a piece of gutta percha, &c.,
this is done "by a covering of caoutchouc."

Third, "combining gutta percha with other materials," in
order to harden it and render it more durable, better adapted for
bearing friction and resisting the effects of the weather. The
gutta percha is boiled for an hour or more in a bath of caustic
alkali, and mixed in certain proportions with oxides of iron and
lead, glue and bituminous matter.

[Printed, 4d. No Drawings. See Mechanics' Magazine, vol. 48, p. 328.]

A.D. 1847, October 21.—N° 11,917.

FORSTER, THOMAS. — " Improvements in combining gutta
" percha with certain materials, and in the application thereof to
" waterproofing fabrics, and in the moulding various articles
" therefrom, in finishing the surface of articles made from gutta
" percha, or gutta percha combined with other materials; and in
" cleansing gutta percha;" and these are, in reference to this
subject, first, combining gutta percha with animal charcoal, ground

whalebone, hydrate of sulphur, fragrant essential oils, musk, tonquin beans, orris root, or gum benzoin.

Second, combining gutta percha with ground bones, horns, hoofs, whalebone, or shavings of these matters, or animal charcoal, hydrate of sulphur, with or without perfumes, or colouring matter.

Third. To cleanse gutta percha " I first cut up the blocks into " small pieces with a knife worked by an eccentric motion, or " otherwise." " These pieces I then pass cold through a pair " of crushing rollers they are then well washed in water at 80°; " not warmer, and then put while wet into a cold masticating " pan " similar to one described in No, 10,092, Old Law.

[Printed, 8d. Drawing. See Repertory of Arts, vol. 11 (*enlarged series*), p. 303; Mechanics' Magazine, vol. 48, p. 450; and Patent Journal, vol. 4. p. 574.]

A.D. 1847, November 4.—N° 11,940.

WESTHEAD, JOSHUA PROCTOR.—(*A communication.*)—" Improvements in the manufacture or treating of india rubber;" and these are, "manufacturing or treating india rubber by subjecting " it to dry and moist heat, and sulphurous acid gas, or products " of burning sulphur," and "treating india rubber in waterproof " fabrics by subjecting such fabrics to heat, steam, and air." The goods or articles are put into a chamber, the air of which is brought to 180° Fahrenheit, and sulphurous acid gas admitted and circulated by a fan for about an hour and a half, and the heat of the chamber raised to 220°; steam is then admitted into the chamber, which is now brought to about 280°, and which takes about two hours; "the steam is allowed to flow off; and the pro-" cess is completed by again causing heated air to flow through " the vessel" or chamber, "which dries and hardens the india " rubber."

[Printed, 10d. Drawings. See Repertory of Arts, vol. 11 (*enlarged series*), p. 345; London Journal (*Newton's*), vol. 32 (*conjoined series*), p. 347; and Patent Journal, vol. 4, p. 600.]

A.D. 1847, December 30.—N° 12,007.

HANCOCK, THOMAS, and PHILLIPS, REUBEN.—" Improve-" ments in the treating or manufacture of gutta percha, or any of " the varieties of caoutchouc;" and these consist in dissolving gutta percha or any of the varieties of caoutchouc, or reducing them to a soft, pulpy, or gelatinous state after they have undergone the process of "vulcanization" or "conversion;" also in treating unvulcanized solutions or preparations of these substances, so as to bring them to a vulcanized state; also in improvements in moulds employed in the manufacture of articles from these substances. The terms "vulcanizing" and "converting," as applied to these matters, are now well known as designating certain improvements in the manufacture of caoutchouc, whereby it is rendered less liable to be affected by variations of temperature; and the improved solutions, when dried, partake more or less of the same property. The first-named process is described in the Specification of a Patent, No. 9952, Old Law, and the second in the Specification of a Patent, granted to Alexander Parkes, No. 11,147, Old Law. In operating on these substances when in a vulcanized or converted state, take the waste or cuttings of these materials and pass them between rollers, or otherwise reduce them to shreads or sheets, and boil them in oil of turpentine until they are dissolved, keeping the mass well stirred during the operation. Other solvents may be used, such as coal naphtha, and other essential oils; but the necessary temperature in such cases cannot well be attained without employing closed vessels, oil of turpentine is therefore preferred. Instead of operating upon the cuttings or waste vulcanized or converted caoutchouc, take a solution of unvulcanized or unconverted caoutchouc, and mix sulphur with it, in the proportion of from 8 to 12 parts of sulphur to 100 parts of dry caoutchouc, and then submit the mixture to a temperature of about 300°, or from that to the boiling point of oil of turpentine, for a period varying from 15 to 30 minutes, and a somewhat similar result is obtained; or the caoutchouc, the solvent, and the sulphur may be treated in the same manner, without previously disturbing the caoutchouc; but it is preferred to employ the vulcanized or converted waste, the appropriating of which to a useful purpose being the chief object had in view.

These vulcanized solutions are applied to a great variety of purposes, and for coating or saturating leather, cloth, felt, and other fabrics, wood, metal, paper, plaster casts, and other articles to be protected from air and wet, and as cements; also for pouring or pressing into moulds. Colors are mixed with these vulcanized solutions, and they are so used for coating, colouring, printing, &c. Boiled oils, japan, varnishes, gums, resins, pitch, asphalte, metallic oxides, earths, wood and cork dust, and fibrous and other substances are mixed with these solutions, and the results applied to various purposes.

Making moulds of materials capable of being dissolved or melted at temperatures so low as not to be injurious to the manufactured material, such as "Darceys' alloy" or "compound of gum, glue, " &c."

[Printed, 4*d*. No Drawings. See Mechanics' Magazine, vol. 49, p. 45; and Patent Journal, vol. 5, p. 202.]

A.D. 1848, April 27.—N° 12,136.

BARLOW, WILLIAM HENRY, and FORSTER, THOMAS.—" Im-
" provements in electric telegraphs, and in apparatus connected
" therewith; and these are, in reference to this subject, :—When gutta percha is not alone used for covering telegraphic wires, it is combined with cowrie or New Zealand gum, and flowers or milk of sulphur. Eight parts, by weight of gutta percha in a suitable kneading machine heated to about 120° F., have added to them one part, by weight of flowers or milk of sulphur, and one part, by weight of the above gum in powder. This makes "what is con-
" sidered the best compound," but "we do not confine ourselves
" thereto, and other matters may be mixed with gutta percha."

[Printed, 2*s*. 2*d*. Drawings. See Repertory of Arts, vol. 13 (*enlarged series*), Mechanics' Magazine, vol. 49, p. 497; Artizan, vol. 7, p. 82.]

A.D. 1848, May 11.—N° 12,153.

HANCOCK, CHARLES.—" Certain improved preparations and
" compounds of gutta percha, and certain improvements in the
" manufacture of articles and fabrics composed of gutta percha
" alone, and in combination with other substances;" and these are, employing " glass moulds to give a polish to the exterior, or
" parts of the exterior, of shoes and galoshes made in whole or
" in part of gutta percha."

Employing other "improved preparations and compounds of
" gutta percha." Gutta percha, previously boiled with muriate of lime, is passed between heated cylinders while rosin is sifted on; or solutions of the two are made and mixed; this is employed "where complete electric insulation is desirable." Gutta percha, shellac, and borax are mixed and compounded.

[Printed, 10*d*. Drawing. See !Mechanics' Magazine, vol. 49, p. 490. Artizan, vol. 7, p. 83; and Patent Journal, vol. 6, p. 76.]

A.D. 1848, July 10.—N° 12,206.

LORIMER, ANTHONY. — "Improvements in combining gutta "percha and caoutchouc with other materials;" and these are said to be, first, "the means of cleansing gutta percha preparatory "to compounding and using the same." And a series of cutters are shown by which it may be cut into shavings; these shavings are afterwards torn in a machine, by three revolving bars with spikes (the bottom of this machine "is made of wire gauze to let "the small dust fall through"), and afterwards treated in a "welding trough" or masticator. When the shavings are required very pure, they are boiled "for about ten minutes in "water acidulated with oxalic acid."

Second, "combining gutta percha with" the following matters: —"Burned clay, burned flint, broken articles of porcelain, earthen- "ware, and china, marble, Portland, Cornish, and other stones, "crushed and sifted; also the oxide of zinc and the oxide of "copper, the hydrate of lime and oxalate of lime; also a compound "of lime slacked with oxalic acid dissolved in water."

Third, "combining caoutchouc" with oxide of zinc and the "oxalate of lime; also the compound produced by slacking lime "with oxalic acid and water."

[Printed, 10*d*. Drawing. See Repertory of Arts, vol. 13, (*enlarged series*), p. 171; London Journal (*Newton's*), vol. 34 (*conjoined series*), p. 26; Mechanics' Magazine, vol. 50, p, 47; Artizan, vol. 7, p. 133; and Patent Journal, vol. 6, p. 146.]

A.D. 1848, July 29.—N° 12,223.

HANCOCK, CHARLES.—"Improvements in apparatus and "machinery for giving shape and configuration to plastic sub- "substances;" and these are, first, "the apparatus for moulding "hollow wares," "as far as regards the base chuck and the "shifting moulds or pattern pieces connected therewith." The "base chuck has dovetails cut lengthwise in its four faces" "for "the reception of four mould pieces," "having dovetailed fillets "to correspond." The moulds or pattern pieces are flat on "their inner faces, and provided with fillets to slide into the "dovetailed grooves of the chuck," so that all that is required when a change of pattern is necessary "is to withdraw one set of "patterns and substitute another."

Second, "the apparatus for moulding hollow wares," whether "used with or without the parts thereof relating to cooling."

This apparatus consists of a hollow female mould, into which a male mould is made to press. The material to be moulded is put into the hollow mould, and the male mould presses upon it, while an arrangement causes the female mould to rotate, while, at the same time, either hot water or cold water or steam passes up into the interior of the hollow female mould.

Third, "the apparatus for preparing plastic materials in so far
" as regards the combination therein, of a vertical presser, with a
" horizontal bed filled with hot water or steam, whether such table
" is fixed or movable."

Fourth, "the apparatus for moulding plastic substances into
" continuous lengths with supporting cores of wire, cord, and
" other like tenacious substances, and the several modifications
" thereof, in so far as regards the combination of a die box and
" a cylinder with piston, each working or operating in directions
" at right angles to or more or less tangential to the other."

Fifth, "the modification of the apparatus which forms the
" subject of the preceding claim, whereby it is adapted to the
" production of short lengths of plastic materials of any required
" form with interior supporting cores."

Sixth, the improved apparatus for forming plastic substances
" into balls, in so far as respects its application to other sub-
" stances than metals." This improved apparatus consists of a pair of rollers made to rotate in close contact with one another. In the periphery of each roller a number of semicircular hollows are cut out, corresponding with a similar set of hollows in the periphery of the other roller, "so that when two such hollows are
" brought together face to face they form an entire circle or
" sphere." The plastic substance is supplied to the rollers from a feeding table. Although gutta percha is not named in this Specification, it is the plastic substance to which this invention is specially directed.

[Printed, 1s. 8d. Drawings. See Mechanics' Magazine, vol. 50, p. 116; Artizan, vol. 7, p. 154; and Patent Journal, vol. 6, p. 176.]

A.D. 1848, September 4.—N° 12,262.

RICARDO, John Lewis.—" Improvements in electric telegraphs
" and in apparatus connected therewith;" and these are, in reference to this subject :—" In place of using gutta percha it is pre-
" ferred to use that material combined with gum cowrie, or New
" Zealand gum and flowers, or milk of sulphur" in the pro-

proportions of one part by weight of the flowers or milk of sulphur, one part by weight of the gum, and eight parts by weight of the gutta percha.

[Printed, 6d. Drawing. See Repertory of Arts, vol. 14 (*enlarged series*), p. 1; London Journal (*Newton's*), vol. 34 (*conjoined series*), p. 159; Mechanics' Magazine, vol. 50, p. 232; Artizan, vol. 7, p. 159; Patent Journal, vol. 6, p. 216; and Engineers' and Architects' Journal, vol. 12, p. 118.]

A.D. 1849, January 11.—N° 12,407.

NICKELS, CHRISTOPHER.—" Improvements in preparing and " manufacturing india rubber (caoutchouc);" and these are, first, " constructing the kneading rollers with flanches," and causing the kneading rollers, "with or without flanches" to work out of " the centre of the cylinder or trough." The " machinery is similar " to that" described in the Specification of Patent No. 7213, Old " Law, only the masticating roller has flanches " " by which the " india rubber is prevented from coming against the ends of the " fixed trough or cylinder." There is also another arrangement of kneading machine, the kneading roller of which "is placed and " works excentrically within the trough or cylinder," and it may have flanches or otherwise.

Second, " manufacturing india rubber by combining sulphur or " matters containing sulphur or products of sulphur by grinding, " kneading, or masticating the same in a manner suitable for " making elastic thread or sheets and other articles, and yet " retaining the property of piecing up and of kneading or masti- " cating;" also " combining sulphur fumes with india rubber," and masticating the rubber combined, as above, " with phos- " phorous." The rubber is masticated with the sulphur, &c. in the usual manner, the rollers being heated. The sulphur fumes are combined with the rubber by passing them from a retort into the masticator. In applying fumes of sulphur, "hydrogen passed " into the machine will be advantageous; or, in place thereof, " phosphorous in small particles, or vapour thereof used in very " small quantities, will be found highly beneficial." After masticating, the products are to be submitted to pressure (hydraulic is preferred), and the moulds heated externally to about 220° to 250°.

[Printed, 1s. Drawings. See Repertory of Arts, vol. 15 (*enlarged series*), p. 224; London Journal (*Newton's*), vol. 35 (*conjoined series*), p. 21; and Mechanics' Magazine, vol. 51, p. 45.]

A.D. 1849, April 26.—Nº 12,585.

SIMPSON, GEORGE, and FORSTER, THOMAS.—" Improve-
" ments in the manufacture or treating solvents of india rubber
" and other gums or substances;" and these are, first, manufacturing chloride or bichloride of carbon, and applying the same for
dissolving india rubber, gutta percha, and other gums or gum
resinous substances not soluble in water, thus obtaining new
" solutions of those substances." This is effected as follows:—
Bisulphuret of carbon is distilled from a retort or still having
a steam jacket, and passes to the bottom of a vessel heated
similarly, and containing pentachloride of antimony; from the
top of this second vessel a pipe leading to a condenser receives
the chloride of carbon. The product is rectified by distilling with
lime, and the resins are dissolved by it "in like manner to that
" heretofore resorted to when using the solvents heretofore
" employed." India rubber is changed by the chloride, and
is not so readily effected by cold, &c.

Second. "Treating coal oil with chloride of lime." In place of
pentachloride of antimony, having a solution of chloride of lime,
passing the vapour of the coal oil with steam into it, and condensing as before.

[Printed, 6d. Drawing. See Repertory of Arts, vol. 14 (*enlarged series*),
p. 344; London Journal (*Newton's*), vol. 35 (*conjoined series*), p. 332; and
Patent Journal, vol. 8, p. 80.]

A.D. 1849, April 26.—Nº 12,591.

BURKE, WILLIAM HENRY.—" Improvements in the manufac-
" ture of air-proof and water-proof fabrics, and in the preparation
" of caoutchouc and gutta percha, either alone or in combination
" with other materials, the same being applicable to articles of
" wearing apparel, bands, straps, and other similar useful purposes;" and these are, in reference to this subject, treating
" caoutchouc or caoutchouc and gutta percha combined with "
precipitated sulphuret of antimony, mixing by means of a masti-
cater, submitting it to pressure, and afterwards to heat. It is
stated that rubber so prepared is superior to that vulcanized by
free sulphur. Sheets of considerable length may be made by
spreading the material from the masticator on cloth saturated
with chalk, &c., which allows the sheet to be separated from the

cloth after it is heated. It may be spread on leather, &c., &c., mixed with colors, or otherwise, and heated.

[Printed, 4d. No Drawings. See Repertory of Arts, vol. 14 (*enlarged series*), p. 365; London Journal (*Newton's*), vol. 35 (*conjoined series*), p. 384; Mechanics' Magazine, vol. 51, p. 430 ; and Patent Journal, vol. 8, p. 69.]

A.D. 1849, May 1.—N° 12,597.

DALTON, JOHN.—"A certain improvement or certain improve-"ments in printing calicoes and other surfaces." These are, in reference to this subject, in applying gutta percha to the web or lapping of a printing cylinder or machine, dissolving five pounds of the gutta percha in one gallon of "benzole, naptha, "spirit of turpentine, camphine, bisulphuret of carbon or other "proper solvents," but, preferring benzole or bisulphuret of "carbon" on account of their "being exceedingly volatile."

[Printed, 4d. No Drawings. See Mechanics' Magazine, vol. 51, p. 448 ; and Patent Journal, vol. 8, p. 94.]

A.D. 1849, June 7.—N° 12,643.

PAYNE, EDWARD JOHN.—(*A communication.*)—" Improvements " in marine vessels, in apparatus for the preservation of human life, " and in moulding, joining, and finishing hollow and solid figures, " composed wholly or in part of certain gums or combinations of " certain gums" "and in apparatus and machinery to be used for " the purposes above mentioned;" and these are in reference to this subject, take gutta percha in the state it is imported and reduce it to small scraps, half fill a kettle with these scraps, pour in water till within six inches of the top, add from four to ten per cent. of common salt, and from 2½ to 5 per cent. of oil of vitrol, put on the lid, boil for an hour; the mixture is taken out with a ladle. This compound is pressed in presses constructed on the principle of a common cheese press, and between two highly polished iron plates, and afterwards it is brushed. To increase the strength and toughness of the material, the cake, slightly warmed, is passed over an anvil and beaten with hammers or passed in a soft state between a pair of flanged rollers, and thus cut into strips which are laid side by side, boiled until they adhere, and twisted into a rope, again boiled and pressed into a cake, and the brushing may now be repeated or not, and the plates cut up to suit the moulds, which should be heated to about 75° F., and wetted with soapy water, and are then ready to receive the boiling plates or cakes taken from the boiler by means of a spoon or ladle. Some qualities require cooling by immersing the moulds in cold water "dissolving, treating, and combining " gutta percha, india-rubber, gummy copal, gummy damar, resin, " shellac, tar, pitch, linseed oil, sugar of lead, white of lead, " litharge, alum, and spirits of turpentine, all or any of them, " and producing thereby waterproofing compounds, varnishes, " and paints to be employed for coating and covering the surfaces " of articles, and as cements for joining articles, and whether " combined with colouring matters or not." Four compounds are described and the proportions in which the substances are to be employed are given. "In any of the compounds wherein " india-rubber is employed combined with gutta percha, the " india-rubber is to be placed first in the kettle with the gummy " copal and linseed oil, the gutta percha is then added when the " india-rubber is on the point of being dissolved; and when " gummy dammar is employed, it is added when the india-rubber " and gutta percha are on the point of being dissolved; gummy " copal being always introduced first."

[Printed, 1s. 2d. Drawings. See Mechanics' Magazine, vol. 51, p. 571; and Patent Journal, vol. 8, p. 128.]

A.D. 1850, March 2.—N° 12,986.

RICHARDS, THOMAS, TAYLOR, WILLIAM, and WYLDE, JAMES, the younger.—"Improved rollers to be used in the " manufacture of silk, cotton, woollen, and other fabrics." These are, in reference to this subject:—"The india-rubber tubes or " pipes by which the rollers are to be covered, after having been " subjected to the vulcanizing or metallo-thionizing process, are " to be boiled for a time, varying from four to six hours, in an " alkaline solution (preferring caustic soda or caustic potass), to " which we add flower of sulphur. The alkalies have a tendency " to render the caoutchouc more solid, while the sulphur gives " to the surface a certain degree of roughness, which renders it " better adapted for the operation of drawing."

[Printed, 6d. Drawing. See London Journal (*Newton's*), vol. 37 (*conjoined series*), p. 174; Mechanics' Magazine, vol. 53, p. 199; and Patent Journal, vol. 9, p. 274.]

A.D. 1850, April 23.—N° 13,062.

SIEMENS, ERNST WERNER.—"Improvements in electric tele- " graphs," and these are very numerous, and in the manufacture of coated wire for electric telegraph purposes. These are, in reference to this subject, "in preparing line wire suitable for " being laid under ground," the wire is coated with a combination of gutta percha and sulphur, gutta percha entirely freed from water is mixed with sulphur in "very fine powder by means of " rollers, and then to affect their chemical combination by heating " the mixture in a steam chamber." This compound has great hardness.

[Printed, 3s. 6d. Drawings. See Mechanics' Magazine vol. 53, p. 356; Practical Mechanics' Journal, vol. 5, p. 25; and Patent Journal, vol. 10, p. 69.]

A.D. 1850, May 7.—N° 13,069.

GERARD, GUSTAVE EUGENE MICHEL.— " Improvements in " dissolving caoutchouc (india rubber) and gutta percha." These are said to be "mixing with the solvent, of whatever nature it " may be, a certain quantity of alchohol," and afterwards "mace- " rate the caoutchouc or gutta percha;" " they will expand a very " little, and at the end of twenty-four hours it will become of the " state of paste, and may be moulded into any required form." The solvents mixed with the alcohol, and which are preferred, are " sulphuret of carbon, sulphuric ether, naphtha, essential oils of " coals of turpentine, and chloroform."

[Printed, 4d. No Drawings. See Repertory of Arts, vol. 16 (*enlarged series*), p. 34; London Journal (*Newton's*), vol. 41 (*conjoined series*), p. 88; Mechanics' Magazine, vol. 53, p. 379; and Patent Journal, vol. 10, p. 95.]

A.D. 1850, June 6.—N° 13,103.

NEWTON, WILLIAM EDWARD.— (*A communication.*)— " Im- " provements applicable to boots, shoes, and other coverings for " or appliances to the feet;" and these are, in reference to this subject, "making that kind of shoes known as clogs " " of " india-rubber sponge," "moulded of the desired form with the " upper part of the sole."

" I compound with the india-rubber prepared in the usual " manner for vulcanizing one quarter of a pound of sugar or " resin to one pound of india-rubber, and after the compound " has been worked and treated in the usual manner, I form the " clog in a mould, and subject it to the curing or vulcanizing " process by heat by which it is rendered spongy and light." In place of using sugar or resin, employing other substances which will evolve gas in quantities during the curing.

[Printed, 4d. No Drawings. See London Journal (*Newton's*), vol. 41 (conjoined *series*), p. 89; Mechanics' Magazine, vol. 53, p. 476; and Patent Journal, vol. 10, p. 208.]

A.D. 1850, July 9.—N° 13,170.

NEWTON, ALFRED VINCENT.—(*A communication.*)—" Improve-
" ments in the preparation and manufacture of caoutchouc or
" india rubber ;" and these are, using " gum lac or shellac in its
" various forms in the preparation or manufacture of caoutchouc
" or india rubber, with or without the application of artificial
" heat." Any of the kinds of lac are combined with india rubber in various proportions, according to what purpose the result is to be applied, and either by grinding or by their solvents. When the compound is intended to be used in certain manufactures, sulphur in small quantity is mixed with it. The fabric thus made with, or dusted with sulphur, is deprived of its tackiness by exposure to the sun. A cement is made by mixing "one
" part of gum lac or shellac with two parts of caoutchouc, by
" grinding or triturating them together in the usual manner, and
" I add a sufficient quantity of camphine or other solvent of
" caoutchouc to render the compound of the proper consistency.
" I generally mix with the cement a small quantity of finely
" divided sulphur, say two or three ounces of sulphur to one
" pound of the composition used." Sometimes this compound is used to make thin fabrics, and generally, when used in thick fabrics or masses, the compound is submitted to a high degree of heat, say about 270° F.

In heating, following the processes described in Specification of Patent, No. 10,027, Old Law, " earths, oxides, or carbonates,
" or salts of lead, or zinc, or other metals," may be mixed with this compound.

[Printed, 4d. No Drawings. See London Journal (*Newton's*), vol. 39, (conjoined *series*), p. 434; Mechanics' Magazine, vol. 54, p. 58 ; and Patent Journal, vol. 10, p. 210.]

A.D. 1851, January 16.—N° 13,453.

BUCHHOLZ, GUSTAV ADOLPH.—" Of improvements in print-
" ing, and in the manufacture of printing apparatus, and also in
" folding and cutting apparatus ;" and these are, in reference to

this subject, the gutta percha used for inking rollers, in preference, is "softened by the action of an acid." "The soft gutta percha which I use for receiving impressions from matrixes" also "I prefer to soften in the following manner:—

I take gutta percha in a divided state and macerate it until all " the acid is removed, after which I wash it in water, and it is " then ready for use."

[Printed, 6s. 6d. Drawings. See Mechanics' Magazine, vol. 55, p. 77; and Patent Journal, vol. 11, p. 263.]

A.D. 1851, March 4.—N° 13,542.

NEWTON, ALFRED VINCENT.—(*A communication from Mr. Goodyear.*)—"Improvements in the preparation of materials for " the production of a composition or compositions applicable to the " manufacture of buttons, knife and razor handles, inkstands, " door knobs, and other articles where hardness, strength, and " durability are required;" and these are, first, treating caoutchouc or gutta percha, or caoutchouc and gutta percha combined, by mixing them with sulphur and heating them to a high temperature, or mixing them with sulphur and other substances and heating them. The other substances mentioned are magnesia, lime, or the carbonates or sulphates of magnesia or lime, or "calcined French chalk or other magnesian earth," "gum, lac, or " shellac," "rosin, oxides or salts of lead or zinc of all colors, and " other similar substances, both mineral and vegetable, may be " added in small quantities to either of the compounds." These compounds are mixed by a masticating machine, and rolled into sheets and manufactured into the articles desired. "The com" pounds or compositions after heating or curing will attain a " hard and stiff character resembling tortoise shell, horne, bone, " ivory, or jet."

Second, applying these compositions when hardened by heating, or before heating by moulding, shaping, and afterwards heating, also uniting them to iron or other metals, &c., which will bear heat, and afterwards heating.

The degree of heat required depends upon the size or thickness of the article, but in ordinary cases the heat should be raised to about 260° or 270° F., and exposed to such heat about 4 hours; as a general rule, however, the heat should range from 250° to 300° F., and the time of exposure from 2 to 6 hours.

By a Disclaimer and Memorandum of Alteration enrolled the 21st day of February 1853, the following observation is made :—
"It should be stated that further experience has shown that
" although foreign matters may be introduced into these compounds,
" their use should be sparing, as they tend to weaken and otherwise
" injure the compounds;" and likewise " but in no case do I claim
" to use a less quantity of sulphur than four ounces to every pound
" of gutta percha."

[Printed, 4d. No Drawings. See London Journal (Newton's), vol. 40 (conjoined series), p. 9; Mechanics' Magazine, vol. 55, p. 219; and Patent Journal, vol. 11, p. 276.]

A.D. 1851, August 14.—N° 13,721.

MOULTON, STEPHEN.—" Certain improvements in the prepa-
" ration of gutta percha and caoutchouc, and in the application
" thereof;" and these are combining gutta percha alone or mixed with caoutchouc "with the acids of sulphur of a lower
" degree of oxygenation than sulphuric acid in combination with
" suitable bases," preferring "a hyposulphite which can be used
" alone or combined with the salts of the acids of sulphur, or
" with the sulphurets," by making a mixture of sulphite or hyposulphite of lead or of zinc, and the artificial sulphuret of lead or zinc with gutta percha, alone, or combined with caoutchouc, and submitting them to a high temperature. Also "using Paris white
" or chalk in the mixture ;" also " combining therewith carbonate
" of magnesia." These mixtures are treated in the same manner as set forth in the Specification of Patent No. 11,567, Old Law.

[Printed, 4d. No Drawings. See London Journal (Newton's), vol. 40 (conjoined series), p. 363; Mechanics' Magazine, vol. 56, p. 158; and Artizan, vol. 10, p. 66.]

A.D. 1851, September 4.—N° 13,738.

DUNCAN, JOHN WALLACE.—" Improvements in engines for
" applying the power of steam or other fluids for impelling pur-
" poses, and in the manufacture of appliances for transmitting
" motion ;" " and these are," in reference to this subject—
" The manufacture of wheels and bosses (used in machinery
" for preparing and spinning fibrous materials) of gutta percha
" and other substances, masticated and combined by machinery."
The gutta percha in its native state "is cut into shreds of a
" fibrous character," and " submitted to a machine similar to that

" known as Calvert's Patent Cotton Opening or Cleaning
" Machine," to teaze out the dirt. The gutta percha and similar
analogous substances, as "catimundo," may be used alone; but
a combination is described as employed, of cannel coal, gutta
percha, alone, or combined with "tintowa" (jintawan?), or
"catimundo." These are ground in a masticator; heat is applied,
and for this purpose "the gaseous products of the combustion of
" coke" are employed. The heat gradually encreases till it rises
to 350° F.

[Printed, 2s. 4d. Drawings. See Mechanics' Magazine, vol. 56, p. 237.]

A.D. 1852, January 12.—N° 13,894.

DUTHOIT, ALCIDE MARCELLIN.—"An improved chemical
" combination of certain agents for obtaining a new plastic pro-
" duct;" and this may be made of "common oxide of zinc,
" purified oxide of zinc, amianthus, fusible spar (or sulphate of
" barytes), and other analogous substances, with purified and
" bleached gutta percha." The gutta percha is "purified and
" bleached" by means of dissolving in pure naphtha, or benzole,
or sulphuret of carbon. These substances are mixed singly and
in different proportions with the gutta percha solution, according
to the object for which they may be required. To give elasticity
" for certain applications," caoutchouc is added in certain proportions.

[Printed, 4d. No Drawings. See Mechanics' Magazine, vol. 57, p. 59.]

A.D. 1852, July 20.—N° 14,230.

RIDER, EMERY.—(*A communication.*)—" Improvements in the
" manufacture or treatment of india rubber and gutta percha, and
" the application thereof;" and these are, first, preparing " gutta
" percha by preliminary heating," so "that the volatile and
" oleaginous fluids" are "expelled." This is preferred to be
done " by means of hot metal rollers," or " in a stove heated by
" steam or hot air."

Second, "producing a new material, permanently elastic, not
" liable to be affected by any change or degree of temperature.
After preparing the gutta percha as above, it is, " either alone, or
" in combination with caoutchouc, mixed with the well-known
" ingredients," cured or vulcanized. Hyposulphite of lead or
" zinc is preferred.

[Printed, 4d. No Drawings. See Mechanics' Magazine, vol. 58, p. 116.]

A.D. 1852, September 18.—N° 14,299.

POOLE, MOSES.—(*A communication from Mr. Goodyear.*)—" Im-
" provements in combining caoutchouc and other matters ;" and
these are, " combining of a product of coal tar, caoutchouc, and
" sulphur, and subjecting the same to heat ;" and it is stated
that no claim is made " to the application of heat to caoutchouc
" combined with sulphur, when the product of coal tar described,
" or of the vegetable or mineral pitch, is not combined therewith."
" The product of coal tar or of vegetable or mineral pitch " " is
" obtained by boiling the coal tar (which is produced in the
" manufacture of coal gas) for two and a half to three hours, or
" until it is little less hard than resin, and about the consistency
" of Burgundy pitch." "This product of coal tar may be used
" in large proportions with caoutchouc, and thus produce an
" extensive saving in the production of what is known 'as vul-
" canized india rubber, as well also in the production of hard
" substances in the character of horn and whalebone; and such
" manufactures may have combined therewith white lead and
" colouring maters."

[Printed, 4d. No Drawings. See Repertory of Arts, vol. 21 (*enlarged series*),
p. 293; and Mechanics' Magazine, vol. 58, p. 277.]

A.D. 1852, September 30.—N° 14,306.

POOLE, MOSES.—(*A communication from Mr. Goodyear.*)—" Im-
" provement in the manufacture of combs ;" and these are
manufacturing " combs by the application of the hard substance
" of a tortoiseshell or ivory-like texture, produced by combining
" sulphur and india rubber, and subjecting them to heat." The
material, it is said, is described, under No. 13,542, Old Law. The
hard substance is improved by rolling when it is at a temperature
of 300° Fahrenheit ; or combs may be cut out of sheets before
heating, and afterwards changed by heating. To give the substance " a tortoiseshell or ivory-like texture, it is found desirable
" gradually to raise the temperature," and retain it at a certain
temperature during given periods or lengths of time.

[Printed, 4d. No Drawings. See Mechanics' Magazine, vol. 58, p. 297.]

A.D. 1852, November 7.—N° 14,348.

POOLE, MOSES.—(*A communication from Mr. Goodyear.*)—" Im-
" provements in the elastic ribs, sticks, and fillets used in the

" manufacture of umbrellas and parasols, and various other
" articles, in substitution of whalebone and steel heretofore em-
" ployed;" and these are, manufacturing of elastic ribs, sticks, and
fillets used in "the manufacture of umbrellas and parasols, and
" various other articles (in substitution of whalebone and steel
" heretofore employed), from hard and elastic substances pro-
" duced by combining india rubber and sulphur, and subjecting
"- the same to the requisite heat;" employing a composition, such
as is described in No. 13,542, Old Law and it is stated that it is
preferred, in manufacturing some of the articles, to employ the
material already hardened, while with others they are made out
of the plastic materials, and hardened afterwards.

[Printed, 4d. No Drawings.]

PATENT LAW AMENDMENT ACT, 1852.

1852.

A.D. 1852, October 1.—N° 6.

POOLE, MOSES. — (*A communication from Mr. Goodyear.*)—
" Improvements in the manufacture of guns and pistols."

This consists, in reference to this subject, in making a compound
of "india-rubber combined with sulphur, with or without other
" materials." "Two parts by weight of india-rubber, and one
" part by weight of sulphur" prepared "though colouring and
" other matters may be combined " " such as shellac, gutta percha,
" coal tar, or pitch, deprived of water, and white lead, oxide of
" zinc, and other colouring matters, and even other matters may
" be added." The heat is applied to the articles made or coated
" gradually in about half an hour to 230° of F., and after half
" an hour gradually increasing the heat for the remainder of six
" hours up to 295° to 305° F.," if a large quantity of foreign

matters be in the compound the heat may be raised more quickly. In place of using sulphur in the compound, "substances con-
" taining or giving off vapour of sulphur on the application of
" heat may be used."

[Printed, 4d. No Drawings.]

A.D. 1852, October 1.—N° 16.

POOLE, MOSES.—(*A communication from Mr. Goodyear.*)—
" Improvements in the manufacture of telescope and other
" tubes."

This consists, in reference to this subject, in making a compound, in preference, consisting of two parts by weight of india-rubber and one part of sulphur, other matters, such as gum lac, gutta percha, pitch, and coal tar, deprived of water by heat, white lead, oxide of zinc, or other coloring matters may be used, and even others. The tubes preferably in metal or plaster moulds are gradually heated up to 230° F., say in about half an hour, and in about half an hour gradually raised to 295° to 305° F., in the remainder of six hours; or the heat may be raised more quickly if the compound contain much foreign matter. The use of sulphur is recommended, " yet matters containing or giving off
" sulphur by heat in the process may be employed."

" In making such tubes the compounded materials are first
" made into sheets, and then introduced and retained in metal or
" plaster moulds during the process of heat, taking care that the
" edges come closely together or overlap, to insure a good joint,
" or, when the material is of sufficient substance, it may be sim-
" ply bent into a tube-like form, and the mould dispensed with,
" or a mandril may be used, the sheet or material enclosing it at
" all parts, and the edges caused to overlap, or otherwise, to
" insure a good joint." " In using a mandril, it is first covered
" with paper to facilitate its delivery after the heating process."
" This substance will be found very useful, amongst many
" other purposes, for receiving and insulating wires for electric
" telegraphs."

[Printed, 4d. No Drawings.]

A.D. 1852, October 1.—N° 19.

POOLE, MOSES.—(*A communication from Mr. Goodyear.*)—
" Improvements in moulding articles when india-rubber, com-
" bined with other materials, are employed."

This consists, in reference to this subject, in combining one part by weight of sulphur with two parts by weight of india-rubber, other materials, such as pigments or colouring matters may be used as well as sulphur. Moulds of several parts are used. The combined india-rubber is rolled into sheets which are pressed upon the moulds, and the cores filled up with sand or other fine granular matter which will bear the necessary heat, by this means the sheets are caused to be pressed with every part of the mould; the moulds are then heated gradually for about half an hour up to 233° F., and kept at that temperature for about two hours, the heat is then gradually raised during the remainder of six hours from 295° to 305° F.; "the lower of these two temperatures appearing to produce the more tough or horny character, and the latter temperature producing more the character of whale-" bone."

[Printed, 4d. No Drawings.]

A.D. 1852, October 1.—N° 24.

POOLE, MOSES.—(*A communication from Mr. Goodyear.*)— " Improvements in making covers for and in binding books and " portfolios, and in making frames for pictures and glasses." These are, first, combining india-rubber and "sulphur, and " subjecting the same to heat, to the making of the covers of " books and portfolios, and to the making of frames for pictures " and glasses;" second, connecting "the leaves of books together " with india-rubber combined with sulphur, and converting or " vulcanizing the same by heat."

The india-rubber compound is rolled into thin sheets, which " are placed on thick paperboard or strong woven fabric," " the " india rubber being turned over at the edges, according to the " size and character of the book or portfolio, or the covers and " back are made wholly of sheets of the compounded materials, " by using thicker sheets of the compound, with fibre or woven " fabric adhering to the inner surfaces, and having shaped them, " they may be pressed into a mould to obtain the desired device " or character; and the process of heat may be conducted whilst " the compound is between the surfaces of the moulds, or " otherwise, "then producing the device by pressure between dies or " engraved surfaces." "The hinges are produced by vulcanized " india-rubber alone, applied to the surfaces of a woven fabric." In the second part of the invention the leaves of the book at the

back "are roughened and coated with india-rubber cement con-
"taining sulphur for producing vulcanization." "Straps of
"woven fabric may be applied at intervals, extending across the
"hinge for the purpose of strengthening the back and hinge
"of the book," and heat "till the change called vulcanization
"is produced, which will generally result in about fifteen minutes
"by applying heat of about 265° Fahrenheit by a metal or other
"surface." "In making the frames for pictures and glasses,"
"the compounds above described" are either used "as veneers,
"after the sheets are vulcanized, to cover the surfaces of wood
"frames, or else mould them solid to the design or device desired."

[Printed, 4d. No Drawings.]

A.D. 1852, October 1.—N° 27.

MACINTOSH, JOHN.—(*Provisional protection only.*)—"Im-
"provements in packing for steam engines and other machinery."
These are, "making and using a composition in the following
"manner:"—"Cuttings of vulcanized india rubber or gutta
"percha (or it may be the materials of which such manufactures
"are composed) are burned, and produce a black and partially
"fluid product, which is mixed with charcoal, black lead, and
"lampblack."

[Printed, 4d. No Drawings.]

A.D. 1852, October 1.—N° 28.

POOLE, MOSES.—(*A communication from Mr. Goodyear.*)—
"Improvements in coating metal and other substances with a
"material not hitherto used for such purposes." This consists in
reference to this subject in "coating the exterior surfaces of rods,
"tubes, and wire, and cords or bands, by enclosing them within
"the compounded materials" "produced by combining india-
"rubber with sulphur, with or without other materials, and so
"that the edges of the material overlap, or the articles are other-
"wise closed over, in all parts of their exterior surfaces, with
"the hard substance;" also, "coating of other hollow articles of
"metal, such as insulating instruments, with such material," in
preference, composed of 2 parts of india-rubber and 1 part of
sulphur, "and then subjecting them to a high degree of heat till
"the desired result is obtained." The compound may contain
"a large proportion of pitch or coal tar, deprived of water."

[Printed, 4d. No Drawings.]

A.D. 1852, October 1.—N° 30.

POOLE, MOSES.—(*A communication from Mr. Goodyear.*)—" Im-
" provements in the manufacture of trunks, cartouch and other
" boxes, knapsacks, pistol holsters, dressing, writing, and other
" cases, and sword and other sheaths;" and these are, employing,
in manufacturing the above articles, "a hard substance, produced
" by combining india rubber with sulphur, with or without other
" materials, and subjecting the same to heat after it has been
" made into the desired articles," " the compound to be used
" being rolled into sheets;" the sheets are "formed into the
" articles above mentioned, by spreading " them " upon forms or
" in moulds, according to the shape and nature of the article,
" more particularly where the article is to be wholly of the com-
" position. Wood or sheet metal are considered best for forms,
" and solid metal is considered best for moulds," " to keep the
" covering in contact with the form, and, to facilitate the heating,
" the articles are placed in cases or frames, and surrounded with
" impalpable powder of talc or soap-stone, when the sheets are
" in the interior of a mould or shape sand is placed in the interior,
" and heat is " applied gradually.

[Printed, 4d. No Drawings.]

A.D. 1852, October 1.—N° 33.

POOLE, MOSES.—(*A communication from Mr. Goodyear.*)—" Im-
" provements in the manufacture of pails, tubs, baths, buckets,
" measures, drinking and other vessels, basins, pitchers, and
" jugs, by the application of a material not hitherto used in such
" manufactures;" and these are, applying "a compound sub-
" stance and process of moulding " in manufacturing these
articles. The compound substance is "india rubber combined
" with sulphur, with or without other materials, and then subject-
" ing them to a degree of heat, till the materials are converted;
" and for the purpose of making the lighter articles above men-
" tioned it is preferred that the composition should simply
" consist of india rubber and sulphur, as other materials, except
" they be coloring matters, only tend to injure the composition
" for such finer purposes." " In making the articles above men-
" tioned the composition is made into sheets, and suitable sheet
" metal moulds are used for the purpose, which are to be lined
" with the sheets, taking care that the edges are well brought
" together, and in order that the composition may retain its form

"within the mould, sand, or other fine heavy material is to be
"filled in." The moulds, of sheet metal, with the articles therein,
"are then to be heated (to convert the compounded materials
"into a hard substance); for this purpose the heat should be
"raised gradually." "It may be stated that in many large
"articles it is desirable, in place of the composition only, to
"employ the composition between surfaces of woven fabrics; and
"in order to give strength and stiffness to the upper or other
"parts, hoops of metal may with advantage be applied, in which
"cases such hoops are to be covered over with the substance
"and incorporated therein, so as to form one with the vessel to
"which such hoop or hoops may be applied."

[Printed, 4d. No Drawings.]

A.D. 1852, October 1.—N° 37.

POOLE, MOSES.—(*A communication from Mr. Goodyear.*)—"Im-
"provements in covering and sheathing surfaces with a material
"not hitherto used for such purposes;" and these are, the manufacture of sheets for covering and sheathing surfaces from a compound of india-rubber and sulphur, with or without other matters. "The same is to be rolled into sheets of the dimensions
"desired, and when the sheets are not large enough for the pur-
"poses desired, different breadths are cemented together in the
"usual way before heating." "The compound may be connected
"to a fabric or fleece which will bear the heat." The heat is applied "gradually, say to 230° of F. in about half an hour,
"retaining that heat for about one and a half hours, and then
"increasing it gradually up to 295° to 305° F. in the remainder
"of six hours." "Where the compound contains a considerable
"quantity of foreign matter the heat may be raised more quickly."
"If very tough sheets are desired, then the heat is stopped from
"rising up to 295°." Such sheets may be reduced in thickness,
"and extended (when not combined with fabrics) by subjecting
"them to pressure between hard and smooth rollers, the sub-
"stance being at a temperature about 300° Fahrenheit when
"rolled."

Printed, 4d. No Drawings.]

A.D. 1852, October 1.—N° 43.

POOLE, MOSES.—(*A communication from Mr. Goodyear.*)—"Im-
"provements in harness and in horse and carriage furniture;"

and these are, manufacturing the above articles, in the manner described, "of india rubber combined with sulphur, with or with-
" out other matters." In No. 13,542, Old Law, the hard material therein mentioned was described to be used in combination with articles of metal in making parts of harness and parts of carriages, such as saddle-trees, terrets, bits, stirrups, martingale rings, and dasher irons. "Now this invention consists of employing this
" hard material in making various articles where no metal is
" used, or where metal is only used as an accessory or furniture
" to the article so made." "As much as may be to dispense with
" the use of metal and leather, when making those parts which
" have heretofore been of metal, or of metal and leather combined,
" and to substitute the substance above mentioned." "In
" making the parts of harness and carriage furniture," "the
" substance or compounded material may be made very tough
" and leatherlike by not carrying the heat beyond 290° to 293°
" of Fahrenheit; but where the compounded materials are in-
" tended to be" a "substitute for iron or metal, then the heat
" is to be raised from 295° to 305° of Fahrenheit ; but if largely
" composed of foreign matters the heat may be raised more
" quickly."
[Printed, 4d. No Drawings.]

A.D. 1852, October 2.—N° 163.

POOLE, MOSES.—(*A communication from Mr. Goodyear.*)—" Im-
" provements in the manufacture of tables, sofas, bedsteads,
" stands, chairs, and other articles of furniture, and the frames
" and bodies of musical instruments;" and these are, the appli- cation of the hard substances produced from india-rubber and sulphur by heat to the manufacture of the above articles. This compound is used alone or mixed with other substances, such as gum, shellac, gutta percha, coal tar, tar or pitch deprived of water, white lead, oxide of zinc, &c.

" In constructing these articles," "when the furniture is made,
" of iron, it is necessary to use the sheets of composition before
" being heated. The articles, either in parts or in whole, are
" wound and covered over in like manner to gun barrels and
" other articles." "They are then heated in the usual manner
" in contact with impalpable talc or soap-stone, and not in moulds.
" Many articles of furniture, and many parts of articles, may be
" made wholly of the compound, being made hollow, or partly

" hollow, in form of shells, and filled in with wood, or strengthened
" in the interior by braces of iron."

[Printed, 4d. No Drawings.]

A.D. 1852, October 2.—N° 168.

MACINTOSH, JOHN.—" Improvements in compositions to be
" used as paints;" and these are, " using india rubber decom-
" posed by heat in combination with oils or fatty matters saponi-
" fied by metallic salts, and using lime for thickening the paint
" or liquid produced;" "and this may be effected" "by suspend-
" ing the same before a fire, and" " causing the substance to
" decompose and run in a fluid state into a suitable receiver
" below, or it may be decomposed by heat in a vessel. The
" fluid thus obtained is to be combined with metallic soap, and
" thickened with lime, and the same may be coloured by the use
" of pigments." "This paint" " is not liable to crack or blister
" in hot climates."

[Printed, 4d. No Drawings.]

A.D. 1852, October 8.—N° 305.

TYLER, JOHN TALBOT.—" Improvements in hats, and in the
" preparation of plush or other covering used in the manufacture
" of hats." This consists, in reference to this subject, in using a
solution made by dissolving " 14 ozs. of caoutchouc in a solvent
" composed of the two parts of coal tar naptha to one part of
" oil of turpentine or in either of these substances by itself."

[Printed, 4d. No Drawings.]

A.D. 1852, October 12.—N° 355.

WARREN, PETER.—" An improved material, applicable to many
" purposes for which papier-maché and gutta percha have been or
" may be used." Straw, of any fibrous substance, is cut into
" short lengths, passed through crushing rollers, in some cases
using water, and afterwards boiled "in a strong alkaline lye or
" solution of caustic alkali, such as soda, potash, &c." "until
" a pulpy mass is produced;" pass it through a rag engine, and
partially dry the pulp, in which state it is rolled or "pressed into
" sheets, or moulded into other forms, and oiled or treated with
glutinous matter and baked. Pigments may be introduced into
the pulp in the rag engine. Pulp from rags may be combined
with the pulp above.

[Printed, 4d. No Drawings.]

A.D. 1852, October 16.—N° 419.

JOHNSON, JOHN HENRY.—(*A communication.*)—",Improvements
" in the manufacture and applications of hyposulphite and similar
" compounds of zinc;" and these are, first, "the systems or
" modes of producing the hyposulphite and bisulphuret of zinc."
These are a solution of caustic potash or soda, and to which sulphur has been added, is evaporated to concentration and saturated
with sulphurous acid gas, a hyposulphite of the alkali is thus
obtained; when cool, this solution is added to a solution of salt
of zinc, acetate preferred, a precipitate falls, "which may be called
" the hyposulphite of zinc." When the saturation with the sulphurous acid gas is dispensed with the precipitate "may be
" termed bi-sulphuret of zinc." Either of these precipitates are
collected on a filter, dried, and "reduced to an impalpable
" powder."

Second, "the system or mode of treating caoutchouc, by incor-
" porating or combining with it" the substances prepared as
above. These are well worked up together, "and subjected to a
" temperature of from 120° to 150° centigrade," "and from three
" to five hours."

[Printed, 4*d*. No Drawings.]

A.D. 1852, October 20.—N° 459.

HARRISON, CHARLES WEIGHTMAN, and HARRISON, JOSEPH
JOHN.—" Improvements in protecting insulated telegraphic
" wires;" and these are, in reference to this subject, first, protecting "insulated telegraph wires by coating or covering them
" with a composition," which is caoutchouc dissolved in naphtha,
and to which may be added creosote; these are mixed in certain
proportions, and aftewards incorporated with a certain weight of
shell-lac; it "may be applied while warm to coat the gutta percha
" or other insulator."

Second, "by coating or covering them spirally with strips or
" ribbons of caoutchouc, and applying over this a coating of the
" composition or varnish first described."

[Printed, 6*d*. Drawing.]

A.D. 1852, October 23.—N° 500.

COOLEY, ARNOLD JAMES.—" Improvements in the manu-
" facture of artificial leather. These are as follows:—Gutta
percha, or any like substances, alone or mixed, is reduced to frag-

ments; the purer parts are selected and heated in a vessel alone or mixed with "oil of turpentine, pyrogenous oil of turpentine, "rectified mineral or coal naptha, bitumen, benzole, bisulphuret "of carbon, pine oil, resin oil, caoutchoucine, or any similar sol- "vents or liquids, either singly or in mixtures of two or more," and passed through strainers. This gutta percha, previously prepared "under any of the now existing patents," is made into a paste "and kept heated, and agitated and mixed with "from 25 to "400 per cent. more or less" of "carbonate or sesqui-carbonate "of soda, Scotch soda, soda ash, common culinary salt, or chlo- "ride of sodium, or of any other salt or salts or saline matter "freely soluble in water, or of powdered carbonate or sesqui- "carbonate of ammonia, or of any other like substance freely "soluble in water, and volatilizable by a moderate heat; or of "powdered sugar, gum, British gum, or roasted starch, or of any "other like saccharine or gummy substance or substances freely "soluble in water;" "mix the said saline matters, salts, gums, "or sugars, either one, or mixtures of two or more of them, with "the before described purified and softened gutta percha, or "other hydrocarbons or materials, by means of pounding, stir- "ring, or grinding together in any suitable or convenient vessel "or apparatus, either alone or with the addition thereto, as may "be required, of from fifteen to fifty per cent. of the above-men- "tioned oils." "To increase the capacity of the said composition "to resist heat and to harden the same," "add to the prepared "dough or paste, before the addition of the powdered saline, "saccharine, or gummy substances," "asphaltum or solid bitu- "men or shell-lac; and when" it is desired "to render it "more elastic or flexible," "add caoutchouc thereto, previously "dissolved or reduced to a dough or paste by means of heat "and the addition of the essential oils," "or, instead thereof," "add powdered sulphate of baryta, or heavy spar hydrate of lime "or slaked lime, finely powdered caustic or quick lime, calcined "magnesia, or carbonate of magnesia, sulphate of lead, sulphuret "of lead or hyposulphite of lead, any one, or a mixture of any "two or more of these substances to the before-described dough "or paste; and promote admixture and union of the said com- "bined materials, by exposing the same to a heat of from one "hundred and eighty degrees to three hundred degrees (more or "less)." "For certain purposes wool, (perfectly carded without "oil,) or of carded cotton, silk, flax, hemp, &c.," "wood dust,

" cotton dust or refuse, saw dust, wood dust, cork dust, raspings
" or cuttings of cork, filings or drillings of iron, steel, copper,
" and other metal, pounded glass, flints, or quartz, or siliceous
" sand, either singly or in the form of mixtures of two or more
" of them," " to impart any particular color to the compositions,
" mix therewith any of the ordinary pigments or stains."
The mass is formed into sheets or skins by passing it between
" rollers or cylinders of metal, stone, wood, or paper, or any com-
" bination of the same, the surfaces of the said rollers or cylinders
" being polished, grained, or figured."

"Or blocks or lamps are put into sheets or skins by means of
" knives or saws;" or "sheets" "are formed" "by spreading
" it on the surface of an endless band of metal, parchment,
" leather felt, gutta percha, india rubber, canvass, calico, or any
" other textile fabric or suitable material, in a common spreading
" machine, adhesion between the band and the then preparing
" artificial leather being prevented by keeping the surface of the
" former moistened with water or oil, or with a weak solution of
" soft soap or sugar."

These articles are treated in a great variety of ways, depending upon how they were prepared and the nature of the object to which they are to be applied, in a manner somewhat resembling the like operation with animal leather. Those prepared with salts are steeped, &c. in water, &c., and are manipulated till "their
" pores open and they become sufficiently soft and flexible."
When ammonia, its compounds, or a volatile substance is employed, the skins, &c. are exposed to a current of hot air, &c.

[Printed, 6d. No Drawings.]

A.D. 1852, October 27.—N° 539.

LE GRAS, Louis Napoleon, and GILPIN, William Lawrence.—(*Provisional protection only.*)—" A compound having
" the properties of gutta percha." It "consists in" "the pro-
" duction of a compound possessing the properties of gutta
" percha, and suitable as a substitute for it." "This compound
" is made by taking gums or glutinous matter, asphalte, bitu-
" minous or pitchy matters, and oily or oleaginous and fatty
" matters, such as may be found in the United Kingdom of
" Great Britain and Ireland, compounding them well together,
" and drying, hardening, softening, or elasticating them accord-
" ing to the particular uses to be subserved thereby.

[Printed, 4d. No Drawings.]

A.D. 1852, November 3.—N° 622.

LEY, GEORGE WILLIAM.—(*Provisional protection only.*)—"The
" manufacture of a material to be used for certain purposes,
" instead of wood, leather, millboard, or oilcloth." It consists
" in combining gutta percha with dry peat dust, or turf dust, in
" the proportion of about one part of the former to about three
" parts of the latter. Heat is required to effect this combination.
" The material, may be formed into sheets, blocks, or other forms
" by rolling or pressing."

[Printed, 4d. No Drawings.]

A.D. 1852, November 3.—N° 623.

LEY, GEORGE WILLIAM.—(*Complete Specification, but no Letters
Patent.*)—" A method of imitating carvings in wood." It consists
" of attaching shavings of wood to the surface of a plastic material
" by the pressure of metal or wood moulds, similar to those used
" in manufacturing papier maché ornaments," as follows :—Take
" gutta percha in a manufactured state," and " heat and knead "
it " through heated metal rollers, or in a heated mortar with a
" pestle; and while in this state of partial fusion, gradually sift
" over the surface a certain quantity of dry bog peat dust or turf
" dust, repeating the operation and kneading in the dust with
" the gutta percha, so as completely to mix or incorporate the
" one with the other. The proportion of dust to gutta percha
" will depend upon the purpose to which the material is to be
" applied, and the pressure to which it is to be subjected, as well
" the heat at which the material is to be worked." "Take this
" material in a heated or plastic state, and press it into a metal
" or wood mould " " with sufficient force to obtain an impres-
" sion of the moulding. When the material is cool, trim and
" remove it from the mould, and apply a coating of liquid india-
" rubber cement, and repeat this coating, if necessary, once or
" twice, allowing each coating to dry between ; " next take some
" shavings of an ornamental or other wood, produced by an
" ordinary steel plane or scraper, and having applied on one side
" of them a similar coat or coatings of liquid india-rubber
" cement," place these shavings with the cemented surface
" downwards upon the moulding, arranging them so that they
" shall match each other as nearly as possible, and be of sufficient
" length and breadth to enter into the hollows of moulding, at,

" the same time taking care to make the grains of the shavings run
" one way," then " press the moulding, now covered with shavings
" as before, whereby it becomes perfectly developed, and resembles
" carving in wood."

[Printed, 4d. No.Drawings.]

A.D. 1852, November 5.—N° 656.

DUNDONALD, Admiral, the Earl of.—" Improving bituminous
" substances, thereby rendering them available for purposes to
" which they never heretofore have been successfully applied."
This consists, in reference to this subject as follows :—The bituminous substance gas pitch is melted in pans, and a certain amount of resinous matter added to it, together with a certain amount of viscous or unctuous oil of tar, or similar oil, by preference " saturated with caoutchouc," and " stir the whole until
" the solution becomes amalgamated." These mixtures may have grit, sand, &c. mixed with them. " Rude works, such as these, may
" be performed by means of factitious bitumens and pitch," but
" the natural cohesive bitumen of Trinidad or New Brunswick,
" which has gradually been deprived of its volatile components "
is preferred. These are ground, sifted, and masticated with about one tenth their weight of unctuous oil, rolled and thoroughly washed " in tepid water." This mixture, with the addition of
" gummy and resinous matters (open to public use), constitutes
" a preparation of great flexibility."

[Printed, 4d. No Drawings.]

A.D. 1852, December 20.—N° 1111.

WILKINSON, WILLIAM.—" Improvements in the manufacture
" of paper and pasteboard, and in the production of a substance
" applicable for veneers, pannels, and to many purposes to which
" gutta percha and papier mâché are applicable. These are,
" take the beards of barley, rye, and other grain which grows
" with a similar beard, and steep the beards, and mix them with
" bone size, or other like glutinous matters, and pass the whole
" through rollers. The paper thus produced may be used, after
" being dried, as it comes from the rollers, or it may be bleached
" at any part of the process. In the manufacture of pasteboard,
" add a portion of bonedust and sawdust; for veneers, panels,
" &c., take sawdust of various-coloured woods, which mixed with

" glutinous matters, forms an artificial board of various colours,
" and being passed between engraved rollers, or being submitted
" to pressure under an engraved or figured die, produces an
" embossed surface."

[Printed, 4d. No Drawings.]

1853.

A.D. 1853, January 1.—N° 8.

JOHNSON, JOHN HENRY.—(*A communication.*)—(*Provisional protection only.*)—" Improvements in the manufacture of oils,
" and the treatment thereof for lubricating purposes." It con-
sists in " destroying the unpleasant smell of certain descriptions
" of oils, more particularly those produced from resin or analogous
" substances, and in the improving such oils. The purified oil
" has an unpleasant odour, which in same cases renders it dis-
" agreeable to use. This may be changed by the addition of
" alcohol, such as is obtained at an extremely cheap rate by an
" invention recently introduced in France by M. Bouis, being
" formed from the residuum left after the obtainment of
" oleaginous matter from certain seeds. By the addition of a
" small quantity of caoutchouc this oil may be made applicable
" for the lubrication of rubbing surfaces in machinery, loco-
" motives, waggons, &c." The caoutchouc in its raw state is cut
up and steeped, pressed, dried, and dissolved "in from 50 to a
" 100 times " its " weight of the oil, and after from 20 to 48 hours
" immersion or thereabouts the temperature is raised considerably
" and kept at the higher degree by a hot water bath. By pro-
" longing the time of immersion a lower temperature may be
" used. The slimy fluid thus produced serves to form the required
" mixture by adding the requisite proportions of oil."

[Printed, 4d. No Drawings.]

A.D. 1853, January 5.—N° 22.

GÉRARD, GUSTAVE EUGÈNE MICHEL. — "Improvements in
" manufacturing and treating caoutchouc." This consists, in
" reference to this subject, as follows :—It is stated that this

" invention is based upon the discovery that caoutchouc in any
" shape submitted to a temperature of about two hundred and
" twenty degrees to two hundred and forty degrees Fahrenheit,
" during a certain time, is susceptible of receiving and retaining
" a greater extension than in its natural state, and heat is applied
" to the caoutchouc in any form or shape for the above purpose."

The caoutchouc, either alone or mixed with dissolving and
" colouring matters," is formed into sheets by passing it down
between two rollers heated from 220 to 240° F. The sheets may
pass over a third cylinder. The sheet is received on to an endless
cloth. The caoutchouc is better fitted for the manufacture of
sheets and tubes when mixed with "twenty-five to forty per cent.
" of red or yellow ochre, chalk, oxide of zinc," &c. " and ten
" per cent. of essential oil or waste caoutchouc melted by the
" direct action of the fire." Caoutchouc thread "required to
" lengthen or reduce in size," is stretched "to its greatest natural
" length," and in this state is submitted to the above temperature.
" For heating the caouthouc thread a hot solution of carbonate
" of potash" may be substituted for water or steam, " by which
" the strength of the thread will be increased."

[Printed, 4d. No Drawings.]

A.D. 1853, February 15.—N° 395.

NORMANDY, ALPHONSE RENE LE MIRE DE.—(*Partly a communication.*)—"Improvements in the manufacture of articles
" made of gutta percha;" and these are, first, " decolorizing
gutta percha by means of " animal charcoal." The gutta percha
cleaned by known means is dissolved by preference in bisulphuret
of carbon, and the solution is filtered through animal charcoal.
The vessel with the solution is placed above and connected with
a vessel containing the charcoal, the charcoal vessel again is connected with a receiver and the receiver and vessel with the solution
are connected together by a tube which enters into the upper
part of each.

Second, "the manufacture of films or layers of gutter percha,"
as follows :—Pour the solution obtained above into a vessel, for
example, a bell jar, which move about until its sides are completely covered, drain the excess of the solution off. On the
evaporation of the bisulphuret of carbon, the sheet or film readily
comes off.

[Printed, 6d. Drawing.]

A.D. 1853, February 16.—N° 410.

NEWTON, ALFRED VINCENT.—(*A communication.*) — (*Provisional protection only.*)—" Improvements in the manufacture of
" printing surfaces." This consists, in reference to this subject,
" in mixing gutta percha and india-rubber with metals or the
" oxides of metals reduced to a granulated state." The metals
" or oxides of the metals " " are peroxide of iron, peroxide of anti-
" mony, or the two combined; also copper oxide and the oxides of
" lead and zinc. In cases where the composition is required to
" keep for a long period it is desirable to use india-rubber and
" gutta percha combined." "When the metallic substances
" above enumerated are used, the composition is capable of being
" worked up again and again for the purpose of being remoulded;
" but when this is not required, plumbago, or the flowers of the
" earth (as clays, ochres, and the crude metallic ores of zinc, tin,
" lead, copper, iron, antimony, &c.) may be mixed in with the
" plastic gum, and the flowers of the metals proper and of
" earthen and glass ware" may be employed.

[Printed, 4*d*. No Drawings.]

A.D. 1853, February 24.—N° 467.

JOHNSON, WILLIAM.—(*A communication.*)—" Improvements
" in the treatment or manufacture of caoutchouc." "*First*, to
" the treatment of the raw juice of the caoutchouc tree in such
" manner that the juice shall remain in a fluid state without
" deterioration. *Second*, to the after treatment of such fluid
" matter for the production of a new article, or raw material of
" manufacture. Shortly after the milk or juice is collected it is
" strained, and has then added to it a quantity of the concen-
" trated liquor of ammonia, *or other ammoniacal matter, or any*
" *combination of nitrogen and carbon.*" "The mixture is then
" well mixed, when it will remain in a white fluid state, capable
" of transportation and use as a preserved material, if kept in
" air-tight receptacles." For the production of a new article of
" manufacture from this composition, it is run out on a suitable
" surface, and submitted to slow evaporation."

This Patent was assigned by William Johnson to Samuel
Thompson Armstrong, and leave was granted to him to file along
with the Specification a Disclaimer, No. 467*, in which the matter
printed above in italic is disclaimed.

[Specification of Patent, 4*d*; Disclaimer, 4*d*. No Drawings.]

A.D. 1853, February 26.—N° 496.

DUNDONALD, Admiral, the Earl of.—"Improvements in pro-
"ducing compositions or combinations of bituminous, resinous,
"and gummy matters, and thereby obtaining products useful in
"the arts and manufactures." These are "increasing the dura-
"bility of gutta percha, caoutchouc, and other gums, deposited
"in humid places, by means of their admixture or coating with
"unctuous oil of petroleum or tar," and also the forming of
compounds of these gums with rosin, shellac, or other indurated
and brittle gums and resins.

[Printed, 4d. No Drawings.]

A.D. 1853, March 9.—N° 598

PIDDING, WILLIAM.—"Improvements in treating sheets of
"caoutchouc or gutta percha, so as to render the same fit for
"ornamental coverings." These are as follows :—Take "a sheet
"of india rubber (caoutchouc), of such thickness as may be re-
"quired; stretch it, by any known means, to from eight to sixteen
"times (more or less as desirable) its original superfice." "Then
"print thereon a design or pattern, by any mode of printing,
"whether block printing or by cylinder. This design or pattern
"is made to show on its surface equidistant dots, or dots printed
"according to the design to be used." "Each of these dots must
"be perforated by any known means." "Into each of the holes
"perforated in the caoutchouc as aforesaid" "introduce a
"stud, or other formed substance, angular, sexagonal, octagonal,
"or otherwise shaped, of any convenient size, or of any suitable
"material, as electro-plated substances, silica, glass, glazed
"metal, or other substance. On withdrawal of the stretching
"press or frame, the sheet of india rubber will collapse to, or
"nearly to, its size before stretching." "This fabric will be
"found fit for covering shoes, boots, ottomans, carpets, orna-
"mental hangings, and for useful and ornamental purposes."
"Closer adhesion of the caoutchouc and ornaments" is effected
"by boiling the fabric in water, where desirable." "Or instead
"of studs," "insert into the holes aforesaid threads of any ma-
"terial, drawn as minutely as possible, previously soaked in
"gelatine, or any proper adhesive substance, and allowed to dry;
"then cut into the required lengths."

[Printed, 4d. No Drawings.]

A.D. 1853, March 16.—N° 656.

NICKELS, EDWARD.—(*A communication.*)—" Improvements in
" preparing lubricating matters ;" these are, " employing india
" rubber and gutta percha (together or separately), combined by
" heat with oily and fatty matters for the purpose of lubricating
" the moving parts of machinery," "Tar, pitch, or bituminous
" matters may be added." The india rubber and gutta percha are
" rolled or pressed into thin sheets or films, placed together or
" separately in any suitable vessel, together with sufficient oil to
" cover them, and heat gradually applied thereto, which should
" be raised to the boiling point, and continued till the india
" rubber or gutta percha are dissolved, when a further quantity
" of oils or fatty matters, and other matters, if any are to be used,
" may be added and combined therewith, without the further ad-
" dition of heat beyond what is necessary to melt any fatty
" matters which may be added. The matters in all cases are
" to be well mixed by stirring when in the fluid or melted
" state." A great variety of compounds may be made in this
" manner."

[Printed, 4*d*. No Drawings.]

A.D. 1853, April 7.—N° 842.

NICKELS, CHRISTOPHER.—" Improvements in machinery for
" masticating, kneading, or grinding india-rubber, gutta percha,
" and other matters ;" these are " using two rollers in each
" machine, the rollers are formed with screws on their surfaces,
" in place of the teeth or projections heretofore employed, and the
" rollers work parallel with each other." The rollers work within
a trough, which may, when desired, "have a steam jacket, if the
" matters, or any of them, which are being acted on require a
" greater heat than is consequent on the process itself." In
kneading or treading gutta percha, it is desirable " to use a steam
" pipe to allow steam to flow into the trough for a short time
" after the machine has been standing for a time; but when
" the machine is continued in work, the heat resulting from
" the process is found sufficient for gutta percha and for india
" rubber, and for compounds or mixtures containing those
" matters."

[Printed, 1*s*. Drawings.]

A.D. 1853, April 14.—N° 906.

DUNCAN, JOHN WALLACE.—" Certain new combinations of
" gutta percha with other materials, and the method of applying
" such for use." This consists, in reference to this subject as
follows :—compounding gutta percha with Canada balsam, or the
balsam of the pinus balsamea, or that from the pinus larix or
styrax from the liquid amber styraciflua, or other analogous
balsams, in such proportions, and with or without certain proportions of shellac or other resinous or bituminous substances,
according to the nature of the article to be cemented, so that the
compound will bear sufficient heat without decomposing or becoming greasy on the surface. A cement is prepared as follows :"
—" Forty pounds of gutta percha, three parts caoutchouc, three
" parts shellac, fourteen parts Canada balsam or Venice turpen-
" tine, thirty-five parts of balsam from the liquid amber styraci-
" flua or styrax, four parts of gum mastic, and one part oxide of
" lead. For cementing and joining leather, a cement is "com-
" pounded" of "sixty parts of gutta percha, ten parts of shellac,
" two parts of caoutchouc, twenty parts of Venice turpentine, and
" eight parts of styrax." "A cement adapted for uniting wood
" or caulking ships is composed of" "about fifty-five parts of
" gutta percha, fifteen parts of shellac, twenty-five parts of Venice
" turpentine, and five parts of pitch." "To unite rigid sub-
" stances, such as metals, glass, stone, and earthenware, a cement
" is compounded of forty-five parts of gutta percha, twenty parts
" of shellac, five parts of gum mastic, half a part of oxide of lead,
" three parts of styrax, twenty-six and a half part of Venice tur-
" pentine, mixing metallic powders, such as cast-iron borings,
" with this cement improves it for fixing iron railways to stone
" work, and such like purposes." " To cement and unite small
" particles of material, such as leather shavings, silk waste, hair
" and the like," " compound a cement of twenty parts of caseum,
" fifteen parts of glutin, five parts of coagulated (or livery) lin-
" seed oil, one part of the oxide of lead, twenty-five parts of
" Venice turpentine, and thirty-four parts of gutta percha. About
" eight per cent. of gum ammoniacum may be introduced with
" advantage in the cement, instead of a like portion of the
" gluten. The above proportions may be varied, but those given
" are found to be the best for the several purposes described."
Masticating machines are described, consisting of double cased

cylinders in which are rotating cylinders; these cylinders are arranged for hot water and steam and have teeth.
[Printed, 1s. Drawings.]

A.D. 1853, April 30.—N° 1051.

BARRETT, BARNABAS.—" Improvements in the treatment of
" natural and artificial stone, and of articles composed of porous
" cements or plaster, for the purpose of hardening and coloring
" the same." This consists, in reference to this subject, in using a compound of gutta percha dissolved in coal tar naphtha, or other suitable solvent in the proportion of three parts by weight of gutta percha to eight parts of the solvent.
[Printed, 4d. No Drawings.]

A.D. 1853, May 4.—N° 1095.

GOODYEAR, CHARLES.—"Improvements in combining india
" rubber with certain metals;" these are, in the manufacture of articles combining with "the hard compound made of india
" rubber and sulphur in the proportion of two of rubber to one
" of sulphur (with or without other matters), subjected to heat " the heat is raised in about half an hour to 230° F., kept up at that for two hours and raised gradually up to 295° to 305° during the remainder of the six hours " thin surfaces of gold, silver, or other
" metal, exterior or interior of the article of the hard compound."
" Supposing it to be desired to ornament or coat, or partly to
" coat, a cup or vessel with an exterior coating of open gold
" work," "take thin sheet metal, and cut therefrom the device
" required, and then, by stamping or otherwise, make it of such
" form as to fit the mould in which the cup or vessel, the com-
" pound of india rubber, is to be formed, and having introduced
" the metal, whether composed of one or more pieces, the plastic compound of india rubber is to be introduced and pressed into
" form in the mould, by which the metal will become imbedded or partially imbedded in the plastic compound."
[Printed, 4d. No Drawings.]

A.D. 1853, May 6.—N° 1121.

NICKELS, CHRISTOPHER.—" Improvements in machinery for
" masticating, kneading, or grinding india rubber, gutta percha,
" and other matters. These consist "in causing cylindrical or

" conical rollers, having projections, teeth, indents, or grooves,
" to be arranged to work " so that these projections, &c. "do not
" enter into each other," and the forms of the projections, &c.
" may for this purpose be varied, and the rollers may work at a
" like or different speed." In carrying out this, two rollers, cut
with angular grooves or projecting parallel ribs, are shown, placed
in a trough or box; and it is stated that it has been found " de-
" sirable to use a steam pipe to allow steam to flow into the trough
" for a short time after the machine has been standing for a
" time; but when the machine is continued in work the heat
" resulting from the process is found sufficient for gutta percha
" and for india rubber, and for compounds or mixtures con-
" taining those matters."

[Printed 1s. Drawings.]

A.D. 1853, May 21.—N° 1260.

SCOUTETTEN, HENRI JOSEPH.—"An improved plastic com-
" pound applicable to various ornamental and useful purposes,"
" composed of vegetable and mineral substances;" "the number
" and quantity of each varies according to the purpose for which
" the material is required." The substances may be "gutta
" percha, caoutchouc, pitch, resin, wax, gum lac, oxyde of iron,
" golden sulphur of antimony, ultra marine, chrome, zinc white,
" &c." Hollow cylinders heated by steam crush the substances
into a mass. The paste resulting is compressed in moulds "com-
" posed of gutta percha, containing a twentieth part of caout-
" chouc." "Each mould should be bound with iron." "This
" paste may also be composed chemically. In this case the gutta
" percha, caoutchouc, and pitch are dissolved in sulphuret of
" carbon. When the solution is complete, and the combination
" well effected, the solution is purified, the sulphuret of carbon is
" drawn off, and a mass is obtained which may be heated dry in
" close vessels." "If it be desired to make pipes, boot soles,
" straps, &c., add to the above substances, held in solution in the
" sulphuret of carbon, carded cotton," "a mass is obtained which
" is heated dry, and passed under rollers." "Under other cir-
" cumstances, and according to known processes, the cotton is
" replaced by linen, canvas, silk, wool, or any other textile sub-
" stance. The paste thus prepared may be colored by adding one
" or more of the oxydes indicated." "To render paper or stuffs
" impermeable, the caoutchouc and the gutta percha must be

"separately dissolved in sulphuret of carbon, in the proportion
" of eight of gutta percha for one hundred of sulphuret of carbon
" well purified. The solution is left to rest during eight days,
" and the white of eggs is added to it. When the impure matters
" are deposited, it is poured forth to obtain an almost colorless
" liquid."

[Printed, 4d. No Drawings.]

A.D. 1853, June 9.—N° 1414.

BROOKES, WILLIAM.—(*A communication.*)—" Improvements
" in treating fabrics suitable for floorcloths, covers, and such
" like articles;" these consist " in coating fabrics with saponified
" fatty matters, metallic salts, and dissolved or decomposed india
" rubber, combined together." The proportions to answer well,
are, 50 lbs. of saponaceous matter or soap dissolved in 15 gallons
water at 250 F. to which has been added 25 lbs. sulphuret of
zinc. " The mode of decomposing india rubber which it is pre-
" ferred to adopt is obtained by putting india rubber in small
" pieces into oil (by preference, olive oil), and heating it to a
" temperature of about 300° Fahrenheit until complete solution
" is effected." The india-rubber solution is added to the above
composition in the proportion of ½ a pint of the india rubber
solution at 220° F. to the gallon of composition.

" Colouring matters, and also thickening matters, may be mixed
" with the compounds. The matters which have been found to
" answer well as thickening are whiting, cream of lime, and lamp
" black, to be added to the above in such proportions that, whilst
" it is in a plastic condition by the heat applied to it, it may be
" applied by a brush."

[Printed, 4d. No Drawings.]

A.D. 1853, June 16.—N° 1461.

CHRISTOPHER, WILLIAM, and GIDLEY, GUSTAVUS.—
" Improvements in abstracting sulphur and other matters from
" vulcanized indian-rubber';" these are " removing sulphur from
" vulcanized india-rubber manufactured articles, and also from
" refuse or spoiled vulcanized india-rubber cuttings, parings, or
" old manufactured articles, and of redissolving the same for new
" purposes." This is effected by " macerating the vulcanized
" india rubber in a hot solution of carbonated alkali, or in a
" solution of hydrate of lime, or in hot water in which caustic

" lime is suspended, till, through the action of the alkali or of the
" lime, the requisite quantity of sulphur is abstracted; that is,
" either as much sulphur withdrawn as reduces the relative pro-
" portions of the sulphur and the caoutchouc to those required
" for any special purpose, or so far removes the sulphur as to
" leave the residual material in a condition to be acted on by the
" usual solvents or softeners of caoutchouc, so as to adapt it for
" reformation into manufactured articles, and of being revul-
" canized with sulphur or another material if required." "To
" render vulcanized manufactured articles or the refuse more soft
" and pliable, they may be advantageously washed in a solution
" of water and fullers' earth."
[Printed, 4d. No Drawings.]

A.D. 1853, June 20.—N° 1508.

DEFEVER, CHARLES LOUIS.—(*Provisional protection only.*)—
" An improved preparation for lubricating machinery." It consists of a composition " principally of colza oil and caoutchouc or
" india rubber, which is dissolved therein by being submitted
" to a high temperature." "The oil is heated in a suitable
" vessel to the required temperature, and when the caoutchouc is
" added it will in a short time be completely dissolved; after
" which, while the mixture is still hot, it must be filtered so as to
" remove the impurities. The preparation will then be fit for
" use."
[Printed, 4d. No Drawings.]

A.D. 1853, July 2.—N° 1592.

BROOMAN, RICHARD ARCHIBALD.—(*A communication from
François Perroncel.*)—" Certain machinery for converting caout-
" chouc into circular blocks or cylinders, and for manufacturing
" the same into sheets." " The caoutchouc is first freed from
" impurities and foreign matters by any process now adopted for
" such purpose, and is then fed in between two iron cylinders
" or rollers, heated by currents of steam, hot water, or other heat-
" ing medium. The rollers are caused to revolve and give out, on
" the opposite side, a thick sheet of caoutchouc, which is led on
" to a small roller termed the gathering roller, the axis of which
" is free to rise in a slot in the frame of the apparatus, while it is
" prevented rising too rapidly by means of a weighted lever

" pressing on the upper surface thereof. Immediately under the
" gathering roller is a hollow fixed roller, heated in the inside."
" Both the gathering roller and fixed roller are caused to revolve,
" and the caoutchouc winds itself round the upper gathering
" roller in the form of a solid mass or cylinder; the pres-
" sure exerted on the gathering roller, together with the heat
" from the fixed heated roller, causing adhesion between the
" several thicknesses, at the same time the pressure forces or
" squeezes out any globules of air that may exist in the caout-
" chouc." "When a cylinder of sufficient size has been thus
" obtained, it is transferred to another machine, together with the
" gathering roller; or it may be mounted upon a separate axis.
" It is then caused to revolve in front of a fixed knife or blade,
" which slices or cuts off a continuous length of the caoutchouc in
" sheets varying in thickness with the setting of the knife, which
" slides in a bed, and can be regulated as required."

[Printed, 8d. Drawing.]

A.D. 1853, July 15.—N° 1690.

GOODYEAR, CHARLES.—" Improvements in the manufacture
" of brushes and substitutes for bristles;" these are, "forming
" the handles and backs of brushes by combining india rubber
" with sulphur, with or without other matters, and subjecting the
" compound to heat till the same is changed into a hard sub-
" stance; and the making of substitutes for bristles consists of
" forcing such compound through perforations in metal plates,
" so as to obtain the same, when subjected to heat, in a state to
" be used as bristles." "The best compound for the purpose
" is two parts india rubber, and one part sulphur." "The
" temperature of the bath is to be raised gradually to about
" 230° of Fahrenheit in about half an hour, at which heat it is
" desirable to retain the compound for about one and a half
" hours, when the heat is again to be raised gradually to 295° to
" 305° of Fahrenheit, say in about four hours."

[Printed, 4d. No Drawings.]

A.D. 1853, July 15.—N° 1693.

GOODYEAR, CHARLES.—" Improvements in the manufacture
" of pens, pencils, and instruments used when writing, marking,
" and drawing;" these are employing india rubber (caoutchouc)

" in constructing or making pens, pencils, and instruments used
" when writing, marking, and drawing," by combining "india
" rubber with sulphur, with or without other matters," and
subjecting "the same to heat to obtain a hard substance;" also
combining "slate, powder, or matters ('porcelain for white slates')
" with india rubber," and thus obtaining "sheets or surfaces,"
" to be written on with ordinary slate pencil, and for making
" artificial slate pencil;" also forming or making "the articles
" or parts of the articles above mentioned by employing such
" compounds."

The india-rubber compound is held between glass surfaces and heated in the bath gradually to 230° F. in about half an hour and kept so for 1½ hours, then brought gradually to about 295° to 300° F. for 4 hours.

[Printed, 4d. No Drawings.]

A.D. 1853, July 15.—N° 1694.

GOODYEAR, CHARLES.—" Improvements in preparing india
" rubber;" these are, "subjecting india rubber in a divided
" state to an alkaline or acid process to cleanse the same of im-
" purities." The india-rubber is cut in gieces, "by preference, in
" thin slices, which are put into a washing or fulling machine
" with water thickened with lime, flour, or other fine matter, for
" preventing the pieces of india rubber adhering when they are
" beaten, by which means some of the impurities are separated."
" The pieces of india rubber are next subjected to chopping or
" cutting to reduce the same to a grannular state, which is
" believed to be best done by means of machinery similer to what
" is used in paper making, employing solutions of potash or lime
" or strong acid, which will decompose the bark and foreign
" matters."

[Printed, 4d. No Drawings.]

A.D. 1853, August 13.—N° 1904.

JOHNSON, JOHN HENRY.—(*A communication from Louis François Alexandre Deseille*).—(*Provisional protection only.*)—
" Improvements in the manufacture or treatment of gutta percha,
" and in the application thereof." This consists, in reference to this subject, of " a peculiar preparation of gutta percha for render-
" ing it either solid or liquid, and consists in the application of a
" carburet of hydrogen for liquifying it, and of any colouring

" powder, which is kneaded into it when it is required to be
" solidified." "The carburet is prepared from oil of tar." "By
" the aid of this liquid gutta percha may be readily dissolved,
" either warm or cold." For solidifying gutta percha, a coloring
powder is kneaded into it, and the mass is then passed between
suitable rollers.

[Printed, 4d. No Drawings.]

A.D. 1853, August 26.—N° 1982.

DE VARROC, EUGENE.—"Certain means of depriving caout-
" chouc of all unpleasant odour, and of imparting to it various
" agreeable perfumes." This consists, first, in exposing caoutchouc
or articles coated with it " in baths containing in solution, infu-
" sions, essences, decoctions, extracts, &c., of such vegetable
" matters as flowers, plants, and roots." The plants, roots, and
flowers are verbena, flowers of lavender, " the root of the whorl-
" flowered bent grass," camomile flowers, elder flowers, elder
root, " root of Florentine iris or fleur de lis " in powder, ginger
root, essence of birch tree, essences "composed with camphor
" on an alcohol base; also camphogenic acid, as it is called by
" Mr. Dumas, may be employed." "Tamarind leaves, black tea-
" leaves, leaves of various laurels, and orange trees, and sage,
" all of which may enter into the different solutions as bases, or
" combined with other leaves, grains, berries, and fruits which
" would be too tedious to enumerate here, but which nevertheless "
are claimed as contributing to the results. " Decoctions of these
" substances are made of certain strengths and are mingled
" together in given proportions; in some instances alcohol is
" added, and also small quantities of hydrochloric and sulphuric
" acid, and English honey and essential oil of lavender;" second,
" subjecting caoutchouc, or articles costed with caoutchouc, to
" the action of currents of air or vapours;" third, "immersing
" the caoutchouc, or articles coated with caoutchouc, in baths
" containing solutions of lime." " For some purposes two of the
" processes are combined."

[Printed, 10d. Drawings.]

A.D. 1853, August 30.—N° 2007.

GOODYEAR, CHARLES.—(*Partly a communication.*)—(*Provisional protection only*).— " Improvements in combining india

" rubber with other matters for writing, marking, and drawing."
It consists in "combining plumbago (black lead) with india
" rubber and sulphur, and subjecting the same to heat, in order
" to produce a change by which a compound is obtained, which
" when made up into pencils, or other form, is suitable for
" writing, marking, and drawing."

[Printed, 4d. No Drawings.]

A.D. 1853, August 30.—N° 2008.

GOODYEAR, CHARLES.—" Improvements in rules, graduated
" scales, and measuring instruments." These are making the
above of the hard substance obtained by mixing "india rubber
" and sulphur with or without other matters," and subjecting the
mixture to heat, in preference, as follows :—" Mix two parts by
" weight of india rubber, and one part by weight of sulphur,
" with or without a small quantity of coloring matter ;" " add
" no other foreign matter." " Roll the compound into sheets of
" the thickness desired, and subject such sheets to heat between
" surfaces of glass or of oiled metal, applying the heat gradually,
" bringing up the temperature to about 300° of Fahrenheit in
" about six hours, which may be done in any convenient man-
" ner." " The sheets having been allowed to cool are then cut
" and worked into the desired forms for rules, graduated scales,
" and measuring instruments desired. In order to give greater
" strength, particularly (to) those which are jointed, insert strips of
" thin metal finely perforated, or of wire cloth, in the middle of
" the india rubber compound, from which the instruments are
" formed. This is done before heating, and serves not only to
" strengthen but also to assist in forming the joints of such
" rules and measuring instruments, the sheet of metal being
" left without perforation at the parts which are to form the
" joint."

[Printed, 4d. No Drawings.]

A.D. 1853, August 30.—N° 2009.

GOODYEAR, CHARLES.—" Improvements in the manufacture
" and ornamenting or coating of articles when compounds con-
" taining india rubber are used." These are "ornamenting or
" coating articles composed of india rubber and sulphur (with
" or without other matters) by electro deposits of metal thereon,"

The surfaces to be coated "must be rendered conductive." This
may be done by dusting plumbago or powered metal "over the
" matter when in a plastic state, and pressing it into the sur-
" faces when moulding, and by retaining the same in moulds
" till the process of heat has been performed." " In addition to
" so applying plumbago or powdered metal, and pressing it into
" the surfaces, some plumbago or powdered metal may be com-
" bined with the india rubber when in a plastic state," or " com-
" bine the plumbago or powdered metal with india-rubber cement,
" and apply a coat or coatings to the surfaces or parts of the
" surfaces where electro deposits of metal are to take place."
Also, " driving in pins of metal about the parts desired to be
"‑coated, in addition to applying plumbago over the surface.
" according to the device desired to be obtained in deposited
" metal, by which means the coating of metal which is produced
" will be held secure by reason of the pins."
[Printed, 4d. No Drawings.]

A.D. 1853, October 18.—N° 2404.

RIDER, EMORY.—(*Partly a communication.*)—" Improvements in
" the manufacture or treatment of gutta percha, being improve-
" ments upon the invention secured to him by Letters Patent,
" dated the 20th day of July 1852." These are, improvements
in No. 14,230, Old Law, for " treating gutta percha by the action
" of heat, so as to expel the volatizable ingredients therefrom,
" and render the same fit for the processes of vulcanization," and
consists in "adding to the raw gutta percha a small quantity of
" sulphur, or any equivalent of sulphur, before subjecting the
" gutta percha to the preliminary heating process," by which
means " a lower temperature produces an effect equal to that of
" a higher temperature when the gutta percha alone is treated."
" One part of sulphur, or the equivalent thereof, added to eighty
" parts of gutta percha when separated from its solid impurities,
" is suitable for effecting this purpose." " The sulphur or hypo-
" sulphite of lead or zinc, or the artificial sulphuret of lead, or
" other equivalent of sulphur, should be thoroughly mixed or
" incorporated with the gutta percha by passing the gum and the
" dryers repeatedly between metallic rollers heated to a tempera-
" ture sufficient to make the gutta percha very soft, and easily
" kneaded or worked." " The incorporated material having been
" ground, is then placed in a strong metal vessel or vessels, care

" being taken, however, that the material does not occupy more
" than one third of the capacity of the vessels, so as to leave due
" allowance for the swelling or expansion of the material when
" under the action of heat." The material is then exposed to a
" temperature of about two hundred and ninety degrees Fahren-
" heit, for a space of about three hours."
[Printed, 4d. No Drawings.]

A.D. 1853, October 19.—N° 2406.

GIDLEY, Gustavus, and MUSCHAMP, John Bell.—(Provisional protection only.)—"An improvement in making india-
" rubber solution for waterpoofing cloths or other articles without
" the offensive smell produced by the use of naptha, turpentine,
" oils, &c." It is as follows:—" Procure a vessel in the shape
" of a bell, composed of iron or any other wire interwoven like the
" meshes of a net; into this put the quantity of rubber required;
" then set fire to one of the pieces; in a short time the oily or
" fatty matter exudes through the holes into a receiver placed
" under. Then take twelve pounds and put it into an iron or other
" vessel, place it over a fire, adding india rubber, gutta percha,
" or any gums required; after it is dissolved add sulphur and
" common salt or saltpetre, the quantity of which will depend
" upon the nature of the work required. Then spread it upon
" the cloth, and, if required, on both sides," "place it upon a
" table heated, which draws it through," "then proceed to put
" on " "different colours."
[Printed, 4d. No Drawings.]

A.D. 1853, October 21.—N° 2430.

JOHNSON, John Henry.—(A communication from Jacques Lefevre.)—(Provisional protection only.)—"Improvements in the
" treatment or manufacture of gutta percha, and in the applica-
" cations thereof." This consists, in reference to this subject, as
follows;—"The raw material is cleansed and purified by being
" passed through a mill having indentations or teeth formed
" within a fixed chamber, and similar indentations on the surface
" of a revolving cone working inside this chamber; the gutta
" percha is passed between these toothed surfaces, and falls on two
" toothed rollers beneath and between which it is drawn by the
" revolutions." The stringy or tough parts are fumigated and
" rendered white, so that it may receive any color required "

" For liquifying gutta percha, carburet of hydrogen is employed.
" From the distillation of pit coal an oil is obtained, which is well
" washed and allowed to rest 48 hours on a (" base salifiable ")
" salt base; it is then distilled." " One application of this
" liquified gutta percha is the construction of printing rollers,
" which are composed of equal parts of glue, treacle, and dissolved
" gutta percha ; but these proportions may be varied according
" to the nature of the ink employed." "Liquid gutta percha
" thus prepared, mixed with gluten, gum lac, and copale, makes
" a varnish which adheres with great affinity to glass or metals,
" preserving the latter from oxidation or from the action of
" acids. For applying the same to wood, a certain amount of
" pitch is added. The gutta percha may be solidified by being
" heated whilst in a soft state, having added to it a solution of
" the gutta percha obtained by the carburet of hydrogen as above
" described, when the mass is passed through rollers to render it
" perfectly homogenous."

[Printed, 4d. No Drawings.]

A.D. 1853, November 15.—N° 2648.

FRY, JOSEPH.—" Improvements in preparing solvents for india-
" rubber and gutta percha, and in rendering waterproof fabrics
" free from odour." These are, first, " distilling the solvents of
" india rubber and gutta percha with those matters present or
" combined therewith," " introduce india rubber or gutta percha
" with the solvent into a still, and then distil over the solvent;"
" four to six ounces of india rubber or gutta percha (according to
" the state of impurity of the solvent) dissolved in each gallon is
" sufficient for the purpose." " The solvents usually employed
" for such purposes are turpentine and coal naptha, or coal oil,
" and either of these may be taken in the crude state, and have
" dissolved therein india rubber or gutta percha, and then
" distilled ; or the crude solvent may be distilled, first, without
" india rubber or gutta percha being present, and afterwards be
" combined with india rubber or gutta percha, and again distilled
" or rectified." " Removing the odour of articles fabricated of
" india rubber or gutta percha, in which solvents have been
" used," " by submitting them to the free action of steam on all
" parts of the surfaces, preferring that the steam chest or chamber
" should be of iron, and it is desirable also to line the whole interior
" with flannel, dry at the commencement of the process."

[Printed, 4d. No Drawings.]

A.D. 1853, December 1.—N° 2798.

JOHNSON, JOHN HENRY. — (*A communication from Charles Eugène François Guibal and Louis Philippe Bernard Edouard Cumenge.*)—" Improvements in the treatment or manufacture of
" caoutchouc." This invention relates " to a system or mode of
" preventing the waste by evaporation of the volatile ingredients
" employed for dissolving the caoutchouc, preparatory to, or in
" the course of its manufacture, and consists in traversing webs
" of cloth containing layers of soft caoutchouc through closed
" chambers, having a refrigerating top and a heated bottom
" over which the cloth is traversed." " The heat produces the
" evaporation required, and the vapour on coming in contact
" with the cold top of the chamber, is condensed, and runs into
" suitable gutters, whence it pours into a main trough or other
" receptacle."

[Printed, 6*d*. Drawing.]

A.D. 1853, December 1.—N° 2799.

JOHNSON, JOHN HENRY.—(*A communication from Charles Eugène François Guibal.*)—" Certain applications of vulcanized
" india rubber." These applications are to " curry combs, brushes
" of all kinds, and artificial cloth." The caoutchouc is mixed with
" a composition of sulphur and oxyde of zinc, and formed into a
" sheet, which is then moulded by suitable moulds into the form
" required, being heated by steam stoves or other means." " In
" manufacturing curry combs, the india rubber is moulded on
" one side into a rough surface, and the other side left plain for
" the attachment of a stiff and rigid handle or back, which is
" fitted with a strap to secure it to the hand." " In making
" tooth and other brushes, the bristles or hairs are replaced by
" the employment of a series of tufts of india rubber formed
" like bristles." " These tufts are inserted into the foundation or
" back of the brush when in the mould, such back being com-
" posed also of india rubber, and attached to any suitable holder,"
" The cloth composed of this material may be made either single
" or double, that is, with one or two faces. In the manufacture
" of single cloth, a cotton, wool, or other fabric is employed, which
" is thinly coated with india rubber, incorporated with any
" material conducive to its eventual vulcanization. The layer is
" then rendered adhesive by heating, and a nap of any kind of

" color desired is laid on to its surface, the adhesion to which is
" afterwards rendered complete by pressure." " The same pro-
" cess is simply repeated for double-faced cloth ;" " in addition
" to the vulcanizing mixture, coloring powders are employed,"
" The dark colours are black ; carbonate of lead may be employed;
" and for the lighter tints, oxide of zinc is used. For reds, blues,
" &c., vermillion, ultramarine, &c. may be employed."
[Printed, 6d. Drawing.]

A.D. 1853, December 16.—N° 2933.

GOODYEAR, CHARLES. — (*Partly a communication.*) — " Im-
" provements in the treatment and manufacture of india-rubber."
These are, " combining vulcanized or changed india-rubber with
" raw or unvulcanized india-rubber." "The old or waste vul-
" canized or changed india-rubber is first reduced to a finely
" divided state before it is mixed and combined with india-rubber
" which has not been vulcanized." "This reduction may be done
" in any convenient manner;" but it is preferred to employ " a
" paper engine for the purpose, and to treat the india-rubber
" therein in like manner to that in which rags and other matters
" are reduced to pulp." " If the vulcanized india-rubber consists
" of pieces of sheets, they may be at once introduced into the
" engine with water, and reduced to a fine state of division. If
" the vulcanized or changed india-rubber is in lumps or blocks "
then "reduce them by cutting them into slices." "When the
" vulcanized india-rubber has been reduced to as fine a state of
" division as may be," "mix the same with raw india-rubber by
" masticating them together." "The combined product of india-
" rubber and vulcanized india-rubber" obtained "is then to have
" mixed with it as much sulphur (or matters which will give off
" products of sulphur on applying heat,) as would be used for
" vulcanizing the quantity of raw or fresh india-rubber that is
" contained in the combined mass, and the compound is then in
" a state suitable to be rolled into sheets or made up into articles
" and subjected to the process of heat."
[Printed, 4d. No Drawings.]

A.D. 1853, December 16.—N° 2936.

WAITHMAN, ROBERT WILLIAM.—" Improvements in belts or
" bands for driving machinery for use in mines and for other

" purposes." These are, in reference to this subject, using "cer-
"tain substances and compounds for coating and cementing"
tubes, and also "for coating the exteriors of bands woven solid,
"of linen or other fibrous materials." These substances, &c.
are as follows:—A composition, formed of india-rubber and
ground peat or bark; gutta percha or caoutchouc dissolved in
gas tar.

[Printed, 4d. No Drawings.]

A.D. 1853, December 31.—N° 3045.

SOREL, STANISLAS TRANQUILE MODESTE.—"Certain im-
"proved compositions, to be employed as substitutes for caout-
"chouc, gutta percha, and certain fatty bodies." This consists,
in reference to this subject. The principal bases of the compositions are the following substances,—"colophony, or common
"resin; bitumen, or natural pitch, or the pitch obtained from
"gas works; fixed resin oils; gutta percha; hydrated lime and
"water;" "natural or vulcanized coautchouc;" "pipe clay, or
"other like argillaceous earths;" "soft or hard alkaline soap;"
"bees'-wax." Various compositions are made by mixing more
or less of these substances together, and in different proportions,
according to the result required.

[Printed, 4d. No Drawings.]

1854.

A.D. 1854, January 5.—N° 23.

WHITE, DAVID BLAIR.—"Improvements in the manufacture of
"waterproof fabrics, and of waterproof bags and other articles."
This consists as follows:—A composition of two pounds of
common dark resin of commerce dissolved in five gallons coal tar
oil, and one pound eight ounces of pitch solution, and four ounces
of india-rubber solution is in some instances added thereto.
Steep the canvas or material in this for about five days; take it
out, and while damp rub into it oxide or oxichloride of lead, or
lime, or both; when dry "repeat the operations," only using a
stronger solution, say "five pounds of resin to five gallons of

" oil." In the manufacture of the bags, in addition to the above,
it is preferred to give them a " coating of a mixture of pitch and
" india-rubber solution." They may also be covered with canvas
saturated with tar oil, the interior washed with " chloride of lime
" or other soluble chloride," and in some instances lined "with
" thin sheet gutta percha, as manufactured by the Gutta Percha
" Company."

[Printed, 4d. No Drawings.]

A.D. 1854, February 3.—N° 275.

MEEUS, PIERRE JOSEPH.—" Improvements in the manufacture
" of threads from or with gutta percha, and in ornamenting the
" same." These are, first, " by cutting thin sheets of gutta
" percha into strips, and twisting such strips either singly or two
" or more together with the aid of heat and compression, so as to
" form round threads." Second, " by twisting or twining a strip
" or strips of gutta percha round a thread or core of textile ma-
" terial or metal, or by passing such thread or core through a
" solution of gutta percha." Third, " ornamenting gutta-percha
" threads " " by the direct application thereto of metal leaf, metal
" powder, or other substance in powder, either before or after such
" threads have been woven or otherwise worked into fabrics."

[Printed, 4d. No Drawings.]

A.D. 1854, February 6.—N° 292.

TRUMBLE, PETER. — " Improvements in paper hangings."
This consists, in reference to this subject, in " manufacturing
" paper hangings with oil colors instead of water colors," as
follows :—" Take the same description of paper as is commonly
" used by paper stainers," and " coat or cover the surface thereof
" with a composition made with the following ingredients, matters,
" or substances ; namely, a solution of india rubber, tallow, japan,
" or boiled oil, soap, and size ;" 2 ozs. solution of india rubber,
2 ozs. tallow, 1 pint japan or boiled oil, ¾ths lb. soap, and 2 galls.
clear size. " These ingredients are well mixed and incorporated
" together " " in any convenient manner."

[Printed, 4d. No Drawings.]

A.D. 1854, February 22.—N° 427.

ASSANTI, DAMIANO. — " A means of rendering porous sub-
" stances waterproof." This consists, in reference to this subject

as follows :—Take " one part by weight of dry gutta percha, cut
" it up into small pieces, and add four parts of sulphuret of
" carbon;" "keep this mixture at a temperature of about 77°
" Fahrenheit, and agitate it at least six times in twenty-four
" hours. In two days the solution will be ready for use." The
solution is placed in any suitable closed vessel which will admit
of being heated in a water bath. Other solvents of the gutta
percha may be used.

[Printed, 4d. No Drawings.]

A.D. 1854, February 24.—N° 442.

RYDER, WILLIAM, and RYDER, JAMES. — "An improved
" composition applicable to coating metals." "Dissolve two
" pounds of gutta percha and four pounds of common resin, or
" tar, or pitch, and one ounce of gum shellac, in four gallons of
" coal naptha; these ingredients are placed in a suitable vessel,
" and heated to about one hundred and sixty degrees Fahrenheit,
" until the solids are completely dissolved." "It may in some
" cases be preferable to substitute asphaltum for the common
" resin, tar, or pitch above mentioned, and impure benzine or
" other volatile hydrocarbons obtained from bituminous shales or
" schists may be substituted for the coal naptha." "When this
" improved composition is applied as a paint, colouring matter
" must be added to give the required tint or colour."

[Printed, 4d. No Drawings.]

A.D. 1854, March 27.—N° 705.

FORTY, ARTHUR EDWARD, and HAYNES, WILLIAM.—(*Provisional protection only.*)—" A new composition of materials suitable
" for mouldings, and for most purposes for which leather and
" gutta percha have been or may be employed."—This consists in reference to this subject "in forming a composition of the
" more fleshy parts of hides and leather (known as curriers'
" shavings), tan, gutta percha, or caoutchouc, or gutta percha
" and caoutchouc and shellac;" and the composition is prepared
as follows :—" Take curriers' shavings and tan, and reduce them
" to small particles by a tearing machine;" "separate dust and
" other refuse matter from the leather shavings and tan by rubbing
" them over a perforated plate," and "continue rubbing them
" until they become soft and spongy; this mixture is then dried,
" and thoroughly saturated with a solution of oil and spirits of

" turpentine;" "next mix in a separate vessel gutta percha or
" caoutchouc, or gutta percha and caoutchouc and shellac,
" reduced into small particles, and boil the whole in water,"
" which heat to from 190° to 230° Fahrenheit, and stir the mass
" the whole time it is kept boiling." "Then evaporate the water,
" and add the mixture of leather cuttings, tan, oil, and turpen-
" tine in proportions varying with the qualities the composition
" may be ultimately required to assume, and cause the whole
" mass to become thoroughly amalgamated in a masticating or
" other suitable machine." " Prepare a solution of gum, com-
" mon salt, and sulphate of ammonia, dissolved and boiled in
" water, and knead and work the composition therein for from 15
" to 30 minutes." ."The composition is thus formed, and may
" be reduced to sheets by passing it through heated rollers."
"When the new composition is required to be of a yielding
" nature," "add a portion of carbonate of soda, and saccharine
" or gummy matter, to the solution of gum, salt, and sulphate
" of ammonia." " When the composition is required to be hard,
" add a greater quantity of the leather shavings and tan."

[Printed, 4d. No Drawings.]

A.D. 1854, March 27.—N° 706.

ARCHEREAU, HENRI ADOLPHE. — (*Provisional protection only.*)—" Certain improvements in treating powders of charcoal,
" coke, coal, peat, and generally all matters obtained by the car-
" bonization of mineral, vegetable, and animal substances, & in
." applying the said powders to useful purposes." These consist in
" forming from the carbonaceous substances above mentioned a
" plastic material of variable consistencies, and possessing many
" properties in common with gutta percha." "The powder is
" mixed in different proportions, according to the use of the
" matter, with one or more of the following substances: coal tar
" or natural 'resin of Bastenner,' residue of coal tar, pitch,
" resinous and bituminous substances, gums, oils, varnishes,
" glues, fatty and ceramic substances, and is then subjected to a
" heat which renders the substance viscous or liquid." "To
" obtain a substance which can be laminated and drawn out in a
" moderate temperature, mix about 100 parts residue of coal tar
" or 'natural coal tar of Bastenner,' with 150 to 200 parts of
" coal powder, and a little linseed oil, if required." "The articles
" made of this substance may be galvanized, or covered with a

" film of metal." To produce a harder material, "mix with the
" coal powder either talc or pulverized earth, silica, alumina, or
" any other substance suitable for that purpose."

[Printed, 4d. No Drawings.]

A.D. 1854, March 30.—N° 736.

WILLIS, EDWARD COOPER.—(*Provisional protection only.*)—
" An improved mode of manufacturing gutta percha into sheets."
" It relates to the manufacture of sheets of gutta percha suitable
" for medical purposes." In " sheets hitherto prepared for such
" purposes," " great tenacity has been obtained in the direction
" of the grain or fibre, but when subject to strain in the opposite
" direction the sheets would readily split into ribbons, and their
" use has consequently been abandoned." In order to remove
this objection, "take sheets of purified gutta percha, such as are
" now procurable in the market, and of the one eighth of an inch
" (more or less) in thickness," and " subject them for a time to
" a bath of heated coal-tar, naptha," then " remove the sheets,
" and subject them to a rolling operation in the direction of their
" length and breadth, until they are reduced to the desired thick-
" ness." "Next drive off the naptha by exposure to the air or
" otherwise, and the sheets will then be ready for use."

[Printed, 4d. No Drawings.]

A.D. 1854, April 24.—N° 939.

NEWTON, WILLIAM EDWARD. — (*A communication.*)—"The
" application of a new or improved material or substance to the
" construction of certain parts of machinery." This material may
consist as follows :—" One part by weight of sulphur to two parts
" by weight of india rubber or gutta percha, or one part by weight
" of india rubber and of gum shellac to one part by weight of
" sulphur," applying the necessary heat. When lightness is required, introduce "cork dust or chips, sawdust, cotton waste, or
" other vegetable fibre, in   proportion, say, of about one part
" by weight, more or less, to two parts of the other combined
" ingredients." Sometimes " from seventy-five to one hundred
" per cent." "of plumbago or black lead is added during the
" manufacture of the component parts of the material."

[Printed, 4d. No Drawings.]

A.D. 1854, May 2.—N° 984.

NEWTON, WILLIAM EDWARD.—(*A communication.*)—(*Letters Patent void for want of Final Specification.*)—" Improvements in
" moulding, preparing, and finishing articles and fabrics made of
" compounds of caoutchouc, gutta percha, and other substances."
—These consist as follows :—" The sheets or masses of caoutchouc
" or other material are first softened with naptha, spirits of turpen-
" tine, or other solvent, and then pressed into forms or moulds,
" in which is placed tin or other metal foil of about the substance
" of writing paper; the foil is pressed into the mould with the
" india rubber or other material, and is taken out of the mould
" with the article which is formed therein by pressure or other-
" wise. The foil is left upon the article, which is then submitted
" to the second process, viz., that of curing or preparing and
" finishing. For this purpose the articles are heated in any con-
" venient and suitable manner to a temperature of about 300°
" Fahrenheit, during which process the foil will prevent the
" article from getting out of shape, and when the process is
" finished the foil may be easily removed from the article." " For
" flexible articles and fabrics no foil will be required, and it will
" only be necessary to submit the articles to the finishing process."
" For dark articles or fabrics they may be dipped in a hot bath
" of nitro-muriatic acid for about half a minute, after which
" they are immersed in an alkaline solution to neutralize the
" acid." " This process will affect the color, and therefore if the
" articles be of a light color," " expose them to the action of
" chlorine gas for about half an hour, after which they will be
" found quite prepared and finished."

[Printed, 4d. No Drawings.]

A.D. 1854, May 23.—N° 1155.

JOHNSON, WILLIAM.—(*A communication.*)—(*Provisional protection not allowed.*)—" Improvements in the treatment of organic
" matters, and in the application of the products thereof."—It
relates "to the obtainment and manufacture of various useful
" products, more particularly of the caoutchouc and gutta-percha
" class, &c. Gluten, fibrine, lignine, gelatine, albumen, caseine,
" and gum dextrine," and other organic compounds, are to be
treated with " cholic, tannic, gallic, mimotannic, and generally
" similar acids." " Such new compounds may be used for all or

" most of the purposes for which gutta percha and caoutchouc
" can be employed; they can also be vulcanized, and may be
" mixed with caoutchouc and gutta percha."
[Printed, 4d. No Drawings.]

A.D. 1854, July 28.—N° 1665.

JOHNSON, RICHARD.—" Improvements in coating and insu-
" lating wire." These are " coating or covering wire with gutta
" percha, caoutchouc, tar, pitch, asphaltum, resin, or wax, in coal
" naptha, or in any other suitable fluid." "These solutions may
" be prepared in various ways." The wire can be coated in various
ways with solutions of the above substances mixed together "in
" various proportions," but preference is given to a mixture made
as follows :—" One volume of tar solution, one volume and a half
" of gutta percha solution, half a volume of caoutchouc solution;
" or, one made of one volume of coal tar solution, and one volume
" and a half of a solution of gutta percha, containing five pounds
" ten ounces per ten gallons of coal naptha."
[Printed, 4d. No Drawings.]

A.D. 1854, July 31.—N° 1687.

NEWTON, ALFRED VINCENT.—(*A communication.*)—" An im-
" proved mode of extracting sulphur from compounds of india
" rubber and sulphur." In preference, the following is the mode
pursued :—The vulcanized rubber is reduced into as small pieces
as it can be, and steeped "in camphine from two to fourteen
" days," depending on the nature of the compound; after this it
is put into a still with camphine, and heat applied for from three
quarters of an hour to two hours. As the camphine distils, a
fresh supply is kept up. "With the camphine should also be put
" from fifteen to twenty-five per cent. of sulphuric ether, and
" about five per cent. of alcohol, to be gradually added as the
" camphine is added." "After the sulphur has been extracted
" and the gum restored to its natural condition (which is easily
" recognized by workmen experienced in the working of india
" rubber and allied gums, notwithstanding its soft state), it
" is removed from the still, put into flat pans, and dried by
" exposure to natural or a gentle artificial heat." "When thus
" restored, the gum can be re-vulcanized or used for a variety of
" purposes, like the native gum." "The object of using alcohol
" in the above process is to prevent the gum when restored from

" being tacky, as it is termed, but when the tacky condition of
" the gum is not objectionable the alcohol may be dispensed
" with; and as the object of using alcohol is to prevent the gum
" from being tacky when restored, any equivalent chemical agent,
" such as fusel oil, may be substituted, but alcohol has been
" ascertained by experiment to be the best." "The office of the
" sulphuric ether is to extract the sulphur from the gum, which
" it does by reason of its affinity therefor; any other chemical
" agent having equivalent properties, such as chloroform, natron,
" kali, or benzole, may therefore be substituted for the sulphuric
" ether; but with this as with the other agents, those first speci-
" fied are preferred, on account of efficiency and economy," &c., &c.

[Printed, 4d. No Drawings.]

A.D. 1854, August 5.—N° 1719.

STANSBURY, Charles Frederick.—(*A communication from Robert Arthur.*)—"Improved air-tight vessels."

In carrying out this, in sealing the covers a cement may be made by adding 1½ ozs. of gutta percha to 1 lb. of common resin melted and kept so until all the gutta percha is dissolved.

For vessels intended for transportation the gutta percha is increased to 3 ozs. to 1 lb. of resin.

[Printed, 8d. Drawing.]

A.D. 1854, August 8.—N° 1739.

OGG, Alexander.—" A new composition applicable to the
" cementing of leather," made as follows:—"Take a bottle
" containing two ounces and a half of bisulphate of carbon,"
to which add "one half of an ounce of gutta percha, one eighth
" of an ounce of common resin, and one eighth of an ounce of
" asphaltum, and leave this mixture until these materials or
" ingredients have become dissolved by the bisulphate of carbon.
" Then take another bottle containing two ounces and a half of
" bisulphate of carbon," to which add "one half of an ounce of
" gutta percha, one eighth of an ounce of common resin, and
" one eighth of an ounce of asphaltum." "These materials or
" ingredients, being left to become dissolved by the bi-sulphate
" of carbon," are afterwards mixed with the contents of the first
" bottle." "The whole composition thus formed becomes ready
" for use in the course of a few hours, sooner or later, according

" to the state of the atmosphere at the time when it is made."
" It should be kept in a bottle well corked."
[Printed, 4d. No Drawings.]

A.D. 1854, August 14.—N° 1767.

STONEHAM, JAMES TOLPUTT.—(*Provisional protection only.*)
—" Improvements in the mode or method of rendering woven
" fabrics waterproof, and in the substance or composition used
" for the purpose." This consists, in reference to this subject, in
making "a composition of tar, oil, resin, bees' wax, and caout-
" chouc, or solvents of caoutchouc," and mixing the same "with
" any felted fibrous matter." "In some cases, especially with
" very low kinds of fabrics, instead of the felted fibrous matter,"
" use paper, the same width and length of the cloth or fabric to
" be waterproofed."
[Printed, 4d. No Drawings.]

A.D. 1854, August 18.—N° 1819.

JOHNSON, WILLIAM.—(*A communication.*)—" Improvements
" in moulding or shaping articles of vulcanized caoutchouc."
These are in making snuff-boxes, knife handles, combs, or similar
articles. "The moulds are previously prepared by having their
" interior surfaces slightly coated with tallow or other similar
" fatty or oily matter." "When a sufficient quantity of material
" has been placed in the mould to give the required thickness to
" the article to be shaped, the mould is closed and placed in or
" under a powerful press." "The mould having been sufficiently
" pressed is removed from the press, and placed between two
" thick plates of red-hot iron, and the mould between these red-
" hot plates is then again introduced into the press, and the
" pressure is increased in proportion as the mould gets heated.
" When these red-hot plates have imparted sufficient heat to
" the mould, it is withdrawn from the press and plunged into
" cold water, and allowed to remain there until cool. The article
" is then taken out of the mould, perfectly shaped to the form
" and contour of the mould, and having a high degree of com-
" pactness, solidity, and polish." "To manufacture articles of
" variegated colours, veined, striped, or marbled, scraps or figures
" cut out of colored india-rubber are first introduced into the
" mould, or mineral colors or other colored substances may be
" employed, and the filings or waste scraps, to form the body of

"the article, are then introduced above them," and other layers are introduced. "It is proposed to apply this process of mould-
"ing to the joining or soldering of articles composed of hard
"vulcanized india-rubber. For this purpose the broken parts are
"first scraped off, and dust or powder of hard vulcanized india-
"rubber is introduced between the scraped surfaces. The whole
"is then submitted to a high degree of heat and pressure."
[Printed, 4d. No Drawings.]

A.D. 1854, August 18.—N° 1820.

JOHNSON, WILLIAM.—(*A communication.*)—(*Letters Patent void for want of Final Specification.*)—It relates to applying and using "hard rubber" "in the manufacture of hat bodies." The material, when soft, is moulded to the shape required, and vulcanized on the mould. The compound preferred is made up of two pounds of rubber to one pound of sulphur. "Sulphurized
" gutta percha may also be used for a similar purpose."
[Printed, 4d. No Drawings.]

A.D. 1854, August 31.—N° 1908.

DUNLOP, JOHN MACMILLAN.—(*Partly a communication.*)—
"Improvements in machinery or apparatus for preparing, clean-
"ing, and cutting india-rubber and gutta percha." The machine for preparing and cleaning consists of a vessel divided by a partition, in which is caused to revolve a cylinder, the periphery of which is covered with knives, and beneath which is fixed a series of knives keyed into a stationary framing. The vessel has a continuous supply of clean water, &c. In cutting cylindrical blocks of the above substances, "imparting rotary motion thereto
"while cutting, by means of a surface roller or rollers." The cylindrical blocks are mounted upon a roller, in preference, "by
"pressure, and with or without heat or steam." A roller, called
"the surface roller," is placed behind the cylinder covered with the material, which moves it forward to the cutting knife, upon which a stream of water is directed. The arrangements are such that, "should the surface roller " "fail in causing" the cylinder of material to rotate, "its advance towards the knife will also be
"arrested." Below the knife is a wheel, "the periphery of
"which is in contact with the cylindrical block," and "in such
"a position that the centres of the two continue on the same
"plane during the cutting of the material."
[Printed, 1s. Drawings.]

A.D. 1854, October 18.—N° 2231.

COOKE, BENJAMIN FRANKLIN.—(*Provisional protection only.*)
—"An improved mode of caulking ships, applicable also to the
" rendering of roofs waterproof." This consists, in reference to
this subject, in using " an elastic caulking material " "known as
" sponge gum," which "is usually made by introducing alum
" into the ingredients of vulcanized india-rubber, whereby the
" compound is rendered cellular after it has been subjected to
" heat in the well-known manner." "To reduce the cost of the
" india-rubber or other gum used in this elastic compound," it
is advisable to mix therewith fibrous materials or cork cuttings,
" in quantity not sufficient seriously to impair its persistent and
" elastic qualities."

[Printed, 4d. No Drawings.]

A.D. 1854, November 9.—N° 2384.

ROSS, GEORGE.—(*A communication.*)—"Improvements applic-
" able to the manufacture of articles of caoutchouc, or of compo-
" sitions of which caoutchouc forms a component part." These
are working up and moulding " into any desired shape scraps
" and waste pieces of cured or vulcanized rubber," and also " in
" the application of heat, either to india-rubber in its native state,
" or to rubber with the substances commonly used in vulcanizing
" rubber, or to rubber which has once been vulcanized by means
" of steam, the rubber or compound while thus heated being
" pressed into moulds or dies, which come in contact with the
" rubber or compound to be acted upon." "By this means the
" process of curing rubber is greatly facilitated, and vulcanized
" rubber, which has hitherto resisted all attempts to remould it
" may be readily pressed into any desired shape." " By thus
" treating rubber, also many foreign articles, such as scraps of
" cloth, sulphur, white lead, coal or wood tar, or any adhesive
" substance, may be so combined with it as to produce a sub-
" stance which has all the valuable properties of vulcanized india
" rubber, although the greater bulk of it is composed of other
" and cheaper materials." "The induration of the rubber or
" substance thus formed is regulated at pleasure by admitting
" cold water around the moulds and dies in place of the steam,
" and thereby checking the curing of the rubber at any desired
" stage of the process." " The different substances of which the

" articles are to be composed, such as old pieces of vulcanized
" rubber, scraps of cloth, sulphur, white lead, coal tar, &c., are
" first ground or kneaded together, by being passed through
" calender rolls, or by any of the methods commonly practised,
" and then placed in the moulds."

[Printed, 1s. Drawings.]

A.D. 1854, November 10.—N° 2394.

RIMMEL, EUGENE.—(*A communication from Hippolyte Magen.*)
" Improvements in combining matters to be employed in coating
" fabrics and leather, and for other uses, in substitution of india
" rubber." These consist in combining the following matters,
" so as to produce suitable compounds for coating fabrics and
" leather, and for other uses, in substitution of india rubber;"
" for which purposes there are to be melted in rain or in distilled
" water a quantity of alum and sulphate of iron, and then soap
" (made of seal oil and potash by preference) is added. The mix-
" ture is allowed to cool, and is then washed well with pure water.
" The mixture is heated and evaporated briskly to a pasty state.
" Linseed oil, which has been boiled or thickened separately,
" whilst still hot, is mixed therewith, and then some raw or
" unboiled oil is added." "This, when for coating fabrics or
" leather, is to be first applied, and then a second coating is to
" be used, of a compound of the above, thinned with linseed oil;
" and when the colour of the compound is desired to be varied
" from those natural to the compounds, whitening and coloring
" matters, combined with turpentine or essential oil, are added."
" In making more solid compounds, more sulphate of iron is used
" with sulphur, and heat is applied for a longer time."

[Printed, 4d. No Drawings.]

A.D. 1854, November 15.—N° 2418.

BROOMAN, RICHARD ARCHIBALD.—(*A communication.*)—
" Improvements in the manufacture of thread from gutta-percha
" and similar gums; in gilding, silvering, and ornamenting the
" same, before or after being manufactured into fabrics; and in
" machinery and apparatus employed therein." These are " the
" manufacture of thread from gutta percha, caoutchouc, and
" other similar gums," as follows :—" Surround a thread of silk

" with a strip of gutta percha," "place it on a hot plate," plunge
" it in cold water," "then, holding the end of the gutta percha
" and of the silk," "draw them out through the fingers or
" through a draw-plate." "The operation is repeated from the
" point where the gutta percha ceased, until the whole of the silk
" is covered, and the joints are made good, if necessary, by heat
" applied by the hand, or by an iron." To produce a thread of
" gutta percha as above, take a strip or rod of gutta percha, and
" draw it out in a similar manner to the above. To produce "a
" gutta percha thread round a textile thread," the following
apparatus is employed:—" Construct a box, which may be her-
" metically closed, except at the bottom, which is pierced with a
" number of holes, so as to form a draw-plate, with apertures of
" the number and degree of fineness required. Having placed
" through the apertures some threads, say silk threads, with the
" reels placed in the upper part of the box, gutta percha, softened
" by heat, is put in the box, which it is made to about half fill,
" and the box is filled up with hot water. The cover of the box
" is hermetically fixed at the edges, but contains through the
" centre a pipe, which communicates with a hydraulic pump.
" When the threads are drawn through the apertures in the
" bottom of the box, pressure is applied by means of the hydraulic
" pump." "To make drawn threads of gutta percha without
" core," "make use of a metal box traversed by tubes, similar
" to a tubular boiler, and this box is heated by water, air or
" steam. Rods or pieces of gutta percha are passed through
" the tubes in the box, and are received upon a cylinder which
" is made to dip in cold water, from which the threads are wound
" upon another cylinder, which, being of larger diameter, or
" revolving at greater speed, draws out the thread to the fine-
" ness required." "In order to gild or silver the threads or
" fabrics of gutta percha, instead of employing small sheets of
" gold or silver leaf, cause the gold or silver leaf to be wound
" with sheets of paper, as usual between each layer, into a roll of
" any desired length; and for the purpose of gilding or silver-
" ing gutta percha after being softened by heat, it is first formed
" into a roll, and both the gutta percha roll and the gold or
" silver leaf roll are simultaneously unrolled against each
" other."

[Printed, 6d. Drawing.]

A.D. 1854, November 23.—N° 2479.

DUVIVIER, Henri Jules, and CHAUDET, Henri.—"Im-
"provements in treating gutta percha." These are treating
"gutta percha with one or more of the following substances,
"namely, chloride, bromide, iodide, and fluoride of sulphur, boron,
"silica, arsenic, and phosphorous, or sulphide of phosphorous,
"preferring the chloride of sulphur. To a solution of gutta
"percha in bisulphide of carbon, from two to fifteen per cent. of
"chloride of sulphur diluted with bisulphide of carbon is added.
"If any of the other substances are substituted for the chloride
"of sulphur then fifteen to fifty per cent. are added. The
"compound of gutta percha differs in properties with the per-
"centage of the admixture in being more or less elastic; and
"more or less acted on by heat or cold; articles steeped in these
"solutions and liable to be damaged by the acid vapours formed
"during the operation, then carbonate of soda should be mixed
"with the solution of gutta percha in quantity sufficient to
"neutralize the acid formed."

[Printed, 4d. No Drawings.]

A.D. 1854, December 29.—N° 2753.

FANSHAWE, Henry Richardson, and FANSHAWE, John
Americus.—"Certain improvements in the manufacture of
"various kinds of waterproof garments." These are, in reference
to this subject, the use of the following compounds :—1st. "Mas-
"ticated india-rubber, ten parts; asphaltum, three parts; pure
"mineral naptha, fifty parts; and the best vegetable black, one
"part." 2nd. "Masticated india-rubber, ten parts; asphaltum,
"three parts; pure mineral naptha, ten parts, and vegetable black,
"one part." 3rd. Masticated india-rubber, ten parts, sulphur,
three quarters to one and a half, vegetable black, one part; and
pure mineral naptha, fifty parts. 4th. "Masticated india-rubber,
"ten parts; sulphur, three quarters to one and a half, according
"to the texture treated; vegetable black, one part; pure mineral
"naptha, ten parts."

[Printed, 4d. No Drawings.]

1855.

A.D. 1855, January 12.—N° 90.

BROOMAN, RICHARD ARCHIBALD. — (*A communication.*)—
" Certain means of devulcanizing india-rubber and other similar
" gums, or of treating such gums after having been vulcanized."
The vulcanized rubber is ground, and the sulphur "extracted by
" boiling it with alkaline leys, soaps, and mixtures of alkalies
" with essential or fixed oils, grease, rosin, naptha, bisulphuret of
" carbon, ether, &c. After applying these, "the rubber is then
" washed and dried." If the vulcanized rubber contain "chalk,
" white lead, metals, oxides," &c., these may be separated by
" acetic or pyroligneous acid," &c. ; and " to give clearness to the
" gum it may be further treated with a solution of cyanide of
" potassium, hypochloride of lime or other like deoxidizing sub-
" stance." The "devulcanization or change" is effected by sub-
" stances which are "solvents of the native gums in connection
" with the employment of heat." The substances may be
" naptha, bicarburet of sulphur," &c., but "spirits of turpentine"
are preferred. If the product is required to be solid, the vapour
of the turpentine is applied. If a soft or liquid product is required, the rubber is subjected to heated turpentine. When this
latter is employed, "in order to prevent the mass from being
" tacky," introduce alcohol or a small quantity of sulphur into
" the solution."

[Printed, 4*d*. No Drawings.]

A.D. 1855, February 6.—N° 283.

AUDEMARS, GEORGE.—" Improvements in obtaining and treat-
" ing vegetable fibres." The fibre particularly mentioned is from
" the mulberry tree," and after this is obtained by boiling with
carbonate of soda and soap, washing with hot water acidulated
with nitric acid, drying by pressure, afterwards soaking in a
mixture of ammonia and alcohol, and bleaching "by chloride of
" lime or otherwise," hackling, &c. ; it is " spun like cotton ;"
or " it may be converted into an explosive compound by the
" action of nitric acid, and then dissolved in a mixture of alcohol
" and ether, then mixed with a solution of caoutchouc, and drawn

" out into fine threads or filaments." The caoutchouc in small pieces is steeped in ammonia then dissolved in 10 parts of ether.
[Printed, 4d. No Drawings.]

A.D. 1855, February 28.—N° 448.

PENNEY, HENRY.—(*Letters Patent void for want of Final Specification.*)—"An improved mode of treating vulcanized or
" cured india rubber." It consists as follows:—"Cut up the
" material into small pieces, and steep it in coal tar naptha, or
" other solvent of india rubber, in order to swell it. When the
" material has thus been deprived of its elasticity, remove it from
" the naptha or other spirit and drain or dry it; next, submit it
" to heat, and thereby reduce it to a fluid state. When the
" naptha has been completely driven off, add to the fluid material
" a small quantity of spirits of turpentine or other spirit, which
" is then volatized by the heat."
[Printed, 4d. No Drawings.]

A.D. 1855, March 7.—N° 506.

JOHNSON, JOHN HENRY.—(*A communication from Charles Morey.*)—(*Provisional protection only.*)—"Improvements in the
" manufacture of hard india-rubber and of articles composed of
" that material." It consists in "hardening the soft india rubber
" or articles composed of soft india rubber by immersing them in
" a bath of melted sulphur contained in an open vessel."
" Should the color or elasticity of the articles require modifying,
" a little shellac, lamp black, oxide, or other substances may be
" incorporated with the soft caoutchouc during its preparation."
[Printed 4d. No Drawings.]

A.D. 1855, March 14.—N° 577.

GOODYEAR, CHARLES, junior.—"Improvements in the plates
" of artificial teeth." Making them of "india rubber and gutta
" percha compounds, combined with sulphur," and "whilst in
" the moulds" causing "the materials and the moulds to be
" subjected to heat for about six hours" gradually raising "the
" heat up to about 230° of Fahrenheit, say, in about half an hour
" and then, unless there be a considerable quantity of foreign
" matter present, the heat may be raised as quickly as may be to
" about 295° of Fahrenheit."

To obtain a suitable colour mixing with 1 lb. of caoutchouc or gutta percha or both in suitable proportions and suitably combined with coloring matter, as vermillion, oxides of iron, or any coloring matter standing the heat.
[Printed, 4d. No Drawings.]

A.D. 1855, March 26.—N° 667.

HILL, HENRY CHARLES.—" Improvements in the manufacture " of waterproof flocked cloth and other fabrics." First, preparing waterproofing material by masticating, either with or without solvents, vulcanized, and ordinary india rubber in proportions which vary according to the " pliability or softness required in " the cloth," &c. to be coated. The result is "reduced to any " consistency by adding naptha, bisulphuret of carbon, camphine, " turpentine, or other solvent." " In some cases " ordinary " caoutchouc may be dispensed with." The cloths, &c. are coated with the preparation and "cured" by submitting them to a temperature from one hundred to three hundred degrees Fahrenheit, preferring heated air for this purpose.

Second, " Curing and rendering inodorous waterproof fabrics " by means of a current or currents of heated air or steam," and " the mechanical arrangements for effecting the same." These arrangements are by induction and eduction pipes for the hot air or steam into a chamber in which the cloths, &c. are supported on stands, &c.

Third, perfuming the goods, by passing the heated air first through a chamber containing perfume or scent.

Fourth. " Flocking surfaces coated or covered with sulphurized, " metalized, mineralized, or other prepared india rubber or gutta " percha, combined with prepared india rubber or gutta percha."

Fifth, Preparing fibrous materials, and applying the same to the manufacture of flocked cloth, &c. The fibrous materials, such as woollen or cotton flock, ground sponge, sawdust, hair, &c., &c., are dyed, or stained, and masticated with the india-rubber compounds, and applied by a solvent to the cloth, or the flocking materials may be sifted on to prepared cloth, &c.
[Printed, 4d. No Drawings.]

A.D. 1855, March 27.—N° 677.

GOODYEAR, CHARLES.—(*A communication.*)—" A new method " of moulding india rubber and gutta percha," either separate or

" combined together, or with other matters by forcing such
" matters when in a plastic state into moulds." "The machine
" employed is constructed in a similar manner to the machines
" now employed for coating telegraphic wires with gutta
" percha."

[Printed, 4d. No Drawings.]

A.D. 1855, April 3.—N° 745.

CORNIDES, Louis.—" Certain improvements in saturating and
" coating or covering leather, paper, and textile fabrics, so as to
" render the same on the coated or covered surfaces thereof im-
" pervious to water." This consists, in reference to this subject,
in making "a solution of caoutchouc in rectified sulphuric æther,
" made by mixing 16 parts purified sulphuric æther with one
" part caoutchouc." Making a solution of caoutchouc in coal
naphtha benzole, spirits of turpentine and other known solvents,
for example, "mixing 16 parts of spirits of turpentine with two
" or four parts gutta percha, or the following:—Sixteen parts
" spirits of turpentine, two or four parts gutta percha, half or one
" part caoutchouc, or any other composition or solution, with
" or without combination of gutta percha, india-rubber, gum,
" resins, bitumen, or other flexible materials." Also, an apparatus "consisting of a close chamber, communicating with a
" closed drying chamber, and such drying chamber communica-
" ting with a condenser, so that the evaporated aether, volatile
" oil or spirit, is not allowed to escape, but is condensed and
" recovered." Employing drying oils, with or without gums, or
resins, or colors, fish-oil colours, tar, with or without colors.
Coat the paper, &c. with gum, &c., and when dry apply another
coat, and so on till the required thickness is obtained; apply the
still moist surface to the fabrics, and pass them between rollers;
then moisten the paper, and draw it off. Sugar and gelatine in
equal proportions may be substituted for the gum. Fourth,
preparing leather with a solution of gutta percha and common
resin dissolved in certain proportions in naptha, &c. Applying
graphite and other metallic or mineral powders in a dry state to
the coating transferred as above, "whilst such coating is in a half
" dry or green state."

[Printed, 10d. Drawing.]

A.D. 1855, April 18.—N° 855.

JOHNSON, John Henry.—(*A communication.*)—(*Provisional protection only.*)—"Improvements in machinery or apparatus for " moulding and casting fusible or plastic materials, and in cover- " ing or coating articles with such materials." It consists as follows:—" The india rubber, if such be the material employed, " is contained in a horizontal cylinder, and is kept in a " melted or plastic state therein, by means of a steam or hot- " water jacket round such cylinder." "The plastic or melted " india rubber is forced out of one end of the cylinder into any " suitable mould, by means of a piston or plunger, on the end " of a screwed shaft or piston rod, which rod works through " a fixed nut, and is rotated by a suitable fly-wheel."
The mould is in a cage or frame, placed on a table which is raised or lowered by a vertical wheel.

[Printed, 4*d*. No Drawings.]

A.D. 1855, April 19.—N° 875.

JOHNSON, John Henry.—(*A communication.*)—"Improve- " ments in the manufacture of articles of hard india-rubber or " gutta percha, or compounds thereof, and in coating or covering " articles with the like materials." These relate to the manu- facture of a number of articles from a compound formed of caoutchouc or gutta percha, either "incorporated with sul- " phur before moulding, or the pure gums may be dissolved " in spirits or carburet of sulphur, and the moulds filled with the " solution, or pure gums may be used, and submitted while in " the mould to the sulphur bath," as described in Nos. 9952, and 11,135, Old Law, and No. 506, A.D. 1855. In other cases the material may be vulcanized in sheets or other forms, or the refuse dust of such material may be treated as described in No. 1819, A.D. 1854. The articles may be colored or variegated by spreading the dust of hard india rubber before adding the scraps or parings. Gutta percha may be employed alone or combined with caoutchouc, as described in Nos. 11,032, and 11,455, Old Law. Imitation whalebone may also be made by mixing two pounds of caoutchouc or gutta percha or both combined, with one pound of sulphur and proceeding as described in No. 9952, Old Law. It is proposed to coat metals, wire, tubes, &c., with pure india rubber or gutta percha and submit them to a sulphur

bath, for hard vulcanization or "into a solution of india rubber
"or gutta percha formed by the carburet of sulphur or into any
"other solution of india rubber or gutta percha, and then
"vulcanized hard."

[Printed, 4d. No Drawings.]

A.D. 1855, May 10.—N° 1053.

NEWTON, ALFRED VINCENT.—(*A communication.*)—"An im-
"proved mode of preparing colors for printing and staining
"fabrics." This consists in using "liquid uncoagulated caout-
"chouc, whether mixed or uncombined with other substances, as
"a vehicle for the application of coloring matter and the means of
"rendering it more or less liquid," by evaporation, or by gums,
&c. as thickeners.

[Printed, 4d. No Drawings.]

A.D. 1855, May 17.—N° 1116.

JOHNSON, WILLIAM.—(*A communication.*)—"Improvements in
"the manufacture, treatment, and application of oily, resinous,
"and gummy substances and soaps." One of the objects of this
invention is to produce substances which resemble gutta percha
and caoutchouc. For this purpose the oils from distilling resin
are mixed with albumen, fibrine, caseine, starch, &c., &c. A
compound resembling leather is made of rosin oil, olive or linseed
oil, turpentine, catechu, starch, all mixed in certain proportions,
and "the mass so produced is then mixed with hot gutta percha."
Other compounds are produced.

[Printed, 4d. No Drawings.]

A.D. 1855, May 21.—N° 1149.

JOHNSON, JOHN HENRY.—(*A communication.*)—"Improve-
"ments in the process of vulcanising and rendering hard, india-
"rubber and gutta percha, and in the application of those mater-
"ials, when hard, to the construction of parts of machinery or
"apparatus employed in the preparation and manufacture of
"fibrous materials and textile fabrics." These are, in reference
to this subject, "the vulcanizing and rendering hard sheets and
"articles of india rubber and gutta percha upon surfaces of glass,
"either engraved or plain, whereby a highly ornamental or
"polished surface will be imparted to the india rubber or gutta

" percha during the process of vulcanizing and hardening the
" the same."

[Printed, 4d. No Drawings.]

A.D. 1855, June 4.—N° 1268.

GODEFROY, PETER AUGUSTIN. — "Improvements in the
" treatment of gutta percha." These consist "in combining
" the shells of the fruit of the cocoa-nut tree (cocos nucifera) in a
" finely ground or communicated state with gutta percha," by
" which considerable "economy" is obtained, as well as "dura-
" bility," and "it will stand a greater degree of heat, and is
" considerably more elastic.

[Printed, 4d. No Drawings.]

A.D. 1855, July 11.—N° 1555.

BIELEFELD, CHARLES FREDERICK.—" Improvements in the
" manufacture of saddle-trees." These consist, in reference to
this subject of matters combined in various proportions, and they
" may be used alone, or may be spread" on "strong canvass."
The matters to be combined may consist of " tanogelatin, sulphur
" balsam, gum thus, and gutta percha, with a suitable solvent of
" gutta percha, preferring Venice turpentine for such purpose."
" When using strong canvass, the compound of tanogelatin and
" gutta percha is what is preferred." Sulphur balsam is a solution of sulphur in fixed oils usually consisting of 2 ozs. of flowers
of sulphur and 8 ozs. of linseed oil. The plastic compound,
having been roughly formed by hand or by pressure, is whilst hot
introduced into the mould and well pressed therein, and, when
set, it is to be removed and dried.

[Printed, 4d. No Drawings.]

A.D. 1855, July 21.—N° 1654.

GOODYEAR, CHARLES.—(*Partly a communication.*)—(*Provisional protection only.*)—" Improvements in the surfaces used
" for printing." It consists in employing a compound of india
rubber and sulphur with or without other matters, and subjected
to a high temperature "to obtain the change into hard material."
For some purposes "a compound of india rubber, sulphur, and
" powder of lithographic stones or oxide of zinc subjected to a
" high temperature is used."

[Printed, 4d. No Drawings.]

A.D. 1855, July 23.—N° 1664.

GOODYEAR, CHARLES.—(*A communication.*)—(*Provisional protection only.*)—"An improvement in manufacturing moulded
" articles made of compounds of india rubber." It consists in
" introducing water or fluid into the mould with the compound
" of india rubber, by which means, when the mould containing
" the compound of india rubber is subjected to heat to produce
" the change in the india-rubber compound the water or fluid
" will be expanded into steam or vapour, which by its pressure
" will force the india-rubber compound into all parts of the
" mould, and cause it to fit the interior of the mould with great
" accuracy."

[Printed, 4d. No Drawings.]

A.D. 1855, August 7.—N° 1787.

JOHNSON, JOHN HENRY.—(*A. communication from Austin S. Day.*)—" Improvements in the manufacture of india-rubber." The
" caoutchouc or other raw gums " is first " cut or torn with any
" suitable machinery into small shreds or pieces, and is then well
" washed in water in the ordinary manner," and "placed in an
" air-tight vessel." "The air and noxious gases are exhausted
" from the caoutchouc or other gum by means of an air pump,"
&c.; and "when a sufficient vacuum is produced in the air-
" tight vessel, a solution of caustic alkali, composed of caustic
" soda or potash is admitted." "When these gums have
" remained a sufficient time under the action of the caustic
" alkali, the solution is drawn off;" and the gum is removed
" from the air-tight vessel, and placed in a vat filled with water,
" where it is kept well stirred and agitated, in order to detach the
" particles of cut caoutchouc or other gum from each other."
" As soon as this occurs, the greater specific gravity acquired by
" the foreign porous substances while subjected to the previous
" action of the caustic alkali causes them to sink to the bottom
" of the cistern, whilst the pure gum is left floating on the
" surface."

[Printed, 8d. Drawing.]

A.D. 1855, August 27.—N° 1937.

SAUTELET, EMILE CONSTANTIN FRITZ.—" An improved im-
" permeable cloth or fabric for sheltering, covering, and pre-

" serving in various purposes." It consists in manufacturing
" an impermeable cloth or fabric by the combination of loose or
" unwoven wool or hair," "from tanneries and similar places,"
" with caoutchouc, or gutta perch, or other similar elastic or
" flexible gum." The caoutchouc is soaked with an ordinary
solvent, oil of turpentine, coal oil, sulphuret of carbon, or other
suitable solvent, ground between cylinders or otherwise, and made
into a paste which is spread upon the wool or hair. Other substances, such as lime, zinc white, white lead, sulphur, or colors
may be added.

[Printed, 4d. No Drawings.]

A.D. 1855, August 30.—N° 1960.

STANSBURY, CHARLES FREDERICK.—(*A communication from M. H. Merrian & Joseph B. Crosby.*)—(*Provisional protection only.*)
—"A machine for splitting leather and for analogous purposes.
It consists, first, "of a disc cutter, having a simultaneous
" rotary and reciprocating movement relative to the machine in a
" plane at right angles to the axis of rotation;" second, "of an
" endless apron passing over an elevated bed and roller, combined
" with another roller having a greater speed than that of the
" apron" for feeding the leather, india rubber, &c. to the above
cutter; third, obtaining an increased feed or draft by having one
of the surface rollers with "a greater surface speed in some
" portions of it than others."

[Printed, 4d. No Drawings.]

A.D. 1855, September 1.—N° 1971.

BUTCHER, MATTHEW, and NEWEY, THOMAS HENRY.—
" An improvement or improvements in the manufacture of bob-
" bins used in winding, twisting, and weaving fibrous substan-
" ces." This consists in "manufacturing bobbins used in
" winding, twisting and weaving fibrous substances of gutta
" percha, hardened by the introduction of grit or sharp sand,
" aluminous earth, or other solid capable of hardening the
" same."

[Printed, 6d. Drawing.]

A.D. 1855, September 1.—N° 1974.

JOB, ALFRED MORTIMER, and TOMLINSON, EDWIN.—(*Provisional protection only.*)—"A new article to be called 'india

" 'rubber leather cloth,' applicable to covering roofs, floors,
" trunks, and for other similar purposes." It consists " in com-
" bining particles of leather" with india rubber or gutta percha,
" or with both." Also mixing metal dust or filings with the
same.

[Printed, 4d. No Drawings.]

A.D. 1855, September 15.—N° 2090.

FORD, ALFRED.—" Improvements in preparing solutions of
" caoutchouc, gutta percha, and like gums for waterproofing and
" other useful purposes." The oil of turpentine or naptha is
agitated with a caustic alkali or alkaline earth, separately or combined, for some days, and the whole allowed to subside. The
supernatent fluid is drawn off, and may be passed through
charcoal, &c. The solvent thus purified "readily" dissolves
" india rubber, vulanized india rubber, gutta percha, or any
" mixtures of the same," "first reduced to shreds." Vulcanized
india rubber is steeped in these solvents for some time, and
bruised or torn up and heated; the excess of solvent may be
condensed. Solutions so prepared may be mixed with oxides, &c.
and colouring matters, and with oxides or salts of copper, singly
or otherwise, " as a coating for iron ships' bottoms."

[Printed, 4d. No Drawings.]

A.D. 1855, October 22.—N° 2359.

PARKES, ALEXANDER.—" Certain preparations of oils for, and
" solutions used when waterproofing, and for the manufacture of
" various articles by the use of such compounds." Adding to
oils, such as linseed, rape, &c., chloride of sulphur, the effect
of which is to render them insoluble in naptha, or sulphuret of
carbon, their usual solvents.

Oils, so changed, have the character of vulcanized india rubber.

Combining india rubber or gutta percha with the oils and
adding chloride of sulphur.

Using a "solution of gun cotton (collodion) alone, or with
" gums or resins that will set transparent with it or with colour."

These compounds are applied to waterproofing, &c., &c., and
the purposes to which india-rubber alone is employed.

"Gun cotton substances are rendered less inflammable" by
adding substances such as " phosphate of ammonia and mag-

" nesia, iodide of cadmium, per-iodide of mercury, oxalate of lime,
" talc, alum."

[Printed, 4d. No Drawings.]

A.D. 1855, November 12.—N° 2547.

JOHNSON, JOHN HENRY. — *(A communication from Henri Victor Wacrenier.)—(Provisional protection only.)*—" Improve-
" ments in the manufacture or preparation of hard india rubber,
" and in the application thereof to the construction of parts of
" textile and other machinery." This consists, in reference to this subject, in manufacturing hard india rubber, " mixing with
" the india rubber and sulphur the shells or scales of oysters,"
&c. in powder.

[Printed, 4d. No Drawings.]

A.D. 1855, November 27.—N° 2679.

JOHNSON, JOHN HENRY.—*(A communication from Henri Victor Wacrenier.)* — " Improvements in the manufacture or
" preparation of india-rubber and gutta percha, and in the ap-
" plication thereof." These are, " mixing with gutta percha or
" india rubber " calcined shells or other cheap substances of a like
" nature reduced to powder;" adding sulphur; constructing of hard india-rubber or gutta percha "rollers and cylinders and
" coupling or clutch boxes of spinning machines," " plate bolsters,
" footsteps, collars and bearings for the spindles of spinning ma-
" chines," the "bearings of driving and other shafts." the "back
" spindles of doubling and twisting machines," " bobbins, reels,
" and spools used in spinning machines;" also constructing racks, ratchets, and gearing of hand and power looms and spinning frames of hard india-rubber. In preference, the caoutchouc is first vulcanised, reduced to powder, then moulded in heated moulds.

[Printed, 4d. No Drawings.]

A.D. 1855, December 7.—N° 2759.

LATTA, ANTOINE.—*(Provisional protection only.)*—" Preparing
" gutta percha in combination with other substances applicable
" to various purposes." It consists, " in mixing gutta percha
" with other substances, and obtaining useful products." The mixtures are made of gutta percha, flour of brimstone, coal, gum lac, cotton, and they are vulcanized.

[Printed, 4d. No Drawings.]

A.D. 1855, December 29.—N° 2944.

FORD, ALFRED.—(*Provisional protection only.*) — "Preparing
" and dissolving in naptha or oil of turpentine vulcanized india
" rubber for the purposes of waterproofing, and all or any of the
" other purposes for which the same, not so prepared and dis-
" solved, is now applicable. Vulcanized india rubber is cut into
pieces and placed in a boiler, and subjected to heat under pressure,
until, by the action of the gas within, it is sufficiently softened,
when it is taken out, and " worked up with French chalk, sul-
" phur, charcoal, lamp-black, black-lead, or some other metallic
" oxide."

[Printed, 4d. No Drawings.]

1856.

A.D. 1856, January 18.—N° 141.

DODGE, NATHANIEL SHATTSWELL.—(*A communication.*)—
" Improvements in treating vulcanized india rubber or gutta
" percha." These are, reducing these substances " to a soft,
" plastic, or liquid state by means of alcohol and bisulphuret of
" carbon," to allow them to be re-manufactured. The refuse
material is reduced to small pieces and treated in a close vessel
for about two hours with a mixture of absolute alcohol and bisulphuret of carbon, " in the proportion of a quarter of a pound
" weight of the former to ten pounds weight of the latter, to one
" hundred pounds weight of the material."

[Printed, 4d. No Drawings.]

A.D. 1856, January 23.—N° 178.

JOHNSON, WILLIAM.—(*A communication.*)—(*Letters Patent
void for want of Final Specification.*)—" Improvements in the
" treatment and application of fatty, resinous, and gummy sub-
" stances, and in the manufacture of pastes, greases, and soaps."
It consists in combining " gluten, starch, or flour, or the farina-
" ceous, slimy, or gummy matters of vegetables, with resins, fats,
" soaps, greases, oils, wax, pitch, and bituminous substances, for
" the advantageous application of the compounds so obtained to

" various useful purposes; and, for example, in the manufacture
" of soaps, greases, and pastes, and of compounds containing
" gutta percha or caoutchouc," &c.

[Printed, 4d. No Drawings.]

A.D. 1856, February 4.—N° 305.

TURNER, WILLIAM ALLEN.—(*Provisional protection only.*)—
" An improved preparation or mixture to be used in the manu-
" facture of compounds of india rubber or caoutchouc." It
relates, "to the manufacture of compounds of india rubber,
" known and distinguished as vulcanized india rubber." Take
" genuine bismuth, ordinary lead, virgin tin, and sulphur, in
" about the following proportions,' namely, of genuine bismuth,
" 5 parts, ordinary lead, 3 parts; these are melted separately and
" mixed together with half their weight of sulphur." In using
" the above mixture, mix 10 pounds of the same with 30 pounds
" of india rubber or caoutchouc."

[Printed, 4d. No Drawings.]

A.D. 1856, February 27.—N° 500.

JOHNSON, JOHN HENRY.—(*A communication from Charles Vincent Steinlen.*)—(*Provisional protection only.*)—" Improve-
" ments in the treatment of hard india rubber for the purpose of
" rendering the same applicable to the manufacture of pens,
" tubes, springs, and other similar articles." The vulcanized
sheets are cut into strips: these strips are softened by exposure
to heat, and passed between heated polished steel, or iron rollers,
again heated and made into the article required.

[Printed, 4d. No Drawings.]

A.D. 1856, February 29.—N° 524.

TURNER, WILLIAM ALLEN.—" Improvements in the manu-
" facture of elastic tubing." These relate " to tubing made of
" india rubber or caoutchouc and gutta percha, either separately
" or in combination, and is designed for the purpose of rendering
" such tube capable of withstanding a pressure," and consists in
covering a helix or a series of rings of metal with the aforesaid
elastic material, and, if necessary, subjecting the tubing so made
to the ordinary vulcanizing process or to the process described in
No. 305, A.D. 1856.

[Printed, 4d. No Drawings.]

A.D. 1856, March 12.—N° 596.

PALMER, CHRISTOPHER RICHARD NORRIS. — (*Provisional protection only.*)—"A new telegraph and improved telegraph or "signal apparatus, parts of the invention, apparatus, or manu-"facture being applicable to other purposes." This consists, in reference to this subject, "for constructing condensing or ex-"hausting cylinders for use on telegraph purposes in buildings" using "gutta percha cast in moulds;" "also gutta precha mixed "(when in a liquid or soft state) with very fine marble powder or "other suitable earthy or metallic dust or plaster of Paris. This "material I apply for moulding many articles now made of gutta "percha alone."

[Printed, 10d. Drawings.]

A.D. 1856, May 26.—N° 1257.

JEUNE, FREDERICK CHARLES.—"An improved manufacture "of floorcloth." This consists as follows:—Mixing in a masticator "india rubber (consisting in part of the cuttings and "waste of vulcanized india rubber) and gutta percha," afterwards adding "ground cedar wood or other vegetable dust;" and, lastly, adding "fibrous substances in length, such as cocoa-nut "fibre, hemp, cotton waste, and hair." This compound is afterwards rolled into sheets, which are submitted to dry or steam heat, "to about the temperature of three hundred degrees "Fahrenheit, when they are painted."

[Printed, 4d. No Drawings.]

A.D. 1856, June 2.—N° 1299.

GIDLEY, GUSTAVUS, and CHRISTOPHER, WILLIAM.— "Reducing the bottle or imported india rubber to a transparent "liquid state, so that it may be used as a transparent varnish or "solution for mixing with colors." The india rubber is cut into pieces, and boiled with an alkaline solution, carbonate of soda preferred, for forty or sixty hours, and then for four or five hours in water; afterwards it is "dissolved in like manner to that "heretofore practised when using crude india rubber."

[Printed, 4d. No Drawings.]

A.D. 1856, June 27.—N° 1512.

FORD, ALFRED.—(*Complete Specification but no Letters Patent.*) —"Preparing and dissolving in naptha or oil of turpentine vul-

" canized india rubber, for the purpose of waterproofing, and for
" all or any of the other purposes for which the same, not so pre-
" pared and dissolved, is now applicable, and especially for the
" coating of iron ships' bottoms." The rubber is cut into small
pieces, and placed in a boiler having a stirrer; heat is applied
under pressure, but not exceeding " 300 degrees of Fahrenheit ; "
" and when the india rubber shall be reduced to the consistence
" of dough," it is mixed with French chalk, and passed through
rollers, " after which it is capable of being dissolved in naptha or
" turpentine in the manner of ordinary rubber."

[Printed, 4d. No Drawings.]

A.D. 1856, July 16.—N° 1674.

DUNCAN, THOMAS.—" A combined and compound engine for
" applying motive power, and for measuring fluids." This con-
consists, in reference to this subject, as follows :—In constructing
the above it is proposed to make "the work piston" of "a com-
" position formed by mixing together gutta percha and black-
" lead."

[Printed, 10d. Drawing.]

A.D. 1856, July 25.—N° 1764.

BOUSFIELD, GEORGE TOMLINSON.—(*A communication.*)—
(*Letters Patent void for want of Final Specification.*)—" Improve-
" ments in the manufacture of vulcanized india-rubber thread."
This consists as follows :—" The india rubber compound, having
" been properly masticated or ground, is, whilst hot, rolled into a
" sheet between rollers, and is immediately divided into thread by
" rollers (one or both being grooved), and the thread is then vul-
" conized by heat." " Or, in place of cutting the sheets whilst
" in a hot and plastic state, as above explained, the rolled out
" sheets may be subjected to artificial freezing or cold, so as to
" set or harden the sheets, when they may be cut in like manner
" to that heretofore practised in cutting india rubber, and the
" thread thus produced may be then vulcanized, as is well under-
" stood."

[Printed, 4d. No Drawings.]

A.D. 1856, July 26.—N° 1781.

YEADON, SAMUEL, and CHAPMAN, GEORGE.—" Improve-
" ments in the construction of reeds for weaving, and in machi-

" nery or implements and materials to be used in such construc-
" tion." This consists, in reference to this subject, in " the com-
" position and preparation of the cement," and " the use and
" application of such cement in uniting the parts of reeds." The
cement, in preference, is composed of " pitch, gutta percha, and
" caoutchouc," in proportions varying " according to the quality
" of the reeds intended to be made."

[Printed, 1s. 6d. Drawings.]

A.D. 1856, July 28.—N° 1785.

RITCHIE, GEORGE.—(*Provisional protection only.*)—" Improve-
" ments in the manufacture of boots and shoes from materials
" not hitherto used for that purpose." This consists in making
the heels and soles of boots and shoes wholly or in part of " gutta
" percha, india rubber," &c., mixed with a hard mineral substance by preference "corundum" ground or broken into small
pieces.

[Printed, 4d. No Drawings.]

A.D. 1856, August 30.—N° 2020.

GOODYEAR, CHARLES.—"An improvement in combining
" gutta percha and asphalte or pitch." Instead of employing
masticating machines, the substances are introduced into a close
vessel with water, and the temperature raised; they melt, and are
further mixed by stirring. "When in a comparatively fluid state,
" they may be further combined with sulphur, india rubber, or
" both," and with other matters, as oxide of lead.

[Printed, 4d. No Drawings.]

A.D. 1856, September 3.—N° 2043.

METCALF, JOHN.—(*Provisional protection only.*)—" Improve-
" ments in the manufacture and treatment of tar oil, for dissolv-
" ing india rubber, gutta percha, gums, and gum resins, and also
" in deodorizing all fabrics, wood, or any article impregnated with
" tar oil, or the products from coal tar." This consists as follows :—To every gallon of " dead oil, crude oil, creosote, or heavy
" oil of tar obtained from coal tar by distillation," add "about
" two lbs. weight" of sulphuric acid, and " half a pound " of
common salt, and agitate the whole; allow it to settle; draw
off the liquid " without disturbing the pulpy precipitate; " add to

the oil caustic soda, and lime, to neutralize any acid in it; separate the soda and lime, and put the oil in a still; and "distil in
" the usual manner until two thirds of the whole has distilled
" over." The whole of the above operations may be repeated
upon the distillate. "All kinds of fabrics" "impregnated with
" india rubber, &c.," are deodorized by "any alkali or alkaline
" earth."

[Printed, 4d. No Drawings.]

A.D. 1856, September 8.—N° 2096.

NEWTON, ALFRED VINCENT.—(*A communication from Henry Davenport.*)—" Improved machinery for cutting india rubber and
" other substances into threads or narrow strips." The fillet of
india rubber is strained over a pair of rollers, to which rotary
motion is communicated for the purpose of presenting the whole
surface gradually to rotary shears or cutters. " These cutters
" are carried by a frame, which slides on transverse guides on the
" table of the machine, situate about midway between the tension
" rollers. By means of a screw shaft, which receives a slow axial
" motion through a train of gearing driven from one of the ten-
" sion roller shafts, the position of the cutter frame is shifted
" laterally, so that the shears, commencing to cut at the edge of
" the endless sheet, will slowly move inwards and cut up the
" rotating sheet (as it passes between the cutting edges) into a
" long continuous thread or strip. The strip, as it is formed, is
" conducted away to a suitable reel. Nipping rollers are also
" provided for holding the sheet of india rubber or other substance
" up to the cutters."

[Printed, 10d. Drawing.]

A.D. 1856, September 20.—N° 2215.

FORD, ALFRED.—" Improvements in dissolving vulcanized india
" rubber for waterproofing and like purposes." These are as
follows: The material, waste or otherwise, is cut up into small
pieces, which are soaked " in oil of turpentine, or naptha spirit,
" either prepared according " to the process given in No. 2090,
A.D. 1855, or otherwise; then transferred to a vessel heated by
a steam jacket, with a still head and means of stirring. After
some time the vulcanized india rubber becomes dissolved, and
" is ready to draw off."

[Printed, 4d. No Drawings.]

A.D. 1856, October 3.—N° 2317.

JOHNSON, WILLIAM.—(*A communication.*)—" Improvements in
" the treatment, preparation, or manufacture of sheet caoutchouc,
" and in the combination thereof with cloth and other fabrics."
This consists in reference to this subject in "desulphurizing"
vulcanized caoutchouc by boiling the sheets in caustic alkali, and
afterwards in salt pickle to neutralize the alkali, afterwards washing. These sheets are then ground with emery, sand paper,
&c., so as to roughen the surfaces and give them "a velvety"
appearance.

[Printed, 4d. No Drawings.]

A.D. 1856, October 20.—N° 2460.

LORIMIER, ANTHONY.—" An improvement in re-working vul-
" canized india rubber." This consists " in preparing the pieces
" or waste of vulcanized india rubber, by crushing the same
" between pressing rollers, then subjecting it to a considerable
" degree of heat, and whilst so heated causing it to be stirred, by
" which means the mass is progressively brought into a fluid state.
" The mass is then allowed to cool; but before becoming cold a
" solution of india rubber is added, by which an india-rubber
" cement is produced, which may be used for spreading on fabrics
" and surfaces for the purposes of rendering the same water and
" air proof."

[Printed, 4d. No Drawings.]

A.D. 1856, November 20.—N° 2746.

FONROBERT, CHARLES FRANÇOIS JULES.—(*Partly a communication.*)—(*Provisional protection only.*)—" Improvements in
" the manufacture of boots and shoes." This consists " in cover-
" ing the soles of boots and shoes with a composition of gutta
" percha and tar." Two parts by weight of gutta percha to one
of coal tar mixed together by heat.

[Printed, 4d. No Drawings.]

A.D. 1856, December 3.—N° 2865.

RIDER, EMORY.—" Improvements in the manufacture or treat-
" ment of gutta percha." These are, the mode of "treating
" gutta percha by the addition to sixty-six parts of that gum of
" one part of sulphur, or an equivalent thereof, and one part of

" litharge, prior to the exposure of the same to the action of 235°
" to 245° Fahrenheit, for the purpose of expelling the volatilizable
" ingredients therefrom, and the after process of vulcanization
" of gum so prepared by subjecting the same to a heat of 255° to
" 265° Fahrenheit."

[Printed, 4d. No Drawings.]

1857.

A.D. 1857, January 1.—N° 10.

LORIMIER, ANTONY.—"An improvement in preparing the
" surfaces of printers' inking rollers, and other articles, when
" vulcanized india-rubber is used." This consists as follows:—
For a roller for distributing ink on a table, a tube of soft vulcanized
india rubber is drawn on the stock of a roller, and in this state it
is passed through a metal ring, which is "at a blood-red heat,"
several times; then coat it "with dissolved vulcanized india
" rubber," prepared as described in No. 2460, A.D. 1856. For
inking type, scraps of vulcanized india rubber, with a little solvent, "are granulated between crushing rollers," and mixed with
" a quantity of "dissolved vulcanized india rubber," prepared as
above. This mixture is put into a mould, with "a stock or core
" previously coated with dissolved india rubber," it is pressed,
and submitted for some hours to the temperature of boiling water,
and finished by passing it "through a heated ring, and coating it
" with dissolved india rubber" as above. "Printers' balls or
" dabbers" are prepared in a similar manner.

[Printed, 4d. No Drawings.]

A.D. 1857, January 8.—N° 67.

HUGHES, EDWARD JOSEPH.—(*A communication.*)—" Improve-
" ments in the manufacture and application of compounds resem-
" bling gutta percha and coautchouc, from flour, fibrine, gelatine,
" and other vegetable and animal substances." These consist in
" combining fibrin, starch, gluten, or substances containing
" them, such as flour, with gelatine, resins, fats, oils, and sub-
" stances containing tannine." Examples are given of mixtures,
and the proportions of such substances are also given. One

mixture consists of wheaten flour, gutta percha, colophane, catechu, glue or gelatine, combined by heat. Another mixture, consists of flour, colophane, caustic alkali of a certain strength, melted soap. The proportions of the ingredients may be altered according to the product required, and the compounds may be improved by exposure "to the action of hydrogen, sulphurous " gas, sulphuretted hydrogen, nitrous gas, or ammonia." These compounds may be combined with fibres of all kinds, and a vast number of other substances. And they may be improved for some purposes by adding to them silicates, sulphates, or resinates of lime, linseed oil, varnishes, &c., and may be spun like glass, producing silky fibres.

[Printed, 4d. No Drawings.]

A.D. 1857, January 30.—N° 275.

ELLIS, THOMAS.—(*Provisional protection only.*)—"Certain im-
" provements in the preparation of india-rubber and gutta percha,
" by combining therewith other materials."—Combining with
" india-rubber or gutta-percha certain metallic bodies, such as
" iron, copper, steel, or other amalgams of metal."

[Printed, 4d. No Drawings.]

A.D. 1857, February 20.—N° 500.

JEUNE, FREDERICK CHARLES.—(*Provisional protection only.*)—
" An improved manufacture of artificial leather."—This consists
" in preparing an elastic compound composed of masticated india-
" rubber, or india-rubber combined with gutta-percha, and mixed
" with sulphuret of antimony and woollen dust or waste," "and
" spreading it upon thin cotton cloth, then subject the same to
" heat." "The fabric is then ready to receive japan varnish."

[Printed, 4d. No Drawings.]

A.D. 1857, March 3.—N° 626.

NEWTON, WILLIAM EDWARD.—(*A communication.*)—"A pre-
" paration of materials for coating roofs, or other portions of
" buildings, to render them impervious to wet." This consists in using and applying for the above purposes "lime in combination " with india-rubber, gutta percha, and shellac solutions." The caoutchouc, gum, shellac, and gutta percha are dissolved in suitable solvents, and mixed in given proportions in one case to form

what is termed "puzzolan," "pulverized glass, quicklime pulverized and sifted, and plaster of Paris or marble dust, or any kind of clay well vitrified and pulverized, or any equivalent substances;" and in another called "'smalt,'" "vitrified glass, sand, flint, gravel, pounded earthenware, or any equivalent pulverized substances." "The use of lime is indispensable."

[Printed, 4d. No Drawings.]

A.D. 1857, March 20.—N° 777.

NINCK, JEAN.—(*Provisional protection only.*)—" Improvements in placing sets or partial sets of teeth, gums, and palates on plates."—It consists in the "use of gutta percha, india rubber, sulphur of zinc, vermilion, and proto-oxide of gold, in such proportions that the heat renders the amalgamation both hard and elastic," for the above purposes.

[Printed, 4d. No Drawings.]

A.D. 1857, March 28.—N° 870.

DEPLANQUE, LOUIS ETIENNE.—" An improved composition for sharpening and setting fine-edged cutting instruments," made by combining "certain vegetable and mineral substances with vulcanized caoutchouc." Several compositions are given consisting of caoutchouc, and two other substances. The substances named are, "emery, smoke black, plumbago, vegetable charcoal, zinc white, yellow ochre, red ochre, pumicestone, sulphur, marble, silex, millstone, brick, &c." The "substances reduced to powder and sifted are mixed with the vulcanized caoutchouc by the ordinary processes, and the composition is then moulded and otherwise formed into the desired shapes."

[Printed, 4d. No Drawings.]

A.D. 1857, April 4.—N° 948.

JOHNSON, JOHN HENRY. —(*A communication from Anna Chadbourne Morey, Widow of Charles Morey.*)—" Improvements in the manufacture of hard india rubber." These are, first, mixing "with the raw india rubber" sulphur, finely powdered coal, or fine wood sawdust, preferring "mahogany or rosewood" in certain proportions. "The vulcanizing process is begun with steam at $3\frac{8}{10}$ ths atmospheres" and brought to "about $4\frac{8}{10}$ ths atmospheres." Second, using "moulds of hard india rubber," making such "hard india rubber moulds from plaster casts of the

"articles to be moulded in the usual way, but in two halves, for
"the greater convenience of moulding." "A number of these
"moulds can be fitted into a frame worked by a powerful press,
"the material to be moulded being cut into a suitable form before
"being put into the moulds."

[Printed, 4d. No Drawings.]

A.D. 1857, April 6.—N° 959.

BOUSFIELD, GEORGE TOMLINSON.—(*A communication.*)—
"Improvements in treating india-rubber and gutta percha, in
"order to render the same impermeable to illuminating and other
"gases." These are, applying linseed or other siccative oil,
"in a heated state to the surfaces of tubes or vessels of vulcanized
"india rubber or gutta percha when in a heated state, or to the
"surfaces of tubes or vessels of india rubber or gutta percha
"combined with sulphur."

[Printed, 4d. No Drawings.]

A.D. 1857, April 13.—N° 1039.

NEWTON, WILLIAM EDWARD.—(*A communication.*)—"Im-
"provements in the construction of boats, buoys, floats, or other
"buoyant vessels." These are, "the method of making boats
"or other vessels of gutta percha, or of gutta percha mixed with
"glue, so that the air chambers or other parts, if separately
"formed, may, together with the boat body, be united and com-
"pleted at one pressure, or (if the braces, knees, thwarts, sup-
"porters, or other accessories to the boat proper are solid), that
"the whole, with the inner and outer forms, may be all made or
"completed together at one time and at one pressure."

[Printed, 10d. Drawings.]

A.D. 1857, April 29.—N° 1210.

JOHNSON, JOHN HENRY.—(*A communication from Poe Edouard
Lemettais and Michel Boniere the younger.*)—" Improvements in
" apparatus for distilling, applicable also to the extraction of oils,
" coloring matters and essences, and to the purification of gums,"
and gutta percha is one of the substances described as treated as
follows :—" Enclose this substance in the case or chamber," and
then "introduce the sulphuret of carbon, or any other suitable
" agent; then heat the apparatus by a current of steam, previously

" produced, at the required temperature. Care should be taken
" previously to place a filter in the interior of the apparatus, in
" order to retain all impurities, and to allow nothing to pass but
" soluble matter." If necessary, "assist the solution by means
" of an agitator of some kind, placed in the centre of the cylinder,
" and driven by external mechanism," &c.

[Printed, 1s. Drawing.]

A.D. 1857, May 2.—N° 1245.

MARLAND, JOHN.—" Improvements in cop tubes used in
" spinning." These are, in reference to this subject "in the
" making of cop tubes of a combination of gutta percha and
" charcoal." Preferring 2 parts of charcoal to 3 parts of gutta
percha.

[Printed, 4d. Woodcut.]

A.D. 1857, May 8.—N° 1302.

TAYLER, CALEB.—" Improvements in the manufacture of sheets
" of material suitable for covering floors, and for other useful
" purposes." These consist, first, "in the combination of caout-
" chouc, gutta percha, and jintawan, in variable proportions, by
" means customarily practised, and incorporating therewith certain
" vegetable matters, either in a fibrous or in a divided state like
" sawdust, adding particular mineral and colouring ingredients,
" when desired." Second, "in manufacturing such compound
" material into sheets by the application of machinery usually
" employed, making the same to any required thickness."

[Printed, 4d. No Drawings.]

A.D. 1857, May 18.—N° 1397.

NEWTON, WILLIAM EDWARD.—(*A communication.*)—"Im-
" provements in the manufacture of boots, shoes, and other
" coverings for the feet." These are, "cementing the inner sole
" and welt, on to an outer sole, a sole and heel formed in one
" entire piece," and "composed of vulcanized india rubber or of
" any of the compounds of india rubber that are susceptible of
" being vulcanized."

The cement is prepared by grinding together 1 lb. of rubber,
¼ lb. of plaster of Paris, ¼ lb. of litharge, 2 ounces of sulphur and
½ pint of camphine, the heat required is from 220° to 250° F.

[Printed, 6d. Drawing.]

A.D. 1857, May 27.—N° 1497.

CODET-NÉGRIER, Jean Léonard.—"Improvements in the
" manufacture of boots, shoes, harness, and other articles." These
are, in reference to this subject "a cement" made of india rubber,
gutta percha, and gum lac dissolved in sulphuret of carbon,
sulphuric ether, or by clarified essential oils, and sulphur may be
added. These are mixed in certain proportions and in a certain
manner, and the "gum lac is dissolved by means of camphine or
" by pure alcohol or used in fine powder."

[Printed, 8d. Drawing.]

A.D. 1857, May 27.—N° 1504.

DANNE, Louis Joseph Almidor.—(*Provisional protection
only.*)—" Manufacturing gutta percha glue, and applying the said
" glue to various new purposes." This consists "in melting
" gutta percha with rosin in a suitable pan, and mixing with it,
" when in a fluid state, if required, some hard powdered material,
" such as glass, sand, emery, pumice stone, &c. The propor-
" tions of the several compound materials are to be modified
" according to the nature of the applications of this glue."

[Printed, 4d. No Drawings.]

A.D. 1857, June 18.—N° 1708.

DAY, Horace Hollister.—(*A communication.*)—"Improve-
" ments in preparing and vulcanizing india rubber, gutta percha,
" or other analogous gums." These are, "mixing with the
" matter, when prepared for being vulcanized, a substance which
" will prevent the cellular and spongy character, by absorbing the
" sulphurous acid gas as fast as it is generated." "The material
" which is proposed to be employed for affecting this object is,
" by preference, ordinary pipe-clay (alumine); but other sub-
" stances capable of absorbing the gas may be employed."

[Printed, 4d. No Drawings.]

A.D. 1857, June 19.—N° 1710.

SOREL, Stanislas Tranquille Modeste.—"New chemical
" compositions, producing either house paintings, cement, or
" plastic paste to be moulded." Obtained by combining the
following substances in suitable proportions :—First, "chloride
" of zinc, or any other chloride which is amorphus with the

" latter," either chloride of iron or of manganese; second, a tar-
trate; third, muriatic acid; fourth, a feculent or amylaceous substance; fifth, water; sixth, oxide of zinc. " The said substances
" are combined in various proportions, according to the nature of
" the products required. Any of the aforesaid substances may
" be replaced by others possessing similar properties; any of
" them could be omitted, and new ones could be added."
" These new compositions can replace in a great many cases
" plaster, alabaster, marble, ivory, caoutchouc, gutta percha,
" gelatine, pasteboard, papier mâché, and several other sub-
" stances."

[Printed, 4d. No Drawings.]

A.D. 1857, June 19.—Nº 1717.

DAY, HORACE HOLLISTER. — (*A communication.*) — "An im-
" proved method of treating or purifying gutta percha," which
" consists in subjecting it to the action of a liquor which dissolves
" out the etheric oil," and at the same time, "acting upon the
" woody matter, disengages the sand and other foreign matters
" held therewith." The liquor consists of a certain amount of
" caustic potash and water, to which is added an ether formed
" from a solution of chloride of lime in alcohol," "about four
" ounces of chloride of lime in eight ounces of alcohol." The
gutta percha is placed in the liquor, and the whole "is brought
" to the boiling point, and kept in that state for eight or ten
" hours." The gutta percha is taken out, and rolled under
water, "and may be vulcanized in the usual way." By adding
a fresh supply of ether, "the liquor may be used for several
" parcels of gutta percha."

[Printed, 4d. No Drawings.]

A.D. 1857, June 20.—Nº 1728.

RICHARDSON, BENJAMIN. — " Improvements in manufac-
" turing and ornamenting articles of flint glass." In these improvements one is :—" In order to ornament such articles made of
" flint glass, parts or the whole of the surfaces thereof are to be
" coated, by preference, with a solution of gutta percha or india
" rubber, or it may be with other compositions, not acted on by
" acid; and from such coated surfaces parts of the coating are
" to be removed by any suitable tool, so as to produce thereon
" the desired ornamental device." " The gutta percha com-

" position preferred is 1 part of gutta percha, 3 parts turpentine
" or other solvent, 4 parts bees-wax and 1 part tallow or suet.
Or 1 part india-rubber, 8 parts naptha, 4 parts of bee's wax, 1
" part rosin, 1 part tallow or suet."

[Printed, 4d. No Drawings.]

A.D. 1857, August 20.—N° 2213.

SPILL, George.— (*Provisional protection only.*)—" Improve-
" ments in treating fabrics employed in the manufacture of hats,
" caps, and bonnets, and for other purposes, and also other
" fabrics, so as to render the same impervious to moisture and
" grease."

It consists as follows :—" Dissolve india rubber or gutta percha
" to a pasty consistency in coal tar, naptha, or other suitable
" solvent, adding thereto powdered sulphur, and spread in a thin
" film the mixture thus obtained upon the fabric ;" " then subject
" such fabrics to a high temperature, sufficient to change the
" nature of the compound, and prevent its decomposition by its
" contact with grease, as also to cause it to retain its permanent
" elasticity," &c.; or " apply as a coating bees'-wax, dissolved, or
" in a liquid state, produced by heat, or a solution of gelatine,"
to which "afterwards apply infusion of nutgalls."

[Printed, 4d. No Drawings.]

A.D. 1857, August 20.—N° 2214.

CHAMBERLAIN, Amos Pierce.— " Improvements in ma-
" chines for cutting corks and other substances." These consist
of a " system of knife and carriage," " also applicable for cutting
" india rubber, caoutchouc, paper, and other substances." " The
" knives are turned by means of a strap or leather band, or any
" other well-known manner for giving a fast motion; the strap
" or band is attached around the pulley."

[Printed, 10d. Drawing.]

A.D. 1857, September 5.—N° 2323.

KING, John.—(*A communication.*)—(*Provisional protection only.*)
—" Improvements in the manufacture of boots and shoes, and in
" machinery for that purpose."

These consist as follows :—Before placing " the upper leather
" and insole " in a machine, their edges are coated with a cement
prepared by dissolving gutta percha and caoutchouc in certain

proportions "in bisulphuret of carbon and mixing the solutions;" and they are pressed together in a machine, &c. "The heel is
" filled with a composition of gutta percha, white resin, or gal-
" lipot, or turpentine, scraps or raspings of leather and drying
" oil, heated and mixed together, &c."
[Printed, 4d. No Drawings.]

A.D. 1857, September 7.—N° 2334.

PARKER, BENJAMIN.—(*Provisional protection only.*)—"A new
" elastic composition for coating, cementing, bedding, and other-
" wise protecting bodies, also applicable to the construction or
" formation of articles to which it may be suitable."

The elastic composition consists of india rubber, coal or other suitable tar, pulverised chalk, or other suitable material, sulphur, and flax or cotton waste, or other suitable material mixed in certain proportions, and formed into sheets, &c., and hardened by heat. "The hardening process is further aided by the assistance
" of sulphuric, muriatic, or any other suitable acid applied in
" conjunction therewith in any suitable manner."
[Printed, 4d. No Drawings.]

A.D. 1857, October 19.—N° 2674.

NEWTON, WILLIAM EDWARD.—(*A communication.*)—"Im-
" provements in the manufacture of drawing rollers." These are as follows :—

The "electricity developed" by india-rubber, "rendering it
" unsuitable for the" above "purpose;" "to divest the india
" rubber (or gutta percha) of this power," it is incorporated with
" a portion of plumbago or black lead previous to vulcanizing."
A composition of "india rubber, magnesia, sulphur, and black
" lead" in certain proportions is described. A tube is formed on a mandril of layers of cloth. Over these is the composition temporarily covered with cloth while being heated. After vulcanization "this tube is cut into short sections, which are secured
" to the drawing roll by any suitable cement."
[Printed, 6d. Drawing.]

A.D. 1857, October 26.—N° 2713.

DE CLIPPÈLE, CHARLES.—"Improvements in the manu-
" facture of boots and shoes, harness, and driving straps, which

" improvements are applicable to uniting various materials
" together, and also for waterproofing."

These are, in reference to this subject, making a composition or cement of " sulphuret of carbon 1¾ pints, gutta percha about " 9½ ozs. muslin a sufficient quantity," the muslin is only employed in certain cases.

[Printed, 4d. No Drawings.]

A.D. 1857, November 14.—N° 2866.

MACINTOSH, JOHN.—" An improvement in preparing tele-
" graphic wire which is coated with gutta percha, in order to
" render it more capable of resisting heat, and in laying down
" telegraph wires in the sea." This consists, in reference to this subject, as follows:—To render the gutta percha more capable of resisting heat the wire with the gutta percha coating as it is expressed from the die, in place of passing, as is usual, through a long trough containing water, this trough is divided "into two
" parts; the division next the covering machine I make about
" six or seven feet long, and I fill it with commercial sulphuric
" acid " (oil of vitriol); "the other part of the trough contains
" water as heretofore." The covered wire may be coiled up and dipped in the acid and allowed to remain ten seconds then removed and plunged into water. " In place of sulphuric acid I
" sometimes employ chloride of sulphur mixed with a solvent by
" sulphuret of carbon, to which from two to four per cent. of
" chloride of sulphur has been added, is very suitable for the
" purpose." The covered wire passes " through this mixture
" after it has come from the water trough and when its surface
" is free from water." The immersing time is "about two
" seconds."

[Printed, 4d. No Drawings.]

A.D. 1857, December 17.—N° 3097.

BLIZZARD, WILLIAM.—(*Provisional protection only.*)— " Im-
" provements in the treatment of india rubber, by a new process
" for the manufacture of a chrystaline and colourless varnish for
" waterproofing all kinds of textile fabricks and papers without
" smell, and without in any degree altering their appearance;
" and for making divers varnishes and paints."

This consists in dissolving india-rubber or caoutchouc in a
" resinous spirit, such as naphtha, camphine, turpentine, rozin,

" benzene, also caoutchine " which solution may be further
" decolorized, if required," and applied as above.

[Printed, 4d. No Drawings.]

1858.

A.D. 1858, February 6.—N° 220.

CANDELOT, LOUIS FULGENCE. — " Divers anti-nitrous ce-
" ments." These are first, melting colophany 14 or 15 lbs., yellow
or white wax at least 1 lb., stearine 2 lbs., in 6 lbs. " painter's or
" boiled oil." The solution thus obtained is removed from the fire,
when 26 or 25 lbs. turpentine is added, in which is dissolved,
" liquid india-rubber, at most 1 lb.," " dissolved in the cold state."
" The smell of turpentine is done away with by adding a spoonful
" of sulphuric ether for each quart." " When gutta percha is
" used instead of india-rubber I melt it together with the colo-
" phony, the wax and the steerine ;" when " the whole is melted
" the oil is added, and the vessel taken from the fire and the
" turpentine poured in." It is found useful to strain the solution
through a metallic or hair sieve and the following powder is
sifted into this solution through a sieve, No. 50. " Glass or silex
" 25 lbs., chalk 9 lbs., grey oxide of zinc 8 lbs., talc (or preferably
" sulphur) 6 lbs., pulverulent slack lime 2 lbs.," and it " may have
" 1 or 2 lbs. of colophony or resin added to it, which has been
" previously broken and screened." A second, third, and fourth
cement or paste is made much in the same way as above, in which
either india-rubber or gutta percha or both, in small quantities,
are ingredients.

[Printed, 4d. No Drawings.]

A.D. 1858, February 12.—N° 274.

MACINTOSH, JOHN.—" An improvement in treating articles
" of gutta percha made or formed in dies or moulds, also certain
" articles of gutta percha made by expressing through dies, and
" also articles of gutta percha made by pressing rollers." This
consists in immersing the article whether it be of gutta percha
alone or mixed with foreign matter, such as india-rubber or bitumen
in a bath of sulphuric acid, preferring " the concentrated acid of
" commerce," for " a period varying from a few seconds to several

" minutes" it is then taken out and all acid removed by cold water. " If the appearance of the surface is not so much an object " as the hardening the material to a considerable depth, the " period of the immersion may be increased,". Pure gutta percha takes less time than mixtures. By this process "blocks made " from a mixture of inferior india-rubber with a small portion of " gutta percha" are rendered suitable "for erasing pencil marks." In a former patent, No. 2866, A.D. 1857, "amongst other things " " telegraph wires coated with gutta percha were submitted to " sulphuric acid and water as a means of rendering them less " liable to injury from tropical and like temperatures."

[Printed, 4d. No Drawings.]

A.D. 1858, March 3.—N° 419.

PARKER, BENJAMIN.—(*Provisional protection only.*)— " The " manufacture of materials for coating, cementing, bedding, and " otherwise protecting bodies, and which is also applicable to the " construction or formation of various articles." 48 lbs. of ground chalk or its equivalent, is mixed with a solution formed by dissolving 10 lbs. of india-rubber with 40 lbs. of "coal or " other suitable tar, sufficient to form a thin pastey solution " when about ½ lb. of sulphur and about 20 lbs of flax, cotton waste or other material are incorporated, and the whole triturated is formed into sheets by rollers, &c. after which the material is " hardened by steam of a sufficiently high temperature" in "a " suitably constructed chamber, and which hardening process " is further aided by the assistance of sulphuric, muriatic or " any other suitable acid applied in conjunction therewith in " any suitable manner."

[Printed, 4d. No Drawings.]

A.D. 1858, March 17.—N° 543.

GOODERHAM, JOHN.— (*Provisional protection only.*)—" Im- " provements in shoemaker's wax." Dissolve about twenty parts gutta percha by heat, and mix with it about fifty eight parts pitch, about five parts soap, about six parts rosin, about five parts bees'-wax, about one part palm oil, and about five parts tallow, "adding the one after the other, and maintaining " the heat at such a temperature while mixing." "It is not " absolutely essential to add the bees'-wax soap, palm oil or " tallow, but I much prefer to do so."

[Printed, 4d. No Drawings.]

A.D. 1858, April 10.—N° 777.

PARMELEE, SPENCER THOMAS.—" The manufacture of im-
" proved belting for machinery or other purposes." "'Two or
" more layers of woven material, such as cotton or linen canvass
" cut into strips of the required dimensions" "previously spread
" or coated on both sides with india-rubber gutta percha, or a
" combination of both," "prepared in the ordinary manner by
" being ground and compounded with the requisite materials for
" that purpose." These strips or layers are laid together as many
plyes as the thickness required, either " by hand labour upon a long
" table or by means of a two cylinder machine so constructed
" with guides as to bring the different plies parallel one to the
" other and press the same into close union." The belting thus
formed is afterwards " submitted simultaneously to heat and
" pressure " as follows, first, by placing it " between two revolving
" cylinders united by an endless metallic band, in such manner as
" to admit of the belting being passed between the periphery of
" one of the rollers enclosed within a heated chamber and the
" endless metallic band, the said cylinders being provided with
" one or more grooves corresponding to the required width of the
" band." Second, in lieu of the above, employing "a metallic
" press, the bed of which is grooved internally in width, corre-
" sponding with the belting, or furnished with shifting plates
" grooved in like manner, in which a portion of the belting is laid,
" and covered with a metallic surface plate, so as to surround that
" part of the belt within the press; pressure by means of screws,
" and heat, by steam or otherwise, is then applied till the belting
" is sufficiently cured, when the next portion thereof has to be
" placed within the press for a like purpose, and operated on in
" like manner." Third, "the belting or otherwise with inter-
" vening metallic bands or strips of the same width as the belting,
" may be coiled or wound upon a shaft or cylinder, and secured
" thereto, and the requisite pressure supplied through the madium
" of a cumferetial (circumferential?) clasp or band and moveable
" side plates; the belting may then be subjected to heat as afore-
" said, by placing the apparatus within a chamber for that
" purpose."

[Printed, 1s. 4d. Drawings.]

A.D. 1858, May 8.—N° 1036.

NEWTON, ALFRED VINCENT.—(*A communication.*)—" An improved manufacture of hard and waterproof fabric and the application of the same to the construction of boots, parts of carriages and of furniture, portmanteaus, and travelling cases, and vessels of capacity." " Woven wire cloth or pierced sheet metal is coated on both sides with india-rubber vulcanite compound in a plastic state." " If the wire cloth is coarse, and it is desired to cover it cheaply, it is placed between two sheets of the compound, and the whole is passed together between calender rollers." " When a smooth surface is desired the wire cloth is to be more thickly coated." This is made into the above named articles using vulcanite rubber as a cement and when put together the articles are vulcanized at "a temperature of about two hundred and seventy degrees," " to obtain a polish on flat surfaces," "the fabric is to be moulded between plates of glass or tin and submitted to the vulcanizing process while still in contact with the glass or tin."

[Printed, 4d. No Drawings.]

A.D. 1858, May 14.—N° 1090.

MACINTOSH, JOHN—" Improvements in insulating telegraphic wires." These are, in reference to this subject, gun cotton is dissolved in a solvent, in preference consisting " of equal parts of wood spirit and coal naptha," and "gutta percha, india-rubber and other substances may be added to the solution." The wire is coated with this mixture and over this coating is one " of india-rubber, or of india-rubber mixed with other substances, and afterwards I submit the wire so coated to the action of sulphuric acid, or of chloride of sulphur and a solvent by which the coating will become so changed as to be no longer liable to be injured by tropical heat or like temperatures." The coated wire is in the sulphuric acid "about twenty seconds, but this varies according to the quality of the india-rubber; if it is kept in for too long a time it becomes charred." "In place of sulphuric acid, bi-sulphuret of carbon mixed with from two to four per cent. of chloride of sulphur may be employed." When this process is employed the water trough is not used."

[Printed, 4d. No Drawings.]

A.D. 1858, June 9.—N° 1298.

MOSELEY, DAVID.—"Improvements in machinery used in the
"manufacture of vulcanized india-rubber thread." These are,
first, "the use and application of a roller to support the roller
"on which the sheet of vulcanized india-rubber is lapped, and to
"answer the purpose of the 'doctor' usually employed to remove
"the surplus shellac or other cement," "which is now squeezed
"out by the pressure between the lap and the roller in the trough."
"In the usual mode of operation the sheet of vulcanized india-
"rubber passes under a rod or roller placed in the trough, and
"the surplus shellac is removed by an instrument called a
"'doctor.'"
Second, "covering the roller" on "which the sheet of vulcanized
"india-rubber is lapped with a coating of vulcanized india-rubber
"or gutta percha," "to protect the wood from injury by the
"cutters, and to prevent the roller from warping by the action of
"the water used in cutting the india-rubber."

[Printed, 6d. Drawing.]

A.D. 1858, June 18.—N° 1377.

BLIZZARD, WILLIAM.—(*Provisional protection only.*)—" Im-
" provements in india-rubber, gutta percha, and drying and other
" oils." These are, in reference to this subject, manufacturing
from india-rubber and gutta percha a transparent solution. "The
" agents I use for the different purposes are sometimes plain
" water or water and sodo (soda?) dissolved therein, to which is
" sometimes added a little quicklime, and afterwards submitted
" to different degrees of temperature, at other times temperature
" alone is sufficient." It is also proposed "to combine the solu-
" tion with any of the resinous or spirit gums, such as copal,
" animal shellac, lac damor, mastic, sandrach, cowrie, &c."

[Printed, 4d. No Drawings.]

A.D. 1858, June 21.—N° 1393.

HENSON, HENRY HENSON.—" Preserving or waterproofing
" ropes, strands, cordage, cables, and other similar articles," by
saturating "the fibre, the ropes or other similar articles when manu-

"factured, or during or previous to the process of their manufac-
"ture" with any or some of the following materials : "1st, boiled
"tallow, mixed or unmixed with arsenic and palm oil; 2nd, weak
"solution of glue, albumen, or gelatine, and subsequently tannin,
"and fat; 3rd, gutta percha and resin; 4th, india-rubber and
"resin; 5th, a solution of Venice turpentine; 6th, common
"japan; 7th, 'kamptulicon' or mixture of granulated wood or
"cork with caoutchouc or gutta percha put on the surface of the
"rope, &c.; 8th, silicate solutions, as silicate of soda or potash
"alone or in combination with other materials, afterwards to be
"subjected if desired to a heat above 212° Fahr. to render the
"silica insoluble and the rope, &c. flame proof; 9th, silicate
"and oil; 10th, vulcanite or caoutchouc and tar; 11th, marine
"glue or caoutchouc and shellac; 12th, acetate of alumina;
"13th, alumina and compounds of lead; 14th, tannin and
"similar treatment to that of leather; 15th, tannin and subse-
"quent treatment with acetate of alumina; 16th, tannin and
"fat; 17th, solutions of india-rubber; 18th, solutions of gutta
"percha."

[Printed, 4d. No Drawings.]

A.D. 1858, July 16.—N° 1609.

PUTNAM, CLARK SAMUEL.—"Improvements in the apparatus
"for hardening vegetable gums, oils, and other substances
"susceptible of being hardened by steam." A retort shaped
circular boiler, is described which may be fitted into the top of a
circular stove, and to the top of the boiler the vulcanizing chest
is fitted by flanges. "To this apparatus the self regulating appa-
"ratus may or may not be attached. This consists of a chamber
"conveniently located, connected and communicating with the
"steam chest through the medium of two pipes. In this
"chamber, over the mouth of one of these pipes a valve is seated
"whose stem passing out through the top of the chamber
"supports a lever carrying an adjustable weight. When the
"temperature is too high, as will be indicated by a thermometer
"placed in a tube formed in the steam chest, the pressure of the
"steam will open the valve and steam will enter when the pres-
"sure in the chest and chamber are equal, and the water in the
"chamber will through this pipe pass into the chest, and thence

" into the boiler. To this lever may also be attached devices for
" regulating the draught of the fire."

[Printed, 6d. Drawing.]

A.D. 1858, July 26.—N° 1687.

GODEFROY, PETER AUGUSTIN. — " Improvements in the
" cleansing of gutta percha." The gutta percha is placed in a
case or chamber, "the corners of said chamber being used only,
" the centre part not obtaining the same friction," the gutta
percha "is forced by hydraulic steam, or other power against"
a granulator or rasp near the upper part of the machine, which
reduces "the gutta percha to shavings or small particles whereby
" the impurities are separated and washed away falling into a
" tub or tank," being previously washed and thrown off the
granulator or rasp by a flow of water issuing from a semi-circular
pipe attached to the rasp. The gutta percha as it falls into the
tub or tank, is kept in continual commotion by means of an agitator within the tub or tank, worked by bevil wheels. "The
" gutta percha is then taken from the tub or tank and sub-
" mitted to the masticator," and is ready for use.

[Printed, 10d. Drawing.]

A.D. 1858, July 30.—N° 1728.

DODGE, NATHANIEL SHATTSWELL. — (A communication.)—
" Improvements in treating waste vulcanized india-rubber."
These are first, "disintegrating or reducing the waste vulcanized
" india-rubber" (by grinding) to as finely a divided state as
possible, and then boiling the reduced rubber in water " for about
" 48 hours but the duration of such operation is dependent on
" the nature of the materials to be treated;" "a soft plastic or
" gummy material is obtained suitable for re-manufacture."

Second, disintegrating or reducing such waste india-rubber,
and passing it through 'mullers' or rollers heated or not, so as
to bring it into a sheet shape, and "subsequently mixing or
" incorporating it with asphalte, coal tar, resin, pitch, shellac, or
" other similar resinous or bituminous substance, whereby a
" new and useful material is obtained." The proportions of
these materials may be more or less varied but good results were
obtained by mixing ten parts of the rubber manipulated as above
" with two parts of the resinous or bituminous substance; but

" when coal tar is used four parts of coal tar may be combined
" with ten parts of rubber."

[Printed, 4d. No Drawings.]

A.D. 1858, August 5.—N° 1778.

LUIS, JOZÉ.—(*A communication.*)—" A new waterproof tube
" without seams or rivets, and in the apparatus connected there-
" with." This consists as follows :—First, the tube of tissue to
be coated internally is passed over a rack which is fixed, in which
are two pipes one for conveying steam the other for carrying it off.
A hollow conical piston is screwed to the end of the rack after the
tissue tube has been passed over it, the rack has also a circular
collar fixed to it. A cylindrical box of copper or iron containing
the material for coating the tube, less in diameter than the tube,
opens lengthways by means of a hinge, adapts itself on a circular
collar and shuts one of the ends, two very thin rods of copper sliding along the box keeps it shut, and also permits of its being
easily opened. Two rings are attached, and to these a cord is
fastened, by this cord the box is made to slide on the circular
collar which pushes the matter contained in the box. After
having passed the tissue tube on the rack and screwed on the
piston, the matter is put in fusion in the box by the steam jets in
the rack, the tissue is drawn on the box, the box is made to slip
in a contrary direction, thus forcing it to abandon a portion of the
matter in the tube. The tube is drawn on the piston (whatever
be its length) which presses the matter on the sides of the tissue.
" The matter can also be spread on the sides by fixing the box
" and making the collar moveable." The box may be dispensed
with and the matter may be introduced in the tube in small quantities and placing it along the rack. Second, the outside of the
tube is coated by drawing the tube somewhat in a similar manner
to the above through a box in which the coating matter is in a
state of fusion or dissolved by chemical agents, but this latter
plan is "less satisfactory." The composition of the coating is
gutta percha, from 30 to 40 parts, and india-rubber, from 70 to 60
parts. " Other ingredients can be added to change the properties,
" such as coal tar," which " added in small portions gives a
" stiffness to the tubes."

[Printed, 4d. No Drawings.]

A.D. 1858, August 9.—N° 1811.

SMITH, WILLOUGHBY.—"An improved compound for coating "or insulating electric telegraph wires and coating other surfaces." One fifth by weight of Stockholm or wood tar, and about the same weight of resin, are put into a vessel with a jacket or a series of pipes, by preference, heated by steam, when properly melted the whole is passed through a wire gauze strainer "into another "vessel similarly heated;" three fifths by weight of gutta percha, having, by preference, been previously cleansed in the ordinary way, and reduced into thin pieces or shreds is then put into the heated vessel and mixed with the resin and tar. In this second vessel are stirrers so as to mix the whole uniformly. The above proportions may, to some extent, be varied.

[Printed, 4d. No Drawings.]

A.D. 1858, August 13.—N° 1853.

JOHNSON, JOHN HENRY.—(*A communication from Austin G. Day.*)—"Improvements in the treatment of crude india-rubber, "gutta percha, or other vulcanizable gums, and in the manu-"facture therefrom of what are usually called hard rubber "articles." These are first, "the general system or mode of "treating crude india-rubber, gutta percha, or other vulcanizable "gums, and the manufacture from gums so treated of hard "rubber articles" as follows:

Second, in place of cutting or tearing the raw gum into small shreds and washing it in the ordinary way as described in No. 1787, A.D. 1855, "passing the crude gum in masses of from "ten to thirty pounds weight through toothed rollers having a "slipping motion" abundantly supplied with water, thus forming the material into long sheets.

Third, "the application and use of alternative pressure and "vacuum in the cleansing process of raw gums," instead of "exhaustion in connexion with the usual pressure of the atmo-"sphere" as described in No. 1787, A.D. 1855. The pressure is thirty, forty-five or more pounds on the square inch. The solution may be of carbonated alkali, in place of caustic. If caustic is used the strength need not exceed 12° to 20° Baumé, when carbonate is used "the strength should be 15° to 25° Baumés' "hydrometer."

Fourth, "the mixing and grinding together of two parts or "thereabouts by weight of caoutchouc or gutta percha, or other

" vulcanizable gum, and one part of sulphur, when such com-
" position is preparatory to the running of the heat."

Fifth, "removing the heat for vulcanizing flexible and elastic
" hard gum compounds" from a temperature of about 275° F.,
to 300° F., and upwards.

Sixth, " equalizing the temperature in the heating apparatus
" by mechanical means, such as a double acting pump, a rotary
" fan, &c., which shall draw out the steam and air from one end
" of the cylinder and transfer the same into the head of the
" opposite end."

[Printed, 8d. Drawing.]

A.D. 1858, August 24.—N° 1924.

MACINTOSH, JOHN.—" Improvements in insulating telegraphic
" wires or conductors." These are, in reference to this subject,
" when using soft East India-rubber and similar india-rubber,
" I mix it with an equal weight of shellac ground to a fine
" powder, and without the addition of a solvent;" preferring to
use the shellac "known as seed black." The india-rubber cleansed
in the usual manner, is repeatedly passed through crushing rollers,
" and after each passage through the rollers it is dusted over
" with the shellac powder," and this is repeated until the requisite
quantity of shellac has been incorporated with the rubber.
" When using india-rubber of a superior quality to the East
" India-rubber, I employ less shellac, as also when gutta percha
" is substituted; in any case the quantity of shellac should not
" be so great as to cause the compound to crack when bent."

[Printed, 4d. No Drawings.]

A.D. 1858, September 1.—N° 1987.

WARNE, WILLIAM.—" Improvements in the construction of
" elastic pavements and linings for walls and in the manufacture
" of elastic mats, brushes, and pads for packing furniture."
These are, "tubes or hollow cells are used made of india-rubber,
" or india-rubber and its compounds rendered permanently elastic
" by sulphur, or sulphur compounds and heat." " In construct-
" ing an elastic pavement or lining for a wall of a lunatic asylum
" or other building," "the numerous cells or tubes of which a
" pavement or lining is to be composed, are arranged side by
" side, and are fixed at right angles to the surface on which they
" are applied" presenting a honeycomb appearance. " In pre-

" paring the materials for a pavement or for a lining, the side
" of the several tubes or cells are cemented together and then
" subjected to heat to produce the change, and they are then
" affixed in their places. In making elastic mats, brushes, and
" pads for packing furniture, similar constructions of india-rubber
" cells are used. In some cases one or both surfaces produced
" by the ends of the cells are covered by a sheet or surface of
" india-rubber or india-rubber compounded with other materials
" and combined with sulphur affixed before subjecting the cells
" to the process of heat to produce the change."
[Printed, 6d. Drawing.]

A.D. 1858, October 1.—N° 2191.

BRADBURY, Henry.—*(Provisional protection only.)*—" Im-
" provements in producing printing surfaces from engraved
" plates." These are, in reference to this subject, making a composition for the above purpose " the composition consists of gutta
" percha and animal grease or oil, or vegetable oil (by preference,
" lard or olive oil is used). The gutta percha is combined with
the grease or oil by means of heat. The composition is kneaded
" and washed in warm water, and then the water is completely
" pressed out."
[Printed, 4d. No Drawings.]

A.D. 1858, October 9.—N° 2251.

HOPE, Lewis.—*(A communication.)*—" Improvements in electric
" telegraph cables." These are, in reference to this subject,
" india-rubber or gutta percha or a compound of these substances
" is ground or masticated together with about one-half the weight
" thereof of sulphur, and when in a plastic state the compound
" is," by ordinary or suitable apparatus applied to cover conducting wires for telegraphs. In preference, the wire is copper,
coated with tin, deposited from a solution of that metal. A considerable portion of the wire thus covered with the compound is
wound upon a reel and introduced into a vessel and heated to
about three hundred degrees Fahrenheit until the coating is
changed or converted into the hard or semi-hard compound.
[Printed, 4d. No Drawings.]

A.D. 1858, October 12.—N° 2270.

WRAY, Leonard.—" New and improved compounds for the
" coating or insulating of submarine electric telegraph wires, and

" which are also applicable to the coating or insulating of electric
" telegraph wires laid underground." "I take two and half
" parts by weight of india-rubber (caoutchouc) cleansed accord-
" ing to the mode well known in the trade, and add to it one
" and a half parts of shell-lac in a melted state, and I well and
" thoroughly mix and incorporate them together by means of
" grinding or mixing rollers heated by steam or otherwise. I
" then add to this mixture one part of flour of glass, and con-
" tinue the grinding or mixing by the heated rollers until the
" whole becomes a sufficiently homogeneous mass; or, I take
" four parts of cleansed india-rubber, one part of gutta percha
" (cleansed by modes well known in the trade), reduced to a
" plastic state by means of heat, and when these are well mixed
" and incorporated together by the grinding, masticating, or
" mixing rollers, heated by steam, or otherwise, I add two parts
" each of shell-lac and flour of glass, grinding and mixing them
" as before, until the compound is brought into a sufficiently
" homogeneous condition. Or I take two parts of either vegetable
" caoutchouc, or mineral caoutchouc (bitumen) or gutta percha, or
" either separately, or one or more combined, and I add thereto
" one part of powdered flint, flour of glass or other suitable
" siliceous or aluminous matter, such as purified kaolin, and I
" combine them together by means of heated masticators, or
" grinding or mixing rollers, as before described." The above
proportions may be varied as required.

[Printed, 4d. No Drawings.]

A.D. 1858, October 14.—N° 2288.

COWPER, CHARLES.—(*A communication from Gustavus Cuppers.*)—This invention consists " in the manufacture of articles
" of hard vulcanized india-rubber and gutta percha and similar
" gums, by partially hardening and repairing or perfecting the
" same one or more times, and then completing the hardening
" or vulcanizing process " as follows :—" When half a pound of
" sulphur is mixed with one pound of india-rubber, and the heat
" is about from 290° to 300° F., the time for leaving it (the article)
" in the mould will be about one hour. If less sulphur be mixed
" with the rubber or less heat used, the time must be increased
" proportionally. If the heat is greater than about 300°, less
" than an hour will be required." The mould is then allowed to
cool, and removed from the article, which by this time is partially

hardened. "Any blisters, holes, or other imperfections on the
" surface are now moistened by a liquid compound, or solution
" of india-rubber or gutta percha, and are filled up and smoothed
" with the original compound," and pressed again in the mould,
which is made water tight during the heating by means of strips
of india-rubber between the joints, or otherwise, and again re‐
placed in the heat; it is left "from about one half an hour
" to three hours, when the compound will still be partially
" hardened;" when removed from the mould, if the article is still
imperfect, the mending and heating is repeated. If otherwise,
the article is placed loosely in a box without the mould; this box,
with the loose articles, is then hermetically closed, and the harden‐
ing of the articles is completed, which may require six or eight
hours' heat. When the article is to be highly ornamented, two
moulds are used. "The mould for the main body of the rubber
" is used for the purpose of repairing imperfections." "The
" mould for the main body of the rubber is used for the purpose
" of repairing imperfections." "The article is then removed
" from the heat, and from the mould, and is deposited in
" another mould" containing the finer impressions; it is then
firmly pressed, and heated in the mould until the hardening is
completed.

[Printed, 4d. No Drawings.]

A.D. 1858, October 18.—N° 2321.

WEST, CHARLES.—" Improvements in the mode of insulating
" and covering wire." These are, in reference to this subject,
first, to make a perfect solid tube of india-rubber, fixing "imme‐
" diately under the reel from which the india-rubber is wound
" on the wire, another small reel covered with flannel or some
" spongy substance saturated with mineral ether or other solvent
" of india-rubber, during the whole time of the working of the
" machine by any convenient means."

Second, causing the surfaces of the strips of india-rubber to co‐
here by submitting the covered wire to moist heat, in preference, by
plunging it into heated water. If a higher temperature is desired
than "that of ordinary boiling water, the water may have common
" salt, alum, or any other salt dissolved in it, so as to raise the
" temperature of the boiling point of the liquid."

[Printed, 4d. No Drawings.]

A.D. 1858, October 27.—N° 2394.

WRAY, LEONARD.—(*Provisional protection only.*)—" The prepa-
" ration and application of a substitute for gutta percha, caout-
" chouc, and similar substances." The substance is " called 'susu
" poko,' signifying in English 'tree milk,'" and is from a tree
" growing in the Malayan Peninsula, and on the islands of the
" Malayan and Eastern Archipeligo." The crude product; " I
" first free it from all impurities " " by certain simple and well-
" known methods ;" it may " be benefitted by compression."
" I also harden and materially change the character of this
" cleansed product by means of chloride of sulphur, or by other
" suitable chemical substances." To dissolve and "render it fit
" for manufacturing purposes in that form, I treat it with naptha,
" bisulphuret of carbon, oil of sassafras, and other suitable solvents,
" also heat." It is also prepared by the methods used for gutta
percha and india-rubber, and in some cases it is mixed with " either
" one or more of them. It may also be combined with lac, shell-lac,
" with pulpy and with fibrous matters, with siliceous, and, indeed,
" with a great number of other substances."
[Printed, 4d. No Drawings.]

A.D. 1858, October 29.—N° 2413.

KIRRAGE, WILLIAM.—" An improved elastic combination of
" materials impervious to atmospheric influences, as a substitute
" for hard woods, metal, leather, or felting, and for other pur-
" poses." When the material when in use will not be heated
above 200° F., 12 lbs. of india-rubber is masticated with 4 lbs. of
gutta percha, 25 lbs. of Stockholm or coal tar, 60 lbs. of fine
powdered chalk, 4 lbs. of hemp or other fibre, and 10 lbs. of
sulphur. The materials are moulded, rolled, cut, or stamped out
as required, and if they are to be elastic, exposed to the action of
steam, from thirty to fifty pounds pressure on the square inch,
for from three to three and a half hours ; if they are to be hard for
polishing, for six hours to steam of greater pressure or higher
temperature. Instead of steam, the compound " may be exposed
" to a temperature of 300° for a longer or shorter period, according
" to the degree of hardness required." As a substitute for
heavy leather, 16 lbs. of india-rubber, 25 lbs. of tar, 48 lbs. of
finely powdered chalk, 16 lbs. of hemp, and 10 lbs. of sulphur
are formed into a compound, and moulded and hardened as

above. "For driving bands, &c., the compound is rolled into bands of half the thickness required; "strands of hemp are " then introduced the whole length, and the compound is rolled " down, making the two thicknesses one solid body." When employed before hardening for lining cisterns, &c., the compound may if preferred have the sulphur left out. A compound which may be exposed to great heat and pressure is made with 20 lbs. india rubber, 25 lbs. of tar, 25 lbs. of fine powdered coke, 25 lbs. of Stourbridge or other fire clay, 10 lbs. of sulphur, 5 lbs. of fine emery and 5 lbs. steel fillings are treated as above. If the compound is to imitate whalebone, ivory, jet, &c., 14 lbs. gutta percha, 4 lbs. of shellac, seedlac, or sticlac, 25 lbs. of tar, 60 lbs. of fine chalk, and 12 lbs. of sulphur are masticated, formed into articles as above and hardened as above described. Coloring matters may be employed to give any required tint.

[Printed, 4d. No Drawings.]

A.D. 1858, November 2.—N° 2449.

DODGE, NATHANIEL SHATTSWELL.—(*A communication.*)— " Improvements in treating waste vulcanized india rubber." These are, first, "restoring waste vulcanized india-rubber by " submitting it to the action of heat, steam, or of steam and " water combined before or after such rubber has been disinteg- " rated, laminated, or reduced in any suitable manner.

Second, " combining or incorporating of fibrous materials with " waste vulcanized india-rubber either previous to or when in a " plastic state, such condition being the result either of the " before mentioned or other means of treatment, for the purpose " of adding strength and stability to the same."

Third, the employment and use of restored "waste vulcanized " india-rubber in combination with fibrous materials in manufac- " turing " fabrics or other articles without any farther treatment, or the resulting material or product may be mixed and incorporated " with asphalte, resin, pitch, coal tar, shellac or other bituminous " or resinous substance," and the compound passed " between " rollers or mullers until thoroughly mixed."

[Printed, 4d. No Drawings.]

A.D. 1858, November 17.—N° 2582.

VASSEROT, CHARLES FREDERIC.—(*A communication from Louis Xavier Beuchot.*)—(*Provisional protection only.*)—" A water-

" proof coating."—" Dissolving in a water bath a certain quantity
" of gutta percha with some essence of turpentine. After com-
" plete dissolution, I add a sixth of its weight of resin and a fifth
" of wax."

[Printed, 4d. No Drawings.]

A.D. 1858, November 19.—N° 2616.

HANCOCK, WALTER.—"Improvements in the manufacture of
" electric telegraph wires and cables." These are in reference to
this subject, in place of gutta percha, making "a compound
" composed of gutta percha or of india-rubber or of an admix-
" ture of gutta percha and india-rubber combined with one or
" more of the following substances, namely, shellac, resin, Venice
" turpentine or other similar non-conducting resinous substance."
" This compound or admixture is made by means of a masticating
" machine."

[Printed, 4d. No Drawings.]

A.D. 1858, November 19.—N° 2618.

HENSON, HENRY HENSON.—"Waterproofing fabrics or mate-
" rials." This consists in "the use in connection with any fabric
" treated with adhesive materials of solutions of hydrated pro-
" toxide of lead and sulphate or acetate of alumina or both if
" desirable or any soluble salt of alumina, or a mixture of a
" solution of slicate of soda or silicate of potash and hydrated
" oxide of lead, or a mixture of solutions of nitrate of lead,
" acetate of lead, and sulphate of alumina or soda, alum, man-
" ganese alum, or any of the double sulphates, or the elements or
" the equivalents thereof," by "immersion, pressure, or exhaus-
" tion, either before or after the fabrics are subjected to any
" application of caoutchouc."

[Printed, 4d. No Drawings.]

A.D. 1858, November 23.—N° 2661.

WARNE, WILLIAM JAQUES, JAMES ARCHIBALD, and
FANSHAWE, JOHN AMERICUS. — "An improved fabric
" applicable for covering floors, and walls and for other analogous
" purposes." India rubber or gutta percha, or both combined,
are reduced by rollers to a plastic state and mixed with "fibrous
" or filamentous materials sawdust, and ground cork with the
" addition of the sulphate of lime, sulphate of zinc, sulphur or its

" equivalent;" when well mixed the plastic material is spread evenly upon one or both sides of a textile or woven fabric which may have been soaked in tar, resin, or some other preservative It is "then submitted to the action of steam or hot air, as in the " ordinary process of vulcanizing."

[Printed, 4d. No Drawings.]

A.D. 1858, December 30.—N° 2997.

DUNCAN, JOHN WALLACE.—In this invention relating to telegraphs cables, &c. the following has reference to this subject, " When the balsams of the pine or terebenthine tribe are extrac- " ted by heat, (such as tar), before applying it to compound with " gutta percha," &c. " to make cement for telegraph conductors, " I agitate the tar in a vessel of water, mixed or not with metal " to free it from the acids or their salts, which act injuriously " upon certain metallic foils." Gutta percha treated as described in No. 13,738, Old Law; " and while still hot, I compound it with " thick livery drying or linseed oil, and masticate or blend the " compound well together at a temperature varying from 250° to " 600° F." "When a convolute envelope of lead foil or 'Betts' " 'metal,' is applied to a cable near the outside, I use a bi-sul- " phuret of carbon with an excess of sulphur and make a thick " solution of gutta percha combined with shellac and apply it " with the covering hot upon the outer camia of the cable, and " cause it to pass through a hot pipe," surrounded by fire to vulcanize the coating. Instead of the metallic uniting medium for connecting the wires together using " a cement consisting of " shellac, or any combination of it, with rosin or gutta percha, " combined with fine metal powder." "For submarine cables " to be used in deep water I prefer to use " a cement for covering the same, composed of " twenty parts of viscid boiled drying oil " with twenty parts of resin, and 60 parts of gutta percha or " twenty parts of coagulated drying oil, ten parts of resin, and " seventy parts of gutta percha, or a much less proportion of oil " and rosin, may be used or it may be other suitable cement," but that described in No. 906, A.D. 1853, "page 4, line 25, " suits very well, and may be mixed or not with very fine cast- " iron powder."

[Printed, 1s. Drawings.]

1859.

A.D. 1859, January 21.—Nº 193.

CHILDS, James.—"An improvement in applying heat in the
" manufacture of artificial gums and teeth, and other articles
" composed of india rubber or gutta percha combined with
" sulphur." This consists when making "artificial gums and
" teeth of a composition of india-rubber or gutta percha and
" sulphur, the moulded gums or teeth, or a combination of gums
" and teeth, are secured between plaster of Paris casts or moulds
" of the mouth they are intended to fit, and in this state they
" are placed in a suitable vessel capable of being externally heated,
" and this I prefer to do by gas jets, though heat may be other-
" wise applied. The vessel (which is provided with a man-hole)
" is in connection with a steam boiler, so that it can be kept full
" of steam, and such steam when in the vessel is then further
" heated up to the high degree of heat requisite for producing
" the well known hardening effect consequent on high tempera-
" tures being applied to india-rubber and gutta percha when
" combined with sulphur. In like manner other articles of
" india-rubber or gutta percha combined with sulphur may, when
" held in suitable moulds or forms be introduced into a vessel
" which is then filled with steam and heated externally. In place
" of, or in addition to the steam being heated in the vessel in
" which the articles are placed, it may, after it leaves the boiler
" be heated in its way to and before getting into the vessel."
 [Printed, 10d. Drawing.]

A.D. 1859, January 22.—Nº 201.

MOSELEY, David.—"Improvements in the manufacture of
" india rubber thread." These are dispensing in this manufacture "with the dissolving and spreading of the india-rubber
" in order to produce sheets of the required thickness; and in
" producing such sheets, by cutting from solid cylindrical blocks."
The india-rubber cleansed or otherwise prepared, and combined
with sulphur or other ingredients in the usual manner or in its
natural state, is masticated, placed in a strong metal cylinder and
pressed into a solid cylindrical block, allowed to cool, and cut

into a thin sheet. This sheet may then be vulcanized. This
sheet "in its natural state vulcanized or otherwise prepared
" must then be lapped on to a roller," and put into a lathe, and
cut into threads by the ordinary apparatus. "In some cases
" sheets of india-rubber in its natural state may be acted upon
" with chloride of sulphur in order to protect them from the
" influence of the atmosphere."

[Printed, 4d. No Drawings.]

A.D. 1859, February 1.—N° 293.

HENRY, MICHAEL.—(*A communication from Moissant and Company.*)—(*Provisional protection only.*)—"The manufacture and use-
" ful applications of certain bituminous products and compounds
" of bitumen with other matters, and treating and applying cer-
" tain bitumen or bitumens for such purposes." This consists in
reference to this subject as follows; the natural bitumen found
in the West Indies called "chapapote," is distilled in retorts
such as are used for gas with heads passing into the receivers.
The oils condensed are washed in sulphuric acid and water,
and separated from the water are treated with "torefied clay,"
drawn off from it "and gradually redistilled by surcharged
" steam." "The raw oils and those given off by the first opera-
" tions may be used for the manufacture of illuminating gas
" without requiring purification." Oils drawn off at 82 centri-
grade among other purposes may be used "for dissolving india-
" rubber."

[Printed, 4d. No Drawings.]

A.D. 1859, February 17.—N° 446.

CATTELL, THOMAS.—"Improvements in treating and purify-
" ing gutta percha." The gutta percha in preference, cleansed
" by well known mechanical processes" is "exposed to the action
" of volatile solvents of two classes, in the proportion of one part
" by weight to about 15 parts of solvent." 1st. Solvents requiring heat, as "coal tar, naptha, and its rectified products; also
" other hydrocarbon, turpentine, and resin spirit." 2nd. Solvents
which do not require heat as "bi-sulphuret of carbon and chloro-
" form." In using the first class of solvents, "I add at the
" same time the gutta percha, and the solvent are brought in
" contact, one ounce of alcohol, holding thirty drops of gly-

" cerine in solution to each gallon; or one ounce of alcohol
" holding thirty grains of soap in solution; or one ounce of
" pyroxilic spirit, holding thirty drops of glycerine in solution;
" or one ounce of commercial nitrate of the oxide of ethyl in the
" same proportion," in a close vessel with an agitator heated by
water or steam to about 110° F., agitating for about an hour
until the gutta percha is dissolved, allowing the whole to stand
for twenty-four hours " when if not sufficiently defecated and
" decolorized I decant off the greater bulk of the gutta percha
" solution into another vessel, and further add, accompanied by
" agitation either of the solutions, preferring the first solution
" already mixed with the solvent." The gutta percha may be
recovered from its solutions in either of three ways; 1st. "Con-
" gelation." A benzole solution exposed to a temperature of
32° F., or lower becomes a solid mass which is either pressed, or
submitted to centrifugal force or "filtration in vacuo." 2nd.
" Distillation." " In direct contact with water or free steam,"
condensing the solvent. 3rd. " Precipitation," by adding to a
benzole solution, " about an equal measure of alcohol, methylated
" or not, and preferred to be about 65° over proof, or pyroxylic
" spirit (preferably anhydrous) or fusil oil," stirring for a few
seconds and drawing off the solvent from the gutta percha.

[Printed, 4d. No Drawings.]

A.D. 1859, March 7.—N° 589.

PATRICK, HUGH WILLIAM.—(*Provisional protection only.*)—
" Improvements in an apparatus for chemical and dental labora-
" tories," &c. A portion of the apparatus described relates to
this subject and consists of a digester which may be of any shape,
but an oval or egg like shape is preferred "made of wrought or
" cast iron with a double chamber in the upper portion of it, or
" with a single chamber in a portable head, the doors of which in
" either case to close perfectly tight and secure, as the lower
" portion of the digester, when steam is required, may have
" water placed in it, and a safety valve or thermometer or bottle
" so fixed as to know the heat and pressure of steam let into the
" chambers for vulcanizing or hardening " india rubber or gutta
percha or any substance "having that tendency with its appli-
" cation allowed if required to enter the chamber or chambers;
" or the digester may be parted near the top, midway or any

" distance from the top, above either with a complete closed or
" open work parting, or not at all, and can be used at any time
" without water as a dry heat or hot bath with or without sand
" or any like material or substance."
[Printed, 4d. No Drawings.]

A.D. 1859, March 8.—N° 608.

BELLING, BENNETT MITCHELL.—(*Provisional protection only*.)
—" Improved apparatus for hardening india-rubber for the bases
" of teeth." This consists of a rectangular or other shaped
chamber, in preference, of wrought iron, furnished with perforated
shelves, and standing upon feet " in order to admit air." " It is
" enclosed at the upper part, but furnished with an escape pipe
" and stop-cock, for the purpose of regulating the escape of heated
" air and products evolved in or admitted to the chamber." It is
heated by a series of jets at the lower part or below, or " instead of
" gas, spirits or other inflammable or combustible matters may be
" employed to heat the chamber, by burning therein or by the
" products being conducted thereinto." " The bases or artificial
" gums in a soft state, enclosed in plaster moulds within metal
" boxes are placed on the shelves of the heat chamber." "The
" apparatus is furnished with a thermometer to indicate the heat
" of the interior of the chamber. The bases having been sub-
" jected for a sufficient length of time in the chamber, and to the
" proper degrees of heat, the hardening required will be effected."
[Printed, 4d. No Drawings.]

A.D. 1859, March 16.—N° 668.

CLARK, JAMES.—" Improvements in the manufacture of fabrics
" in which compounds containing india rubber are used." These
are first, applying in a cloth " a succession of coatings one on
" the other, the succeeding guages or instrument being set at a
" greater distance from the bed on which the fabric is suppor-
" ted." When the fabric is to be vulcanized sulphur is used in
the compound of india-rubber.

Second, making endless fabrics for calico printers, &c. by a
succession of layers of the same fabric cemented by india rubber
cement which may contain sulphur to admit of the same being
vulcanized; the fabric is so wound that the end of the outer
layer comes opposite the end of the inner layer.

Third, combining finely ground or powdered cork with sulphur and india-rubber solvent, sulphur, one part, india-rubber four parts, ground cork wood, ten parts by weight, spreading and moulding, and heating to vulcanize the same.

Fourth, applying an endless elastic cloth or fabric to the beds of spreading or coating machines. In place of the endless elastic fabric the cylinder itself may be coated with like elastic materials, and used without an endless cloth.

Fifth, " combining the fibres of silk, cotton, wool, flax or other
" fibrous materials with woven felted or other fabrics, so as to
" produce in a continuous manner combined fabrics " and coated with one or more coatings of the composition, in or out of the machine. These are vulcanized when required.

Sixth, vulcanizing the fabric known as " Clarks patent felt " by combining sulphur with the rubber used in the manufacture and submitting the patent felt to the action of heat.

[Printed, 8d. Drawing.]

A.D. 1859, March 21.—N° 716.

WARNE, WILLIAM, FANSHAWE, JOHN AMERICUS, JAQUES, JAMES ARCHIBALD, and GALPIN, THOMAS.— (*Letters Patent void for want of Final Specification.*)—" An im-
" proved compound or preparation of materials," for insulating wires, &c. This consists in reference to this subject as follows:—
" We propose to dissolve or soften the caoutchouc or gutta percha
" by means of suitable solvents as is well known, & then add the
" required proportion of bituminous matter, which may either
" be separately dissolved, previously to being added, or it may be
" mixed in a solid state with the caoutchouc or gutta percha, and
" the mass of ingredients dissolved in the same solvent with or
" without the addition of heat. The caoutchouc and bituminous
" matters may be dissolved or ground up with animal or vegetable
" oils, with the addition of heat, the grinding operation being
" continued until the mass becomes homogeneous. During the
" operation the earthy matters may be added, so as to become
" intimately blended with the other ingredients."

[Printed, 4d. No Drawings.]

A.D. 1859, March 25.—N° 755.

COWPER, CHARLES.—(*A communication from Robert Jefferson Bingham.*)—(*Provisional protection only.*)—" Improvements in

" telegraph cables." These are, "the copper wire somewhat
" thicker than those usually employed for telegraphic cables, is
" first covered with a coating of gutta percha or other insulating
" substance, and thence with a mixture composed of caoutchouc
" gum lac, tar, and cork reduced to powder or saw dust in such
" proportions that the cable shall remain sufficiently flexible and
" but slightly heavier than the water in which it is immersed;
" gutta percha may be mixed with or substituted for the caout-
" chouc." "For those parts of the cable which approach the
" shore or in any part where a wearing action is to be feared the
" same mixture is made use of, with this exception, that the cork
" or sawdust is in such cases replaced gradually by emery
" corundum, silix, or some other similar hard substances."

[Printed, 4d. No Drawings.]

A.D. 1859, April 7.—N° 865.

MOSELEY, DAVID.— " Improvements in the manufacture of
" cards for carding cotton and other fibrous materials."

These are, " manufacturing card backs of a fabric of cotton or
" linen warp threads, and woollen weft threads, united to a sheet
" of native india-rubber, either in its natural state, or subjected
" to the influence of chloride of sulphur." "When it is requisite
" to increase the strength, elasticity and durability of the card
" backs, I subject the sheet of native india-rubber, after it is
" cemented to the cloth or otherwise, to the influence of chloride
" of sulphur;" afterwards, washing with a weak solution of
quicklime or a solution of caustic alkali, then exposing it to the
air, finally washing it with water."

[Printed, 4d. No Drawings.]

A.D. 1859, April 8.—N° 882.

HOOPER, WILLIAM.—" Improvements in re-working or re-
" manufacturing compounds of india-rubber and sulphur."
These are, "the combining raw india-rubber and sulphur or
" matters containing sulphur (with or without other substances)
" with the ground product of waste or old converted sulphur
" compounds of india-rubber, and subjecting the same to high
" degrees of heat to convert or change the same into elastic and
" hard compounds." "A convenient mixture (though the pro-
" portions may be varied) is obtained by combining at the rate of

"thirty parts by weight" of the ground waste product, "ten parts by weight of raw india-rubber, seventeen to twenty parts by weight of sulphur, and four parts by weight of lime, or of magnesia or of silicate of magnesia." These are masticated together and moulded and heated in the moulds, but "not so much heat is required as when using raw india-rubber and sulphur."

[Printed, 4d. No Drawings.]

A.D. 1859, April 14.—N° 942.

SINNOCK, WILLIAM.—" Improvements in submarine and sub- terranean electric telegraph cables, and in machinery for the manufacture thereof." For this purpose "taking the electric conductor of wire or strand of wires, and either insulated with india-rubber or gutta percha or other suitable material, or with- out any such insulation, I apply one or more layers of fibrous material completely saturated, either previously or in the process of application to the electric conductor, with a compound of insulated materials consisting of india-rubber, gutta percha, and bitumen; these layers of fibre thus rendered insulating may be arranged around the conductor, either spirally, longitu- dinally, or otherwise (the former I prefer) and this may be effected mechanically, by any of the ordinary machines here- tofore employed for such purposes."

[Printed, 8d. Drawings.]

A.D. 1859, April 25.—N° 1040.

WARNE, WILLIAM, FANSHAWE, JOHN AMERICUS, JAQUES, JAMES ARCHIBALD, and GALPIN, THOMAS.— "Improved compounds, applicable for packing the joints of steam or other pipes, which compounds are also applicable for packing or lining parts of machinery in general, or parts of ships, bridges, tanks or railways." The object being "to produce a compound which will be able to resist any degree of heat to which it is liable to be exposed in use."

"The following are the proportions which we should prefer to use to produce a cement or compound of this description, viz., caoutchouc or india-rubber, two parts; gutta percha, one part; hydrochlorate of ammonia, one part; sulphur, one part; iron filings or borings, ten parts. This compound may be modified

" by altogether dispensing with the use of gutta percha, and
" employing in lieu thereof an equivalent quantity of caoutchouc
" or some gelatinous substance, or a larger quantity of gutta
" percha than that above set forth, may, if required, be employed,
" and an equivalent portion of the caoutchouc dispensed with;
" the propriety of adopting modifications of this description will
" depend very much upon the relative cost of caoutchouc and
" gutta percha or the other materials employed in place thereof.
" Instead of a portion of the iron filings or borings an equivalent
" portion of pulverized iron pyrites may be sometimes employed
" with advantage, and when iron pyrites is employed the sulphur,
" or a portion of it, may be omitted. When a brass or copper
" cement is required, filings or turnings of these metals or
" analogous alloys must of course be used in place of the iron
" turnings, and copper pyrites may also be employed in place of
" a portion of the metallic copper or brass. Cements of this
" kind, will not, however, possess much elastic strength or
" resistance to tension, this property not being required for
" cementing or packing joints of pipes.

" A cement or compound for packing the joints of cold water
" or other pipes that are not liable to be exposed to a high degree
" of heat may with advantage contain a larger proportion of the
" elastic gum. A compound suitable for these purposes may
" contain of caoutchouc or india-rubber, four parts; gutta percha
" one part; hydrochlorate of ammonia, one part; sulphur, one
" part; iron filings, turnings, or borings, ten parts. This com-
" pound may be modified in the same way as the other, and the
" metallic sulphurets or ores of the metals may be employed
" instead of the pure metal, or they may be added to the com-
" pound. The earthy sulphates of lime, baryta, or strontia,
" may also be added with advantage for some purposes. For a
" compound applicable for packing the glands or pistons of
" engines or machines, we take of caoutchouc or india-rubber-
" 5 parts, gutta percha, two parts; sulphur, one part; pulverized
" plumbago, or black lead, or of red hematite, one part; silicate
" of magnesia, steatite or soapstone, one part; and of the filings
" or borings of copper, zinc; lead, spelter, tin, or any of their
" alloys, ten parts. When these ingredients are well mixed
" together, so as to form a homogenous mass, the compound will
" be found to possess some very valuable properties when used
" as packing for glands or pistons."

" By augmenting the proportion of caoutchouc or other elastic
" gum, the elasticity and tensile strength of the compound will
" be increased, and then the compound may be used for purposes
" where the qualities or properties are required. When the
" cement is liable to be exposed to the direct action of fire or to
" very high degree of heat we mix with the other ingredients
" some fibrous asbestos." The several ingredients being well
mixed, the compound is rolled out and cut or stamped into the
forms required. The articles are soaked in hot or cold water to
oxidize the metallic particles. "The above articles containing
" sulphur may or may not be subjected to heat in order to pro-
" duce the change commonly known as vulcanization." For some
discriptions of packing aluminous and calcareous matters may be
added.

[Printed, 4d. No Drawings.]

A.D. 1859, May 12.—N° 1194.

WARNE, WILLIAM, FANSHAWE, JOHN AMERICUS, JAQUES, JAMES, ARCHIBALD, and GALPIN, THOMAS.—
"An improved compound or preparation of materials" for insulating wires, &c. This consists, in reference to this subject, as follows, the compound " is composed of caoutchouc or gutta
" percha, or both these materials, combined with coal tar pitch,
" bituminous or resinous substances, to which are to be added
" animal or vegetable oils, animal or vegetable charcoal, earthy
" matters, such as silicate of magnesia, rottenstone, plumbago,
" the sulphates of lime baryta, and strontia and other earths."

" In order to harden the compound we sometimes find it con-
" venient to add to the other ingredients a suitable quantity of
" the solid residuum obtained after the distillation of turpentine
" and various hydrocarbons, rangoon tar, rosin oil, and other
" analogous substances." The following proportions give satis-
" factory results :—" When no gutta percha is employed in the
" compound we take ten pounds of caoutchouc, five pounds of
" coal tar pitch, and fifteen pounds of French chalk (silicate of
" magnesia)."

" When gutta percha is used with the other materials, the
" following proportions will be found useful, viz., eight and a
" half pounds caoutchouc, one and a half pounds gutta percha,
" five pounds coal tar pitch, five pounds of plumbago, three
" pounds of oxide of lead, five pounds of silicate of magnesia."

" These materials are put into a suitable vessel and brought into
" a plastic state by means of heat, they are then ground and well
" mixed together."

[Printed, 1s. Drawing.]

A.D. 1859, May 13.—N° 1203.

JOHNSON, JOHN HENRY.—(*A communication from Austin G. Day.*)—" Improvements in machinery or apparatus for treating
" india-rubber and other similar gums." These are for breaking down and cleansing the above substances employing rollers arranged either "in pairs, or sets of three working together by
" the aid of suitable toothed gearing," and " covered with quad-
" rangular, pyramidal teeth arranged in rows parallel with the
" axis and also at right angles thereto, that is, in a series of
" parallel rings. The teeth of one roller work in the intervals
" between the parallel rings of teeth on the next roller, so as to
" admit of a slipping motion, which is accomplished by driving
" each roller faster than the preceding one." During the breaking down process, a stream of water is directed upon the rollers, and the bark, &c. washed away may be partly removed by hand. The broken or comminated gum on leaving the rollers is subjected to the action of a watery solution of caustic or carbonated alkali by exhaustion above or by exhaustion and compression as described in No. 1853, A.D. 1858, and when "thoroughly charged
" with the alkaline liquor, it is removed therefrom or the liquor is
" drawn off and the mass is well washed with water and again
" passed through the herein-before described toothed rollers." The mass is then placed in an iron cylinder which is exhausted to
" a practical vacuum," the alkaline solution is then let in, pressure is put on by means of a force pump, twenty to thirty-five pounds to the square inch, after from fifteen to sixty minutes the mass is removed from the cylinder and thoroughly washed with water in the squeezing rollers using the above rollers for grinding and mixing rubber and incorporating it with sulphur or other ingredients " as also for rolling it into sheets the same
" rollers are used but with smaller pyramidal teeth than when
" intended for breaking up crude gums."

[Printed, 10d. Drawing.]

A.D. 1859, May 18.—N° 1239.

CHILDS, JAMES.—"Improvements in hardening and vulca-
" nizing compounds of sulphur with india-rubber and gutta

" percha." These are in place of using the ordinary modes of heating these mixtures to produce the change, namely, dry heat or steam heat, placing "articles formed of india-rubber and gutta " percha compounded with sulphur in a close vessel together with " a hydrated substance, such as gypsum or lime, but without " free water, and then exposing the vessel and its contents to a " heat sufficient to produce the change required in the compound. " The hydrated substance during the process generates steam " sufficient to maintain an atmosphere of steam in the close " vessel, but will not under any ordinary heat generate so much " steam as to endanger the safety of the vessel."

[Printed, 6d. Drawing.]

A.D. 1859, May 23.—N° 1274.

DODGE, NATHANIEL SHATTSWELL.—(*A communication from Hiram Lyman Hall.*)—" Improvements in finishing, coloring, and " varnishing india-rubber goods, and similar manufactures." These are first in, sizing or preparing the surfaces of these goods for the reception of varnishes and colors, employing "starchy, " glutinous, alluminous, bituminous, resinous, or gummy sub- " stances." In practice common starch dissolved in water has been found to answer as well as any other size. Economy is secured by first adding to it color, but higher class goods are first sized and the colors or varnishes afterwards applied "and " dried in suitable drying chambers, the temperature being " regulated to suit the particular varnish employed ranging from " 90° to 280° Fahrenheit."

Second. For the above purposes using a varnish obtained by boiling "linseed oil together with sulphur until the two sub- " stances are thoroughly combined." A good result has been obtained with from "one pound of flour of sulphur to one gallon " of oil."

Third. For the above purposes "combining, say, four pounds " of oxide of lead, two pounds lamp black, five ounces of flour of " sulphur and ten pounds of india-rubber gum, with any suitable " solvent, and boiling the mass in a suitable vessel, until the " substances become dissolved and combined together in a liquid " state, or, if desired, india-rubber gum alone may be used, " dissolved by boiling it in any well-known solvent applicable as " a size before applying colouring matter, or as a varnish or " finish for the goods."

[Printed, 4d. No Drawings.]

A.D. 1859, May 26.—N° 1300.

PATRICK, HUGH WILLIAM.—"A new substance or material to be used in lieu of ivory and other like substances." "I have found in actual practice that a good result has been obtained from the following proportions and combinations of ingredients namely, amber, 12 ozs." Australian gum kowrie, 3 ozs.; gum anime, $\frac{1}{2}$ oz.; and gum copul, 5 ozs., in solution in naphtha methylated spirit, chloroform, or essential oils or other suitable solvent, according to the particular substance to be treated; these are mixed with seven ozs. of meerschaum, 1 oz. paper pulp and $\frac{1}{2}$ oz. " of the fluorate of selicia (fluoride of silicon?);" or the paper pulp and fluoride "may be replaced by the same quantities of the chlorides of zinc, or half the quantity of cream of tartar, or 3 ozs. of asbestos may be substituted for the chloride of zinc and cream of tartar. When bleached india rubber or gutta percha are used in the above combinations I also propose to add an equal quantity of sulphur." Colors may also be added.

[Printed, 4d. No Drawings.]

A.D. 1859, June 3.—N° 1368.

JOHNSON, JOHN HENRY.—(*A communication from William James Cantelo.*)—"Improvements in reducing solid substances to powder, and in the machinery or apparatus employed therein." These are "placing the ends of blocks of the material or substance to be reduced opposite to and in contact with each other, and presenting them simultaneously and at the exact point or line of junction to the cutting edge of a circular or reciprocating saw or rasp, so that the cut will be effected in the line of junction, and will cause the simultaneous reduction of each of the blocks, which after every through cut are again brought together in readiness for the succeeding cut." The apparatus may consist "of an ordinary circular saw and saw brush, the latter being provided with guide rails, between which, slides in a direction to and from the saw, a box containing the two blocks of material to be operated upon. This box is slotted transversely in the line of the plane of the saw to admit of the saw cutting through the blocks, and it is further provided with slides worked by a right and left screw spindle, which slides by turning the spindle in a proper direction, approach each other and force the contiguous ends of the blocks of material together after each cut."

This apparatus is applicable among other things which are named "to the reduction of gutta percha."

[Printed, 8d. Drawing.]

A.D. 1859, June 15.—N° 1437.

NEWTON, ALFRED VINCENT.—(*A communication from Thomas J. Mayall.*)—" Improvements in the manufacture of polishing " wheels, sticks, and tools." These are " preparing hard flexible " compounds " as afterwards described and " applying them " when in the green or soft state to the moulding " of the above and other tools, and " when curved in the form of sheets to the " coating or covering of such tools." " To about 15 lbs. of emery " reduced to a fine powder, or its equivalent grit " (powdered glass, fine sand, &c.) " add 1lb. of india rubber or gutta percha " and 5 ozs. of sulphur and mix the same together in a suitable " masticating apparatus. When thoroughly combined place the " composition thus formed in metallic moulds, and submit it to " great pressure therein, after which, subject the filled moulds to " a temperature of from 260° to 300° Fahrenheit for form fifteen " minutes to four hours." " In order to ensure elasticity and " toughness in the manufactured compound, or after the com- " position has undergone the curing operation, olive oil is to be " added to the mixture of materials while in the green or uncured " state, in the proportion of ½ lb. of olive oil to the quantities of " rubber, sulphur, and emery above named, and well mixed to- " gether." " These tools may be composed of the polishing " compound throughout, or they may have a wooden or other " base, and be merely coated with the hardened compound, either " before or after it has been subjected to the curing operation."

[Printed, 6d. Drawing.]

A.D. 1859, August 4.—N° 1801.

WALTON, FREDERICK.—" Improvements in the manufacture " of ornamental fabrics suitable for book binding and other " uses and in machines employed in such manufacture." These are, in reference to this subject, " the fabric I usually " employ as the base of the fabric is an ordinary stout calico " and the composition I consider most suitable for the purpose " is composed in the following manner:—Two pounds weight " of india-rubber is dissolved in one gallon of naptha and there

" is mixed therewith 5 lbs. of fibre. The fibre most suited for
" the purpose is what is known as fustian cutters flock. This is
" mixed with the india-rubber solution by means of suitable
" mixing apparatus; and there is also added to the composition
" a pigment or pigments, or colouring matter, such as are usually
" employed for colouring india-rubber, in order to bring the
" composition as nearly as may be to the colour the fabric is to
" have when finished. The thin paper employed to form the
" surface of the fabric should be unsized, and of the colour which
" it is desired to give to the surface of the fabric."

[Printed, 8d. Drawing.]

A.D. 1859, August 5.—N° 1809.

NEWTON, WILLIAM EDWARD.—(*A communication from Jonathan H. Green.*)—(*Provisional protection only.*)—" An improve-
" ment in billiard and bagatelle cues." This consists in the
" tip of the cue, and is in the employment for this purpose of
" a compound composed of gutta percha or india-rubber, vulca-
" nized or not vulcanized, with pulverized or comminuted chalk,
" or siliceous or calcareous substance or glass, to which may be
" added or not, as may be desired, oxide of zinc or of lead, or
" other metallic substance; the proportions which have been
" found best in practice are about three parts of the chalk or
" other substance to one part of gutta percha or india-rubber.
" This compound must be well mixed and rolled out to a suitable
" thickness."

[Printed, 4d. No Drawings.]

A.D. 1859, August 9.—N° 1840.

BOUSFIELD, GEORGE TOMLINSON.—(*A communication from John Murphy.*)—" A new and useful method of manufacturing
" the vulcanized compounds of vulcanized gums." These are
" first, " the manufacture of hard stock of the vulcanizable gum
" by blending it with sulphur or its equivalent, and vulcanizing
" the compound until it is hard."

Second. " The reduction of the hard stock to powder."

Third. " The formation of a compound of the ground stock
" and raw gum by blending the two together."

Fourth. " The vulcanization of the compound formed by the
" preceding operations; the several operations constituting the

" process being effected in the order herein stated," and " whether
" the materials be so proportioned and the vulcanization be so
" conducted as to produce hard compound for hard goods or
" soft compound for soft or very flexible goods."

The hard stock is reduced " to powder by grinding it in a
" heated state between rollers or by any other means which will
" produce this result," preferring however, to use the ordinary
grinding mill consisting of two hot horizontal rollers, revolving
with different velocities both for blending and grinding; " effec-
" ting the change commonly called vulcanization, by heating the
" vulcanizable compounds in any ordinary steam heater, as these
" means are well known in the art to which this invention apper-
" tains." In manufacturing hard stock from raw gum, taking
the gum after it has been cleansed from foreign matters in the
usual way, " and grinding or kneading," the same in a heated
state with sulphur until the two are thoroughly blended and
formed into a putty like mass. The proportions are " thirty
" pounds of gum and from fifteen to forty pounds of sulphur as
" may be found necessary."

[Printed, 4d. No Drawings.]

A.D. 1859, August 9.—N° 1842.

LAWRENCE, FREDERIC LOUIS.—" Improvements in coloring
" and hardening elastic gums for dental purposes." These are
" coloring to the required tint the elastic gums used by dentists
" and hardening them for the purpose of being used in lieu of
" gold or bone at present in use. I take caoutchouc sulphur,
" oxide of zinc, and cinnibar (vermillion) in certain proportions
" and pass them together through grinding rollers or masticating
" apparatus until thoroughly incorporated or blended. The
" proportions which are believed to be most suitable are at the
" rate of about $3\frac{1}{2}$ lbs. of caoutchouc, $1\frac{1}{4}$ lbs. of sulphur, 1 lb. of
" vermillion, $9\frac{1}{2}$ lbs. of oxide of zinc, but these proportions may
" be varied. The compound is to be moulded as heretofore when
" using compounds of caoutchouc for dental purposes, and sub-
" jected to heat as is well understood, to obtain the desired hard-
" ness; after which it is polished by any known means, and then
" placed in a closed glass vessel containing alcohol or other suit-
" able liquid, and subjected to solar light, which brings the
" required flesh colour to the surface. By this means the ma-

" terial will be found better suited to answer the purpose of bone
" or gold."
[Printed, 4d. No Drawings.]

A.D. 1859, August 25.—N° 1941.

CHAMBERLAIN, Amos Pierce.—" Improvements in ma-
" chinery or apparatus for cutting cork, part of which improve-
" ments is also applicable to cutting paper, caoutchouc, and
" other substancees." These are, in reference to this subject, " a
" system of revolving cutters made from very thin steel plates, fas-
" tened to the end of a spindle or axle-tree and held between discs
" of cast iron or other suitable material of a less diameter."
These are accurately adjusted on a frame of cast iron or other
suitable material. The carriage holding the material to be cut is
provided with slides and guides so as to present the same at
right angles to the cutters. This carriage with its slides and
guides is passed under the cutters, the carriage being provided
with a groove to receive the lower edge of the knife or cutter and
keep it steady during the cut, " or the guides and carriage may
" be constructed in two separate pieces and so arranged and
" connected (by means of springs) that when they are not under
" the cutters they touch each other throughout their whole length
" except a short portion at each end, which is bevilled off so as
" to let the carriage come under the cutters without touching the
" edge of the same, and as soon as the said bevilled part has
" arrived under the cutters, the pressure of the sides of the
" cutters separates the two parts of the carriage and allows of a
" free passage of the same past the cutters." When the material
has been " cut into strips crosswise, these strips are handed over
" to the other side of the machine and at the other end of the
" same spindle is another cutter with the same adjustment of
" carriage, slides and guides provided with a notched guide so
" arranged as to cut successively and lengthwise of the grain any
" thickness of strips."
[Printed, 1s. 4d. Drawings.]

A.D. 1859, August 31.—N° 1991.

CHATTERTON, John.—" Improvements in the manufacture
" of tubes of gutta percha and other substances capable of being
" moulded in a similar manner when in a plastic state, and also

" in coating wire and other cores with such substances." These
are, first, "in place of depending on the water contained in the
" trough, into which a tube passes as it is forced through the die
" filling the tube as heretofore, the apparatus is arranged to
" introduce water or liquid into the interior of the tube through
" the core or mandril upon which the tube is formed, the pressure
" of the water being regulated to give to the tube the necessary
" internal support, and when it is desired to introduce a liquid or
" semi-liquid matter between the interior of a tube of gutta percha
" or other similar materials and a wire or core therein," such is
" introduced through the core or mandril at the die into the
" interior of the tube around the core as the tube is made, the
" liquid or semi-liquid being introduced at such pressure as may
" be desired." " In moulding tubes of india-rubber and com-
" pounds thereof, rollers are sometimes employed in place of
" ordinary dies, and then according to this invention water or
" liquid is introduced into the tube as it is made by a nozzle or
" hollow mandril entering between the rollers."

Second, "lowering the temperature of the water or liquid em-
" ployed to harden tubes of gutta percha or other substances
" capable of being moulded in a similar manner when in a plastic
" state by means of ice or by the use of freezing or cooling mix-
" tures," and this is " also applicable when coating wire or other
" cores with such substances."

[Printed, 8d. Drawing.]

A.D. 1859, September 12.—N° 2079.

GISBORNE, FREDERIC NEWTON, and MAGNUS, LAZARUS
SIMON.—(*Provisional protection only.*)—" Improvements in tele-
" graph cables." These are, in reference to this subject, longitudinal strands are arranged so as to surround the wire, and the
said "longitudinal surroundings and buildings" are covered
" with a preservative compound of india-rubber, shellac, resin,
" and vegetable wax, with pitch, so as to give the cable a smooth
" and regular exterior surface."

[Printed, 4d. No Drawings.]

A.D. 1859, September 24.—N° 2170.

DAFT, THOMAS BARNABAS.—" Improvements in coating metal
" conductors suitable for electric telegraphs." These are, in

reference to this subject, the metal conductor coated with brass is covered with india-rubber or india-rubber compound, then over this yarn saturated with india-rubber solution is wrapped, then lay longitudinal strands of similarly prepared yarn " and again " another spiral wrapping of yarn as above, and over the whole " I put a coating of india-rubber or india-rubber compound. " I then, as the finishing coating of india-rubber or india-rubber " compound is given to the cable, render the outside unadhesive " by means of French chalk or otherwise, as is well understood, " and when the india-rubber has been compounded with sulphur, " previous to applying it to the cable, as I prefer that it should " be, I proceed to vulcanize it while it is either embedded in " French chalk or otherwise protected from adhering together " either by steam, water, or dry heat, as is well understood. If " sulphur is not compounded with the india-rubber, it should be " vulcanized by immersion in a vulcanizing bath."

[Printed, 4d. No Drawings.]

A.D. 1859, October 5.—N° 2262.

NEWTON, WILLIAM EDWARD.—(*A communication from Seth W. Baker.*)—" Improvements in blankets used for printing calicoes " and other fabrics, and in the mode of washing or cleansing the " same." These are, in reference to this subject, using an elastic blanket and dispensing "with the use of grays between it and " the fabric to be printed." "The compositions of which the " improved blanket is made can of course be varied, but good " results may be obtained by using the following ingredients, " vizt., eight pounds of india-rubber or gutta percha, four pounds " of zinc, three quarters of a pound of sulphur, and half a pound " of magnesia. These substances are to be mixed or ground " together and the composition rolled into a sheet in any of the " modes well known by india-rubber manufacturers. The ends " are to be united so as to form an endless band, and the sheet " may then be cured or vulcanized in the usual manner. A " roughened selvage is then formed upon the blanket, or the " whole surface may be roughened by any suitable means."

[Printed, 1s. 4d. Drawings.]

A.D. 1859, October 5.—N° 2269.

MACINTOSH, JOHN.—" Improvements in coating metallic con-" ductors for electric telegraphs." These are, " I prefer to use

" at the rate of about fifty parts by weight of gutta percha,
" twenty-five parts by weight of naphthaline, and twenty-five
" parts by weight of lamp-black, though other portions may be
" used. I apply heat of about 170° of F. to the naphthaline
" which melts it, and I introduce and mix therewith the gutta
" percha." "The fluid is run off from the impurities and then
" mixed with the lamp black." "When the materials are pure,
" or comparatively pure, they may be mixed by masticating
" machinery, as when mixing gutta percha with other materials.
" In some cases I combine lamp black with india-rubber for
" external coatings on insulated wires or electric conductors, and
" I use as much lamp black with the india-rubber, as the india-
" rubber will take, and yet retain a plasticity such as will enable
" it to be applied by rollers, or by being forced through dies as a
" coating to a previously insulated or coated wire or other electric
" conductor, or in place of india-rubber being used alone, gutta
" percha may be combined therewith."

[Printed, 4d. No Drawings.]

A.D. 1859, October 8.—N° 2295.

CHILDS, JAMES.—" Improvements in the manufacture of arti-
" ficial gum." These are, in reference to this subject, in the
above manufacture "I prefer to use a compound consisting of
" 6 or 8 parts by weight of caoutchouc, 2 parts by weight of
" sulphur, 6 parts by weight of vermillion, 12 parts by weight
" of silicate of magnesia, or 6 or 8 parts by weight of caoutchouc,
" 2 parts by weight of sulphur, 5 parts by weight of vermillion,
" 12 parts by weight of sulphate of lime." " Other proportions
" of these matters may be used and magnesia may be employed
" in place of silicate of magnesia," and other light or white sub-
" stances as well as other coloring matters may be used in place
" of or in combination with those mentioned above, such as
" oxides of zinc." The gums are moulded and " enclosed in
" plaster, and submitted to the hardening process."

[Printed, 4d. No Drawings.]

A.D. 1859, October 24.—N° 2430.

SEAGER, ROBERT.—" Improvements in compounds of india-
" rubber and gutta percha." These are, " the combining pre-
" pared fibres of leather with india-rubber and with gutta percha "
as follows :—Leather cuttings are soaked in an alkaline ley,

preferring soda (about one pound of soda of commerce to three gallons of water), for about three days, then removed from the ley, pressed, steamed, and again pressed, or they are steamed for about an hour and pressed "to separate the ley and moisture " completely therefrom," and then passed through a fine sieve, generally about one hundred holes to the square inch. The fibrous parts of the leather are then fit "to be combined with " india-rubber or gutta percha or a combination of these sub- " stances" in proportions which may vary; about equal proportions of these substances are found to be a good compound; in a less flexible article "more of the leather fibre may be employed. " These substances are mixed in a masticating machine using " sufficient heat."

[Printed, 6d. No Drawings.]

A.D. 1859, October 31.—N° 2477.

TURNER, JAMES ALFRED.—" Improvements in rendering paper " waterproof." These are, in reference to this subject, making " a composition of caouchouc, gutta percha, resin, benzene, " caoutchine or any ground mineral dissolved by naptha, cam- " phine, turpentine, or other well known solvents.".

[Printed, 4d. No Drawings.]

A.D. 1859, November 3.—N° 2497.

TURNER, JAMES ALFRED.—(*Provisional protection only.*)— " Improvements in rendering paper waterproof." These are, in reference to this subject, making "a composition of caoutchouc, " gutta percha, resin, and any ground mineral dissolved by " naptha, turpentine, or other well known solvents."

[Printed, 4d. No Drawings.]

A.D. 1859, November 21.—N° 2637.

PITMAN, JOHN TALBOT. — (*A communication from Asahel Knowlton Eatin.*)—" An improved method of curing india-rubber " or gutta percha compounds." This consists in the use of a metallic bath for the purposes of vulcanization, " so constituted as " to fuse at or below the lowest degree of temperature required in " vulcanization and capable of being elevated readily to the " highest temperature required in the process." The preparations of india-rubber or gutta percha and sulphur or "any " vulcanizing agent or agents immersed in such a bath when at

"its fusing point are thoroughly vulcanized in from two to five
" hours according to the temperature maintained." "The compo-
" sition of the bath may be varied to meet any required case."
" It will perhaps be well usually to make use of an alloy 50 parts
" of bismuth, 31 of lead, and 19 of tin, fusing at about 203
" degrees Fahrenheit." "When the articles will bear a higher
" temperature than 212° in the early stage of the process a bath
" of higher fusing point may be used," by "increasing the pro-
" portion of tin and lead and by the addition of zinc or other
" metal." A bath of mercury might be used but is expensive
and when used openly the vapors evolved would be objectionable,
but mercury may be used " in small proportions for increasing the
" fusibility of alloys." "The articles may, if desired, be trans-
" ferred from one bath to another successively in order to avoid
" the necessity of materially raising the temperature of a single
" bath."

[Printed, 4d. No Drawings.]

A.D. 1859, November 22.—N° 2643.

DAFT, THOMAS BARNABAS.—" An improvement in coating
" sheathing metal." This consists in coating Muntz's or such
like yellow metal cleaned with acid or other means with india-
rubber combined with sulphur. The compound is made into thin
sheets which are laid on sheets of yellow metal and " subjected
" to heat whilst pressed in contact with the clean metal surface."
" If I wish to cover sheets of iron " or other metal "with india
" rubber I first coat them with Muntz's or such yellow metal."
Sometimes the metal is coated on both sides with the india-rubber
compound and in some cases two sheets of yellow metal are
" united by means of a sheet of india-rubber."

[Printed, 4d. No Drawings.]

A.D. 1859, December 2.—N° 2734.

NEWTON, ALFRED VINCENT.—(*A communication from George
August Engelhard and Horace Hollester Day.*)—(*Provisional protection only.*)—" An improved mode of treating india-rubber,
" gutta-percha, and analogous gums." This consists in subjecting lumps of these substances to a stream of chlorine in an
air-tight vessel; " the gum thus treated begins to swell and
" becomes converted into a white brittle mass," which is well

washed with water to free it from chlorine "dissolved in one of
" the well known solvents of these gums, such as bi-sulphuret of
" carbon, chloroform, benzole, or naphtha, or other essential oil,"
the solution is evaporated, and the new substance "applied to
" the articles to which it is designed to be attached by moulding,
" dipping, and by other modes." A more rapid way of pro-
" ducing this change is to pass a stream of chlorine through a
" solution of the gum dissolved by one of the above solvents
" until the solution becomes yellow. At this stage "the material
" is flexible and limp, like leather;" if required hard like "'vul-
" canite' the action of the chlorine is continued until such effect
" is produced." The solvent is removed by evaporation or by
adding alcohol which "causes the gum combined with the chlorine
" to precipitate," by adding water to the solution the solvent
separates from the alcohol and may be used over again. The
precipitated gum is washed with alcohol, "pressed and dried,
" when it forms a .white and hard mass. In dissolving india-
" rubber, gutta percha, and other allied gums, they are cleaned,
" cut in small pieces, placed in a vessel with chloride of carbon.
" The perfect solution takes place in the space of from one to
" two days, and may be facilitated by warming."

[Printed, 4d. No Drawings.]

A.D. 1859, December 6.—N° 2762.

NEWTON, WILLIAM EDWARD.—(*A communication from Rudolph Franz Heinrich Havemann.*)—" An improved mode of treating
" gums, such as india-rubber or gutta, percha for the manufacture
" of various articles." This consists in "subjecting gum, such
" as india-rubber or gutta percha, to the action of chlorine" as
follows :—Lumps of those gums are exposed to a stream of chlorine
in an air-tight vessel, the chlorine being renewed as it is absorbed
they begin to swell and turn into a white brittle mass from which
the chlorine is washed by water, when " it is dissolved in one of
" the well known solvents of those gums, such as bi-sulphuret of
" carbon, benzole, chloroform, &c.," and the solvent evaporated;
the substance after drying becomes perfectly white and hard, like
ivory. To produce the change quicker the gum is dissolved in one
of the above solvents and a stream of chlorine is passed through
the solution until it becomes of a yellow color "when the combi-
" nation of the gum with the chlorine is perfected." "The
" solvent is now removed by evaporation at a moderate tempera-

" ture not sufficiently high to reach the boiling point of the
" solvent or it may be done by treating the mixture with alcohol
" which combines with the solvent, and causes the gum combined
" with the chlorine to precipitate." The precipitate is washed
" with alcohol, " pressed and dried, when it forms the same
" white and hard mass which has been mentioned above."

[Printed, 4d. No Drawings.]

A.D. 1859, December 10.—N° 2809.

CHATTERTON, JOHN, and SMITH, WILLOUGHBY.—" Im-
" provements in insulating telegraphic conductors and in the
" treatment of gutta percha." These are, in reference to this
subject, in some cases closing the pores or mechanical defects
of gutta percha by submitting it when in a thin sheet or in a
divided state, " by preference at that stage of the manufacture
" when it has been torn up and washed." It is put into an air-
" tight vessel. From the vessel a pipe passes to an air pump
" which is worked until as good a vacuum is obtained as the
" pump will produce, a vacuum of twenty six or twenty-seven
" inches answers the purpose well. The pipe connecting the
" pump and the air pump is furnished with a cock and when the
" vacuum is complete, the communication between the two is
" closed by turning the cock. Above the vessel a tank contain-
" ing the insulating fluid is fixed and is connected with it by a
" pipe, in which also a stop-cock is fitted. For the insulating
" fluid, Stockholm tar we believe to be most suitable and, by
" preference, it is slightly warmed, say to about 70° or 80° Fah-
" renheit, the raising the temperature to a degree which might
" soften the gutta percha being carefully avoided. When the
" vacuum is complete the tar is allowed to descend from the
" tank into the vessel by opening the stop-cock, and care is taken
" to prevent the tank becoming empty which would allow air to
" enter the vessel. When the vessel contains as much tar as will
" run into it, through another pipe connected with the vessel a
" further quantity of tar is forced by a pump until a pressure is
" produced within the vessel. A pressure of 500 lbs. to the inch
" answers well. The pipe connecting the pump with the vessel
" is fitted with a safety valve, which allows the tar to escape
" when this pressure is exceeded. The pressure is maintained for
" about ten minutes and is then taken off."

[Printed, 4d. No Drawings.]

A.D. 1859, December 15.—N° 2857.

HANCOCK, Charles. — "Improvements in insulating tele-
" graphic conductors, and manufacturing cables for telegraphic
" purposes." These are, in reference to this subject, tubes or
tapes or other binders for the covering of the wires may if required "be coated with a cement or solution in order to give
" adhesive property to the surface and for this purpose I prefer a
" cement consisting of a compound of masticated india-rubber
" dissolved in a solvent composed of oil, gold size, and coal tar
" naptha."

[Printed, 4d. No Drawings.]

A.D. 1859, December 28.—N° 2956.

MAGNUS, Lazarus Simon, and SINNOCK, William.—
" Improvements in preparing yarn, twine, cords, and strands, and
" other fibrous materials to render the same more suitable for
" submarine telegraph cables and other uses." These are, in
carrying out the above using " twelve and a half parts by weight
" of india-rubber or gutta percha, or of the two combined,
" preferring the best india-rubber and the best sheet gutta percha
" or gutta percha in a state of purity, such as is now used in
" making the best sheets; twenty-five parts by weight of vege-
" table or other wax, preferring Australian vegetable wax;
" twelve and a half parts by weight of resin, fifty parts by weight
" of the best vegetable pitch. These matters or substances are put
" into a suitable vessel, and heat applied thereto, and they are
" kept well stirred till they are intimately blended. We prefer a
" vessel heated by steam so as to maintain the mixture at a heat
" of about two hundred and twenty degrees of Fahrenheat. The
" composition above described is used by preference at a tempera-
" ture of about two hundred and twenty degrees of Fahrenheat."

[Printed, 4d. No Drawings.]

A.D. 1859, December 28.—N° 2962.

ROSTAING, Charles Sylvester.—"Improvements in com-
" bining and mixing gutta percha with mineral and vegetable
" substances capable of altering its quality in such a manner as
" to produce hard resistant, unalterable, and imputrescible com-
" pounds diversely coloured." These are, first, the " preliminary
" purification of gutta percha " as follows :—Boiling the crude
gutta percha in soft water (rain or river water) and constantly

moving and dividing it, and while hot flatting it to the thickness of ordinary paper, then washing in cold water, boiling or steeping " in a decoction of radix saponaria alba or soap wort," again forming into thin sheets, and, finally, washing with cold water.

Second, completely purifying gutta percha. The above partially purified gutta percha is boiled with a lye of caustic soda, or of soda and potash, for several hours, flatted to press the lye out as much as possible, re-boiled in soft water, flatted, washed in cold water, finally dried.

Third, "preparing several colors and mineral combinations " employed either mixed with the colors" prepared as described in No. 3060, A.D. 1856, or separately to furnish several new compositions.

The processes are given for making what is called "artificial " silicate of zinc" and "a second mineral combination composed " of silicate of alumina and of zinc." "A third mineral combi- " nation, composed of a mineral known as talc or steatite (silicate " of magnesia), rose colored by oxyde of cobalt." "A fourth " mineral combination prepared with blende or native sulphuret " of zinc combined with kaolin or with felspar." These combi- nations, colored or not, are "mixed with the gutta percha and " other matters."

Fourth, a "vegetable combination composed of tannin, gutta " percha, benzone, balsam of tolu or essential oil."—"This " combination reduced to thin sheets is mixed in varying pro- " portions with the compositions of gutta percha and color."

Fifth, "a second vegetable combination" composed of gutta percha made soft by heat, and adding little by little pulverized " catechu. Camphine or benzine may be added to facilitate the " admixture but these bodies communicate an odour." Other vegetable extracts "may be substituted for tannin and catechu."

[Printed, 1s. 4d. Drawings.]

A.D. 1859, December 29.—N° 2978.

NEWTON, WILLIAM EDWARD.—(*A communication from John H. Cheever.*)—" Improvements in machine belting or banding " and in the machinery and process of making the same." These are first, in "machinery for manufacturing ordinary india-rubber " or gutta percha belting or banding." The sheet of either of these substances that is to form the outside of the belt is coated with cement or is sticky on one surface is wound together with a cloth upon a supply roll and passes through two revolving circular cutters susceptible of lateral adjustments upon their shafts. The remaining portion of the wide strip is wound upon a roller together with a sheet of cloth. The sheet of rubber or gutta percha forming the inner portion or body of the belt is wound on a roller alternately with a sheet of cloth. "The cloth is fed along "to two sets of revolving circular cutters which cut off the "desired width of strip for the body of the belt. The strips to "form the inner and outer portions of the belt being thus cut off "are then fed over rolls, the outside strip being the lower, and "thence between two other rollers which unite the two strips." The sheet "then passes between two rollers, the lower one having "cams while the upper one works between these cams upon the "upper surface of the belt," forming the belt into a gutter shape and thence to a roller with two tapering surfaces and a thin circular disc which completes the overlapping or covering of the inner strip by the outer one. The belt is formed by being drawn down or cramped partly around the periphery of a roller.

Second, "imparting a smooth and finished surface to the belt "or band." A "strip or sheet of india-rubber or of gutta percha "or of cloth covered with rubber or of gutta percha, (the latter "being the stronger and better) is to be vulcanized" at about 280°. This vulcanized strip or sheet is sprinkled "with soapstone "dust or black lead or other similar substances," and the driving belt or band having been made up in any proper manner previous to vulcanization is then rolled tightly up with it and vulcanized by a steam boiler or dry heat, &c. but at a higher temperature than usual. The desired effect may also be produced by placing the belt extended between two sheets of vulcanized rubber or gutta percha instead of rolling as above. Another mode is to enamel a sheet of cloth or paper with similar materials as above and roll it up tightly with the belt or band and vulcanize it as above. "The ordinary patent leather or enamelled leather or "cloth composition" may be employed.

Third, "the production of a new kind of belting and banding "and the machinery and process for forming the same." The centre of the belt is formed of a thick cotton, &c. fabric woven of the intended width of the belt and of different thicknesses as required. Both or one side of the belt is covered by "grinding "or driving" it in "with any composition of vulcanizable india- "rubber or gutta percha." The machine for grinding or driving in the material consists of pressure rollers revolving in opposite directions with arrangements for cutting off the superfluous material, &c.. The belt is afterwards vulcanized.

Fourth, a new machine for manufacturing the new and improved 'solid belting,' by which the sides and edges of the cotton duck, or other fabric of which the inner portion of the belt is composed are covered with or encased within a coating of india-rubber or gutta percha at one operation and also by which any number of belts of the same or of different widths can be formed at a time. This consists of an arrangement of rollers, cutters, and circular formers, &c.

[Printed, 1s. 8d. Drawings.]

1860.

A.D. 1860, January 6.—N° 47.

HOOPER, WILLIAM.—(*Provisional protection only.*)—" Im-" provements in re-working compounds of india-rubber and " sulphur, and in insulating telegraphic wires or conductors." These are, reducing such compounds "to a pulp by grinding them " with naptha or solvent" and adding to this mixture raw india rubber and sulphur. In this state the mixture is moulded or otherwise brought to the form desired and is afterwards exposed to heat to cure it, as is ordinarily practised. Coating "the wire " with a layer of copper or other metal before applying the com-" pound containing sulphur." "In some cases I coat copper " wire with collodion" or with tannate of gelatine tannin and collodion, or tannin and shelac, combined or separate, and then with a compound of india-rubber, and sulphur and subject the whole to heat. In preference the wire is first coated with ordinary rubber and then with the compound, and on applying heat the whole becomes vulcanized or hardened. In some cases cotton or fibre is round the wire, over it is placed the compound which is then converted. Before exposing wires or conductors coated with the compound to heat the same is covered with strands of fibre or wire. To make a joint between two lengths of a metallic conductor which has been previously insulated by vulcanite, " I solder or " otherwise connect the ends of the metal conductors and coat " the joint with india-rubber uncombined with sulphur" and round this a quantity of sulphur compound, and over this a sheet of vulcanized india-rubber. These parts are to be well bound

together or clamped during the heating "for converting the
" sulphur compound of india-rubber which has been introduced
" between the lapping surfaces." "In place of interposing a
" composition of india-rubber and sulphur between the native
" india-rubber and the vulcanized india-rubber the two latter are
" placed directly in contact with each other, the surfaces which
" come in contact being coated with naptha or solvent or with a
" solution of india-rubber, sulphur being by preference mixed
" with the solvent or solution."

[Printed, 4d. No Drawings.]

A.D. 1860, January 14.—N° 109.

CHATTERTON, John, and SMITH, Willoughby.—"To
" improve the pliability and durability of tubes and other articles
" made of gutta percha, india-rubber or compounds of the same
" by immersing and soaking them for some hours in a heated
" insulating liquid not being a solvent of gutta percha or india-
" rubber which will fill the pores of such substance." A tank is
used with a jacket of steam or hot water; Stockholm tar is preferred as the insulating liquid heated to between 80° and 90° F.,
time allowed 10 to 12 hours, the superflous liquid is removed by
passing through a die or suitable box. In some cases the tar is
mixed with "about $\frac{1}{4}$ of its weight of clean resin."

[Printed, 4d. No Drawings.]

A.D. 1860, February 7.—N° 325.

NEWTON, William Edward.—(*A communication from John
H. Cheever.*)—"Rendering waste 'vulcanized,' 'hermized,' and
" 'changed' or 'converted' india-rubber, and india-rubber
" compounds useful, and capable of being re-worked for the
" manufacture of a great variety of articles of trade and com-
" merce." This consists, "in reducing waste vulcanized, hermized
" or changed india-rubber or its compounds into fine particles,
" and subjecting them with or without heat by incorporation,
" impregnation, or other method of effecting the required ad-
" mixture to the action of the products derived from heating,
" melting, burning, or distilling native, or vulcanized, or changed
" india-rubber, and applied either separately or combined with
" other substances, and whether the rubber be vulcanized or
" hermized, or not, and whether combined with other substances
" or not."

First, the simplest method is to melt the rubber and "for

" ordinary purposes, the proportion of four ounces of melted
" rubber to one pound of vulcanized rubber will answer."

Second, it is found that one ounce of the liquid product from distilling india-rubber or changed india-rubber " to one pound of
" the powder will be a good average, and also that if heat ranging
" from 200° F., and upwards be applied for a few minutes only
" it will greatly facilitate the softening of the vulcanized rubber
" powder."

Third, producing the same result, but more expeditiously " by
" passing the vapors of either or all of these oily products through
" the powdered vulcanized india-rubber."

[Printed, 4d. No Drawings.]

A.D. 1860, February 22.—N° 472.

LEMOINE, FRANÇOIS HYPOLITE.—" Improvements in the
" manufacture of waterproof papers and pasteboards of every
" description." These are, in reference to this subject, gutta percha is employed for the above purpose " alone or mixed with
" substances such as white pitch and gum lac." The material is heated in a steam oven so as to make it plastic.

[Printed, 8d. Drawings.]

A.D. 1860, March 5.—N° 604.

BRIDGES, WILLIAM.—" Improvements in the manufacture of
" elastic bands." These are first, " the bands are cut of an
" oblong form, by preference, with two sides parallel, the ends
" being rounded, though they may be of an elliptical or oval
" form," using cutters shaped accordingly. " By these means
" there need be but a very small quantity of material cut to
" waste in the interior of the smallest band, when several are
" cut one from within the other, as a straight single cut will in
" such cases be sufficient for the making of such band, there
" being a small portion cut out at the ends of such straight cut."
" In place of cutting oblong bands one within the other, all the
" bands made from a sheet may be made in the manner in which
" the innermost one above described is cut."

' Second, to make oblong flat elastic bands, producing a hollow form of vulcanized or cured india-rubber of an oblong section and of a thickness of material corresponding with the width of the intended bands, and in order to produce oblong elastic bands thin slices or cuttings as compared with the thickness of the material will be cut from the end or ends of the hollow form,

" or the same form may be made solid, and thin slices cut there-
" from be also cut in the centre, as before explained."

[Printed, 6d. Drawing.]

A.D. 1860, March 10.—N° 646.

LUIS, Jozé.—(*A communication from Jean François Joseph Lecocq.*)—(*Provisional protection only.*)—" An improved calcarious " varnish." This consists " principally of 1st, oxyde of calcium ;
" 2nd, gutta percha, or india-rubber; 3rd, a solvent for the gutta
" percha or india-rubber. The oxydes of calcium, which may be
" employed are plaster and lime; chalk can also be employed,
" but with less advantage. The gutta percha and india-rubber
" employed must be as pure as possible. The principal solvents
" are coal tar, oil of turpentine, sulphuret of carbon, and benzine.
" The proportions may vary according as it is desired to obtain
" a liquid, thick, or pasty varnish. A drying oxyde can be
" introduced, if required. The varnish is melted at a gentle
" heat and strained through a fine cloth."

[Printed, 4d. No Drawings.]

A.D. 1860, April 16.—N° 946.

RICHARD, ALBERT C.—(*Provisional protection only.*)—" The
" manufacture of machine belting and apparatus connected
" therewith." The canvas coated with india-rubber or other elastic gums or their compounds, and with a cotton cloth lining is passed over a metal roller under a series of adjustable revolving knives by which it is cut into as many longitudinal strips as is desired. The strips thus cut are by the same mechanism wound up each separately with linings adapted to their several widths, on suitable hollow shafts ready to be made up into belts. Two strips one above the other, the lower strip double the width of the upper, are passed through suitable guides to bring the narrow strip as near as can be on the middle of the wider strip, they are passed together between two welding rollers. The compound strip issuing from between the welding rollers is now formed partly into a belt by folding the sides of the widest strip over or around the narrow inner strip in such a manner as to cause the " edges to meet each other on the centre of the narrow strip." When the belt is further finished and firmly consolidated it "is
" placed for heating or vulcanizing between two polished surfaces
" which I form of plate glass, of slabs of stone or slate solidly

"cemented to hollow metal boxes, or I vulcanise the belt between
"surfaces, which I form by coating any heat-conducting bodies
"of suitable form with any hard or vitreous enamel susceptible
"of a high polish." When it is desired to vulcanize several
belts at one operation, enamelled bars of a similar thickness as
the belts are employed. "Heat is applied to the belts in any of
"the well-known manners."

[Printed, 4d. No Drawings.]

A.D. 1860, April 30.—N° 994.

SILVER, HUGH ADAMS, and BARWICK, JAMES.— (*Letters Patent void for want of Final Specification.*)—" Improvements in
"moulding india-rubber and other like gums in cells for galvanic
"batteries and in insulators for telegraph wires." These are in reference to this subject placing "india-rubber, gutta percha, or
"other similar gums together with sulphur in metal moulds,"
"bringing the moulds and contents by means of an oven or other-
"wise to a temperature of about 400° Fahr.," and suddenly cooling the same. The article is formed of hardened gum alone or of metal or metal cloth coated with the gum on one or both sides or in such parts as may be desired.

[Printed, 4d. No Drawings.]

A.D. 1860, May 29.—N° 1317.

SCHIELE, CHRISTIAN. — (*A communication from Ferdinand Wendelin Kleist*).—" Improvements in the manufacture of lubri-
"cants." These are, in reference to this subject, "the dissolving
"of caoutchouc at a lower degree of temperature than has hither-
"to been used for the purpose of producing a solution capable
"of improving the lubricating qualities of oils or other fatty
"substances with which it is mixed." "Caoutchouc by prefer-
"ence of the best quality" usually sold in sheets is "to be cut
"up in minute pieces, and should be dried in a stove or by the
"sun, until all the white specks have disappeared from its
"surface" it is then put into "fatty paraffin oil, or other oils
"procured from coals," and submitted to a low temperature, well stirring up at first and afterwards at intervals, until the small pieces can be easily crushed between the fingers. The jelly like solution is rubbed by means of a pestle through a finely perforated
"half spherical receptacle." The previous heating must now be continued until it becomes a perfectly clear solution "which will

" dissolve in olive oil in any required proportion by merely
" shaking it. The paraffin oil used above is best when of a gravity
" from 0·852 to 0·895," taking from 15 to 18 parts in weight of it
to 1 part in weight of caoutchouc. "The room in which" the
dissolving process "takes place must never be heated to a higher
" temperature than 122° Fahrenheit, or the process may be con-
" ducted in the cold but a longer time will be required to
" complete it. When quite dissolved, I sometimes strain or
" sieve the solution through a fine brass sieve having pre-
" viously mixed it with some olive or other fatty oil, and let it
" stand in a warm place for clearing."

[Printed, 4d. No Drawings.]

A.D. 1860, June 25.—N° 1546.

HOOPER, WILLIAM. — "Improvements in re-working com-
" pounds of india-rubber and sulphur, and in insulating tele-
" graphic wires or conductors." These are reducing such
compounds "to a pulp by grinding them with naptha or other sol-
" vent" and adding to this mixture raw india-rubber and sulphur
or matters which give off sulphur and moulding and exposing to
heat. The sulphur of the compound is found to act injuriously
on the conductors, and to prevent this, coating the copper wire
or other conductor with a coating of "a solution of shellac or
" other gum resin combined with oxide of zinc or other suitable
" oxide" or with cotton or fibrous substance saturated with the
above varnish, or "a layer of paper or fibre saturated with tannate
" of gelatine or tannin and collodion, or tannin and shellac, with
" or without oxide of zinc or of other metal;" or " I apply col-
" lodion and oxide of zinc or of other metal, with or without one
" or more of the aforesaid substances. I then insulate with
" india-rubber and protect the india-rubber with a compound of
" india-rubber and sulphur," and apply heat "to convert or cure
" the compound of india-rubber." "To make a joint between
" two lengths of a metallic conductor which have been previously
" insulated and coated with india-rubber vulcanite," &c. " I
" solder the ends of the metal conductors together and protect
" the joint from the action of sulphur," and coat the joint with
india-rubber uncombined with sulphur to insulate the same, then
over or around this I apply a suitable compound of india-rubber
and sulphur and over this I put a sheet of vulcanized india-rubber
" and submit the whole well clamped together to heat." The
surfaces of vulcanized or cured india-rubber used in making joints

are rendered more suitable for the purpose by searing the edges or surfaces which are to be joined with a heater. In some cases the wires or yarns of the two ends of the cable should be placed correctly side by side, and lapped round with a wire or thread or yarn, the ends of the wires or yarns should then be bent back and again bound round and the compound formed and applied and fixed by heat as above described.

[Printed, 4d. No Drawings.]

A.D. 1860, June 27.—N° 1560.

MACINTOSH, JOHN.—"Improved compounds for coating or insulating submarine or other telegraphic wires; also in rendering the gutta percha or india-rubber coatings of telegraphic wires impervious." This consists in mixing gutta percha or india-rubber with paraffine or stearic acid. The proportions may vary, but in preference "the composition should consist of 75 parts by weight of gutta percha or india-rubber or of the two combined, to 25 parts by weight of paraffine or stearic acid," mixed by masticating or grinding machinery. Telegraphic cables are made "more impervious and durable by surrounding them with yarn fillets, or ribbons made of cords, strands of hemp or other fibrous materials saturated with paraffine or stearic acid in combination with or without india-rubber." This is effected in a vessel heated to about 150° Fahrenheit. "A coating of india-rubber or compounds of india-rubber suitably prepared is put over the "fibrous materials," and an outer coating of india-rubber or compounds of india-rubber is put on and vulcanized or cured as is described in No. 2866, A.D. 1857.

[Printed, 4d. No Drawings.]

A.D. 1860, July 19.—N° 1750.

WOODCOCK, ALONZO BUONAPARTE.—"Improvements in the manufacture of moulded articles of vulcanized india-rubber." These are, "heretofore vulcanized india-rubber in the form of scrap or waste, or otherwise has been reduced by rollers or by grinding to the state of powder or dust, and such powder or dust has been mixed with comparatively large proportions of native or unvulcanized india-rubber and sulphur, and such compounds have been made up into articles and have been subjected to heat to vulcanize the same; and in some cases in place of native india-rubber, india-rubber solution has been

"used;" the patentee has discovered "that by mixing a large
" proportion of the ground or powdered vulcanized india-rubber
" with a small proportion of native or unvulcanized india-rubber
" that a plastic compound is obtained which admits of being
" immediately moulded;" and this moulded article retains its
form though it be forthwith delivered from the mould, and vulcan-
canized "(without any addition of sulphur) in or upon a mould
" the article produced has a like character to a similar one
" made directly from native india-rubber and sulphur." The
proportions believed best are 80 per cent. of the grained or powdered vulcanized, to 20 per cent. of native or unvulcanized.

[Printed, 4d. No Drawings.]

A.D. 1860, July 23.—N° 1777.

NOIROT, JEAN BAPTISTE JULES.—"An improved method of
" manufacturing india-rubber tubes and various articles." This
consists "in vulcanizing the rubber in two operations, and in
" working and shaping it between the first and second operations
" as hereafter explained." As an example "in manufacturing
" tubes of any length," forming them "in lengths of about two,
" three, four, or five yards" placing them "upon mandrils or
" rods and rolling them in cloths as is ordinarily done;" then
subjecting them to the semi-vulcanization, after which the mandril
and cloths are removed and the lengths are united by fusing the
ends, thus obtaining "a tube of any length required, say twenty,
" fifty, and one hundred yards," and rolling "the tube upon a
" drum or otherwise" and completing the vulcanization.

[Printed, 4d. No Drawings.]

A.D. 1860, August 3.—N° 1873.

PITMAN, JOHN TALBOT.—(*A communication from Messrs. Bourn,
Brown, & Chaffee.*)—"An improved process in the vulcanization
" of india-rubber and other similar substances under pressure."
This is said to consist in "the use of the mould press, the lubri-
" cating and strengthening materials in combination for forming
" and vulcanizing mats or other similar articles under pressure,
" substantially as follows," first, forming a metallic die or mould
by plaining or removing in a similar manner from the flat surface
of the metal, the spaces necessary to receive and form the raised
portions of the mat when moulding. A hoop may be secured
around its edge to form the outer ridge or border of the mould.
" The face of the mould is then moistened with soap and water,

" or other suitable lubricating material, and the flat face or sheet
" of the material to be impressed is placed upon it. The surface
" of the chest next the die to a certain depth, say $\frac{1}{16}$ part of an
" inch should consist of good material, the remainder may be
" composed of poorer." A cotton or other fabric is laid on the
back, the whole placed in a press and subjected to a steam heat
at "80 pounds pressure to the square inch, the vulcanization is
" effected in seven or eight minutes, and in like proportion as
" will easily be ascertained by practice. Withdrawn from the
" press the mat while hot is removed from the mould by pulling
" it off by means of the cloth."

[Printed, 4d. No Drawings.]

A.D. 1860, August 3.—N° 1875.

PITMAN, JOHN TALBOT.—(*A communication from Messrs. Bourn, Brown, and Chaffee.*)—"An improved press." "Constructing a
" press with an upper and lower stationary bed plate, having be-
" tween them mounted one or more revolving screws, or in any
" other manner effecting the same object, a follower, which is
" operated so that while removing the pressure on one side of the
" follower it can be communicated to new matter on the other, and
" in having the bed plates and follower hollow." To furnish the
heat necessary for vulcanizing the india-rubber or other material
under the action of the press, steam is admitted by pipes, into
the bed plates and follower. "The substance to be vulcanized
" is placed upon moulds or dies formed in part and counterpart
" in two corresponding metallic plates, or in any other way, and
" between the two plates is pushed in between the follower and
" one of the bed plates when the pressure and heat are applied
" for the necessary length of time. When ready to be removed
" the other side of the follower receives another set, and the
" pressure in being withdrawn from the finished matter is im-
" mediately applied to the new without loss of time, so that one
" charge is constantly under treatment."

[Printed, 6d. Drawing.]

A.D. 1860, August 13.—N° 1957.

NEWTON, ALFRED VINCENT.—(*A communication from John Haven Cheever.*)—"An improved mode of treating waste vul-
" canized india-rubber." This consists as follows :—The waste
rubber "is first ground into a coarse powder," and "steeped in
" or mixed with vegetable tar, or with the tarry or pitchey pro-

" ducts derived from the distillation of resin when producing
" resin oil," preferring what is "known in the United States of
" America as pine oil." The mixture of oil and ground rubber
having remained " from about four to five days, the superfluous tar
" or oil is run or strained off, and there is then to be added to the
" now softened rubber, by kneading new or green vulcanizable
" rubber, in any desired proportion, to suit the quality, as respects
" tenacity, of the compound desired." When thoroughly amalgamated and the compound moulded or otherwise made into goods,
the goods are cured " in the ordinary manner, but it is preferred
" to submit the goods to the curing heat while under pressure,
" whereby great elasticity will be secured."

[Printed, 4d. No Drawings.]

A.D. 1860, August 13.—N° 1959.

NEWTON, ALFRED VINCENT.—(*A communication from John
Haven Cheever.*)—" Improvements in the mode of and machinery
" for manufacturing hose pipes." These are first, "to expedite the
" operation and improve the quality of the manufacture," "the
" following arrangement of mechanism is employed :"—" A hori-
" zontal mandril (the outer diameter of which corresponds to the
" inner diameter of the hose to be made) is provided to receive
" strips of vulcanizable rubber cloth, which are to be laid heli-
" cally thereon. These strips are wound upon spools, which are
" mounted in a rotating traversing frame surrounding the man-
" dril. A traverse motion is given to the frame by means of a
" carriage which supports it, and the spools will thus be caused
" to lay the strips helically around the mandril with the edges of
" the same strips abutting. When the mandril has received the
" required number of layers, it is to be removed from the ma-
" chine and carried to the curing chamber, the heat of which will
" by melting the rubber ensure the proper cementation of the
" joints."

Second, another mode is, "to draw over a mandril a woven
" tube, and by means of a series of adjustable pressing rollers set
" radially around the mandril to press india-rubber vulcanizable
" compound thereon, the rubber being fed by hand on to the
" woven tube in front of the rollers as the mandril is drawn
" between them. This machine may also be used to give solidity
" to india-rubber cloth hose made in any way."

Third, "manufacturing hose pipes, which will admit of being
" rolled up flat on a barrel for easy transport, and will com-

"bine great strength and lightness. The hose pipe is made of "two strips of strong woven cloth" coated "with rubber, which "strips are secured together at the edges by rivets or sewing." The strips may be coated on one or both sides with india-rubber or gutta percha and united by sewing or rivetting, any desired numbers of layers being used to constitute the sides of the hose. The hose can be vulcanized or not as desired.

Fourth, manufacturing "strong hose without seams," "first "cover a tolerably thin woven tube with a sheet of india-rubber "or gutta percha," and then "turn it inside out" as usual. Over this tube is then drawn a woven tube of little larger diameter and in like manner any number may be added. Another mode is to wind a tube of rubber or gutta percha or of fibrous materials coated with these materials, or other waterproof lining, with twine cord or other suitable thread of sufficient fineness closely around the periphery of the same. Another mode is to slip over the mandril a tube of india-rubber or gutta percha, and over this is drawn a woven tube which is then coated with a cement, and this is covered by hand or machinery with strands of thread, twine or cord. If desired this surface may be again covered with a suitable cement or a tube of india-rubber or gutta percha. In place of the woven tube above, sheets of cotton or other material coated with a cement may be wrapped round the india-rubber, &c. tube. The whole may be vulcanized on the mandril. Another mode is to wind upon a tube of rubber or gutta percha on a mandril, strands, and if desired coating them with cement or with a tube of rubber or gutta percha. In manufacturing seamless tubes without a woven fabric for a base, this is also accomplished by covering the mandril with "plastic rubber, and this coating being "dusted over with burnt flour or other dust, which will amalga- "mate in the curing process, or moistened with a thin rubber "cement, the woven tube is drawn over the rubber coating." After the curing the mandril is drawn out. Another mode of carrying out the above is to cover a mandril with a thin sheet of vulcanizable rubber or gutta percha, this is vulcanized or not, and this is coated or covered much as before. For pipes as a substitute for lead ones, the woven tube is omitted and a larger quantity of sulphur, together with metallic oxide, &c., and rags, &c. are ground together, rolled into sheets and formed upon a mandril and cured at a temperature of $270°$ F.

Fifth, treating fabrics that are to form the base of those pipes by "a kyanizing or other well-known process for preserving "vegetable fibres preparatory to being coated with compounds." The substances used in the kyanizing process are "corrosive sublimate, chloride of zinc, pyrolignite of iron, oil of tar, and other bituminous, pitchy, and resinous matters."

[Printed, 2s. Drawings.]

A.D. 1860, August 13.—N° 1961.

NEWTON, ALFRED VINCENT.—(*A communication from John Haven Cheever.*)—"Improvements in the manufacture of driving "bands, and in the machinery to be employed in such manufac-"ture." These are, first, "in making the ordinary belting it is "proposed to use mechanical instead of hand labour. To this "end the covering cloth coated on both sides with vulcanizable "cement is passed between a system of vertical grooved rollers "which turn up the edges thereof preparatory to folding them "over. Before these rollers come into action a band of filling "material of the width of the band to be made of one, two, or "more plies of cloth coated with vulcanizable cement is brought "down from a feed roll and laid upon the covering cloth. The "folding rollers then act and turn the cloth over it. To prevent "the covering cloth closing prematurely upon the filling cloth, "a guard is provided for keeping up the edges until the cloth "in travelling comes near to the bite of a pair of transverse "pressing rollers. These rollers then compress the overlapping "parts of the band upon the filling piece, and the band then "shows a central seam along its whole length." A narrow strip of rubber is brought down upon this seam, and finally the band passes into a box of powdered soapstone or other powder. The band is ready for the curing process.

Second. An improvement in No. 2978, 1859. In making solid belting much difficulty has been experienced in perfectly covering the edges of the belt or band; to obviate this it is proposed to remove the lateral rollers used for spreading the first coating of rubber on the edges of the band, and in lieu thereof to increase the nip of the pressing rolls. When the band has received its second or outside coat, it is requisite to trim the edges, which is effected by stationary cutters pressed up laterally to their work by suitable springs. A series of rollers work the rubber into the edges of the woven fabric. In curing, the roll of belt is wound up loosely and set on one end on a heated plate with some smooth surface intervening; the roll is then reversed.

Third. In finishing or surfacing the bands made as above by

grinding or polishing down the surface of the belts, either by hands or by machinery, but preferably by machinery, or by imparting to them a smooth surface during the process of vulcanizing or curing by passing them into a chamber between a series of hollow rolls which are heated, the latter of which finish the vulcanization. Or by dusting over the bands previous to vulcanization with some non-adhesive substance like soapstone, rolling them up tightly and vulcanizing them in a steam heater, &c. Or they are wound upon a roller and passed gradually between two slabs or plates of glass heated by steam in a chamber. Or by " the use of flexible sheet metal composed of an alloy of tin and " lead, interposed between the coils of the bands before it is " submitted to heat."

[Printed, 1s. 8d. Drawings.]

A.D. 1860, August 25.—N° 2052.

TRUMAN, EDWIN THOMAS.—" An improved method of cleansing and purifying gutta percha and other like substances and " their compounds, and an improved apparatus to be employed " therein." This consists, first, " the masticating or kneading " " of gutta percha and other like substances and their compounds " " by means of a masticator or other similar apparatus " acting upon the material whilst it is in contact with hot water " for the purpose of cleansing or purifying the gutta percha or " other material, and at the same time masticating or kneading " it into a homogeneous mass."

Second. "A masticator made entirely of 'pot' or other suitable earthenware, stone, or stoneware, immersed and made to " work in hot water. The earthen or stoneware or stone pre" vents any coloration of the gutta percha or other substance, " and enables me to obtain it clean and of its natural colour. " For delicate uses, I find when metal masticators are employed " that they injuriously affect the color."

[Printed, 8d. Drawing.]

A.D. 1860, September 1.—N° 2116.

HARRISON, CHARLES WEIGHTMAN. — " Improvements in " electric telegraphs." These are, in reference to this subject, " preventing the decay of the outer or protecting wires of " electric cables by surrounding them with fibrous materials " saturated with a compound" consisting of "1 lb. of gutta " percha or india-rubber dissolved in 4 gallons of tar oil, and

" 24 lbs. of resin dissolved in 12 gallons of bone or Dippel's
" oil; these are well mixed and heated together in an iron
" vessel." The fibrous material "is then dipped in the hot
" liquid until thoroughly saturated," when it may be wound
around each of the outer or protecting wires previous to their
being laid on the cable.

[Printed, 10d. Drawing.]

A.D. 1860, September 6.—N° 2152.

BURKE, WILLIAM HENRY, the elder, and BURKE, WILLIAM
HENRY, the younger.—" A method of preparing fabrics composed
" of or containing caoutchouc to enable them to resist the action
" of colours and varnishes containing oil." This consists in
coating the above fabrics " with a solution of shell-lac or other
" like suitable gum, or with size.". The fabric to which this invention is said "more particularly to apply is that known as
" Clark's patent felt." It is better " to dissolve the shell-lac or
" other gum in water aided by ammonia, instead of dissolving it
" in spirit, though it may be used dissolved in spirit." It is preferred "to use a solution of gelatine as one size, the gelatine being
" dissolved in water, though flour paste, or gluten in solution,
" and, in fact, any other size acting as a stop to the color to be
" afterwards applied may be employed."

[Printed, 4d. No Drawings.]

A.D. 1860, October 8.—N° 2439.

CLARK, WILLIAM.—(*A communication from Louis Boulet, Auguste Sarazin, and Louis Hamy.*)—" Improvements in cleaning or
" separating gutta percha from extraneous matters and in appa-
" ratus for the same." These are " treating gutta percha with a
" heated alkaline solution " and " apparatus constructed and
" arranged for the purpose." For about one hundred weight of
gutta percha one hundred and twenty gallons of water are placed
in a vessel, the whole boiled, and a gallon of soda solution, about
20° Baumé, is added, then the gutta percha in large pieces as imported or cut in pieces is introduced, and when it has become soft
the machine is set in motion, which consists of " upright shafts
" mounted parallel to each other in a suitable chamber or vessel,
" each shaft having radial prongs or arms which interlock with
" each other by the rotation of the shaft." " At first it is driven
" about seventy or eighty revolutions per minute, but the speed
" may be increased in proportion as the gutta percha becomes

" comminated." In about half an hour the grosser particles of dirt, &c. having separated and fallen to the bottom of the vessel, the gutta percha is skimmed off the surface of the water, and placed in another or similar apparatus and treated as before, and so on three or four times " according to the state of purity to " which it is desired to reduce the gutta percha." " Ultimately " it is washed in like manner in clean water to remove any trace " of alkaline solution." " The gutta percha may then be kneaded, " masticated, or rolled into sheets, or otherwise worked."

[Printed, 8d. Drawing.]

A.D. 1860, November 2.—N° 2689.

NEWTON, WILLIAM EDWARD.—(*A communication from Rudolph Franz Heinrich Havemann.*)—" An improvement in preparing " compounds of india-rubber, gutta percha, and allied gums." " This consists, " in preparing (a compound) by the admixture of " lime, aqua-ammonia and sal-ammoniac with india-rubber, " gutta percha, or any of their allied gums, or two or more of such " gums, after such gum or gums have been treated with chlorine " by either of the two processes described in No. 2762, A.D. 1859, " but it is preferred to use that process in which the gum is reduced " to a solution before being subjected to the action of the chlo- " rine." The gum after treatment in a plastic state has "aqua- " ammonia or liquor ammonia " added to it " in the proportion " of about one-eighth of a drachm to every pound of gum, and " after grinding or stirring the mass about till a thorough mix- " ture is effected, one-eighth of a drachm of powdered sal-am- " moniac (hydrochlorate of ammonia) together with half a pound " of pure lime (oxide of calcium) in a finely powdered state are " added to each pound of gum." After thorough mixing and grinding, the compound is placed in a mould, pressed "until it " is incapable of further condensation, when it is removed from the " press and mould," and "exposed to heat of about 240° F. until " it becomes perfectly hard. The compound will then be com- " pact and white, and of a texture and appearance resembling " ivory, and will withstand the action of all varieties of climate, " hot or greasy water, and of acids."

[Printed, 4d. No Drawings.]

A.D. 1860, December 11.—N° 3035.

STEVENS, CHARLES.—(*A communication from J. Chapa and Lacaze.*)—(*Provisional protection only.*)—" An impermeable anti-

" sulphuric coating for leather." This consists of "two coatings
" composed of the following ingredients." "1st, coating india-
" rubber dissolved in sulphuret of carbon to saturation. It must
" be dissolved in a bottle or other suitable receptacle closed with
" a glass stopper." "2nd, coating gutta percha dissolved in a
" solution of sulphuret of carbon to saturation; likewise dissolved
" in a flask or other receptacle closed as before with a glass
" stopper." " The matters used must be as pure as possible."
[Printed, 4d. No Drawings.]

A.D. 1860, December 19.—N° 3121.

BROOMAN, RICHARD ARCHIBALD.—(*A communication from J. D. Duhousset and P. E. Thomas.*) — " Improvements in
" treating caoutchouc, and the employment of a product obtained
" thereby for lubricating and coating bodies." These are, heating
caoutchouc in a hermetically closed vessel having an agitator "to
" convert it into a viscous semifluid substance denominated
" 'hévéone' to be used pure or mixed with fatty or other
" matters." Sometimes it may be heated in a distilling apparatus, and the coil or serpentine from it is refrigerated. If
" thick 'hévéone' be desired, the carburets of hydrogen that are
" given off from the caoutchouc may be partially condensed,
" the condensed portions being afterwards rectified and added to
" other hévéone which may be required in a more fluid state."
[Printed, 4d. No Drawings.]

1861.

A.D. 1861, January 10.—N° 62.

MOULTON, STEPHEN.—" Improvements in the manufacture
" of india rubber applicable to springs, valves for machinery,
" and other purposes." It is stated " the process of curing
" or changing the character of the india-rubber, by treating or
" compounding it with sulphur, or with sulphur chemically com-
" bined with other substances, being now generally understood" it
need not be described, but the processes described in Nos. 10,027
and 11,567 Old Law, " are very suitable for carrying out my pre-
" sent improvements, which consist in embedding steel or other
" metal of suitable forms," and in moulding the same with the
manufactured india-rubber, the same " being afterwards 'cured'

" or rendered permanently elastic by heat, or otherwise, as is well
" understood."

[Printed, 8d. Drawing.]

A.D. 1861, January 31.—N° 263.

CHATTERTON, JOHN.—"Improvements in treating gutta
" percha, india-rubber, and compounds containing one or both
" of those substances, and in machinery and apparatus employed
" therein." These are, first, washing " dirt, woody fibre, and
" other impurities capable of being removed by water " from the
above substances, as follows; "causing heated water, by prefer-
" ence at from 180° to 200° Faht., to flow in a continuous stream
" or streams or in jets into and through the masticators " while
at work. Or the water is applied at intervals, employing any
suitable form of apparatus, or an " apparatus invented for the
" purpose," consisting of " a small hopper-bottomed cistern at a
" suitable height over and above the masticators," in which is
fitted " a V-shaped trough called a tumbler, having a pivot at
" each end, and hung in suitable bearings, slightly out of the
" centre; the tumbler is fixed, so as to turn over when the water
" which flows into it reaches to the height to make the front the
" heavier, when it discharges its contents into the cistern, and
" then through proper conducting pipes to the masticator, to
" flush the whole inside of it completely."

Second, using "hot water instead of cold in the tanks of the
" machines known as 'tickers'" in cleansing the above substances. In preference, the tanks are oval, divided down the
centre by a plate with a space at each end. Agitators or paddles
drive the material round the tank, and sometimes a series of rolls
fixed in a similar tank are employed; hot water completely covers
the lower rolls, and partially the top rolls. The material is drawn
from one set of rolls to another as long as required. In some
cases, a dividing plate or knives is fixed in front of these rolls.

[Printed, 4d. No Drawings.]

A.D. 1861, February 19.—N° 414.

TURNER, ARCHIBALD.—" Improvements in preparing warps
" for the manufacture of elastic fabrics." These are, in reference to this subject, " cutting all the india-rubber threads or
" strands intended to form one warp or two warps from one and
" the same sheet of india-rubber, which, of course, is made of
" one uniform length," "there being little or no waste or odd

" pieces when the strands are of uniform length." "In order
" to cut the short rubber into strands of the requisite thickness,
" one extremity of the sheet of rubber should be secured in a
" groove or recess made for the purpose on a cylinder." "By
" this means I shall obtain a narrow piece or band of rubber,
" which may be called a head, with a given number of threads of
" uniform length pendant therefrom." It is "loosely placed on
" a cylinder or roller, from which it is drawn off by the head or
" uncut end on to a beam cylinder or warping mill, and from
" this it is again drawn off by the other end or tail, and is wound
" tightly on the warp roller or beam, so that the warp may be
" placed in the loom with the india-rubber or elastic strands, all
" stretched to the same tension." Sometimes the sheet is cut
throughout into separate threads, and these threads are clamped
and held by a clamp, the faces of which are covered with india-
rubber, or some other suitable material. The threads are passed
round a series of tension rollers, so "that the tension throughout
" the warp will be rendered uniform."

[Printed, 8d. Drawing.]

A.D. 1861, February 22.—Nº 446.

TRUMAN, EDWIN THOMAS.—" Improvements in masticators or
" machines employed in the mastication of gutta percha, india-
" rubber, and other similar substances." These are, first, "con-
" structing masticators with apertures in the case thereof, for the
" passage of the roller made to rotate therein, of such diameter
" as to allow of such roller or axle turning freely in such aper-
" tures, without coming in contact with the case."
Second, " mounting rollers in masticators upon independent
" axles," which pass through the case and are supported and
revolve in bearings outside the case. The masticators are made
" of earthenware, stone, glass, or other brittle material, and the
" above improvements are made in order to prevent the breaking
" off of particles of the ware," owing to the roller being thrown
out of truth.

[Printed, 4d. No Drawings.]

A.D. 1861, February 23.—Nº 467.

DUNLOP, JOHN MACMILLAN.—" Improvements in machinery
" suitable for cutting india-rubber fillets." These are, " the
" machinery is arranged to cut fillets from circular flat discs of
" india-rubber by cutting from the peripheries towards the centres

" of the discs." A circular cutter or knife. " is fixed on an axis,
" and by preference on a horizontal axis (though that is not
" essential), so that the circular knife or cutter will revolve in a
" vertical plane. The axis is driven by an endless strap or band
" acting on a drum or pulley, and from this axis rotary motion
" is, by suitable gearing, communicated to a roller, which, by
" constantly acting on the periphery or peripheries of the disc
" or discs which is or are being cut, gives a uniform surface speed
" to such disc or discs notwithstanding the diameter of the disc
" or discs constantly becoming less and less, and the cut is made
" by the edge of the circular knife or cutter at the part near where
" the roller is pressing on the disc or discs, that is, at a point
" between the place of contact of the roller and the centre of the
" disc or discs, according to the thickness which is being cut off.
" The axis on which the disc or discs of india-rubber is or are
" placed, is moved progressively towards the pressing and ac-
" tuating roller by gearing, which receives motion suitable for
" keeping the periphery or peripheries of the disc or discs in
" contact with the actuating roller."

[Printed, 10*d*. Drawing.]

A.D. 1861, February 28.—N° 513.

HAY, WILLIAM JOHN.—" An improved glue or composition
" suitable for covering the caulking of ships and other like
" purposes, for uniting wood and other substances, for filling up
" seams, and for use as a waterproof glue or composition gene-
" rally," consisting of " resin oil, together with asphalte, natural
" bitumens, and some or all of the other ingredients " afterwards
mentioned. The following proportions of the ingredients may
be used, but they may be considerably varied according to the
purpose to which the glue or composition is applied. Take of
asphalte or natural bitumen, 20 cwt.; vegetable pitch, 5 cwt.;
resin oil, 5 cwt.; caoutchouc, $17\frac{1}{2}$ lbs. Or take of asphalte or
natural bitumen, 20 cwt.; resin oil, $7\frac{1}{2}$ cwt.; caoutchouc, 26 lbs.
Or take of asphalte or natural bitumen, 20 cwt.; black or yellow
resin, $2\frac{1}{2}$ cwt.; vegetable pitch, 5 cwt.; resin oil, 5 cwt.; caoutchouc,
$17\frac{1}{2}$ lbs. Or take of asphalte or natural bitumen, 20 cwt.;
vegetable tar, 5 cwt.; resin oil, 3 cwt.; caoutchouc, $10\frac{1}{2}$ lbs.

[Printed, 4*d*. No Drawings.]

A.D. 1861, March 6.—N° 569.

SILVER, HUGH ADAMS, and GRIFFIN, HENRY.—This con-
sists, first, in manufacturing insulators and other articles in india-

rubber required to retain a shape once given to them, of two or more sheets of india-rubber compound with a core or layer of cloth or other suitable stiffening material interposed, "for the " purpose of supporting such articles during the process of curing " or manufacture."

Second, " protecting hard rubber ebonite, and vulcanite goods, " while being cured or vulcanized " by " employing a separate " hood for each separate article, or by placing several articles " under one and the same hood, or in one oven, or sometimes in " the manufacture of insulators we dispense with the hood and " use chalk or other material instead."

Third, " moulding insulators of india-rubber or india-rubber " compound " of " a single shape or form of the intended in- " sulator, over and upon which form the insulator in a soft state " is applied; the process of curing or vulcanizing causes the " shape thus given to the insulator to be retained. Or we mould " hard india-rubber insulators and other articles in moulds made " of French chalk or other like suitable pulverized material," and " fill up the internal part with the same material."

Fourth, constructing cellular fabrics from sheets or plates of india-rubber or india-rubber compound of the thickness of the intended article, "by cutting parallel slits in and through the " sheet without removing any portion thereof, the slits in every " line or plane alternating with those in the next line in such " manner that the slits in one line shall come opposite to uncut " or solid pieces in the next line, then by drawing the sides of " the sheet in a direction opposite to that of the line of slits a " cellular fabric will be produced." " In curing the cellular " fabrics we fill the cells or spaces with French chalk or other " pulverized materials."

Fifth, "forming articles partly of hard rubber or ebonite or " vulcanite and partly of soft vulcanized rubber," by "suitably " preparing the india-rubber compounds to assume respectively " the soft vulcanized and the hard rubber states, as is well " understood by the workers in india-rubber; and we unite the " two compounds so prepared in the soft state, and then cure " or vulcanize " them.

Sixth, "varnishes for hard india-rubber, ebonite, or vulcanite " goods, which we prefer to apply to goods in their soft state, " prior to their being cured or vulcanized, though they may be " applied after the manufacture of the goods;" they consist of the following compositions in or about the following proportions :

"We take of india-rubber 30 parts, of naptha 120 parts; or
" india-rubber 30 parts, vegetable black 1 part, and naptha 120
" parts; or india-rubber 30 parts, bitumen 15 parts, and naphtha
" 120 parts; or bitumen 30 parts, and naphtha 50 to 100 parts;
" or gutta percha 30 parts, and naphtha 120 parts; or gutta
" percha 30 parts, vegetable black 1 part, and naphtha 120 parts;
" or india-rubber 30 parts, shellac 10 parts, and naphtha 120
" parts; or india-rubber 30 parts, resin 5 to 20 parts, & naphtha
" 120 parts; or india-rubber 30 parts, resin 5 to 10 parts; bi-
" tumen 5 to 10 parts, and naphtha 120 parts; or we employ
" a varnish consisting wholly of boiled linseed oil."

[Printed, 6d. Drawing.]

A.D. 1861, March 14.—N° 637.

TRUMAN, EDWIN THOMAS.—"Improvements in masticators
" or apparatuses for preparing gutta-percha caoutchouc and other
" similar substances." These are, in "substituting for the solid
" roller or rollers now used in masticators an axle or spindle
" furnished with arms which project from it inside the case and
" carry a roller or bar which is so adjusted that there is space
" between it and the axle or spindle, and also between it and the
" masticator case; the roller or bar is made to revolve with the
" axle or spindle." Instead of one roller or bar, two or more
are sometimes used, and the number of arms or fixed discs are
increased on the axle or spindle for carrying the rollers or bars.
For some purposes employing a "skeleton drum with a central
" spindle, the blades of which are fixed or are free to revolve in
" the bearings whereby they are connected to the central
" spindle."

[Printed, 4d. No Drawings.]

A.D. 1861, March 20.—N° 697.

BROOMAN, RICHARD ARCHIBALD.—(*A communication from
Corneille Lambert Charles Casimir Gobert.*)—(*Provisional protection only.*)—"Improvements in preparing caoutchouc, adapted
" especially to dental purposes." These are "red caoutchouc"
is dissolved "in sulphuret of carbon, ether, chloroform, or other
" solvent," varying in quantity "from about one-quarter of the
" weight up to an equivalent weight of caoutchouc," introducing
" one of the following decoloring substances, sulphate of baryta,
" of manganese, of strontian, of antimony, calcined alumina, cal-

" cined or precipitated silex; phosphate of lime, or carbonate of
" baryta," " alone or mixed with oxide of zinc " so as " to reduce
" or tone down the red in the caoutchouc " to " a flesh color tint ;
" sometimes a little carmine is added." The product is a paste
for the moulding of dental pieces, &c.; if required " more supple
" and malleable a small quantity of ordinary caoutchouc solution
" is added." The moulded article is hardened by heating in a
closed vessel " from about 300° to about 335° Fahr." for three-
quarters of an hour. " Caoutchouc prepared in the ordinary
" manner would require, to attain an equal degree of hardness,
" at least one hour and a quarter." " The flesh color will be
" improved by exposing the ' piece ' or other articles either directly
" or in an alcoholic bath to solar rays for a period varying with
" the intensity of the light."

[Printed, 4d. No Drawings.]

A.D. 1861, April 15.—N° 924.

MILLER, THOMAS.—This invention consists, in reference to
this subject, in "machinery for preparing india-rubber and other
" similar gums for insulating telegraphic wires." " This I effect
" by means of a cutting machine having its knife set or placed
" and cutting in a longitudinal direction with the block of ma-
" terial from which the sheet or strips is or are to be cut. The
" knife may either be made to advance to the block when cutting
" or vice versâ. The reciprocating knife may be either the whole
" length of the block of rubber or other gums, or any portion
" of its length; if of the whole length, the framing which sup-
" ports the knife with its driving apparatus when cutting, will
" have no longitudinal traversing or reciprocating motion, but
" when the reciprocating knife is only a portion of the length of
" block, the frame which supports or carries the knife will have
" so much of a traversing or reciprocating motion as will make
" the knife cut freely over both ends of the block, or the knife
" may be an irregular shaped oval or a circular revolving one
" fixed in a spindle running flush over and mounted in a tra-
" versing frame similar to that last described. These knives may
" either make a cut vertically or horizontally." " When making
" vertical cuts from the block set in edge, I secure such blocks to
" the platform by atmospheric pressure by pumping the air from
" under the block by means of an air pump operated in any con-
" venient manner." " These sheets are then wound on a man-

" dril and cut into strips by means of a knife mounted in a
" self-acting slide rest, which has a traversing and to-and-fro
" motion alternately." Another mode is "after the rubber, or
" rubber with its compounds" has been efficiently masticated,
one or more blocks of the same are placed in an annular space in
a heated press and pressed until a solid ring is produced. This
ring, in preference, " of a rectangular cross section, is mounted in
" a cylinder ring or pulley fixed on a shaft, and set to turn or
" revolve in bearings, or in centres, and driven at the required
" speed in any suitable manner." "This annular block may
" likewise be secured on to a cylinder or ring which may be made
" hollow by atmospheric pressure in a similar manner to that
" before described." "If I want a strip equal to the circum-
" ference of the ring only, I mount a suitable knife in a self-
" acting slide rest in such a manner that the requisite thickness
" of strip or ribbon is taken off the circumference to the width
" required; a second knife fixed in a slide on the above-men-
" tioned slide rest, and set at about right angles to the former
" knife, is made to cut the proper width of ribbon or strip, either
" of the cuts may be made first, as may be found necessary."
Modifications of the foregoing machinery for cutting strips or
ribbons of india-rubber are further described. The ribbons and
strips are "taken to a water bath or baths of corresponding length,
" heated to the necessary temperature, and are then cleansed from
" dust and other extraneous matter which may have adhered to
" them."

[Printed, 4s. 2d. Drawings.]

A.D. 1861, May 3.—N° 1114.

GODEFROY, PETER AUGUSTIN.—(*Provisional protection only.*)
—"An improvement in the manufacture of gutta percha." This
consists in adding to gutta percha, after it has been thoroughly
masticated and while still in "the masticator from five to ten
" per cent., more or less, of rosin in a semi-fluid state; this I
" amalgamate for an hour or more," the result is preferably for
insulating telegraph wires.

[Printed, 4d. No Drawings.]

A.D. 1861, May 8.—N° 1166.

HUNT, JOHN ROLFE.—"Improvements in the manufacture of
" gutta percha and compounds thereof, with other matters and

" substances." These are "the combination or admixture of
" vulcanized india-rubber and arrowroot with gutta percha."
" I prefer using new, fresh made, and pure, vulcanized india-
" rubber, but in some cases I mix the same with old and waste
" vulcanized india-rubber, freed as much as possible from any
" admixture of black lead, French chalk, or other deteriorating
" matters." One pound of vulcanized india-rubber is passed
through suitable rollers with 2 parts of gutta percha, this matter
is sprinkled with coal tar naptha or other suitable solvent, and
four ounces of arrowroot are worked into it, when it is rolled into
sheets; or it may be first passed through iron sieves.

[Printed, 4d. No Drawings.]

A.D. 1861, May 10.—N° 1192.

GODEFROY, Peter Augustin.—(*Provisional protection only.*)
—" An improvement in the treatment of india-rubber." This
consists in immersing it in bisulphide of carbon or chloride of
sulphur, the strength varying with the thickness of the goods;
drying the india-rubber in air and treating it as follows :—" Ve-
" getable oil (any galipoli) is taken, and to every quart of it is
" applied one-eighth, more or less, of the pure sulphuric acid
" which is held in complete combination." " The india-rubber
" is immersed from ten to fifteen minutes more or less," rinsed
in hot water and placed in a boiler or steam chamber heated up
to 212° or 300° F. according to the thickness of the india-rubber.
" The time of boiling or steaming is from one to four hours.
" The goods having undergone this process and being dried, are
" finished and fit for use."

[Printed, 4d. No Drawings.]

A.D. 1861, May 11.—N° 1204.

TOOTH, William Henry.—This invention consists, in reference to this subject, of a machine which may be employed for
cutting up or reducing waste vulcanized india-rubber in order to
facilitate the removal therefrom of the sulphur that has been used
in the vulcanizing process consisting " principally of a metal
" roller composed of a number of serrated discs or circular saws
" strung upon a spindle, with thin washers between them to
" keep them a certain distance apart. This cylinder is mounted

" in horizontal bearings, and rotates opposite to a pair of adjust-
" able feeding or holding rollers, which may be constructed in
" the same manner as the serrated roller above mentioned. This
" pair of feeding or holding rollers is mounted in bearings in a
" moveable block, which is provided with adjusting screws or
" other analogous contrivances, whereby the feeding rollers may
" be moved forward to or backward from the acting roller as
" may be required." The "materials are fed in between the
" holding rollers which carry them forward to the acting or
" reducing roller, the surface speed of which is greater than that
" of the holding rollers," and the effect will therefore be that the
materials " will be torn up by the teeth of the acting roller while
" held by the holding or feeding rollers."

[Printed, 2s. 10d. Drawings.]

A.D. 1861, June 3.—N° 1387.

JEUNE, WILLIAM RICHARD.—"Improvements in the manu-
" facture of kamptulican." These are, the india-rubber cleaned
and rolled out roughly is soaked in coal naptha or other solvent
for about 12 hours until quite soft, and for every pound of rubber
3 lbs. of ground cork are mixed up or incorporated with it, but
the proportions may be varied. The prepared mixture is then
passed between iron or wood rolls adding more cork dust. When
it is passed through larger rolls between two sheets of calico, and
the sheet thus formed is wound on to a mandril, from which it
is afterwards unwound and suspended in a close stove into which
an inch jet of steam is passed, the fire heat being kept up as well;
the heat is kept up at about 200° F., and "kept under steam for
" about two hours, there being a suitable escape from the stove."
The steam is shut off and the fire heat continued until the solvent is thoroughly evaporated. The sheets are then taken down,
passed through tight rolls, the two sheets of calico are stripped off
either in passing or after passing through the rolls, and the sheet
after the calico has been removed is finally passed through the
rolls. When desired one of the woven fabrics only is removed,
or "two coarse woven fabrics may be employed, and the product
" obtained split by a splitting machine into two sheets of kamp-
" tulicon each having a strong woven back."

[Printed, 4d. No Drawings.]

A.D. 1861, June 4.—N° 1410.

BUFF, HEINRICH LUDWIG. — (*Provisional protection only.*)— Treating fatty and oily matters, so as to produce what the patentee calls artificial caoutchouc. The fatty or oils matters are first treated with nitric acid, then a substance which will decompose nitric acid is added, such as starch, flour or sawdust; " the oxalic " acid formed is then washed out," and the residue " treated with " reducing agents such as sulphurous acid or compounds of " sulphur, which properly treated will give off sulphuretted " hydrogen, iron, zinc, or other metals producing hydrogen with " dilute sulphuric acid or hydrochloric acid in order to remove " any oxide of nitrogen, and destroy any other compounds formed " by the previous treatment." After well washing " the oily and " fatty matters are distilled by superheated steam, or in any other " convenient manner." " The residue in the still is the black " elastic compound which resembles caoutchouc and which is " soluble in fatty oils and hydrocarbons, such as oil of turpentine, " and the hydrocarbons of coal tar."

[Printed, 4d. No Drawings.]

A.D. 1861, June 11.—N° 1489.

STEVENS, CHARLES.—(*A communication from Joseph Chapa and Ernest Lacaze.*)—" An improved impermeable varnish for " leather." This consists of the varnish or varnishes afterwards described, " to be used either together or separately or mixed " with paint or other varnishes, and to be employed for coating " any fabric, article, or substance which it may be desirable to " protect from acids, dampness, or render waterproof." " The " first coat, which may also be used separately, consists of a 100 " parts of india-rubber and 400 parts of sulphuret of carbon" mixed in a close vessel. " The second coat consists of 100 parts " of gutta percha dissolved in 400 parts of sulphuret of carbon. This solution must also be made in a close vessel." A mixture of the two liquids can be made and used together.

[Printed, 4d. No Drawings.]

A.D. 1861, June 18.—N° 1566.

Mc KAY, MURDOCH.—" An improvement or improvements in " the manufacture of cements or adhesive solutions for joining

" or connecting together surfaces or articles of leather, wood,
" paper, or other similar materials." This consists in " dissolving
" gutta percha in the bisulphuret of carbon, or its chemical con-
" stituents," as follows :—The solution is made in an open vessel
in order that the bisulphuret of carbon may " take up a sufficient
' quantity of oxygen," but it should not be exposed too long.
Where great strength is wanted employing " a saturated solution
" of the gutta percha, which would be almost a plastic cement."
The compound material joined by this cement " will be thoroughly
" waterproof," a single coating " having the power of effectually
" waterproofing any material upon which it may be laid." " The
" proportions of each ingredient employed will depend upon the
" strength or tenacity required in the cement or solution."

[Printed, 4d. No Drawings.]

A.D. 1861, June 19.—N° 1580.

WILLIAMS, JOHN FISHER.—" Improvements in compounds of
" india-rubber and gutta percha with other substances." These
are, combining the residuum of a dark or black color " obtained
" when distilling palm oil or other vegetable oils, which is usually
" done by the aid of superheated steam," " with india-rubber or
" gutta percha, or both these substances, with or without sulphur,
" chalk, fibre, cork, or other materials, according to the purposes
" to which such india-rubber and gutta percha compounds are to
" be applied." " When making a compound as a substitute for
" leather, &c., about 8 lbs. of india-rubber, 8 lbs. of gutta
" percha, 8 lbs. of the black or dark residuum, 4 lbs. of fibrous
" materials, 6 lbs. of sulphur, 20 lbs. of powdered chalk," are
gradually mixed together in a masticating machine with heat,
rolled into sheets or moulds, and vulcanized. This compound
may be varied. For compounds for packing high pressure steam
and hot-water joints, " about 16 lbs. of india-rubber, 6 lbs. of dark
" or black residum, 30 lbs. of steel or iron or other metal filings,
" according to the nature of the articles, 6 lbs. of sulphur," are
employed. If the packings are required for low temperatures
more of the residuum may be used, also chalk may be added.
When making kamptulicon it is preferred to employ, " 6 lbs. of
" gutta percha, 12 lbs. of india-rubber, 6 lbs. of black or dark
" residuum, 4 lbs. of ground cork, 2 lbs. of chalk, 1 lb. of hair,
" using sulphur or not according as the product is or is not to

" be vulcanized." It has been found "advantageous to employ
" a small proportion of oxide of zinc, as a better surface is
" thereby obtained."

[Printed, 4d. No Drawings.]

A.D. 1861, June 28.—N° 1651.

FORD, ALFRED.—(*Provisional protection only.*)—"Improvements
" in the manufacture of waterproof felt." These are first, "mixing
" hair or wool, hemp or cotton fibre, with india-rubber and gutta
" percha in such a way as to produce a light pulpy dough capable
" of being rolled out with the aid of water, into sheets of a felt-
" like appearance." A certain quantity of india-rubber and gutta
percha is mixed " with naptha or turpentine in a machine usually
" employed for such purpose " until of a very soft plastic state,
and mixing with it the above substances. If it is desired to make
the dough unusually light, cork or some vegetable fibre is added
to it. The dough is passed through wetted rollers, for "getting
" it into sheets and giving to it a felt-like surface."

Second, "the application of such felt-like material to the manu-
" facture of caps and hats in particular, and to other useful
" purposes."

[Printed, 4d. No Drawings.]

A.D. 1861, July 18.—N° 1806.

WEST, CHARLES.—(*Provisional protection not allowed.*)—" Im-
" provements in the mode of insulating and covering wire."
These are, driving " off the moisture in the india-rubber previous
" to its being placed upon the wire. This I readily accomplish
" by subjecting the strips of ribbands of pure india-rubber, after
" they are cut from the bottle to a process of dessication or
" evaporation." " In cases where I may deem it expedient to
" consolidate the rubber on the wire by my process of boiling,"
described in No. 2321, A. D., 1858, " the dessication or driving
" off the moisture under the present process will prepare the
" rubber for consolidation by boiling."

[Printed, 4d. No Drawing.]

A.D. 1861, July 31.—N° 1906.

FLANDERS, JOSEPH FOLLANSBEE.—This invention consists,
in reference to this subject, in machinery for dividing or splitting

sheets of india-rubber, or gutta percha. "The knife or cutting in-
" strument consists of an endless metal band extended over a
" pair of pullies with a sharp cutting edge, which is kept in
" motion as the skin is fed forward," " supported upon an endless
" travelling cloth or table, to which a progressive motion is given
" by means of suitable gearing actuated by the driving shaft."
A modification of this plan consists in placing the sheet " on a
" rotating cylinder, which will carry it forward as the cutting
" operation proceeds," or it " may be placed upon a flat hori-
" zontal table which may be moved forward by a rack gearing or
" otherwise," or causing it "to bear against a vertical bar over
" which it may be drawn by means of a holding roller or cylinder
" the knife being made to act vertically instead of horizontally,
" as in the former instances." To maintain or hold the sheet
" firmly against the gauge roll during the cutting operation,"
" subdividing either the supporting roller or the guage roller into
" a number of contiguous small rollers, all of which will be sus-
" ceptible of independent action without interfering with the
" others." "These pressing rollers are kept up to their work
" by springs, or by being made to bear against an elastic bed
" roller. The subdivided pressing or gauge rollers may be placed
" above the travelling endless supporting sheet, or the pressing
" or guage roller may be made in one length, and supporting
" sheet and roller may be subdivided into sections, with separate
" rollers and travelling endless belts."

[Printed, 10d. Drawings.]

A.D. 1861, October 8.—N° 2506.

FORD, ALFRED.—"An improved method of forming water-
" proof fabrics by combining paper with woven or piece fabrics."
The combining solution is made "by dissolving india-rubber in
" mineral naptha, turpentine, or some of the present known and
" approved solvents, and of a suitable consistence, either alone
" or in combination with gum resin. I prefer gum damar and
" gutta percha, in the proportion of about one part to four of
" solid india-rubber, reduced by spirit in the proportion of one
" part of solid to eight of fluid; but I do not bind myself to any
" particular proportions."

[Printed, 4d. No Drawings.]

A.D. 1861, October 9.—N° 2515.

BAGGS, Isham, and PARKES, James Thomas.—(*Provisional protection only.*)—" Certain improvements in the manu-
" facture and treatment of india-rubber and vulcanite, as applied
" to various purposes." These are, first, colouring these substances " by incorporating or combining coloured glass, pipe-clay,
" and other suitable colouring substances or agents with the
" india-rubber or vulcanite." The materials thus prepared are baked, submitted to the action of concentrated sulphuric acid or any other chemical substance which may be capable of preventing the injury usually resulting from high temperatures upon the materials, and finally treated with chloride of lime or "a sub-
" stance or substances possessing analogous properties," which restores or bleaches the portions which have been altered or decomposed by the action of the sulphuric acid or other chemical substance, and develops the proper effects of the colouring matter. The surfaces may then be consolidated by a suitable varnish or
" coal tar, naptha, or bisulphide of carbon, or any other chemical
" solvent."

Second. Treating "small pieces, fragments, or particles of
" powdered glass with hydrofluoric acid," gaseous or liquid, so as to destroy the edges and reflective parts of such fragments, and to make them cover or colour such materials better.

Third. Combining metals or their alloys in a state of minute division with india-rubber or vulcanite prepared as above.

Fourth. Fixing scales or plates of vulcanite upon vulcanized india-rubber or india-rubber fabrics, so as to represent the scales or plates upon the heads or skins of reptiles, &c.

Fifth. Vulcanizing india-rubber by subjecting it " to great
" pressure either of steam, air, gas, or vapour."

[Printed, 4d. No Drawings.]

A.D. 1861, October 16.—N° 2574.

FORSTER, Thomas. — " Improvements in re-working waste
" vulcanized india-rubber." These are, " combining waste vul-
" canized india-rubber with gutta percha and sulphur," as follows :—The waste rubber is " reduced by crushing rollers or
" otherwise, and is then mixed with gutta percha and sulphur." Pigments may be added. " A useful compound is formed by
" combining vulcanized rubber at the rate of 75 lbs. of vul-
" canized waste rubber with 25 lbs. of gutta percha and 35 lbs.

" of sulphur to the above 100 lbs. when intended to produce a
" hard gum; (if for soft goods 5 lbs. of sulphur only)." The
materials are incorporated finally in a hot masticator, and the
compound is moulded, cut, &c., in the usual way, and converted
or cured by heat. The above proportions may be greatly varied.

[Printed, 4d. No Drawings.]

A.D. 1861, November 5.—N° 2779.

BOWRA, EDWARD.—" Improvements in the manufacture of
" elastic fabrics." These are, first, " the manufacture of elastic
" fabrics composed of india-rubber, gutta percha, or other elastic
" gums combined with chloride of sulphur and dry hypochloride
" of lime, and the covering of linen, woollen, silken, or other
" fabrics," as afterwards described. " Take 50 lbs. of clean
" masticated india-rubber, gutta percha, or other elastic gums,
" and add to this 25 oz. of chloride of sulphur and 25 oz. of dry
" hypochloride of lime, and well work them in at a temperature
" of 60 degrees F.," and when properly amalgamated roll them
into sheets with cold rollers," " then elongate such sheets into a
" suitable form or pattern, and apply sheets of cloth " as above
" in transverse forms or otherwise," and when properly adhered
" place such goods or sheets so combined into a heated chamber
" or steam chest at 100° F. for two hours, and by this process
" it becomes perfectly, equally, and permanently vulcanized "
" without injury to the colors or finish of such fabrics." " The
" same cold process and same mixtures are used for solid india-
" rubber, gutta percha, or other gums, with more or less of the
" chloride of sulphur and dry hypochloride of lime as may be
" required."

Second, "the combination or covering of elastic cloths with
" the refuse or cuttings of leather or other fibrous material and
" waste vulcanized india-rubber, gutta percha, or other elastic
" gums, and chloride of sulphur and hypochlorate [hypochlo-
" ride ?] of lime."

Such cloths are ventilated when required by perforations by
means of rolls or other mechanical means.

[Printed, 4d. No Drawings.]

A.D. 1861, November 7.—N° 2800.

SHEPHARD, WILLIAM ALBERT.—" Improvements in prepar-
" ing and treating gutta percha and india-rubber." These are,

first, "preparing and purifying gutta percha." The gutta percha is first washed and cleansed, thoroughly masticated, placed in an iron vessel, and the air exhausted. Fumes of sulphur are "admitted into the vacuum, or a small quantity of
" sulphur may be ground with the gum before it is placed in the
" vacuum vessel," say "from one to one and a half, and some-
" times two ounces of sulphur to every ten pounds of the gum,
" according as the gum is good or poor, but care must be taken
" that not sulphur enough is added to produce vulcanization."
Thus prepared, the gutta percha is exposed to a heat varying from 300° to 450° F., admitting air "which has passed through
" highly heated tubes or through a bath prepared by means of
" pumice stone saturated with the prussiate of potash or other-
" wise prepared to answer the purpose," or the heat is applied
" directly to the gutta percha in vacuo, which is preferable."
Gutta percha thus prepared is next combined with sulphur or certain compounds of sulphur, such as the hyposulphite of lead, &c., but sulphur is much preferred; with the gutta percha and fibrous materials thus prepared various ingredients are mixed, as
" prepared chalk or Paris white, carbonate of lead, oxide of
" zinc, carburet of iron or graphite, magnesia, vegetable oils
" boiled to a proper consistency, emery, pitch, different kinds of
" tar, gums, coloring, and other materials, according to the kind
" of goods."

Second, the method of mixing the various ingredients "sepa-
" rately with separate portions of gutta percha, and then to grind
" together and mix these partial compounds thoroughly into
" one."

Third, the vulcanizing of gutta percha goods prepared and compounded as above, and the use of a bath for so doing, consisting of a solution of bisulphide of carbon in combination with bromine and chlorine in certain proportions.

[Printed, 4d. No Drawings.]

A.D. 1861, December 9.—N° 3081.

MENNONS, MARC ANTOINE FRANÇOIS.—(*A communication from François Debons and Theobald Denny.*)—(*Provisional protection only.*)—"Improvements in the production of relief designs
" on metallic surfaces and general printing, gaufering, and
" embossing purposes." In carrying this out a number of solu-

tions are employed, one of which consists of "rectified benzine,
" 20 ozs., caoutchouc, as pure and white as possible, in sufficient
" quantity to saturate and leave an excess undissolved. To the
" resulting viscid solution is added a mixture of rectified oil of
" naphtha, 7 ozs., essence of turpentine, 3 ozs.; incorporated
" thoroughly. The mass is then heated for about fifteen minutes
" to from 70° to 80° (Centigrade), and left to cool." This solution is strained through any suitable close tissue, and incorporated
with finely ground zinc white or other like powder; the quantity
is such that after allowing it "to repose after thorough incorpora-
" tion a deposit to the depth of about half an inch may be found
" at the bottom of the solution." This white varnish "is pre-
" served in long-necked bottles, and should be well shaken when
" about to be used."

[Printed, 4d. No Drawings.]

A.D. 1861, December 27.—N° 3247.

FAJOLE, Jean Joseph Hector, and AGOSTINI, Pascal
Achille.—(*Provisional protection only.*)—"An improved com-
" position or improved compositions suitable for painting, var-
" nishing, and coating," consisting of "15 litres (about 26 pints)
" essence of turpentine; 250 grammes (about 8 oz. 12 dr.)
" caoutchouc; 250 grammes (about 8 oz. 12 dr.) sulphate of
" zinc; 1,000 grammes (about 2 lbs. 3 oz. 4 dr.) copal resin; or
" sulphuric ether to which rectified alcohol is added may be sub-
" stituted for the turpentine, preferring to take 2,000 grammes
" (or about 4 lbs. 6 oz. 8 dr.) thereof. We recommend that the
" ingredients should be dissolved in a warm state." For painting generally filtering the product and saturating or combining it
with colouring matters. Sometimes mixing "with empyruematic
" oil of gas, or the fat unctuous oils of coal tar, and other gas
" yielding matters instead of using essence of turpentine."

[Printed, 4d. No Drawings.]

1862.

A.D. 1862, January 17.—N° 123.

MYERS, Thomas, and MYERS, Edward.—"An improved
" composition for preventing rust on bright steel, iron, brass, or

" metal surfaces." This consists in combining " ten pounds of
" gutta percha, twenty pounds of mutton suet, thirty pounds of
" beef suet, half a gallon of sweet oil, two gallons of neats' foot
" oil, one gallon of oil of thyme, and half a pint of rose pink, or
" any other suitable perfuming and coloring matter. These
" ingredients must be gently simmered until the whole is dis-
" solved and well mixed together; and when cold the composition
" is ready for use." These proportions may be varied.

[Printed, 4d. No Drawings.]

A.D. 1862, January 21.—N° 158.

MARTIN, ALFRED JOSEPH.—"Improvements in the treatment
" of fusel oil, and for various applications of the same to useful
" purposes." These are, first, mixing " together the oil distilled
" from Trinidad or any other pitch or asphaltum " " with fusel
" oil in such proportions as shall produce a mixture to produce
" by the hydrometer 960°;" distilling off " about three parts of
" the whole quantity, or as much as is found upon trial to yield
" a good illuminating oil."

Second, with every gallon of fousel oil mixing or dissolving
1 or 2 lbs. of resin and distilling to dryness.

Third, an iron pipe, partly filled with rough pieces of iron,
about 4 inches in diameter is placed across a furnace, " this pipe
" is bifurcated at one end, while the other end is connected with
" a worm immersed in cold water." One of the branch pipes is
connected with a steam boiler, and the other branch is connected
with a boiler of fousel oil, and the steam and fousel oil together
passing through the red hot tube produce " propylic alcohol "
which is condensed. These oils it is said are used for different
purposes, among which are named " solvents for gums, gum resins,
" caoutchouc and gutta percha."

[Printed, 6d. Drawing.]

A.D. 1862, January 29.—N° 236.

HARBY, JAMES BENJAMIN. — Impregnating or coating the
yarn or textile fabric or fibres employed in the manufacture of
electric telegraph cables with a composition of solution of caoutchouc, resin, and powdered chalk, the proportions of the materials
being varied according to the pliability required when the composition is set. In some cases I mix with the composition arsenic
or other poison to guard against the attacks of fish, insects, and

animals; also coating complete cables and the separate wires of telegraph cables with the following composition applied in a heated state. "Caoutchouc 1 part, resin 3½ parts, arsenic $\frac{1}{16}$th " part."

[Printed, 4d. No Drawings.]

A.D. 1862, March 1.—N° 560.

GABRIEL, MAURICE, and GABRIEL, ARNOLD.—(*Provisional protection only.*)—"Improvements in the bases of artificial teeth." These are, in reference to this subject, forming a compound of 7 parts india-rubber, 2 parts sulphur, 2¼ parts phosphate of lime, and 2 parts of phosphate of soda. The compound is then moulded and hardened by well-known processes. The above proportions "can be varied as circumstances may require."

[Printed, 4d. No Drawings.]

A.D. 1862, April 16.—N° 1105.

CARTWRIGHT, MATTHEW.—(*Provisional protection only.*)— " Improvements in the manufacture of models and of plates or " pieces for artificial teeth, and in combining or amalgamating " india-rubber and gutta percha with metals for the manufacture " of artificial plates or pieces, and for other purposes." In making models for the above purpose india-rubber composition is inserted in the cavities occupied by the wax, and the flasks containing the moulds "are again put together, heated, pressed, and " the india-rubber vulcanized in the ordinary manner." When an elastic model is required, "soft and hard rubber are used " alternately, or hard rubber in combination with cotton, or any " other material capable of rendering it elastic." In combining india-rubber and gutta percha with metals, the india-rubber or gutta percha is reduced to a liquid state and the metals, say gold, mixed therewith.

[Printed, 4d. No Drawings.]

A.D. 1862, April 26.—N° 1232.

SPILSBURY, FRANCIS GYBBON, and EMERSON, FREDERICK WILLIAM.—(*Provisional protection only.*)—"Improvements in " the treatment of fusel oil, and for various applications of the " same to useful purposes." These are first, "mixing fusel oil " with any hydrocarbon, such as petroleum, rock oil, kerosene

"oil, paraffine oils, turpentole, naptha, or the heavy oils remain-
"ing from the distillation of paraffine oils or of naptha, or of
"benzole from coal tar, turpentine, or other similar substances."
The proportions vary from 10 to 400 %$_o$ of the oils to the fousel
oil used, and drawing off as much as will come over under
500° F.

Second, dissolving or mixing "rosin bitumen, coal paraffine, or
"napthaline or fat, tallow, or oil with fusel oil," and distilling as
above.

Third, passing "fusel oil by itself, or any of the aforesaid mix-
"tures through a red hot tube which splits the oil up into pro-
"pylic and other alcohols with certain oils." All or any of these
oils so produced may, it is said, among other purposes which are
named, be used, "as solvents for gums and caoutchouc."

[Printed, 4d. No Drawings.]

A.D. 1862, May 14.—N° 1460.

BRANT, JOHN CHARLES.—(*Provisional protection only*.)—This
invention consists, in reference to this subject, in making a
cement, in preference, by taking "one part of magnetic oxide of
" iron or manganese" and making it "into a stiff paste with oil
" of turpentine or any other essential oil. I then put into an
" iron pot 2 parts of Swedish pitch, and heat it over a fire, and
" mix in the oxide with it; I then gradually add to it one part or
" more, if desired, of pure gutta percha cut into small pieces; the
" whole is then brought to boil, and is kept constantly stirred till
" it is well mixed together; the mixture is then removed from
" the fire, and is kept stirred until nearly cold; it is then poured
" on plates previously covered with water, and when set it is fit
" for use."

[Printed, 4d. No Drawings.]

A.D. 1862, May 28.—N° 1597.

KIDD, JOHN HOWARD.—" An improved manufacture of com-
" positions applicable for waterproofing fabrics, for coating and
" protecting various articles, and for various other purposes."
This consists first, of "a composition formed by the combination
of oxydized oil and a base formed of wax, mutton suet, and resins,
and such coloring matters as may be required." " Oxydized oil "
is made by boiling " cod-fish or linseed oil or both " " with oxide

" of lead, zinc, or other oxide," and exposing the same "for some
" time in thin films on extensive surfaces to the action of the air,
" and is thus further oxydized and converted into a substance of
" a semi-resinous nature." This oxydized oil is mixed with wax,
mutton suet, and resins termed "the base of my compositions,"
in varying proportions "according to which it is to be applied and
" the quality of the article desired;" coloring matters are also
added. The composition is melted or "solved" by heat, and is
applied hot to the fabric, "or it is moulded in that state into the
" required articles." Naptha or a volatile solvent need not be
used, although in some instances "it may be employed, and par-
" ticularly in some cases when used as a varnish."

Second, "combining india-rubber or gutta percha with the com-
" pound herein-before termed the base of my improved composi-
" tion, namely, wax, mutton suet, and resins" made "either with
" or without volatile solvents; the proportions in which they may
" be combined will vary according to the purpose required."

[Printed, 4d. No Drawings.]

A.D. 1862, May 31.—N° 1651.

NEWTON, WILLIAM EDWARD. — (*A communication from
William Elmer.*)—In the treatment of cloth and other textures,
leather, or animal tissues, at one part of the process an elastic
coating is prepared consisting of caoutchouc and gutta percha,
singly or combined, formed into a perfect solution, " which is
" placed under pressure in a suitable apparatus, and heat is
" gradually applied and raised to about 300° F." During the
time "dichloride of sulphur or sulphur liquified in some other
" form is admitted into the apertures in contact with the solution,
" drop by drop, or in very small quantities, and the solution in the
" meantime is kept in constant motion until sufficient sulphur has
" been introduced to form an elastic sulphide or sulphite of caout-
" chouc and gutta percha." If the solvent contained no oxygen
nor hydrogen, as the bisulphide of carbon, CS_2, then no
other substance is needed in conjunction with the dichloride of
sulphur; but if the solvents contained "either hydrogen or
" oxygen, then, upon the introduction of the chloride of sulphur
" an acid is instantly formed, to neutralize which will require the
" presence of an alkali." "The elastic sulphide is a semifluid,
" which when filtered through animal charcoal is devoid of all

" unpleasant odours, and possesses (when evaporated to the solid
" state) all the characteristics of vulcanized caoutchouc or gutta
" percha." The article thus coated is then passed between
" metallic revolving cylinders, one of which is heated to a tem-
" perature, according to the thickness of the coating, from 250° to
" 300° Fahrenheit."

[Printed, 6d. No Drawings.]

A.D. 1862, June 12.—N° 1749.

LÈRENARD, Auguste Aimé.—" A new and improved cement
" or mastic for making joints of steam, water, or gas pipes or
" chambers." This consists, first, in "employing india-rubber
" more or less vulcanized to make a cement or paste fit" for the
above purposes, "by combining and mixing by a suitable tritura-
" tion, vulcanized or non-vulcanized india rubber in various pro-
" portions with powdered mineral or earthy substances, among
" others, and especially with a powdered hydraulic cement, fire
" clay, and flowers of sulphur."

Second, " the formation of sheets of various thicknesses by
" mixing in the cement some hemp or other textile material cut
" in small pieces, and cutting rings, square bands, or strips from
" the said sheets for making joints. The sheets or rings can be
" vulcanised by the usual process when cut to shape."

Third, " using the same cement, in a softer or more liquid state,
" that is to say, containing less powdered cement and sulphur, to
" make joints with strips of hemp daubed up or coated with this
" india-rubber solution."

[Printed, 4d. No Drawings.]

A.D. 1862, July 2.—N° 1924.

DE LA BASTIDA, Eugène.—(*A communication from Albert
Cohen and Charles Vaillant.*)—" A new method of manufacturing
" india-rubber articles by the simultaneous combination of pres-
" sure and vulcanization." Plates heated by steam are arranged
so that the bottom plate is by preference a fixture and " the top
" is made to rise and fall by means of a screw, hydrostatic pres-
" sure, or any other convenient means." Long pipes are formed
in the usual way of sulphur, compound of india-rubber, or of such
compound and strong woven fabric and placed in a mould, which
mould with the tube is placed upon the press table and the top

brought close down by pressure and vulcanized by means of the steam-heated press plates; then raise the top plate and open the mould and introduce another part of the same tube, and so on until the tube is all vulcanized; to make greater lengths, leaving a piece of the ends of the tube or pipe out of the mould and unvulcanized, to one end of which attach or join in the unvulcanized end of another piece and put the joined unvulcanized part into a short mould and vulcanize it. Telegraph wires or cables are made and vulcanized in a similar manner, as are driving bands for machinery.

[Printed, 4d. No Drawings.]

A.D. 1862, July 17.—N° 2049.

DAFT, THOMAS BARNABAS.—"Improvements in the manufacture of vulcanized india-rubber thread." The india-rubber cleaned, ground and mixed with a proper quantity of sulphur and "spread or rolled to about the thickness of the diameter of " the thread required to be made, is cut up into strips of the full " length of the sheets, and of a suitable width for the apparatus." The sheets or strips, well seasoned, have "a dusting of powdered " 'French chalk,' which may be lightly rubbed on the surfaces " in order to prevent adhesion in the process of reeling or wind- " ing the strips upon feeding pullies." A pair of steel grooved rollers about two inches diameter and two inches long on the face or barrel are mounted in suitable frames; the rollers are formed with corresponding semicircular grooves, varying, say, from the 10th to the 50th, of an inch in diameter; these are brought together in preference to form slightly elliptical openings so as to form threads which are slightly elliptical, as there is "a minute " tendency under vulcanization of the thread to flatten a fraction " in the depth or thickness way of the sheet." The strips are fed into the rollers from an overhead pulley, and converted into threads, which pass through the bottom of the machine, or they are carried under one of the rollers; in either case they are conducted to separate reels; but, in preference, they are conducted to a receiving metal drum of about three feet diameter, upon which they are taken up loosely, and at the same time are dusted with French chalk, or the lower part of the receiving drum works " in a trough containing a mixture of the kind calculated to sepa- " rate the threads and fill up the interstices between them." The loaded drum may stand for a day before subjecting the thread to the curing process. "Rollers of about two inches on the barrel, "with $\frac{1}{16}$ inch grooves and blunt cutting edges in proportion" would give about 25 threads.

[Printed, 10d. Drawing.]

A.D. 1862, July 28.—N° 2131.

DEVLAN, PATRICK SARSFIELD.—(*Provisional protection only.*) —In telegraph cables, in reference to this subject, coating the wires to be insulated, with "a composition consisting of about "eight pounds of paper or other fibrous pulp, half a pound of "caoutchouc or gutta percha, with one pound of resin or there- "abouts."

[Printed, 4d. No Drawings.]

A.D. 1862, July 29.—N° 2149.

DEVLAN, PATRICK SARSFIELD.—(*Provisional protection only.*) —An improved composition which is to be employed for many purposes which are named. The proportions preferred are "about eight pounds of fibrous pulp to half a pound of caout- "chouc or gutta percha, and one pound of resinous gum, "although such proportions may be varied without materially "differing in effect." "Plumbago may also, if required, be "mixed therewith."

[Printed, 4d. No Drawings.]

A.D. 1862, September 27.—N° 2634.

HENRY, MICHAEL.—(*A communication from the Société Chartier et Compagnie*).—"New and improved application of petroleum "and its products, certain agents produced by combining the "same with other substances and certain modes of treating "caoutchouc, gutta percha, and their compounds and substances "similar thereto." These are, in reference to this subject, as follows:—Petroleum distilled yields a clear colourless liquid "boiling at about 154°;" a second liquid "boiling at about "203°;" a third "heavier clear colourless liquid distilling at "about 320°." These three products combined are called "'mixed' petroleum." First, dissolving and purifying caout- chouc and recovering or separating the same from cloth, &c. "Rectified or refined petroleum is used, but the mixed petroleum

" is preferred." "In preparing the mixed petroleum, for this
" object, there should be a predominent proportion of the first
" of its three components."

Second, vulcanizing caoutchouc, " by taking rectified or refined
" petroleum or the 'mixed petroleum,' saturated with sulphur,"
" and "combining it with chloride or bromide of sulphur."
" Where vulcanized caoutchouc is to be dissolved in petroleum
" it should first be boiled in a carbonate of soda solution."

Third, " devulcanizing caoutchouc (especially when vulcanized
" in white) " by reducing the caoutchouc to small pieces,
macerating it in a retort, in preference, with the first distillate
from petroleum, distilling off a large portion of the liquid,
heating the residue in a close vessel to from 212° to 356°,
till the disintegrated vulcanized caoutchouc " becomes smooth,
cohesive, elastic, and soluble in petroleum," finally the petroleum
is separated by distillation.

Fourth, making varnishes.— Instead of turpentine, in preference, using 97½ parts petroleum, in which are dissolved ½ part
caoutchouc and 2 parts Bordeaux turpentine. A damp-proof
varnish, in preference, using 70 parts, white linseed oil paint,
20 parts Bordeaux turpentine, 2 parts " Baruel's zumatic drier,"
7½ parts rectified petroleum (or mineral essence or spirit of
petroleum) ½ part caoutchouc. " Gallipot or colophany may be
" substituted for the turpentine."

[Printed, 6d. No Drawings.]

A.D. 1862, October 14.—N° 2769.

CARTWRIGHT, MATTHEW. — " Improvements in plates for
" artificial teeth." These are, in reference to this subject, dissolving india-rubber or gutta percha and grinding the same with
gold leaf or finely precipitated gold "to combine the metal with
" the gum used ; " also, "forming plates for artificial teeth by
" coating a model of the plate to be produced with] successive
" layers of gutta percha alone or combined with other substances
" until a sufficiently thick plate has been formed," each coat is
allowed to become hard " before applying the next, and then
" submit the finished plate to any curing process that may be
" necessary to make it sufficiently hard for wear."

[Printed, 4d. No Drawings.]

A.D. 1862, October 16.—N° 2794.

RÈMIÉRE, HENRI AMABLE.—" An improved horse collar."
This consists, in reference to this subject, as follows :—The vulcanized india-rubber used in this manufacture is prepared as
follows :—" To one part of the best Java india-rubber
" I add about twenty parts of flower of sulphur, from eight to
" ten parts of white zinc, about five parts of chloride of calcium,
" and from five to ten parts of black lead. The ingredients vary
" in proportion as the india-rubber is more or less pure. The
" whole is then subjected to heat, and mixed in the usual way,
" after which it is exposed to a temperature of from 50 to 60
" degrees Reaumur." When the moulds are filled, "the moulds
" with their contents are subjected to a temperature of 150 to
" 200 degrees Reaumur for about two hours."

[Printed, 8d. Drawing.]

A.D. 1862, October 18.—N° 2815.

FULLER, JOHN.—" An improvement in treating india-rubber
" used on a wire or wires for insulating the same." The india-
rubber on the wire is " treated with naphtha or other solvent,
" water or other matter," that will " render the surface damp or
" adhesive, then powdering, or otherwise applying sulphur, and
" exposing the rubber so treated to heat in order to cure the
" same. Or before curing more india-rubber may be applied to
" the sulphured india-rubber, and the curing may be effected
" after the additional india-rubber has been applied."

[Printed, 4d. No Drawings.]

A.D. 1862, October 21.—N° 2835.

BROOMAN, RICHARD ARCHIBALD.—(*A communication from
Adolph Baldamus.*)—" Improvements in waterproofing and in
" recovering products employed therein." These are " rendering
" materials more or less waterproof, and in recovering the volatile
" solvents used." " Caoutchouc, gutta percha, resins or metallic
" soaps (obtained by combining metal dissolved in acid with the
" fatty matter of soap in solution) are dissolved in bisulphide of
" carbon, ether, or other like volatile solvent," and sulphur added
or not. " The solution of any one or more of the substances
" named," is placed " in a vessel closed air-tight or nearly so,
" and after immersing the materials therein," they are drawn

o 2

" through an air-tight channel into another vessel," the communication between the two vessels is shut off and to the second vessel heat is applyed, preferring, that derived from hot water, " steam, or hot air, to evaporate the bisulphide of carbon or other " volatile solvent used." The vapour is condensed by any of the ordinary methods and the solvent collected " may be used over " and over again." Instead of distilling the solution by heat from the second vessel it is recovered by exhausting, and then condensing it from the second vessel. "The density of the solu- " tion of the water-proofing agents determining the extent or " degree of water-proofing to be imparted to the materials under- " going the operation."

[Printed, 4d. No Drawings.]

A.D. 1862, October 28.—Nº 2904.

DUNCAN, CHARLES STEWART.—"An improved compound or " material for coating or covering metallic and vegetable sub- " stances to preserve them from corrosion or decay." The com- pound is to be made as follows :—Using " marine glue, gutta " percha, india-rubber, shellac, copal, mastic, vegetable or mineral " pitch or tar, or resin, or iodine, or sulphur, or creosote, or " asphalte bitumen and coal tar in combination with one or more " of the following substances :—"Alumina, schist, quartz, slate, " silex or flint, marble or pozzolano, sand, sandstone, cement " (natural or artificial), chalk, glass, emery, tripoli, white oxide " of zinc or of lead, or the litharge, or red oxide of lead, in every " case reduced to a fine and nearly impalpable powder, in pro- " portions varying from one-fourth part to five parts of these " powdered materials to one part or more of the before-mentioned " plastic substances. The materials are then to be heated, so as " to reduce them to a plastic or semi-liquid state." The remain- der of the Specification refers to the application of this and other compounds to various materials.

[Printed, 4d. No Drawings.]

A.D. 1862, November 6.—Nº 3006.

GRIFFIN, HENRY.—" An improved method of securing india- " rubber cylinders on rollers and blocks upon spindles and other " bodies on which they are to be mounted." These are, first, coating or clothing such spindle or other body " with a composi-

" tion of india-rubber for forming what is known as ebonite or
" hard rubber, and in then adding on such composition to com-
" plete the article to the thickness required, ordinary or pure
" india-rubber, or rubber known as cut sheet rubber (that is to
" say, sheets of rubber cut from a solid block), or rubber pre-
" pared for being vulcanized," and subject the whole " to heat
" in order to 'cure' the composition."

[Printed, 4d. No Drawings.]

A.D. 1862, December 12.—N° 3331.

HANCOCK, CHARLES, and SILVER, STEPHEN WILLIAM.—
" Certain compounds and substances applicable for electric insu-
" lation and other purposes." It is stated that india-rubber
" cannot of itself be rendered so thoroughly plastic as to pass
" through the dies ordinarily used for covering telegraphic wires
" or conductors," and to obviate this it is proposed to combine
it " with a milk or gum the produce of a tree called Sapota
" Mulieri, or bullet tree, which is found in British Guiano and
" elsewhere, and to which the term ballata has been occasionally
" applied," and which possesses similar insulating properties to
caoutchouc. The caoutchouc and ballata are combined by mastication, rolling, or solution, as is well understood. The following
compound is suitable for a soft vulcanized substance :—2 lbs.
caoutchouc, 1 lb. ballata, and 9 ozs. of sulphur, vulcanized by
heating from 260° to 280° F. from 2 to 6 hours. For a hard
vulcanized substance 2 lbs. caoutchouc, 1 lb. ballata, and $\frac{1}{4}$ lb.
sulphur, heated from 260° to 300° F. from 4 to 8 hours. The
following compounds are suitable for substances not to be vulcanized :—No. 1. 3 lbs. ballata, 3 lbs. caoutchouc, 2 lbs. vulcanized caoutchouc pulverized or ground to powder. No. 2. 2 lbs.
ballata, 6 lbs. caoutchouc, 2 lbs. colcother. No. 3. 3 lbs. ballata,
and 1 lb. of caoutchouc. No. 4. 3 lbs. of ballata, 1 lb. of shellac,
parrafine, or rosin, pitch, tar, marine glue, gum copal, gum mastic, or other gum insoluble in water. No. 5. India-rubber, gutta
percha, and ballata in equal proportions. No. 6. Gutta percha
and ballata. The compounds before-mentioned when in a plastic
state can be moulded into various articles, in preference, in metal
moulds. Besides vulcanizing ballata and its compounds as above,
it is vulcanized " by the cold or chloride of sulphur process which
" is well understood by caoutchouc manufacturers." In some
cases first insulate the wire with the several plastic compounds,

or some of them, through dies, covering them with tapes and fillets of caoutchouc, and finally submitting them to steam or heated vapour.

[Printed, 4d. No Drawings.]

A.D. 1862, December 16.—N° 3355.

WARDEN, GEORGE COCKBURN.—(*A communication from Adolph Baldamus.*)—(*Provisional protection only.*)—This invention consists, in reference to this subject, in a cement to be used for several purposes which are named. The cement "is composed " of the following materials in or about the following proportions, " that is to say, seven parts of gutta percha, two parts of resin, " and one part of solution of caoutchouc mixed by dissolving " them together under heat."

[Printed, 4d. No Drawings.]

A.D. 1862, December 22.—N° 3415.

GÉRARD, GUSTAVE EUGÈNE MICHEL.—" Improvements in " the fabrication of threads from vulcanized india-rubber, and " the apparatus connected therewith." These are, first, " the " cutting of bands or sheets of vulcanized india-rubber into " threads in such a manner that the said threads are united by " a sort of selvage at each end formed by the uncut extremity of " the said band or sheet of india-rubber."

Second, the apparatus consisting of thin circular cutting blades, threaded upon a metal spindle, mounted on centre points, and capable of making from 500 to 2,000 revolutions per minute. " These blades are separated by washers, or between blades, also in " steel, and of which the thickness varies according to the size of " the thread to be cut, and which are from 2 to 6 lines smaller " than the cutting blades." Under this spindle, parallel to it and touching the outer extremities of the blades is a cylinder of from $1\frac{1}{2}$ to $3\frac{1}{2}$ inches in diameter; this cylinder, in preference, is of half supple india-rubber, but may be made of hardened rubber, wood, bronze, zinc, " or other metal may be solid or composed of " a number of thin washers screwed one against the other, and " having the appearance of a solid cylinder, is so adjusted as to " be removed at will from its contact with the spindle, and to be " approached again so as to touch the blades." "The cutting " blades trace a slight groove on the cylinder by their rapid rota- " tion, which serves to increase the regularity of the cutting.

"Two small cylinders may be employed, also parallel to each "other, and serving the same purpose, namely, for rendering "more certain the complete separation of all the threads." The sheet to be cut is placed above the spindle between it and the cylinder; a short length is allowed to pass to permit of its being held. The spindle is set in motion, the blades being kept wet by means of a brush on which soapy water drops; the cylinder or cylinders are approached so as to touch the extremity of the blades, and the rotary motion is communicated also to them. The sheet is drawn by the cylinder or cylinders, or by the workman, or by a row of small cylinders; and at a few lines before the end of the sheet the pressure is withdrawn; the selvage is left. If the pressure remains the threads are separated.

[Printed, 4d. No Drawings.]

1863.

A.D. 1863, January 8.—N° 67.

HULL, LIVERAS. — "Having reference to the treatment of "ground caoutchouc, and for the purpose of rendering it elastic "or improving its elasticity, as well as imparting to such caout-"chouc other useful properties." This consists in "the appli-"cation of carbon spirits" as afterwards described, "and chlo-"ride of sulphur to ground caoutchouc," for the above and other purposes. Carbon spirits is the light fluid known by that name in commerce, "whose specific gravity generally varies from "·650 to ·750. It is now made from the 'rock oil' which is pro-"duced from the oil wells of Pensylvania and Canada." In practice one measure of the chloride of sulphur is mixed with forty of the carbon spirits, but these proportions "may be some-"what varied and yet productive of like results." Into this mixture the ground caoutchouc is immersed "for about one "minute, after which it should be removed and suffered to dry." "The action of the mixture not only prevents the caoutchouc "from becoming tackey, but neutralizes the tackey properties "when present. It also restores the lost elasticity, and imparts "to the caoutchouc all the useful characteristics which it receives "from the ordinary processes of vulcanizing without any of "their disadvantages."

[Printed, 4d. No Drawings.]

A.D. 1863, January 27.—N° 232.

HENSON, Henry Henson.—"Improvements in fabrics for
" covering floors, walls, roofs and other surfaces or objects, which
" fabrics are also partly applicable to the manufacture of water-
" proof articles." These are, in reference to this subject, in
carrying out the above, first, making " a combination of india-
" rubber, gutta percha, or substances having similar properties,
" and cork dust, peat dust, ground leather, ground tan, flock,
" oxydized oil, boiled oil, gums, resins, umber, litharge or other
" similar or fibrous materials." The following are the proportions
in which the materials, are preferred to be used, " 112 lbs. of the
" india-rubber or gutta percha, with 336 lbs. of the fibrous
" or other materials, mixed together by the aid of about 224 lbs.
" of any suitable solvent, or by any of the known modes of masti-
" cation, but I in no way limit myself to the above proportions."
Second, a combination of " india-rubber, gutta percha, or similar
" substances with other materials such as pigments." Third, a
combination of " Trinidad pitch, india-rubber, gutta percha and
" cork." Fourth, " india-rubber, gutta percha, or similar sub-
" stances " with " the admixture of such materials as are capable
" of receiving dies, such as flock, cocoa-nut fibre dust, leather
" waste, ground tan, hair, wool, or any similar material," in
preference, in the before mentioned proportions. Fifth, " a
" mixture of gutta percha or india-rubber with French chalk,
" flock, woollen dust, cotton or silk waste or any mineral, vege-
" table or metallic dust or similar substances. Such mixture
" may be composed of about 112 lbs. of india-rubber or gutta
" percha, and about 336 lbs. of the fibrous or non-plastic materials
" employed, and these may be mixed together by any suitable
" solvent, but I do not limit myself to these proportions."

[Printed, 6d. No Drawings.]

A.D. 1863, February 10.—N° 365.

CARTWRIGHT, Matthew.—" Improvements in combining
" plastic substances with metals." These are, " combining by
" grinding together, a solution of india-rubber, or gutta percha,
" and metal leaf or metal in a state of finely divided powder."
" Instead of a solution of india-rubber or gutta percha I some-
" times use campticon, parkesine, dissolved amber, gum copal,
" or other suitable vehicle, or two or more of these substances

" combined. After grinding the materials together I sometimes
" subject them to heat for the purpose of hardening and in some
" cases of curing them."

[Printed, 4d. No Drawings.]

A.D. 1863, February 18.—N° 448.

BOUSFIELD, GEORGE TOMLINSON.—(*A communication from Daniel Hayward.*)—" Improvements in boots and shoes, and in
" preparing india-rubber for such and other uses." These are, in reference to this subject, in " improved heel stiffeners, commonly
" called 'counters.' " " Any suitable compound of india-rubber
" is employed which, when vulcanized will have the required
" stiffness combined with the necessary resiliency; this compound
" after being ground upon the ordinary heated rolls is spread in
" a sheet of from $\frac{1}{10}$ to $\frac{1}{4}$ inch in thickness upon cotton, the
" thickness of the rubber and of the cloth varying with the size
" of the required stiffener;" pieces are cut from this sheet and placed in a mould the shape of the heel, cloth side inwards, and vulcanized. Any "compound of rubber, sulphur, and metallic
" oxides, and salts that will vulcanize and preserve a proper
" degree of elasticity and strength will answer for both the sole
" and the heel stiffener," but that preferred for its great cheapness and its strength "is produced by a peculiar treatment of
" the waste scraps and rags of cloth covered with un-
" vulcanized rubber, which are made at nearly all india-rubber
" manufactories." Hitherto this material has not been ground to a uniform consistence on account of the tenacity of the fibre causing blistering and swelling when it is vulcanized, and it is here proposed to destroy that tenacity, for which purpose, 1,000 lbs. of the rags or other fibrous india-rubber articles are boiled from 10 to 12 hours in a mixture of 8 hhds. of water and 75 lbs. of sulphuric acid, by "copper steam pipes in the bottom of a
" wooden tank;" removing the acid, in preference, by steam under a pressure of from 75 to 125 lbs. and from 3 to 6 hours; and after being dried the rags are ground. For the purpose of mixing with the rubber rags thus prepared and ground, the following ingredients are incorporated and ground in the usual manner, 8 lbs. fresh or crude rubber, 4 parts plaster of Paris, 4 parts litharge, 4 parts whiting, $\frac{6}{16}$ parts sulphur; and this compound is mixed in equal parts by weight of the ground rubber

rags, and the whole incorporated by grinding; the result may be vulcanized without blistering or swelling.

[Printed, 10d. Drawing.]

A.D. 1863, February 20.—N° 464.

SIEMENS, CHARLES WILLIAM.—"Improvements in insulating " and supporting telegraph line wires." These are, in reference to this subject, sending out to the countries where "the india-
" rubber or gutta percha trees or varieties of the same abound,
" metallic or other vessels capable of being hermetically sealed;
" these vessels being attached to the tree receive the juice through
" a connecting tube, as far as is practicable under exclusion from
" contact with the surrounding air. These vessels, when filled
" with juice, are hermetically closed by means of a screw stopper
" or otherwise, and are then shipped to this country. I prefer
" to give these vessels a rectangular prismatic form with a screw
" stopper at one end for convenience of stowage."

[Printed, 1s. Drawing.]

A.D. 1863, February 24.—N° 505.

HOOPER, WILLIAM.—"Improvements in insulating and pro-
" tecting telegraphic and other wires and rods and in machinery
" connected therewith." These are, in reference to this subject, a continuous sheet of india-rubber or compound of the same is cut "from a block of the material caused to rotate in front of a
" knife, and afterwards I divide this sheet into tapes or narrow
" strips by a series of cutting edges, the interval between which
" is the width of the tape required. I apply these tapes to the
" wire or rod usually by lapping it around the same" and " vul-
" canize the same by any of the well-known methods." The compounds of india-rubber are as follows:—" India-rubber and
" sulphur (or a substance having a similar action) combined, by
" preference, with tar, or any of the articles usually employed
" with india-rubber and sulphur;" or "combine india-rubber
" with gutta percha, prepared tar, French chalk, silica, oxide of
" zinc, shellac, or any one or more of the articles usually em-
" ployed;" or such compounds, may be, by rollers or by some suitable surface, made into sheets, and by cutters or dividers these sheets are made into strips. Similar cutters or dividers are employed, "to cut lengths of cotton or other cloth into tapes for

" lapping round the aforesaid tapes. To cause vulcanized
" india-rubber to unite, I coat the surface with india-rubber
" solution, and ignite the same to produce tackiness;" over the
surface so prepared, I lay a coating of india-rubber and sulphur
or sulphur compounds, and bind the same with cloth or other
suitable material, and submit the same to heat, in a chamber in
the form of a tube or tubes heated by steam. " In the case of
" vulcanized india-rubber or compound, I sometimes immerse
" the joints in a tar and sulphur bath, or a bath of metal, or other
" bath of suitable temperature."

[Printed, 4d. No Drawings.]

A.D. 1863, March 31.—N° 824.

HUGHES, EDWARD THOMAS.—(*A communication from James Hodgskin.*)—" An improved composition for rendering cloth,
" paper, and similar articles transparent and waterproof." This
composition consists, " of one part by measure of linseed oil, one
" part by measure of india-rubber cement, and six parts by
" measure of benzine," in some cases using an " additional pro-
" portion of benzine." " The india rubber cement spoken of is
" the article generally and technically known in the trade by that
" name, and is a saturated solution of india-rubber in naptha,
" camphine, or other solvent." " The linseed oil should be
" boiled before being mixed with the other ingredients, though
" if this is not done it can be dried by an application of
" sufficiently strong heat." " Some other essential oil or solvent
" might be used instead of benzine," but " the use of benzine is
" preferred to any other solvent at present known."

[Printed, 4d. No Drawings.]

A.D. 1863, April 7.—N° 873.

GILBEE, HENRY.—(*A communication from Jacques Mathevon.*)—
(*Provisional protection only.*)—" A new composition for dressing
" and preserving silk, cotton, and woollen tissues and fibres, and
" also mixtures of the same." This composition consists of
Brazilian tapioca, fig juice, pearl moss (called in French, mousse
perlée), vulcanized caoutchouc, the juice of mulberry leaves. No
proportions of the materials are given, but it is said that the preparation and the proportions vary.

[Printed, 4d. No Drawings.]

A.D. 1863, April 21.—N° 985.

FORD, ALFRED, and RIGG, RICHARD.—"Reforming and re-"using old or waste vulcanized india-rubber." This consists, first, "the pressing of vulcanized india-rubber when in a state of "fine division, and without any previous annealing or amalga-"mating into moulds, for the purpose of its being subsequently "submitted to the action of heat."

Second, "the re-moulding and re-vulcanizing old or waste "vulcanized india-rubber without the aid of the new or un-"vulcanized india-rubber."

The pieces of vulcanized india-rubber are boiled in a strong alkaline solution, or otherwise treated, and by means of grinding or crushing rollers, reduced to powder. The powder, "alone or in "conjunction with other bruised or powdered substances, such "as sulphur, zinc, black lead, or other pigment powders, or "earths," is put into suitable moulds, and pressed "by means "of hydraulic or other suitable pressure, so as to give to the "mass the necessary amount of solidity. We then submit the "same to the action of steam pressure, as employed in ordinary "vulcanizing, so as to aglutinate and conform the whole."

[Printed, 4d. No Drawings.]

A.D. 1863, April 21.—N° 988.

SIMPSON, EDWIN LINDSEY.—"An improvement in waterproof "compounds and in fabrics prepared therewith." This consists in melting "together in a covered vessel two parts of gutta percha "in three parts of camphene or naphtha over a slow fire, and, if "wanted for delicate tints" the fluid is thinned "by adding more "camphene or naphtha." Next preparing "a drying oil by con-"centrating or boiling linseed oil or other suitable vegetable oil "until it attains the consistency of a jelly, and when it is cool "enough to do so without danger of ignition," to four gallons of this concentrated oil adding "one ounce of purified benzine, "three gallons of camphene or naphtha, and three gallons of the "composition first prepared," then adding such colours as it is desired "to impart to the fabric if any," and applying "the com-"position to such fabrics" as it is desired "to render waterproof "or impervious to air by spreading one or more coats, as may be, "with a brush or otherwise," and "afterwards apply a finishing "or coat or mixture composed as follows:"—"Take one gallon

" of linseed or other drying oil, four ounces of red lead or their
" equivalents," and "boil them together until it will 'string' two
" or three inches, and when it has cooled sufficiently to allow it,"
add "one quart of camphene or naphtha and one quart of the
" gutta percha liquid before prepared." "Any designed color
" may be obtained by adding to this varnish the proper colouring
" pigments." The waterproof fabrics are produced without
sulphur, and the offensive odour is avoided. A coating of flocks
may be imparted to them or otherwise.

[Printed, 4d. No Drawings.]

A.D. 1863, June 16.—N° 1506.

JENNINGS, JOSIAH GEORGE, and LAVATER, MANUEL LEOPOLD JONAS—"Improvements in moulding and vulcanizing " articles of india-rubber." These are, first, in moulding and vulcanizing articles of india-rubber, such as mats in common use, employing a frame with four or other convenient number of sides; to this is adapted a bottom and a top with a number of projections upon it for the perforations of the article. The dough is put into the frame, and the projections on the lid are forced by a press, and the frame and its contents are subjected to heat until the rubber is vulcanized, and a perforated block is thus produced, which is cut into slices by a knife; each slice forms a mat or similar article. In place of the projections being all carried in the lid, there are holes in the lid, and pieces corresponding with these holes pass through them, forcing the india-rubber through holes in the bottom.

Second, in place of proceeding as above, employing a roller, to the periphery of which are attached studs of the form of the perforations desired, conveniently fixed by screws revolving in contact with another roller. The dough thus moulded may be removed and vulcanized, but it is preferred to vulcanize it whilst in the hollows of the roller, and this is done by admitting steam, or other heated fluid to the interior of the roller. Or in place of a roller or cylinder, employing a drum with four or more flat sides, mounted on trunnions; each of the sides is prepared with studs, and sulphurized rubber is pressed by means of a press against one of the sides of the drum, so as to fill the spaces, and turned round, another side is filled, and so on. Heat into the interior of the drum, the material is vulcanized as the work goes on.

[Printed, 4d. No Drawings.]

A.D. 1863, June 16.—N° 1512.

BROOMAN, RICHARD ARCHIBALD.—(*A communication from Joseph Jules Anthoine and François Etienne Hyppolite Brossette.*)—
"Protecting or preserving the silvering or quicking on glass, and
" in the manufacture of glass vessels for silvering or quicking."
This consists, in reference to this subject, in making a composition
" of gutta percha or caoutchouc dissolved in essence of turpentine
" in a water bath," to this solution, adding "colophany or other
" gum to constitute a species of varnish without oil." Another composition is made "of gutta percha or caoutchouc dissolved
" in turpentine rectified and filtered, and of the consistence of
" varnish."

[Printed, 8*d*. Drawing.]

A.D. 1863, June 25.—N° 1603.

KIRRAGE, WILLIAM.—" Using apo elastikon hyphasma as a
" new and improved cloth for floors, roofs, walls, tanks and other
" linings, being impervious to damp, and of great strength
" and durability." Forming "a material to be called apo
" elastikon hyphasma" which may be used as above, by masticating india-rubber or gutta percha, or both, then adding a proportion of the residue from cotton seed oil in preference "as
" being cheap, tough, and without smell. To this mass I add for
" some purposes a portion of sterine pitch. I then work in the
" masticators as much vegetable fibre or other matter as will
" convert it into a strong felt." The mass is then taken from the masticators, passed through a set of mixing rollers, adding as much farinaceous matter preferring husks from rice, ground fine, if a light ground is required, otherwise any other of the farinaceous substances are used to suit the colours as will render it in a fit state for the finishing roller through which it is passed, "heated
" hot, to bring it to the thickness, length and width required."
The material is then fit for printing. If the material is required more stiff and hard after the addition of the fibrous matter as above, "I add as much common chalk or talk as the masticators
" will receive without breaking up the mixture, I then remove it
" to the mixing rollers and put in as much steatite or French
" chalk as will get it in a fit state for the finishing rollers. I
" then roll it out to the length, width and thickness required."

[Printed, 4*d*. No Drawings.]

A.D. 1863, July 1.—N° 1635.

SNELL, WILLIAM.—*(A communication from Jules Wiese.)*—*(Provisional protection only.)*—"An improved waterproof material." This consists in making "of a material or substance called
" elastic fabrine (or 'gounne indéchirable') composed of gutta-
" percha, new or waste caoutchouc, or any other kind of elastic
" gummy matter mixed with hair, wool, fur, flax, hemp, cotton
" or other fibrous matter impervious to moisture, in various
" proportions."

[Printed, 4d. No Drawings.]

A.D. 1863, July 4.—N° 1668.

BONNEVILLE, HENRI ADRIEN.—*(A communication from Gustave Eugène Michel Gérard.)*—"Improvements in the manu-
" manufacture of telegraph wires, and in the apparatus connec-
" ted therewith." These are, in reference to this subject, the outward covering of the wire is india-rubber, which "may be
" mixed with gum lac for the purpose of hardening it in the
" proportion of from 10 to 300 parts of lac for 100 of india-
" rubber. This envelope presents some analogy to gutta-percha,
" but is much superior as it is not like it subject to alteration."

[Printed, 4d. No Drawings.]

A.D. 1863, July 10.—N° 1721.

MENNONS, MARC ANTOINE FRANÇOIS.—*(A communication from Diodor Briansky.)*—"Preserving and protecting the silver-
" ing of mirrors.". This consists, in reference to this subject, making the following compositions:—

No. 1. Caoutchouc, 3 lbs.; dissolved in naptha, 7 lbs.

No. 2. Caoutchouc, 3 lbs.; naptha, 5 lbs.; to this solution, heated to ebullition, is added by small portions benzine, 2 lbs.

No. 3 is composed of an oil varnish, with which is incorporated a quantity of minium, zinc white, or other metallic pigment. The mixture being thoroughly ground up, is brought to the requisite degree of fluidity by the addition of four parts of essence of turpentine, and one part of caoutchouc solution No. 1.

No. 4. Linseed oil, $1\frac{1}{2}$ lbs.; essence of turpentine, $1\frac{1}{2}$ lbs.; Tallow, $1\frac{1}{2}$ lbs.; zinc white, $1\frac{1}{4}$ lbs.; minium, $1\frac{1}{4}$ lbs.; bi-oxide of iron, $\frac{3}{4}$ of a lb.; slaked lime, $\frac{3}{4}$ of a lb.; Portland cement, $\frac{1}{2}$ lb.; beeswax, $\frac{1}{4}$ lb.; gutta percha, $\frac{1}{4}$ lb.; sulphate of lead, $\frac{1}{4}$ lb.

" These ingredients being ground up are heated together until
" the volume of the mass is reduced by about one fifteenth. The
" product of this operation being cooled is again ground up
" and reduced by essence of turpentine to the consistence of
" syrup."

[Printed, 4d. No Drawings.]

A.D. 1863, August 7.—N° 1950.

MULHOLLAND, FREDERICK GEORGE.—(*Provisional protection only.*)—This consists, in reference to this subject, over each junction of a gas or water pipe passing "a hollow collar rimmed
" (singly or doubly) inside" to retain an elastic composition in position where required, and through a cup or orifice therein the compound is poured in a fluid or semi-fluid state. In preparing the composition, "ordinarily and preferentially" using "the
" following materials in varying proportions to suit the climatic
" temperature of the countries or localities wherein pipe laying
" works are to be executed."

" For low temperatures and for high temperatures—

Vulcanized india-rubber	60·2 to	80·0	per Centum.
Resin and tallow -	- 35·0 ,,	10·0	,,
Shoddy or fluff -	- 3·5 ,,	7·5	,,
Prepared phosphorus	- 1·5 ,,	2·5	,,
	100·0	100·0	

" or I introduce or use other compounds or compositions having
" similar elastic and preservative properties."

The ingredients are exposed " in a proper vessel for 4 or 5
" hours to a temperature of from 260° F. to 290° F. and when
" the other materials are thoroughly incorporated and slightly
" cooled I add the prepared phosphorus to prevent the decom-
" position of the caoutchouc therein."

[Printed, 4d. No Drawings.]

A.D. 1863, August 28.—N° 2127.

MULET, LOUIS ALEXANDRE.—(*Provisional protection only.*)—Shoeing horses and other animals. These are, in reference to this subject, using "hardened india-rubber, gutta-percha, and
" other such like materials, in combination with pulverized silica,
" iron or steel filings, or other granulated metals, sand, and

" pounded glass, the proportions of which are to be varied
" according to the different degree of hardness or elasticity
" required."

[Printed, 4d. No Drawings.]

A.D. 1863, September 9.—N° 2224.

BOUSFIELD, GEORGE TOMLINSON.—(*A communication from Amos Taylor.*)—(*Provisional protection only.*)—In rollers to be used for spinning and manufacturing, having on their shaft or spindle two discs placed "at a distance apart, corresponding to
" the width of the intended roll." A composition of gutta percha, india-rubber, or other elastic materials capable of being vulcanized, compounded with sulphur and other materials, "is
" either spread on cloth or made into sheets to be cut into strips
" to be wound around the shaft or spindle until the formation of
" the roll is completed. When strips of cloth are used, the last
" or outer layer forming the outer surface of the roll should be
" of the prepared sheet without cloth." The under layers, or composition forming the under body of the roll, have less sulphur than the outer layer, " so that when the same degree of heat
" is applied to both in the vulcanizing process, there will remain
" an elasticity in the under or inner part of the roll, while the
" outer surface will be as rigid as may be required, the electricity
" being diminished under the action of the heat applied in pro-
" portion as the proportion of sulphur is increased in the com-
" position." The heat required is about 270° F., but this varies according to the proportion of sulphur in the compounds. The flanges may be dispensed with.

[Printed, 4d. No Drawings.]

A.D. 1863, September 26.—N° 2367.

SPILL, GEORGE, BRIGGS, THOMAS JAMES, and SPILL, DANIEL.—" Improvements in the manufacture of driving straps
" or bands and of flexible tubes or hose." These are in place of
" coating with various materials woven bands, the bands are saturated with metallic salts or any other antiseptic solutions, preferring chloride of zinc; if the band is thick it is better to employ exhaustion and pressure, and dried, it is placed in an exhausted chamber, and a solution of " 1 part of water, 2 parts
" gelatine, and 4 parts of saccharine matter," heated to fluidity, is forced in under a pressure varying from two to 20 atmospheres

according to the thickness of the band. The vessel is heated by steam pipes to 200° F. The band is then passed between rollers, and when cold and dry, it is soaked in a decoction of any astringent, preferring "5 parts of tanin from bark to 95 parts of " water, from one to six days, according to its thickness," then washed and dried. The surface is rough, and to obviate this it is coated with a vulcanizing compound of india rubber or gutta percha, preferring "one part of india rubber and one part of " oxide of zinc, to which we add 6 per cent. of sulphur, and four " cwt. of ochre to colour it," and it is heated in a close vessel by steam to about 275° F. for about 4 to 6 hours, or in place of vulcanizing by heat, when the band is coated, it may be "dipped " in bisulphide of carbon, containing about 2½ per cent. of " chloride of sulphur." In place of the gelatine and saccharine solution above, there may be substituted a solution of gutta percha or india-rubber or oxidized oil or "parkesine," or mixture of those materials, and the smooth coating may also be communicated as above, or by "oxidized oil or parkesine" in preference, compounded with india rubber and sulphur. Tubes made as above, after passing through the rollers, are expanded "by air or " other fluid. The vulcanizing process is conveniently performed " when the tube is mounted on a mandril."

[Printed, 4d. No Drawings.]

A.D. 1863, September 26.—N° 2373.

NORRIS, LUCIUS HENRY.—(*A communication from Lyman Holl.*)—"Improvements in the manufacture of india-rubber and " gutta percha compounds." These are, combining vulcanized india-rubber waste with gutta percha and tar. "Other ingredients " may be added, such as native india-rubber, sulphur, lead, mag- " nesia, chalk also coloring and other matters," as required; some of such compounds are vulcanized. A compound for spreading on fabrics for coating belting for driving machinery is made of "30 lbs. gutta percha, as free from wood and other im- " purities as may be, and formed into shavings or thin sheets or " cuttings; 60 lbs. of vulcanized india-rubber waste reduced to " powder; 15 lbs. of tar, Stockholm by preference." "These are " well mixed and blended by a masticating machine or otherwise, " as is well understood in manufacturing compounds of india- " rubber;" "5 lbs. of flowers of sulphur, 12 lbs. litharge, 15 lbs.

" oxide of zinc," may be mixed and combined with the previous compound, and made into articles and " converted or vulcanized " by heat in the ordinary manner." " Articles of the original " compound may be converted by the process known as the cold " process, using bisulphite (bisulphide?) of carbon, with or with- " out bromine or chlorine."

[Printed, 4d. No Drawings.]

A.D. 1863, September 29.—N° 2386.

MULHOLLAND, FREDERICK GEORGE.—This invention consists, in reference to this subject, " in the preparation of the " several compounds described for electric insulation and other " purposes." First composition is composed of " shellac, from " 30 to 40 parts, naptha 90 to 100 parts, and muriatic acid from " a moiety of to 1 whole part." These ingredients are to be mixed and intimately incorporated together in a suitable vessel, and heat applied thereto; the foregoing composition is combined with "caoutchouc solution, 80 or 90 parts; shellac solution, 10 to " 20 parts," and "$1\frac{1}{2}$ to $2\frac{1}{2}$ parts of phosphorus, prepared by " subjecting same to a temperature of from 40° to 50° F. during " a period of from 6 to 8 hours." The wires cleaned in the acid bath, coated with the shellac solution, are carefully overlapped with india-rubber tapes, coated with the aforesaid composition, passed through dies, and vulcanized " by the well-known cold or " chloride of sulphur process." Any number of the conductors prepared as aforesaid, "are strained or imbedded " " in a composi- " tion made by mixing from 80 to 100 parts of vulcanized caout- " chouc, 20 to 25 parts of resin, 30 to 35 parts of coal tar, 10 to " 15 parts of shoddy or fluff, with from 3 to 5 parts of phos- " phorus, combining these materials by subjecting them for from " 5 to 8 hours to a temperature of about 280° F.;" the cable is then passed "through rollers flat grooved to the size determined." The cable or flat rope, "constructed as aforesaid, is passed " through a trough or vessel containing a protective composition " prepared at a temperature at from 47° to 55° F. in the follow- " ing proportions:"—" Shellac solution about 100 parts, caout- " chouc solution from 20 to 25 parts, red lead 20 or 30 parts, " and phosphorus 5 to 7 parts."

[Printed, 6d. No Drawings.]

A.D. 1863, October 21.—N° 2579.

CLARKSON, THOMAS CHARLES.—This invention consists, in reference to this subject, in making " a solution of india-rubber " mixed with or without sulphur, chloride of lime, or antimony." This is used in making saddles and coverings for the head, and other articles.

[Printed, 1s. Drawings.]

A.D. 1863, November 18.—N° 2893.

JENNINGS, JOSIAH GEORGE, and LAVATER, MANUEL LEOPOLD JONAS.—" Improvements in the manufacture of tubes, " rings, and cords of india-rubber, and in covering telegraph " wires." These are, in reference to this subject, in cutting tapes or strips; the bevelled edges of the tapes or strips are not produced by the knives or cutters, but are obtained from parallel sides of a block, the knife being caused to cut at an angle to these sides (by preference at an angle of 45°). "Elastic bands or rings " of india-rubber may be produced by cutting off slices of the " thickness desired for the band or ring from tubes made with " strips cut from parti-coloured blocks." Tubes are produced by first lapping on a mandril a strip of plain rubber, then a particolored strip, and exterior to this another plain strip, or a mandril is covered "in succession with several strips of rubber, each of a " different color;" and rings are cut from these tubes. These tubes "may either be cut into slices previous to being vulcanized, " or the tubes may be first vulcanized, and then cut up into rings " or bands." In producing a cord of india-rubber suitable for a spring, a band is cut " of suitable substance and square in sec- " tion;" this is passed when very plastic through rollers which press down the angles, and the band is frozen to set it in the round form; this is best done by passing the band as it comes from the rolls through a fluid, such as salt and water, kept below the freezing point of water by "freezing mixtures or other- " wise." "A band so made, when thawed and vulcanized, will " retain its round form. Before vulcanizing, however, we prefer " to cover the cord with a strip of india-rubber, either parti- " colored or otherwise, which is lapped around it. The cord may, " however, if preferred, be at once vulcanized without being so " coated."

[Printed, 4d. No Drawings.]

A.D. 1863, November 27.—N° 2985.

CLARK, James.—" Improvements in machinery or apparatus
" for cutting strips or threads of india-rubber or other materials."
These are, first, "cutting india-rubber strips or threads by self-
" acting mechanism instead of by hand, as heretofore."

Second, "the use or employment of two or more cutting knives,
" either circular or of the ordinary kind, for cutting india-rubber
" strips or threads," as follows :—The sheet of material is wound
on a drum, and caused to revolve in the ordinary way. A shaft
extending from one end of the machine to the other is made " to
" revolve either by separate driving, or by being geared to the
" shaft of the drum holding the rubber, or to the spindle or shaft
" by which the drum is turned." The aforesaid shaft "has a
" long groove, and carries an excentric, which revolves with and
" traverses along the shaft. The said eccentric is connected with
" the slide of the cross slide rest, and moves the cutter to and
" from the rubber or material to be cut." Or instead of an
eccentric a cam is employed, " which acts upon a roller on the
" slide, and moves the slide and cutter forwards, the back or
" return movement being caused by the operation of one or more
" springs." The slide rest carrying the cutter is moved longitudinally by a screw having fixed to it at one end a ratchet wheel
with a number of teeth in proportion to the distance the slide rest
has to traverse for each cut, and at one end of the shaft carrying
the eccentric or cam there is a plate and crank pin carrying a rod
mounted with a catch or ratchet which rides on the teeth of the
ratchet wheel when the cutter is "moving forwards to cut the
" rubber or material, but seizes the wheel and moves it the dis-
" tance of a tooth when the cutter is moving back, thus turning
" the screw and moving the slide rest onwards the distance
" required for the next strip or thread. The cutter may be either
" the ordinary knife fixed to the slide rest, or a revolving cutter
" fixed to a spindle working in bearings or on centres on the
" slide of the slide rest, and having motion imparted to it from a
" separate revolving drum." Two or more cutters may work at
suitable distances from each other, and traverse "from one end
" of the machine to the other, or one or more cutters may be
" made to traverse from one end of the rubber or material
" towards the centre, and when the cutter or cutters traverse from
" each end they must be connected to separate slide rests, and

" be acted upon by separate eccentrics or cams, and one-half of
" the length of the screw must be right, and the other half left-
" handed, or two separate screws may be used."

[Printed, 10d. Drawing.]

A.D. 1863, December 10.—N° 3116.

BOUSFIELD, GEORGE TOMLINSON.—(*A communication from Thomas Mayall.*)—"Improvements in the manufacture of india-
" rubber and gutta percha compounds." These are, "the com-
" bination of fibres of leather with india-rubber or gutta percha,
" separately or combined with litharge, with or without the use
" of any of the other ingredients mentioned," "when the com-
" pound is subjected to artificial heat to produce the product"
described. The proportions are as follows, "four pounds of the
" fibres of leather, one pound of india-rubber or gutta percha,
" separately or combined, with two pounds of litharge, and two
" ounces of sulphur," mixed by a process well "known to
" manufacturers of india rubber or gutta percha," and spread
upon cloth or run into sheets and vulcanized quickly between
metal plates. "The proportions of the ingredients specified may
be varied," and magnesia or lime, or a carbonate or sulphate of
" magnesia or lime, or calcined French chalk, or other magnesian
" earths, or white lead, or zinc, or oxide of metal may be used
" with or without litharge in this compound, but litharge alone
" is preferred."

[Printed, 4d. No Drawings.]

A.D. 1863, December 16.—N° 3183.

HUMFREY, CHARLES.—"Improvements in dissolving india-
" rubber." These are as follows, " light spirit of petroleum
" dissolves india-rubber with 'great facility," but on evaporating
this " solution the deposited gum remains stickey, its elasticity is
" destroyed, and in other respects it is unfit for use." The
cause of this appears to the inventor to be owing to the petroleum
spirit being a hydrate, and in order to deprive it of its water of
hydration, 100 gallons of the spirit sp. gr. about 725° are mixed
with 10 gallons of "sulphuric acid of a strength not less than
" 1,840, and brought into contact by violent agitation," allowed
to stand for some time, the acid drawn off by a stop cock from
the bottom, the acid operation again repeated, and the spirit is
drawn into a close vessel, avoiding exposing it to air, especially

damp air; "about 2 or 3 lbs. of protoxide of lead and 1 lb. of
" peroxide of manganese in fine powder must then be added to
" 100 gallons, about, of spirit, and the mixture must be well and
" repeatedly agitated." The spirit "is fit for use and will become
" bright by a few hours resting." Or 100 gallons of petroleum
spirit of the quality above recommended is repeatedly agitated in
a close iron vessel with about 25 lbs. of freshly calcined chloride of
calcium in fine powder; after settling, the clear spirit is drawn off
into a similar vessel, and again treated as above with " chloride
" of calcium, and finally, must be distilled from calcined chloride
" of calcium. This process requires considerable time, several
" days at the least, and on the whole" the first process is
preferred.

[Printed, 4d. No Drawings.]

1864.

A.D. 1864, January 12.—N° 81.

TWILLEY, FREDERICK HENRY, and LAINÉ, ARMAND.—
(*Provisional protection not allowed.*)—A waterproof adhesive compound applicable for uniting the surfaces of many substances
which are named. This is made by dissolving gutta percha " of
" the best quality, pink and not white, and easily broken," in
bisulphuret of carbon, "perfectly purified, and freed from sulphur
after evaporation;" "if desired, any of the following ingredients
" may be mixed with the gutta percha in different proportions,
" viz., caoutchouc, resin, gum lack in powder, colphony, arcanson,
" pitch, tar, or wax, benzoine, turpentine, chloroform, and ether."
The proportions vary with the quality of the gutta percha, "but
" 1 of gutta percha, and 10 of bisulphuret of carbon, is the best
" proportion." The gutta percha cut in small pieces is immersed
in the bisulphuret, in air-tight vessels, and agitated to facilitate
solution. When perfectly dissolved it is "poured through a
" strainer or cloth, or it can be left to settle and drawn off clear."

[Printed, 4d. No Drawings.]

A.D. 1864, March 5.—N° 562.

HUMFREY, CHARLES.—" Improvements in vulcanizing india-
" rubber." These are, "the substitution of petroleum spirit and

" petroleum products" described, " as a solvent for chloride of
" sulphur, in the place of bisulphuret of carbon, spirit of turpen-
" tine and camphine, which are ordinarily used for that purpose."
It is said that the ordinary petroleum spirit and products contain
water, which decompose chloride of sulphur into hydrochloric and
hyposulphurous acids, rendering the solution unfit for the above
purpose, and to get rid of the water the petroleum spirit or product is agitated strongly and for some time with about 10 per
cent. of concentrated sulphuric acid, allowed to settle, the petroleum run into a dry still; to every 100 gallons of petroleum
products, 5 lbs. " of dry caustic lime in fine powder is then added,
" together with a small quantity of peroxide of manganese, and
" distilled over in the usual way;" the product is "perfectly
" anhydrous, and can be used as a solvent for chloride of sulphur
" for vulcanizing india-rubber."

[Printed, 4d. No Drawings.]

A.D. 1864, March 9.—N° 598.

BOUSFIELD, GEORGE TOMLINSON.—(*A communication from Amos Taylor.*)—In rollers to be used in machinery for spinning and manufacturing, having on their shaft or spindle circumferential flanges and bearings. The flanges are on said shaft at a distance apart corresponding to the width of the roll required. A com- position of gutta percha, india-rubber, or other elastic materials capable of being vulcanized, compounded with sulphur and other materials, is either spread on cloth or made into sheets to be cut into strips to be wound around the shaft or spindle until the formation of the roll is completed. When strips of cloth are used, the last or outer layer forming the outer surface of the roll should be of the prepared sheet without cloth. The under layers or composition forming the under body of the roll have less sulphur than the outer layer, " so that when the same degree of
" heat is applied to both in the vulcanizing process, there will
" remain an elasticity in the under or inner part of the roll,
" while the outer surface will be as rigid as may be required, the
" elasticity being diminished under the action of the heat applied
" in proportion as the proportion of sulphur is increased in the
" composition." The heat required is about 270° F., but this varies according to the proportion of sulphur in the compounds. The flanges may be dispensed with.

[Printed, 6d. Drawing.]

A.D. 1864, April 2.—N° 819.

SILVER, STEPHEN WILLIAM.—(*A communication from John Thornborrow Manifold.*)—(*Provisional protection only.*)—" Certain " machinery for extracting the juice of the sapota mulleri, or " bullet tree." Two or more rollers are arranged "so as to be " capable of adjustment by screws, and of being driven at suitable " distances from each other," and at varied speeds. The bark of the above tree "is then introduced between the rollers from a " table or feeding board placed on one side of the rollers, and " after passing through them is received on another table or dis- " charge board placed on the other side." The milk, gum, or juice, called " ballata " expressed, passed through strainers with holes of different sizes, is collected in a tank or other suitable apparatus. The whole may be arranged in a punt or truck for transport.

[Printed, 8d. Drawing.]

A.D. 1864, April 2.—N° 820.

SILVER, STEPHEN WILLIAM.—(*A communication from John Thornborrow Manifold.*) — (*Provisional protection only.*) — "The " preparation of the milk, gum, or juice of the sapota mulieri " or bullet tree." This milk, gum, or juice, usually called " ballata," is mixed " with wood naphtha, alcohol, rum, or other " liquids or substances containing alcohol, whereby coagulation " takes place, and a solid or coagulated mass or compound is the " result."

[Printed, 4d. No Drawings.]

A.D. 1864, April 21.—N° 1007.

JENNINGS, JOSIAH GEORGE, and LAVATER, MANUEL LEOPOLD JONAS.—" Improvements in pumps, and in the con- " truction of flexible pipes or hose, and in the apparatus employed " therefor." These are, in reference to this subject, in construct- " ing flexible pipes or hose, applying " the india-rubber cement to " the yarns and not to the covered core. This arrangement admits " of the braiding machine being stopped at any time, and for any " length of time without injury to the india-rubber covering of " the core." In preference, for this purpose, arranging at the eye of the machine, or where the yarns meet around the core, a mushroom-shaped disc with a hole at the centre for the passage of the core. The yarns as they pass to the eye to be plaited in,

rub over this disc, the disc being smeared with cement; there are means for scraping down any excess of cement taken up by the yarns. An outer covering of india-rubber compound is applied over the braiding; and the vulcanizing process is conducted as heretofore. For making flexible gas tubing employing "india-
"rubber vulcanized by means of hyposulphite of lead, or by
"means of sulphuret of lead, the hyposulphite or sulphuret is
"mixed with the india-rubber in the same manner as when
"sulphur is employed and the compound exposed to heat as
"usual." This rubber does not contain free sulphur. In making glazed tubing substituting for the india-rubber a mixture of india-rubber and hyposulphite or sulphuret of lead.

[Printed, 1s. 8d. Drawings.]

A.D. 1864, April 28.—N° 1072.

GHISLIN, THOMAS GOULSTON.—" Improvements in the treat-
" ment and application of seaweed." These are, combining seaweed " with various gummy, resinous, bituminous, fatty,
" gelatinous, and earthy matters, and fibrous substances," and applying the compound to a number of purposes named. As an example, for flooring purposes, using " 10 per cent. of india-rubber,
" 10 per cent. of foots of varnish, 10 per cent. of foots of oil, and
" 5 to 10 per cent. of Burgandy pitch, combined with from 10 to
" 15 per cent. of the commoner and cheaper kinds of bituminous
" or resinous substances," " 50 per cent. ground seaweed," sometimes adding " any required quantity of fibrous and earthy
" matters to give the required tenacity and consistency," these
" are incorporated in a masticator and the mass passed between
" cylinders." Sometimes prepared seaweed is masticated with gutta percha " to the extent of 30 to 60 per cent. or even more of
" gutta percha with a corresponding proportion of pulverized sea-
" weed." " For a portion of the gutta percha, I sometimes substi-
" tute an equivalent proportion of india-rubber dissolved in a
" solvent." In preference, the above proportions are employed although others may be used. Among the substances also named which may be amalgamated in the compounds are paraffin and oily or fatty substances, shearings of woollen cloth, cotton and flax waste, liquid silicates of potash and soda, pulverized chalk, talc, " metallic oxides, gelatine, farina, alum, tungstic acid, powdered charcoal, and other analogous substances."

[Printed, 4d. No Drawings.]

A.D. 1864, May 5.—N° 1135.

HENSON, HENRY HENSON.—"Improvements in armour and other plating and sheathing for ships or vessels, partly applicable to other purposes." These are, in reference to this subject, as follows:—on the metal or sheathing of ships having thin layers of wood and cementing on to the wood or spreading on the same india-rubber combined with sulphur, and heating from 230° to 300° F. Coating roughened, smooth or perforated metal plates of ships with the ebonite composition and heating from 230° to 300" F.

[Printed, 1s. Drawing.]

A.D. 1864, May 13.—N° 1218.

BATEMAN, DANIEL.—In the manufacture of card cloth, &c., a cement is employed consisting of "gutta percha, 55 parts; india-rubber, 10 parts; bisulphuret of carbon, 20 parts; gum lac, 5 parts; bisulphide of mercury, 5 parts; carburet of iron, 5 parts; all by weight. These ingredients being properly amalgamated."

[Printed, 4d. No Drawings.]

A.D. 1864, June 4.—N° 1394.

COLES, GEORGE, JAQUES, JAMES ARCHIBALD, and FAN-SHAWE, JOHN AMERICUS.—Machinery or apparatus for producing thin strips, threads, or filaments from various substances, such as, "a thin sheet of india-rubber or caoutchouc, or gutta-
" percha, or any compound or preparation " thereof; "mounting
" the axle of the cutting discs and the axle of the supporting
" roller so that either the cutting discs may be capable of being
" lifted by the workman away from the sheet or brought into con-
" tact therewith, or the sheet with the supporting roller may be
" lowered away from and out of contact with the cutting discs, or
" brought up against them, as may be required, in order that the
" cutting operation may be either arrested or commenced or con-
" tinued at any time without stopping the machine."

[Printed, 10d. Drawing.]

A.D. 1864, June 23.—N° 1577.

TURNER, ARCHIBALD, and CLARK, JAMES.—(*Provisional protection only*.)—Apparatus for vulcanizing india-rubber, peculiarly

adapted for the cold process. The machine "is self-acting and is
" provided with a drum, roller, or pulley, whereby the rubber is
" carried forward, into and through a vessel containing the chemi-
" cal solutions which are allowed to act upon the rubber for a given
" and determinate space of time." " The rubber passes under a
" pulley or drum in the solution vessel." Varying speeds are
given to the rollers, drums, or pulleys, this is effected by cone
pullies or other contrivances.

[Printed, 4d. No Drawings.]

A.D. 1864, July 19.—N° 1804.

DE BRIOU, HENRY EDWARD FRANCIS.—A composition for
preserving metals, ships' bottoms, &c., consisting of vulcanized
" india rubber 750 parts, mineral pitch 250 parts." The india-
rubber cut into small pieces is melted over a slow fire and the
mineral pitch is added and melted and the whole well mixed and
stirred is left boiling for two or three hours, then the fire is put
out.

[Printed, 4d. No Drawings.]

A.D. 1864, August 4.—N° 1940.

GÉRARD, GUSTAVE EUGÈNE MICHEL.—"Improvements in
" apparatus for cutting sheets or bands of vulcanized india
" rubber and other substances into threads." This is said to be an
improvement upon No. 3415, A.D. 1862, and consists in mounting
a shaft on two mandril heads, which shaft carries a number of
circular steel cutting blades for cutting sheets of india rubber into
threads, these blades are separated by washers, the thickness
varying according to the size of the threads to be cut. Immediately under this blade shaft is a cylinder covered with half
supple india rubber, wood, horn, zinc, or pewter, against which
the knives or cutting blades come in contact. Parallel and in a
line with this cylinder are four rollers, two for feeding in the
sheet of india rubber to be cut on one side of the cylinder and
two on the other side for drawing off the thread after being cut.
The sheet of india rubber to be cut is in the first place rolled on
to a large roller, which revolves in a trough of water so that
while unrolling the sheets are constantly wetted, the sheet then
passes over a quick threaded fixed screw to prevent the sheet
having a zig-zag movement, from whence it is drawn by and

under the first feeding in roller and over the second; these
feeding in rollers having a slower surface speed than the roller in
the water trough to prevent folds being formed in the sheet
while passing between the cutting plates and hard rubber cylinder; the sheet then arrives between the cutting blade shaft
(such shaft being wetted by water to keep the blades cool) and
the hard rubber roller where it is cut into threads. Between
each cutting blade the teeth of a comb are applied which serves
for withdrawing and throwing off the threads from between the
blades which might by accident break whilst being cut. The
threads which are cut from the sheet are then seized by the
drawing off rollers which revolve at a greater surface speed than
the hard rubber cylinder to prevent the threads being carried
away by the contact and friction of the blades. The feeding in
rollers, hard rubber cylinder and drawing off rollers are all
mounted in a frame which is caused to rise and fall by the action
of a pedal and levers so as to approach or withdraw from the
cutting blades the hardened rubber cylinder as well as the other
rollers. After the threads have been taken out by the drawing
rollers they are rolled on to reels and the uncut part of the sheet
falls on to a platform which has a to-and-fro movement given to
it by a rack and pinion which forms it into folds similar to a
cloth folding machine.

[Printed, 1s. 4d. Drawings.]

A.D. 1864, August 9.—N° 1982.

CLARK, WILLIAM.—(*A communication from Alexander Marie
Quinet and Achille Baudouin*).—" Improvements in the manu-
" facture of india-rubber balls and other elastic recipients, and
" in the valves applied to the same." These are, in reference to
this subject, first, for closing balls employing india rubber valves
composed of a base of such material perforated at the centre, and
furnished with a tongue piece, also of india-rubber, which is
caused to adhere to the internal face of said base piece for a
portion only of its surface the remaining part forming a valve,
closing the orifice before mentioned. This valve also has the
advantage of being vulcanized at the same time as the recipient
to which it may have been previously applied, and so unites the
whole together. The valve may further, in certain cases and
particularly with balls, consist of a single tongue, "applied on
" the inside of the hole in the ball."

Second, utilizing the vulcanization of balls or recipients "to
" produce on their external surface in a different color to that of
" the ball, suitable inscriptions or designs, or geographical maps,
" either sunk or in relief, without said designs being engraved in
" the vulcanizing moulds," by the "introduction of intermediate
" linings into said moulds having the designs formed on their
" concave surfaces, either hollow or in relief, the designs being
" produced by the action of the sulphurets on the vulcanized
" india-rubber to which they are applied."

[Printed, 8d. Drawing.]

A.D. 1864, September 13.—N° 2236.

RITCHIE, JOHN HORATIO, junior.—Bolts for constructing ships or vessels. This consists in covering such bolts "either
" entirely or partially, with a compound of sulphur and caout-
" chouc or caoutchouc and gutta percha, or a compound in
" which these are principal ingredients, such compound being
" changed by the process known as vulcanization." The composition of the vulcanite or ebonite, in preference, is such
" that it shall at the same time be tough as well as hard.
" A compound of caoutchouc masticated with $\frac{4}{10}$ths to $\frac{5}{10}$ths its
" weight of sulphur laid on the bolt in a plastic state, and tightly
" bound thereto with tape or other material and exposed to a
" heat of 300° Fahrenheit for from three hours to four hours
" answers the purpose well."

[Printed, 6d. Drawing.]

A.D. 1864, September 15.—N° 2256.

LAVATER, MANUEL LEOPOLD JONAS.—(*Provisional protection only*.)—" Improvements in the manufacture of driving straps or
" belting, and of tubes of vulcanized india-rubber, and also in
" the manufacture of the helical coils of wire commonly inserted
" in vulcanized india-rubber tubes, also in desulphurizing articles
" of vulcanized india-rubber." These are in reference to this subject, in driving straps or belting, a number of cords or threads kept parallel by passing through the teeth of reeds, are drawn through rollers on a leading cloth, and receive at same time a coating of india-rubber dough, embedding them on one side. This sheet is wound upon a drum and is again passed through rollers to receive a coating of dough upon the other side. This is done by passing through rollers, stripping off the leading

cloth at the same moment introducing another leading cloth on the first coated surface. "Both leading cloths may be " left if preferred." "The whole is then tightly wound on a " metal cylinder and may be vulcanized in a chamber by steam, " but dry heat is preferred." Several sets of parallel cords or threads may be treated as above at one time. If the straps are to be covered with canvas, "this is done by cutting the straps " before vulcanizing, then a strip of coated canvas is overlapped " on the strap and the whole vulcanized as before;" or "an un- " vulcanized strap cut at right angles," "may be braided over," " then the braid is covered with india-rubber cement and vul- " canized." In place of parallel cords, the core of the belt is a braided fabric. A tube is made by causing the mandril to be coated " to pass through a hollow axis, on the exterior of which is " an arm carrying the axis of a bobbin, around which is wound " the strip of india-rubber compound, the bobbin can thus be " caused to revolve around the mandril, and so wind around it " the strip of india-rubber compound." When the tube so coated is to be braided, this arrangement may be applied to a braiding machine. When the tube or hose is to have a coil of wire within it, that, forms the mandril; if wire is not used a tubular flexible mandril may be employed, being inflated, whilst being coated. Before the strip of india-rubber compound is wound on to the mandril, the bevilled edges of the strip are coated with a solvent as is usual.

"In order to remove any free sulphur from articles of vulcanized " india-rubber, I subject them, whilst moistened with or im- " mersed in water, to the action of beaters or rubbers, so as by " mechanical means to free the articles from the sulphur," in place of using chemical means.

[Printed, 4d. No Drawings.]

A.D. 1864, October 7.—Nᵒ 2477.

KEMP, HENRY, and KEMP, FRANCIS JOHN.—This invention consists, in reference to this subject, in preparing a compound to be used for hardening leather, as follows :—Caoutchouc or gutta percha is dissolved in naptha, and tar from distilling wood is dissolved in methylated spirit of about 60° above proof, or pure spirits of wine; to one gallon of the tar to one quart of spirit, more or less is used, and the compound is made " of equal parts of

" tar and the dissolved india-rubber in the proportion of four to
" eight ounces of india rubber to a gallon of the solvent."
Another compound is made of " india-rubber, shell-lac, and tar."

[Printed, 4d. No Drawings.]

A.D. 1864, October 12.—N° 2516.

STORY, ROBERT.—*(Provisional protection only.)*—Manufacturing india rubber thread. Hitherto, it is said, a solvent, such as naptha, has been used to soften the rubber, previous to its being passed through the rollers, to secure uniformity of thickness and quality; and to avoid expense and disagreeable smell attending same, india-rubber or caoutchouc of the ordinary quality employed in this manufacture, is passed " between rolls, preferably arranged
" to run at the same speed, one or both of which are heated by
" steam or other means to a temperature sufficient to soften the
" rubber, and to continue passing it between the said rolls until
" the sheets are formed into the required size, thickness, and
" quality. 'Rubber' of the usual kind passed between rolls
" heated by steam, in manner well understood, to 250° Faren-
" heit's thermometer on their surface or surfaces, will produce
" economically good sheets fit for cutting into threads by any of
" the means now used for that purpose."

[Printed, 4d. No Drawings.]

A.D. 1864, October 26.—N° 2656.

FONTAINEMOREAU, PETER ARMAND Le Comte de.— *(A communication from Henri Lemaistre and Company.)*—" An
" improved composition for uniting iron with wood and leather
" with leather, for waterproofing textile fabrics, paper, and cord-
" age, for moulding, and for various other purposes." The composition above referred to consists " of about 12 ounces of gutta
" percha for every pint and three-quarters of sulphate (sulphide?)
" of carbon."

[Printed, 4d. No Drawings.]

A.D. 1864, October 28.—N° 2675.

PARKES, ALEXANDER.—This consists, in reference to this subject, in the preparation of balata to be used separate or mixed with dissolved gun cotton. The gum ballata dissolved is mixed with chloride of sulphur, usually not more of the chloride than

five per cent., first diluting the chloride of sulphur "with an
" equal bulk or more of mineral naptha or bisulphide of carbon
" to prevent too violent an action." Gun cotton is dissolved to
a pasty mass in wood naptha, distilled from fused chloride of
calcium (a gallon of naptha distilled with from two to six pounds
chloride of calcium) gives three quarts of solvent for the gun
cotton. The ballata above prepared may be mixed with the dissolved gun cotton.

[Printed, 4d. No Drawings.]

A.D. 1864, November 11.—N° 2801.

LEES, WILLIAM LINGHAM.—A cement composed of two ounces
of india-rubber dissolved in about "one pint of mineral or coal
" tar naptha, or petrolene." The materials are placed in a vessel
with a lid, and allowed to stand until the india-rubber is perfectly
dissolved. One ounce of powdered shellac is placed in a large
bottle or vessel which can be closed and shaken, with a quarter
of a pint of wood naptha, or methylated spirit, the solution is
complete in about three or four hours. One pound of glue or
other gelatinous matter, such as gelatine or isinglass is dissolved
by heat "in two-thirds of a pint of ale, or a mixture of ale and
" linseed oil in the proportions of eight parts of ale to one or
" two parts of linseed oil." The ale is strong and frequent
stirring is required. When this glue solution is still warm the
shellac solution is well stirred into it, and the india-rubber solution is then well stirred in. If the odour of the solvents is objectionable a small quantity of the essential oil of thyme or other
fragrant essential oil is added. When the compound required is
to be harder more shellac than the above is used, say five or six
times. When the cement is to be used where it will be exposed
to the weather, in preference, employing a larger proportion of
linseed oil, as the said linseed oil effectually protects the cement
against atmospheric influences.

[Printed, 4d. No Drawings.]

A.D. 1864, December 15.—N° 3110.

HANCOCK, CHARLES and SILVER, STEPHEN WILLIAM.—
This invention, in reference to this subject, consists "in employ-
" ing an admixture of the milk of caoutchouc and the milk of
" balata." "These substances are mixed together in equal pro-

" portions by stirring one into the other in suitable vessels, the
" air being excluded from the mixture until required for use, as
" exposure to the air has a tendency to produce coagulation,
" which causes some difficulty in the after working." A flexible
compound is the result, but great elasticity is obtained when two-
thirds of caoutchouc is used to one-third ballata. "When pig-
" ments, powders, sulphur, or coloring matter are to be combined
" with the milk," they are first ground or mixed in water or in
" flour paste, size, or gum," and then combined with the mixture
or combination of the gums. "The sheets of ballata and caout-
" chouc may be cut into tapes and fillets, or formed into rings
" and other forms, by processes which are well understood by
" caoutchouc manufacturers. A compound substance applicable
" to various useful purposes may be made by mixing with the
" milk of caoutchouc or with ballata milk, or with the two com-
" bined, ground powder, or elastic pulverized dust of vulcanized
" india-rubber."

[Printed, 4d. No Drawings.]

A.D. 1864, December 17.—N° 3136.

HALL, HIRAM LYMAN.—"Improvements in the manufacture of
" elastic fabrics." This consists, in reference to this subject,
upon an elastic substance applying a sheet or sheets of india-
rubber by pressure in any convenient manner, and "grooving,
" corrugating, crimping, channelling, or otherwise figuring by
" means of pressure, one or both the outer surfaces of the sheet
" or sheets of vulcanized india-rubber employed.

[Printed, 8d. Drawing.]

1865.

A.D. 1865, January 20.—N° 176.

STEVENS, BENJAMIN FRANKLIN.— (*A communication from
Simon Stevens.*)—"Improvements in vulcanizing compounds, and
" vulcanized fabrics." These are, first, a "vulcanizing compound
" of vegetable oil and sulphur;" the oil may be "linseed or other
" similar oil," instead of free sulphur as generally used. Second,
" the vulcanized preparation or compound prepared by combining
" the vegetable oil and sulphur with india-rubber, gutta percha,

" or other similar gums, oxide or carbonate of lead, lamp black,
" Paris white, or any other colouring matter usually employed,
" avoiding such as have an offensive odour." The oil is first
boiled to about the consistency of honey, and to each quart of
oil is added about one pound of sulphur. This vulcanizing
compound is added in variable proportions, according to the
nature of the manufactured article, " the greater the proportion
" of the compound the harder will be the rubber. The mixture
" is then subjected to steam heat at a temperature of 320°
" Fahrenheit for about four or five hours."

Third, " the production of waterproof fabrics by applying the
" herein-described vulcanized preparation or compound to
" fabrics " heated from 260° to 270° F. for about 12 hours.

Fourth, applying a coat of flocks to fabrics first prepared with
the above compound; while the coat is in an adhesive state, the
flocks are applied "by sifting in excess, rolling or pressing the
" same, then removing the excess," or otherwise, and heated as
above.

[Printed, 4d. No Drawings.]

A.D. 1865, February 11.—N° 398.

FONTAINEMOREAU, PETER ARMAND le Comte de.—(*A communication from Léon Désire Innocent and François Perroncel.*)—
(*Provisional protection only.*) — " Certain improvements in the
" manufacture of caoutchouc." These are, making "artificial
" caoutchouc capable of resisting acids and a high temperature,
" and of replacing oil cloth and varnished or plain leather, and
" other similar products," by taking 56 lbs. of caoutchouc, 12 lbs.
of gutta percha, or about 67 lbs. of caoutchouc if gutta percha is
not used, in small pieces, " 67 lbs. powdered cork or sawdust; 11
" lbs. of flower of sulphur " adding " about 67 lbs. of any dissolv-
" ing agent, such as sulphur of carbon or turpentine." In about
10 or 24 hours the whole is in a state of paste, and is passed through
heated rollers to obtain sheets. The sulphur is replaced " by a com-
" pound of sulphured chlorine, such as the chlorides and sulphites
" of sulphur, lime, zinc, lead, or by the basis with which the above
" agents are formed." The sheets formed with the above agents
are passed " slowly in a bath heated to about 122° F.," composed
" of about 22 gallons of distilled or rain water, 56 lbs. of alum,
" 12 lbs. of sulphate of iron, copper, or zinc, 2 lbs. of alumina."

To obtain them black they are again immersed in a bath containing "gall nut, tan, or any other substance causing tan." The sheets are vulcanized in a boiler heated to from 266° to 302° F. from 1½ to 3 hours. When vulcanized, if rough, they are pumiced over. If to be varnished or printed, a brush lays on the following solution; 3 gallons of water at 95° F., "7 lbs. of sulphate of iron, " copper, or zinc, 45 lbs. of alum, 2 lbs. of sulphate of alumina, " 23 lbs. of alkaline soap; the iron and alumina salts can be re- " placed by every kind of salt producing non-soluble salts with " alkaline soaps;" add 23 lbs. of hard siccative oil, heat, wash, the compound, dry it, add 23 lbs. of soft siccative oil, heat, add 7 lbs. of benzine or other agent, to enable it to spread on the sheets.

[Printed, 4d. No Drawings.]

A.D. 1865, February 14.—N° 413.

HARTON, GEORGE.—Waterproofing skins, hides, and leather, " by placing them in a close vessel exhausting the air, and forcing into it a solution of india-rubber or gutta percha, "with " the addition to either solution of a small quantity of copal, " gum-cowrie, or other known and suitable resinous gum in- " soluble in water, or of a small quantity of wax or spermaceti."

[Printed, 4d. No Drawings.]

A.D. 1865, March 9.—N° 656.

COLLINS, BENONI.—(*Provisional protection only.*)—" Cutting " sheets of india-rubber and like materials into strips or threads. This consists "in simultaneously cutting and unwinding the " part cut from the roll, by which I am enabled to cut several " strips or threads, or to cut the entire width of the roll into " strips or threads at one operation," by using "as many cutters " as there are strips or threads required to be cut at the same " operation, which cutters are placed at such distance apart as is " necessary to give the width of the strips or threads required; " and these cutters are simultaneously advanced against the " materials upon the drum or roller, so as to cut, say the depth " of one or two layers; then the ends of the cut layers are un- " wound from the roll, and delivered to arrangements which will " draw off or unwind the threads or strips from the roll at the " surface speed at which it is driven, or thereabouts." "Streams

" or jets of water are directed against the cutting edges when in
" operation, as usual."

[Printed, 4d. No Drawings.]

A.D. 1865, April 15.—N° 1068.

CLARK, WILLIAM.—(*A communication from Henry Loewenberg and Emile Granier.*)—" Improvements in the manufacture of a
" compound or material to be used as a substitute for india-
" rubber." These are, " the use of resinous or balsamic substances
" (as copal, pitch, tar, or their equivalents) with sulphur or its
" vapor, and the application of heat in combination with gluish
" or gelatinous substances either with or without other ingredients
" for the purpose of vulcanizing or solidifying such gluish or
" gelatinous substances or compositions, in order to impart to
" them qualities similar to vulcanized india-rubber." The proportion in which these substances are mixed depends upon the quality and nature of the materials used. " The following proportions gives a good result; glue or gelatinous substances, 4 lbs.;
" nut-gall, or gallic or tannic substances, 3 ozs.; glycerine or
" oils, or their equivalents, 8 ozs.; acid, either acetic, pyroligneous,
" or other similar, 1 lb." The acetic acid is diluted in about five
" parts of water, and it is added " to the glue in such quantity
" as to cover the same. When the glue is dissolved, the other
" ingredients are added."

[Printed, 4d. No Drawings.]

A.D. 1865, May 5.—N° 1257.

MAYALL, THOMAS JEFFERSON.—" Improvements in the manu-
" facture or treatment of india-rubber or gutta percha, or com-
" pounds thereof, applicable to the production of sterotype plates
" and other forms." These are, taking " india-rubber or gutta
" percha or compounds thereof when combined with sulphur and
" in a semi or partially ' converted ' state, produced by the action
" thereon of the sulphur, aided by heat, and then in this partially
" ' converted ' state " applying " such matters under pressure and
" heat to the surface to be stereotyped or copied," and continuing
" the pressure and heat until perfect conversion is obtained."
By the terms 'conversion' and 'converted' is meant, "that state
" of the material which is otherwise called ' vulcanized' or
" ' cured.' " Six ozs. of sulphur or thereabouts are ground in with every pound weight of the india-rubber or gutta percha.

[Printed, 4d. No Drawings.]

A.D. 1865, May 9.—N° 1283.

MAYALL, THOMAS JEFFERSON.— First. Forming door and other mats of india-rubber, gutta percha, or compounds thereof, with points or projections of such material standing up from the surface, by moulding the same in dies, having projections to pass into the backs or under sides of the points or projections in the material forming the mat. When the required form is given "to " the india-rubber, gutta percha or compound thereof it is to be " ' converted,' ' vulcanized ' or ' cured ' as is well understood."

Second. Forming such points or projections of cocoa nut or other fibre, or the refuse or clippings of india-rubber or gutta percha, &c., which are held in position by a layer of india-rubber, gutta percha or a compound thereof, or a sheet of other suitable material connected or otherwise held to the back thereof.

Third. Mats made as follows :—Taking a sheet of india-rubber, gutta percha, or a compound of such matters combined with sulphur, applying to one side a sheet of canvas or other cloth, punching or piercing this sheet with a number of holes. Tufts of hair or other suitable material formed as required are then placed in holes in a die; to and around the looped ends projecting through the die string is applied; a backing with holes corresponding with the tufts in the die is applied over these projecting tufts, string, wire, or other holding material is passed through the loops, then apply a solution of cement, over this a sheet, and finally the article is placed in a die or mould, ramming into the holes of the die or mould powdered soapstone or other material, placing on the other part of the die or mould and vulcanizing by heat and pressure.

[Printed, 1s. 10d. Drawings.]

A.D. 1865, May 11.—N° 1309.

MAYALL, THOMAS JEFFERSON.—" Improvements in the manu-
" facture of hose and other flexible tubing, which improvements
" are also applicable in uniting surfaces of india-rubber, gutta
" percha, or of compounds thereof to each other, or to woven or
" other fabrics or material for other purposes." These are applying to one surface of a sheet of india-rubber or gutta percha with which sulphur has been mixed previous to vulcanization, a layer of cement " obtained by mixing shellac with india-rubber, gutta
" percha or a compound thereof, dissolved by camphine or other

" suitable solvent," in preference, are combined "in the following
" proportions, say, 8 lbs. of india-rubber, gutta percha or a com-
" pound thereof, ground with 2 lbs. of pure gum shellac, and
" then dissolved in highly rectified camphine in quantity adapted
" to the degree of consistency desired to be obtained," but not
confined to these proportions. To obtain increased strength
" several layers or thicknesses of the woven or other fabric or
" material may be laid one on the other and united together by
" the aid of the cement referred to." Both surfaces of the woven
or other fabric or material may be treated "as explained to one of
" them."

[Printed, 4d. No Drawings.]

A.D. 1865, May 11.—N° 1313.

PARKES, ALEXANDER.—"Manufacture of parkesine or com-
" pounds of pyroxyline, and also solutions of pyroxylin known
" as collodion." This consists, in reference to this subject, in employing as solvents of the pyroxiline "nitro benzole, analine, and
" glacial acetic acid." In making parkesine with these new
solvents the proportion of materials are varied; when flexibility
is required, more oil than pyroxyline is employed, say from 150 to
200 parts of oil, cotton seed or castor oil preferred, to 100 parts
of pyroxyline. Nitro benzole and analine are solvents of gutta
percha and india-rubber as well as for pyroxyline, gun cotton,
by using these solvents, employing " these and a variety of other
" gums and resins in the manufacture of parkesine better than
" by the solvents heretofore used." "A compound of 100 parts
" gutta-percha or india-rubber softened by or dissolved with nitro
" benzole or analine, with 100 parts of pyroxiline" makes a
" good insulating material for telegraph wire, and it can be put
" on the wire in the way usually adopted with gutta percha."

[Printed, 4d. No Drawings.]

A.D. 1865, July 29.—N° 1962.

ABEL, FREDERICK AUGUSTUS.—Compounds for waterproofing
and insulating " consisting of india-rubber whether in its natural
" state or vulcanized, or gutta percha made to combine by the
" aid of heat with paraffin or beeswax or with a mixture of both."
The proportions may be variously modified, stearine or spermacetti
or other solid substances may be also used; but it is preferred to
use paraffin and beeswax, either alone or mixed. "In preparing

" such compounds for this purpose instead of mixing, masticating
" or incorporating the india-rubber with the paraffin or beeswax
" in definite proportions," placing the india-rubber or gutta percha
in a bath of paraffin or beeswax, heated, by preference, to a temperature of from 120° to 150° F. when gutta percha is employed, and from 220° to 250° F. when india-rubber is employed; and when by the absorption of a certain quantity of the paraffin or beeswax the india-rubber or gutta percha has become soft and adhesive, "it is removed from the bath and formed into bands or
" ribbons."

[Printed, 4d. No Drawings.]

A.D. 1865, August 4.—N° 2025.

MULHOLLAND, FREDERICK GEORGE.—This consists, in reference to this subject, in compositions " prepared and admixed
" in or about the following proportions :—

"Asphalt or bitumen	- -	10 to 25 Parts.
Plumbago	- - -	10 ,, 15 ,,
Caoutchouc	- - -	50 ,, 75 ,,
Naptha or benzine	-	100 ,, 125 ,,
Sulphur	- - -	10 ,, 13·5 ,,
Siliceous acid	- -	3·5 ,, 4·75 ,,
Phosphoric acid	-	5 ,, 10 ,,
Bisulphide of carbon	-	5 ,, 10 ,,

Sometimes it is necessary to omit or dispense altogether with one or more of the ingredients herein described, or vary same by increasing or decreasing the several proportions relatively.

[Printed, 4d. No Drawings.]

A.D. 1865, September 30.—N° 2516.

MILLER, JOHN WILLIAM MOORE.—Waterproofing hides and leather. This consists in reference to this subject, in making a waterproof solution " composed of six to eight ounces of india-
" rubber dissolved in one gallon of rosin oil, cotton oil, poppy
" oil, cod oil, or any of the fixed and drying oils. The other
" solution consists of one pound of gum thus or frankincense to
" a gallon of methylated spirit or methylated 'finish' as it is
" termed in commerce. I prefer to mix these two solutions
" together, and to every gallon of these mixed fluids I add one
" ounce of vegetable or Japan wax rendered fluid by heat," but

"not too hot or hot enough to set fire to the whole." "I then
"add from half a pint to a pint of best spirits of turpentine to
"every gallon, and one fluid ounce of nitro-benzole."

[Printed, 4d. No Drawings.]

A.D. 1865, October 6.—N° 2568.

SMITH, HENRY FRANCIS.—"An improved composition or
" material to be employed in waterproofing or rendering woven
" fabrics impervious to moisture." This consists as follows, to
about a gallon of linseed oil, either in a raw, boiled, or previously
oxidized state, add about two pounds of a resin of any description
and about two pounds of caoutchouc or india-rubber previously
dissolved in mineral naptha "when raw oil is used in order to
" give the compound its drying properties add two pounds of
" litherage, litharge, or similar preparations of lead or other well-
" known dryers." Coloring matters may be added. This composition permeating woven fabrics renders them "impervious to
moisture" and prevents them from "becoming rotten." Linseed oil is named from its better drying properties in preference
to other vegetable oils. In preference the oils are oxidized before
their application as above and this "may be effected by well-
" known means and in such instances the addition of litharge
" or other 'driers' as before given is not necessary."

[Printed, 4d. No Drawings.]

A.D. 1865, October 12.—N° 2630.

LERENARD, AUGUSTE AIMÉ.—This consists, in reference to
this subject, in making india-rubber cements as follows :—"To
" make 36 lbs. of mastic, I take about 12 lbs. of solution of
" indian-rubber, 6 lbs. of rag paper pulp, 12 lbs. of plastic clay
" 4 lbs. red ochre or other colouring material, and 2½ lbs. of
" flour of sulphur; total 36½ lbs." The mixing is between
rollers heated inside by steam "some solution of india-rubber is
" first poured between the rollers then some pounded paper pulp,
" again indian-rubber solution and then again paper pulp, and so
" on until the whole quantity of both these materials is mixed to-
" gether," the clay in a plastic state is mixed between the rollers
together with the mixture already made, then the red ochre or
any other colouring matter; when thoroughly mixed the sulphur
is added and the whole thoroughly incorporated. "For water or
" gas joints sulphur must not be added to the mixture, and

" for gas joints more paper pulp must be added. This cement
" may be used generally as a waterproofing or anti-hygrometric
" coating, but for such purpose it is composed of indian-rubber
" and clay only."

[Printed, 10d. Drawing.]

A.D. 1865, October 14.—N° 2653.

MAC MILLAN, WILLIAM JARDINE COMBE, MASON, JAMES, and SCARBOROUGH, JOHN VICKERS.—This invention consists, in reference to this subject, in compositions for preserving and keeping clean the bottoms of iron vessels or of iron structures exposed to the action of the atmosphere or water. "Take equal
" parts of resin and gutta percha, dissolve in bi-sulphuret of
" carbon, naptha or other solvent, bring the solution to the con-
" sistency of varnish." A coating is also made of equal pro-
" portions of gutta-percha and phosphorus. A third "anti-
" fouling coating" is made as follows, "take of phosphorus
" 0·125 parts, of gutta percha 500 parts, bi-sulphuret of carbon
" 2·000 parts, dissolve, after being in solution, add turpentine
" 0·250 parts, all by weight."

[Printed, 4d. No Drawings.]

1866.

A.D. 1866, January 31.—N° 300.

LAKE, WILLIAM ROBERT. — (*A communication from Frank Marquard.*) — "Improvements in working and treating india-
" rubber, gutta percha, and other similar gums." These are, first, treating a solution of these gums (about two pounds of the gum in about thirty-two pounds of chloroform) " with caustic
" ammonia gas or chloride of ammonia," preferring "caustic
" ammonia gas to bleach the rubber or other gum operated on." When thoroughly bleached the charging with the gas is suspended. In the Provisional Specification a stream of chlorine may also be used as a bleaching agent.

Second, agitating the rubber, &c. after bleaching with hot water until the gum is entirely freed from the bleaching agent used.

Third, treating such gums "by a distilling operation either "simultaneously with or after the washing operation in hot "water," so as to save the chloroform in a condenser as it evaporates from the gum for again using.

Fourth, treating such gums after the above manipulations re-dissolving it in a small quantity "of chloroform or other sol"vent and mixing with it phosphate of lime or the carbonate of "zinc" to give a body to it.

Fifth, subjecting such gums "to pressure in hot moulds to "harden and solidfy the gums" and this compound "may then "be put in the lathe or other mechanism to be worked and "shaped into all manner of forms and devices."

[Printed, 4d. No Drawings.]

A.D. 1866, February 8.—N° 394.

DE BRIOU, HENRY EDWARD FRANCIS.—This invention consists in reference to this subject, in making compositions for different purposes, as follows :—66 lbs. of vulcanized india-rubber cut into small pieces are placed in a large open kettle heated by a fire underneath and heated to about 360° F. with constant stirring until the contents are in a liquid state; then add 20 lbs. of vegetable pitch or asphaltum (the former by preference) and continue the stirring until it is melted and thoroughly mixed, afterwards add 10 lbs. of shellac and 10 lbs. of common rosin and in a similar manner incorporate these with the other ingredients. These proportions may be varied but the above composition is preferred; five lbs. of this composition and one gallon of bi-sulphide of carbon are put together in a close vessel, and turned about daily; in 8 or 10 days "the composition will be completely "dissolved and fit for use as a paint and otherwise." "When it "is desired that the composition shall resist the attacks of marine "animals it is compounded with poisonous materials" by stirring into 25 lbs. of the vulcanized india-rubber composition 1 oz. of "hydrocyanic acid and chlorine (chloride of cyanogen)," 2 ozs. "chlorocyanide of mercury" and 2 ozs. "Ferrocyanide of copper." Sometimes replacing the cyanide of mercury by prussian blue in the proportion of 3 ozs. for 25 lbs. of vulcanized india-rubber composition. Also, mixing with 25 lbs. vulcanized india-rubber composition, 5 ozs. Arsenite of copper, and 2 ozs. bi-cyanide of mercury. The above proportions may be varied.

[Printed, 4d. No Drawings.]

A.D. 1866, February 8.—N° 397.

FELT, NATHANIEL HENRY.—(*A communication from John Gillingham Felt.*)—Stiffenings for the heels of boots and shoes; they are made "of a composition of india-rubber, sulphur, and ground " rags or other fibres." The proportions may be varied, but the compound is preferred to consist of one part by weight of the sulphur compound of india-rubber "to two parts by weight of " fibrous materials, by preference of cotton or linen rags, ground " to a pulp, but other fibrous substances may be similarly pre-" pared and used." "These materials are intimately mixed in " an ordinary masticator or otherwise, and the compound is " moulded into form, the bottom and curved back of a stiffening " for a heel being formed in one piece; or the composition may " be rolled or formed into sheets, and the parts cut out and placed " in moulds, and subjected to heat in order to vulcanize or cure " the india-rubber compound, as is well understood when making " and curing other articles in which sulphur compounds of india-" rubber are used."

[Printed, 6*d*. Drawing.]

A.D. 1866, February 16.—N° 499.

WHITEHEAD, JAMES HEYWOOD. — Making india-rubber fabrics as follows, "the yarns or threads of which the warp and " weft of a fabric are to be composed are both or either of them " coated with a vulcanizing compound," consisting of "india-" rubber (8 parts) dissolved in naptha (28 parts), and well mixed " with powdered sulphur (1 part)," and "when woven the fabric " is to be subjected to heat, as is well understood, in order to " produce the change known as curing or vulcanization." In some cases the fabrics composed of coated yarns or threads after being woven and before being subjected to heat, are spread over with a further coating of a vulcanizing compound, and then vulcanized by heat. The threads are passed through the vulcanizing compound as often as is required.

[Printed, 4*d*. No Drawings.]

A.D. 1866, March 12.—N° 748.

MACINTOSH, JOHN.—Impervious compounds. These are in reference to this subject, as follows, 25 parts by weight of caoutchouc, gutta percha, or balata, 75 parts by weight of paraffin or stearic acid, with 25 parts by weight of coal tar naptha for the solvent, "are brought into a homogeneous plastic state by means " of mixing rollers, or in the masticator;" or brought into a plastic state by means of heat. This compound "may be rolled " or spread by suitable machinery into sheets, or moulded or " formed into articles, and vulcanised in the same way as india-" rubber."

[Printed, 4d. No Drawings.]

A.D. 1866, March 24.—N° 871.

BUCKINGHAM, JAMES.—(*Provisional protection only.*)—"The " application and use of a certain material to be employed in " admixture with india-rubber, oils, resins, or bituminous matters, " which combinations may be applied to various useful purposes." This consists "in the application and use of the material called " 'solid paraffine' in admixture with india-rubber, or resins, or " bituminous matter, or vegetable oils, the 'solid paraffine' being " used in any quantity, according to the thickness of the solution " required."

[Printed, 4d. No Drawings.]

A.D. 1866, April 2.—N° 934.

VAUGHAN, EDWARD PRIMEROSE HOWARD.—(*A communication from Sydney Rupert Pontifex.*)—Solidifying the juice or sap of the bullet tree, known as balata juice and analogous products. "The " juice or sap from the bullet tree is ordinarily obtained either by " passing the bark between pressure rollers, or by the operation " of 'tapping.'" In the latter case the juice is free from fibres, but in the former, fibres are frequently in the juice. To separate these fibres the juice is passed through felt, cocoa-nut fibre matting, or some other suitable fibrous material by pressure. The juice, fresh, or after fermentation of itself, or by adding ferments, or after adding to the juice, pure or fermented, acetic, citric, tartaric, or other analogous organic acid, or one of the alkalies, or rennet, wood naphtha, or methylated spirit to curd or coagulate the solid particles thereof, air is forced into or through the juice by means of a fan or any blowing apparatus, or by means of churning apparatus, paddles, or centrifugals, &c., but with access of air, when the solid particles separate steam or hot water may be introduced into it, or "the solid particles may be collected and removed into another receptacle, in which the steam or hot water may be caused to operate upon them;" complete coagulation ensues, any acid, &c. removed, and the mass taken out and pressed is ready for shipment. If the solid matter contained in the juice has not been sufficiently extracted therefrom, it is evaporated with stirring, oil may be at the bottom of the pan to prevent the juice or sap touching the pan, and finally, the juice evaporated in large shallow steam boxes which can be shifted into the sun's rays. Wood naphtha or methylated spirit alone or combined, precipitates the solid matter from the juice or sap. The proportions necessary are about $1\frac{1}{2}$ gallons of naphtha or spirit to 1 gallon of the sap; the solid matter is taken out and the liquid distilled for the spirit.

[Printed, 4d. No Drawings.]

A.D. 1866, April 13.—N° 1044.

JAMES, HENRY BENSON.—Compositions for attaching sheathing. This consists, in reference to this subject, of a composition prepared "by taking about two pounds of solution either of india-"rubber or of gutta percha, one pound of red lead in the usual "condition as ordinarily sold, one and a half pounds of varnish "or of varnish and mastic, the whole heated and made to the "consistency of soft putty, and applied while hot." The above proportions may be varied.

[Printed, 4d. No Drawings.]

A.D. 1866, May 3.—N° 1257.

BOURNE, STEPHEN.—"Improvements in treating india-rubber "and india-rubber compounds and also india-rubber fabrics." These are "removing the odour and flavour from the same, by "heating them in the presence of charcoal, by preference, animal "charcoal." "The method of applying the animal charcoal will "vary according to the nature of the article to be treated." An arrangement by which the article to be deodorized is heated between layers of charcoal is desirable. Within vulcanized articles a temperature of 120° to 150° F., "may be safely employed and "continued for three or four hours;" with partially vulcanized "articles a temperature of 180° F. may be used, and to fully "vulcanized articles 212° F. or even higher" may be applied and continued for six hours or more, and this will be necessary when the article is stout. "At the end of the operation the articles are " at once removed, and the charcoal shaken off or otherwise re- " moved." The same charcoal may employed, say six or more times, and is finally restored by re-burning.

[Printed, 4d. No Drawings.]

A.D. 1866, May 8.—N° 1305.

MOSELEY, CHARLES. — "Improvements in machinery and " apparatus used in the manufacture of sheets of india-rubber." These are said to be "the taking up motion" and also the apply- ing of a "stream of water to the back of the cutting knife of " machines for cutting india-rubber into sheets" as described. Two levers are fixed upon the centres of two rollers, one of these rollers revolving in a fixed bearing; "the other rests upon the " block of india-rubber to be cut into sheets; this roller rises " or falls according to the diameter of the block. As the block " revolves it comes in contact with the cutting knife, as usual, " which by an oscillating motion cuts from it a sheet which passes " over guide rollers. As the block revolves it gives a motion to " the roller bearing on it, which by means of straps and pulleys " gives a rotatory motion to the roller, over which passes the " sheet of india-rubber, and as the roller bearing on the block of " india-rubber has a surface speed corresponding to that of the " block, which decreases as the block decreases in diameter, the " sheet of india-rubber is kept at one exact tension. The same " effect may also be produced by self-acting cone pulleys to give " a positive motion to the drawing roller corresponding to the " decreasing surface speed of the block. It is necessary in cutting " india-rubber to have a stream of water running upon the face " of the knife to reduce friction; but to produce a smooth surface " upon both sides of the sheet, a stream of water is applied to the " back of the knife in addition to that at the front."

[Printed, 8d. Drawing.]

A.D. 1866, May 21.—N° 1431.

DUNLOP, JOHN MACMILLAN.—"Improvements in machinery " for cutting india-rubber." These are, "the combined arrange- " ment by which a worm is made to gear with and actuate the " cutter slide by a rack, and then to separate from such rack and " admit of the cutter slide being moved back, and combined

" therewith the stopping of the lathe and the actuating the ordi-
" nary ratchet wheel by the moving back of the cutter slide," as
follows :—To cut into thread sheet india-rubber it is "wound
" round a cylinder, and the succeeding coils are cemented together
" with cement as heretofore. An ordinary lathe is employed to
" which is applied a block shaft parallel with the bed of the lathe;
" this shaft receives motion by a band or strap from the overhead
" shaft, or it might be driven from the head-stock of the lathe.
" The back shaft by a screw or worm gives motion to a worm
". wheel on another or cross shaft at right angles to the back
" shaft, such cross shaft having a worm or screw thereon which
" takes into and gives motion to a rack fixed on the cutter slide,
" or such cross shaft may give motion to an intermediate shaft
" between it and the slide which carries the knife or cutter up to
" the cylinder on which the sheet india-rubber is wound so as to
" cut in a direction from the surface of the india-rubber up
" towards the centre of the cylinder on which it is wound. One
" end of the cross shaft is arranged to drop so that the screw or
" worm descends away from the teeth of the rack (or intermediate
" motion) of the cutter slide so soon as the cutter has cut through
" the coils of india-rubber on the cylinder. Immediately after
" the dropping of the worm or screw out of gear a cam or an
" eccentric is brought into action to move back the cutter slide.
" On the dropping of the worm or screw out of the teeth of the
" rack or intermediate motion a partial rotation is given to a cross
" shaft, by which not only is the cam or eccentric brought into
" action as above mentioned, but the lathe is stopped by throwing
" off the band or strap from the fast to the loose pulley on the
" over head shaft, and by putting on a break. The same motion
" which moves the cutter slide back by means of the eccentric or
" cam gives the traverse of the cutter slide by its screw and
" ordinary division wheel, which are caused to rotate a distance
" requisite for cutting the thickness of thread desired."

[Printed, 1s. Drawings.]

A.D. 1866, June 19.—N° 1649.

BOUSFIELD, GEORGE TOMLINSON.—(*A communication from Charles McBurney.*)—" An improved process of utilizing waste
" vulcanized india-rubber and manufacturing hard rubber there-
" from." This consists, first, in utilising "waste scraps or
" worn-out articles of vulcanized rubber, such as old boots, car-

" springs, &c., &c.," as follows :—These articles are reduced to powder by some means and the powder is moistened with water, on standing for a few weeks this product is ready for use, when, twenty pounds of this prepared powder and two to four pounds of crude rubber are well combined by grinding rolls, after which they are gradually mixed with from "three to five pounds of oil," " such as cotton seed oil, olive oil, castor oil, palm oil, or cocoa-" nut oil," this compound is more perfectly prepared by submitting it "to a low steam heat (not exceeding 230° Fahrenheit) for " from four to ten hours," forms a valuable product "which " may be extensively used in connection with other rubber " compounds." The proportions above given may be varied.

Second, in making "hard rubber or vulcanite" which is composed chiefly of the best quality of gum (or at least more than half its weight of the best gum) the other ingredients being " sulphur, litharge, white lead, magnesia, and lampblack in " various quantities," now it is proposed to take twenty pounds of the compound " above described, four pounds best crude " rubber, four to six pounds sulphur, one or two pounds lamp-" black, from one quarter to one pound calcined magnesia, and " for some purposes one or more pounds litharge or white lead. " The proportion of all these articles may vary or some of them " may be omitted in some cases."

[Printed, 4d. No Drawings.]

A.D. 1866, June 22.—N° 1667.

HUNT, EDMUND.—" Improvements in dissolving or treating " rubber, gutta percha, copal, and similar gums or resins, and " their compounds." These are, "the employing of an acid or " alkaline substance which is an oleagenous fluid at any tem-" perature below 300 degrees Fahrenheit for dissolving or treat-" ing difficultly soluble gums or resins, such us rubber, gutta " percha, or copal and their compounds, and especially the recover-" ing or renovating of vulcanized or mineralized rubber by means " substantially as follows :"—In the case of vulcanized rubber, the rubber, by preference, reduced to small particles is treated with oleic acid, which if necessary should "be freed from sulphuric " acid by washing with water;" heat aids the action, but not above 300°, 240° F. preferred. Agitation or stirring also hastens the dissolving action. To separate the rubber from the oleic acid the solution is allowed to cool, methylated spirit added, precipitates the rubber, and the rubber is washed once or twice in fresh spirit, boiled " in a very weak solution of caustic soda, " and afterwards in pure water." The result on " being dried " and heated to the ordinary ' curing ' temperature has thereby " restored to it the properties of ordinary vulcanized rubber." Before curing it may " be manufactured into various forms, alone " or in combination with new rubber and dissolved in benzine " and similar volatile fluids it may be used for waterproofing."

[Printed, 4d. No Drawing.]

A.D. 1866, July 12.—Nº 1826.

MOSELEY, JOSEPH.—Manufacturing of card cloth. This consists, in reference to this subject, taking " equal portions by weight " of india-rubber or any preparation of india-rubber and cotton " waste or other suitable fibrous substances, these ingredients, " either with or without a solvent, are intimately mixed or com- " bined together by passing them through friction rollers, and " the compound so prepared is then rolled out into sheets by " passing between other rollers either heated or not heated as " may be required."

[Printed, 4d. No Drawings.]

A.D. 1866, September 20.—Nº 2418.

CRUMP, CHARLES.—(*Provisional protection only*.)—Solvent for gutta percha, tetrachloride of carbon. " Tetrachloride of carbon " may also be used in conjunction with linseed or other oils, " rendered drying in the usual manner as a solvent " for gutta percha, or as a substitute for alcohol. Caoutchouc also is to a " considerable extent soluble therein, so that it may be used in " place of bisulphide of carbon or other liquids now employed " by india-rubber manufacturers."

[Printed, 4d. No Drawings.]

A.D. 1866, October 3.—Nº 2541.

FORSTER, THOMAS.—Elastic mats and coverings for floors. This consists, in the reference to this subject, first, " the making " of elastic mats and coverings for floors the parts of which are " of tubes or other forms of different heights, so that parts of " the surfaces of such mats and coverings shall be at different

" levels, and thus more effectively serve to wipe or scrape boots
" or shoes." The mixture used is composed of india-rubber
10 lbs., oxide or zinc 5 lbs. sulphur 1 lb., and ground rags
2½ lbs, or any of the suitable compounds of india-rubber;
and " in place of using one uniform proportion of india-
" rubber compound for making up the tubular parts or forms
" by which the perforated cellular character is produced,"
using "various coloured preparations of india-rubber of like or
" different shapes or forms, and in building up or forming the
" desired cellular structure," employing " different coloured
" pieces of india-rubber compound, and put them together in
" such manner as to produce various patterns, or what may be
" termed mosaic work."

Second, "ornamenting the mats or other coverings for floors
" by cementing on them veneers or thin sheets of coloured india-
" rubber, so as to form a pattern or what may be termed ' mosaic
" 'work.' As most colors are much deteriorated during the
" process of vulcanization it is necessary to use a large quantity
" of color to a small portion of rubber, using, by preference, in
" all cases sulphurets, such as those obtained with arsenic, zinc,
" antimony, and mercury, also the oxides of zinc and chro-
" mium."

[Printed, 1s. Drawings.]

A.D. 1866, October 19.—N° 2707.

SIMPSON, EDWIN LINDSEY.—" An improved process for the
" preparation of india-rubber and kindred gums." This consists
as follows, first, a " compound of vegetable oil, sulphur, and benzoin." The sulphur is reduced to powder; two ounces of the
gum are mixed with one pound of sulphur, and to each quart
of the oil boiled are added one pound of the prepared sulphur.
This mixture heated moderately, the result is a semi-fluid or
semi-solid material having ." a honecomb or spongy appearance "
forming the vulcanizing compound.

Second, combining the material made as above with india-
rubber, gutta percha, or other similar gums, two ounces of the
compound, one pound of india rubber or gutta percha, eight
ounces litharge, and " to increase the quantity at the expense of
" the quality" adding " about eight ounces of whiting."

Third, coating fabrics with the above preparation.

Fourth, combining the above vulcanizing compound with india-rubber or gutta percha in the following proportions for a material for dental purposes. To one pound of rubber, &c., adding ten to fourteen ounces of the compound, twelve ounces believed to be the "proper quantity for general purposes," grinding between warm rolls, coloring by means of chrome red or lake pink, rolling into thin sheets. When the dentist form the plate it is heated for about four hours to 320° F.

Fifth, forming the same as above into various articles of commerce known as hard rubber.

Sixth, applying the same to fabrics.

Seventh, the rubber or gutta percha when applied to fabrics as above mentioned, "may be 'flocked' in the usual manner of " flocking similar coated fabrics."

[Printed, 4d. No Drawings.]

A.D. 1866, November 7.—N° 2886.

DARLOW, WILLIAM, and SEYMOUR, PHILIP WILLIAM.— A new magnetic compound. This consists, in reference to this subject, " when it is required to produce an elastic or flexible com-
" pound, we employ gums, india-rubber, gutta percha, or their
" compounds, and combine with them as large a proportion of
" the magnetic element as the composition will bear without be-
" coming what is termed 'rotten.' The proportions that have
" been found most suitable for this kind of compound are from
" one and a half to one and three quarters pound of the magnetic
" element to each pound of the gum or adhesive substance, but
" we do not confine ourselves to these exact proportions, as they
" will depend upon the quality or kind of gums used." The gums, india-rubber, or gutta percha are reduced to a pasty or fluid consistency by any of the well-known methods, "when the steel
" fillings or other magnetic element of the compound is introduced
" and well incorporated therewith; then after such incorporation
" of the two elements of the compound it is either rolled into
" sheets or moulded into any required shape, and, if required,
" vulcanized."

[Printed, 4d. No Drawings.]

A.D. 1866, November 13.—N° 2966.

MOSELEY, CHARLES.—(*Letters Patent void for want of Final Specification.*)—" Machinery for the manufacture of india-rubber

" thread." The "solid cylindrical block or hollow cylinder of
" india-rubber, vulcanized or otherwise prepared, or in its natural
" state," is "put upon a mandril or centre, and receiving a slow
" rotary and lateral or progressive motion is cut upon its outer
" surface by a series of knives having a quick rotary, oscillating
" or sliding motion, and by a knife having a reciprocating motion
" given by steam or other power, thus producing a series of
" threads or filaments of india-rubber."

[Printed, 4d. No Drawings.]

A.D. 1866, November 16.—N° 3012.

DUNLOP, JOHN MACMILLAN, and CROSSLEY, FRANK.—
" Improvements in machinery for cutting india-rubber." These
are, "in order to cut sheet india-rubber into thread it is lapped
" around a mandril, and mounted in a lathe with a self-acting
" slide rest. A cutter moving from the circumference of the roll
" of india-rubber towards the centre or mandril cuts off threads
" from its end. After each cut the tool is caused to move back
" rapidly, and before the next cut commences it is traversed a
" short distance," by this invention "to give the forward and
" backward movement to the tool a rocking shaft is employed to
" a sliding arm on which the tool holder is linked," receiving
" its motion by means of two curved tails upon it, which are acted
" on by studs on the faces of two wheels, one on either side of the
" curved tails; the studs act on the two tails alternately so as to
" produce the rocking movement; the wheel which produces the
" inward motion of the cutter carries several (usually six) studs
" and moves slowly, and so it gives a slow motion to the tool.
" The wheel which produces the outward motion carries usually
" but one stud and moves rapidly, and so gives a rapid return
" motion to the tool." The feed motion is "given by means of a
" cam on the axis of the last-mentioned wheel, which acts on the
" lever of a clutch, and clutches for a time a spur wheel to it
" which drives the feed screw. The length of time during which
" the clutch is held in so as to drive the feed motion is regulated
" by a disc in connection with the feed screw; the disc has
" notches in it at regular intervals, into which a projection on the
" clutch lever drops, and when this lever is raised by the cam it
" cannot return until the feed screw has travelled so far as to enable
" it to fall into the next notch on the divided plate or disc." Or

in place of this arrangement, on the axis of the feed screw is mounted "a star wheel, and on the axis which in the former "arrangement carried the cam and clutch is mounted a locking "disc and pin for locking and driving the screw alternately."

[Printed, 1s. 8d. Drawings.]

INDEX OF SUBJECT MATTER.

[The numbers refer to the pages on which the Abridgments commence. The names printed in *Italic* are those of the persons by whom the inventions have been communicated to the Applicants for Letters Patent.]

Albuminous substances. See Compounds of gutta percha, &c.; Compounds of india-rubber, &c.

Alcohol. See Solvents, &c.

Ale. See Solvents, &c.

Alkalies. See Compounds of india-rubber, &c.

Alum. See Compounds of gutta percha, &c.; Compounds of india-rubber, &c.

Aluminium, acetate of. See Compounds of india-rubber, &c.

Ammonia. See Solvents, &c.

Aniline. See Solvents, &c.

Antimony, sulphuret of. See Vulcanizing.

Arcanson. See Compounds of gutta percha, &c.

Arsenic. See Compounds of india-rubber, &c., (poisonous materials); Vulcanizing.

Asbestos. See Compounds of gutta percha, &c.; Compounds of india-rubber, &c.

Asphalte. See Compounds of gutta percha, &c.; Compounds of india-rubber, &c.

Ballata. See also Compounds of gutta percha, &c.; Compounds of india-rubber, &c.
    Hancock and Silver, 213.
    Silver (*Manifold*), 233.
    Silver (*Manifold*), 233.
    Parkes, 240.
    Hancock and Silver, 241.
    Macintosh, 252.
    Vaughan (*Pontifex*), 253.

Balsams. See Compounds of gutta percha, &c.

Bands and belts. See also Thread and string, &c.:
    Westhead, 5.
    Nickels, 13.
    Alsop and Forster, 22.
    Clark, 24.
    Burke, 44.
    Harrison and Harrison, 61.
    Scoutetten, 73.
    Waithman, 84.
    Johnson (*Steinlen*), 111.
    Parmelee, 129.
    Kirrage, 140.
    Newton (*Cheever*), 168.
    Bridges, 172.
    Richard, 173.
    Newton (*Cheever*), 181.
    Miller, 191.
    West, 197.
    Lerenard, 207.
    De la Bastida (*Cohen and Vaillant*), 207.
    Hancock and Silver, 213.
    Gérard, 214.
    Hooper, 218.
    Bousfield (*Taylor*), 225.
    Spill, Briggs, and Spill, 225.
    Mulholland, 227.
    Jennings and Lavater, 228.
    Clark, 229.
    Bousfield (*Taylor*), 232.
    Coles, Jaques, and Fanshawe, 235.

INDEX OF SUBJECT MATTER.

Bands and belts—*cont.*
   Gerard, 236.
   Lavater, 238.
   Hancock and Silver, 241.
   Collins, 244.
   Abel, 247.

Benzole. *See* Solvents, &c.

Bitumen. *See* Compounds of gutta percha, &c., (asphalte); Compounds of india-rubber, &c., (asphalte).

Bones; Borax; Boron. *See* Compounds of gutta percha, &c.

Bromine. *See* Compounds of gutta percha, &c.; Compounds of india-rubber, &c.

Camphine; Camphor. *See* Solvents, &c.

Carbon, bisulphide and chlorides of. *See* Solvents, &c.

Casein. *See* Compounds of gutta percha, &c.; Compounds of india-rubber, &c.

Catechu. *See* Compounds of gutta percha, &c.

Catimundo:
   Duncan, 50.

Cementing, preparations of india-rubber and gutta percha for. *See* Coating and cementing.

Chapapote. *See* Solvents, &c

Charcoal. *See* Compounds of gutta percha, &c.—charcoal, (animal) and charcoal (vegetable).

Chlorides, vulcanizing by means of. *See* Vulcanizing (chlorides, &c.; and sulphur, chloride or hypo-chloride of).

Chlorine. *See* Compounds of gutta percha, &c.; Compounds of india-rubber, &c.

Chloroform. *See* Solvents, &c.

Clamminess or stickiness, removing:
   Hancock, 17.
   Forster, 19.
   Newton, 48.
   Newton, 91.
   Brooman, 99.
   Hull, 215.
   Humfrey, 230.

Clay. *See* Compounds of gutta percha, &c.

Cleansing. *See* Preparing, &c.

Chromium. *See* Compounds of india-rubber, &c.

Coal; Coal tar. *See* Compounds of gutta percha, &c.; Compounds of india-rubber, &c.

Coal tar, oil of. *See* Solvents, &c.

Coating and cementing, preparations of india-rubber and gutta percha for. *See also* Solvents, &c.:
   Fabrics and paper;
   Peal, 1.
   Johnson, 1.
   Clark, 2.
   Macintosh, 2.
   Weise, 3.
   Hancock, 4.
   Pickersgill, 8.
   Hancock, 10.
   Hancock, 11.
   Bethell, 12.
   Keene, 14.
   Fanshawe, 15.
   Hancock, 16.
   Hancock, 17.
   Newton, 19.
   Forster, 19.
   Brockedon and Hancock, 30.
   Moulton, 32.
   Hancock, 33.
   Forster, 37.
   Westhead, 38.
   Hancock, 38.
   Burke, 44.
   Poole (*Goodyear*), 57.
   Poole (*Goodyear*), 58.
   Scoutetten, 73.
   Brookes, 74.
   De Varroc, 78.
   Gidley and Muschamp, 81.
   Fry, 82.

INDEX OF SUBJECT MATTER. 265

Coating and cementing—*cont.*
  Fabrics and paper—*cont.*
    Johnson (*Guibal*), 83.
    Waithman, 84.
    White, 85.
    Trumble, 86.
    Assanti, 86.
    Stoneham, 93.
    Rimmel (*Magen*), 96.
    Fanshawe and Fanshawe, 98.
    Hill, 101.
    Cornides, 102.
    Bielefeld, 105.
    Ford, 108.
    Ford, 110.
    Ford, 112.
    Metcalf, 114.
    Ford, 115.
    Lorimier, 116.
    Jeune, 118.
    Spill, 124.
    De Clippéle, 125.
    Blizzard, 126.
    Candelot, 127.
    Parker, 128.
    Parmelee, 129.
    Newton, 130.
    Henson, 131.
    Luis, 134.
    Vasserot (*Beuchot*), 141.
    Henson, 142.
    Clark, 147.
    Moseley, 149.
    Walton, 156.
    Daft, 160.
    Turner, 163.
    Turner, 163.
    Newton (*Engelhard and Day*), 164.
    Hancock, 167.
    Magnus and Sinnock, 167.
    Newton, (*Cheever*), 168.
    Lemoine, 172.
    Luis (*Lecocq*), 173.
    Newton (*Cheever*), 179.
    Newton (*Cheever*), 181.
    Harrison, 182.
    Burke and Burke, 183.
    Brooman (*Duhousset and Thomas*), 185.
    Jeune, 194.
    Mc Kay, 195.
    Ford, 198.
    Bowra, 200.
    Fajole and Agostini, 202.
    Harby, 203.
    Brant, 205.
    Kidd, 205.
    Newton (*Elmer*), 206.
    De la Bastida (*Cohen and Vaillant*), 207.
    Brooman)*Baldamus*), 211.
    Warden (*Baldamus*), 214.
    Henson, 216.
    Bousfield (*Hayward*), 217.
    Hughes (*Hodgskin*), 219.
    Gilbee (*Mathevon*), 219.

Coating and cementing—*cont.*
  Fabrics and paper—*cont.*
    Simpson, 220.
    Kirrage, 222.
    Snell (*Wiese*), 223.
    Bousfield (*Taylor*), 225.
    Spill, Briggs, and Spill, 225.
    Norris (*Holl*), 226.
    Bousfield (*Mayall*), 230.
    Bousfield (*Taylor*), 232.
    Jennings and Lavater, 233.
    Bateman, 235.
    Lavater, 238.
    Fontainemoreau (*Lemaistre and Co.*), 240.
    Stevens (*Stevens*), 242.
    Mayall, 246.
    Mayall, 246.
    Abel, 247.
    Smith, 249.
    Lerenard, 249.
    Whitehead, 252.
    Bourne, 254.
    Hunt, 257.
    Simpson, 259.
  Leather;
    Peal, 1.
    Macintosh, 2.
    Fleetwood, 3.
    Keene, 14.
    Hancock, 17.
    Wright, 18.
    Forster, 19.
    Brockedon and Hancock, 30.
    Hancock, 33.
    Burke, 44.
    Duncan, 71.
    De Varroc, 78.
    Ogg, 92.
    Rimmel (*Magen*), 96.
    Cornides, 102.
    Newton, 121.
    Codet-Négrier, 122.
    King, 124.
    Candelot, 127.
    Parker, 128.
    Gooderham, 128.
    Stevens (*Chapa and Lacaze*), 184.
    Brooman (*Duhousset and Thomas*), 185.
    Stevens, (*Lacaze*), 195.
    Mc Kay, 195.
    Brant, 205.
    Newton (*Elmer*), 206.
    Clarkson, 228.
    Kemp and Kemp, 239.
    Fontainemoreau (*Lemaistre and Co.*), 240.
    Harton, 244.
    Miller, 249.
  Metals;
    Hancock, 4.
    Hancock, 33.
    Hancock, 38.
    Poole (*Goodyear*), 56.

INDEX OF SUBJECT MATTER.

Coating and cementing—cont.
  Metals—cont.
    Poole (Goodyear), 87.
    De Vavroc, 88.
    Johnson (Lefevre), 81.
    Ryder and Ryder, 87.
    Johnson, 102.
    Ford, 103.
    Deal, 112.
    Yanlen and Chapman, 113.
    Caudelot, 127.
    Parker, 128.
    Newton, 130.
    Macintosh, 132.
    Smith, 132.
    Macintosh, 132.
    Hope, 137.
    Wray, 137.
    West, 139.
    Hancock, 143.
    Duncan, 145.
    Warne, Fanshawe, Jaques, and Galpin, 146.
    Cowper (Bingham), 146.
    Sinnock, 146.
    Warne, Fanshawe, Jaques, and Galpin, 152.
    Warne, Fanshawe, Jaques, and Galpin, 152.
    Chatterton, 163.
    Gisborne and Magnus, 163.
    Daft, 163.
    Macintosh, 163.
    Daft, 164.
    Chatterton and Smith, 166.
    Hancock, 167.
    Hooper, 170.
    Silver and Barwick, 174.
    Hooper, 175.
    Macintosh, 176.
    Harrison, 182.
    Brooman (Duhoussot and Thounes), 185.
    Moulton, 185.
    Hay, 185.
    Miller, 192.
    Godefroy, 192.
    West, 197.
    Myers and Myers, 202.
    Harby, 203.
    Brunt, 205.
    Leronard, 207.
    De la Bastide (Cohen and Vaillant), 207.
    Devlan, 209.
    Cartwright, 210.
    Rémaître, 211.
    Fuller, 211.
    Duncan, 212.
    Griffin, 212.
    Hancock and Silver, 215.
    Siemens, 216.
    Hooper, 218.
    Brooman (Authoine and Brossette), 221.
    Bonneville (Gérard), 225.
    Mennons (Friemsby), 226.

Coating and cementing—cont.
  Metals—cont.
    Mulholland, 224.
    Mulholland, 227.
    Jennings and Lavater, 228.
    De Brion, 228.
    Ritchie, 228.
    Fontainemoreau (Lemaistre and Co.), 240.
    Parkes, 247.
    Abel, 247.
    Leronard, 249.
    Mac Millan, Mason, and Scarborough, 252.
    James, 254.
  Other materials;
    Peal, 1.
    Macintosh, 2.
    Fleetwood, 3.
    Bethell, 16.
    Hancock, 20.
    Brockedon, 22.
    Hancock, 55.
    Hancock, 56.
    Ley, 64.
    Duncan, 71.
    Barrett, 72.
    De Vavroc, 78.
    Johnson (Lefevre), 81.
    Stansbury (Arthur), 92.
    Metcalf, 114.
    Richardson, 122.
    Caudelot, 127.
    Parker, 128.
    Brooman (Duhoussot and Thounes), 165.
    Hay, 185.
    Silver and Griffin, 186.
    Mc Kay, 194.
    Brunt, 203.
    Kidd, 205.
    Duncan, 212.
    Griffin, 212.
    Brooman (Authoine and Brossette), 222.
    Twilley and Laird, 231.
    Benson, 238.
    Fontainemoreau (Lemaistre and Co.), 240.

  Paper. See Fabrics.

Coke. See Compounds of india-rubber, &c.

Colcothar. See Compounds of india-rubber, &c.

Collodion. See Compounds of gutta percha, &c.; (gun-cotton).; Compounds of india-rubber, &c. (gun-cotton).

INDEX OF SUBJECT MATTER.

Colouring matters, blending with india-rubber, &c. See Compounds of gutta percha, &c., (pigments); Compounds of india-rubber, &c., (pigments).

Compounds of gutta percha with various ingredients. See also Vulcanizing, &c.; Fibres, mixing, &c.; Jistawan, &c.:

   Albuminous substances;
      Duncan, 71.
      Johnson (Lefevre), 81.
      Johnson, 90.
      Johnson, 110.
   Alum;
      Payne, 45.
      Wray, 137.
      Ghislin, 264.
   Arsenson;
      Twilley and Lainé, 261.
   Asbestos;
      Warne, Fanshawe, Jaques, and Galpin, 160.
      Patrick, 165.
   Asphalte;
      Hancock, 25.
      Hancock, 32.
      Hancock, 38.
      Cooley, 61.
      Ryder and Ryder, 87.
      Ogg, 92.
      Goodyear, 134.
      Wray, 137.
      Warne, Fanshawe, Jaques, and Galpin, 140.
      Sinnock, 160.
      Warne, Fanshawe, Jaques, and Galpin, 162.
      Duncan, 212.
      Henson, 216.
   Bafista;
      Hancock and Silver, 213.
   Balsams;
      Duncan, 71.
      Rostaing, 167.
   Bitumen. See Asphalte.
   Bones (ground);
      Forster, 37.
   Borax;
      Hancock, 40.
   Boron;
      Duvivier and Chaudet, 98.
   Bromine;
      Shephard, 200.
      Norris (Holt), 205.

Compound of gutta percha, &c. —cont.

   Caseine. See Albuminous substances.
   Catechu;
      Johnson, 104.
      Hughes, 117.
      Rostaing, 167.
   Charcoal (animal);
      Forster, 37.
      Warne, Fanshawe, Jaques, and Galpin, 140.
   Charcoal (vegetable);
      Marland, 131.
      Warne, Fanshawe, Jaques, and Galpin, 162.
      Macintosh, 161.
      Shiver and Griffin, 188.
      Ghislin, 264.
   Chlorine;
      Newton (Englehard and Day), 104.
      Newton (Hassmann), 105.
      Newton (Hassmann), 144.
      Shephard, 200.
      Norris (Holt), 205.
      Lake (Marquard), 260.
   Clay. See Earths.
   Coal;
      Latta, 140.
   Coal tar;
      Vernebert, 114.
      Lais, 134.
      Kirmage, 140.
      Warne, Fanshawe, Jaques, and Galpin, 162.
      Shephard, 200.
   Collodion. See Gun-cotton.
   Copper, oxides or salts of;
      Lorimer, 41.
      Newton, 69.
      Ford, 101.
   Cork;
      Hancock, 20.
      Hancock, 34.
      Newton, 69.
      Henson, 131.
      Warne, Jaques, and Fanshawe, 140.
      Cowper (Bingham), 168.
      Williams, 184.
      Ford, 197.
      Henson, 216.
      Fontainemoreau (Innocent and Perronet), 243.
   Earths. See also Pigments.
      Silicates;
      Brockman, 22.
      Hancock, 29.
      Brockedon and Hancock, 30.

INDEX OF SUBJECT MATTER.

Compounds of gutta percha, &c. —*cont.*
  Earths—*cont.*
    Hancock, 38.
    Lorimer, 41.
    Payne, 45.
    Newton (*Goodyear*), 49.
    Moulton, 50.
    Duthoit, 51.
    Cooley, 61.
    Newton, 68.
    Sorel, 85.
    Butcher and Newey, 107.
    Johnson (*Wacrenier*), 109.
    Palmer, 112.
    Ritchie, 114.
    Newton, 118.
    Danne, 122.
    Day, 122.
    Candelot, 127.
    Blizzard, 131.
    Wray, 137.
    Kirrage, 140.
    Warne, Jaques, and Fanshawe, 142.
    Warne, Fanshawe, Jaques, and Galpin, 148.
    Cowper (*Bingham*), 148.
    Warne, Fanshawe, Jaques, and Galpin, 150.
    Warne, Fanshawe, Jaques, and Galpin, 152.
    Childs, 153.
    Patrick, 155.
    Newton (*Mayall*), 156.
    Newton (*Green*), 157.
    Newton (*Baker*), 161.
    Rostaing, 167.
    Newton (*Cheever*), 168.
    Luis (*Lecocq*), 173.
    Williams, 196.
    Bowra, 200.
    Shephard, 200.
    Duncan, 212.
    Henson, 216.
    Hooper, 218.
    Kirrage, 222.
    Mennons (*Briansky*), 223.
    Norris (*Holl*), 226.
    Bousfield (*Mayall*), 230.
    Ghislin, 234.
    Lake (*Marquard*), 250.
    Simpson, 259.
  Emery;
    Brooman, 22.
    Brockedon and Hancock, 30.
    Ritchie, 114.
    Danne, 122.
    Cowper (*Bingham*), 148.
    Newton (*Mayall*), 156.
    Shephard, 200.
    Duncan, 212.
  Fatty substances. *See* Wax or Tallow.
  Fibrin. *See* Albuminous substances.

Compounds of gutta percha, &c. —*cont.*
  French chalk;
    Brooman, 22.
    Newton (*Cheever*), 168.
    Henson, 216.
    Hooper, 218.
    Kirrage, 222.
    Bousfield (*Mayall*), 230.
  Gelatin. *See* Glue.
  Glass (powdered). *See* Silicates.
  Glue, gelatin, isinglass, or size;
    Hancock, 36.
    Johnson (*Lefevre*), 81.
    Johnson, 90.
    Bielefeld, 105.
    Hughes, 117.
    Newton, 120.
    Ghislin, 234.
  Gluten. *See* Albuminous substances.
  Gold, oxide of;
    Ninck, 119.
  Gums;
    Hancock, 25.
    Forster, 36.
    Forster, 37.
    Hancock, 38.
    Barlow and Forster, 40.
    Hancock, 40.
    Ricardo, 42.
    Payne, 45.
    Newton (*Goodyear*), 49.
    Cooley, 61.
    Dundonald, 69.
    Duncan, 71.
    Scoutetten, 73.
    Johnson (*Lefevre*), 81.
    Ryder and Ryder, 87.
    Forty and Haynes, 87.
    Newton, 89.
    Johnson, 90.
    Cornides, 102.
    Bielefeld, 105.
    Latta, 109.
    Johnson, 110.
    Newton, 118.
    Codet-Négrier, 122.
    Blizzard, 131.
    Wray, 137.
    Kirrage, 140.
    Hancock, 142.
    Duncan, 143.
    Cowper (*Bingham*), 148.
    Patrick, 155.
    Lemoine, 172.
    Ford, 198.
    Shephard, 200.
    Henson, 216.
    Hooper, 218.
    Brooman (*Anthoine and Brossette*), 222.
    Twilley and Lainé, 231.
    Bateman, 235.
    Harton, 244.

INDEX OF SUBJECT MATTER. 269

Compounds of gutta percha, &c.
—*cont.*
  Gums—*cont.*
    Mayall, 246.
    James, 254.
  Gun cotton, or collodion ;
    Macintosh, 130.
    Parkes, 247.
  India-rubber ;
    Hancock, 20.
    Brooman, 22.
    Hancock, 29.
    Brockedon and Hancock, 30.
    Hancock, 33.
    Burke, 44.
    Payne, 45.
    Newton (*Goodyear*), 49.
    Moulton, 50.
    Duthoit, 51.
    Rider, 51.
    Cooley, 61.
    Newton, 68.
    Nickels, 70.
    Duncan, 71.
    Scoutetten, 73.
    Sorel, 85.
    Forty and Haynes, 87.
    Johnson, 90.
    Johnson, 91.
    Goodyear, 100.
    Cornides, 102.
    Johnson, 103.
    Job and Tomlinson, 107.
    Turner, 111.
    Jeune, 112.
    Yeadon and Chapman, 113.
    Ritchie, 114.
    Goodyear, 114.
    Jeune, 118.
    Newton, 118.
    Ninck, 119.
    Taylor, 121.
    Codet-Négrier, 122.
    King, 124.
    Candelot, 127.
    Macintosh, 127.
    Luis, 134.
    Hope, 137.
    Wray, 137.
    Kirrage, 140.
    Hancock, 142.
    Warne, Jaques, and Fanshawe, 142.
    Cowper (*Bingham*), 148.
    Sinnock, 150.
    Warne, Fanshawe, Jaques, and Galpin, 150.
    Warne, Fanshawe, Jaques, and Galpin, 152.
    Turner, 163.
    Turner, 163.
    Magnus and Sinnock, 167.
    Chatterton and Smith, 171.
    Newton (*Havemann*), 184.
    Chatterton, 186.

Compounds of gutta percha, &c.
—*cont.*
  India-rubber—*cont.*
    Hunt, 192.
    Williams, 196.
    Ford, 197.
    Ford, 198.
    Forster, 199.
    Cartwright, 204.
    Newton (*Elmer*), 206.
    Hancock and Silver, 213.
    Warden (*Baldamus*), 214.
    Henson, 216.
    Cartwright, 216.
    Hooper, 218.
    Kirrage, 222.
    Mulet, 224.
    Bousfield (*Taylor*), 225.
    Spill, Briggs, and Spill, 225.
    Norris (*Holl*), 226.
    Twilley and Lainé, 231.
    Bateman, 235.
    Ritchie, 238.
    Fontainemoreau (*Innocent and Perroncel*), 243.
    Darlow and Seymour, 260.
  Iron, oxides of ;
    Hancock, 36.
    Newton, 68.
    Scoutetten, 73.
    Goodyear, 100.
    Warne, Fanshawe, Jaques, and Galpin, 150.
    Brant, 205.
    Mennons (*Briansky*), 223.
  Isinglass. *See* Glue.
  Lampblack ;
    Macintosh, 161.
  Lead, acetate of ;
    Payne, 45.
    Newton (*Goodyear*), 49.
  Lead, carbonate of ;
    Payne, 45.
    Newton (*Goodyear*), 49.
    Shephard, 200.
    Bousfield (*Mayall*), 230.
    Stevens (*Stevens*), 242.
  Lead, oxides of ;
    Hancock, 36.
    Payne, 45.
    Newton (*Goodyear*), 49.
    Newton, 68.
    Duncan, 71.
    Goodyear, 114.
    Rider, 116.
    Warne, Fanshawe, Jaques, and Galpin, 152.
    Newton (*Green*), 157.
    Duncan, 212.
    Henson, 216.
    Simpson, 220.
    Mennons (*Briansky*), 223.
    Norris (*Holl*), 226.

Compounds of gutta percha, &c.
—cont.
  Lead, oxides of—cont.
    Bousfield (*Mayall*), 230.
    Stevens (*Stevens*), 242.
    James, 254.
    Simpson, 259.
  Lead, sulphate of;
    Cooley, 61.
  Leather, particles of;
    Job and Tomlinson, 107.
    King, 124.
    Henson, 216.
  Lime;
    Newton, 118.
    Candelot, 127.
    Blizzard, 131.
    Childs, 153.
    Luis (*Lecocq*), 173.
    Newton (*Havemann*), 184.
    Mennons (*Briansky*), 223.
    Bousfield (*Mayall*), 230.
  Lime, carbonate of. *See* Earths.
  Lime, sulphate of. *See* Earths.
  Linseed, rape, or neat's-foot oil;
    Payne, 45.
    Nickels, 70.
    Duncan, 71.
    Johnson, 104.
    Bielefeld, 105.
    Parkes, 108.
    Johnson, 110.
    Hughes, 117.
    Bousfield, 120.
    King, 124.
    Duncan, 143.
    Warne, Fanshawe, Jaques, and Galpin, 148.
    Warne, Fanshawe, Jaques, and Galpin, 152.
    Myers and Myers, 202.
    Simpson, 220.
    Mennons (*Briansky*), 223.
    Stevens (*Stevens*), 242.
    Crump, 258.
  Litharge. *See* Lead, oxides of.
  Metallic oxides, not otherwise particularised. *See also* other sub-heads.
    Hancock, 38.
    Newton (*Goodyear*), 49.
    Newton, 68.
    Ford, 108.
    Newton (*Cheever*), 179.
    Brant, 205.
    Ghislin, 234.
  Metallic powders;
    Parkes, 27.
    Hancock, 29.
    Cooley, 61.
    Newton, 68.
    Duncan, 71.
    Cornides, 102.

Compounds of gutta percha, &c.
—cont.
  Metallic powders—cont.
    Job and Tomlinson, 107.
    Palmer, 112.
    Ellis, 118.
    Duncan, 143.
    Warne, Fanshawe, Jaques, and Galpin, 150.
    Newton (*Baker*), 161.
    Cartwright, 204.
    Cartwright, 210.
    Henson, 216.
    Cartwright, 216.
    Mulet, 224.
    Norris (*Holt*), 226.
    Darlow and Seymour, 260.
  Mimo-tannic acid. *See* Catechu.
  Minium. *See* Lead, oxides of.
  Musk;
    Forster, 37.
  Naphthaline;
    Macintosh, 161.
  Neat's-foot oil. *See* Linseed oil.
  Nitrogen, binoxide of;
    Hancock, 33.
  Oils. *See also* Linseed, rape, or neat's foot oil.
    Forster, 37.
    Hancock, 38.
    Nickels, 70.
    Forty and Haynes, 87.
    Johnson, 110.
    Candelot, 127.
    Bradbury, 137.
    Duncan, 143.
    Warne, Fanshawe, Jaques, and Galpin, 148.
    Warne, Fanshawe, Jaques, and Galpin, 152.
    Newton (*Mayall*), 156.
    Williams, 196.
    Shephard, 200.
    Myers and Myers, 202.
    Henson, 216.
    Kirrage, 222.
    Spill, Briggs, and Spill, 225.
    Ghislin, 234.
    Simpson, 259.
  Oils (fragrant essential);
    Forster, 37.
  Orris root;
    Forster, 37.
  Peat dust (dry);
    Ley, 64.
    Ley, 64.
    Henson, 216.
  Petroleum or tar, oil of;
    Dundonald, 69.
    Nickels, 70.
    Henry (*Société Chartier et Compagnie*), 209.

INDEX OF SUBJECT MATTER.

Compounds of gutta percha, &c.
—*cont.*
  Phosphorus;
    Duvivier and Chaudet, 98.
    MacMillan, Mason, and Scarborough, 250.

  Pigments;
    Brooman, 22.
    Brockedon and Hancock, 30.
    Forster, 37.
    Hancock, 38.
    Burke, 44.
    Payne, 45.
    Cooley, 61.
    Scoutetten, 73.
    Johnson (*Deseille*), 77.
    Ryder and Ryder, 87.
    Goodyear, 100.
    Ford, 108.
    Ninck, 119.
    Tayler, 121.
    Kirrage, 140.
    Patrick, 155.
    Rostaing, 167.
    Forster, 199.
    Shephard, 200.
    Myers and Myers, 202.
    Henson, 216.
    Simpson, 220.
    Kirrage, 222.
    Spill, Briggs, and Spill, 225.
    Norris (*Holl*), 226.
    Stevens (*Stevens*), 242.
    Simpson, 259.

  Pitch. *See* Tar.

  Plaster of Paris. *See* Earths.

  Plumbago;
    Duncan, 113.
    Newton, 125.
    Warne, Fanshawe, Jaques, and Galpin 150.
    Warne, Fanshawe, Jaques, and Galpin, 152.
    Newton (*Cheever*), 168.
    Shephard, 200.
    Devlan, 209.
    Bateman, 235.

  Rape oil. *See* Linseed oil.

  Red lead. *See* Lead, oxides of.

  Resins;
    Hancock, 25.
    Hancock, 38.
    Hancock, 40.
    Payne, 45.
    Newton (*Goodyear*), 49.
    Dundonald, 69.
    Duncan, 71.
    Scoutetten, 73.
    Sorel, 85.
    Ryder and Ryder, 87.
    Stansbury, (*Arthur*), 92.
    Ogg, 92.

Compounds of gutta percha, &c.
—*cont.*
  Resins—*cont.*
    Cornides, 102.
    Johnson, 104.
    Johnson, 110.
    Hughes, 117.
    Danne, 122.
    King, 124.
    Candelot, 127.
    Gooderham, 123.
    Henson, 131.
    Smith, 135.
    Vasserot (*Beuchot*), 141.
    Hancock, 142.
    Duncan, 143.
    Warne, Fanshawe, Jaques, and Galpin, 152.
    Turner, 163.
    Turner, 163.
    Magnus and Sinnock, 167.
    Chatterton and Smith, 171.
    Harrison, 182.
    Godefroy, 192.
    Kidd, 205.
    Devlan, 209.
    Devlan, 209.
    Brooman (*Baldamus*), 211.
    Warden (*Baldamus*), 213.
    Henson, 216.
    Brooman (*Anthoine an Brossette*), 222.
    Twilley and Lainé, 231.
    MacMillan, Mason, and Scarborough, 250.

  Sawdust;
    Hancock, 20.
    Hancock, 38.
    Cooley, 61.
    Newton, 89.
    Taylor, 121.
    Henson, 131.
    Warne, Jaques, and Fanshawe, 142.
    Cowper (*Bingham*), 148.
    Fontainemoreau (*Innocent and Perroncel*), 243.

  Seaweed;
    Ghislin, 234.

  Shellac. *See* Gums.

  Silicates;
    Cooley, 61.
    Newton, 68.
    Butcher and Newey, 107.
    Hughes, 117.
    Newton, 118.
    Danne, 122.
    Candelot, 127.
    Wray, 137.
    Warne, Fanshawe, Jaques, and Galpin, 152.
    Patrick, 155.
    Newton (*Green*), 157.
    Rostaing, 167.
    Duncan, 212.

272 INDEX OF SUBJECT MATTER.

Compounds of gutta percha, &c.—cont.
  Silicates—cont.
    Henson, 216.
    Hooper, 218.
    Kirrage, 222.
    Mulet, 224.
    Ghislin, 234.
  Size. *See* Glue.
  Soap:
    Johnson, 110.
    Gooderham, 128.
    Brooman (*Baldamus*), 211.
  Soap-stone. *See* French chalk.
  Sodium, chloride of ;
    Payne, 45.
    Cooley, 61.
    Gidley and Muschamp, 81.
  Soluble salts, or saccharine or gummy substances (in general). *See also* specific sub-heads.
    Cooley, 61.
    Johnson (*Lefevre*), 81.
  Starch ;
    Johnson, 104.
    Johnson, 110.
  Stearine. *See* Wax or tallow.
  Sugar of lead. *See* Lead, acetate of.
  Sulphuric acid. *See* Vitriol, oil of.
  Susu poco ;
    Wray, 140.
  Tallow. *See* Wax.
  Tar, vegetable ;
    Payne, 45.
    Nickels, 70.
    Scoutetten, 73.
    Johnson (*Lefevre*), 81.
    Sorel, 85.
    Ryder and Ryder, 87.
    Johnson 110.
    Yeadon and Chapman, 113.
    Goodyear, 114.
    Gooderham, 128.
    Smith, 135.
    Kirrage, 140.
    Duncan, 143.
    Cowper (*Bingham*), 148.
    Chatterton and Smith, 166.
    Magnus and Sinnock, 167.
    Chatterton and Smith, 171.
    Shephard, 200.
    Brant, 205.
    Hooper, 218.
    Norris (*Holl*), 226.
    Twilley and Lainé, 231.
    Kemp and Kemp, 239.
  Tonquin beans ;
    Forster, 37.

Compounds of gutta percha, &c.—cont.
  Tungstic acid ;
    Ghislin, 234.
  Varnishes :
    Hancock, 38.
    Johnson (*Lefevre*), 81.
    James, 234.
  Vegetable powders ;
    Godefroy, 105.
    Johnson, 110.
    Jeune, 112.
    Hughes, 117.
    Taylor, 121.
    Rostaing, 167.
    Hunt, 192.
    Henson, 216.
    Kirrage, 222.
    Ghislin, 234.
  Vitriol, oil of ;
    Payne, 45.
    Macintosh, 126.
    Macintosh, 127.
    Macintosh, 130.
  Wax or tallow ;
    Hancock, 25.
    Nickels, 70.
    Scoutetten, 73.
    Sorel, 85.
    Johnson, 110.
    Richardson, 123.
    Candelot, 127.
    Gooderham, 128.
    Bradbury, 137.
    Vasserot (*Beuchot*), 141.
    Magnus and Sinnock, 167.
    Mackintosh, 176.
    Myers and Myers, 202.
    Kidd, 205.
    Kirrage, 222.
    Mennons (*Briansky*), 223.
    Twilley and Lainé, 231.
    Ghislin, 234.
    Harton, 244.
    Abel, 247.
    Mackintosh, 252.
  Whalebone (ground) ;
    Forster, 37.
  White lead. *See* Lead, carbonate of.
  Zinc, salts of (including the oxide) ;
    Hancock, 33.
    Lorimer, 41.
    Newton (*Goodyear*), 49.
    Duthoit, 51.
    Newton, 68.
    Candelot, 127.
    Warne, Jaques, and Fanshawe, 142.
    Patrick, 155.
    Newton (*Green*), 157.

INDEX OF SUBJECT MATTER.

Compounds of gutta percha, &c. —cont.
  Zinc, salts of—cont.
    Rostaing, 167.
    Shephard, 200.
    Duncan, 212.
    Hooper, 218.
    Mennons (*Briansky*), 223.
    Spill, Briggs, and Spill, 225.
    Norris (*Holl*), 226.
    Bousfield (*Mayall*), 230.
    Lake (*Marquard*), 250.

Compounds of india-rubber with various ingredients. *See also* Vulcanizing, &c.; Fibres, mixing, &c.; Jintawan, &c.:
  Albuminous substances;
    Johnson, 90.
    Johnson, 110.
  Alkalies, salts of the;
    Forster, 19.
    Gidley and Muschamp, 81.
    Blizzard, 131.
    Patrick, 155.
    Newton (*Havemann*), 184.
    Gabriel and Gabriel, 204.
    Ghislin, 234.
  Alum;
    Payne, 45.
    Cooke, 95.
    Wray, 137.
    Ghislin, 234.
  Aluminum, acetate of;
    Hancock, 16.
    Wray, 137.
  Asbestos;
    Warne, Fanshawe, Jaques, and Galpin, 150.
    Patrick, 155.
  Asphalte;
    Hancock, 17.
    Hancock, 38.
    Fanshawe and Fanshawe, 93.
    Dodge, 133.
    Wray, 137.
    Dodge, 141.
    Warne, Fanshawe, Jaques, and Galpin, 148.
    Sinnock, 150.
    Warne, Fanshawe, Jaques, and Galpin, 152.
    Hay, 188.
    Silver and Griffin, 188.
    Duncan, 212.
    Henson, 216.
    De Briou, 230.
    Mulholland, 248.
    De Briou, 251.

Compounds of india-rubber, &c. —cont.
  Ballata;
    Hancock and Silver, 213.
    Hancock and Silver, 241.
  Bitumen. *See* Asphalte.
  Bromine;
    Norris (*Holl*), 226.
  Casein. *See* Albuminous substances.
  Chlorine;
    Newton (*Engelhard and Day*), 164.
    Newton (*Havemann*), 165.
    Newton (*Havemann*), 184.
    Norris (*Holl*), 226.
    Lake (*Marquard*), 250.
  Chromium, oxides of;
    Forster, 258.
  Coal;
    Johnson (*Morey*), 119.
    Kirrage, 140.
  Coal tar;
    Poole (*Goodyear*), 52.
    Poole (*Goodyear*), 53.
    Poole (*Goodyear*), 54.
    Poole (*Goodyear*), 56.
    Poole (*Goodyear*), 59.
    Dundonald, 65.
    Sorel, 85.
    Ross, 95.
    Parker, 125.
    Parker, 128.
    Dodge, 133.
    Luis, 134.
    Kirrage, 140.
    Dodge, 141.
    Warne, Fanshawe, Jaques, and Galpin, 152.
    Mulholland, 227.
  Coke. *See* Coal.
  Colcothar;
    Hancock and Silver, 213.
  Collodion. *See* Gun cotton.
  Copper, oxides or salts of;
    Ford, 108.
  Cork;
    Hancock, 20.
    Hancock, 27.
    Parkes, 27.
    Hancock, 38.
    Newton, 89.
    Henson, 131.
    Warne, Jaques, and Fanshawe, 142.
    Clark, 147.
    Cowper (*Bingham*), 148.
    Jenne, 194.
    Williams, 196.
    Ford, 197.
    Henson, 216.
    Fontainemoreau (*Innocent and Porroncel*), 243.

Compounds of india-rubber, &c.
—cont.
- Earths. See also Pigments.
  - Hancock, 11.
  - Hancock, 16.
  - Hancock, 17.
  - Hancock, 27.
  - Parkes, 27.
  - Hancock, 29.
  - Brockedon and Hancock, 30.
  - Moulton, 32.
  - Hancock, 38.
  - Lorimer, 41.
  - Payne, 45.
  - Newton, 48.
  - Newton (*Goodyear*), 49.
  - Moulton, 50.
  - Dundonald, 65.
  - Newton, 68.
  - Brookes, 74.
  - Goodyear, 76.
  - Sorel, 85.
  - White, 85.
  - Coke, 95.
  - Johnson (*Morey*), 100.
  - Goodyear, 105.
  - Sautelet, 106.
  - Johnson (*Wacrenier*), 109.
  - Johnson (*Wacrenier*), 109.
  - Ford, 110.
  - Ford, 112.
  - Ritchie, 114.
  - Newton, 118.
  - Deplanque, 119.
  - Newton, 121.
  - Day, 122.
  - Parker, 125.
  - Newton, 125.
  - Candelot, 127.
  - Parker, 128.
  - Wray, 137.
  - Kirrage, 140.
  - Warne, Jaques, and Fanshawe, 142.
  - Warne, Fanshawe, Jaques, and Galpin, 148.
  - Cowper (*Bingham*), 148.
  - Hooper, 149.
  - Warne, Fanshawe, Jaques, and Galpin, 150.
  - Warne, Fanshawe, Jaques, and Galpin, 152.
  - Childs, 153.
  - Patrick, 155.
  - Newton (*Mayall*), 156.
  - Newton (*Green*), 157.
  - Daft, 160.
  - Newton (*Baker*), 161.
  - Childs, 162.
  - Luis (*Lecocq*), 173.
  - Newton (*Havemann*), 184.
  - Brooman (*Gobert*), 190.
  - Williams, 196.
  - Bowra, 200.
  - Harby, 203.
  - Gabriel and Gabriel, 204.
  - Lerenard, 207.

Compounds of india-rubber, &c.
—cont.
- Earths—cont.
  - Rèmiére, 211.
  - Duncan, 212.
  - Henson, 216.
  - Bousfield (*Hayward*), 217.
  - Hooper, 218.
  - Kirrage, 222.
  - Mulet, 224.
  - Norris (*Holl*), 226.
  - Clarkson, 228.
  - Bousfield (*Mayall*), 230.
  - Humfrey, 230.
  - Ghislin, 234.
  - Hancock and Silver, 241.
  - Mulholland, 248.
  - Lerenard, 249.
  - Lake (*Marquard*), 250.
  - Bousfield (*McBurney*), 256.
  - Simpson, 259.

Emery. See Pumice powder, &c.

Fibrin. See Albuminous substances.

Fig juice;
- Gilbee (*Mathevon*), 219.

French chalk. See Magnesium, silicate of.

Fuller's earth;
- Hancock, 17.
- Wray, 137.

Gelatin. See Glue.

Glue, gelatin, isinglass, or size;
- Trumble, 86.
- Johnson, 90.
- Hancock, 167.
- Ghislin, 234.
- Lees, 241.
- Hancock and Silver, 241.

Gluten. See Albuminous substances.

Gold, oxide of;
- Ninck, 119.

Gums;
- Weise, 3.
- Forster, 19.
- Parkes, 27.
- Forster, 36.
- Hancock, 38.
- Payne, 45.
- Newton, 48.
- Newton (*Goodyear*), 49.
- Poole (*Goodyear*), 53.
- Poole (*Goodyear*), 54.
- Poole (*Goodyear*), 59.
- Harrison and Harrison, 61.
- Dundonald, 65.
- Dundonald, 69.
- Gidley and Muschamp, 81.
- Forty and Haynes, 87.
- Newton, 89.
- Johnson, 90.

INDEX OF SUBJECT MATTER.

Compounds of india-rubber, &c.
—cont.
  Gums—cont.
    Johnson (*Morey*), 100.
    Cornides, 102.
    Newton, 104.
    Newton, 118.
    Moseley, 131.
    Blizzard, 131.
    Henson, 131.
    Dodge, 133.
    Macintosh, 136.
    Wray, 137.
    Dodge, 141.
    Hancock, 142.
    Cowper (*Bingham*), 148.
    Patrick, 155.
    Gisborne and Magnus, 160.
    Silver and Griffin, 188.
    Ford, 198.
    Fajole and Agostini, 202.
    Hancock and Silver, 213.
    Henson, 216.
    Hooper, 218.
    Brooman (*Anthoine and Brossette*), 222.
    Bonneville (*Gérard*), 223.
    Mulholland, 227.
    Bateman, 234.
    Kemp and Kemp, 239.
    Lees, 241.
    Hancock and Silver, 241.
    Harton, 244.
    Mayall, 246.
    Miller, 248.
    Lerenard, 249.
    De Briou, 251.
    James, 254.
  Gun cotton, or collodion;
    Macintosh, 130.
    Parkes, 247.
  Gutta percha;
    Hancock, 20.
    Brooman, 22.
    Hancock, 29.
    Brockedon and Hancock, 30.
    Hancock, 33.
    Burke, 44.
    Payne, 45.
    Newton (*Goodyear*), 49.
    Moulton, 50.
    Duthoit, 51.
    Rider, 51.
    Poole (*Goodyear*), 53.
    Poole (*Goodyear*), 54.
    Poole (*Goodyear*), 59.
    Nowton, 68.
    Nickels, 70.
    Gidley and Muschamp, 81.
    Sorel, 85.
    Forty and Haynes, 87.
    Johnson, 90.
    Johnson, 91.
    Goodyear, 100.
    Cornides, 102.
    Johnson, 103.

Compounds of india-rubber, &c.
—cont.
  Gutta percha—cont.
    Job and Tomlinson, 107.
    Turner, 111.
    Jeune, 112.
    Yeadon and Chapman, 113.
    Ritchie, 114.
    Jeune, 118.
    Newton, 118.
    Ninck, 119.
    Tayler, 121.
    King, 124.
    Candelot, 127.
    Macintosh, 127.
    Luis, 134.
    Hope, 137.
    Wray, 137.
    Kirrage, 140.
    Hancock, 142.
    Warne, Jaques, and Fanshawe, 142.
    Cowper (*Bingham*), 148.
    Sinnock, 150.
    Warne, Fanshawe, Jaques, and Galpin, 150.
    Warne, Fanshawe, Jaques and Galpin, 152.
    Macintosh, 161.
    Turner, 163.
    Turner, 163.
    Magnus and Sinnock, 167.
    Chatterton and Smith, 171.
    Newton (*Havemann*), 184.
    Chatterton, 186.
    Hunt, 192.
    Williams, 196.
    Ford, 197.
    Ford, 198.
    Forster, 199.
    Cartwright, 204.
    Newton (*Elmer*), 206.
    Hancock and Silver, 213.
    Warden (*Baldamus*), 213.
    Henson, 216.
    Cartwright, 216.
    Hooper, 218.
    Kirrage, 222.
    Mulet, 224.
    Bousfield (*Taylor*), 225.
    Spill, Briggs, and Spill, 225.
    Norris (*Holl*), 226.
    Bateman, 235.
    Ritchie, 238.
    Fontainemoreau (*Innocent and Perroncel*), 243.
    Darlow and Seymour, 260.

Isinglass. *See* Glue.

Lampblack;
  Brookes, 74.
  Johnson (*Morey*), 100.
  Ford, 110.
  Deplanque, 119.
  Dodge (*Hall*), 154.
  Macintosh, 161.

s 2

Compounds of india-rubber, &c.
—cont.
  Lamblack—cont.
    Stevens (Stevens), 242.
    Bousfield (McBurney), 256.
  Lead, acetate of;
    Payne, 45.
  Lead, carbonate of;
    Newton, 19.
    Payne, 45.
    Newton, 48.
    Newton (Goodyear), 49.
    Poole (Goodyear), 52.
    Poole (Goodyear), 53.
    Poole (Goodyear), 54.
    Poole (Goodyear), 59.
    Johnson (Guibal), 83.
    Ross, 95.
    Sautelet, 106.
    Bousfield (Mayall), 230.
    Stevens (Stevens), 242.
    Bousfield (McBurney), 256.
  Lead, oxides of;
    Payne, 45.
    Newton, 48.
    Newton (Goodyear), 49.
    Newton, 68.
    White, 85.
    Johnson (Morey), 100.
    Newton, 121.
    Warne, Fanshawe, Jaques, and Galpin, 152.
    Dodge (Hall), 154.
    Newton (Green), 157.
    Duncan, 212.
    Henson, 216.
    Bousfield (Hayward), 217.
    Mennons (Briansky), 223.
    Norris (Holl), 226.
    Mulholland, 227.
    Bousfield (Mayall), 230.
    Humfrey, 230.
    Stevens (Stevens), 242.
    Smith, 249.
    James, 254.
    Bousfield (McBurney), 256.
    Simpson, 259.
  Leather, particles of;
    Job and Tomlinson, 107.
    Henson, 216.
  Lime;
    Newton, 118.
    Hooper, 149.
    Childs, 153.
    Luis (Lecocq), 173.
    Newton (Havemann), 184.
    Bousfield (Mayall), 230.
  Lime, carbonate of. See Earths.
  Lime, sulphate of. See Earths.
  Linseed, rape, or neat's-foot oil;
    Hancock, 16.
    Wright, 18.
    Payne, 45.

Compounds of india-rubber, &c.
—cont.
  Linseed, rape, or neat's-foot oil
    —cont.
    Nickels, 70.
    Parkes, 108.
    Johnson, 110.
    Bousfield, 120.
    Warne, Fanshawe, Jaques, and Galpin, 148.
    Warne, Fanshawe, Jaques, and Galpin, 152.
    Henry (Société Chartier et Compagnie), 209.
    Hughes (Hodgskin), 219.
    Mennons (Briansky), 223.
    Lees, 241.
    Stevens (Stevens), 242.
    Miller, 248.
    Smith, 249.
    Crump, 258.
  Litharge. See Lead, oxides of.
  Magnesium, carbonate of;
    Moulton, 32.
    Newton (Goodyear), 49.
    Moulton, 50.
    Bousfield (Mayall), 230.
  Magnesium, oxide of;
    Moulton, 32.
    Newton (Goodyear), 49.
    Johnson (Morey), 100.
    Newton, 125.
    Hooper, 149.
    Newton (Baker), 161.
    Childs, 162.
    Norris (Holl), 226.
    Bousfield (Mayall), 230.
    Bousfield (McBurney), 256.
  Magnesium, silicate of;
    Hancock, 17.
    Hancock, 27.
    Hooper, 149.
    Warne, Fanshawe, Jaques, and Galpin, 150.
    Warne, Fanshawe, Jaques, and Galpin, 152.
    Patrick, 155.
    Daft, 160.
    Childs, 162.
    Henson, 216.
    Kirrage, 222.
    Bousfield (Mayall), 230.
  Metallic oxides (not otherwise particularised). See also specific subheads;
    Hancock, 38.
    Newton, 48.
    Newton, 68.
    Johnson (Morey), 100.
    Ford, 103.
    Newton (Cheever), 179.
    Bousfield (Hayward), 217.
    Ghislin, 234.

INDEX OF SUBJECT MATTER. 277

Compounds of india-rubber, &c. —*cont.*

Metallic powders;
Parkes, 27.
Hancock, 29.
Newton, 68.
Cornides, 102.
Job and Tomlinson, 107.
Turner, 111.
Ellis, 118.
Kirrage, 140.
Warne, Fanshawe, Jaques, and Galpin, 150.
Newton (*Baker*), 161.
Williams, 196.
Baggs and Parkes, 199.
Cartwright, 204.
Cartwright, 210.
Henson, 216.
Cartwright, 216.
Mulet, 224.
Norris (*Holl*), 226.
Clarkson, 228.
Darlow and Seymour, 260.

Minium. *See* Lead, oxides of.

Moss;
Gilbee (*Mathevon*), 219.

Mulberry leaves, juice of;
Gilbee (*Mathevon*), 219.

Muriatic acid;
Mulholland, 227.

Neat's-foot oil. *See* Linseed oil.

Nitrogen, binoxide of;
Hancock, 33.

Oils. *See also* Linseed, rape, or neat's-foot oil;
Hancock, 38.
Nickels, 70.
Brookes, 74.
Defever, 75.
Trumble, 86.
Forty and Haynes, 87.
Stoneham, 93.
Johnson, 110.
Candelot, 127.
Warne, Fanshawe, Jaques and Galpin, 152.
Newton (*Mayall*), 156.
Hancock, 167.
Godefroy, 193.
Williams, 196.
Henson, 216.
Kirrage, 222.
Mennons (*Briansky*), 223.
Spill, Briggs, and Spill, 225.
Ghislin, 234.
Bousfield (*McBurney*), 256.
Simpson, 259.

Paraffin (solid). *See* Wax.

Peat;
Waithman, 84.
Henson, 216.

Compounds of india-rubber, &c. —*cont.*

Petroleum or tar, oil of;
Dundonald, 69.
Nickels, 70.
Henry (*Société Chartier et Compagnie*), 209.
Hull, 215.
Humfrey, 230.
Humfrey, 231.

Phosphoric acid;
Mulholland, 248.

Phosphorus;
Mulholland, 224.
Mulholland, 227.

Pigments;
Hancock, 10.
Keene, 14.
Hancock, 16.
Parkes, 27.
Hancock, 29.
Brockedon and Hancock, 30.
Hancock, 38.
Burke, 44.
Payne, 45.
Poole (*Goodyear*), 52.
Poole (*Goodyear*), 53.
Poole (*Goodyear*), 54.
Poole (*Goodyear*), 54.
Poole (*Goodyear*), 57.
Gérard, 66.
Brookes. 74.
Goodyear, 79.
Gidley and Muschamp, 81.
Johnson (*Guibal*), 83.
Fanshawe and Fanshawe, 98.
Goodyear, 100.
Newton, 104.
Sautelet, 106.
Ford, 108.
Gidley and Christopher, 112.
Ninck, 119.
Tayler, 121.
Kirrage, 140.
Patrick, 155.
Walton, 156.
Laurence, 158.
Childs, 162.
Brooman (*Gobert*), 190.
Baggs and Parkes, 199.
Forster, 199.
Fajole and Agostini, 202.
Henson, 216.
Ford and Rigg, 220.
Kirrage, 222.
Mennons (*Briansky*), 223.
Spill, Briggs, and Spill, 225.
Norris (*Holl*), 226.
Jennings and Lavater, 228.
Hancock and Silver, 241.
Stevens (*Stevens*), 242.
Smith, 249.
Leronard, 249.
Forster, 258.
Simpson, 259.

278 INDEX OF SUBJECT MATTER.

Compounds of india-rubber, &c. —*cont.*

  Pitch. *See* Tar.
  Plaster of Paris. *See* Earths.
  Plumbago;
    Hancock, 17.
    Newton, 68.
    Goodyear, 78.
    Goodyear, 79.
    Newton, 89.
    Ford, 110.
    Deplanque, 119.
    Newton, 125.
    Warne, Fanshawe, Jaques, and Galpin, 150.
    Warne, Fanshawe, Jaques, and Galpin, 152.
    Devlan, 209.
    Rèmiére, 211.
    Ford and Rigg, 220.
    Bateman, 235.
    Mulholland, 248.
  Poisonous materials;
    Harby, 203.
    De Briou, 251.
  Potassium, arseniate of;
    Forster, 19.
  Pumice powder, fine emery, powdered glass, or other similar gritty substances;
    Hancock, 11.
    Brockedon and Hancock, 30.
    Dundonald, 65.
    Newton, 68.
    Goodyear, 76.
    Goodyear, 105.
    Ritchie, 114.
    Newton, 118.
    Deplanque, 119.
    Candelot, 127.
    Wray, 137.
    Kirrage, 140.
    Cowper (*Bingham*), 148.
    Newton (*Mayall*), 156.
    Newton (*Green*), 157.
    Duncan, 212.
    Mulet, 224.
    Hancock and Silver, 241.
    Mulholland, 248.
  Rape oil. *See* Linseed oil.
  Red lead. *See* Lead, oxides of.
  Resins;
    Hancock, 27.
    Parkes, 27.
    Hancock, 38.
    Payne, 45.
    Newton (*Goodyear*), 49.
    Dundonald, 65.
    Johnson, 66.
    Dundonald, 69.
    Sorel, 85.
    White, 85.
    Stoneham, 93.
    Cornides, 102.

Compounds of india-rubber, &c. —*cont.*

  Resins—*cont.*
    Johnson, 110.
    Richardson, 123.
    Blizzard, 126.
    Candelot, 127.
    Henson, 131.
    Dodge, 133.
    Hancock, 142.
    Warne, Fanshawe, Jaques, and Galpin, 152.
    Gisborne and Magnus, 160.
    Turner, 163.
    Turner, 163.
    Magnus and Sinnock, 167.
    Chatterton and Smith, 171.
    Harrison, 182.
    Hay, 188.
    Silver and Griffin, 188.
    Ford, 198.
    Harby, 203.
    Kidd, 205.
    Devlan, 209.
    Devlan, 209.
    Henry (*Société Chartier et Compagnie*), 209.
    Hancock and Silver, 213.
    Warden (*Baldamus*), 213.
    Henson, 216.
    Brooman (*Anthoine and Brossette*), 222.
    Mulholland, 224.
    Mulholland, 227.
    Ghislin, 234.
    Smith, 249.
    De Briou, 251.
  Sawdust;
    Hancock, 20.
    Hancock, 27.
    Parkes, 27.
    Hancock, 38.
    Newton, 89.
    Hill, 101.
    Johnson (*Morey*), 119.
    Tayler, 121.
    Henson, 131.
    Warne, Jaques, and Fanshawe, 142.
    Cowper (*Bingham*), 148.
    Fontainemoreau (*Innocent and Perroncel*), 243.
  Seaweed;
    Ghislin, 234.
  Shellac. *See* Gums.
  Size. *See* Glue.
  Soap;
    Brookes, 74.
    Sorel, 85.
    Trumble, 86.
    Johnson, 110.
    Brooman (*Baldamus*), 211.
  Soap-stone. *See* Magnesium, silicate of.

INDEX OF SUBJECT MATTER. 279

Compounds of india-rubber, &c.
—*cont.*
  Starch;
    Johnson, 110.
  Stearine. *See* Wax.
  Sugar of lead. *See* Lead, acetate of.
  Sulphuric acid. *See* Vitriol, oil of.
  Susu poco;
    Wray, 140.
  Tallow. *See* Wax.
  Tapioca;
    Gilbee (*Mathevon*), 219.
  Tar, vegetable;
    Hancock, 4.
    Wright, 18.
    Hancock, 27.
    Payne, 45.
    Poole (*Goodyear*), 52.
    Poole (*Goodyear*), 53.
    Poole (*Goodyear*), 54.
    Poole (*Goodyear*), 56.
    Poole (*Goodyear*), 59.
    Nickels, 70.
    White, 85.
    Stoneham, 93.
    Ross, 95.
    Johnson, 110.
    Yeadon and Chapman, 113.
    Parker, 125.
    Henson, 131.
    Dodge, 133.
    Kirrage, 140.
    Dodge, 141.
    Cowper (*Bingham*), 148.
    Gisborne and Magnus, 160.
    Magnus and Sinnock, 167.
    Chatterton and Smith, 171.
    Newton (*Cheever*), 178.
    Hay, 188.
    Hancock and Silver, 213.
    Hooper, 218.
    Norris (*Holl*), 226.
    Ghislin, 234.
    Kemp and Kemp, 239.
    De Briou, 251.
  Tungstic acid;
    Ghislin, 234.
  Varnishes;
    Hancock, 38.
    Payne, 45.
    Ghislin, 234.
    James, 254.
  Vegetable powders;
    Johnson, 110.
    Jeune, 112.
    Deplanque, 119.
    Tayler, 121.
    Silver and Griffin, 188.
    Hunt, 192.
    Henson, 216.
    Gilbee (*Mathevon*), 219.
    Kirrage, 222.

Compounds of india-rubber, &c.
—*cont.*
  Vegetable powders—*cont.*
    Ghislin, 234.
    Hancock and Silver, 241.
  Vitriol, oil of;
    Godefroy, 193.
    Baggs and Parker, 199.
    Humfrey, 230.
    Humfrey, 231.
  Wax or tallow;
    Wright, 18.
    Nickels, 70.
    Sorel, 85.
    Trumble, 86.
    Stoneham, 93.
    Johnson, 110.
    Richardson, 123.
    Candelot, 127.
    Gisborne and Magnus, 160.
    Magnus and Sinnock, 167.
    Macintosh, 176.
    Kidd, 205.
    Kirrage, 222.
    Mulholland, 224.
    Ghislin, 234.
    Harton, 244.
    Abel, 247.
    Miller, 249.
    Macintosh, 252.
    Buckingham, 253.
  White lead. *See* Lead, carbonate of.
  Zinc, salts of (including the oxide);
    Brockedon, 22.
    Hancock, 33.
    Lorimer, 41.
    Newton, 48.
    Newton (*Goodyear*), 49.
    Poole (*Goodyear*), 53.
    Poole (*Goodyear*), 54.
    Poole (*Goodyear*), 59.
    Gérard, 66.
    Newton, 68.
    Johnson (*Guibal*), 83.
    Johnson (*Morey*), 100.
    Goodyear, 105.
    Sautelet, 106.
    Deplanque, 119.
    Candelot, 127.
    Warne, Jaques, and Fanshawe, 142.
    Patrick, 155.
    Newton (*Green*), 157.
    Laurence, 158.
    Childs, 162.
    Brooman (*Gobert*), 190.
    Williams, 196.
    Mennons (*Debons and Denny*), 201.
    Fajole and Agostini, 202.
    Rèmiére, 211.
    Duncan, 212.
    Hooper, 218.

Compounds of india-rubber, &c.
—*cont.*
  Zinc, &c.—*cont.*
    Ford and Rigg, 220.
    Mennons (*Briansky*), 223.
    Spill, Briggs and Spill, 225.
    Norris (*Holl*), 226.
    Bousfield (*Mayall*), 230.
    Lake (*Marquard*), 250.
    Forster, 258.

Copper. See Compounds of gutta percha, &c.; Compounds of india-rubber, &c.

Cork. See Compounds of gutta percha, &c.; Compounds of india-rubber, &c.

Cutting and reducing into small pieces. See Preparing, &c.

Cutting sheets into bands and belts. See Bands and belts.

Cutting sheets into strips, threads, &c. See Thread and string, &c.

Deodorizing:
  Johnson, 1.
  Martin, 6.
  Hancock, 33.
  Johnson, 66.
  De Varroc, 78.
  Fry, 82.
  Hill, 101.
  Metcalf, 114.
  Blizzard, 126.
  Candelot, 127.
  Cattell, 145.
  Myers and Myers, 202.
  Newton (*Elmer*), 206.
  Simpson, 220.
  Kirrage, 222.
  Lees, 241.
  Bourne, 254.

Earths. See Compounds of gutta percha, &c.; Compounds of india-rubber, &c.

Elasticity, retaining; treating india-rubber so as to obviate the tendency to unduly stiffen and soften:
  Macintosh, 2.
  Pickersgill, 8.
  Nickels, 8.

Elasticity, &c.—*cont.*
  Hancock, 10.
  Fanshawe, 15.
  Moulton, 32.
  Spill, 124.
  Hull, 215.
  Bousfield (*Hayward*), 217.

Emery. See Compounds of gutta percha, &c.; Compounds of india-rubber, &c.

Ether. See Solvents, &c.

Eupion. See Solvents, &c.

Fabrics. See Coating and cementing, &c.

Fatty substances. See Compounds of gutta percha, &c.; Compounds of india-rubber, &c.

Fibres, mixing with india-rubber, gutta percha, &c.:
  Hancock, 4.
  Hancock, 13.
  Hancock, 27.
  Parkes, 27.
  Hancock, 29.
  Brockedon and Hancock, 30.
  Hancock, 38.
  Cooley, 61.
  Scoutetten, 73.
  Forty and Haynes, 87.
  Newton, 89.
  Johnson, 90.
  Stoneham, 93.
  Cooke, 95.
  Ross, 95.
  Audemars, 99.
  Hill, 101.
  Sautelet, 106.
  Latta, 109.
  Jeune, 112.
  Hughes, 117.
  Jeune, 118.
  Tayler, 121.
  Parker, 125.
  De Clippéle, 125.
  Parker, 128.
  Kirrage, 140.
  Dodge, 141.
  Warne, Jaques, and Fanshawe, 142.
  Clark, 147.
  Sinnock, 150.
  Patrick, 155.
  Walton, 156.
  Seager, 162.
  Hooper, 170.

Fibres, &c.—*cont.*
    Newton (*Cheever*), 179.
    Williams, 196.
    Ford, 197.
    Bowra, 200.
    Shephard, 200.
    Cartwright, 204.
    Lérenard, 207.
    Devlan, 209.
    Devlan, 209.
    Henson, 216.
    Simpson, 120.
    Kirrage, 222.
    Snell (*Wiese*), 223.
    Mullholland, 224.
    Mulholland, 227.
    Bousfield (*Mayall*), 230.
    Ghislin, 234.
    Stevens (*Stevens*), 242.
    Mayall, 246.
    Lerenard, 249.
    Felt (*Felt*), 252.
    Moseley, 258.
    Forster, 258.
    Simpson, 259.

Fibrin. *See* Compounds of gutta percha, &c.; Compounds of india-rubber, &c.

Fig juice. *See* Compounds of india-rubber, &c.

Fillets. *See* Bands.

Filtering. *See* Preparing, &c.

Flexibility, retaining. *See* Elasticity retaining, &c.

French chalk. *See* Compounds of gutta percha, &c.; Compounds of india-rubber, &c.

Fuller's earth. *See* Compounds of india-rubber, &c.

Gelatin. *See* Compounds of gutta percha, &c.; Compounds of india-rubber, &c.

Glass (powdered). *See* Compounds of gutta percha, &c.

Glue; Gluten; Gold, oxide of; Gums; Gun cotton. *See* Compounds of gutta percha, &c.; Compounds of india-rubber, &c.

Gutta percha, substitutes for. *See also* Ballata; Chapapote; Jintawan; Susu poco:
    Warren, 60.
    Le Gras and Gilpin, 63.
    Wilkinson, 65.
    Sorel, 85.
    Archereau, 88.
    Johnson, 104.
    Hughes, 117.
    Sorel, 122.
    Wray, 140.

Hardening gutta percha or india-rubber by means of caustic alkali:
    Hancock, 36.
    Richards, Taylor, and Wylde, 46.

India-rubber, substitutes for. *See also* Ballata; Chapapote; Jintawan; Susu poco:
    Sorel, 85.
    Rimmel (*Magen*), 96.
    Johnson, 104.
    Parkes, 108.
    Hughes, 117.
    Sorel, 122.
    Wray, 140.
    Buff, 195.
    Clark (*Loewenberg and Granier*), 245.

Iron. *See* Compounds of gutta percha, &c.

Isinglass. *See* Compounds of gutta percha, &c.; Compounds of india-rubber, &c.

Jintawan, treating and combining with india-rubber and gutta percha:
    Hancock, 25.
    Hancock, 29.
    Brockedon and Hancock, 30.
    Hancock, 33.
    Duncan, 50.
    Tayler, 121.

Lampblack. *See* Compounds of gutta percha, &c.; Compounds of india-rubber, &c.

Lead. *See* Compounds of gutta percha, &c.; Compounds of india-rubber, &c.; Vulcanizing.

282 INDEX OF SUBJECT MATTER.

Leather. *See* Coating and cementing, &c.; Compounds of gutta percha, &c.; Compounds of india-rubber, &c.

Lime; Lime, carbonate of; Lime, sulphate of. *See* Compounds of gutta percha, &c.; Compounds of india-rubber, &c.

Lime, hydrosulphuret of. *See* Vulcanizing.

Linseed oil. *See* Compounds of gutta percha, &c.; Compounds of india-rubber, &c.

Liquid ammonia. *See* Solvents, &c.

Litharge. *See* Compounds of gutta percha, &c.; Compounds of india-rubber, &c.

Magnesium, carbonate, oxide, and silicate of. *See* Compounds of india-rubber, &c.

Masticating. *See* Preparing, &c.

Mercury, sulphide of. *See* Solvents, &c.; Vulcanizing.

Metallic oxides; Metallic powders. *See* Compounds of gutta percha, &c.; Compounds of india-rubber, &c.

Metals. *See* Coating and cementing, &c.

Mimo-tannic acid. *See* Compounds of gutta percha, &c.

Minium. *See* Compounds of gutta percha, &c.; Compounds of india-rubber, &c.

Moss. *See* Compounds of india-rubber, &c.

Moulding:
    Nickels, 8.
    Hancock, 11.
    Parkes, 16.

Moulding—*cont.*
    Forster, 19.
    Brooman, 22.
    Hancock, 25.
    Hancock, 27.
    Parkes, 27.
    Hancock, 29.
    Brockedon and Hancock, 30.
    Hancock, 36.
    Forster, 37.
    Hancock, 38.
    Hancock, 40.
    Hancock, 41.
    Nickels, 43.
    Payne, 45.
    Newton (*Goodyear*), 49.
    Poole (*Goodyear*), 54.
    Poole (*Goodyear*), 54.
    Poole (*Goodyear*), 55.
    Poole (*Goodyear*), 57.
    Poole (*Goodyear*), 57.
    Ley, 64.
    Newton, 68.
    Goodyear, 72.
    Scoutetten, 73.
    Johnson (*Guibal*), 83.
    Newton, 90.
    Johnson, 93.
    Johnson, 94.
    Ross, 95.
    Goodyear, 100.
    Goodyear, 101.
    Johnson, 103.
    Bielefeld, 105.
    Goodyear, 106.
    Johnson (*Wacrenier*), 109.
    Palmer, 112.
    Lorimier, 117.
    Deplanque, 119.
    Johnson (*Morey*), 119.
    Macintosh, 127.
    Newton, 130.
    Cowper (*Cuppers*), 133.
    Kirrage, 140.
    Childs, 144.
    Moseley, 144.
    Belling, 147.
    Clark, 147.
    Hooper, 149.
    Newton (*Mayall*), 156.
    Chatterton, 159.
    Childs, 162.
    Newton (*Engelhard and Day*), 164.
    Hooper, 170.
    Silver and Barwick, 174.
    Hooper, 175.
    Woodcock, 176.
    Pitman (*Bourn Brown and Chaffee*), 177.
    Pitman (*Bourn, Brown and Chaffee*), 178.
    Newton (*Cheever*), 178.
    Newton (*Havemann*), 184.
    Moulton, 185.
    Silver and Griffin, 188.

Moulding—*cont.*
    Brooman (*Gobert*), 190.
    Williams, 196.
    Forster, 199.
    Gabriel and Gabriel, 204.
    Cartwright, 204.
    De la Bastida (*Cohen and Vaillant*), 207.
    Rèmiére, 211.
    Hancock and Silver, 213.
    Bousfield (*Hayward*), 217.
    Ford and Rigg, 220.
    Jennings and Lavater, 221.
    Clark (*Quinet and Baudouin*), 237.
    Fontainemoreau (*Lemaistre and Co.*), 240.
    Mayall, 246.
    Lake (*Marquard*), 250.
    Pelt (*Felt*), 252.
    Macintosh, 252.
    Darlow and Seymour, 260.

Mulberry leaves, juice of. *See* Compounds of india-rubber, &c.

Muriatic acid. *See* Compounds of india-rubber, &c.

Musk. *See* Compounds of gutta percha, &c.

Naphtha. *See* Solvents, &c.

Naphthaline. *See* Compounds of gutta percha, &c.

Neat's foot oil. *See* Compounds of gutta percha, &c.; Compounds of india-rubber, &c.

Nitro-benzole. *See* Solvents, &c.

Nitrogen, binoxide of. *See* Compounds of gutta percha, &c.; Compounds of india rubber, &c.

Oils. *See* Compounds of gutta percha, &c.; Compounds of india-rubber, &c.; Solvents.

Oleic acid. *See* Solvents, &c.

Orris root. *See* Compounds of gutta percha, &c.

Paints made from decomposed india-rubber:
    Macintosh, 60.

Paper. *See* Coating and cementing, &c.

Peat. *See* Compounds of gutta percha, &c.; Compounds of india-rubber, &c.

Petroleum. *See* Compounds of gutta percha, &c.; Compounds of india-rubber, &c.

Phosphoric acid. *See* Compounds of india-rubber, &c.

Phosphorus; Pigments; Pitch; Plaster of Paris; Plumbago. *See* Compounds of gutta percha, &c.; Compounds of india-rubber, &c.

Poisonous materials. *See* Compounds of india-rubber, &c.

Porous gutta percha or india-rubber. *See* Sponge.

Potassium, arseniate of. *See* Compounds of india-rubber, &c.

Preparing gutta-percha (treating the raw material):
    Cleansing;
        Brooman, 22.
        Hancock, 25.
        Parkes, 27.
        Hancock, 29.
        Hancock, 33.
        Hancock, 36.
        Forster, 37.
        Hancock, 40.
        Lorimer, 41.
        Duncan, 50.
        Rider, 51.
        Normandy, 67.
        Scoutetten, 73.
        Johnson (*Lefevre*), 81.
        Forty and Haynes, 87.
        Dunlop, 94.
        Johnson (*Lemettais and Boniere*), 120.
        Day, 123.
        Godefroy, 133.
        Smith, 135.
        Johnson (*Day*), 135.

INDEX OF SUBJECT MATTER.

Preparing gutta percha—*cont.*
  Cleansing—*cont.*
    Wray, 137.
    Cattell, 145.
    Newton (*Engelhard and Day*), 164.
    Rostaing, 167.
    Truman, 182.
    Clark (*Boulet, Sarazin, and Hamy*), 183.
    Chatterton, 186.
    Shephard, 200.
  Cutting and reducing into small pieces;
    Hancock, 29.
    Brockedon and Hancock, 30.
    Hancock, 33.
    Forster, 37.
    Lorimer, 41.
    Payne, 45.
    Duncan, 50.
    Macintosh, 56.
    Cooley, 61.
    Assanti, 86.
    Dunlop, 94.
    Ford, 108.
    Dodge, 110.
    Godefroy, 133.
    Smith, 135.
    Johnson (*Cantelo*), 155.
    Newton (*Engelhard and Day*), 164.
    Forster, 199.
    Twilley and Lainé, 231.
  Masticating;
    Hancock, 20.
    Brooman, 22.
    Hancock, 25.
    Brockedon and Hancock, 30.
    Hancock, 33.
    Forster, 37.
    Lorimer, 41.
    Burke, 44.
    Newton (*Goodyear*), 49.
    Duncan, 50.
    Nickels, 70.
    Duncan, 71.
    Nickels, 72.
    Forty and Haynes, 87.
    Dunlop, 94.
    Jeune, 112.
    Jeune, 118.
    Godefroy, 133.
    Hope, 137.
    Wray, 137.
    Kirrage, 140.
    Hancock, 142.
    Duncan, 143.
    Newton (*Mayall*), 156.
    Macintosh, 161.
    Seager, 162.
    Macintosh, 170.
    Truman, 182.

Preparing gutta percha—*cont.*
  Masticating;
    Clark (*Boulet, Sarazin, and Hamy*), 183.
    Chatterton, 186.
    Truman, 187.
    Truman, 190.
    Miller, 191.
    Godefroy, 192.
    Williams, 196.
    Forster, 199.
    Shephard, 200.
    Henson, 216.
    Kirrage, 222.
    Norris (*Holl*), 226.
    Ghislin, 234.
    Macintosh, 252.
    Simpson, 259.
  Straining and filtering;
    Hancock, 25.
    Cooley, 61.
    Candelot, 127.
    Smith, 135.
    Cattell, 145.
    Luis (*Lecocq*), 173.
    Hunt, 192.
    Newton (*Elmer*), 206.
    Twilley and Lainé, 231.

Preparing india-rubber (treating the raw material):
  Cleansing;
    Hancock, 4.
    Hancock, 10.
    Hancock, 33.
    Defever, 75.
    Brooman (*Perroncel*), 75.
    Goodyear, 77.
    Forty and Haynes, 87.
    Newton, 91.
    Dunlop, 94.
    Johnson (*Day*), 106.
    Johnson (*Day*), 135.
    Wray, 137.
    Moseley, 149.
    Johnson (*Day*), 153.
    Newton (*Engelhard and Day*), 164.
    Chatterton, 186.
    Henry (*Société Chartier et Compagnie*), 209.
    Hunt, 257.
  Cutting and reducing into small pieces;
    Clark, 2.
    Fleetwood, 3.
    Weise, 3.
    Siever, 6.
    Hancock, 10.
    Keene, 14.
    Freeman, 14.
    Fanshawe, 15.
    Hancock, 17.
    Wright, 18.
    Burke, 20.

INDEX OF SUBJECT MATTER. 285.

Preparing india-rubber—*cont.*

  Cutting and reducing into small pieces—*cont.*
    Brockedon and Hancock, 30.
    Hancock, 33.
    Macintosh, 56.
    Johnson, 66.
    Goodyear, 77.
    Goodyear, 84.
    Newton, 91.
    Dunlop, 94.
    Penney, 100.
    Johnson (*Day*), 106.
    Stansbury (*Merrian and Crosby*), 107.
    Ford, 108.
    Ford, 110.
    Dodge, 110.
    Gidley and Christopher, 112.
    Ford, 112.
    Ford, 115.
    Chamberlain, 124.
    Moseley, 131.
    Chamberlain, 159.
    Newton (*Engelhard and Day*), 164.
    Schiele (*Kleist*), 174.
    Tooth, 193.
    Forster, 199.
    Henry (*Société Chartier et Compagnie*), 209.
    Jennings and Lavater, 221.
    De Briou, 236.
    De Briou, 251.

  Masticating;
    Hancock, 10.
    Fanshawe, 15.
    Forster, 19.
    Hancock, 20.
    Brockedon and Hancock, 30.
    Hancock, 33.
    Nickels, 43.
    Burke, 44.
    Newton (*Goodyear*), 49.
    Dundonald, 65.
    Nickels, 70.
    Nickels, 72.
    Goodyear, 84.
    Forty and Haynes, 87.
    Dunlop, 94.
    Fanshawe and Fanshawe, 98.
    Hill, 101.
    Jeune, 112.
    Bousfield, 113.
    Jeune, 118.
    Dodge, 133.
    Hope, 137.
    Wray, 137.
    Kirrage, 140.
    Hancock, 142.
    Moseley, 144.
    Hooper, 149.
    Johnson (*Day*), 153.
    Newton (*Mayall*) 156.

Preparing india-rubber—*cont.*

  Masticating—*cont.*
    Laurence, 158.
    Seager, 162.
    Hancock, 167.
    Macintosh, 176.
    Chatterton, 186.
    Truman, 187.
    Truman, 190.
    Miller, 191.
    Williams, 196.
    Forster, 199.
    Hancock and Silver, 213.
    Henson, 216.
    Kirrage, 222.
    Norris (*Holl*), 226.
    Ghislin, 234.
    Felt (*Felt*), 252.
    Macintosh, 252.
    Simpson, 259.

  Straining and filtering;
    Clark, 2.
    Macintosh, 2.
    Hancock, 13.
    Hancock, 15.
    Parkes, 16.
    Johnson, 68.
    Defever, 75.
    Candelot, 127.
    Luis (*Lecocq*), 173.
    Schiele (*Kleist*), 174.
    Hunt, 192.
    Mennons (*Debons and Denny*), 201.
    Pajole and Agostini, 202.
    Newton (*Elmer*), 206.

Pumice powder. See Compounds of india-rubber, &c.

Purifying. See Preparing, &c.

Rape oil; Red lead; Resins. See Compounds of gutta percha, &c.; Compounds of india-rubber, &c.

Sawdust; Seaweed. See Compounds of gutta percha, &c.; Compounds of india-rubber, &c.

Sheet india-rubber or gutta percha, making:
    Hancock, 4.
    Pickersgill, 8.
    Nickels, 8.
    Hancock, 10.
    Hancock, 11.
    Nickels, 13.
    Hancock, 17.
    Forster, 19.

INDEX OF SUBJECT MATTER.

Sheet india-rubber, &c.—*cont.*
  Brockedon, 22.
  Rewley, 25.
  Brockedon and Hancock, 30.
  Moulton, 32.
  Hancock, 38.
  Nickels, 43.
  Burke, 44.
  Poole (*Goodyear*), 54.
  Poole (*Goodyear*), 54.
  Poole (*Goodyear*), 55.
  Poole (*Goodyear*), 57.
  Poole (*Goodyear*), 57.
  Poole (*Goodyear*), 58.
  Poole (*Goodyear*), 59.
  Cooley, 61.
  Ley, 64.
  Gérard, 66.
  Normandy, 67.
  Pidding, 69.
  Nickels, 70.
  Brooman (*Perroncel*), 75.
  Goodyear, 79.
  Johnson (*Guibal*), 83.
  Goodyear, 84.
  White, 85.
  Forty and Haynes, 87.
  Willis, 89.
  Johnson, 103.
  Johnson, 104.
  Johnson (*Steinlen*), 111.
  Jeune, 112.
  Bousfield, 113.
  Johnson, 116.
  Tayler, 121.
  Parker, 126.
  Macintosh, 127.
  Parker, 128.
  Dodge, 133.
  Johnson (*Day*), 135.
  Warne, 136.
  Moseley, 144.
  Johnson (*Day*), 153.
  Daft, 164.
  Newton (*Cheever*), 179.
  Clark (*Boulet, Sarazin, and Hamy*), 183.
  Silver and Griffin, 188.
  Miller, 191.
  Hunt, 192.
  Jeune, 194.
  Williams, 196.
  Ford, 197.
  Flanders, 197.
  Bowra, 200.
  Lerenard, 207.
  Daft, 208.
  Griffin, 212.
  Gérard, 214.
  Bousfield (*Hayward*), 217.
  Hooper, 218.
  Kirrage, 222.
  Bousfield (*Taylor*), 223.
  Norris (*Holl*), 228.
  Bousfield, (*Mayall*), 230.
  Bousfield (*Taylor*), 232.
  Ghislin, 234.

Sheet india-rubber, &c.—*cont.*
  Gérard, 236.
  Story, 240.
  Hall, 242.
  Fontainemoreau (*Innocent and Perroncel*), 243.
  Mayall, 246.
  Felt (*Felt*), 251.
  Macintosh, 252.
  Mosely, 253.
  Dunlop, 255.
  Moseley, 258.
  Forster, 258.
  Simpson, 259.
  Darlow and Seymour, 260.
  Dunlop and Cressley, 261.

Shellac. See Compounds of gutta percha, &c.; Compounds of india-rubber, &c.

Silicates. See Compounds of gutta percha, &c.

Size; Soap; Soapstone. See Compounds of gutta percha, &c.; Compounds of india-rubber, &c.

Sodium, chloride of. See Compounds of gutta percha, &c.

Softening of gutta percha by the action of an acid:
  Buchholz, 48.

Softening, special treatment to obviate. See Elasticity, retaining.

Solutions. See Solvents, &c.

Solvents, &c.:
  Alcohol used in conjunction with a solvent;
    Johnson, 1.
    Weise, 3.
    Forster, 36.
    Gerard, 47.
    Johnson, 66.
    Newton, 91.
    Brooman, 99.
    Dodge, 110.
    Codet-Négrier, 122.
    Cattell, 145.
    Patrick, 155.
    Newton, (*Engelhard and Day*), 164.
    Newton (*Havemann*), 165.
    Fajole and Agostini, 202.
    Kemp and Kemp, 239.
    Lees, 241.
    Miller, 248.
    Hunt, 257.

INDEX OF SUBJECT MATTER.

Solvents, &c.—*cont.*
  Ale used in conjunction with a solvent;
    Lees, 241.
  Aniline;
    Parkes, 247.
  Benzole;
    Dalton, 45.
    Duthoit, 51.
    Cooley, 61.
    Newton, 91.
    Cornides, 102.
    Blizzard, 126.
    Cattell, 145.
    Turner, 163.
    Newton (*Engelhard and Day*), 164.
    Newton (*Havemann*), 165.
    Rostaing, 167.
    Luis (*Lecocq*), 173.
    Mennons (*Debons and Denny*), 201.
    Spilsbury and Emerson, 204.
    Hughes (*Hodgskin*), 219.
    Simpson, 220.
    Mennons (*Briansky*), 223.
    Twilley and Lainé, 231.
    Mulholland, 249.
    Hunt, 257.
    Simpson, 259.
  Camphine;
    Dalton, 45.
    Newton, 48.
    Newton, 91.
    Hill, 101.
    Newton, 121.
    Codet-Négrier, 122.
    Blizzard, 126.
    Turner, 163.
    Rostaing, 167.
    Hughes (*Hodgskin*), 219.
    Simpson, 220.
    Mayall, 246.
  Camphor treated with sulphurous acid gas;
    Parkes, 27.
  Carbon, bisulphide of;
    Parkes, 16.
    Parkes, 27.
    Hancock, 29.
    Dalton, 45.
    Gerard, 47.
    Duthoit, 51.
    Cooley, 61.
    Normandy, 67.
    Scoutetten, 73.
    Assanti, 86.
    Ogg, 92.
    Duvivier and Chaudet, 98.
    Brooman, 99.
    Hill, 101.
    Johnson, 106.
    Santelet, 106.
    Dodge, 110.

Solvents, &c.—*cont.*
  Carbon, bisulphide of—*cont.*
    Johnson (*Lemettais and Boniere*), 120.
    Codet-Négrier, 122.
    King, 124.
    De Clippóle, 126.
    Macintosh, 126.
    Macintosh, 130.
    Duncan, 143.
    Cattell, 145.
    Newton (*Engelhard and Day*), 164.
    Newton (*Havemann*), 165.
    Luis (*Lecocq*), 173.
    Stevens (*Chapa and Lacase*), 184.
    Brooman (*Gobert*), 190.
    Gedefroy, 192.
    Stevens (*Lacase*), 195.
    McKay, 196.
    Beggs and Parkes, 199.
    Shephard, 200.
    Newton (*Elmer*), 206.
    Brooman (*Baldamus*), 211.
    Spill, Briggs, and Spill, 225.
    Norris (*Holl*), 228.
    Twilley and Lainé, 231.
    Bateman, 235.
    Fontainemoreau (*Lemaistre and Co.*), 240.
    Fontainemoreau (*Innocent and Perroncel*), 243.
    Mulholland, 249.
    MacMillan, Mason, and Scarborough, 250.
    De Briou, 251.
  Carbon, chlorides of;
    Simpson and Forster, 44.
    Newton (*Engelhard and Day*), 164.
    Crump, 258.
  Chapapote;
    Henry (*Moissant and Co.*), 146.
  Chloroform;
    Gerard, 47.
    Newton, 91.
    Cattell, 145.
    Patrick, 155.
    Newton (*Engelhard and Day*), 164.
    Newton (*Havemann*), 165.
    Brooman (*Gobert*), 190.
    Twilley and Lainé, 231.
    Lake (*Marquard*), 250.
  Coal tar, oil of;
    Macintosh, 2.
    Hancock, 4.
    Hancock, 10.
    Bethell, 12.
    Hancock, 13.
    Hancock, 15.
    Forster, 36.
    Hancock, 38.

Solvents, &c.—cont.
  Coal tar, oil of—cont.
    Simpson and Forster, 44.
    Gerard, 47.
    Cooley, 61.
    Johnson (*Deseille*), 77.
    Johnson (*Lefevre*), 81.
    Fry, 82.
    Waithman, 84.
    White, 85.
    Johnson, 91.
    Sautelet, 106.
    Metcalf, 114.
    Spill, 124.
    Cattell, 145.
    Luis (*Lecocq*), 173.
    Schiele (*Kleist*), 174.
    Harrison, 182.
    Baggs and Parkes, 199.
    Fajole and Agostini, 202.
    Martin, 203.
    Spilsbury and Emerson, 204.
  Ether, sulphuric ;
    Gerard, 47.
    Newton, 91.
    Brooman, 99.
    Audemars, 99.
    Cornides, 102.
    Codet-Négrier, 122.
    Candelot, 127.
    Brooman (*Gobert*), 190.
    Fajole and Agostini, 202.
    Brooman (*Baldamus*), 211.
    Twilley and Lainé, 231.
  Eupion ;
    Parkes, 16.
  Liquid ammonia ;
    Sievier, 6.
    Johnson, 68.
    Audemars, 99.
    Newton (*Havemann*), 184.
    Lake (*Marquard*), 250.
  Mercury, bisulphide of ;
    Bateman, 235.
  Naphtha ;
    Parkes, 16.
    Brooman, 22.
    Bewley, 25.
    Parkes, 27.
    Hancock, 38.
    Dalton, 45.
    Gerard, 47.
    Duthoit, 51.
    Tyler, 60.
    Harrison and Harrison, 61.
    Cooley, 61.
    Barrett, 72.
    Fry, 82.
    Ryder and Ryder, 87.'
    Willis, 89.
    Newton, 90.
    Johnson, 91.
    Fanshawe and Fanshawe, 98.

Solvents, &c.—cont.
  Naphtha—cont.
    Brooman, 99.
    Penney, 100.
    Hill, 101.
    Cornides, 102.
    Ford, 108.
    Ford, 110.
    Ford, 112.
    Ford, 115.
    Richardson, 123.
    Spill, 124.
    Blizzard, 126.
    Macintosh, 130.
    Cattell, 145.
    Patrick, 155.
    Walton, 156.
    Turner, 163.
    Newton (*Engelhard and Day*), 164.
    Hancock, 167.
    Hooper, 170.
    Hooper, 175.
    Silver and Griffin, 188.
    Hunt, 192.
    Jeune, 194.
    Ford, 197.
    Ford, 198.
    Baggs and Parkes, 199.
    Mennons (*Debons and Denny*), 201.
    Spilsbury and Emerson, 204.
    Fuller, 211.
    Hughes (*Hodgskin*), 219.
    Simpson, 220.
    Mennons (*Briansky*), 223.
    Mulholland, 227.
    Kemp and Kemp, 239.
    Lees, 241.
    Mulholland, 248.
    Smith, 249.
    Mac Millan, Mason, and Scarborough, 250.
    Whitehead, 252.
    Macintosh, 252.
  Nitro-benzole ;
    Parkes, 247.
    Miller, 248.
  Oil (animal) ;
    Wright, 18.
    Warne, Fanshawe, Jaques, and Galpin, 152.
    Harrison, 182.
  Oils (essential) ;
    Hancock, 38.
    Cooley, 61.
    Brooman, 99.
    Codet-Négrier, 122.
    Patrick, 155.
    Newton (*Engelhard and Day*), 164.
    Rostaing, 167.
    Martin, 203.
    Spilsbury and Emerson, 204.
    Brant, 205.
    Lees, 241.

INDEX TO SUBJECT MATTER. 289

Solvents, &c.—*cont*.
  Oil (volatile);
    Martin, 6.
  Oleic acid;
    Hunt, 257.
  Turpentine, oil of;
    Peal, 1.
    Johnson, 1.
    Clark, 2.
    Fleetwood, 3.
    Weise, 3.
    Hancock, 4.
    Hancock, 10.
    Hancock, 13.
    Keene, 14.
    Hancock, 15.
    Hancock, 16.
    Parkes, 16.
    Wright, 18.
    Brooman, 22.
    Bewley, 25.
    Hancock, 25.
    Parkes, 27.
    Hancock, 38.
    Dalton, 45.
    Payne, 45.
    Gerard, 47.
    Tyler, 60.
    Cooley, 61.
    Johnson, 66.
    Fry, 82.
    Forty and Haynes, 87.
    Newton, 90.
    Brooman, 99.
    Penney, 100.
    Hill, 101.
    Cornides, 102.
    Johnson, 103.
    Johnson, 104.
    Bielefeld, 105.
    Sautelet, 106.
    Ford, 108.
    Ford, 110.
    Ford, 112.
    Ford, 115.
    Richardson, 123.
    King, 124.
    Blizzard, 126.
    Candelot, 127.
    Vasserot (*Beuchot*), 141.
    Hancock, 142.
    Cattell, 145.
    Warne, Fanshawe, Jaques, and Galpin, 152.
    Turner, 163.
    Luis (*Lecocq*), 173.
    Ford, 197.
    Ford, 198.
    Mennons (*Debons and Denny*), 201.
    Fajole and Agostini, 202.
    Spilsbury and Emerson, 204.
    Brant, 205.
    Henry (*Société Chartier et Compagnie*), 209.
    Brooman (*Anthoine and Brosette*), 222.

Solvents, &c.—*cont*.
  Turpentine, oil of—*cont*.
    Mennons (*Briansky*), 223.
    Twilley and Lainé, 231.
    Fontainemoreau (*Innocent and Perroncel*), 243.
    Miller, 248.
    Mac Millan, Mason, and Scarborough, 250.
  Vapour of the solvent;
    Hancock, 17.
    Parkes, 27.
    Johnson (*Guibal and Cumenge*), 83.

Sponge or porous india-rubber or gutta percha:
  Hancock, 25.
  Hancock, 33.
  Newton, 47.
  Cooke, 95.
  Warne, Fanshawe, Jaques, and Galpin, 150.
  Silver and Griffin, 183.

Starch. *See* Compounds of gutta percha, &c.; Compounds of india-rubber, &c.

Stearine. *See* Compounds of gutta percha, &c.; Compounds of india-rubber, &c.

Stickiness. *See* Clamminess, &c.

Straining. *See* Preparing, &c.

Stiffening, special treatment to obviate. *See* Elasticity, retaining.

Strips. *See* Bands.

Substitutes. *See* Gutta percha; India-rubber.

Sugar of lead. *See* Compounds of gutta percha, &c.; Compounds of india-rubber, &c.

Sulphur. *See* Vulcanizing.

Sulphur, abstracting from vulcanized india-rubber:
  Christopher and Gidley, 74.
  Newton, 91.
  Brooman, 99.
  Johnson, 116.
  Tooth, 193.
  Henry (*Société Chartier et Campagnie*), 209.
  Lavater, 238.

I.R.   T

290 INDEX TO SUBJECT MATTER.

Sulphur, chloride of. *See* Vulcanizing.

Sulphurets. *See* Vulcanizing.

Sulphuric acid. *See* Compounds of gutta percha, &c.; Compounds of india-rubber, &c.

Sulphurous acid gas. *See* Vulcanizing.

Susu poco. *See also* Compounds of gutta percha, &c.; Compounds of india-rubber, &c.
    Wray, 140.

Tallow. *See* Compounds of gutta percha, &c.; Compounds of india-rubber, &c.

Tapioca. *See* Compounds of india-rubber, &c.

Tar. *See* Compounds of gutta-percha, &c.; Compounds of india-rubber, &c.

Thread and string of gutta percha, india-rubber, &c.
    Dumeste, 5.
    Hartley, 7.
    Nickels, 8.
    Hancock, 11.
    Parkes, 16.
    Alsop and Forster, 22.
    Brooman, 23.
    Clark, 24.
    Newton, 24.
    Hancock, 33.
    Forster, 36.
    Nickels, 43.
    Gérard, 66.
    Meeus, 86.
    Brooman, 96.
    Bousfield, 113.
    Newton (*Davenport*), 115.
    Macintosh, 127.
    Moseley, 131.
    Moseley, 144.
    Turner, 186.
    Dunlop, 187.
    Miller, 191.
    Daft, 208.
    Gérard, 214.
    Jennings and Lavater, 228.
    Clark, 229.
    Coles, Jaques, and Fanshawe, 235.

Thread and string—*cont.*
    Gérard, 236.
    Storey, 240.
    Collins, 244.
    Dunlop, 255.
    Moseley, 260.
    Dunlop and Crossley, 261.

Tonquin beans. *See* Compounds of gutta percha, &c.

Tungstic acid. *See* Compounds of gutta percha, &c.; Compounds of india-rubber, &c.

Turpentine. *See* Solvents, &c.

Varnishes. *See* Compounds of gutta percha, &c.; Compounds of india-rubber, &c.

Varnishing. *See* Coating, &c.

Vegetable powders. *See* Compounds of gutta percha, &c.; Compounds of india-rubber, &c.

Vitriol, oil of. *See* Compounds of gutta percha, &c.; Compounds of india-rubber, &c.

Vulcanizing, by means of:
    Antimony, sulphuret of;
        Hancock, 33.
        Burke, 44.
        Moulton, 50.
        Scoutetten, 73.
        Jeune, 118.
        Forster, 258.
    Arsenic, trisulphide of (orpiment);
        Hancock, 25.
        Parkes, 27.
        Brockedon and Hancock, 30.
        Hancock, 33.
        Moulton, 50.
        Forster, 258.
    Chlorides, nitrites, nitrates, fluorides, bromides, iodides, and phosphurets of the earths and metals;
        Parkes, 27.
        Brockedon and Hancock, 30.
        Duvivier and Chaudet, 98.

INDEX TO SUBJECT MATTER. 291

Vulcanizing by means of—*cont.*
  Lead, hyposulphite of;
    Moulton, 32.
    Moulton, 50.
    Rider, 51.
    Cooley, 61.
    Rider, 80.
    Shephard, 200.
    Jennings and Lavater, 233.
    Fontainemoreau (*Innocent and Perroncel*), 243.
  Lead, sulphuret of;
    Moulton, 32.
    Moulton, 50.
    Cooley, 61.
    Ryder, 80.
    Jennings and Lavater, 233.
    Fontainemoreau (*Innocent and Perroncel*), 243.
  Lime, hydrosulphuret of;
    Hancock, 33.
    Moulton, 50.
    Fontainemoreau (*Innocent and Perroncel*), 243.
  Mercury, sulphides of;
    Bateman, 235.
    Forster, 258.
  Sulphur;
    Hancock, 17.
    Newton, 19.
    Brockedon, 22.
    Brooman, 22.
    Keene, 24.
    Hancock, 27.
    Hancock, 33.
    Forster, 37.
    Hancock, 38.
    Barlow and Forster, 40.
    Ricardo, 42.
    Nickels, 43.
    Richards, Taylor, and Wylde, 46.
    Siemens, 46.
    Newton, 46.
    Newton (*Goodyear*), 49.
    Poole (*Goodyear*), 52.
    Poole (*Goodyear*), 52.
    Poole (*Goodyear*), 52.
    Poole (*Goodyear*), 53.
    Poole (*Goodyear*), 54.
    Poole (*Goodyear*), 54.
    Poole (*Goodyear*), 55.
    Poole (*Goodyear*), 56.
    Poole (*Goodyear*), 57.
    Poole (*Goodyear*), 57.
    Poole (*Goodyear*), 58.
    Poole (*Goodyear*), 58.
    Poole (*Goodyear*), 59.
    Goodyear, 72.
    Goodyear, 76.
    Goodyear, 76.
    Goodyear, 78.
    Goodyear, 79.
    Goodyear, 79.
    Rider, 80.
    Gidley and Muschamp, 81.

Vulcanizing by means of—*cont.*
  Sulphur—*cont.*
    Johnson (*Guibal*), 83.
    Goodyear, 84.
    Sorel, 85.
    Newton, 89.
    Johnson, 90.
    Johnson, 94.
    Ross, 95.
    Fanshawe and Fanshawe, 98.
    Johnson (*Morey*), 100.
    Goodyear, 100.
    Bielefeld, 105.
    Goodyear, 105.
    Sautelet, 106.
    Johnson (*Wacrenier*), 109.
    Johnson (*Wacrenier*), 109.
    Latta, 109.
    Ford, 110.
    Turner, 111.
    Johnson (*Steinlen*), 111.
    Turner, 111.
    Ford, 112.
    Bousfield, 113.
    Goodyear, 114.
    Ford, 115.
    Lorimier, 116.
    Rider, 116.
    Lorimier, 117.
    Deplanque, 119.
    Johnson (*Morey*), 119.
    Bousfield, 120.
    Newton, 121.
    Codet-Négrier, 122.
    Day, 122.
    Day, 123.
    Spill, 124.
    Parker, 125.
    Newton, 125.
    Candelot, 127.
    Parker, 128.
    Newton, 130.
    Moseley, 131.
    Henson, 131.
    Putnam, 132.
    Dodge, 133.
    Johnson (*Day*), 135.
    Warne, 136.
    Hope, 137.
    Cowper (*Cuppers*), 138.
    Kirrage, 140.
    Dodge, 141.
    Warne, Jaques, and Fanshawe, 142.
    Duncan, 143.
    Childs, 144.
    Moseley, 144.
    Patrick, 146.
    Belling, 147.
    Clark, 147.
    Hooper, 149.
    Warne, Fanshawe, Jaques, and Galpin, 150.
    Johnson (*Day*), 153.
    Childs, 153.
    Dodge (*Hall*), 154.

Vulcanizing, by means of—*cont.*
  Sulphur—*cont.*
    Patrick, 155.
    Newton (*Mayall*), 156.
    Newton (*Green*), 157.
    Bousfield (*Murphy*), 157.
    Laurence, 158.
    Daft, 160.
    Newton (*Baker*), 161.
    Childs, 162.
    Pitman (*Eatin*), 163.
    Daft, 164.
    Newton (*Cheever*), 168.
    Hooper, 170.
    Newton (*Cheever*), 171.
    Bridges, 172.
    Richard, 173,
    Silver and Barwick, 174.
    Hooper, 175.
    Woodcock, 176.
    Noirot, 177.
    Pitman (*Bourn, Brown, and Chaffee*), 177.
    Pitman (*Bourn, Brown, and Chaffee*), 178.
    Newton (*Cheever*), 178.
    Newton (*Cheever*), 179.
    Newton (*Cheever*), 181.
    Moulton, 185.
    Silver and Griffin, 188.
    Hunt, 192.
    Williams, 196.
    Baggs and Parkes, 199.
    Forster, 199.
    Shephard, 200.
    Gabriel and Gabriel, 204.
    Cartwright, 204.
    Lerenard, 207.
    De la Bastida (*Cohen and Vaillant*), 207.
    Daft, 208.
    Henry (*Société Chartier et Compagnie*), 209.
    Rémiére, 211.
    Fuller, 211.
    Brooman (*Baldamus*), 211.
    Griffin, 212.
    Hancock and Silver, 213.
    Gérard, 214.
    Bousfield (*Hayward*), 217.
    Hooper, 218.
    Gilbee (*Mathevon*), 219.
    Ford and Rigg, 220.
    Jennings and Lavater, 221.
    Mulholland, 224.
    Bousfield (*Taylor*), 225.
    Spill, Briggs, and Spill, 225.
    Norris (*Holl*), 226.
    Clarkson, 228.
    Bousfield (*Mayall*), 230.
    Bousfield (*Taylor*), 232.
    Jennings and Lavater, 233.
    Henson, 235.
    De Briou, 236.
    Gérard, 236.
    Clark (*Quinet and Baudouin*), 237.

Vulcanizing, by means of—*cont.*
  Sulphur—*cont.*
    Ritchie, 238.
    Lavater, 238.
    Hancock and Silver, 241.
    Stevens (*Stevens*), 242.
    Fontainemoreau (*Innocent and Perroncel*), 243.
    Mayall, 245.
    Mayall, 246.
    Mayall, 246.
    Abel, 247.
    Mulholland, 248.
    Lerenard, 249.
    De Briou, 251.
    Felt (*Felt*), 252.
    Whitehead, 252.
    Macintosh, 252.
    Bourne, 254.
    Bousfield (*McBurney*), 256.
    Hunt, 257.
    Forster, 258.
    Simpson, 259.
    Darlow and Seymour, 260.
    Moseley, 260.
  Sulphur, chloride or hypochloride of;
    Parkes, 27.
    Brockedon and Hancock, 30.
    Duvivier and Chaudet, 99.
    Parkes, 108.
    Macintosh, 126.
    Macintosh, 130.
    Wray, 140.
    Moseley, 144.
    Moseley, 149.
    Macintosh, 176.
    Godefroy, 198.
    Bowra, 200.
    Newton (*Elmer*), 206.
    Henry (*Société Chartier et Campagnie*), 209.
    Hancock and Silver, 213.
    Hull, 215.
    Spill, Briggs, and Spill, 225.
    Mulholland, 227.
    Jennings and Lavater, 228.
    Humphrey, 231.
    Turner and Clark, 235.
    Fontainemoreau (*Innocent and Perroncel*), 243.
  Sulphuret of an alkali;
    Hancock, 36.
    Moulton, 50.
  Sulphurous acid gas;
    Westhead, 38.
    Nickels, 43.
    Hughes, 117.
  Zinc, sulphide, sulphite, or hyposulphite of;
    Moulton, 50.
    Rider, 51.
    Johnson, 61.
    Brookes, 74.

Vulcanising by means of—*cont.*
   Zinc, sulphide, sulphite, or hyposulphite of;
      Rider, 80.
      Ninck, 119.
      Rostaing, 167.
      Fontainemoreau (*Innocent and Perroncel*), 243.
      Forster, 258.

Waterproof coating, preparations for. *See* Coating and cementing, &c.; Solvents, &c.

Wax. *See* Compounds of gutta percha, &c.; Compounds of india-rubber, &c.

Whalebone. *See* Compounds of gutta percha, &c.

White lead. *See* Compounds of gutta percha, &c.; Compounds of india-rubber, &c.

Zinc. *See* Compounds of gutta percha, &c.; Compounds of india-rubber, &c.; Vulcanizing.

LONDON:
Printed by GEORGE E. EYRE and WILLIAM SPOTTISWOODE,
Printers to the Queen's most Excellent Majesty.

PATENT OFFICE.

LIST OF WORKS printed by order of THE COMMISSIONERS OF PATENTS FOR INVENTIONS, and sold at the PATENT OFFICE, 25, Southampton Buildings, Chancery Lane, London.

I.

1. SPECIFICATIONS of PATENTS for INVENTIONS, DISCLAIMERS, &c., enrolled under the Old Law, from A.D. 1617 to Oct. 1852, comprised in 13,561 Blue Books, or 691 thick vols. imp. 8vo. Total cost price about 600*l*.

2. SPECIFICATIONS of INVENTIONS, DISCLAIMERS, &c., deposited and filed under the Patent Law Amendment Act from Oct. 1, 1852, to June 30, 1875, comprised in 76,851 Blue Books, or 2,440 thick vols. imp. 8vo. Total cost price, about 2,460*l*.

II.

INDEXES to PATENTS of INVENTION under the Old Law, from A.D. 1617 to October 1852:—

1. CHRONOLOGICAL INDEX. 2 vols. (1554 pages.) Price 30*s*.; by post, 33*s*. 2*d*.

2. ALPHABETICAL INDEX. 1 vol. (647 pages.) Price 20*s*.; by post, 21*s*. 5*d*.

3. SUBJECT-MATTER INDEX. 2 vols. (970 pages.) Second Edition, to which is prefixed a key of Terms and Phrases. 1857. Price 2*l*. 16*s*.; by post, 2*l*. 18*s*. 8*d*.

4. REFERENCE INDEX of PATENTS of INVENTION, pointing out the Office in which each enrolled Specification may be consulted and the Books in which Specifications, Law Proceedings connected with Inventions, &c. have been noticed. 1 vol. (710 pages.) Second Edition. 1862. Price 30*s*.; by post, 31*s*. 5*d*.

I.R. U

5. APPENDIX to the REFERENCE INDEX, containing abstracts from such of the early Patents and Signet Bills as describe the nature of the Invention. 1 vol. (91 pages.) Price 4s.; by post, 4s. 6d.

INDEXES of APPLICATIONS for PATENTS and PATENTS GRANTED under the Patent Law Amendment Act, 1852.

CHRONOLOGICAL INDEXES :—

For 1852 (Oct. 1—Dec. 31) and 1853. (258 pages.) Price 11s. by post 12s.

		s.	d.		s.	d.
1854 (167 pages), price	6	0; by post	6	9
1855 (188 „)	„	6	6	„	7	2
1856 (189 „)	„	6	6	„	7	2
1857 (196 „)	„	6	6	„	7	2
1858 (188 „)	„	6	0	„	6	8
1859 (196 „)	„	6	6	„	7	1
1860 (209 „)	„	7	0	„	7	7
1861 (215 „)	„	7	0	„	7	7
1862 (237 „)	„	7	6	„	8	2
1863 (220 „)	„	7	0	„	7	7
1864 (222 „)	„	7	0	„	7	7
1865 (230 „)	„	7	0	„	7	7
1866 (239 „)	„	7	0	„	7	8
1867 (254 „)	„	7	6	„	8	2
1868 (274 „)	„	8	0	„	8	8

(*For continuation see* CHRONOLOGICAL AND DESCRIPTIVE INDEXES.)

ALPHABETICAL INDEXES :—

For 1852 (Oct. 1—Dec. 31) and 1853. (181 pages.) Price 13s. by post 13s. 8d.

		s.	d.		s.	d.
1854 (119 pages), price	7	0; by post	7	7
1855 (129 „)	„	7	6	„	8	1
1856 (143 „)	„	8	0	„	8	7
1857 (153 „)	„	8	0	„	8	8
1858 (148 „)	„	8	0	„	8	7
1859 (188 „)	„	10	0	„	10	7
1860 (203 „)	„	10	6	„	11	1
1861 (222 „)	„	10	6	„	11	2
1862 (240 „)	„	11	6	„	12	2
1863 (218 „)	„	11	0	„	11	8
1864 (220 „)	„	11	0	„	11	8
1865 (236 „)	„	11	6	„	12	2
1866 (243 „)	„	11	6	„	12	2
1867 (258 „)	„	12	0	„	12	8
1868 (291 „)	„	13	0	„	13	10
1869 (272 „)	„	13	0	„	13	9
1870 (242 „)	„	12	0	„	12	8
1871 (52 „)	„	2	0	„	2	1½

(*For continuation see* CHRONOLOGICAL AND DESCRIPTIVE INDEXES.)

SUBJECT-MATTER INDEXES:—
For 1852 (Oct. 1—Dec. 31). (132 pages.) Price 9s.; by post, 9s. 7d.

		s.	d.		s.	d.
1853 (291 pages), price	16	0	; by post	16	11
1854 (311 „)	„	16	6	„	17	6
1855 (311 „)	„	17	0	„	17	11
1856 (335 „)	„	18	6	„	19	7
1857 (367 „)	„	19	6	„	20	8
1858 (360 „)	„	19	6	„	20	6
1859 (381 „)	„	20	0	„	20	11
1860 (405 „)	„	22	0	„	23	0
1861 (442 „)	„	23	0	„	24	1
1862 (465 „)	„	23	0	„	24	1
1863 (432 „)	„	22	0	„	23	0
1864 (446 „)	„	23	0	„	24	1
1865 (474 „)	„	23	0	„	24	1
1866 (465 „)	„	23	0	„	24	4
1867 (508 „)	„	25	0	„	26	2
1868 (632 „)	„	30	0	„	31	5
1869 (587 „)	„	28	0	„	29	$2\frac{1}{2}$
1870 (509 „)	„	28	0	„	29	2

(*For continuation see* CHRONOLOGICAL AND DESCRIPTIVE INDEXES.)

DESCRIPTIVE INDEXES (Abridgments of Provisional and Complete Specifications).

For 1867. In the following quarterly parts:—
1. Quarter ending 31st March. (228 pages.) Price 1s. 8d.; by post, 2s. 1d.
2. Quarter ending 30th June. (224 pages.) Price 1s. 8d.; by post, 2s. 1d.
3. Quarter ending 30th September. (196 pages.) Price 1s. 8d.; by post, 2s.
4. Quarter ending 31st December. (232 pages.) Price 1s. 8d.; by post, 2s. 1d.

For 1868. In the following quarterly parts:—
1. Quarter ending 31st March. (236 pages.) Price 1s. 8d.; by post, 2s. 1d.
2. Quarter ending 30th June. (218 pages.) Price 1s. 8d.; by post, 2s. 1d.
3. Quarter ending 30th September. (194 pages.) Price 1s. 8d.; by post, 2s.
4. Quarter ending 31st December. (224 pages.) Price 1s. 8d.; by post, 2s. 1d.

CHRONOLOGICAL AND DESCRIPTIVE INDEXES (containing the Abridgments of Provisional and Complete Specifications, with an Alphabetical Index of Names).

For 1869. In the following quarterly parts:
1. Quarter ending 31st March. (226 pages, with 7 pages Index of Names = 233 pages.) Price 1s. 8d.; by post, 2s. 1d.
2. Quarter ending 30th June. (234 pages, with 8 pages Index of Names = 242 pages.) Price 1s. 8d.; by post, 2s. 1d.
3. Quarter ending 30th Sept. (200 pages, with 7 pages Index of Names = 207 pages.) Price 1s. 8d.; by post, 2s. 1d.
4. Quarter ending 31st Dec. (212 pages, with 7 pages Index of Names = 219 pages.) Price 1s. 8d.; by post, 2s. 1d.

For 1870. In the following quarterly parts:—
1. Quarter ending 31st March. (222 pages, with 7 pages Index of Names = 229 pages.) Price 1s. 8d.; by post, 2s. 1d.
2. Quarter ending 30th June. (208 pages, with 7 pages Index of Names = 215 pages.) Price 1s. 8d.; by post, 2s. 1d.
3. Quarter ending 30th Sept. (168 pages, with 6 pages Index of Names = 174 pages.) Price 1s. 8d.; by post, 2s.
4. Quarter ending 31st Dec. (182 pages, with 6 pages Index of Names = 188 pages.) Price 1s. 8d.; by post, 2s.

CHRONOLOGICAL AND DESCRIPTIVE INDEXES (containing the Abridgments of Provisional and Complete Specifications), with Indexes of Names and Subject Matter.

For 1871. (792 pages, with 77 pages Indexes of Names and Subject Matter = 869 pages). Price 19s.; by post, 20s. 9d.

For 1872. (876 pages, with 92 pages Indexes of Names and Subject Matter = 968 pages). Price 19s.; by post, 20s. 11d.

For 1873. (928 pages, with 126 pages Alphabetical and Subject-matter Indexes = 1,054 pages). Price 19s.; by post, 21s.

For 1874 (954 pages, with 52 pages Alphabetical Index, and 103 pages Subject-matter Index* = 1109 pages). Price 20s. 8d.; by post, 22s. 8d.

For 1875. Published on Friday in each week, and forwarded, post free, to Subscribers. Terms 30s. per annum. Subscriptions received at the Sale Room of the Patent Office, where also single copies may be obtained at 4d. each, except the No. [31] containing the Alphabetical Index for the year and the concluding No. [52] (containing the Subject-matter Index for the year), which are 2s. each. Post Office Orders to be made payable at the Post Office, Chancery Lane, to Mr. Bennet Woodcroft, Clerk to the Commissioners of Patents.

III.

ABRIDGMENTS (in Classes and Chronologically arranged) of SPECIFICATIONS of PATENTED INVENTIONS, from the earliest enrolled to those published under the Act of 1852.

These books are of 12mo. size, and each is limited to inventions of one class only. They are so arranged as to form at once a Chronological, Alphabetical, Subject-matter, and Reference Index to the class to which they relate. Inventors are strongly recommended, before applying for Letters Patent, to consult the classes of Abridgments of Specifications which relate to the subjects of their inventions, and by the aid of these works to select the Specifications they may consider it necessary to examine in order to ascertain if their inventions are new. The *preface* of each volume explains (in most cases) the scope of the series of Abridgments which it contains.

The following series of Abridgments do not extend beyond the end of the year 1866. From that date the Abridgments will be found in chronological order in the "Chronological and Descriptive Index" (*see* Section II. of this List of Works). It is intended, however, to publish these Abridgments in classes as soon as the Abridgments of all the Specifications from the earliest period to the end of 1866 have appeared in a classified form. Until that takes place the Inventor (by the aid of the Subject Matter Index for each year) can continue his examination of the Abridgments relating to the subject of his invention in the Chronological and Descriptive Index.

* The Alphabetical and Subject-matter Indexes may be purchased separately in blue covers, price 2s. each.

The classes already published are,—

1. DRAINS AND SEWERS; INCLUDING THE MANUFACTURE OF DRAIN TILES AND PIPES, price 1s., by post 1s. 2d.
2. SEWING AND EMBROIDERING (*2nd edition*), price 1s. 6d.; by post 1s. 9d.
3. MANURE, price 4d., by post 5d.
4. PRESERVATION OF FOOD, Part I., A.D. 1691-1855, price 4d., by post 5d.—Part II., A.D. 1856-1866, price 6d., by post 7d.
5. MARINE PROPULSION, Parts I., II., & III., A.D. 1618-1857, price 1s. 10d., by post 2s. 1d.—Part IV., A.D. 1857-1866, price 1s. 10d., by post 2s. 2d.
6. MANUFACTURE OF IRON AND STEEL, Parts I., II., & III., A.D. 1621-1857, price 1s. 6d., by post 1s. 8½d.—Part IV., A.D. 1857-1865, price 2s. 6d., by post 2s. 8d.
7. AIDS TO LOCOMOTION, price 6d., by post 7d.
8. STEAM CULTURE, price 8d., by post 9½d.
9. WATCHES, CLOCKS, AND OTHER TIMEKEEPERS, Part I., A.D. 1661-1856, price 8d., by post 9½d.—Part II., A.D. 1857-1866, price 8d., by post 9½d.
10. FIRE-ARMS AND OTHER WEAPONS, AMMUNITION, AND ACCOUTREMENTS, Part I., A.D. 1588-1858, price 1s. 4d., by post 1s. 7½d.—Part II., A.D. 1858-1866, price 2s. 2d., by post 2s. 6d.
11. PAPER. MANUFACTURE OF PAPER, PASTEBOARD, AND PAPIER-MÂCHÉ. Part I., A.D. 1665-1857, price 10d., by post 1s.—Part II., A.D. 1858-1866, price 3s. 8d., by post 3s. 10½d.
12. PAPER. CUTTING, FOLDING, AND ORNAMENTING; INCLUDING ENVELOPES, CARDS, PAPER-HANGINGS, &c., price 8d., by post 10d.
13. TYPOGRAPHIC, LITHOGRAPHIC, & PLATE PRINTING. Part I., A.D. 1617-1857, price 2s. 8d., by post 3s. 3d.—Part II., A.D. 1858-1861, price 2s., by post 2s. 6d.
14. BLEACHING, DYEING, AND PRINTING YARNS AND FABRICS, Part I., A.D. 1617-1857, price 3s. 4d., by post 4s. 1d.—Part II., A.D. 1858-1866, price 8s. by post 8s. 4½d.
15. ELECTRICITY AND MAGNETISM, THEIR GENERATION AND APPLICATIONS, Part I., A.D. 1766-1857, price 3s. 2d., by post 3s. 11d.—Part II., A.D. 1858-1866 (*2nd edition*), price 2s. 8d., by post 3s. 2d.
16. PREPARATION OF INDIA-RUBBER, AND GUTTA-PERCHA (*2nd edition*), price 1s. 2d., by post 1s. 4½d.
17. PRODUCTION AND APPLICATIONS OF GAS, Part I., A.D. 1681-1858, price 2s. 4d., by post 2s. 11d.—Part II., A.D. 1859-1866 (*2nd edition*), price 2s. 4d., by post 2s. 8½d.
18. METALS AND ALLOYS, price 1s. 10d., by post 2s. 3½d.
19. PHOTOGRAPHY, Part I., A.D. 1839-1859, price 8d., by post 10d.—Part II., A.D. 1860-1866 (*2nd edition*), price 10d., by post 11½d.
20. WEAVING, Part I., A.D. 1620-1859, price 4s., by post 4s. 11½d.—Part II., A.D. 1860-1866, price 2s. 8d., by post, 3s. 1d.
21. SHIP BUILDING, REPAIRING, SHEATHING, LAUNCHING, &c., Part I., A.D. 1618-1860, price 2s. 4d., by post 2s. 11d.—Part II., A.D. 1861-1866, price 2s. 6d., by post 2s. 11d.
22. BRICKS AND TILES, Part I., A.D. 1619-1860, price 1s., by post 1s. 3½d.—Part II., A.D. 1861-1866, price 8d., by post 9½d.
23. PLATING OR COATING METALS WITH METALS, Part I., A.D. 1637-1860, price 10d., by post 1s. 0½d.—Part II., A.D. 1861-1866 (*2nd edition*), price 6d. by post 7d.
24. POTTERY, Part I., A.D. 1626-1861, price 10d., by post 1s.—Part II., A.D. 1862-1866, price 6d., by post 7d.
25. MEDICINE, SURGERY, AND DENTISTRY (*2nd edition*), price 1s. 10d., by post 2s. 1½d.
26. MUSIC AND MUSICAL INSTRUMENTS (*2nd edition*), price 1s. 10d., by post 2s. 1½d.
27. OILS, FATS, LUBRICANTS, CANDLES, AND SOAP (*2nd edition*), price 2s. 10d., by post 3s. 4d.
28. SPINNING; INCLUDING THE PREPARATION OF FIBROUS MATERIALS, AND THE DOUBLING OF YARNS AND THREADS, Part I., A.D. 1624-1863, price 24s., by post 25s. 5d.—Part II., A.D. 1864-1866, price 2s., by post 2s. 4d.
29. LACE AND OTHER LOOPED AND NETTED FABRICS, price 10s., by post 10s. 8d.
30. PREPARATION AND COMBUSTION OF FUEL, price 17s., by post 17s. 9d.
31. RAISING, LOWERING, AND WEIGHING (*2nd edition*) price 3s. 8d., by post 4s. 3½d.
32. HYDRAULICS (*2nd edition*), price 4s. 8d., by post 5s. 5d.
33. RAILWAYS (*2nd edition*), price 2s. 6d., by post 2s. 11d.

34. SADDLERY, HARNESS STABLE FITTINGS, &c., price 1s., by post 1s. 2d.
35. ROADS AND WAYS, price 1s., by post 1s. 2d.
36. BRIDGES, VIADUCTS, AND AQUEDUCTS, price 10d., by post 1s.
37. WRITING INSTRUMENTS AND MATERIALS, price 1s. 4d., by post 1s. 7d.
38. RAILWAY SIGNALS AND COMMUNICATING APPARATUS, price 5s. 10d., by post 6s. 1½d.
39. FURNITURE AND UPHOLSTERY, price 2s., by post 2s. 4d.
40. ACIDS, ALKALIES, OXIDES, AND SALTS, price 3s. 8d., by post 4s. 3d.
41. AERONAUTICS, price 4d., by post 5d.
42. PREPARATION AND USE OF TOBACCO, price 10d., by post 1s.
43. BOOKS, PORTFOLIOS, CARD-CASES, &c., price 10d., by post 1s.
44. LAMPS, CANDLESTICKS, CHANDELIERS, AND OTHER ILLUMINATING APPARATUS, price 2s. 6d., by post 2s. 10½d.
45. NEEDLES AND PINS, price 6d., by post 7d.
46. CARRIAGES & OTHER VEHICLES FOR RAILWAYS, price 5s.6d., by post, 6s. 4d.
47. UMBRELLAS, PARASOLS, AND WALKING STICKS, price 10d., by post 11½d.
48. SUGAR, price 1s. 10d., by post 2s. 1½d.
49. STEAM ENGINE, Part I. (in 2 vols.), A.D. 1618–1859, price 9s. 4d., by post 10s. 10½d.—Part II. (in 2 vols.), A.D. 1860–1866, price 4s. 10d., by post 5s.7d.
50. PAINTS, COLOURS, AND VARNISHES, price 1s. 10d., by post 2s. 1½d.
51. TOYS, GAMES, AND EXERCISES, price 1s., by post 1s. 2d.
52. VENTILATION, price 1s. 10d., by post 2s. 0½d.
53. FARRIERY; INCLUDING THE MEDICAL AND SURGICAL TREATMENT OF ANIMALS, price 1s., by post 1s. 1½d.
54. ARTISTS' INSTRUMENTS AND MATERIALS, price 10d., by post 1s.
55. SKINS, HIDES, AND LEATHER, price 1s. 6d., by post 1s. 8½d.
56. PREPARING AND CUTTING CORK; BOTTLING LIQUIDS; SECURING AND OPENING BOTTLES, &c., price 1s. 6d., by post, 1s. 9d.
57. BRUSHING AND SWEEPING, price 1s., by post, 1s. 2d.
58. NAILS, RIVETS, BOLTS, SCREWS, NUTS, AND WASHERS, price 1s. 8d., by post, 1s. 11½d.
59. HINGES, HINGE JOINTS, AND DOOR SPRINGS, price 8d., by post, 9½d.
60. LOCKS, LATCHES, BOLTS, AND SIMILAR FASTENINGS, price 1s. 6d., by post, 1s. 9d.
61. COOKING, BREAD-MAKING, AND THE PREPARATION OF CONFECTIONERY, price 1s. 10d., by post 2s. 1½d..
62. AIR, GAS, AND OTHER MOTIVE POWER ENGINES, price 1s. 10d., by post 2s. 1½d.
63. WATER CLOSETS, EARTH CLOSETS, URINALS, &c., price 10d., by post, 1s.
64. SAFES, STRONG ROOMS, TILLS, AND SIMILAR DEPOSITORIES, price 6d., by post, 7d.
65. WEARING APPAREL. DIVISION I.—HEAD COVERINGS, price 1s. 4d., by post, 1s. 6½d.
66. WEARING APPAREL. DIVISION II.—BODY COVERINGS, price 2s. 4d., by post 2s. 8½d.
67. WEARING APPAREL. DIVISION III.—FOOT COVERINGS (*in course of preparation*).
68. WEARING APPAREL. DIVISION IV.—DRESS FASTENINGS AND JEWELLERY (*in course of preparation*).
69. ANCHORS, price 6d. by post 7d..
70. METALLIC PIPES AND TUBES, price 1s. 8d., by post 1s. 11d.
71. MINING, QUARRYING, TUNNELLING, AND WELL-SINKING, price 1s. 4d., by post 1s. 6½d.
72. MILKING, CHURNING, AND CHEESE-MAKING, price 6d., by post 7d.
73. MASTS, SAILS, RIGGING, &c.; INCLUDING APPARATUS FOR RAISING AND LOWERING SHIPS' BOATS, price 1s., by post 1s. 2d.
74. CASKS AND BARRELS, price 8d., by post 9½d.
75. STEERING AND MANŒUVRING VESSELS, price 1s., by post 1s. 2d.
76. OPTICAL, MATHEMATICAL, AND OTHER PHILOSOPHICAL INSTRUMENTS: INCLUDING NAUTICAL, ASTRONOMICAL, AND METEOROLOGICAL INSTRUMENTS, price 2s. 10d., by post 3s. 2d.

IV.

COMMISSIONERS of PATENTS' JOURNAL, published on the evenings of Tuesday and Friday in each week. Price 2d.; by Post, 3d. Annual Subscription, including postage, 23s. 6d., which may be remitted by Post Office Order, made payable at the Post Office, Chancery Lane, to Mr. Bennet Woodcroft, Clerk to the Commissioners, Patent Office.

CONTENTS OF JOURNAL.

1. Applications for Letters Patent.
2. Grants of Provisional Protection for six months.
3. Inventions protected for six months by the deposit of a Complete Specification.
4. Notices to proceed.
5. Patents sealed.
6. Patents extended.
7. Patents cancelled.
8. Patents on which the third year's stamp duty of 50l. has been paid.
9. Patents which have become void by non-payment of the stamp duty of 50l. before the expiration of the third year.
10. Patents on which the seventh year's stamp duty of 100l. has been paid.
11. Patents which have become void by non-payment of the stamp duty of 100l. before the expiration of the seventh year.
12. Colonial Patents and Patent Law.
13. Foreign Patents and Patent Law.
14. Weekly price lists of printed Specifications, &c.
15. Official advertisements and notices of interest to Patentees and Inventors generally.

V.

1. PATENT LAW AMENDMENT ACTS (15 & 16 Vict. cap. 83, A.D. 1852; 16 Vict. cap. 5, A.D. 1853; and 16 & 17 Vict. cap. 115, A.D. 1853); together with the RULES and REGULATIONS issued by the Commissioners of Patents for Inventions, and by the Lord Chancellor and the Master of the Rolls, under the Acts 15 & 16 Vict. c. 83, and 16 & 17 Vict. c. 115. Price 6d.; by post, 7d.
2. APPENDIX to the SPECIFICATIONS of ENGLISH PATENTS for REAPING MACHINES. By B. WOODCROFT, F.R.S. Price 6s. 6d.; by post, 6s. 11d.
3. INDEX to ALL INVENTIONS PATENTED in ENGLAND from 1617 to 1854 inclusive, arranged under the greatest number of heads, with parallel references to INVENTIONS and DISCOVERIES described in the scientific works of VARIOUS NATIONS, as classified by Professor Schubarth. By B. WOODCROFT, F.R.S. Price 1s.; by post, 1s. 1d.

The foreign works thus indexed form a portion of the Library of the Commissioners of Patents, where they may be consulted.

4. EXTENSION of PATENTS to the COLONIES.—Abstract of Replies to the Secretary of State's Circular Despatch of January 2, 1853, on the subject of the Extension of Patents for Inventions, to the Colonies. Second Edition, with Revised Table. 1861. Price 2s.; by post, 2s. 1½d.
5. PATENT RIGHTS in the COLONIES.—Abstract of Replies to the Secretary of State's Circular Despatch of July 11, 1856, calling for Information as to the form of the application to be made by persons desirous of obtaining Patent Rights in the Colonies, and the expenses attendant on the Grant of such Patent Rights. Price 2s.; by post, 2s. 1½d.
6. COPY of AMERICAN PATENT, SPECIFICATION, and other DOCUMENTS relating to an invention of "A new and useful "improved method of removing incrustation from boilers,'

presented by Davis Embree, of Dayton, Ohio, United States of America, to The Government and People of the United Kingdom of Great Britain and Ireland, 21st April 1865. Price 6*d.*; by post, 6½*d.*

7. SUPPLEMENT to the SERIES of LETTERS PATENT and SPECIFICATIONS, from A.D. 1617 to Oct. 1852; consisting for the most part of Reprints of scarce Pamphlets, descriptive of the early patented Inventions comprised in that Series.

CONTENTS.

1. Metallica; or the Treatise of Metallica, briefly comprehending the doctrine of diverse new metallical inventions, &c. By SIMON STURTEVANT. (*Letters Patent, dated 29th February* 1611.) Price 1*s.* 4*d.*; by post, 1*s.* 5*d.*
2. A Treatise of Metallica, but not that which was published by Mr. Simon Sturtevant, upon his Patent, &c. By JOHN ROVENZON. (*Letters Patent granted A.D.* 1612.) Price 4*d.*; by post, 4½*d.*
3. A Commission directed to Sir Richard Wynne and others to inquire upon oath whether NICHOLAS PAGE or Sir NICHOLAS HALSE was the first inventor of certaine kilnes for the drying of malt, &c. &c. (*Letters Patent, Nos.* 33 *and* 85, *respectively dated* 8*th April* 1626, *and* 23*rd July* 1635.) Price 2*d.*; by post, 2¼*d.*
4. DUD DUDLEY's Metallum Martis; or iron made with pit-coale, sea-coale, &c. (*Letters Patent, Nos.* 18 *and* 117, *respectively dated* 22*nd February* 1620, *and* 2*nd May* 1638.) Price 8*d.*; by post, 8½*d.*
5. Description of the nature and working of the Patent Waterscoop Wheels invented by WILLIAM WHELEE, as compared with the raising wheels now in common use. By J. B. W. Translated from the Dutch by Dr. Tolhausen. (*Letters Patent, No.* 127, *dated* 24*th June* 1642.) Price 2*s.*; by post, 2*s.* 1½*d.*
6. An exact and true definition of the stupendous Water-commanding Engine invented by the Right Honourable (and deservedly to be praised and admired) EDWARD SOMERSET, Lord Marquis of WORCESTER, &c. &c. (*Stat.* 15 *Car. II. c.* 12. *A.D.* 1663.) Price 4*d.*; by post, 4½*d.*
7. Navigation improved; or the art of rowing ships of all rates in calms with a more easy, swift, and steady motion than oars can. By THOMAS SAVERY. (*Letters Patent. No.* 347, *dated* 10*th Jan.* 1696.) Price 1*s.*; by post, 1*s.* 0½*d.*
8. The Miner's Friend; or an engine to raise water by fire, described, &c. By THOMAS SAVERY. (*Letters Patent, No.* 356, *dated* 25*th July* 1698, *and Stat.* 10 *& 11 Will. III. No.* 61, *A.D.* 1699.) Price 1*s.*; by post, 1*s.* 1*d.*
9. Specimina Ichnographica; or a brief narrative of several new inventions and experiments, particularly the navigating a ship in a calm, &c. By JOHN ALLEN, M.D. (*Letters Patent, No.* 513, *dated* 7*th August* 1729.) Price 8*d.*; by post, 9*d.*
10. A description and draught of a new-invented Machine for carrying vessels or ships out of or into any harbour, port, or river against wind and tide, or in a calm, &c. By JONATHAN HULLS. (*Letters Patent, No.* 556, *dated* 21*st December* 1736.) Price 8*d.*; by post, 9*d.*
11. An historical account of a new method for extracting the foul air out of ships, &c., with the description and draught of the machines by which it is performed, &c. By SAMUEL SUTTON, the Inventor. To which are annexed two relations given thereof to the Royal Society by Dr. Mead and Mr. Watson. (*Letters Patent, No.* 602, *dated* 16*th March* 1744.) Price 1*s.*; by post, 1*s.* 1*d.*
12. The letter of Master WILLIAM DRUMMOND for the construction of machines, weapons, and engines of war for attack or defence by land or sea, &c. Dated the 29th September 1626. (*Scotch Patent, temp. Car. II.*) Price 4*d.*; by post, 4½*d.*
13. Contributions to the History of the Steam Engine, being two deeds relating to the erection by Messrs. Boulton and Watt of steam engines on the United Mines at Gwennap, Cornwall, and at Werneth Colliery, near Oldham, Lancashire. From the originals in the Patent Office Library. Price 10*d.*, by post, 10½*d.*

A FREE LIBRARY and READING ROOMS are open to the Public daily, from 10 till 4 o'clock, in the Office of the Commissioners of Patents, 25, Southampton Buildings, Chancery Lane. In addition to the printed Specifications, Indexes, and other publications of the Commissioners, the Library includes a Collection of the leading British and Foreign Scientific Journals, and text-books in the various departments of science and art.

Complete sets of the Commissioners of Patents' publications (each set including more than 3,330 volumes and costing for printing and paper upwards of £3,150) have been presented to the authorities of the most important towns in the kingdom, on condition that the works shall be rendered daily accessible to the public, for reference or for copying, free of all charge. The following list gives the names of the towns, and shows the place of deposit, so far as ascertained, of each set of the works thus presented :—

Aberdeen (*Mechanics' Institution*).
Belfast (*Queen's College*).
Beverley (*Guildhall*).
Birmingham (*Central Free Library—Reference Department, Ratcliff Place*).
Blackburn (*Free Library and Museum, Town Hall Street*).
Bolton-le-Moors (*Public Library, Exchange Buildings*).
Bradford, Yorkshire (*Borough Accountant's Office, Corporation Buildings, Swain Street*).
Brighton (*Town Hall*).
Bristol (*City Library, King Street*).
Burnley (*Office of the Burnley Improvement Commissioners*).
Bury.
Carlisle (*Pub. Free Lib*y, *Police Office*).
Cork (*Royal Cork Instⁿ, Nelson Place*).
Crewe (*Railway Station*).
Darlington (*Mechanics' Institute, Skinnergate*).
Derby (*Free Public Library*).
Dorchester.
Drogheda.
Dublin (*Royal Dublin Soc, Kildare St.*)
Dundalk (*Free Library*).
Falmouth (*Public Liby, Church St.*).
Gateshead (*Mechanics' Institute*).
Gorton (*Railway Station*).
Glasgow (*Stirling's Liby, Miller St.*).
Grimsby, Great (*Mechanics' Institution, Victoria Street*).
Halifax.
Hertford (*Free Pub. Lib*y, *Town Hall*).
Huddersfield (*Improvement Commissioners' Offices, South Parade*).
Hull (*Mechanics' Inst., George St.*).
Ipswich (*Museum Library, Museum Street*).
Keighley (*Mechanics' Inst., North St.*).
Kidderminster (*Public Free Library, Public Buildings, Vicar Street*).
Leamington Priors (*Public Library, Town Hall*).
Leeds (*Public Library, Infirmary Buildings*).
Leicester (*Free Library, Wellington Street*).
Limerick (*Town Hall*).
Liverpool (*Free Public Library, William Brown Street*).

London (*British Museum*).
——— (*Society of Arts, John Street, Adelphi*).
Macclesfield (*Useful Know. Society*).
Maidstone (*Free Library*).
Manchester (*Free Liby., Camp Field*).
Montrose (*Free Library*).
Newcastle-upon-Tyne (*Literary and Philosophical Society*).
Newport, Monmouth (*Commercial Room, Town Hall*).
Northampton (*Museum Buildings, Town Hall*).
Norwich (*Free Library, St. John's, Maddermarket*).
Nottingham (*Free Library*).
Oldham (*School of Arts and Sciences Lyceum*).
Oxford (*Pub. Free Lib., Town Hall*).
Paisley (*Government School of Design, Gilmour Street*).
Plymouth (*Mechanics' Institute, Princess Square*).
Preston, Lancashire (*Dr. Shepherd's Library, the Institution, Avenham*).
Reading (*Literary, Scientific, and Mechanics' Institution, London St.*).
Rochdale (*Free Public Library, Town Hall*).
Rotherham (*Board of Health Offices, Howard Street*).
Salford (*Royal Museum and Library, Peel Park*).
Sheffield (*Free Public Library, Surrey Street*).
Southampton (*Hartley Institution*).
Stirling (*Burgh Library, Town House, Broad Street*).
Stockport (*Museum, Vernon Park*).
Sunderland (*Corporation Museum Athenæum, Fawcett Street*).
Wakefield (*Mechanics' Institution Barstow Square*).
Warrington (*The Museum and Lib*y.
Waterford (*Town Hall, The Mall*).
Wexford (*Mechanics'. Institute Crescent Quay*).
Wigan.
Wolverhampton (*Free Library*).
Wolverton (*Railway Station*).
York (*Lower Council Chamber Guildhall*).

The Commissioners' publications have also been presented to the following Public Offices, Seats of Learning, Societies, British Colonies, and Foreign States:—

Public Offices, &c.

Admiralty—Chatham Dockyard.
    Sheerness ditto.
    Portsmouth ditto.
    Devonport ditto.
    Pembroke ditto.
Artillery Institution, Woolwich.
Board of Trade, Whitehall.
War Office, Pall Mall.
    Small Arms Factory, Enfield.
India Office.
Royal School of Mines, &c., Jermyn Street, Piccadilly.
Dublin Castle, Dublin.
Record and Writ Office, Chancery, Dublin.
Office of Chancery, Edinburgh.
Museum of Science and Art, Edinburgh.

Seats of Learning and Societies.

Cambridge University.
Trinity College, Dublin.
Queen's College, Galway.
Incorporated Law Society, Chancery Lane, London.

British Colonies.

Barbados.
British Guiana.
Canada—Library of Parliament, Ottawa.
   Bureau of Agriculture, Toronto.
   Board of Arts and Manufactures, Montreal.
Cape of Good Hope.
Ceylon.

India—Bengal.
   Bombay.
   Madras.
   N.-W. Provinces.
Jamaica.
Malta.
Mauritius.
New Brunswick.
Newfoundland.
New South Wales.
New Zealand.
Nova Scotia.

Prince Edward Island.
South Australia—Colonial Institute, Adelaide.
Tasmania.
Trinidad.
Victoria—Parliamentary Library, Melbourne.
   Patent Office, Melbourne.
   Public Library, Melbourne.

Foreign States.

Argentine Republic—Buenos Ayres.
Austria—Athenæum, Vienna.
Belgium—Ministère de l'Intérieur, Brussels.
   Musée de l'Industrie, Brussels.
France—Bibliothèque Nationale, Paris.
   Conservatoire des Arts et Métiers, Paris.
Germany—Alsace—Société Industrielle, Mulhouse.
   Bavaria—Königliche Bibliothek, Munich.
   Gotha—Ducal Friedenstein Collection.
   Prussia—Königliche Polytechnische Schule, Aix-la-Chapelle.
    Gewerbe-Akademie, Berlin.
    Königliche Bibliothek, Berlin.
    Königliche Polytechnische Schule, Hanover.
   Saxony—Polytechnische Schule, Dresden.
   Wurtemberg—Bibliothek des Musterlage, Stuttgart.
Italy—Ufficio delle Privative, Rome.
Netherlands—Harlem.
Russia—Bibliothèque Impériale, St. Petersburg.
Spain—Madrid.
Sweden—Teknologiska Institutet, Stockholm.
United States—Patent Office, Washington.
   Astor Library, New York.
   State Library, Albany.
   Franklin Institute, Philadelphia.
   Free Public Library, Boston.
   Library Company, Philadelphia.
   Free Public Library, Chicago.
   Peabody Institute, Baltimore.
   Historical Society, Madison, Wisconsin.
   Cornell University, Ithaca, N.Y.
   Mercantile Library, St. Louis.
   Mechanics' Institute, San Francisco.

Grants of complete series of Abridgments of Specifications have been made to the undermentioned Mechanics' Literary and Scientific Institutions:—

Aberystwith (*Literary and Working Men's Reading Room*).
Alnwick (*Scientific and Mechanical Institution*).
Alton (*Mechanics' Institution*).
Altrincham (*Altrincham and Bowdon Literary Institution*).
Ashburton (*Ashburton Library, East Street*).
Ashby-de-la-Zouch (*Mutual Improvement Society*).
Ashton-under-Lyne, (*Mechanics' Institution*).
Aylesbury (*Kingsbury Mechanics' Institute*).
Bacup (*Mechanics' Institution*).
Ballymoney (*Town Hall*).
Banbridge (*Literary and Mutual Improvement Society*).
Banbury (*Mechanics' Institution*).
Barnstaple (*Literary and Scientific Institution*).
Bath (*Athenæum*).
—— (*City Free Library*).
—— (*Royal Literary and Scientific Institution*).
Batley (*Mechanics' Institution*).
Battle (*Young Men's Christian Association*).
Belfast (*Athenæum*).
—— (*Northern Law Club*).
—— (*People's Literary Institute*).
Berkhampstead, Great (*Mechanics' Institute*).
———————— (*Working Men's College*).
Birkenhead (*Literary and Scientific Society*).
Birmingham (*Bloomsbury Institution*).
—— (*Central Lending Library*).
—— (*Free Library and News Room, Gosta Green.*)
—— (*Graham Street Institution*).
—— (*Law Students' Society.*)
Bodmin (*Literary Institution*).
Bolton (*Mechanics' Institute*).
—— (*School of Art*).
Bournemouth (*Library and Reading Room*).
Bradford, Yorkshire (*Church Institute*).
———————— (*Library and Literary Society*).
———————— (*Mechanics' Institute*).
Braintree (*Braintree and Bocking Literary and Mechanics' Institution*).
Brampton, near Chesterfield (*Local Museum and Literary Institute*).
Breage, Cornwall (*Institution*).
Bristol (*Athenæum*).
—— (*Institution*).

Bristol (*Law Library Society*).
—— (*Library, Queen's Road*).
Bromsgrove (*Literary and Mechanics' Institute*).
Burnley (*Literary Institution*).
—— (*Mechanics' Institution*).
Burslem (*Wedgwood Institute*).
Bury (*Athenæum*).
Bury St. Edmund's (*Athenæum*).
—— (*Mechanics' Institution*).
Calne (*Literary Institution*).
Cardigan (*Mechanics' Institute*).
Carharrack (*Literary Institute*).
Carmarthen (*Literary and Scientific Institution*).
Cheddar (*Literary Institution*).
Cheltenham (*Permanent Library*).
—— (*Working Men's Club*).
Chertsey (*Literary and Scientific Institution*).
Chester (*City Library and Reading Room*).
Chesterfield (*Mechanics' Institution*).
Chichester (*Literary Society and Mechanics' Institute*).
Chippenham (*Literary and Scientific Institution*).
Christchurch (*Working Man's Institute*).
Cockermouth (*Mechanics' Institution*).
Coggeshall (*Literary and Mechanics' Institution*).
Colchester (*Literary Institution*).
—— (*Young Men's Christian Association*).
Compstall (*Athenæum*).
Coventry (*Free Library*).
—— (*Institute*).
—— (*School of Art*).
Crediton (*Working Men's Club*).
Crewe (*Mechanics' Institution*).
Dartmouth (*Mutual Improvement Society*).
Deal (*Deal and Walmer Institute*).
Derby (*Mechanics' Institution*).
Devonport (*Mechanics' Institute*).
Dewsbury (*Mechanics' Institution*).
Diss (*Reading Room and Library*).
Doncaster (*Free Library*).
—— (*Great Northern Mechanics' Institute*).
—— (*Young Men's Christian Association*).
Dorchester (*County Museum and Library*).
—— (*Working Men's Institute*).
Dudley (*Mechanics' Institution*).
Dukinfield (*Village Library and Reading Room*).
Dumbarton (*Philosophical and Literary Society*).
Dumfries (*Mechanics' Institution*).

Dundee (*Young Men's Christian Association and Literary Institution*).
Durham (*Mechanics' Institute*).
Eagley, Bolton-le-Moors (*Library and Institute*).
Ealing (*Mechanics' Institute*).
Earlestown, Newton-le-Willows (*Mutual Improvement Society*).
East Greenwich (*Working Men's Institute*).
East Retford (*Literary and Mutual Improvement Society*).
Ebbw Vale (*Literary and Scientific Institute*).
Edinburgh (*Philosophical Institution*).
——— (*Royal Scottish Society of Arts*).
——— (*Subscription Library*).
——— (*Watt Institution and School of Art*).
——— (*Working Men's Club*).
Egham (*Literary Institute*).
Egremont (*Mechanics' Institute*).
——— (*Workmen's Institute*).
Exeter (*Devon and Exeter Albert Memorial Museum, School of Science and Art, and Free Library*).
——— (*Devon and Exeter Institution*).
Farnham (*Young Men's Association*).
Faversham (*Institute*).
Fowey (*Working Men's Reading Rooms*).
Frome (*Literary and Scientific Institution*).
——— (*Mechanics' Institution*).
Gainsborough (*Literary, Scientific and Mechanics' Institute*).
Garforth, near Leeds (*Working Men's Club*).
Glasgow (*Athenæum*).
——— (*Central Working Men's Club and Institute*).
——— (*Institution of Engineers in Scotland*).
——— (*Mechanics' Institution, Bath Street*).
——— (*Philosophical Society*).
Glastonbury (*Literary Institute*).
Godmanchester (*Working Men's Reading Room*).
Gosport (*Gosport and Alverstoke Literary and Scientific Institution*).
Grantham (*Public Literary Institution*).
Gravesend (*Gravesend and Milton Library and Reading Rooms*).
Guernsey (*Working Men's Association*).
Guildford (*Working Men's Institution*).
Hadleigh (*The Reading Room*).
Halesworth (*Mechanics' Institute*).
Halifax (*Literary and Philosophical Society*).
——— (*Mechanics' Institute*).
——— (*Working Men's College*).
Halstead (*Literary and Mechanics' Institute*).
Haslingden (*Institute*).
Hastings (*Literary and Scientific Institute*).
——— (*Mechanics' Institution*).

Hawarden (*Literary Institution*).
Hebden Bridge, near Todmorden (*Mechanics' Institution*).
Helston (*Reading Room and Library*).
Hemel Hempsted (*Mechanics' Institute*).
Hereford (*Natural History, Philosophical, Antiquarian, and Literary Society*).
Hertford (*Literary and Scientific Institution*).
Heywood (*Mechanics' Institute*).
Hitchin (*Mechanics' Institute*).
Holbeck (*Mechanics' Institution*).
Hollingwood (*Working Men's Club*).
Holt, Norfolk (*Literary Society*).
Holywell Green (*Mechanics' Institution*).
Horncastle (*Mechanics' Institution*).
Huddersfield (*Mechanics' Institution*).
Hull (*Church Institute*).
——— (*Literary, Scientific, and Mechanics' Institute*).
——— (*Lyceum Library*).
——— (*Royal Institution, Albion Street*).
——— (*Young People's Institute*).
Huntingdon (*Literary and Scientific Institution*).
Ipswich (*Working Men's College*).
Kendal (*Christian and Literary Institute*).
——— (*Highgate Mechanics' Institute*).
——— (*Working Men's Institute*).
Kidderminster (*Mechanics' Institute*).
Lancaster (*Mechanics' Institute and School of Science*).
Lee, Kent (*Working Men's Institution*).
Leeds (*Chapeltown Branch Library*).
——— (*Church Institute*).
——— (*Holbeck Branch Library*).
——— (*Hunslet Branch Library*).
——— (*Leeds Library*).
——— (*Mechanics' Institution and Literary Society*).
——— (*Philosophical and Literary Society*).
——— (*Working Men's Institute*).
——— (*Young Men's Christian Association*).
Leek, Staffordshire (*Literary and Mechanics' Institution*).
Leicester (*Law Society*).
——— (*Young Men's Christian Association*).
Leighton Buzzard (*Working Men's Mutual Improvement Society*).
Leith (*Mechanics' Subscription Library*).
Lewes (*Fitzroy Memorial Library*).
——— (*Mechanics' Institute*).
——— (*School of Science and Art*).
Lincoln (*Mechanics' Institute*).
Liverpool (*Institute*).
——— (*Medical Institution*).
——— (*Polytechnic Society*).
Llanelly (*Chamber of Commerce and Reading Room*).
Lockwood (*Mechanics' Institution*).

London (*Albert Working Men's Club, Knightsbridge*).
—— (*Bank of England Library and Literary Association*).
—— (*Beaumont Institute, Mile End*).
—— (*Bedford Working Men's Institute, Spitalfields*).
—— (*Birkbeck Institution, Southampton Buildings, Chancery Lane*).
—— (*Bow and Bromley Road Institute, Bow Road*).
—— (*Bow Common Working Men's Club, Devon's Road, Bow Common*).
—— (*Christchurch Working Men's Club, New Street Lark Hall Lane, Clapham*).
—— (*Clerkenwell Club, Lower Rosoman Street*).
—— (*Holloway Working Men's Club and Institute, Holloway Road*).
—— (*Literary and Scientific Institution, Walworth*).
—— (*London Association of Foremen Engineers and Draughtsmen*).
—— (*London Institution, Finsbury Circus*.)
—— (*London Library, St. James'*).
—— (*St. James and Soho Working Men's Club, Rupert Street, Soho*).
—— (*St. Mary Charterhouse Working Men's Club, Golden Lane*).
—— (*South London Working Men's College, Blackfriars Road*).
—— (*Southwark Working Men's Club, Broadwall, Stamford Street*).
—— (*Working Men's Club, Brixton Hill*).
—— (*Working Men's Club, St. Mark's, Victoria Docks*).
—— (*Working Men's Club and Institute, Battersea*).
—— (*Working Men's Club and Institute Union, Strand*).
—— (*Working Men's Club, Triangle, Hackney*).
—— (*Working Men's College, Great Ormond Street*).
Longwood (*Mechanics' Institution*).
Lowestoft (*Library and Reading Room*).
Lye (*Institution*).
Lymington (*Literary Institute*).
Madeley, Shropshire (*Anstice Memorial, Workmen's Club and Institute*).
Maidstone (*St. Paul's Literary Institute*).
—— *Working Men's Club and Institute*.)
Maldon, Essex (*Literary and Mechanics' Institute*).
Manchester (*Ancoats Branch Free Library*).
—— (*Athenæum*).
—— (*Campfield Free Lending Library*).
—— (*Cheetham Branch Library*).
—— (*Chorlton and Ardwick Branch Free Library*).

Manchester (*Hulme Branch Free Library*).
—— (*Law Library*).
—— (*Mechanics' Institution*).
—— (*Natural History Museum, Peter Street*).
—— (*Owen's College*).
—— (*Portico Library, Mosley Street*).
—— (*Rochdale Road Branch Free Library*).
—— (*Royal Exchange Library*).
—— (*Scientific and Mechanical Society*).
Manningtree (*Manningtree and Mistley Literary and Scientific Institution*).
Mansfield (*Co-operative Industrial Society*).
—— (*Mechanics', Artizans', and Apprentices' Library*).
—— (*Mechanics' Institute*).
Marlborough (*Reading and Mutual Improvement Society*).
—— (*Working Men's Hall*).
Melksham (*Mutual Improvement Society*).
Melton Mowbray (*Literary Institute*).
Mere, near Bath (*Literary Association*).
Middlesborough (*Iron and Steel Institute*).
—— (*Mechanics' Institution*).
Middlewich (*Literary and Scientific Institution*).
Modbury (*Mechanics' Institution*).
Mossley (*Mechanics' Institute*).
Newark (*Mechanics' Institute*).
Newbury (*Literary and Scientific Institution*).
Newcastle-upon-Tyne (*Mechanics' Institution*).
—— (*Working Men's Club*).
New Mills, near Stockport (*Mechanics' Institute*).
Newport, Isle of Wight (*Young Men's Society and Reading Room*).
Northampton (*Mechanics' Institute*).
North Shields (*Free Library*).
Nottingham (*Mechanics' Institution*).
—— (*Subscription Library Bromley House*).
Oldham (*Mechanics' Institution, Werneth*).
Ormskirk (*Public Library*).
Oswestry (*Institute*).
Over, Cheshire (*Working Men's Institute*).
Oxford (*North Oxford Working Men's Club*).
Patricroft (*Mechanics' Institution*).
Pembroke Dock (*Mechanics' Institute*).
Pendleton (*Mechanics' Institution*).

Penzance (*Institute.*).
───── (*Penzance Library*).
───── (*Working Men's Association*).
Perth (*Mechanics' Library, High Street*).
Peterborough (*Mechanics' Institution*).
Plymouth (*Working Men's Institute*).
Pontypool (*Literary Institute*).
Poole (*Literary and Scientific Institution*).
───── (*Mechanics' Institute*).
Port Glasgow (*Public Library*).
Portsea Island (*Young Men's Christian Association*).
Preston (*Institution for the Diffusion of Knowledge*).
Redruth (*Redruth Institution*).
Reigate (*Mechanics' Institution*).
Richmond (*Working Men's College*).
Rotherham (*Rotherham and Masbro' Literary and Mechanics' Institute*).
Royston (*Institute*).
Rusholme (*Public Hall and Library*).
Ryde, Isle of Wight (*Philosophical and Scientific Society*).
───── (*Young Men's Christian Association and Literary Institute*).
Saffron Walden (*Literary and Scientific Institution*).
St. Just (*Institution*).
St. Leonards (*Mechanics' Institution*).
───── (*Working Men's Club*).
Salford (*Working Men's Club*).
Salisbury (*Literary and Scientific Institution*).
Saltaire (*Literary Institute*).
Scarborough (*Mechanics' and Literary Institute, Vernon Place*).
Selby (*Mechanics' Institute*).
Sevenoaks (*Literary and Scientific Institution*).
Shaftesbury (*Literary Institution*).
Sheerness (*Literary Institute*).
Sheffield (*Branch Free Library*).
───── (*Brightside Branch Library*).
───── (*Literary and Philosophical Society, School of Arts*).
───── (*Mechanics' Institution*).
Shepton Mallet (*Reading and Mutual Improvement Society*).
Sidmouth (*Mechanics' Hall*).
Skipton, Yorkshire (*Mechanics' Institute*).
Slough (*Mechanics' Institute*).
Smethwick, Staffordshire (*Library, Reading Room, and Literary Institute*).
Southampton (*Polytechnic Institution*).
───── (*Workmen's Hall*).
Southport (*Athenæum*).
South Shields (*Public Free Library*).
Southwell (*Literary Institution*).
Spalding (*Mechanics' Institute*).
───── (*Christian Young Men's Association*).
Stafford (*Mechanics' Institution*).
Staines (*Literary and Scientific Institution*).

Staines (*Mechanics' Institute and Reading Room*).
Stalybridge, Cheshire (*Mechanics' Institution*).
Stamford (*Institution*).
Stourbridge (*Associated Institute*).
───── (*Church of England Association*).
───── (*Iron Works Reading Room and Library*).
───── (*Mechanics' Institution*).
───── (*Working Men's Institute*).
Stowmarket (*Literary Institution*).
Stratford (*Working Men's Hall*).
Sudbury, Suffolk (*Literary and Mechanics' Institute*).
Sunderland (*Working Men's Club*).
Swansea (*Royal Institution of South Wales*).
───── (*South Wales Institute of Engineers*).
───── (*Working Man's Institute*).
Tavistock (*Mechanics' Institute*).
───── (*Public Library*).
Thornton, near Bradford (*Mechanics' Institute*).
Thornton Heath, Croydon (*Workmen's Club*).
Todmorden (*Mechanics' Institution*).
Truro (*Cornwall County Library*).
───── (*Institution*).
───── (*Royal Institution of Cornwall*).
Tunbridge (*Literary and Scientific Institute*).
───── (*Mechanics' Institute.*)
Tunbridge Wells (*Mechanics' Institution*).
───── (*Society of Literature and Science*).
Turton, near Bolton (*Chapel Town Institute*).
Tynemouth (*Free Public Library*).
Ulverston (*Temperance Hall*).
Uttoxeter (*Mechanics' Literary Institute*).
Uxbridge (*Uxbridge and Hillingdon Reading and Newsroom Institute*).
Wakefield (*Mechanics' Institute*).
Wallingford (*Free Library and Literary Institute*).
Walsall (*Free Library*).
Walsham-le-Willows, Suffolk (*Institute*).
Ware (*Institute*).
Warminster (*Athenæum*).
Watford (*Literary Institute*).
Wellingborough (*Working Men's Club*).
Wellington (*Young Men's Christian Association*).
Wells, Somerset (*Young Men's Society*).
West Bromwich (*Free Library*).
Whaleybridge (*Mechanics' Institute*).
Whitby (*Institute*).
───── (*Museum*).
───── (*Subscription Library*).
Whitehaven (*Mechanics' Institute*).
───── (*Working Men's Reading Room*).

Whitstable (*Institute*).
Wilton (*Literary Institute*).
Winchester (*Mechanics' Institution*).
───── (*Training College*).
Winsford (*Town Hall Reading Room*).
Wirksworth (*Mechanics' Institution*).
Wisbeach (*Mechanics' Institute*).
Witham (*Literary Institution*).
Witney (*Athenæum*).
Wolverhampton (*Law Library*).
───── (*Library*).
Wolverton (*Institute*).
Woodbridge (*Literary and Mechanics' Institute*).
Worcester (*Railway Literary Institute*).
───── ───── (*Workman's Hall*).
Workington (*Mechanics' Institute*).
Yarmouth, Great (*Parochial Library and Museum*).
Yeovil (*Mutual Improvement Society*).
York (*Church Institute*).
───── (*Institute of Popular Science, &c.*).
───── (*North Eastern Railway Library and Reading Room.*)

Presentations of portions of the Works, published by order of the Commissioners of Patents, have been made to the following Libraries:—

Armagh (*Town Clerk's Office*).
Aylesbury (*Mechanics' Institution and Literary Society, Kingsbury*).
Birmingham (*Institution of Mechanical Engineers, Newhall Street*).
Boston, Lincolnshire (*Public Offices, Market Place*).
Cambridge (*Free Library, Jesus Lane*).
Cardiff (*Free Library and Museum*).
Chester (*Mechanics' Institute, St. John Street*).
Coalbrookdale (*Literary and Scientific Institution*).
Coventry (*Watchmakers' Association*).
Dublin (*Dublin Library, D'Olier Street*).
Edinburgh (*Horological Society*).
Ennis (*Public Library*).
Gloucester (*Working Men's Institute, Southgate Street*).
Guernsey (*Public Record Office*).
Guildford (*Mechanics' Institute*).
Ipswich (*Mechanics' Institute, Tavern Street*).
Kew (*Library of the Royal Gardens*).
Leominster (*Literary Institute*).
London (*House of Lords*).
───── (*House of Commons*).
London (*Hon. Soc. of Gray's Inn*).
───── (" " *Inner Temple*).
───── (" " *Lincoln's Inn*).
───── (" " *Middle Temple*)
───── (*Aeronautical Society*).
───── (*British Horological Institute*).
───── (*General Post Office*).
───── (*Guildhall Library*).
───── (*Institution of Civil Engineers*).
───── (*Odontological Society*).
───── (*Royal Society*).
───── (*United Service Museum*).
Manchester (*Literary and Philosophical Society, George Street*).
───── (*Mechanics' Institution, David Street*).
Newcastle-upon-Tyne (*North of England Institute of Mining Engineers*).
Over Darwen (*Free Public Library*).
Oxford (*Bodleian Library*).
Stretford, near Manchester (*Mechanics' Institute*).
Swindon, New (*Mechanics' Institute*).
Tamworth (*Library and Reading Room, George Street*).
Yarmouth, Norfolk (*Public Library, South Quay*).

British Colonies and Foreign States.

British Columbia—Mechanics' Institute, Victoria.
───── Public Library, New Westminster.
France—Academy of Science, Paris.
Germany — Kaiserliche Universitäts und Landes-Bibliothek, Strasburg.
Netherlands—Bibliothéque de l'Ecole Polytechnique de Delft.
Russia—Imperial Technological Institute, St. Petersburg.
Turkey—Literary and Scientific Institute, Smyrna.
United States—American Academy of Arts and Sciences, Boston.
───── American Institute, New York.
United States.—American Society of Civil Engineers, New York.
───── Industrial University Champaign, Illinois.
───── Mechanics' Institute, San Francisco.
───── Mercantile Library Association, Pittsburgh, Pennsylvania.
───── Odd Fellows' Library Association, San Francisco.
───── Smithsonian Institute, Washington.
───── Wabash College, Crawfordsville, Indiana.
───── Young Men's Christian Association, Scranton, Pennsylvania.

PATENT OFFICE MUSEUM, SOUTH KENSINGTON.

This Museum is open to the public daily, free of charge. The hours of admission are as follows :—

Mondays, Tuesdays, and Saturdays, 10 A.M. till 10 P.M.

Wednesdays, Thursdays, and Fridays, from 10 A.M. till 4, 5, or 6 P.M., according to the season.

If any Patentee should be desirous of exhibiting a model of his invention in London, he may avail himself of this Museum, which has been visited since its opening on the 22nd June 1857 by more than 3,640,000 persons. The model will be received either as a gift or loan; if deposited as a loan, it will be returned on demand. Before sending a model it is requested that the size and description of it shall first be given to the Superintendent of the Patent Office Museum. No charge is made for the exhibition of models.

GALLERY OF PORTRAITS OF INVENTORS, DISCOVERERS, AND INTRODUCERS OF USEFUL ARTS.—This Collection, formed by Mr. Woodcroft, and first opened to public view in 1853, is now exhibited in the Patent Office.

Presentations or loans of Portraits Medallions, Busts, and Statues, in augmentation of the Collection, are solicited. They will be duly acknowledged in the Commissioners of Patents' Journal, and included in the next edition of the Catalogue.

All communications relating to the Patent Office, Portrait Gallery, or Museum, and Registry of Designs, to be addressed to B. WOODCROFT, Clerk to the Commissioners of Patents, Superintendent of the Patent Office Museum, and Registrar of Designs, at the Patent Office, 25, Southampton Buildings, Chancery Lane, London, W.C.

LONDON:
Printed by GEORGE E. EYRE and WILLIAM SPOTTISWOODE,
Printers to the Queen's most Excellent Majesty.

November, 1875.

PATENTS FOR INVENTIONS.

ABRIDGMENTS

OF

Specifications

RELATING TO THE

REPARATION OF INDIA-RUBBER AND GUTTA PERCHA.

PART II.—A.D. 1867–1876.

LONDON:
PUBLISHED AND SOLD AT
THE PATENT OFFICE SALE BRANCH,
38, CURSITOR STREET, CHANCERY LANE, E.C.

1884.

PREFACE.

The present volume forms Part II. of the series of abridgments of specifications of inventions relating to the "Preparation of India-rubber and Gutta Percha," and embraces the period from A.D. 1867 to 1876, inclusive. Part I. contains the abridgments of this class from the earliest date (A.D. 1791) to the end of the year 1866.

This series comprises inventions relating to mechanical and chemical processes for preparing, cleansing, bleaching, cutting, dissolving, combining, masticating, vulcanizing, hardening, deodorizing, or otherwise treating india-rubber, gutta percha, or their compounds, or similar substances, or substitutes for them.

It also includes the preparation and recovery of some of the solvents employed in their treatment or manufacture, as well as the utilization of waste and the re-use of old materials.

The series likewise embraces the manufacture from the above materials of thread, tubing, sheets, and driving bands or belts, but otherwise it does not include the application of india-rubber, gutta percha, or similar substances, to any particular articles or fabrics unless there appears to be some improvement in the material or compound used or in the mode of treating the manufactured articles or fabrics so as to alter the character of the material or compound.

A detailed list of the various kinds of inventions comprised in the present series of abridgments is furnished by the subject-matter index at the end of this volume.

It should be borne in mind that the abridgments are merely intended to serve as guides to the specifications, which must themselves be consulted for the details of any particular invention.

At the foot of each abridgment is stated the price at which a printed copy of the specification may be purchased at the Patent Office Sale Branch (38, Cursitor Street, Chancery Lane, E.C.).

By means of the "key" at page 20 of the List of Works at the end of this volume, the reader will be able to find out what series of abridgments contains any other class of inventions to which he may desire to refer.

H. READER LACK.

October, 1884.

INDEX OF NAMES.

[The names printed in *Italic* are those of the persons by whom the inventions have been communicated to the Applicants for Letters Patent.]

Name	Page
Anderson, A.	56
Aspinall, J.	27
Bailey, M.	10
Baker, F. R.	62
———, J. M. B.	85
Banks, J.	64
Barrow, J.	98
Bates, A. M.	23
———, W. H.	23
Bell, W.	86, 91
Blanc, A. J. le	22
Boethius, E.	82
Boggett, W.	6, 12, 55, 69
Boss, M.	35
Bousfield, G. T.	96
Boyden, W. W.	63
Brandely, A. A.	93
Broadhurst, G.	41
Bugg, F. J.	8
Catlow, U.	97
Cattell, T.	73
Challenger, C.	36
Chapman, G. T.	49
Chapman, G. T.	61
Clark, A. M.	33, 71
Coleman, J. J.	49, 50
Coles, G.	15, 16
Connolly, T.	97
Conybeare, H.	85
Cow, P. B., jun.	32, 34
Cowper, P.	96
Crossley, F.	2
Crouzières, J.	38
Danckwerth, L.	101
Davis, O.	61
Day, A. G.	8
Day, A. G.	24, 54, 57
Deiss, A.	105
De Wolf, A. G.	60
Dick, R.	40
Dodge, G. P.	11, 68, 78
Don, T.	65
Dufilhol, A. M.	10
Dunbar, H. P.	99
Eastham, R.	51
Ewing, J. O.	49
Fagan, E.	37
Fanshawe, H. R.	44
———, J. A.	15, 16, 31
Faulkner, H.	23
Fish, W. S.	92
Fixsen, B.	101
Ford, A.	49
Forster, T.	15, 26, 28, 32, 34, 106
Frankenburg, I.	84
Gale, W. J.	63
Galloway, G. B.	58
Gedge, W. E.	38
Gilbee, W. A.	82
Grasser, C.	103
Gray, M.	3, 17, 26, 32
Greenacre, T.	90
Greening, F.	94
Grether, E.	10
Guenin, E.	2, 47

INDEX OF NAMES.

Hacking, T. 74
————, W. H. 74
Halsey, W. H. 13
Hamer, M. 4, 7
Harris, I. B. 29, 55, 62, 67, 70, 76, 80, 89
Harrop, J. 75
Haseltine. G. 83
Haskins, J. 25
Hauer, H. 15
Hawkins, F. 26
Heald, J. 106
Heartfield, J. 26, 28
Heinzerling, C. 97
Henderson, W. C. 93
Hooper, W. 14
Howell, W. 15
Hoyle, R. 97
Huebscher, H. 66
Hunt, B. 25

Ingram, J. G. 23, 87, 89

Jackson, C. 41
————, E. B. 24
Jamieson, A. 76
Jaques, J. A. 15, 16, 31, 64
Jenks, T. 99
Jenney, W. P. 102
Jeyes, J. 7
Jochumsen, N. 60
Johnson, H. A. 61
————, J. H. 15, 37, 46, 48, 50

Kershaw, J. 41

Lake, W. R. ...8, 49, 60, 86, 87, 91, 103
Lavater, M. L. J. 33, 71
Le Blanc, A. J. 22
Lemoine, L. 56
Lévy, D. 104
Liddell, W. H. 29
Liepmann, H. 97
Lippincott, W. H. 102
Lothrop, T. C. 99
Loughton, G. R. V. 24
Luyckx, G. 5

Macbay, A. J. 100
MacCartney, W. N. 45
Macintosh, J. 6, 12, 31, 50, 55, 69, 78
McLellan, G. 98
Mac Millan, C. 28
Mac Millan, W. J. C. 28
Magnus, G. 100
Marsh, J. 30
Mayall, T. J. 20, 21, 22
Menier, H. 107
Meyer, L. O. P. 87
Miller, J. 77
Montaugé, R. E. 93
Mori, F. 99
Moseley, C. ...2, 62, 67, 74, 101
————, J. 2
Moulton, J. 42
————, S. 16
Mudford, G. 69
Murfey, E. D. 48, 50
Myerus, H. 65

Naphegyi, G. 85
Napier, W. D. 92
Newbrough, J. B. 37, 46
Newton, A. V. 95
————, H. E. 100, 107
————, W. E. 102

Paget, F. A. 56
Parnacott, E. J. W. 59, 70
Perkins, W. 11
Phillips, J. E. 30, 34
Pieri, J. P. 87
Pigott, G. W. R. 9
Poisnel, J. M. 13, 14

Quin, J. ...4, 51, 71, 72, 81, 90

Read, H. F. 83
Reed, D. 9
Requa, L. F. 95
Rhodes, S. G. 77
Righter, C. 78
Rigollot, P. 2, 47
Roberts, G. H. 85
Rockliffe, J. W. 91

INDEX OF NAMES.

Name	Page
Rockliffe, W.	91
Rodgers, J.	18
Rogers, J.	16
Rolls, J. G.	68
Rostaing, C. S.	30
Ryding, F.	1
Scaife, R.	105
Scholes, F.	96
Seccombe, J.	88
Sintzenich, E. R.	9
Smart, P.	61
Smith, G. T.	36
———, W. H.	44
Sörensen, S.	42
Spill, D.	48
Sterne, L.	17, 31, 64
Stewart, D.	105
———, L.	46, 51, 57, 59
Stocker, A. S.	19
Struthers, T.	61
Sutherland, M. A.	53
Swindells, J.	41
Talling, R.	88
Tandy, G. G.	5, 11
Taylor, G.	20
Thamsen, P. C.	42
Thomas, F. S.	65
Thompson, J.	23
Thomson, B. L.	97
Thomson, G.	88
Tongue, J. G.	93
Torrey, S. W.	77
Torrey, W. A.	8
Toussaint, C. J.	79
———————, J.	1
Truman, E. T.	39, 45, 81
Turnbull, H. J.	27
Turner, A.	36, 37, 78
Unsworth, J.	78
Venman, H.	72
Wadsworth, J.	18
Walker, J.	39, 54, 58
Warne, C. J.	72
Warren, T. T. P. B.	52
Watson, G.	88
Wilbaux, A.	66
Wilkinson, W.	35
Wise, W. L.	66
Wolf, A. G. de	60
Wolfgang, M. S.	35
Woodcock, F. A.	75
Woodward, H.	102
Wright, R. A.	65
Young, J.	94
Younghusband, G.	91
———————, G. T.	91

PREPARATION OF INDIA RUBBER AND GUTTA PERCHA.

1867.

A.D. 1867, March 11.—No. 688.

RYDING, FREDERICK.—Hardening vulcanite or dental india-rubber and other similar compounds.

The invention consists in applying heat of any required temperature to every portion of the substance to be worked on by means of a bath of melted metal or alloy. The bath consists of a cauldron, into which is to be put any metal or alloy that will melt to about the consistency of butter at the required temperature without being sufficiently fused to cause evaporation or oxidization of the metal. When the metal is sufficiently heated the case containing the vulcanite or other preparation is then plunged into it.

[*Printed, 4d. No Drawings.*]

A.D. 1867, March 26.—No. 878.

TOUSSAINT, JOSEPH.—(*Provisional protection only.*)—Process for uniting cork or leather.

Pure gutta percha is dissolved by heat and a thin coating is put upon the surface of one of the pieces of cork or leather, the uncoated piece is then placed quickly upon the coated piece whilst the coating is warm. India-rubber may be employed in lieu of gutta percha, or mixed with it, and in some cases vegetable and resinous oils may be mixed with either or both. An important feature is conducting the above process with dry heat, of from seventy to ninenty-six degrees of Fahrenheit's thermometer.

"Another mode of conducting the above process is by placing pure gutta percha in powder upon the surfaces of the two pieces of cork or leather to be united, then place them in a stove, and when the powder begins to inflate or expand and give off vapour the coated surfaces of the pieces of material should be quickly pressed together."

[*Printed, 4d. No Drawings.*]

A.D. 1867, April 24.—No. 1193.

CROSSLEY, FRANK. — (*Provisional protection only.*) — "Cutting india-rubber or other materials into strips or thread."

"These improvements consist in so lapping a succession of sheets on the drum of the ordinary thread lathe that two or more knives may be made simultaneously to act on two or more sheets instead of employing one or more knives to act on one sheet only."

[*Printed, 4d. No Drawings.*]

A.D. 1867, April 26.—No. 1212.

GUENIN, EMILE.—(*A communication from Paul Rigollot.*)— "Preparation and application of mustard for curative purposes."

A thin layer of mustard seed or mustard flour is caused to adhere, "by means of any suitable flexible adhesive medium or cement," to paper, linen, cotton, or other fabric, on which it is applied. The adhesive medium or cement is by preference a solution "obtained by dissolving 1 lb. of india-rubber in about 20 lb. of essence of petroleum, coal naptha, sulphuret of carbon, or other suitable volatile solvent."

According to the provisional specification the adhesive medium is "composed of india-rubber, one ounce; sulphuret of carbon, one pound; essence of petroleum, one pound."

[*Printed, 4d. No Drawings.*]

A.D. 1867, April 27.—No. 1219.

MOSELEY, JOSEPH, and MOSELEY, CHARLES.—"Coverings for rollers which are required to be smooth and elastic."

The covering is made in the form of a tube. The "inner
"portion of the covering consists of elastic india-rubber or
"india-rubber and cloth, or of a fibrous compound of india-
"rubber alone or in combination with elastic rubber or
"fibrous compound and cloth combined together. The outer
"surface of the covering is composed of india-rubber mixed
"with any earthy or metallic substances which will in
"vulcanizing cause it to harden sufficiently to make it
"susceptible of being polished, that is to say, the outer
"surface is converted into the composition known as vul-
"canite." "The covering when made is placed in or on a
"mould of the required size so as to produce uniform thick-
"ness and smoothness of surface, and then the process of
"vulcanizing is performed in the usual manner, after which
"the tube or covering is taken from the mould, polished and
"cut to the desired length; the covering is then ready
"for use by placing it on the roller, the surface of which may
"be made adhesive by cement."

[*Printed*, 4d. *No Drawings*.]

A.D. 1867, June 17.—No. 1772.

GRAY, MATTHEW.—"Manufacture of electrical telegraphic
"conductors."

Part of this invention relates to first coating the several wires which are to surround a core wire with a substance adapted in the subsequent twisting of these wires to fill up any space between them.

For this purpose the outer wires pass through a chamber carried by a revolving twisting frame and containing a suitable coating solution. The solution found to answer is composed of gutta percha, bitumen, and tar in proportions such as will be kept in a sufficiently fluid state by the application of heat.

The second part of the invention relates, when coating wires with gutta percha or other insulating substance in a heated state, to means for drawing upon the coated wire at separate parts of its progress through the cooling media before winding it on to the reels to avoid injury to such coating while it is cooling; the fresh coated wire after being in part cooled by cold water in a bath, passes partly round a grooved pulley of size sufficient to act by its holding to draw the coated wire; the grooved pulley has a positive motion given to it.

[*Printed, 2s. 4d. Drawings.*]

A.D. 1867, August 1.—No. 2224.

QUIN, JAMES.—Preparation of hose pipes and woven fabrics.

Firstly, the yarn or woven fabric is steeped in a solution of about five pounds of corrosive sublimate in one hundred quarts of soft water, it is then washed.

Secondly, a mixture is formed "of about ten parts of " caoutchouc, one part of magnesia, two parts of black anti- " mony, one part of sulphur, one half part of asphalt or coal " pitch, four parts of oxide of zinc, four parts of calomel, and " two parts of red oxide of mercury." This compound must be heated, and well mixed and masticated together, and then rolled into a thin sheet and dissolved in about twelve parts of coal naptha or rectified coal tar oil. The solution is laid upon one side of the hose or fabric, and then pressed into the fibres, when dry it is again brushed over with a coating of the compound. When the naptha or tar oil has evaporated the hose or fabric is placed in a strong iron pan, made to receive water or steam, and subjected to a temperature of about 270° Fah. for about fifteen minutes.

Thirdly, the reverse side of the hose or fabric is coated with a solution composed of about one part of creosote or coal tar oil to five parts of red oxide of mercury to prevent the rotting of the outer part of the fabric.

[*Printed, 4d. No Drawings.*]

A.D. 1867, August 7.—No. 2280.

HAMER, MILTON. — Machinery for india-rubber thread cutting.

This invention relates to machines, " in which the india- " rubber is caused to revolve while a cutting tool advances, " retreats, and is traversed so as to sever successive strips of " the material, and consists,—

"Firstly, in causing the said cutter to advance at an " accellerated speed." A cam of increasing radius acts upon suitable rods and levers connected to the sliding frame which carries the cutter.

" Secondly, in an arrangement of self-acting apparatus for
" causing the cutter to traverse for successive cuts." A cam
" gives motion through the medium of rods or levers to one
" of two plates, the one loose and the other fast upon the
" traversing screw. The former of these plates carries short
" levers capable of turning upon centres in one direction.
" When they are moved forward to prepare for a traversing
" by the screw they slip over the other plate, but when they
" are moved in the other direction they bite or clip its surface
" and thus cause the screw to revolve."

" Thirdly, in a method of adapting the cutter for different
" thicknesses of material." The cutter is rendered adjustable by a screw mounted in a nut capable of swivelling in the lever, by which the cutter is forced forward.

[*Printed*, 10d. *Drawing*.]

A.D. 1867, August 21.—No. 2394.

LUYCKX, GUSTAVE.—" Manufacture of waterproof tubes."

A seamless tube constructed of hemp, flax, or other substance is tanned and then impregnated with caoutchouc in solution, which is introduced into the interior of the tube. A tube of caoutchouc prepared but not fully vulcanized is introduced into the seamless tube. The vulcanization of the interior of the caoutchouc tube is then completed by means of a jet of steam, the tube being exposed to the air during this process.

Another method consists in placing the tube of caoutchouc on the mandril of a circular weaving machine, and weaving upon the caoutchouc a covering of hemp, flax, or other substance, and afterward vulcanizing the caoutchouc as before.

[*Printed*, 4d. *No Drawings*.]

A.D. 1867, August 28.—No. 2449.

TANDY, GEORGE GRAINGER.—(*Provisional protection only.*)—Preparing vulcanizable compounds, and manufacturing articles therefrom.

The invention consists, 1st, in "preparing compounds of
"india-rubber and sulphur or other vulcanizable gums or
"resins used for making ebonite or vulcanite, so as to render
"them more plastic than can at present be attained."
"Hitherto little or no solvent has been used in these com-
"pounds in consequence of the great amount of porosity
"resulting from the escape of the vapours generated during
"the process of vulcanization." This is overcome by exposing
the moulded articles to a sufficiently high temperature to
expel the solvent previous to subjecting them to the indurating
process, and "by using petroleum spirit not having a higher
"specific gravity than ·630 (although a higher specific gravity
"may be used) the expulsion is easily effected." "This
"method is particularly applicable to dentists in the formation
"of palates."

2ndly. The dough or paste prepared as above described
may be used to unite ebonite that may have been broken,
"by cleansing or washing the surfaces to be united with
"bisulphide of carbon, petroleum spirit, or other hydro-
"carbon."

Coatings of the colored dough are also applied on surfaces
of black ebonite.

[*Printed, 4d. No Drawings.*]

A.D. 1867, August 29.—No. 2457.

MACINTOSH, John, and BOGGETT, William.—Springs for boots and shoes.

According to one method of making the springs two pieces of unvulcanized sheet india-rubber of the size and shape of the spring required are coated on one side with india-rubber cement. The two cemented sides are then placed together, a strip of tape being inserted between them at their edges to prevent the stitching from giving way. It is preferred to give the springs a ribbed appearance by passing the sheets of india-rubber between ribbed or grooved rollers; or the sheet rubber springs are placed upon a ribbed or grooved metal surface and subjected to pressure whilst warm. The springs are afterwards vulcanized. India-rubber alone or its compounds with sulphur and other materials may be employed but it is preferred to employ the compounds of india-rubber and paraffine or stearic acid described in No. 748, A.D. 1866.

According to another part of the invention the materials, of which the springs are formed, are first made into sheets, which are afterwards cut up to form the springs of the size and shape required. Various methods of forming the sheets are described, in some cases the india-rubber is combined with knitted or looped fabrics, in others the unvulcanized sheet india-rubber is coated with finely divided materials such as flock or powdered pumice stone. Or a coating of flock or other finely divided materials is given to sheet rubber, and when such rubber is vulcanized and coated with cement, it is stretched to the extent of the elasticity required, and any suitable open woven fabric is applied upon the cemented flock.

[*Printed*, 4*d*. *No Drawings.*]

A.D. 1867, September 14.—No. 2604.

JEYES, JOHN.—" Material to be used as a substitute for oiled
" silk, bladders, gut skins, india-rubber, and other water-
" proof materials, and leather."

Blotting, tissue, or thick paper is covered or saturated with a solution of gutta percha, shellac, coal tar, and methylated spirit. The gutta percha, shellac, and tar are mixed at a temperature of about 212 degrees Fahrenheit, and then the spirit is added. For a cheap material gutta perch and shellac are dissolved in petroleum spirit or other hydrocarbon solvent.

As a substitute for leather blotting paper is used in a series of alternate layers in combination with cotton, linen, or other fabric secured together by the application of the above-mentioned solutions.

Paper pulp is also treated with the solutions, and from it sheets of any required thickness are manufactured.

[*Printed*, 4*d*. *No Drawings.*]

A.D. 1867, September 28.—No. 2744.

HAMER, MILTON.—Apparatus for manufacturing india-rubber tubing.

This invention consists in " the production of india-rubber
" tubing by drawing strips of material through guides or

" guides along the strips so as to bring the edges thereof
" together."

[*Printed*, 10*d*. *Drawing*.]

A.D. 1867, October 23.—No. 2977.

BUGG, FREDERICK JOHN.—Manufacture of pressed leather.

According to this invention it is proposed to employ in the manufacture of pressed leather a cementing material which is not soluble in water, and which is by preference prepared by dissolving one pound of india rubber, four ounces of gutta percha, and two ounces of shellac in three gallons of coal-tar naptha.

[*Printed*, 4*d*. *No Drawings*.]

A.D. 1867, November 4.—No. 3108.

LAKE, WILLIAM ROBERT.—(*A communication from Austin Goodyear Day*.)—" Artificial compound chiefly designed for " use as a substitute for india-rubber."

The compound is formed by combining together " one or
" more vegetable fats or oils, one or more mineral oils or
" resins, one or more gum resins, one or more essential or
" volatile oils, either with or without resins, or one or more
" alkalies and sulphur," and then combining this compound with a small proportion of india-rubber or gutta percha, or their equivalents, and vulcanizing the same.

[*Printed*, 4*d*. *No Drawings*.]

A.D. 1867, November 6.—No. 3136.

LAKE, WILLIAM ROBERT.—(*A communication from William Augustus Torrey*.)—Manufacture of waterproof fabrics, and articles formed of the same.

The invention consists in applying to a woven fabric, a compound the principal ingredient of which is india-rubber, and also a compound the principal ingredient of which is gutta percha, separately, " and thereby preserving the elastic
" quality required in belting, hose, packing, and like articles,
" and protecting them against the injurious operations of
" heat, oils, alkalies, and acids, and against injury from other
" causes."

Also in interposing between the inner tube or lining and the outer covering of the hose a layer of any suitable air and waterproof material.

And in winding the fabric upon the mandrel in such a manner that the warp threads will cross or intersect each other.

[*Printed, 8d. Drawing.*]

A.D. 1867, November 8.—No. 3157.

PIGOTT, GEORGE WEST ROYSTON.—Means and apparatus for covering or coating wire with tin, zinc, or other suitable metal or material when in a state of fusion or liquefaction.

Part of this invention relates to "the employment of a
" combination of parkesine, ebonite, or of hard vulcanized
" india-rubber with soft india-rubber, or a combination of
" either of these with cork, asbestos, or talc in either round
" or rectangular blocks of suitable size and in a state of
" compression, for the purpose of discharging or stripping
" from the wire the superfluous fused metal or liquefied
" material, and also to give a more perfect finish and polish
" or smoothness the metallized or coated wire."

[*Printed, 4d. No Drawings.*]

A.D. 1867, December 13.—No. 3542.

SINTZENICH, EDWARD REED.—(*A communication from Daniel Reed.*)—(*Provisional protection only.*)—Treating gutta-percha, india-rubber, Honduras gum, and other allied gums for the production of a preparation applicable for various purposes.

" The treatment consists in dissolving such gums in benzine
" or benzole, or its chemical equivalents, and by adding
" alcohol in sufficient quantity, in separating the purer
" portions of the gum from the barky, resinous, and other
" foreign substances, the gum rising and collecting in the
" form of a curd more or less solid (by the action of the
" alcohol) which is to be redissolved thoroughly in benzine or
" benzole to any consistency for the finer uses." "When the
" gums thus prepared are to be used for coarse purposes, such
" as the treatment of clothes, leather, or woven fabrics, or
" substances to render them waterproof, or when used as a
" cement or coating or solid substance the treatment consists

" in redissolving one part of the curd formed in the first or
" finer process in benzine or benzole, and one part in bisul-
" pheret of carbon or its chemical equivalents, and when both
" are thoroughly dissolved the two solutions are mixed
" together and are ready for use."

When used as a substitute for type fullers' earth is added to the solution, and the substance thus formed is pressed into moulds.

Telegraphic wires or conductors are insulated by one or more coats of the material.

When used for dental and surgical purposes the solution is evaporated either with or without moulds and with or without pigments, fullers' earth, or similar materials.

When the solution is used in conjunction with leather as a substitute for leather, the cuttings of leather ground up, cut or scraped into shred are used with the solution.

[*Printed, 4d. No Drawings.*]

1868.

A.D. 1868, February 4.—No. 373.

GRETHER, ERNEST, and BAILEY, MARK.—(*Provisional protection only.*)—" Machinery for cutting discs or washers of
" india-rubber and other substances."

A number of india-rubber or other cords or cylinders are fitted into tubes, which revolve rapidly round their axes. " All these tubes are placed side by side in one row, and
" whatever projects out of them is cut off by a knife, which is
" caused to vibrate or travel to and fro in front of and in
" close proximity to the tubes." At the back of each tube is a rod, which, after each stroke of the knife, pushes the cord forward a distance equal to the thickness of the discs.

[*Printed, 4d. No Drawings.*]

A.D. 1868, February 18.—No. 526.

DUFILHOL, ADRIEN MARIE.—(*Provisional protection only.*)—
" Method of shoeing horses and other beasts of burden."

Instead of fixing the shoe with nails it is proposed to use
"an intermediate body of cement, at the same time very
"adhesive and very elastic." The cement is composed as
follows:—" Gutta percha 75 per cent., india rubber $10°/_c$, and
"gum lac $15°/_o$, the whole intimately mixed."
[*Printed*, 4d. *No Drawings.*]

A.D. 1868, February 18.—No. 535.

PERKINS, WILLIAM, and TANDY, GEORGE GRAINGER. — A
"compound applicable for insulating electric conductors and
"for such purposes as india-rubber and other vulcanizable
"gums are applicable."
The "compound is produced by the combination of anthra-
"cene (or paranaphthaline) and naphthaline and compounds
"thereof with vulcanizable substances, such as india-rubber,
"gutta percha, gum ballata, and other analogous gums and
"sulphur."
[*Printed*, 4d. *No Drawings.*]

A.D. 1868, February 19.—No. 554.

DODGE, GEORGE POMEROY.—(*Provisional protection only.*)—
"Manufacture of india-rubber valves, valve seats, and other
"similar articles."
The improvements "consist in manufacturing such valves
"or sheets from which the same are to be cut of india-rubber
"with an interior web of elastic woven fabric."
[*Printed*, 4d. *No Drawings.*]

A.D. 1868, February 19.—No. 555.

DODGE, GEORGE POMEROY.—(*Provisional protection only.*)—
"Packing for the stuffing boxes of steam engines and for
"other like purposes."
This invention relates to elastic packing, consisting of
india-rubber combined with fibrous material, either with or
without an elastic core, which packing is usually manufactured by rolling or twisting hemp, jute, or other fibrous
material or woven fabrics into ropes or strands of suitable
diameter.

The improved packing is formed as above described, but instead of finishing off at the exterior with hemp or jute, a coating of good sound cotton, canvas, or duck is put over the hemp or jute.

[*Printed, 4d. No Drawings.*]

A.D. 1868, February 24.—No. 609.

MACINTOSH, JOHN, and BOGGETT, WILLIAM.—" Manu-
" facture and application of elastic goods or fabrics."

This invention relates, first, to means of making a fabric elastic by puckering or gathering it, previous to combining it with india-rubber, or with a composition of india-rubber and paraffine or stearic acid described in No. 748, A.D. 1866. A sheet of stout vulcanised rubber is employed, though the surface of which the points of steel wire staples are passed, and project in transverse rows. When the sheet rubber is distended the points are pressed into the cloth or fabric placed thereon, the sheet rubber is set free, and in contracting draws the fabric held by the points into puckers. The fabric is then coated with india-rubber cement, or with a sheet of unvulcanized rubber in a soft heated state, which, when vulcanized, will expand and contract to the extent allowed by the puckered fabric. Untanned thin soft leather or thin felt may be puckered up in like manner, but as these materials are to some extent elastic in place of being puckered they may be stretched and coated with rubber, or combined with distended sheet rubber as described in No 2457, A.D. 1867. In making leggings, leather or knitted or looped tubular fabrics are drawn on or attached to moulds of the shape of the human leg. The fabric is then coated or dipped in a hot solution of the compound before referred to, or it may be otherwise coated. When dry the dipping may be repeated. The leggings are finished by vulcanizing.

Another part of the invention relates to elastic boot laces made either of rubber, or of the compound above referred to combined if desired with an elastic textile fabric.

The invention also relates to elastic fabrics made by coating fibrous threads or yarns with soft rubber or a solution of rubber, such threads being afterwards employed in the manufacture of knitted, looped, plaited, or braided fabrics.

[*Printed, 4d. No Drawings.*]

A.D. 1868, March 9.—No. 815.

HALSEY, WILLIAM HENRY.—"Process for making articles
" from hard rubber and from other substances capable of
" being moulded in dies, and at the same time inlaying or
" inserting in and attaching to such articles metallic and
" other plates."

The improvements claimed are,—

I. Attaching hinges or joints to articles made from hard
rubber, gutta percha, or from any other substance capable of
being moulded in dies, by forcing such hard rubber or other
substance upon and about or over the hinge plate or equivalent while the article is being moulded, by forming such
joints or hinges with projecting points upon their back surfaces or with bevelled or serrated edges, either singly or in
combination, so that such hinges or joints shall be firmly and
permanently clasped by and secured in the pressed material.

II. Constructing the dies with suitable cavities or recesses
to receive the different parts of any joint or hinge, and hold
them in place while the article is being pressed.

III. Forming and shaping with projecting points or bevelled
or serrated edges one or both of the metallic or other plates,
whether of solid or perforated or open pattern, designed to be
inlaid or inserted, whether in intaglio, or relievo, or otherwise.

[*Printed*, 10d. *Drawing*.]

A.D. 1868, March 17.—No. 906.

POISNEL, JEAN MARIE.—"Manufacture of straps, belts,
" bands, pipes, and other articles of india-rubber or similar
" fabric."

These articles " have been produced by coating a sheet of a
" suitable fabric with a layer of india-rubber on one or both
" sides." The present invention consists " in substituting
" for the sheet of fabric threads or small cords of suitable
" fibrous material covered with india-rubber or compound of
" india-rubber or similar material. These threads or cords
" are woven, plaited, or otherwise combined together so as
" to produce a fabric of the form and size of the article
" required." This fabric may be coated on one or both sides
with a layer of india-rubber or similar material.

[*Printed*, 4d. *No Drawings*.]

A.D. 1868, March 17.—No. 908.

POISNEL, JEAN MARIE.—Manufacture of coverings for the feet to replace wooden shoes or sabots.

India-rubber or india-rubber cuttings containing suitable fibrous material together with well-known agents for producing vulcanization are employed. "This mixture is " masticated and heated, and is moulded or rolled to the " form and thickness required." The upper is first formed upon a suitable shape, and the sole is then applied and fixed with india-rubber cement. The article is then vulcanized.

[*Printed, 4d. No Drawings.*]

A.D. 1868, March 19.—No. 939.

HOOPER, WILLIAM.—Treating india-rubber, and the manufacture therefrom of fabrics and of insulated telegraph conductors.

When the crude india-rubber has been washed and cleaned before masticating, compressing, grinding, or dissolving it, as the case may be, it is placed in a closed heated chamber and the temperature is raised to about 250 degrees Fahrenheit, at which it is maintained for about two hours. The india-rubber is placed in the heated chamber in sheets as it comes from the rollers of the washing machine. " The india-rubber " after this treatment is much easier to masticate or grind." " It also, if compressed without mastication, forms a solid " block," " and may be cut into sheets or threads and elastic " fabrics manufactured therefrom; and also it is more " readily dissolved in solvents than is the crude rubber.

"In the manufacture of insulated telegraphic conductors " where a strand of metal wires is insulated partially or " wholly by means of a vulcanized coating," the central wire of the strand is coated "with india-rubber or a compound of " india-rubber, and into this coating the outer wires of the " strand bed themselves, and a solid strand is thus obtained." It is preferred to use a compound of india-rubber such as can be applied to the wire through a die. The composition found suitable consists of a mixture of india-rubber and oxide of zinc.

[*Printed, 4d. No Drawings.*]

A.D. 1868, March 30.—No. 1077.

JOHNSON, JOHN HENRY.—(*A communication from Henry Hauer, and William Howell*).—The treatment of cork, and the manufacture of a compound therefrom.

This invention consists,—firstly, in treating cork "by " charring or roasting it so that it may be deprived of the " resinous and gummy matter with which the fibrous tissues " are more or less impregnated, after which the cork is " granulated or torn into small fragments."

Secondly, of a compound "composed of the cork charred or " roasted and granulated as above described and caoutchouc " or gutta percha kneaded or worked together so as to become " nearly a homogeneous mass, the composition thus produced " being available for the construction of light soles and heels " for boots and shoes, for being moulded into different forms " and objects for articles of utility and ornament, for being " rolled into sheets, and used for waterproof coverings, floor- " cloths, and for other useful purposes."

[*Printed*, 4d. *No Drawings.*]

A.D. 1868, April 13.—No. 1222.

FORSTER, THOMAS.—"Manufacture of compounds of india- " rubber, gutta percha, balata, parkesine, solid paraffine or " vegetable oils, and vegetable fibre."

The vegetable fibre is first reduced to a fine powder resembling flour, it is then mixed with india-rubber, gutta percha, balata, parkesine, or with solid paraffine or vegetable oils. "Any vegetable fibre, such as cotton, flax, hemp, " manilla jute, or other fibrous material that is capable of " being manufactured into paper, or such as waste paper, " rags, wood, or sawdust may be employed." To reduce the fibre it is first cleansed, then macerated in an acid bath; after which it is removed and while wet exposed to heat, it is then washed, dried, and sieved.

[*Printed*, 8d. *Drawing.*]

A.D. 1868, April 20.—No. 1289.

COLES, GEORGE; JAQUES, JAMES ARCHIBALD; and FAN-SHAWE, JOHN AMERICUS.—Manufacture of elastic bands.

This invention "consists in embossing the faces of the "bands and rounding the edges."

When cylindrical bands are to be produced the strips of rubber to form the bands are laid out flat between the embossing plates and submitted to pressure.

When the bands are made in the form of disc rings these may be strung on a spindle with metal embossing washers between them, and while thereon they may be vulcanized.

[*Printed, 6d. Drawing.*]

A.D. 1868, April 21.—No. 1296.

COLES, GEORGE; JAQUES, JAMES ARCHIBALD; and FANSHAWE, JOHN AMERICUS.—Apparatus for producing thin strips or filaments, intended particularly for dividing sheets of india-rubber into threads.

The sheet of india-rubber is passed between pairs or sets of cutters with square edges, which act on the principle of a pair of shears. It is proposed to use a number of these cutters in combination, so that several threads may be cut simultaneously from the same sheet of india-rubber.

[*Printed, 10d. Drawing.*]

A.D. 1868, April 23.—No. 1336.

ROGERS, JOSEPH.—Utilizing residual products obtained in the treatment of vegetable oils and from the distillation and refining of crude mineral and bituminous products.

A compound, consisting of two parts by weight of the solid residuum resulting from the treatment of vegetable oils, such as cotton seed oil, and one part of the fluid residuum resulting from the rectification of petroleum or of coal oil, is mixed and incorporated with gutta percha or india-rubber or mixtures of the same, for the purpose of obtaining a material suitable for coating telegraphic wires, ships bottoms, metal, wood, masonry, paper, fibrous materials, and woven fabrics.

[*Printed, 4d. No Drawings.*]

A.D. 1868, May 9.—No. 1522.

MOULTON, STEPHEN.—"Treatment of vulcanized or cured "india-rubber for obtaining a substance of a mossy nature "suitable for printers' inking rollers, cushions, and other "articles."

Vulcanized india-rubber is reduced to powder, and then subjected " to a second vulcanizing heat, the powder or dust " being placed (previous to this second vulcanizing) in a suit-" able mould according to the particular form or shape of the " article required."

[*Printed*, 4d. *No Drawings.*]

A.D. 1868, May 27.—No. 1750.

GRAY, MATTHEW.—Manufacture of electric conductors which are covered with insulating composition such as vulcanized india-rubber or its compounds.

This invention consists, firstly, in vulcanizing the successive lengths of the cable as they are joined up in such a manner that the free end for, say, from one to two feet of its length will be left uncured and unchanged, so that the next length can be joined on without difficulty. The vulcanizing vessel is formed with two openings, through which the ends of the cable, when coiled up in the vessel, are allowed to project, so that those portions may not be operated on by the curing process. Or the end of the cable which it is desired to protect may be placed in a tubular vessel contained in the vulcanizing vessel and imbedded in a bad conductor of heat, the tubular vessel may be further protected by a water jacket.

Secondly, when it is required to join two ends that are covered with vulcanized rubber, the insulating compound is cut away for a few inches from each of the ends that require to be joined; the wires are then soldered and covered with uncured rubber compound. " This uncured part of the " insulating compound is then to be placed in a small vul-" canizing vessel, through the sides of which the cable will " project, and hot steam being admitted to the interior of the " vessel the change called vulcanizing will then be effected."

[*Printed*, 8d. *Drawing.*]

A.D. 1868, June 2.—No. 1811.

STERNE, LOUIS.—" Manufacturing driving belts, bands, or " straps from india-rubber and metal united or joined " together during the process of vulcanization."

When a belt is to be made with metal on one side only, a length of rubber prepared for vulcanization and a thin strip of

rubber or other soft material. "The sheet after having been
" operated upon will assume a porous-like texture." Sheet
rubber may be similarly punctured by the aid of piercing
tools fixed in a fly press or otherwise. "Sheet rubber so
" prepared will be useful for various purposes."

[*Printed, 4d. No Drawings.*]

A.D. 1868, June 22.—No. 2015.

TAYLOR, GEORGE.—" Construction of boots and shoes, also
" means to be used in connection with such construction."

A metal mould is made of a shape similar to the sole of the
foot and its length may be from the toe to the inside of the
heel. The mould is made with " indents (say $\frac{3}{16}$ths of an inch
" in diameter at distances of $\frac{3}{8}$ths of an inch apart) in that
" portion which extends from the toe to the commencement
" of the 'waist.' Flanges are formed round the edges of the
" mould." Into the mould is poured liquid caoutchouc,
which, when solidified, dried, and removed from the mould,
presents on one side a series of nipples resulting from the
indents. This india-rubber sole is placed as the under or
intermediate sole of the boot or shoe.

[*Printed, 6d. Drawing.*]

A.D. 1868, July 7.—No. 2151.

MAYALL, THOMAS JEFFERSON.—" Manufacture of sheets of
" vulcanized india-rubber compounds for forming the soles
" of boots and shoes."

Upon a sheet of cotton cloth or other fabric is spread a
layer of pure india-rubber dissolved in naphtha, camphine, or
other solvent, upon this coating is spread the prepared india-
rubber or compound which is to form the vulcanized sheet.
The compound preferred consists of—" Four pounds of the
" rubber, two pounds of whiting, one pound of sulphur, one
" pound of litharge, one half pound of magnesia, one half
" pound of lampblack, and two pounds of clay." When the
compound has been spread by means of an ordinary coating
machine the sheet is again passed between the rolls of the
machine in contact with a sheet of some woven fabric or other
substance, the surface of the rubber being first sprinkled with
French chalk or other suitable material to prevent the

adhesion of the two materials. The pattern of the fabric is by this means impressed upon the surface of the india-rubber compound. The sheet of material is then wound upon a receiving roller and left till vulcanized. The impression cloth is then removed from the vulcanized sheet, leaving a pattern on the latter. The cotton cloth united by the pure rubber solution may then be stripped from the rubber by moistening it with warm water, naptha, or camphine.

[*Printed, 4d. No Drawings.*]

A.D. 1868, July 8.—No. 2159.

MAYALL, THOMAS JEFFERSON.—" Manufacture of gas tubing " and other articles of india rubber."

This invention consists—firstly, of a composition, "com- " posed of linseed oil, and fine litharge, or white lead in the " proportion of one quart of oil to one pound of litharge" well boiled together for coating the interior of india-rubber tubes and other articles.

Secondly, of a composition, consisting of one quart of linseed oil mixed with one half pound of litharge, to which is added a gill of gold size, well boiled together, for coating the exterior surface of tubes and other articles of india-rubber.

Thirdly, of a compound for forming the tubing, consisting of four pounds of india-rubber, two pounds of zinc, three pounds of pipe clay, one pound of shellac, one-quarter of a pound of white resin, and one-half pound of sulphur. " This " compound should be subjected for about two hours to a " temperature of two hundred and sixty degrees Fahrenheit, " more or less."

[*Printed, 4d. No Drawings.*]

A.D. 1868, July 8.—No. 2160.

MAYALL, THOMAS JEFFERSON.—" Electric telegraph cables."

Part of this invention relates to a compound of india-rubber and gutta percha with other ingredients for forming an exterior casing for cables. Upon a sheet of cotton or other fabric is spread a layer of pure rubber dissolved with camphine or other solvent. Over this rubber is applied the vulcanizing compound consisting of "one pound of Para rubber, one " pound of gutta percha, one pound of zinc, two pounds of

"pipeclay, one quarter of a pound of sulphur, one half pound
"of shellac, one half pound of French chalk, and two ounces
"of white resin. This compound should be cured or vulcan-
"ized for about two and one half hours at a temperature of
"about two hundred and fifty degrees Fahrenheit." The
cloth or fabric is then removed from the vulcanized sheet by
wetting it with hot water, camphine, or naphtha.

[*Printed, 4d. No Drawings.*]

A.D. 1868, July 8.—No. 2167.

LE BLANC, ARMAND JULES.—"Manufacture of belts, bands,
"or ropes."

This "invention primarily consists in the manufacture of
"belts, bands, or ropes by means of a fabric, by preference
"of cotton, coated with caoutchouc and rolled on and into
"one another; it is then submitted to strong pressure in
"order to cause the caoutchouc to pass through and into the
"pores of the fabric; the material is subsequently coated with
"caoutchouc and vulcanized."

The "invention further consists in the employment for
"the manufacture of belts, bands, or ropes of all kinds of
"woven tissues or textile fibres woven or twisted, and
"impregnated with caoutchouc, gutta percha, or other
"gummy or resinous materials."

[*Printed, 4d. No Drawings.*]

A.D. 1868, July 9.—No. 2175.

MAYALL, THOMAS JEFFERSON.—Treatment of india-rubber,
gutta percha, or compounds thereof, and the manufacture of
type and other articles therefrom.

In treating india-rubber the patentee combines with 8 lbs.
of that material 5 lbs. of sulphur that has been washed and
2 lbs. of whiting or black or white lead previously dried. The
compound is then mixed or ground together and placed in a
mould of the desired form, pressure is applied so that the
rubber may fully occupy the parts of such mould to the thickness desired. The mould, with the contained rubber, is then
subjected to a progressive heat of from 232° to 296° Fahrenheit.

In treating gutta percha the patentee combines 8 lbs. of
that material cleansed of oil, with 4 lbs of washed sulphur,

and 2 lbs. of whiting or white or black lead previously dried. These matters are combined together by grinding, placed in moulds, pressed and subjected to a progressive heat of from 232° to 290° Fahrenheit.

In treating a combination of india-rubber and gutta percha the patentee adds to 4 lbs. of gutta percha from which the oil has previously been removed, 4 lbs. of india rubber, also 4 lbs. of washed sulphur, and 2 lbs. of whiting or black or white lead previously dried. These matters having been thoroughly combined, are pressed into a mould, and then subjected to a progressive heat of from 232° to 295° Fahrenheit.

[*Printed, 4d. No Drawings.*]

A.D. 1868, July 14.—No. 2223.

THOMPSON, JOHN, and INGRAM, JAMES GEORGE.—" Caps " for feeding bottles."

The caps are formed from vulcanizable india-rubber compounds moulded to form in dies by pressure, and subsequently vulcanized.

[*Printed, 6d. Drawing.*]

A.D. 1868, July 20.—No. 2282.

BATES, WILLIAM HENRY, BATES, ALFRED MASON, and FAULKNER, HUGH. — Manufacture of flexible tubes or hose.

This invention relates to articles made of a compound of textile materials or thin wires and india-rubber gutta percha, or other elastic gum. A core of india-rubber is used, which is capable of being stretched so that by reducing its diameter it may be easily withrawn from the interior of the tube. Upon the core is formed a tube either of sheet rubber, or of compound sheet rubber, or of rubber cloth. The covered core is then placed in a braiding machine supplied with any suitable number of threads or wires according to the intended diameter of the tube and these threads are braided tightly round the core. The core must be coated with india-rubber solution, in which the braiding threads imbed themselves as the operation proceeds. The braided part passes up through a hollow die, whereby any excess of india-rubber solution will be scraped off. From the die the braided core is conducted through one or more heated cylinders or tubes, whereby the solvent will be evaporated, after which it is to be passed through other dies whereby the braided surface will be coated with a solution of india-rubber to any required thickness, and as this coating is laid on the tube must be conducted through heated cylinders to drive off the solvent. "A second " and even more plies of braid and rubber may be laid round " the tube so as to give it additional strength, and after " drawing out the elastic core the article will be ready for " vulcanizing."

[*Printed, 8d. Drawing.*]

A.D. 1868, July 27.—No. 2350.

LOUGHTON, GEORGE RICHARD VEVERS, and JACKSON, EDWARD BLASINI.—"Material for the manufacture of bosses " for flax spinning machinery."

The material consists of from 60 to 80 per cent. of india-rubber and 30 to 50 per cent. of pure golden sulphuret of antimony, which is mixed together into a paste. The bosses are made from this paste and then vulcanized..

[*Printed, 4d. No Drawings.*]

A.D. 1868, July 31.—No. 2404.

DAY, AUSTIN GOODYEAR. — "Artificial compound chiefly " designed for use as a substitute for india-rubber."

The object of this invention is to provide a compound to be used for similar purposes to those for which the compound described in No. 3108, A.D. 1867, was designed.

The present invention consists in combining certain acids with the ingredients which compose the compound described in the prior invention, "for the purpose of enabling the oils " employed therein to better combine together," and also to diminish the quantity of sulphur required.

Various proportions and combinations of the ingredients used may be adopted. The following examples are given:—

For soft or elastic rubber goods, when steam heat is to be employed for vulcanizing, "twenty pounds of linseed oil, " twenty pounds of cotton seed oil, four pounds of coal oil, " twenty-four ounces of sulphuric acid, one pound of bi-car- " bonate of soda, one pound of nitrate of soda, fifteen pounds

" of coal tar, five pounds of asphaltum, five pounds of litharge,
" two pounds of calcined magnesia, and eight pounds of
" sulphur."

If dry heat is to be used for vulcanizing then thirty ounces of sulphuric acid, two pounds of bi-carbonate of soda, four pounds of litharge and two pounds of calcined magnesia are used instead of the quantities of these materials given above.

For semi-hard rubber goods, " twenty-four pounds of
" linseed oil, sixteen pounds of cotton seed oil, four pounds
" of castor oil, twelve ounces of sulphuric acid, twelve ounces
" of nitric acid, one pound of bi-carbonate of soda, one pound
" of sulphate of zinc, one and one half pound of muriate of
" tin, eight pounds of coal tar, eight pounds of asphaltum,
" two pounds of gutta percha, ten pounds of sulphur, and one
" pound of calcined magnesia."

For hard rubber goods—" Thirty-two pounds of linseed
" oil, eight pounds of cotton seed oil, three pounds of castor
" oil, one pound of coal oil, twenty-four ounces of nitric acid,
" six ounces of muriatic acid, one-half pound of bi-carbonate
" of soda, two pounds of muriate of tin, five pounds of coal
" tar, five pounds of asphaltum, one pound of gutta percha,
" and ten pounds of sulphur."

The compound is combined with india-rubber in varying proportions. The whole is then vulcanized.

[*Printed, 4d. No Drawings.*]

A.D. 1868, August 7.—No. 2471.

HUNT, BRISTOW.—(*A communication from John Haskins.*)— Manufacturing india-rubber fabrics, which will resist the passage of water (excepting under pressure) and at the same time be sufficiently pervious to allow of ventilation.

The fabric " is produced by taking sheets of india-rubber
" (of various thicknesses, according to the uses to which they
" are to be applied), and piercing or perforating them all
" over with minute holes or perforations, the size, number,
" and distance apart being also varied according to circum-
" stances, but they must be of sufficient size to allow of air
" and gases passing through, and to be plainly visible on
" holding the fabric up to the light, at the same time that

" they must be sufficiently minute to prevent the passage of
" water, excepting when pressure is applied."

[*Printed, 6d. Drawing.*]

A.D. 1868, August 11.—No. 2505.

GRAY, Matthew, and HAWKINS, Frederick.—" Manu-
" facturing telegraphic insulated wires and cables."

This invention relates, firstly, to covering wire or strands
with an insulating coat of plastic compound, and consists in
using "pairs of pressing or squeezing rollers formed with
" several half-round ring grooves placed side by side, and
" having, as projections that separate the grooves, blunt
" edges or compressing rings." Between these rollers are
passed a number of wires (to be coated) corresponding with
the number of grooves provided in the rollers, and with the
wires are passed two ribbons or fillets of the compound rubber,
one above and the other below the wires.

" Secondly, to combining covered strands or wires into one
" cable; the objects being, first, to facilitate the drawing out
" of the ends of the several wires from the cable to connect
" them with other lengths of wire or with electrical instru-
" ments;" "and, secondly, to effect an economy in the
" vulcanizing process." Over the wires which have been
covered, and while in an uncured state, is dusted French
chalk; flour, or other substance that will destroy the tendency
to adhesion between the coated wires, which are then laid
together to form a cable. The coated wires thus grouped are
enclosed in a coating of plastic compound rubber which may
be applied by lapping or by grooved rollers. The coated cable
is then submitted to heat to produce the "change" required.

Printed, 10d. Drawing.]

A.D. 1868, September 2.—No. 2715.

FORSTER, Thomas, and HEARTFIELD, John.—" Manu-
" facture of porous or spongy substances from india-rubber,
" gutta percha, balata, or their compounds."

This invention " consists in combining with india-rubber,
" gutta percha, balata, or their compounds, ground animal or
" vegetable fibre, together with water or other liquid or

" substance which will generate vapour in the curing process,
" or in some cases charcoal or other absorbent material may
" be used in place of fibre."

The fibre may be previously ground as flock, or it may be ground together with the rubber compound by any of the usual methods, and when perfectly broken up and combined with the rubber the usual quantity of sulphur is added. The mass is then thoroughly wetted, and, after the surface moisture has been dried off, pressed into sheets or blocks approximating to the desired form when finished. Strips or pieces of the mass so formed are subsequently placed in moulds and vulcanized. The moulds generally used are 16 inches by 12 inches, and 3 inches in depth, and the sheet of rubber, which is 1 inch in thickness, is cut into pieces a little less than 16 inches by 12 inches. The piece of compound is fastened by cement to a thin perforated metal plate, which fits loosely into the mould and allows the air to escape from underneath it.

If a sponge with very coarse pores is required sawdust is used, preferably that of soft woods, such as lime, pear, or deal; if the latter it is boiled in caustic soda and water to remove any resin, then well washed, and soaked in acid and water as described in No. 1222, A.D. 1868.

[*Printed, 4d. No Drawings.*]

A.D. 1868, September 14.—No. 2825.

TURNBULL, HENRY JOHN.—Compositions for preserving and keeping clean the bottoms of iron ships, and iron structures exposed to the action of the atmosphere and water.

The composition for preventing the oxidation of the iron consists of gutta percha and resin dissolved in combination with pine varnish.

The anti-fouling composition is a preparation of phosphorus and shellac.

[*Printed, 4d. No Drawings.*]

A.D. 1868, October 6.—No. 3051.

ASPINALL, JOSEPH.—(*Provisional protection only.*)—" Im-
" provements in telegraphic and other ropes or cables,"
" also applicable in hardening the surface of india-rubber
" and gutta percha."

The ropes or cables are enveloped in felt or other fabric saturated with a compound of gutta percha and pitch or rosin. Silica or other similar hard powder is mixed with the gutta percha and pitch or similar composition, or a silicate such as soap-stone is mixed with it, and the silica is afterwards freed by means of an acid, or a solution is applied such as chloride of calcium, which converts the silicate originally employed into a hard stoney substance. The surface of india-rubber and gutta percha is hardened in a similar manner; the surface is washed over with cement or solvent having a silicate such as soapstone mixed with it, an acid or a solution of chloride of calcium or such like salt is then applied.

[*Printed, 4d. No Drawings.*]

A.D. 1868, October 20.—No. 3215.

FORSTER, THOMAS, and HEARTFIELD, JOHN.—"Improve-
" ments in sponging or bath gloves," partly " applicable to
" the joining india-rubber sponge."

In the manufacture of the gloves sheets of india-rubber sponge are employed. The sheets are cut to suitable forms, the edges of the pieces are then cemented with india-rubber cement made with benzole. " When the cement is dry the
" pieces are stuck together, and then to make the joint secure
" they are treated with chloride of sulphur diluted with
" bi-sulphide of carbon, and thus the india-rubber films
" forming the joints are also vulcanized.

" The same method of securely joining pieces of india-
" rubber sponge by uniting them with india-rubber cement
" and subsequently vulcanizing such joint is also applicable
" to the manufacture of other articles."

[*Printed, 4d. No Drawings.*]

A.D. 1868, October 21.—No. 3226.

MacMILLAN, CATHERINE.—(*A communication from William Jardine Combe MacMillan.*)—" Protecting iron ships and
" other submerged surfaces from corrosion and marine
" growths," and " compositions to be so employed."

" A compound of gutta percha and resin in equal pro-
" portions is employed; these materials are boiled together,

" using however only so much heat as is necessary to admit
" for the complete mixture of the ingredients."

" The surface of the iron ship having been thoroughly
" cleaned is heated by means of a coke fire contained in a
" portable basket; the compound is then applied." It is
spread by means of small hand metal-spreading rollers or irons,
these are also heated.

To prevent the adhesion of barnacles and marine growths a
second coating is applied, which is a preparation of phosphorus
and shellac.

[*Printed, 4d. No Drawings.*]

A.D. 1868, October 29.—No. 3309.

LIDDELL, WILLIAM HODGSON.—Treating pig skins.

Part of this invention relates to a " system of buffing
" adapted to closing and filling up the pores of the skin, so
" that the black body used for filling up shall not run through
" to the other side." The black body employed is " a mix-
" ture of dissolved india-rubber, with about a fourth part of
" sugar of lead made into a paste by gum dissolved in oil, or
" spirit, or both, in place of water as hitherto."

[*Printed, 4d. No Drawings.*]

A.D. 1868, November 21.—No. 3543.

HARRIS, ISAAC BLUE.—(*Provisional protection only.*)—
" Manufacture of driving bands."

A core is first formed of woven wire embedded in a sheet of
soft vulcanized india-rubber or gutta percha, or their compounds. One or more layers of this embedded woven wire
may be employed to form the core, the upper face of which is
overlaid with sheet rubber to cover the exposed wire. Round
the core thus formed is lapped a coating of strong cotton
cloth or canvas prepared on one side with the soft rubber or
gutta percha compound, joining the edges of the lapping
cloth on the face of the band, and this joint is covered with
the strip of the compound. The fabric thus formed is submitted to pressure and to the vulcanizing process.

[*Printed, 4d. No Drawings.*]

A.D. 1868, November 23.—No. 3564.

PHILLIPS, JAMES EDWIN.—(*Provisional protection only*).—
" Improvements in sewing machines, parts of which im-
" provements are applicable to other purposes."

Part of this invention relates to the employment of india-rubber, gutta percha, or compounds thereof, in the construction of gearing in the following manner:—For toothed pinions a boss or foundation wheel is cast in metal with a ring or suitable projections, this foundation wheel is placed in a mould, having suitable cavities formed for the teeth, the space in the mould not occupied by the foundation wheel is filled with india-rubber gutta percha or compounds thereof, it is then submitted to heat to " cure " it and cause the compound to adhere to the boss. Wheels of coarse pitch are cast in metal with smaller teeth than those required, a coating of india-rubber is then applied in a manner similar to that above described. In some cases a band of india-rubber, gutta percha or compounds thereof is placed around the teeth and drawn down between them by bolts and nuts or other means.

[*Printed, 4d. No Drawings.*]

A.D. 1868, December 2.—No. 3661.

ROSTAING, CHARLES SYLVESTER. — (*Provisional protection only*).—Construction of electric telegraph cables.

Part of this invention consists of a "plastic compound
" composed of gutta percha melted with from five to ten
" per cent. of tannin, or of catechu, or of a combination of
" gutta percha and caoutchouc melted and thoroughly
" worked together also combined with tannin or catechu,"
used for impregnating textile fabrics serving for the construction of electric cables, or for coating them, or for giving the electric fluid conducting wires, for their better insulation, a coating or varnish more or less thick before winding them round the central cord or core.

[*Printed, 6d. Drawing.*]

A.D. 1868, December 29.—No. 3961.

MARSH, JOHN.—(*Provisional protection only*.)—" Covering
" or capping bottles, jars, and other surfaces."

India-rubber vulcanized or prepared so as to be really elastic or other suitable elastic material is made into small conical, or sugar loaf, or other suitably shaped caps, these are pressed on to and over any corks or stoppers of the bottles, jars, or surfaces to be capped or covered so as to tightly encompass the same. "The india-rubber coverings for bottles are first of " all made in moulds, then put on mandrels, and finished off by " hand, every one single and every cap moulded separately."

[*Printed, 4d. No Drawings.*]

1869.

A.D. 1869, January 13.—No. 101.

STERNE, LOUIS, JAQUES, JAMES ARCHIBALD, and FANSHAWE, JOHN AMERICUS.—(*Provisional protection only.*)—
" Manufacture of elastic rubbers."

This invention relates to articles made of porous rubber, sometimes called rubber sponge. The object is to prevent the articles from getting out of shape. The porous rubber is combined with a framing of some more rigid substance which will maintain its shape, such for instance as solid vulcanized india-rubber or hard rubber. Bars or pieces of this solid substance are arranged "in any convenient manner, as for
" instance in the form of a cross or of a rectangular or oval
" frame or skeleton with cross bars or cells ; the composition
" to form the spongy or porous rubber is placed in the cells
" or interstices between the solid parts, and the whole being
" submitted to the vulcanizing process all the several parts
" will be firmly united together."

[*Printed, 4d. No Drawings.*]

A.D. 1869, February 3.—No. 327.

MACINTOSH JOHN.—" Ornamenting surfaces."

This " invention consists in using a combination of paraffin
" or stearic acid, india rubber, and collodion mixed with
" metallic powders or gold or silver leaf for the ornamenta-
" tion of surfaces, whereby they are rendered waterproof and
" not liable to tarnish or oxidation." In some cases the

compound of india-rubber and paraffin or stearic acid is used as a ground, and the metallic powder or leaf is spread thereon.

[*Printed, 4d. No Drawings.*]

A.D. 1869, February 18.—No. 507.

FORSTER, THOMAS, and COW, PETER BRUSEY, junior.—(*Provisional protection only.*)—"Manufacture of india-rubber "suction and other pipes, and of hose, buckets, bags, and "such like vessels."

The inventors "substitute for the galvanized iron wire coil "used in the manufacture of ordinary suction and other hose "alternate rings or spirals of rubber having two different "quantities of sulphur in them; so that after the operation "of steam vulcanizing every alternate ring or spiral will be "hard, while the intermediate ones will be flexible."

In manufacturing india-rubber hose, buckets, bags, and such like vessels they "substitute for the cotton or linen "fabric ordinarily used for giving strength a material com- "posed of rubber and fibre." This is obtained "by mixing "rubber and vegetable fibre (cotton, linen, and flax, by pre- "ference) with or without sulphur by means of a pair of "rollers moving at unequal speeds until the compound forms "a kind of felted paper impervious to water." This compound is rolled into sheets, which are used in the same manner that the cotton or linen fabric is now used.

[*Printed, 4d. No Drawings.*]

A.D. 1869, February 20.—No. 531.

GRAY, MATTHEW.—"Manufacture of covered electrical con- "ductors."

The object of this invention is to reduce the liability which the conducting strands or wires have to lose their central position in the india-rubber envelope during the vulcanizing process. The conducting wire is enclosed first in pure india-rubber, this is overlaid with a plastic compound of india-rubber and sulphur applied by means of the machine described in No. 2505, A.D. 1868, or by other machinery. A tape or strip of cotton or other suitable fabric is next lapped or coiled helically around the india-rubber and sulphur coating while it is still in a green state. This cloth covering is paid over with a solution of the rubber compound, and the face of a second strip of cloth is prepared with the like solution, this strip of cloth is lapped around the coated wire in the opposite direction to that of the first cloth covering. The conductor thus prepared is submitted to heat in the vulcanizing chamber. The covered conductor is wound on a large hollow iron cylinder or drum (covered on the outside with a soft substance such as cotton) by causing the drum to rotate. This drum is put into the vulcanising chamber. "The drum being hollow " and open at the ends will allow of a smaller drum similarly " laden with a covered electrical conductor being placed " therein, and this second drum may contain a third, and " so on."

[*Printed, 4d. No Drawings.*]

A.D. 1869, April 14.—No. 1157.

CLARK, ALEXANDER MELVILLE. — (*A communication from Manuel Leopold Jonas Lavater.*)—(*Provisional protection only.*) —" Manufacture of india-rubber nipples for feeding bottles."

"The nipple is formed in hollow moulds made in a single " piece of metal, glass, or ceramic material."

India-rubber either pure or a composition "is run in a " state of solution into the mould, which is then inverted to " allow the material to run off. In this manner a thin film " of india-rubber is deposited on the interior surface of the " mould."

The operation is repeated as many times as required until the desired thickness is obtained. The hollow central space within the mould is then filled with silicate of magnesia and the whole submitted to a vulcanizing process.

Or the nipple may be made by hand of vulcanized india-rubber, then placed in the mould, and an elastic mandril introduced into the nipple. The mandril consists of a small tube of india-rubber closed at the end inserted in the nipple. Air is then forced into the elastic mandril by the aid of an insufflator, whereby it is expanded so as to press the nipple against the sides of the mould and maintain it in such position. When the mandril is withdrawn the nipple is filled with talc and the whole subjected to a vulcanizing process.

[*Printed, 6d. Drawing.*]

A.D. 1869, April 24.—No. 1278.

FORSTER, THOMAS, and COW, PETER BRUSEY, junior. — " Compounds containing india-rubber, gutta percha, or " balata."

A compound is made by combining with india-rubber a substance called coorongite. This substance is prepared " by " passing it through and through between rollers over which " water is running until it works into a plastic mass, and " until much of the sand which it contained has been washed " out." It is then passed between hard rollers to crush up the remaining sand, and it is worked up with masticated india-rubber. The compound " may be dissolved in the " ordinary india-rubber solvents, although these solvents " will not dissolve coorongite itself."

Sulphur is also mixed with this compound, and it is exposed to heat and in this way vulcanized. "The compound may " also be vulcanized by other well-known vulcanizing " processes.

" Other substances may be added to the compound of " india-rubber and coorongite, such as gutta percha, balata, " gums, pigments, mineral powders, and other substances " now commonly mixed with india-rubber.

" Gutta percha may also be substituted for india-rubber in " the above-mentioned compounds, and so also may balata."

[*Printed*, 4*d*. *No Drawings*.]

A.D. 1869, May 5.—No. 1386.

PHILLIPS, JAMES EDWIN. — " Improvements in sewing " machines," " parts of which improvements are applicable " to other machinery."

Part of this invention relates to the employment of india-rubber, gutta percha, or compounds thereof, in the construction of gearing in the following manner :—For toothed pinions, a boss or foundation wheel is cast in metal with a ring or suitable projections, this foundation wheel is placed in a mould, having suitable cavities formed for the teeth, the space in the mould not occupied by the foundation wheel is filled with india-rubber, gutta percha or compounds thereof, it is then submitted to heat to " cure " it and cause the compound to adhere to the boss. Wheels of coarse pitch are cast in metal with smaller teeth than those required, a coating of india-rubber is then applied in a manner similar to that above described. In some cases a band of india-rubber, gutta percha or compounds thereof is placed around the teeth and drawn down between them by bolts and nuts or other means.

[*Printed*, 1s. 6d. *Drawings*.]

A.D. 1869, May 10.—No. 1424.

WOLFGANG, MARK SCHMERL.—" Cricket and other balls."

A core is first formed of compressed cork united by means of india-rubber solution, a coating of asbestos is then applied, and bound with canvas, cotton, twine, or other suitable material. This is again covered with asbestos, after which a coating of india-rubber mixed with powdered asbestos is applied. The ball is now submitted to heat to cure the rubber.

[*Printed*, 6d. *Drawing*.]

A.D. 1869, May 15.—No. 1495.

WILKINSON, WILLIAM, and BOSS, MARK.—Embossing, printing, enamelling, and ornamenting various substance, and preparing the materials employed.

Part of this invention relates to transferring printed designs from transfer paper to the surfaces of glass or metal to be embossed the design being printed with Brunswick black and printers' ink mixed together in equal quantities, and any required quantity of pitch may also be mixed therewith, or printers' ink and gutta percha or wax or any combination of these materials.

Another part of the invention relates to a composition for preventing damp or oxidation destroying iron or metallic plates, and consists of two pounds of coal or gas tar, one pound of resin, and one pound of gutta percha.

Another part of the invention relates to a composition applicable to various purposes. It consists of refuse skivings or leather cuttings or old leather torn up and reduced to a fine powder, and india-rubber dissolved in naphtha, a proportionate quantity of cork may be added. It may be heated to any required degree in cylinders " and undergo a similar operation

" to that of india-rubber and gutta percha, and rolled out into
" lengths or sheets," "and may also be rolled upon any
" desired fabric in order to fill up the meshes."

[*Printed, 1s. 4d. Drawing.*]

A.D. 1869, June 28.—No. 1955.

SMITH, GEORGE THOMAS, and CHALLENGER, CHARLES.—
" Composition applicable to the manufacture of floorcloths,
" tarpaulins, railway sheets, and other waterproof fabrics."

1 cwt. of vulcanized india-rubber is ground small, then 4 lbs. of sulphuric acid mixed with 32 lbs. of water are added to it, after the mixture has been well stirred it is covered over for 12 hours; it is then put into a copper with 8 lbs. of naphtha and 3 lbs. of blue vitriol, and boiled down for a sufficient time to incorporate the mass. The mixture is then placed in a tub and washed with cold water; it is then to be passed through rollers and made into sheets, which are to be hung up to dry for two or three weeks. 1 lb. of the dried mixture is added to 1½ lbs. of rags or waste refuse of flax or hemp, and 1½ lbs. of leather ground up, this mixture is passed through rollers several times, ½ lb. of coloring matter being added during the mixing. "The compound or material is then to be passed
" through a series of rollers in order to roll it into small
" sheets, which are then to be placed in a jacket pan until
" sufficient sheets are made to produce a length of cloth;" the sheets are then run through a three-bowl calender to the thickness required.

[*Printed, 4d. No Drawings.*]

A.D. 1869, July 1.—No. 1989.

TURNER, ARCHIBALD. — (*Provisional protection only.*) — Utilizing the waste strips of india-rubber which are cut off from the edges of sheet rubber.

The waste strips are wound " singly on a bobbin from
" which when the bobbin is placed in the cutting machine the
" strip is unrolled and brought under the action of a series of
" circular cutters, which are mounted on a spindle and are
" driven at a high speed. The knives or cutting instruments
" are kept wet, and as the strip is fed forward it is by the
" rapid rotation of the cutters divided up into separate

" threads, the number depending upon the width of the strip,
" and these threads are drawn forward by suitable pressure
" rollers."

[*Printed, 4d. No Drawings.*]

A.D. 1869, August 9.—No. 2379.

TURNER, ARCHIBALD.—(*Letters Patent void for want of Final Specification.*)—Utilizing waste strips of india-rubber, and machinery for cutting sheet rubber into thread.

The waste strips, cut off from the edges of sheet rubber, are wound singly on bobbins, or they may be simply placed in a basket or skip. " The strips are brought singly under the
" action of a series of circular cutters, whereby the strip is
" divided up into a number of threads. A wide sheet of
" rubber (any width) can be cut up into threads in the same
" manner in a machine of the same construction, which
" consists of any convenient number of circular cutters
" according to the width of the strip or sheet to be operated
" upon. These circular cutters are mounted on a spindle,
" and are driven at a high speed. The cutting edges of these
" circular cutters are made to bear against a horizontal bar
" at the end of a weighted or spring lever." " The circular
" knives or cutters are kept wet by causing water to drip
" thereon, and as the strip or sheet of rubber is fed forward
" by a pair of rollers it passes over the horizontal pressing
" bar, which is forced by the weighted lever or spring against
" the cutting edges of the rotary knives."

[*Printed, 4d. No Drawings.*]

A.D. 1869, November 11.—No. 3254.

JOHNSON, JOHN HENRY.—(*A communication from John Ballou Newbrough and Edward Fagan.*)—" The treatment of
" caoutchouc, gutta percha, and analogous gums for the
" production therefrom of articles of utility and ornament."

This invention relates to " producing what is known as hard
" or vulcanized rubber, and consists in combining iodine with
" caoutchouc or analogous gum so as to form a composition
" whereof to mould or shape articles of utility or ornament
" prior to the same being hardened by vulcanizing; the said
" composition being in some cases mixed with clay, kaolin,

"or other mineral substance so as to vary its consistency,
and wolfram or tungsten oxide being used if desired in
combination with the composition so as to prevent the same
from being over vulcanized during the process of incorporating the gum with the iodine by heat and pressure."

"The invention further consists in the application of
bromine to the above composition" through the medium of
one of the following preparations:—One preparation consists
of a solution of bromine in chloroform. A second preparation
is made by dissolving in turpentine one part of iodine and two
parts of bromine. "To make a third preparation sulphur is
boiled in turpentine until the sulphur is decomposed and
settles with part of the oil to the bottom of the vessel
in which the materials are treated; the oil is then poured
off and the residuum gradually dried by moderate heat
after being washed if necessary with sulphuric acid. A
fourth preparation is formed by treating iodine in the same
manner as sulphur is treated in making the third preparation, except that the turpentine need not be boiled, and
refuse out from the manufacture of the third preparation
may be employed." "Also in the manufacture of articles
of utility and ornament by first shaping the same of
unprepared caoutchouc or analogous gum, and then treating
them with a solution of bromine in chloroform."

The invention also relates to a composition for coating
metal and other material, "consisting of caoutchouc or other
analogous gum dissolved in a solution of bromine and
chloroform."

[*Printed*, 6d. *No Drawings.*]

A.D. 1869, November 13.—No. 3274.

GEDGE, WILLIAM EDWARD.—(*A communication from Jules
Crouzières*).—"Composition to be used as a coating for
preserving metal and other surfaces, also as a cement or
luting."

It is "composed essentially of sulphur, coal tar, gutta
percha, white lead, minium or red lead, and spirit of turpentine, to which may be added resin or pitch, either or
both according to the application to be made."

[*Printed*, 4d. *No Drawings.*]

A.D. 1869, December 4.—No. 3513.

WALKER, Joseph.—(*Provisional protection only.*)—Material to be employed for calico printers' washing blankets "and " for other purposes requiring a waterproof material having " an absorbent surface."

"India-rubber when in the soft state, that is to say, " previously to its being vulcanized, is covered on one surface " with powdered cork; the cork by the pressure of rollers " being partially embedded in the india-rubber firmly adheres " thereto." When a considerable degree of absorbency is required the cork is applied in a granular form.

[*Printed, 4d. No Drawings.*]

1870.

A.D. 1870, January 5.—No. 41.

TRUEMAN, Edwin Thomas.—" Machinery for cleansing and " preparing gutta percha, india-rubber, and like substances."

The instruments used for dividing or ploughing the materials operated upon are formed of the shape approximately of a double wedge; this is effected by cutting upon the periphery of a suitable metal spindle or cylinder a double-threaded male screw. The threads are made by preference square and each thread runs in a reverse way to and at intervals crosses the other, the result being that wedge-shaped projections are formed upon the spindle, which is placed inside a suitable metal case and is supported on bearings. The internal surface of the metal case is provided with wedge-shaped projections corresponding to those formed upon the spindle. "The gutta percha or other analogous " material required to be cleansed may be introduced into " the machine by means of a suitable hopper, and the mass " is forced by the action of the rotating dividing instrument " between the spindle and the inside of the case." The machine works in or under water, or while the materials are submitted to the action of streams or jets of water.

In a modification of the machine, instead of cutting or forming the projections in or upon and in one piece with the spindle or internal surface of the case respectively, the projections are formed by cutting the double-threaded screw used as the dividing instrument in several sections; these are fixed on the spindle, and are separated by suitable washers. The machines may be employed without water, and they may be applied for mixing purposes, and for preparing gutta percha and other analogous materials and their compounds with other substances.

[*Printed*, 4d. *No Drawings.*]

A.D. 1870, January 31.—No. 272.

DICK, ROBERT.—"Covering and insulating the wires of
" electric telegraphs."

The improvements are,—" First. The covering, insulating,
" and protecting the conducting wires of electric telegraphs
" with inner coatings formed of vulcanized india-rubber and
" gutta percha solution (the latter as a cement to the former)
" by themselves or in conjunction with coatings of gutta
" percha, as heretofore used."

" Second. The application and use of thin strips of vul-
" canized india-rubber coated with gutta percha solution (as
" a cementing medium) for insulating and covering the
" conducting wires of electric telegraphs."

" Third. The application, construction, and use of sectional
" strips of vulcanized india-rubber coated with gutta percha
" solution (as a cementing medium) with grooves for receiving
" the electric telegraph wires, all for forming the inner
" insulating and protecting coverings of said wires."

" Fourth. The application of a first insulating and roughen-
" ing coating of shellac and sawdust, finely ground vulcanized
" india-rubber, or other equivalent powder material to the
" conducting wires of electric telegraphs for insuring the
" adhesion of the subsequent cementing coating of gutta
" percha solution and vulcanized india-rubber, or of the
" ordinary coatings (as gutta percha or others) heretofore
" applied to such wires."

[*Printed*, 1s. *Drawings.*]

A.D. 1870, February 1.—No. 295.

BROADHURST, George, SWINDELLS, John, and KERSHAW, John.—Manufacture of india-rubber sacks for tobacco and other purposes; also elastic webbing for boot gussets; also a partially cut fabric for rollers; and a pierced or cellular fabric intended for the use of woollen cloth manufacturers.

The sacks are made of a length sufficient to admit of being folded up and turned inside out at the mouth.

The webbing is made by sewing a band or sheet of india-rubber between two woven or other fabrics by the aid of sewing machinery.

The cut fabric is made by fixing vulcanized india-rubber of suitable size and thickness to a travelling platform, with which it is passed under a rapidly revolving circular knife, which makes parallel cuts in the rubber to any required depth.

The pierced or cellular fabric is made by punching small holes in a sheet of india-rubber prepared for vulcanizing, and then vulcanizing it to canvas. For punching the sheet rubber a steel plate pierced with suitable sized holes and fitted with centre punches are employed. The sheet of rubber is passed between the plate and the punches and the points of the punches are forced into the holes by a sharp blow.

[*Printed, 1s. 6d. Drawings.*]

A.D. 1870, March 11.—No. 726.

JACKSON, Charles.—Improvements in vulcanizers, also applicable for regulating the flow of gas for other purposes.

The vulcanizer consists of a boiler heated by gas. The boiler is made of wrought-iron plates and the lid is provided with a metallic joint so as to render india-rubber packing unnecessary. On the pipe which connects the pressure gauge with the boiler is fixed a chamber, into which open the inlet pipe conveying gas to this chamber, and two outlet pipes conveying gas from the chamber to the burners of the vulcanizer. In the chamber is a flat tube closed at one end and bent into a nearly circular figure. The open end of this flat tube communicates with the pipe of the pressure gauge, and the closed end is free to move. On the closed end is a lever carrying two valves, situated respectively opposite the outlet pipes, by which gas is conveyed to the burners. By the pressure of steam in the boiler the flat curved tube in the gas chamber tends to uncoil itself, and, acting on the valves, regulates the supply of gas to the burners.

[*Printed, 1s. 2d. Drawings.*]

A.D. 1870, March 11.—No. 728.

THAMSEN, PETER CHRISTIAN.—(*A communication from Soren Sörensen.*)—" Manufacture of artificial leather."

Leather waste, leather cuttings, leather shavings, or other small bits of leather, either new or old, are reduced to a kind of fibrous pulp by hand labour or by a machine or mill. "This matter or pulp is then kneaded with india-rubber, " which is rendered fluid or dissolved in oils or spirits and " treated with ammonia." It is preferred to dissolve the india-rubber in oil of turpentine. Previous to mixing the pulp with the india-rubber solution it is preferred to treat the pulp with ammonia vapour. When the mixture of pulp and india-rubber solution has been kneaded to an even mass it is pressed in forms, or by rollers, or otherwise into the required shape. It is afterwards dried and pressed and is then ready for use.

In some cases the india-rubber solution is dispensed with, ammonia alone being employed to act upon the leather pulp. " The quality of this artificial leather can be improved by " vulcanizing." For this purpose one part of chloride of sulphur is mixed with forty parts of sulphide of carbon. " In " this liquid the leather remains for 5 or 6 minutes, when the " intended effect has been produced." " The mixed liquid " may also be added to the solution of india-rubber and " ammonia."

[*Printed, 4d. No Drawings.*]

A.D. 1870, March 16.—No. 786.

MOULTON, JOEL.—Manufacture of elastic rolls or tubing for clothes wringers and other purposes.

The first part of the invention consists in the employment of a woven webbing, or one or more strings or strands of any suitable material, covered or saturated with india-rubber or other analogous gum, wound or extended about a shaft and subsequently vulcanized. A plan for preventing the roll from slipping upon its shaft consists in constructing such shaft between its journals in three parts or rods, and introducing the fibres between and about these rods, and subsequently applying about the whole a mass of rubber and vulcanizing it.

According to the second portion of the invention a strip of woven webbing has applied to its opposite sides two strips of thin vulcanized india-rubber, leaving a narrow space in the middle of the webbing upon each side thereof and between such rubber strips. The strip of webbing is then folded in the centre, and a metallic wire is enclosed in the fold. The strip is then wound spirally about a shaft from end to end thereof between its journals and the whole is subjected to the vulcanizing process. A modification of this portion of the invention consists in applying transversely to a sheet or between two sheets of vulcanized rubber a layer or range of strands of fibrous material, and subsequently cutting this sheet into ribbons of the desired width at right angles to the length of the strands and forming the strips as before described. String may be used instead of a metallic wire.

"The first portion of the machinery for manufacturing the
" above rolls consists, first, in a frame suitably constructed
" for holding and rotating a metallic shaft about which the
" elastic material is wound, and in combining therewith a
" series of bunters or hammers for driving the layers or coils
" of rubber in close contact with each other as they are wound
" about the shaft, the machine further being provided with
" means for folding the strips of rubber previous to being
" wound about the shaft, and for introducing into the fold
" thus formed a metallic wire or string."

The machinery for detaching elastic rolls or tubes from the vulcanizing moulds consists of two rotating cylindrical rods, termed "cleavers," " supported horizontally in a suitable
" frame in longitudinal alignment with each other, and in
" such a manner as to be capable of being advanced or
" retracted with respect to each other and the vulcanizing
" mould or shell and its contents."

The last portion of the machinery is "for enveloping an
" elastic roll in its outer case or jacket, which is applied to it

" for the purpose of imparting to it a smooth and perfect
" face." The elastic jacket or tube, destined to give the
finishing surface to the roll, is inserted in an upright hollow
cylinder, a small portion of the jacket being left protruding
from the top of the cylinder. The roll is forced into the
jacket by a plunger actuated by a rack and pinion.

[*Printed, 1s. Drawings.*]

A.D. 1870, March 24.—No. 863.

FANSHAWE, HENRY RICHARDSON, and SMITH, WILLIAM
HENRY.—Treating hides and skins.

Part of the invention relates to treating leather intended
for boot soles, uppers, harness and such like purposes, in
which imperviousness is required by placing it quite dry in an
exhaust vessel, and saturating it with a bituminous compound
of coal tar pitch dissolved in common coal tar spirit. To this
is added india-rubber well masticated twelve per cent., and
gutta percha six per cent. on the weight of the bitumen
employed. When color is an object a solution of shell lac is
employed instead of the bituminous mixture.

Another part of the invention relates to the treatment of
skins such as calf sheep and goat skins with white wax in
turpentine, and afterwards with a composition of bleached
shell lac and liquor ammonia or borate of soda, and a mixture
of stearine with white wax, and what are known as the
metallic oxide colors. "In each or any of the above coatings
" or compositions the black or colouring can be introduced,
" and a small proportion of caoutchouc, or, for great firm-
" ness, gutta percha, may be introduced, the caoutchouc or
" gutta percha to be blended with the solvent of the materials
" forming the coating composition." In some cases as a
finishing coating a compound of bisulphide of carbon and
ter-chloride of sulphur is employed. The inner surfaces of
boot soles and similar articles are coated with a solution on
india-rubber and lac blended by a masticator in the proportions of one hundred parts of rubber and fifteen parts ground
lac dissolved in one of the usual solvents; or of rubber one
hundred parts and of gutta percha twenty parts dissolved as
before stated.

[*Printed, 6d. No Drawings.*]

A.D. 1870, March 25.—No. 878.

TRUMAN, EDWIN THOMAS.—" Treating and preparing gutta " percha and other like substances."

The gutta percha or other material is first cleansed either by the process described in No. 2052, A.D. 1860, or preferably by the process described in No. 41, A.D. 1870, or it may be cleansed by the ordinary cleansing processes hitherto used, and in some instances materials comparatively free from dirt may be used without cleansing.

The material when cleansed, if it requires cleansing, is placed in a machine consisting of a cylindrical metal case, in which works a screw (having by preference) three blades. The case has on the top of it a large open hopper, and it has also an exit opening at one end, towards which the material is forced by the action of the screw. To this opening is attached a bent tube, which conducts the material back into the hopper and so delivers it again to the action of the screw. This operation is repeated over and over again. In an early part of the operation the tube or case is highly heated, the result being that the moisture contained in the pores of the gum is converted into steam and is ready to be liberated directly the gutta percha reaches the opening of the tube leading back into the case. The application of heat is continued until all the moisture is driven off, the heat is then withdrawn and the operation is continued with the tube cool until the air and gas contained in the gum are driven off and the gutta percha passes out of the tube desiccated and consolidated.

[*Printed, 6d. No Drawings.*]

A.D. 1870, April 4.—No. 982.

MacCARTNEY, WILLIAM NEWTON.—" Process for dissolving " or reducing crude or manufactured india-rubber."

This invention is specially applicable for utilizing waste vulcanized or ebonized india-rubber, to reduce which it is immersed in any of the ordinary solvents of crude india-rubber until it has become softened and can be easily cut, torn, or ground into small pieces. It is then placed in a still with variable proportions of camphor to the india-rubber, some india-rubber requiring more and some less of the camphor.

"Heat is then applied and the contents of the still kept in agitation, when the india-rubber will be dissolved, and the solvent passed over either in vacuo or under the pressure of the atmosphere. The liquid solvent which is distilled over from the rubber is suitable for dissolving other waste rubber." If all the camphor is to be exhausted from the india-rubber, alcohol is added to the hot solution. "Upon cooling the alcohol is separated from the india-rubber and is then drawn off, when the camphor may be separated from the alcohol by being thrown down by the addition of water, or by distilling the alcohol."

"Camphor or any of its allied substances, such as artificial camphor, camphine, camphin, oil of camphor, camphoric acid, camphrone, camphol, campholic acid, or any of the camphorates, or camphoric ethers," may be used for the purposes of this invention.

[*Printed*, 4d. *No Drawings.*]

A.D. 1870, April 14.—No. 1095.

STEWART, LAWRENCE.—Wheels for carriages, waggons, carts, and other vehicles.

The wheels are made of vulcanized caoutchouc, known as vulcanite, of which the whole of the wheels are made, or parts only may be made of vulcanite the other parts being of wood metal or other material. When made wholly of vulcanite they are manufactured by pressing the caoutchouc, mixed with sulphur or other material, in a plastic state in moulds of the requisite shape. Each wheel may be moulded in one piece, or several moulds may be employed for forming the wheel in different pieces or divisions. But it is preferred to construct a light framework of any suitable material of the form and dimensions of the wheels required, and to lay the plastic caoutchouc over it to any depth or thickness required. The caoutchouc composition is afterwards vulcanized.

[*Printed*, 10d. *Drawing.*]

A.D. 1870, April 20.—No. 1155.

JOHNSON, JOHN HENRY.—(*A communication from John Ballou Newbrough.*)—A hardening composition called "acid resin," and its employment with india-rubber, gutta percha, gums, and oils.

This invention consists, "firstly, in subjecting turpentine
" to the action of sulphuric or other equivalent acid, and
" applying heat to the mixture until upon cooling the pro-
" duct assumes the consistency of honey, or if the heat be
" further continued the product will be obtained in a brittle
" or pulverizable condition; secondly, in the employment of
" the gelatinous or hard products thus obtained in conjunc-
" tion with caoutchouc or other similar gums, or with gutta
" percha, so as to produce a material capable of being
" moulded and solidified."

Instead of employing turpentine only with the acid " other
" substances may in part be substituted, viz., benzole or
" turpentine, to which about one-fourth part by weight of
" resin or asphaltum has been added."

" Instead of mixing the acid resin with caoutchouc it may
" for certain purposes be mixed with either linseed or rape
" oil, and the product thus obtained when submitted to a
" temperature of from 230° to 300° Fahrenheit will become
" hard. The acid resin may be combined with sulphur,
" iodine, bromine, or phosphorus, and in such combination
" may be employed for the production of compounds with all
" the resinous gums so as to produce a hardened compound
" or compounds."

[*Printed, 4d. No Drawings.*]

A.D. 1870, May 7.—No. 1315.

GUENIN, EMILE.—(*A communication from Paul Rigollot*).
" —Manufacture of mustard and other plasters," and
" machinery for the same."

This invention relates to improvements on No. 1212, A.D.
1867. Referring to that Specification the patentee says,—" I
" there described the mustard flour (deprived of its oil) as
" being caused to adhere to the paper or other surface on
" which it is applied by the aid of a solution of india-rubber
" and a mixture of equal parts of sulphuret of carbon and
" essence of petroleum." "According to the present im-
" provements I substitute benzine for the sulphuret of
" carbon, the solution being prepared in the following
" manner:—I place, for example, about ½ lb. of Para india-
" rubber in sheets (this being the only kind suitable for the
" purpose) previously masticated by passing between toothed

"rollers in a closed apparatus, and digest it at a temperature
"of from 80 to 90 degrees Fahrenheit in about 5 or 6 lbs. of
"benzine having a density of about 17 oz. per pint. This
"operation is continued for twenty-four hours, after which I
"introduce the mass into a tinned metal apparatus provided
"with a stirrer similar to a churn, and well agitate the
"contents, simultaneously with which I add in small quanti-
"ties at a time about 15 lbs. of essence of petroleum." "I
"pass the viscous liquid obtained through a wire sieve when
"it is ready for immediate use."

[*Printed, 10d. Drawing.*]

A.D. 1870, May 16.—No. 1401.

JOHNSON, JOHN HENRY.—(*A communication from Eliza Dexter Murfey.*)—" Manufacture of bearings, slides, and pack-
"ings for steam engines and other machinery."

Paper or other like material is reduced to a pulpy condition and then pressed in a mould until perfectly hard. "In some
"instances the pulp is thoroughly saturated before or after its
"introduction into the mould with paraffine, and is then con-
"densed or subjected to a pressure, the moulds if necessary
"being heated, so that the lubricant is preserved in a liquid
"state until thoroughly absorbed. In many cases it is best
"to add a solution or mixture of rubber caoutchouc, or other
"soluble material, to the pulp, or to add both rubber and
"paraffine, the product being thereby rendered more service-
"able as a bearing."

[*Printed, 4d. No Drawings.*]

A.D. 1870, June 4.—No. 1626.

SPILL, DANIEL.— Compounds for insulating telegraph wires, manufacturing flexible tubing, and other purposes.

Flexible and plastic compounds are produced by combining one or more gums, resins, or gum resins, with camphor, or with caoutchouc and camphor, or with balsams, or fatty or volatile oils. The gums, resins, or gum resins may be dissolved in the cold way by any of their solvents, and then incorporated with gutta percha or caoutchouc, or with diluents, such combinations being made by grinding rolls or masticators, or by heat and stirring alone.

[*Printed, 4d. No Drawings.*]

A.D. 1870, June 18.—No. 1752.

EWING, JOHN ORR, and COLEMAN, JOSEPH JAMES.—
" Treating or preparing certain lubricating oils."

The object of this invention is to impart to refined mineral lubricating oils obtained from crude shale oil, which is distilled from shale at a low red heat, the quality known as "body." This is effected by combining caoutchouc with the oils, by digesting the oils with the caoutchouc by the aid of heat, or by violently agitating the oils and the caoutchouc together, or both these methods may be employed in combination. Other oils may be mixed with the mineral oils.

[*Printed*, 4*d*. *No Drawings*.]

A.D. 1870, October 20.—No. 2761.

FORD, ALFRED.—Coloring india-rubber, gutta percha, and other like waterproof fabrics and materials.

This invention consists in the use of aqueous solutions of aniline colours in the dyeing or coloring of india-rubber, gutta percha, and other waterproof fabrics and materials.

[*Printed*, 4*d*. *No Drawings*.]

A.D. 1870, October 22.—No. 2790.

LAKE, WILLIAM ROBERT. — (*A communication from George Temple Chapman.*) — "Producing a hard, protective or
" ornamental covering or coating of compounds of india-
" rubber or gutta percha upon metal and other surfaces."

The india-rubber or gutta percha is dissolved in one of its solvents; one half pound of sulphur to one pound of india-rubber or gutta percha is then introduced into the solution, the sulphur being first reduced very fine by grinding in one of the solvents of india-rubber or gutta percha. "Allamine,
" feldspar, silex, magnesia, sulphate or carbonate of lime,
" French chalk, slate, lime, pumicestone, gum lac or gum
" shellac, or soapstone may be added." These substances must be ground very fine before mixing with the rubber or gutta percha. The compound is reduced to a homogeneous mass of the consistency of paint and is applied to the surface to be enamelled with a brush or by dipping or pouring. The article is then cured by exposing it to a high degree of artificial heat."

[*Printed*, 4*d*. *No Drawings*.]

A.D. 1870, November 1.—No. 2879.

JOHNSON, JOHN HENRY.—(*A communication from Eliza Dexter Murfey.*)—Boxes and bearings for axles and other shafts, and compositions to be applied thereto.

Part of this invention relates to a slightly elastic bearing especially applicable to the axle boxes of railway vehicles. Upon a sheet of cloth, leather, paper, or other material coated with india-rubber is spread a bearing material or composition consisting of any suitable ingredients. The sheet is then passed between heated rolls which soften the india-rubber and work the powdered bearing material into the plastic india-rubber. The "sheet may be perforated throughout its entire
" extent with fine needles or punches, so that on the applica-
" tion of pressure the material will be forced into the
" perforations. After the sheet is pressed it may be cut
" into strips, pads, or washers for use as substitutes for the
" ordinary metallic bearings."

[*Printed*, 10*d*. *Drawing*.]

A.D. 1870, December 6.—No. 3200.

MACINTOSH, JOHN. — "Compounds for waterproofing
" textile fabrics and other surfaces."

One of the compounds consists of one part by measure of india-rubber paste and six parts of lampblack.

The patentee states that he is "aware that lampblack
" or carbon has been combined with india-rubber, but only in
" small quantities and merely as a coloring matter;" what he claims, in reference to this part of the invention, is "the
" combination of lampblack or carbon with india-rubber
" in large proportions so as to act as a preservative of the
" small proportion of india-rubber employed."

[*Printed*, 4*d*. *No Drawings*.]

A.D. 1870, December 13.—No. 3261.

COLEMAN, JOSEPH JAMES. — "Treating certain mineral
" lubricating oils and paraffin."

The object of the first part of this invention is to impart
" body " to lubricating oils obtained from crude oil distilled from coal, or peat, or from petroleum, rock, or earth oils by

the processes of refining and treatment by acids and alkalies, which oils may be used alone or mixed with other oils. The result being the production of an oil similar in character to the oil prepared from the treatment of shale oil, as described in No. 1752, A.D. 1870.

Body is imparted to the oils mentioned by combining with them a certain portion of caoutchouc by the aid of heat, or by violently agitating the oils and the caoutchouc together, or both these methods may be employed in combination.

The second part of the invention has for its object the imparting to solid paraffin or paraffin wax the qualities of increased tenacity or toughness by combining with the paraffin a portion of caoutchouc. "The combination is effected by
" the aid of heat to reduce the solid paraffin to the liquid state,
" and mechanical agitation or heat alone may be used to
" effect the combination."

[*Printed, 4d. No Drawings.*]

1871.

A.D. 1871, January 14.—No. 104.

STEWART, LAURENCE. — (*Provisional protection only.*) — Wheels for carriages, waggons, carts, and other vehicles made of vulcanite.

This is a further development of No. 1095, A.D. 1870. The present invention consists in employing one or more strands of wire passing longitudinally through the spokes or arms of the wheel, being fastened at or near to the nave, and at the outer end of each spoke the strand is divided and each half of the strand is bent over to a circular arc corresponding to that of the felly of the wheel and in which the wire is enclosed when the caoutchouc either unmixed or admixed and combined with other materials is solidified or vulcanized over it.

[*Printed, 4d. No Drawings.*]

A.D. 1871, February 11.—No. 356.

QUIN, JAMES, and EASTHAM, ROBERT.—"Manufacture of
" india-rubber and other suitable elastic or flexible substances
" into hose or tubing."

At the top of a framing are attached a series of pinions, which gear into racks connected to or forming part of the hanging supports of a roller. Under this roller are arranged two other similar rollers which are mounted in slides and are capable of being moved further apart or nearer together. A mandrel is first coated with india-rubber by taking a piece of sheet rubber of the requisite length, and of a width rather more than equal to the circumference of the mandrel around which it is rolled and a lap joint is formed. This mandrel is then placed in the machine and a piece of woven cloth coated with india-rubber or other cement, and of a sufficient width to form the number of laps required is introduced into the machine with its forward edge in contact with the india-rubber coating of the mandrel. Upon the outer edge of the cloth is placed a piece of sheet rubber of a width rather more than equal to the outer circumference of the finished tube. The top roller being lowered till it presses on the material on the mandrel, a few turns of the rollers effects the required rolling and finishing, and a length of hose pipe is completed at one operation.

[*Printed*, 10d. *Drawing.*]

A.D. 1871, February 28.—No. 537.

WARREN, Thomas Thomas Peter Bruce.—Treating india-rubber and other materials so as to render them suitable for insulating telegraph wires, and applying such insulating materials, and rendering india-rubber so treated suitable for remanufacture.

The object of the first part of the improvements is to obtain the electrical advantages of india-rubber, so as to insure its durability without vulcanizing, or the aid of sulphur, and also to dispense with india-rubber solvents.

The improvements also enable a cheap protective material, which is itself an insulator, to be applied over a thinly insulated wire. The patentee is aware that Letters Patent No. 11,147, A.D. 1846, have been granted to A. Parkes "for " acting upon india-rubber with iodine, bromine, and chlorine, " in the state of vapors, with the addition of vapors of india- " rubber solvents, and for suspending articles of india-rubber " in the same solvents, in which chloride of sulphur and " other 'changing' agents have been dissolved."

The present improvements for rendering india-rubber suitable for insulating telegraph wires are carried out by submitting "the india-rubber insulated wires or telegraph " cores, previously consolidated as herein-after described, to " the action of iodine, bromine, or chlorine, dissolved in such " menstrua as can neither dissolve india-rubber nor exert any " action upon it, or by burying insulated wires in French " chalk with which iodine or bromine has been previously " triturated." The solvents it is preferred to employ are " water, alcohol, wood naphtha, or mixtures of alcohol and " water, to which iodide or bromide of potassium may be " added so as to obtain a more saturated solution."

The conductors, whether iron or copper, may be coated with tin, and a mixture becoming adhesive by heat may be applied so as to ensure the adhesion of the india-rubber to the conductor under the process of consolidating.

The india-rubber coatings when applied spirally or longitudinally are consolidated by being coiled round iron cylinders, which are heated by air, steam, or water applied inside the cylinder, or the wire or coils may be placed in a heated chamber.

For making joints in insulated wires " (the ends of the con- " ductor being united) the insulator is tapered down, and the " surface pared off for a few inches on each side. The " insulator is afterwards applied longitudinally or spirally, " and when completed is tightly bound with tape." Heat is gradually applied. When cooled the tape is removed, and the joint is dipped into melted iodine, or bromine may be painted over it.

In remanufacturing india-rubber which has been treated with iodine or bromine it is submitted to a dry air heat of 280° Fah. for 4 or 6 hours so as to expel the iodine or bromine, it is afterwards mixed with a fresh quantity of india-rubber which is then suitable for ordinary india-rubber manufactures.

[*Printed*, 10*d*. *No Drawings.*]

A.D. 1871, March 10.—No. 640.

SUTHERLAND, Mosher A.—An india-rubber compound adapted for use as steam packing, hose, belting, or other similar purposes.

Foliated or fibrous silicate or massive steatite, preferably asbestos, is compounded in suitable proportions with caoutchouc and sulphur, or other vulcanizing material, and vulcanized in the ordinary manner.

For making hose, belting, or similar articles canvas or other fabric is covered with the compound and vulcanized, and by coating a core of fibrous asbestos (not disintegrated) with this rubber-coated fabric another form of steam packing is produced.

[*Printed, 4d. No Drawings.*]

A.D. 1871, April 15.—No. 1010.

DAY, AUSTIN GOODYEAR.—An elastic compound resembling caoutchouc and designed chiefly for mixing with caoutchouc.

The compound is made by mixing the following substances in about the proportions mentioned:—14 pounds of cotton seed oil, 14 pounds of linseed oil, 8 pounds of asphaltum, 8 pounds of coal tar, and 10 pounds of sulphur. It is preferred to add about one-half pound of camphor.

The tar or asphaltum and the cotton seed oil are first mixed in a suitable boiler under a sufficient heat, the linseed oil is then combined with them and the sulphur is added when the temperature of the compound is about 270° Fah. The sulphur is put in gradually and as it combines with the other substances the temperature is raised to about 310° or from that to 330° Fah.

[*Printed, 4d. No Drawings.*]

A.D. 1871, April 29.—No. 1151.

WALKER, JOSEPH.—(*Provisional protection only.*)—" A cloth " or material from which washing blankets used by calico " printers may be made."

India-rubber in the soft state, that is, previous to vulcanizing, is applied to a groundwork of cotton or linen cloth; the india-rubber surface is afterwards covered with powdered leather, which is partially imbedded in the india-rubber by the pressure of rollers.

[*Printed, 4d. No Drawings.*]

A.D. 1871, April 29.—No. 1155.

HARRIS, Isaac Blue.—Manufacture of india-rubber suction hose.

This invention relates to hose manufactured of india-rubber or india-rubber compounds in combination with canvas or cloth, and consists in a method of protecting the spiral metallic wire or loose rings employed in keeping the flexible materials of the hose distended. The outside covering of india-rubber and canvas, is first applied to the spiral wire or rings in the ordinary manner, a plastic india-rubber tube is then introduced inside the spiral wire ; or rings, and hydraulic, or gaseous, or steam pressure is applied inside this plastic india-rubber tube. By this means the inner tube is forced outwards against the wire or rings and also against the inner surface of the outside covering. The hose is afterwards vulcanized.

[*Printed*, 6d. *Drawing*.]

A.D. 1871, May 6.—No. 1226.

MACINTOSH, John, and BOGGETT, William.—" Methods
" of expanding or treating sheet india-rubber, and employing
" it either by itself or combined with textile or other materials
" in the fabrication of various articles."

One method of expanding india-rubber is to exhaust the air from a vessel over the mouth of which a sheet of rubber has been placed so that the pressure of the atmosphere shall dilate the rubber to the required degree.

Another method is " to lay upon a table a sheet of india-
" rubber and make it air tight at the edges, leaving an
" opening through which air or steam is forced until the
" sheet is sufficiently expanded. Two sheets laid one upon
" the other can in like manner be dilated at one operation,
" forming an inflated bag or tube."

Or the sheet rubber " may be moderately heated and
" stretched out by any suitable mechanical means keeping it
" distending until cold, when it can be cured by the cold
" process or by the vapor of the curative solution." Bags or tubes made as previously described are converted into elastic beds, cushions, and coverlets by laying them upon a frame divided by partitions. A similar frame is then laid on the

bag and the two frames are pressed together while the india-rubber is warm, or before the curative chemical has evaporated, which causes the adhesion of those parts where the partitions meet.

Elastic webbing or fabrics coated with india-rubber may be inflated and employed in making similar goods or articles.

Another method of constructing elastic air beds, cushions, and coverlets is to plait or interweave inflated india-rubber tubes made as previously described with tape or elastic bands.

In some cases the tubular webbing is placed between two strips of india-rubber and passed through warm rollers, the excess of india-rubber is then removed and the tube is turned inside out.

[*Printed*, 4*d*. *No Drawings*.]

A.D. 1871, May 8.—No. 1242.

ANDERSON, ALEXANDER.—(*Provisional protection only*.)—" Manufacture of india-rubber valves for steam engines."

This invention consists in strengthening the vulcanized india-rubber used in steam engines by incorporating with it, when it is being manufactured into sheets or slabs, wire gauze or netting in one or more sheets, or wire in any other convenient form.

[*Printed*, 4*d*. *No Drawings*.]

A.D. 1871, May 10.—No. 1257.

PAGET, FREDERICK ARTHUR.—(*Partly a communication from Louis Lemoine*.)—(*Provisional protection only*.)—" Improve-" ments in springs."

This invention relates particularly to the annular or segmental springs used for the wheels of road locomotives and carriages, and to the annular springs used for buffer and draw springs. It consists in combining prepared cork with india-rubber, preferably vulcanized, and with or without additional springs of steel.

Cork in shreds, discs, segments, or other forms is prepared by soaking it in a solution of molasses and water, or in a concentrated solution of any deliquescent salt. It is then compressed and worked up into regular or irregular forms

with india-rubber heated in the usual way. "Or a sort of net
" of india-rubber may be formed into which the pieces of
" cork may be inserted."

[*Printed, 4d. No Drawings.*]

A.D. 1871, May 17.—No. 1333.

STEWART, LAURENCE. — (*Provisional protection only.*) —
" Wheels for carriages, waggons, carts, and other articles."

" Under the first system of construction the wheels are
" composed of a framework of wire constituting the core of
" the rim or felly, and to which the outer ends of the arms
" also formed of wire are attached, their inner ends being
" attached to the nave. This framework is covered with
" vulcanite in the plastic state and afterwards vulcanized."

Under a second system one or more strands of wire passing longitudinally through the arms of the wheel may be used, these strands being fastened at the nave of the wheel and at the outer end of each arm, the strand proceeding from each arm is divided, and each half is bent over to a circular arc corresponding to that of the felly, and in which the wire is enclosed when the caoutchouc, either mixed or unmixed with other materials such as leather parings, is solidified or vulcanized over it.

Under a third system the wire may be used in separate lengths, and passed through the spokes or arms and felly or other parts besides those at or near to the centre of such parts.

" The spokes and felly of the wheel may be made hollow in
" place of solid, and instead of using a wire core, a core of
" malleable cast iron may be employed, or the central parts
" of the spokes and felly may be made of vulcanite and
" leather parings admixed, whilst the outer part is composed
" of vulcanite."

It is preferred to provide the wheel " with an elastic tyre
" between the wheel proper and the exterior metallic tyre."

[*Printed, 4d. No Drawings.*]

A.D. 1871, May 20.—No. 1364.

DAY, AUSTIN GOODYEAR.—" Protective and insulating covering
" for telegraphic conducting wires and compound for forming
" the same."

The compound is formed by the combination of caoutchouc and a small quantity of other substances herein-after specified with the artificial elastic compound described in No. 1,010, A.D. 1871. " These ingredients are combined in about the " following proportions, viz., caoutchouc twenty pounds, the " aforesaid elastic compound twenty to twenty-five pounds, " and sulphur two and a half pounds." To these substances it is preferred to add three pounds of litharge or other oxide of lead or carbonate of lead. Gutta percha or a mixture of the same and caoutchouc may be used as a substitute for the caoutchouc to some extent.

" The compound when applied to the wire is vulcanized by ", subjecting it to a suitable heat."

The compound " may be employed as a substitute for india-" rubber or gutta percha for many purposes."

[*Printed, 4d. No Drawings.*]

A.D. 1871, May 26.—No. 1413.

WALKER, JOSEPH.—(*Provisional protection only.*)—" Material " to be employed as floorcloth and for other purposes."

The material is made of india-rubber, one part; of naptha, two parts; of powdered leather, three parts. These form a dough, which is spread by means of rollers over the surface of cotton or linen cloth, " forming a felt thereon which may " be faced or covered by cotton or linen cloth if desired; or " cotton or linen cloth may be enclosed or coated on each " surface by the dough."

[*Printed, 4d. No Drawings.*]

A.D. 1871, July 26.—No. 1958.

GALLOWAY, GEORGE BELL.—" Obtaining and applying " motion power."

The "improvements consist in the application of various " principle involved and in part described in" No. 55, A.D. 1865.

Part of the invention relates to the mode of making " elastic tires or rims to render travelling smooth." The patentee describes this part of the invention as follows:—" I " dissolve by the action of steam or heated air or a chemical

" agent the parings of leather, and also spetches to be so
" dissolved, I then add a quantity of india-rubber or other
" combining adhesive substance to combine and temper such
" travelling rims or surfaces with sulphur or other hardening
" substance."

[*Printed*, 6d. *No Drawings.*]

A.D. 1871, August 2.—No. 2035.

STEWART, LAURENCE.—(*Provisional protection only.*)—" Pens
" for writing."

The pens are made of vulcanite or vulcanized caoutchouc
or india-rubber combined or not with gutta percha, asphalte,
or other similar ingredient.

The vulcanite or other material is reduced or rolled to the
form of a sheet, and blanks of the requisite shape are cut,
punched, or pressed out; these are afterwards curved to the
shape of an ordinary writing pen and the points split by
a splitting machine.

[*Printed*, 4d. *No Drawings.*]

A.D. 1871, August 5.—No. 2070.

PARNACOTT, EDWARD JOSEPH WILLIAM.—The manufacture
of flexible elastic waterproof sheets, and the machinery
employed therefor.

In the manufacture of the composition gutta percha is used,
waste pieces of this material may be used, this is subjected to
heat until brought to a soft state; ordinary pitch, Burgundy
pitch, Stockholm tar, ballata, and consolidated oil. These
substances are mixed in a pug mill or masticator, which is
heated by steam. When properly amalgamated the compound
is moulded to a suitable form.

When large sheets are required the compound is moulded
into a cylindrical form having a mandrel through its centre
or axis, this is mounted between centres in a lathe. The
cutting tool is of similar construction to those used on wood
planing machines, and it is carried on a table fitted on to
a slide rest. On the sliding table in bearings is mounted
a loose roller, which works against the face of the material
during the cutting operation.

When small sheets are required the compound is moulded into forms suitable to the purposes for which it is required. "The bottom part of the form is moulded or dovetailed in a "cast-iron plate. When the compound is sufficiently cold, "it is taken from the mould and fixed securely by means of "the plate to the table of a planing machine, which is similar "in construction to an iron planing machine, except that the "cutter is (or cutters are) much broader and of a similar "construction to those used on wood planing machines, and "fixed on a suitable carrier on the cross slide, having a "vertical self-acting motion of the ordinary construction "used for iron planing machines.

[*Printed*, 1s. 4d. *Drawings.*]

A.D. 1871, August 10.—No. 2106.

LAKE, WILLIAM ROBERT.— (*A communication from A. G. de Wolfe.*)—"Machine for covering wire with india-rubber or "compounds of the same or similar substances, and for "manufacturing tubes of such compounds or substances."

The machine has a cylinder for containing the substance or compound in a liquid condition. In this cylinder is a screw of the same diameter or nearly so as the bore of the cylinder. This screw extends through one end of the cylinder, and is supported in bearings, and is rotated by gearing outside of the cylinder. At one end of the cylinder is placed the die through which the substance or compound is forced to form the wire covering or the tubing, and through which the wire and the substance pass when the machine is employed for covering wire. "The said die is arranged at a right angle to "the axis of the cylinder, so that the wire passes transversely "across the end of the screw or at a right angle to its axis."

[*Printed*, 8d. *Drawing.*]

A.D. 1871, August 22.—No. 2207.

JOCHUMSEN, NIELS. — (*Provisional protection only.*) — "Material applicable to the manufacture of valves for pumps "and other purposes."

The material is "composed of india-rubber and brass, "copper, or other practically incorrodible wire cloth or "gauze."

" The invention is carried into effect by placing sheets of
" the said wire cloth or gauze between layers of the india-
" rubber whilst the latter is in a plastic state, and which when
" subsequently vulcanized, rolled, or exposed to a pressure in
" the usual way becomes solidified through the meshes of the
" wire cloth."

[*Printed, 4d. No Drawings.*]

A.D. 1871, August 28.—No. 2256.

DAVIS, Charles, and STRUTHERS, Thomas.—(*Provisional protection only.*)—" Composition for bootsoling, waterproofing,
" insulating, and other purposes."

The ingredients are cane or cocoa-nut fibre cut up fine and mixed with the bottoms of varnish and gutta percha about equal parts of each. The compound is then exposed to a moderate heat for from a quarter to half an hour while being stirred. A small quantity of stone ochre and if required pigments to color it are mixed in with the compound while being stirred.

[*Printed, 4d. No Drawings.*]

A.D. 1871, August 30.—No. 2282.

JOHNSON, Hiram André. — (*A communication from Porter Smart.*)—(*Provisional protection only.*)—" Compound solution
" suitable as a vehicle to mix with pigments and coloring
" matters in the preparation of paint."

" First dissolve about three pounds of pure gum caoutchouc
" or india-rubber (by preference pure Para rubber gum) in
" about forty gallons of benzole of the gravity of seventy-one
" degrees Beaumé, then add thereto about eight ounces
" of sulphuric ether to facilitate the dissolution of the rubber,
" and stir the whole occasionally."

[*Printed, 4d. No Drawings.*]

A.D. 1871, September 16.—No. 2440.

CHAPMAN, George Temple.—" Process for forming a hard
" protective or ornamental covering of india-rubber or gutta-
" percha upon the surface of metal, wood, clay, and other
" materials."

This invention consists in the hardening of india-rubber, gutta percha, and similar gums upon the surfaces of articles and substances, capable of withstanding the necessary degree of heat, by heat alone, dispensing with the use of sulphur or other vulcanizing agent. The raw gum is first reduced to the liquid state by melting or by dissolving with a solvent, it is then applied in any convenient way to whatever object it is desired to furnish with a hard surface, the coating is afterwards hardened by heat in a closed oven.

[*Printed*, 4d. *No Drawings.*]

A.D. 1871, October 24.—No. 2846.

HARRIS, ISAAC BLUE.—"Manufacture of piston packing
" formed of canvas, cloth, or other textile material in com-
" bination with india-rubber or india-rubber compounds
" susceptible of vulcanization."

This invention consists in "submitting cords or ropes of
" india-rubber packing to vulcanization in a coiled state and
" thereby securing for the packing a permanent spiral or
" helical set."

[*Printed*, 6d. *Drawing.*]

A.D. 1871, November 1.—No. 2927.

MOSELEY, CHARLES.—"Manufacture of bowls for calenders and other purposes."

The bowls are made of vulcanized or other compound of india-rubber combined with vegetable or other fibre. This mixture is rolled into sheets, which are afterwards cut into discs and then vulcanized. The discs are placed upon a metallic centre and compressed by hydraulic pressure. " These bowls can be made of any desired hardness or " elasticity by an admixture of magnesia or other earthy " substance or metallic oxides with the india-rubber."

[*Printed*, 4d. *No Drawings.*]

A.D. 1871, November 20.—No. 3133.

BAKER, FRANCIS ROBERT.—(*Provisional protection only.*)—
" Manufacturing pens of ebonite."

Ordinary ebonite is rolled into thin sheets, one side of each sheet is polished, the other side is left in the rough state in which it comes from the rolls. The sheet ebonite is next heated to a temperature of from 100° to 150° Fah., so as to soften it and remove the brittleness from it. While in the soft state blanks of the required shape are cut from it by means of press tools. The blanks are then pierced and slit. A series of these blanks are placed side by side and are clamped together and their edges are polished. "The blanks are next
" warmed on a heated plate so as to make them flexible, and
" while so heated are shaped or raised into pens by press
" tools."

Instead of making the pens from sheet ebonite, they may be made by shaping or moulding ebonite while in a soft state, and afterwards hardening the pens in the way in which ebonite is usually hardened.

[*Printed*, 4d. *No Drawings.*]

A.D. 1871, December 13.—N°. 3376.

GALE, WILLIAM JOSEPH, and BOYDEN, WILLIAM WESLEY.— (*Provisional protection only.*) — " Utilizing waste pieces of
" leather for the production of new and improved materials."

The composition which is prepared in the manner hereinafter described may be used in the manufacture of india-rubber, gutta percha, and parkesine, and for other purposes.

Leather cuttings and scraps are torn into shreds or ground into dust. A quantity of the shreds or dust is subjected to a solution of nitric, sulphuric, or other acid or acids heated sufficiently long to render the mass glutinous when it is washed first in alkaline water to expel the free acid and then in pure water. " In this state the composition is again sub-
" jected to heat, adding to it animal glue or size prepared in
" a solution of nitric, sulphuric, or other acid or acids till it acquires the requisite consistency."

Coal tar is sometimes used instead of or in connection with the animal glue or size. " The material so far prepared is
" then rolled into sheets of the required thickness and size
" or subjected to pressure as found most convenient, and
" subsequently dried."

Or the shreds or dust may be mixed with water, to which is added " a solution of animal glue or size prepared with

" nitric, sulphuric, or other acid or acids, or with coal tar, or
" with both as before described, the whole being subjected to
" the action of heat, and when thorougly amalgamated it is
" washed in water and rolled or pressed into sheets."

A weak alkaline solution is sometimes used instead of acids in the preparation of the pulp.

The invention further consists in vulcanizing the material prepared as above, whereby it is rendered applicable to the purposes to which vulcanized india-rubber is now applied.

[*Printed*, 4*d.* *No Drawings.*]

A.D. 1871, December 19.—No. 3437.

JAQUES, JAMES ARCHIBALD, and STERNE, LOUIS. —
" Making bags and pouches of vulcanized india-rubber by
" means of a moulding process."

" The rubber is prepared in sheets in the usual manner of
" making vulcanized sheet rubber, and is cut up in pieces of
" the required shape to form the sides and other parts of the
" article." " The raw or cut edges of the several parts are
" brought into contact and are pressed together by two
" plates which form the outsides of the mould and which may
" be engraved or cut with any device it may be desired to
" produce on the external surface of the article. A metal or
" other core is placed inside the bag, and when the mould is
" closed and secured the article may be submitted to the
" vulcanizing process in the usual manner."

[*Printed*, 8*d.* *Drawing.*]

1872.

A.D. 1872, January 31.—No. 305.

JAQUES, JAMES ARCHIBALD, and BANKS, JOHN.—Manufacture of surgical instruments intended to be introduced into cavities in the body.

The instruments are made of "a compound of hard and
" soft india-rubber, prepared by mixing metallic sulphurets
" with the native rubber and then submitting the mixture to

" definite degrees of heat so as to produce the desired
" chemical change in the mass." The instruments are made
with a core of the hard compound to give the requisite
rigidity, and the outer surface is formed of soft vulcanized
rubber to impart the required softness and flexibility. These
instruments are cured either in moulds or embedded in
French chalk or other suitable material.

[*Printed, 4d. No Drawings.*]

A.D. 1872, March 15.—No. 793.

THOMAS, FREDERICK SAMSON.—Materials for " making roads,
" ways, and floors."

This invention consists in melting india-rubber, gutta
percha, or alpha gutta by means of and with pitch until they
form one cohesive mass which is allowed to cool and is then
pulverized.

This cohesive powder is mixed with a non-cohesive powder
such as sawdust, coal ashes, pulverized granite, or by preference for roads " fossil ironstone " in a pulverized form. For
the purpose of laying down either of the compounds thus
formed it is heated and laid down while in a heated state.

[*Printed, 4d. No Drawings.*]

A.D. 1872, April 2.—No. 970.

DON, THOMAS, and WRIGHT, ROBERT ALFRED.—(*Provisional
protection only.*)—Substitutes for leather, gutta percha, and
other materials, and manufacturing articles from such substitutes.

Fibrous, ligneous, or textile substances or materials, or pulp
or paper made therefrom are treated with one of the following
agents,—" Cupro ammonium or a solution of copper in
" ammonia, or sulphuric acid, or a caustic alkali." The
material or pulp, after being deprived of the excess of the
agent used, is moulded or shaped into the required form by
pressure, forcing, rolling, or other method.

[*Printed, 4d. No Drawings.*]

A.D. 1872, April 30.—No. 1286.

MYERNS, HENRY.—(*Provisional protection only.*)—" Solution
" for joining vulcanized india-rubber."

"Take (say) three parts of Stockholm pitch, three parts of
American rosin, eight parts oil of turpentine, six parts best
bottle india-rubber, and twelve parts best mineral naptha,
and dissolve them together by gentle heat, or one or more
of the solids may be dissolved separately, after which add
the requisite quantity of the oil of turpentine and mineral
naptha thereto."

[*Printed, 4d. No Drawings.*]

A.D. 1872, May 6.—No. 1374.

WISE, WILLIAM LLOYD.—(*A communication from Heinrich Huebscher.*) — (*Provisional protection only.*) — Musical instruments.

It is proposed to use "hard rubber," or "wood paste
soaked in glycerine" instead of wood for making the
covers, cases, and various parts of musical instruments.

When "hard rubber" is used, "if the covers of harmoniums
are to be made the soft india-rubber is thrust into the
respective moulds and subjected to pressure, the ornaments
or parts to be inserted, which may be composed of German
silver, ivory, mother of pearl, or other material are then
pressed into the soft plastic mass; the rubber is then hardened by the well-known mode of vulcanizing, and finally
the surfaces of the covers containing the ornaments are
ground and polished."

[*Printed, 4d. No Drawings.*]

A.D. 1872, May 8.—No. 1406.

WILBAUX, AMÉDÉE.—"Manufacture of printing surfaces
for printing on paper hangings, stuffs, or other material."

Moulds of the designs to be reproduced are obtained "in
any suitable material with plain surfaces, such designs
being engraved or otherwise formed in such flat surfaces."

Upon the moulds is applied "a sheet, sufficiently thick
according to the relief of the designs, of india-rubber, gutta
percha, or mixtures of these two substances, or of glue,
gelatine, vulcanized oils, artificial preparations or substitutes of india-rubber and gutta percha mixed or not, and
lastly, of leather or of any other know substance capable of
taking the impressions and of afterwards acquiring by

" themselves or by artificial means a degree of hardness
" rendering them capable of resisting the pressure and wear
" involved in printing." " The sheet of india-rubber applied
" upon the mould is first dipped into boiling water so as to
" render it plastic and therefore diminish its coefficient of
" elasticity." These sheets of impressions are attached to
rollers or blocks by india-rubber solution or other means, they
are then submitted to a certain degree of heat to determine
their shrinkage, and are afterwards vulcanized. " Some
" impressions may however be vulcanized before being applied
" to the blocks or rollers."

[*Printed, 4d. No Drawings.*]

A.D. 1872, May 27.—No. 1609.

HARRIS, ISAAC BLUE.—Moulds for the production of india-rubber disc valves and such like articles.

Heretofore these moulds have consisted of two concentric rings laid on a bed plate and covered by the other plate of the steam press, or between two plates clamped together if heated otherwise than by a steam press. The object of this invention is to provide means for readily securing these rings concentrically with each other. The bottom plate of the mould is provided with a centre stud which is notched to receive radial distancing bars, which serve to centre and retain in position the ring forming the inner wall of the mould. The ring forming the outer wall of the mould is secured in a position concentric with the inner ring by means of adjustable stops, which, when the ring is properly centred, are pushed into contact therewith and are then made fast to the bottom plate by clamping screws.

[*Printed, 8d. Drawing.*]

A.D. 1872, May 30.—No. 1637.

MOSELEY, CHARLES.—Condensing the vapours of coal tar naphtha generated in the manufacture of india-rubber.

The invention is applied to a spreading machine.

Upon the drying chest of the machine is fixed a cover or receiver of sufficient capacity for the passage of the cloth which is coated with india-rubber solution by the machine, and for the evaporation of the naptha which is used as a solvent for the india-rubber. Into the top or side of the receiver is inserted a tube or tubes of sufficient capacity to exhaust the vaporized solvent. The tube is connected to a fan or air pump, which draws away the naphtha vapour as it is generated and delivers it into a condenser, from which the air and naptha vapour flow into a vessel. The condensed naptha accumulates at the bottom of the vessel and the air escapes through a pipe.

[*Printed, 8d. Drawing.*]

A.D. 1872, June 13.—No. 1786.

ROLLS, Jesse Gooldsmith.—Adapting and applying the gum or juice of the euphorbia tree to the purpose of an insulator of electricity in substitution for gutta percha and india-rubber, and also to the purposes for which vulcanites are applicable.

The gum or solidified juice is adapted for insulating purposes by pounding, grinding, or reducing, then drying by heat at a low temperature then dissolving by a suitable solvent, and finally hardening it by mixture with paints or by adding shellac or other dryers.

To adapt the gum or juice for use as a vulcanite it is dried and reduced, and afterwards heated and mixed with sulphur in the ordinary manner of forming a vulcanite.

[*Printed, 4d. No Drawings.*]

A.D. 1872, August 17.—No. 2459.

DODGE, George Pomeroy.—(*Provisional protection only.*)—A cement, composed of india-rubber, oil, and other ingredients, for forming the joints of pipes or vessels for containing or conducting fluids.

A portion of waste or other more or less " cured " or vulcanized india-rubber is pulverized or ground between two rolls revolving at different speeds. With the ground india-rubber is mixed from one-fourth to three-fourths of the same quantity of tar oil; other oils will answer. The mixture is then submitted to a steam heat varying from 220° Fah. to a temperature corresponding with 60 lbs. or 70 lbs. steam pressure per square inch. When properly amalgamated the compound is taken out and mixed with suitable earths or metals. "Portland " cement and fire clay are generally used, with sufficient " sulphur to ' cure ' it when applied to a hot joint."

The compound of india-rubber with oil, when mixed under steam heat and pressure, may be used to mix with or adulterate during manufacture the ordinary vulcanized india-rubber and gutta percha.

[*Printed, 4d. No Drawings.*]

A.D. 1872, August 28.—No. 2554.

MACINTOSH, John, and BOGGETT, William.—Manufacture of life preserves, air beds, cushions, and coverlets, and materials employed therefor.

"The object of this invention is to lessen the cost and
" weight of the above-named articles, by employing air-proof
" fabrics consisting of but one cloth in place of the double
" cloths heretofore used." The fabric the patentees prefer to employ is made "by giving a coating of india-rubber to closely
" woven thin cloth, adding upon it a second coat of a mixture
" of one part india-rubber and six parts of lamp black, or
" thereabout, mixed in naptha, in some cases putting in about
" 8 or 10 per cent. of paraffine, or for certain purposes where
" a high temperature is not objectionable, equal parts of
" india-rubber and paraffine." This or other air-proof single cloth is converted into life preservers, by making it into tubes. It is also used (generally converted into tubular lengths) for making air beds, cushions, and coverlets, by interweaving the tubes in the manner described in No. 1226, A.D. 1871. Or the above-mentioned articles may be made by fastening the opposite sides by placing discs of leather or vulcanized sheet india-rubber soaked in melted paraffine at intervals between the two cloths, through which holes are punched for the insertion of metal eyelets, which when pressed together, hold the cloth in its place. To prevent the passage of air the cloth is saturated round the apertures with spirit varnish. The compound of lamp black and india-rubber is not claimed as it is described in No. 3200, A.D. 1870.

[*Printed, 4d. No Drawings.*]

A.D. 1872, August 30.—No. 2582.

MUDFORD, George. — (*Provisional protection only.*) — "Manufacture of straps, driving bands, and belting for
" machinery."

A single strand is first formed by covering a wire with hemp, flax, wool or cotton, then two of such strands are twined into one cord, and cords so formed (in number proportioned to the width and thickness of the strap or band required) are arranged so as to constitute a warp, with which is interwoven a weft composed of the said fibrous material either alone or combined with wire, or of wire alone. The strap or belt so formed is afterwards coated with waterproofing, consisting of tar and resin, or oil and white lead, or other suitable composition, "and the strap or belt is or may be also " covered with india-rubber and afterwards subjected to the " process of vulcanizing."

[*Printed*, 4d. *No Drawings.*]

A.D. 1872, September 28.—No. 2867.

HARRIS, Isaac Blue.—"Material for use as packing for the " piston rods of steam engines, and like uses."

The packing material is formed of india-rubber and sulphur mixed together with soapstone, or steatite, or French chalk in powder. The compound is made into a cord or strand around which a single or double layer of cloth is wound, the object of which is to keep the strand in form while it is subjected to partial vulcanization, and also to keep it from the piston rod when first applied, " until it shall have changed by the heat " of the steam from the soft vulcanized condition to the more " homogenous and consolidated plastic condition." "Instead " of soapstone, or steatite, or French chalk, plumbago or " black lead, or asbestos ground into a powder, or sulphate of " barytes, or equivalent mineral powders may be employed in " combination with rubber and sulphur."

[*Printed*, 4d. *No Drawings.*]

A.D. 1872, November 6.—No. 3292.

PARNACOTT, Edward Joseph William.—Manufacture of artificial fuel.

One combination consists of,—"Clay 7 cwt.; road mud, " 2 cwt.; smudge, fine riddlings of small coal or dust of coke, " 8 cwt.; peat, 8 or 10 lbs.; sawdust, wood turnings, or " shavings, 50 or 60 lbs.; chloride of sodium or common salt,

" about 6 lbs." After these have been properly agglomerated 2 lbs. of dissolved caoutchouc are added, preferably waste pieces, waste gutta percha may also be used. The whole is mixed in a pug mill afterwards pressed into forms in a brick machine, and then dried for use.

Another combination consists of,—Peat and sawdust which are placed in a pug mill and mixed together, a quantity of dissolved caoutchouc or gutta percha is added until the mass arrives at the proper consistency.

A superior fuel is made with peat or turf in combination with slack, small coal, or cinders, with the admixture of a quantity of clay and chloride of sodium and dissolved or powdered caoutchouc or gutta percha.

To improve the fuel after being dried, a quantity of liquid caoutchouc or gutta percha in the form of a spray is thrown over it. This liquid is also injected in the form of spray into boiler or other furnaces.

[*Printed, 4d. No Drawings.*]

A.D. 1872, November 15.—No. 3414.

CLARK, ALEXANDER MELVILLE. — (*A communication from Manuel Léopold Jonas Lavater.*)—(*Provisional protection only.*) —" Machinery for moulding india-rubber and other plastic " materials."

The sheets of rubber from which combs are made are moulded with half round ribs on either side to form the round back of the comb, which is cut out of the sheet. A thin sheet of tin to serve as a mould is placed on each side of the sheet of soft rubber, which is then inserted between a pair of moulding cylinders, having grooves of the desired form made parallel to the axes of the cylinders, the grooves in the two cylinders meeting exactly at each revolution. The cylinders are made hollow and are heated. "By this means the plastic " material is enabled to accurately take the form of the " grooves, and the tin having the exact configuration of the " cylinders serves as a mould during the vulcanization."

[*Printed, 6d. Drawing.*]

A.D. 1872, December 27.—No. 3932.

QUIN, JAMES.—Manufacture of belting, made from woven fabric (cotton duck) and india-rubber.

The "duck" saturated with india-rubber is cut into strips of sufficient breadth when folded to make a belt of the required width, but is left the whole length of the piece of duck. This is folded by hand, covered with sheet rubber, and then passed through a metal die which is supplied with a suitable lubricant, and which smoothes and polishes the surface; and forms the edge square. As it issues from this die it is coiled on to a revolving cast-iron drum, a strip of thin metal (zinc by preference) being coiled up with it. It is then vulcanized while still on the drum.

[*Printed*, 10*d*. *Drawing*.]

A.D. 1872, December 27.—No. 3933.

QUIN, JAMES.—(*Provisional protection only*.)—Manufacture of solid seamless india-rubber tubing.

The india-rubber after mastication is placed into one end of a cylinder which is kept at a proper heat by a steam jacket. The other end of the cylinder is conical and terminates in a die, through which the india-rubber is forced by a piston.

If a wire lining is required the coil of wire is passed through a tube on which the piston rod (which is hollow) works.

"By working at a lower temperature and employing a suitable lubricant, gutta percha tubing may also be made by this machine."

[*Printed*, 4*d*. *No Drawings*.]

A.D. 1872, December 28.—No. 3944.

VENMAN, HEZEKIAH, and WARNE, CHARLES JOHN.— "Manufacture of flexible type inking pads and rollers used "for stamping and printing letters and devices."

A mould is formed of plaster, metal, paper pulp, or other suitable material of the required size and shape, with a loose or separate top and bottom. Into this mould is placed the die, and then the uncured mineralized caoutchouc. Pressure is exerted on the top of the mould and consequently on the india-rubber. Whilst under pressure the india-rubber is cured in the manner usually practised in the manufacture of mineralized india-rubber.

[*Printed*, 4*d*. *No Drawings*.]

1873.

A.D. 1873, February 17.—No. 587.

CATTELL, Thomas.—Methods for purifying gutta percha.

Process No. 1.—Crude gutta percha is treated by the method described in No. 446, A.D. 1859, so far as to dissolve or bring the same into the state of a solution, which is then filtered or strained and subjected to one of the following processes A., B., C. :—

A. The vapor of alcohol either in its methylated or pure state, pyroxylic acid, or amylic alcohol is passed through or into the solution. This step of the process will be accelerated by passing dry steam with the alcohol into the vessel containing the solution. This operation is continued until the purified gutta percha is deposited or separated.

B. The vapour of alcohol is to be added to the solution in a heated condition, in quantity sufficient to effect the deposition or separation of the gutta percha. When, however, any one of the alcohols is added at its ordinary temperature, heat is to be applied until the deposition or separation is effected.

C. The solution is passed into a vessel in a sprey-like form, and currents of steam are simultaneously directed into the vessel so as to come into contact with the spreyed solution. The steam, with the vaporized solvent passes out of the vessel into a condenser and the gutta percha is deposited.

Process No. 2.—The gutta percha in a shaved or shredded condition is placed in a vessel containing water in sufficient quantity to allow the gutta percha to be kneaded along with the solvent. The contents of the vessel are gradually heated until the gutta percha is softened, so that it may be easily strained, and this operation may be repeated until the gutta percha is sufficiently freed from impurities. Should any portion of the solvent employed be present with the gutta percha it may be removed by submitting the gutta percha to a current of steam.

Process No. 3.—The gutta percha in a shaved or shredded condition is placed in a vessel and submitted to a mixture of benzole or other rectified products of coal tar, naptha, and methylated or other alcohols, or petroleum spirit, and methylated or other alcohols, or bisulphide of carbon, and methylated or other alcohols, in equal or nearly equal proportions. The contents of the vessel are to be gradually heated, and the gutta percha is to be kneaded until it becomes so softened as to be capable of being readily forced through strainers. It is then submitted to the action of steam.

Process No. 4.—Instead of adopting any of the steps described in the prior Specification to get rid of the solvent, the heat required for the manufacture of the solution is withdrawn and the solid mass is broken up into small particles which are dropped into an apparatus into which currents of steam are conveyed. The steam and vapor may be condensed and the purified gutta percha will be left in the apparatus. The same result will be obtained by passing the vapor of alcohol into the apparatus.

[*Printed, 4d. No Drawings.*]

A.D. 1873, March 13.—No. 916.

MOSELEY, CHARLES. — "Apparatus for condensing the "vapours of naptha."

This is an improvement on No. 1637, A.D. 1872. Referring to the prior invention, the patentee states, "it is found that "a great proportion of the vapours of naptha instead of "being condensed escape into the atmosphere with the air, "and the object and effect of my present invention, is to "prevent the escape of the naptha vapours." This is accomplished by causing the naptha vapours and air escaping from the condenser to pass through wire gauze sieves or perforated plates and through a body of naptha.

[*Printed, 8d. Drawing.*]

A.D. 1873, March 19.—No. 1015.

HACKING, WILLIAM HENRY, and HACKING, THOMAS.— Machinery for plaiting or folding and measuring woven fabrics.

Part of this invention relates to the material for holding the cloth when plaited and the means used for attaching the same to the machine. For holding the cloth when plaited the patentees employ a strip of thin vulcanized india-rubber moulded on coarse sacking cloth or other suitable mould to give it a rough surface. The rubber is backed with strong canvass and attached to the ordinary holding rail of the machine.

[*Printed, 8d. Drawing.*]

A.D. 1873, March 26.—No. 1119.

WOODCOCK, FREDERICK ALONZO. — " The preparation of " india-rubber."

From india-rubber in its cleaned state is prepared dough or paste of any desired consistence, dispensing with the processes of drying, masticating, and crushing, and also with the finishing dough machine commonly used. The sheets of cleaned india-rubber are allowed to absorb any suitable solvent, sulphur, metallic oxides, sulphurets of metals, or other substances may be added.

The saturated india-rubber or compounds of india-rubber are placed in a machine called a "digester," by which the preparation of the dough is completed. "The digester may
" be described as a closed cylinder, access to the interior
" being by a moveable lid or cover. A piston is provided
" pierced by numerous passages, such passages resembling a
" double cone or other figure through which, on the piston
" traversing the cylinder, the saturated contents are squeezed.
" The motion of the piston will be slow at the first, increasing
" towards the completion of the operation."

It is preferred to connect the piston rod with a hydraulic ram and to work the machine by hydraulic pressure.

[*Printed, 4d. No Drawings.*]

A.D. 1873, March 28.—No. 1166.

HARROP, JAMES.—Apparatus for the manufacture of india-rubber hose, and other tubular articles.

This " invention relates to a method of coiling india-rubber
" or several 'plies' upon each other, and subsequently
" submitting them to a rolling action."

A table is provided with a projecting guard or fence, against which is placed the core of the intended article, and beneath this core one edge of the "ply" to be coiled is placed. " Above the core are two rollers capable of being turned

" upward or downward upon a longitudinal shaft driven by
" the motive power, and carrying gearing which gives motion
" to screws connected to the bearings of the aforesaid rollers,
" which are also caused to revolve by suitable gearing. The
" core and ply having been adapted as above mentioned, the
" two rollers are turned down so as to be brought in contact
" with the former, the guard or fence giving way against
" springs, and the machine being then put in motion, the
" two rollers by their rotation coil the ply upon the core, and
" at the same time move outward bodily to effect the neces-
" sary number of coils. This outward movement may extend
" to any distance after the whole of the ply has been coiled
" to effect a rolling action, after which the motion of the
" machine is reversed and a rolling inward takes place."

[*Printed*, 10d. *Drawing*.]

A.D. 1873, April 16.—No. 1383.

HARRIS, ISAAC BLUE.—" Preparing wire cloth coated with
" india-rubber for the manufacture of washers, piston packing,
" hose, and such like articles."

This invention consists in cutting a sheet or web of wire cloth coated with india-rubber into diagonal strips of any suitable width before the rubber is vulcanized, and with these strips forming washers, valves, cords or ropes for packing, hose and tubing, and such like articles in the same manner as when textile cloth is used to form these articles.

[*Printed*, 8d. *Drawing*.]

A.D. 1873, May 12.—No. 1715.

JAMIESON, ALEXANDER.—(*Provisional protection only*.)—
" Regulating the temperature of vulcanizing apparatus for
" vulcanizing india-rubber used in the manufacture of
" artificial teeth."

The quantity of gas admitted through the tube which supplies the burner under the vulcanizing chamber is regulated by the expansion and contraction of mercury placed in a glass tube or chamber let into the top of the vulcanizing chamber. "When the heat of the steam in the vulcanizing
" chamber has reached the proper temperature, the mercury

" in the gas chamber expands, and closes or partly closes
" the gas tube (which is made to extend down in the mercury
" chamber) to cut off or regulate the supply of gas to
" the furnace, for keeping the vulcanizer at the proper
" temperature."

[*Printed, 4d. No Drawings.*]

A.D. 1873, May 14.—No. 1756.

RHODES, Samuel Gibson, and MILLER, Joseph.—(*Provisional protection only.*)—Manufacture of tobacco pipes and cigar holders.

Caoutchouc, sulphur, and any suitable colouring matter such as French chalk or vermillion are reduced by heat to a soft state and then pressed into a mould of the desired form with a core for forming the inside of the bowl and stem. " The mould being filled with the compound it is brought to " a temperature of about 300 to 350 degrees Fahrenheit. " When brought to a proper degree of softness the mould is " closed and retained in position by a clamp." Afterwards the forms are placed in a vulcanizer, which consists of a metallic vessel heated by gas or other means; " in this " vessel the forms are exposed to a temperature of about 300 " to 350 degrees Fahrenheit, the vessel at the same time is " kept closed and charged with superheated steam at a " high pressure. This operation hardens or vulcanizes the " caoutchouc. After this operation the form is taken from " the mould, cleaned, and dressed."

[*Printed, 4d. No Drawings.*]

A.D. 1873, July 9.—No. 2375.

TORREY, Samuel Whittemore.—(*Provisional protection only.*) —" Preparing textile fabrics, india-rubber, gutta percha, and " other like materials to preserve them from decay."

Cloth or other textile material is saturated with carbolic acid, coal tar, naphtha, or other similar antiseptic by immersion or by pressure of steam in a closed vessel. The india-rubber or gutta percha is treated in the same manner, and may be combined with the textile fabric by passing them together between rollers.

[*Printed, 4d. No Drawings.*]

A.D. 1873, August 29.—No. 2844.

MACINTOSH, JOHN. — Compounds for waterproof fabrics, also applicable to other purposes.

This invention consists in mixing large quantities of carbon in the form of lampblack, soot, or ground charcoal, or their compounds with india-rubber or its compounds in the proportion of about 4 parts by weight of carbon to one part of india-rubber. The mixture is effected by means of heated masticators or mincing rollers and without the india-rubber paste or solvent described in No. 3200, A.D. 1870.

[*Printed, 4d. No Drawings.*]

A.D. 1873, September 16.—No. 3043.

TURNER, ARCHIBALD. — (*A communication from Charles Righter.*)—Manufacture of india-rubber hose and tubing, and the preservation of india-rubber, gutta percha, and rubber fabrics.

This invention consists in treating flexible hose or tubing or the fabrics or materials of which it is made with carbolic acid or its equivalent. Also in treating india-rubber and gutta percha with carbolic acid or its equivalent either during their manufacture or after vulcanization for the purpose of preserving them.

[*Printed, 4d. No Drawings.*]

A.D. 1873, October 17.—No. 3362.

UNSWORTH, JAMES. — (*Provisional protection only.*) — Manufacturing frillings.

This invention consists in the introduction of elastic india-rubber threads into fabrics for the purpose of producing a frilling.

It is proposed to prepare the elastic rubber threads with steatite, which enables the elastic rubber to work in friction with the silk warp.

[*Printed, 4d. No Drawings.*]

A.D. 1873, October 22.—No. 3425.

DODGE, GEORGE POMEROY.—(*Provisional protection only.*)— "Manufacture of india-rubber hose."

The inventor covers canvas or other suitable fabric on one or both sides with a coat of india-rubber unvulcanized; he then cuts up this material to the desired width and size for the intended hose, and he stitches it into shape, and immediately or at the same time nearly covers the stitches on the line of stitches inside or inside and outside the hose with a strip of india-rubber, or fabric covered with india-rubber, using solvent or solvent india-rubber when necessary to secure adhesion. The pipe is then placed on a mandril, by preference French chalk, or other material being previously applied to the interior of the pipe. The whole is then vulcanized in the usual manner.

[*Printed*, 4d. *No Drawings.*]

A.D. 1873, November 19.—No. 3753.

TOUSSAINT, CHARLES ISIDORE.—Manufacture of composite straps or driving bands and other articles, and machinery to be employed in connection therewith.

The first part of the invention relates to composite straps and other articles in which india-rubber, gutta percha, or other resinous and plastic substances are employed. In the case of a strap of six thicknesses a strip of nonvulcanized india-rubber or other suitable substance is enclosed in a seamless cover of textile material, having warp and woof, in the form of a flattened tube, thus obtaining two thicknesses of strap. This strap is then coated with india-rubber, and a second covering of seamless cloth placed around it, thus producing four thicknesses, a similar operation being performed to produce the last two thicknesses. A final coating of india-rubber may be added or not. The strap is then finished by being pressed and vulcanized.

If the strap is to have an odd number of thicknesses the first or odd fold or layer of textile fabric is placed in the centre as a core, and having been coated on both sides with india-rubber it is then covered with successive layers of seamless tissue until the desired thickness is obtained.

When the two outer folds of the strap are worn out they may be removed, and the strap used without them, or a fresh coating of india-rubber may be applied to the inner folds, and a new seamless wrapping substituted for the same.

The invention further relates to a loom for weaving the seamless tissue.

[*Printed 8d. Drawing.*]

A.D. 1873, November 27.—No. 3885.

HARRIS, Isaac Blue.—Manufacture of hose or flexible tubing for conveying oils, beer, spirits, and alkaline and acid liquids, and capable of resisting internal and external pressure.

The inner surface of the tube is made of any of the mixtures of rubber and sulphur that will harden under the curing process "into vulcanite or ebonite, or by preference into a soft "vulcanite or a semi-hard flexible horny substance," this is coated with soft rubber compound, and this again while still in the green state is enclosed in coils of cloth, the tubing is completed by a coating of soft rubber compound, the whole is then submitted to heat.

To adapt the tubing for the transmission of water and steam at a high pressure and to enable it to resist rough usage it is proposed to embed within the hose a coil or coils of wire, which may either form a substitute for the coils of cloth or may be employed together with the same.

[*Printed, 6d. Drawing.*]

A.D. 1873, November 27.—No. 3886.

HARRIS, Isaac Blue.—"Manufacture of tubing, suitable " for distributing gas and other fluids, or as conduits for oils, " beer, spirits, and alkaline and acid liquids."

It is proposed to manufacture india-rubber tubing the internal surface of which shall possess a horny character. For this purpose a compound of sulphur and india-rubber is prepared in the proportions commonly employed in the production of what is known as semi-vulcanite, and this material, when converted into tubing, is submitted to the curing process. The tubing is made thin to ensure its flexibility and it may be strengthened either with an external or an internal coil of wire.

The semi-vulcanite may also be used as an internal facing for a soft rubber tube.

[*Printed, 8d. Drawing.*]

1874.

A.D. 1874, January 6.—No. 63.

QUIN, JAMES.—*(Provisional protection only.)* — "Protecting india-rubber valves, tubes, and other like articles from chemical action."

For valves an elastic cloth is provided, which is saturated or faced with a metallic or vegetable substance such as lead, tin, tinfoil, tea lead, or varnish. The valves and like articles are encased by the cloth, they may also be coated with the substance without the cloth. When so prepared they are placed in moulds and subjected to the usual heat for vulcanizing.

For tubes an inside casing of the same material is applied, but for some purposes a thin casing of metallic foil is provided, this is impregnated with the inner surface of the tube previous to vulcanizing. In all cases when vulcanized they are inseparable.

[*Printed*, 4d. *No Drawings.*]

A.D. 1874, January 9.—No. 124.

TRUMAN, EDWIN THOMAS. — Manufacture of insulated telegraphic conductors, machinery for their manufacture, and the preparation of the materials therefor, parts of the machinery applicable to other purposes.

The first part of this invention relates to apparatus for covering wire or other conductors with gutta percha or other insulating material.

Another part of the invention consists in the formation by moulding of a solid covering applied to those portions of the wire which form the union or joint between the various lengths in which the covered wire is made. It is preferred to unite the ends of the wire in the manner sailors splice a rope, the joint is then covered with gutta percha or other insulating material by placing the uncovered joined wire and the two ends of the disconnected covering in a mould, which should be slightly heated. The mould is in halves united by a hinge, and there is an opening communicating with a filling machine, which forces a continuous supply of heated gutta percha into the mould.

Another part of the invention relates to what is termed "the filling machine," which is similar in its general construction to the machines described in No. 878, A.D. 1870, the improvement consisting in constructing machinery for giving out a regular and uniform supply of gutta percha or other insulating material with two screws, the first delivers the material from a hopper to the second screw, which delivers it to a tube or die.

Another part of the invention relates to machines for washing or cleansing gutta percha and other analogous materials described in No. 41, A.D. 1870. The improvement consists in the use in the machines of openings so provided with means of closing them that they can be closed or partly closed as required.

[*Printed, 6d. No Drawings.*]

A.D. 1874, January 28.—No. 354.

GILBEE, WILLIAM ARMAND. — (*A communication from Emil Boëthius.*)—Cork cutting machinery, partly applicable to other purposes.

The first three parts of these improvements may be employed for such purposes as cutting paper, pasteboard, and india-rubber.

The improvements relate,—Firstly, to a machine for cutting the corkwood or bark into strips. This machine is constructed of two pairs of horizontal feed rollers which carry the sheet cork to be cut into strips towards a revolving circular knife, having a ground edge which is kept sharp by a pair of revolving rollers having leather bands on their peripheries.

Secondly, to a machine for paring or barking the strips of cork made from thick cork wood. Two horizontal rollers are employed, the shafts of which move in adjustable bearings. Above the first of the said horizontal rollers is another roller having its bearings in a moveable frame turning on centres in a line with a horizontal shaft driven by a strap from the main shaft; a circular rotary knife is employed, the shaft of which moves in bearings in a frame on one of the side standards of the machine. The knife is kept sharpened by two whetting rollers attached to a directing bar running in guides at the sides of the said moveable frame. The moveable frame, the shaft, and the whetting rollers attached to the director are so connected together that when the moveable frame is raised or lowered, the knife and the whetting rollers are moved to the right or to the left in proportion as the upper roller is raised or lowered according to the thickness of cork required.

Thirdly, to a machine for cutting the strips of cork into pieces suitable to be made into corks. A guide is employed fixed to a diagonal piece placed like the guide at an angle of forty-five degrees to the machine. A continuous forward and backward motion is communicated to the guide by means of an eccentric. The table receiving the strips of cork is screwed to the said guide and consists of a horizontal plate having a fillet or raised piece at one side with a returned end. An arm is screwed at one end of the table which follows the direction of the said fillet. A plate screwed to the framework inclines over the table and has a fillet similar to that of the table. In each fillet there is a slit to allow of the passage of the knife. A moveable frame pivots at one side on fixed bearings carrying a shaft driven by a strap. At the other end of the frame is a shaft provided with a circular knife. The frame also carries the shafts of the whetting rollers and is connected by means of a rod to a balance lever jointed to the framework of the machine, and resting on an eccentric keyed on the main shaft so as to communicate an intermittent up-and-down motion to the knife. The breadth of the piece of cork cut by the knife is determined by the width of the strip.

[*Printed, 7s. 6d. Drawings.*]

A.D. 1874, April 8.—No. 1223.

HASELTINE, GEORGE. — (*A communication from Henry Franklin Read.*)—(*Complete specification but no Letters Patent.*) —Water meters of the class in which a screw propeller is employed for transmitting the measurement of the water to the indicating dial.

The propeller is made of hard india-rubber, and part of the invention consists in a method of moulding it in a metallic mould, which is composed of spiral segments with straight ends having screw threads cut upon their outer faces, and the interior hollow of the mould formed by these segments is of uniform size and open at each end. The straight ends of the segments are secured together by annular collars to which each segment is fastened by a screw. Spiral slots are formed between the segments and within these slots the vanes of the screw propeller are formed. Caps carrying plungers are screwed upon the threaded ends of the segments when the mould is filled with rubber. The caps are cylinders of a depth to allow them to be screwed over each end of the shell of the mould and to meet in the middle of its length so as to form a case for the spiral openings of the mould. The plungers, being carried within the mould by the screwing on of the caps, serve as pistons to compress the rubber within the mould from both ends alike and out into the spiral openings and in this way form the hub and the projecting vanes at one operation.

Instead of the sectional mould a solid mould may be employed, the moulding chamber being formed in a solid core with spirally-formed grooves in the solid metal of a depth just equal to the projection of the vanes. " In using the solid
" mold a piece of rubber is rolled into the form of a hollow
" cylinder and inserted into the chamber, and the ends of the
" rubber cylinder are sealed with rubber discs after a small
" quantity of water has been put into the said cylinder and
" metallic caps are applied to each end. The mold is then
" subjected to heat which generates steam within the closed
" chamber of the rubber core, and the force thereof drives the
" rubber out into all the spiral grooves, forming thereby the
" vanes with a hollow hub. It is then cooled and screwed
" out of the mold."

[*Printed*, 10d. *Drawing.*]

A.D. 1874, May 9.—No. 1650.

FRANKENBURG, ISIDOR.—" Waterproofing and preparing " leather."

The leather is coated "with a solution of india-rubber in " naphtha combined with chloride, sulphur, and bi-sulphide of " carbon or other chemical agents." The leather is then exposed to the atmosphere and to artificial heat in an oven until the naphtha is evaporated.

[*Printed, 4d. No Drawings.*]

A.D. 1874, May 20.—No. 1794.

BAKER, JOHN MORCOMBE BROMLEY. — Material for the manufacture of horse-shoes applicable also for other purposes.

This invention consists in combining metal borings or turnings with gutta percha or other suitable plastic materials. The gutta percha is first melted and then the borings or turnings are mixed with it, the composition is then run into moulds of the desired shape and size and if necessary it is subjected to pressure whilst warm.

[*Printed*, 4d. *No Drawings.*]

A.D. 1874, June 17 —No. 2106.

CONYBEARE, HENRY, and NAPHEGYI, GABOR.—(*Provisional protection only.*)—Treating the juice of the zapote or chickley tree and producing materials and articles therefrom.

The product of the tree is termed "zapotine" and it may be used as a substitute for caoutchouc, gutta percha, and their compounds, and for other materials.

To render zapotine applicable as a substitute for gutta percha it is dissolved in alcohol or ether, and the alcohol is distilled off.

For adapting the zapotine to the purposes of india-rubber two processes are described:—According to one process the zapotine is passed through or exposed to carbonic acid in a state of gas or otherwise or it is passed through or exposed to compounds containing carbon.

According to another proces 2 lbs. of caoutchouc are combined with 3 lbs. of zapotine. This compound is converted into a material analogous to vulcanized india-rubber by processes similar to those by which india-rubber is converted.

To convert zapotine into a substance similar to vulcanite or hard rubber it is combined with white lead and sulphur.

[*Printed*, 4d. *No Drawings.*]

A.D. 1874, June 24.—No. 2199.

ROBERTS, GEORGE HENRY.—" Apparatus to be employed in
" the manufacture of screws of vulcanite or other analogous
" material."

A mould is employed formed of a number of cores, or spiral segments of metal to form the threads of the screw, each core being in the form of the space between two adjacent threads and having a projecting rim running along one side. These cores are arranged inside a cylindrical mould box so as to form a complete mould of the screw required; they fit against each other, and are received at their lower ends on a piece of metal shaped to fit. The top and bottom of the cylinder are formed in separate pieces. When the parts are all put together, with the exception of the top, the rubber or composition to form the screw is placed in the mould in bulk sufficient to stand somewhat above the mould, the top is then placed on the rubber and forced down so as to force the rubber into the spaces between the cores. The mould with the screw therein is then submitted to heat to cure the screw.

The cores are formed of tin or other readily fusible metal capable of withstanding the heat required to cure the screws, and they are cast in moulds of the form required.

[*Printed, 6d. Drawing.*]

A.D. 1874, June 29.—No. 2250.

LAKE, WILLIAM ROBERT.—(*A communication from William Bell*).—(*Provisional protection only.*)—" Compounds for sur-
" facing textile and other fabrics, which compounds are also
" designed for use as a substitute for wood and other
" material in the production of moulded articles."

The compounds are intended to be used in place of india-rubber, leather, gutta percha, paper, and oiled or painted cloths.

The compounds are composed as follows :—Glue dissolved with vinegar or other suitable liquid ten quarts, glycerine from two and a half to four quarts, cork in fine particles from five to seven quarts, and about an ounce of chromic acid, or an equivalent quantity of bichromate of potassa; the chromic acid being first dissolved in water and then mixed with about one quart of glycerine before being added to the other ingredients. It is preferred to add to the compound either tannic acid or Aleppo gall water. In case Aleppo gall water is added, then one quart of good oil (linseed preferred) is to be mixed with it.

After the article has been formed or coated and is sufficiently dry it is preferred to apply to the surface of the compound employed the following solution—about one ounce of chromic acid (or its equivalent) is first dissolved in a small quantity of water and then added to about a quart of glycerine. This process is termed vulcanizing.

[*Printed, 4d. No Drawings.*]

A.D. 1874, July 8.—No. 2402.

LAKE, WILLIAM ROBERT.—(*A communication from L. Otto P. Meyer.*)—"Compound to form surfaces for the ignition of "safety matches."

The compound consists " of india-rubber or allied gum, " sulphur, and gray sulphuret of antimony, the said com- " pound being vulcanized by heat as in the preparation of " what is known as hard rubber or vulcanite."

[*Printed, 4d. No Drawings.*]

A.D. 1874, August 6.—No. 2727.

PIERI, JACQUES PHILIPPE.—Manufacture of cartridges with cases formed of metal foil and caoutchouc or gutta percha.

The case is composed of a piece of foil rolled up into the form of a tube and with an envelope of caoutchouc or gutta percha or their compounds. It is preferred to use Para caoutchouc mixed with chalk or whiting and gravel. The mass is passed between parallel rollers to reduce it to a very thin sheet, which is spread upon a slab and coated with sandarach gum, talc, or other powdered material; the sheet is then cut into pieces of the required size. Each piece is rolled up with a piece of foil upon a mandril and then introduced into a mould and subjected to vulcanization; or the mould may be dispensed with by binding the cartridge with paper or cloth, which is removed after the vulcanization. The cartridge when withdrawn from the mould is dipped in cold water and then in oil.

[*Printed, 4d. No Drawings.*]

A.D. 1874, August 10.—No. 2762.

INGRAM, JAMES GEORGE.—Manufacture of india-rubber washers or packing pieces.

Around a mandril of any desired size are wrapped layers of india-rubber and canvas in any desired alternation until the required thickness is produced, thus producing a tube in the cross section of which the layers of india-rubber and canvas alternate. This tube is then cut up crosswise into slices so as to produce washers or packing pieces of any desired thickness.

[*Printed, 4d. No Drawings.*]

A.D. 1874, August 26.—No. 2913.

THOMSON, GAVIN, and WATSON, GEORGE.—Manufacture of compound india-rubber sheets or surfaces applicable to various purposes.

One side of the sheet is composed of "india-rubber, "sulphur, lime, or other materials, which admit of being "converted by heat into ebonite, or hard rubber, or vul- "canized only," the other side of the sheet being simply of india-rubber, or compounds of india-rubber or other materials which will not become hard when subjected to heat. The materials are prepared in separate sheets, one with and the other without sulphur, and then united by rollers or otherwise, and subjected to heat together.

[*Printed, 4d. No Drawings.*]

A.D. 1874, September 5.—No. 3048.

TALLING, RICHARD, and SECCOMBE, JAMES.—" Manufac- " ture of material suitable for packing for steam engines, " junction rings or washers, paint varnish, lacquer, cover- " ings for floors, also for roofing and other purposes."

The invention consists in the employment of mica or of minerals of the mica species either separately or in combination with some binding or retaining material, such as vulcanite, caoutchouc, or other gum resin, and in some cases also with hemp, jute, or cotton, or like fibrous substances or with asphalte or other analogous substance for the purposes above mentioned.

A packing is made by combining from ten to eighty per cent. of ground mica with caoutchouc.

For stuffing boxes one pound of india-rubber is incorporated with four pounds of ground mica, to which one ounce of sulphur is added, the compound is cured in the usual manner.

[*Printed, 4d. No Drawings.*]

A.D. 1874, October 7.—No. 3433.

HARRIS, Isaac Blue.—Manufacture of india-rubber mats.

The mats are made with a series of closely set conical or other shaped projections rising from a sheet of rubber forming the ground work of the mat, and made in a piece with it.

The mat is made in a mould consisting of a plate through which a series of conical holes are made. These holes form cells for the plastic india-rubber compound, and they are made completely through the metal to ensure the expulsion of the air. The mould plate is set in a cast iron chase and is placed upon a press plate a layer of cloth being interposed between the press plate and the mould. A sheet of plastic india-rubber is then inserted in the mould and over this a piece of cloth to receive the pressure of the follower plate of the press which forces the plastic material into the conical cells of the mould. The mould is afterwards clamped between plates and submitted to steam heat to vulcanize the mat.

[*Printed, 6d. Drawing.*]

A.D. 1874, October 7.—No. 3437.

INGRAM, James George.—" Manufacture of bands or straps, " and of washers, sheets, rings, discs, tubes, and packing, " and insertion pieces."

This invention consists in the employment in the manufacture of various articles of india-rubber of a layer or layers of perforated sheet metal or wire gauze in combination with layers of india-rubber, and with or without layers of canvas or cloth.

In the case of bands or straps where great strength is required, whether made of india-rubber, gutta percha, or other material, continuous longitudinal rods, bars, or flat strips of hoop iron or other metal are embedded in the interior of the bands or straps.

[*Printed, 4d. No Drawings.*]

A.D. 1874, October 24.—No. 3672.

GREENACRE, Thomas. — "Apparatus for manufacturing
" screws of vulcanite or other analogous material for liquid
" meters."

It is proposed to dispense with moulds in the manufacture
of these screws, and in lieu thereof to cut them out of solid
material. For this purpose a metal screw, of the pitch
required for the vulcanite screw, is mounted in two fixed
standards. This metal screw is capable of revolving freely in
bearings except as controlled in its rotation by the means
hereinafter described. "At one end of the metal screw is
" formed or fixed a socket to receive one end of the piece of
" solid vulcanite or a spindle carrying the same, the other
" end of which may be passed into another socket formed to
" revolve freely in an adjustable standard or ' poppet head,'
" or it may be carried by a centre bearing. Over the metal
" screw is passed a nut, to which is fixed by rigid connections
" properly guided a cylindrical cutter head, which may be
" provided with three sets of cutters mounted therein, in
" which case each set would be of a corresponding number to
" the threads required in the screw, and would be fixed a
" short distance in front of the other and so that the second
" and third sets should each cut a little deeper than the
" cutters immediately in advance of them, the last set of
" cutters being arranged to finish the desired screw, or in
" some cases more sets of cutters or only one cutter may be
" employed, or they may be caused to traverse more than
" once over the vulcanite.

" The nut is by suitable means moved slowly forward so as
" to cause the cutters to traverse the length of the piece of
" solid vulcanite to be cut into screws." In some cases
lengths of solid vulcanite suitable for making two screws at
the same operation are employed.

[*Printed*, 10*d*. *Drawing*.]

A.D. 1874, November 12.—No. 3902.

QUIN, James.—"Protecting india-rubber valves, tubes, and
" other like articles from chemical action."

The patentee describes his invention in the following terms :—

"For valves and such-like articles as may be required to be made insoluble I provide as required by the shape and size an inside shape or groundwork so much less than the object I desire to make. This I make of 'red' or A 'floating rubber,' which possess the quality of both lightness and durability. These I coat or case with a mixture of mineral and vegetable matter for enveloping the valves with or without ground metallic dust or foil in such proportions as the nature and future use of the article may require."

"For pipes, tubes, and such-like articles I provide similar groundwork of red or floating A, cased with and by a similar material and in a similar manner, after which they are vulcanized in the usual way."

[*Printed*, 6d. *Drawing.*]

A.D. 1874, November 28.—No. 4079.

YOUNGHUSBAND, GEORGE, YOUNGHUSBAND, GEORGE THOMAS, ROCKLIFFE, WILLIAM, and ROCKLIFFE, JAMES WILLIAM.—(*Provisional protection only.*)—" Composition suitable for preserving the bottoms of ships, boats, and other similar vessels."

One pound of gutta percha, half an ounce of copper bronze and half an ounce of arsenic are mixed and melted together; the mixture is allowed to cool and it is then cut into sheets.

The bottom of the vessel is cleaned and heated and a coat of liquid gutta percha is applied, and allowed to cool. The surface of this first coating is warmed and the sheets of composition are laid on it whilst still warm.

[*Printed*, 4d. *No Drawings.*]

A.D. 1874, December 16.—No. 4343.

LAKE, WILLIAM ROBERT.—(*A communication from William Bell.*)—Compounds to be used as substitutes for india-rubber, gutta percha, and other materials.

The compounds consist of glue 10 quarts; glycerine from 2½ to 4 quarts; cork, when used from 5 to 7 quarts, but this may be omitted; and about an ounce of chromic acid or an equivalent quantity of bichromate of potassa, the chromic acid being first dissolved in water and then mixed with about 1 quart of glycerine before being added to the other ingredients. It is preferred to add to the compound to be used either tannic acid or Aleppo gall water, one quart of the former, or two quarts of the latter. In case Aleppo gall water is added then one quart of good oil (linseed preferred) is to be first mixed therewith.

After the article has been formed or coated and is sufficiently dry, it is preferred to apply to the surface of the compound used the following solution, about one ounce of chromic acid (or its equivalent) is first dissolved in a small quantity of water and then added to about a quart of glycerine. This process is termed vulcanizing.

[*Printed, 4d. No Drawings.*]

1875.

A.D. 1875, January 1.—No. 9.

FISH, WILLIAM STEBBINS.—" Material applicable for packing
" stuffing boxes of engines, pumps, and other mechanism,
" for packing joints of pipes, boilers, tanks, cylinders, and
" valve chests, and others analogous thereto, also applicable
" for covering floors, roofs, and other surfaces."

The material is formed of a mixture of raw caoutchouc or india-rubber gum and triturated or comminuted asbestos or amianthus. The caoutchouc is kneaded in a masticator and when sufficiently reduced to a pasty condition the asbestos or amianthus is mixed with it, and these are still further operated on by the masticator until the asbestos or amianthus is regularly distributed throughout the pasty caoutchouc. A sufficient quantity of sulphur is also mixed with the compound for the purpose of vulcanization.

[*Printed, 4d. No Drawings.*]

A.D. 1875, February 20.—No. 633.

NAPIER, WILLIAM DONALD. — India-rubber compound for making tooth, and flesh brushes or rubbers.

It is proposed to combine with the india-rubber a sharp polishing powder, such as powdered pumice. " The powder " is worked into the india-rubber compound by means of " kneading rollers, and when the mixture is complete the " brush moulds are filled with it, and the india-rubber is " then cured by the application of heat."

[*Printed*, 4*d*. *No Drawings*.]

A.D. 1875, April 17.—No. 1404.

HENDERSON, WILLIAM CREAM. — (*Provisional protection only*.)—Treatment of " vulcanite," to obtain various colored effects.

India-rubber is combined with color and sulphur is added in such quantity as may be required for the conversion of the india-rubber; the compound is then " cured " or partially " cured " so as to reduce it into particles of the size required. These particles are mixed with the dough of ordinary vulcanite in proportions varying with the effect desired to be produced. This dough is then formed into sheets or moulded, and " cured." Effects are obtained resembling granite and other stones, or marbles.

[*Printed*, 4*d*. *No Drawings*.]

A.D. 1875, April 22.—No. 1477.

TONGUE, JOHN GARRETT.—(*A communication from Raymond Edouard Montaugé, and Auguste Alfred Brandely.*)—" Manu- " facture of corks or stoppers from cork, reduced to powder " and mixed with india-rubber and other materials."

The cork is reduced to dust, the gum and other impurities in the cork being removed by boiling alcohol, and by washing in water. The cork dust is then drained and dried, and from 10 to 20 per cent. of hemp cut the length of about a $\frac{1}{4}$ to $\frac{1}{2}$ inch is added, or the hemp may be omitted. The india-rubber is dissolved in refined sulphuret of carbon and brought into a state of paste, which is put into a mixing apparatus and the cork dust is added thereto. When the materials are well mixed the compound is placed in the apparatus employed to mould it into corks or stoppers.

For certain kinds of stoppers the right is reserved to impart greater rigidity to the composition or paste by making mixtures of wood sawdust or any powders or dust taken from either vegetable, animal or mineral substances.

[*Printed*, 1s. 2d. *Drawings.*]

A.D. 1875, April 27.—No. 1549.

YOUNG, JOHN. — Manufacture of waterproof and airproof fabrics.

This invention relates to the vulcanizing of india-rubber or compounds of india-rubber used for cementing together two textures of animal fibres. The invention also applies where textures of cotton or mixed fibres are used in producing the compound fabric.

The fabrics to be joined are coated on one side with a solution of india-rubber, and the rubber covered sides of the fabrics are run over a roller mounted in a vessel charged with a solution composed of bi-sulphide of carbon and chloride of sulphur or any other liquid vulcanizing agent, and immediately brought together by passing the coated fabrics between a pair of nipping rollers while the two surfaces are tacky. By this means a vulcanized double texture fabric is obtained without employing heat.

[*Printed*, 8d. *Drawing.*]

A.D. 1875, June 4.—No. 2059.

GREENING, FREDERICK. — Compounds to be used as substitutes for india-rubber, for insulating telegraph wires, for the production of waterproof fabrics, and for other purposes.

This invention consists " in submitting mixtures of paraffin,
" shellac, resin, or gum, such for example as copal, also of
" the residues left after effecting the distillation of the
" heavier oils of tar or mixtures of the same with solution
" gun cotton, or with soluble compounds analogous thereto,
" to the action of kreosote obtained from wood tar or of
" mixtures of the same with other solvents of gun cotton,
" which at an elevated temperature effects the combination
" or incorporation of the materials."

[*Printed*, 4d. *No Drawings.*]

A.D. 1875, June 5.—No. 2074.

NEWTON, ALFRED VINCENT.—(*A communication from Leonard F. Requa.*) — "Compound for coating textile fabrics and " rendering them acid and waterproof."

"Crude gum or rubber" is washed in water, and then dried and reduced by the masticating process and by rolling to a comparatively thin or sheet condition. Six pounds of the prepared india-rubber are submerged in two gallons of benzine or other suitable solvent, which will in about ten hours reduce the same to a plastic state. To this are added " fifteen pounds of ground whiting or chalk, five pounds of " oxide of zinc, two pounds of asphaltum, seven ounces " of pulverized sulphur, and two pounds of lampblack. " These ingredients are then subjected to agitation in a " closed vessel till thoroughly mixed and brought to a proper " consistency to be spread upon the fabric." "The coated " material is submitted to a steam heat in a closed chamber " under a pressure of about thirty pounds to the inch to " vulcanize or cure the same."

[*Printed*, 4d. *No Drawings.*]

A.D. 1875, June 5.—No. 2075.

NEWTON, ALFRED VINCENT.—(*A communication from Leonard F. Requa.*) — Manufacture of waterproof bags, cases, and envelopes from textile fabrics and paper coated with india-rubber compounds, the object being to secure the lapped edges of the articles by the coated surface; also deodorizing the same.

The material having been prepared, cut, and folded to the required size the uncoated surface of the lapped portions joins the coated surface, and to secure the connection of the parts of the lapped portions are rolled with a cold roller. Bags thus prepared are then put into a suitable box one upon the other and vulcanized by steam.

In order to deodorize the bags, leaf mint is placed among and between the bags in the curing chamber, so that the heat from the moist steam seizes upon the mint leaves, and impregnating them produces an evaporation from the leaves which permeates the bags. This effect is enhanced by the employment in connection with the mint leaves of copperas.

[*Printed*, 6d. *Drawing.*]

A.D. 1875, July 9.—No. 2482.

BOUSFIELD, GEORGE TOMLINSON.—(*A communication from Francis Scholes, and Peter Cowper.*)—(*Provisional protection only.*)—" Machine for the manufacture of rubber belting."

"At one end of a long table is mounted a frame holding " two or more horizontal bars," upon each of which is placed a pair of adjustable discs. A smaller frame, similarly arranged, but with one bar less in it, is placed immediately in front of the frame just mentioned and in rear of a pair of rolls, the lower of which is carried in proper bearings and driven by suitable means. The upper roll is placed between grooved uprights. Beyond these rolls are placed long adjustable guides, which serve to fold the cover piece over those in the centre. Next to these come one or more pairs of rolls, having small guides provided to each; another pair of rolls, also provided with guides, is placed near the end of the table.

"The several pieces which are to make up the belt pass
" over the horizontal bars in the end frame and between the
" discs, which are arranged so as to bring them exactly one
" over the other and centrally with the cover piece, which
" passes over the bottom bar and straight to the first pair of
" rolls, the filling pieces being taken through the second
" frame so as to keep them separate from each other till they
" reach the rolls, which press them with the centre part of
" the cover piece firmly together. The belt thus half formed
" passes on to the folders, which by their peculiarly curved
" inner surfaces turn over and inwards the extra width of the
" cover piece, till on issuing from the folders the belt is
" formed, and is thoroughly pressed together between the
" pair or pairs of rolls beyond the folders.

"Between the centre and last pairs of rolls is arranged a
" reel carrying the rubber strip which is to be placed upon
" the joined edges of the cover piece; this is conducted from
" the reel to an adjustable guide through which it passes to
" the last pair of rolls, means being provided for damping
" the strip with benzine." The belt passes in a receptacle filled with French chalk, and is afterwards vulcanized.

[*Printed*, 4d. *No Drawings.*]

A.D. 1875, July 12.—No. 2495.

HEINZERLING, Christian, and LIEPMANN, Henry.—Recovering and utilizing refuse caoutchouc and gutta percha.

The refuse caoutchouc or gutta percha is first disintegrated by any convenient means, it is then subjected to a treatment first with acids and then with alkalies, it is next washed with water and dried. The material is next subjected to a treatment with either turpentine, naphthaline, sulphide of carbon, petroleum, or petroleum spirit.

A solution of caoutchouc or gutta percha is thereby obtained, which solution may be distilled or concentrated and employed in the preparation of cements or in the manufacture of waterproof articles.

When the solution is employed in the preparation of inflexible caoutchouc or vulcanite, the residuum after concentration may either be mixed with new caoutchouc and then vulcanized, or it may be directly used by admixing it with resins.

[*Printed*, 4d. *No Drawings.*]

A.D. 1875, July 15.—No. 2547.

CATLOW, Urban, and HOYLE, Robert.—Stoppers for bottles, and purifying and protecting the same and other articles.

Part of this invention relates to eliminating the smell from india-rubber by washing it in a boiling solution of caustic alkali, preferably a strong solution of Canadian black ash, and then in one of ordinary washing soda.

[*Printed*, 6d. *Drawing.*]

A.D. 1875, September 7.—No. 3138.

THOMSON, Benjamin Lumsden, and CONNOLLY, Thomas.—" Protecting ships or vessels and other submerged or par-" tially submerged surfaces."

To the sides of the vessel or other surfaces are applied suitably prepared sheets of copper, zinc, yellow metal, or other similar metals or alloys, with the interposition between such sheets and the sides of the vessel or other surfaces of a layer or layers of insulating adhesive compounds. " This

" compound consists of caoutchouc combined with any
" sulphide of antimony or other suitable poisonous compound
" so as to secure at the same time both poisonous and vulcan-
" izing properties." To this may be added a variable
quantity of silica or French chalk. Over this layer of compound is applied a second layer of sheets consisting of caoutchouc combined with litharge, oxide of zinc, silica, and other suitable substances to act as strongly adhesive protective and insulating material. Heat is applied to the sheets of metal by which the inner layer of compound will become vulcanized.

[*Printed*, 4*d*. *No Drawings.*]

A.D. 1875, October 15.—No. 3578.

MacLELLAN, GEORGE.—Compound of caoutchouc with other substances.

The object of the invention is to produce a material heavier and less brittle than ordinary vulcanite.

It may be carried into effect in two ways, first, by disintegrating the waste of india-rubber cloth manufacture, or old india-rubber cloth, the result of which is the production of a mass of india-rubber with the fibres of textile material mixed with it. With this, if there is not sufficient sulphur, the requisite quantity of sulphur and colouring matter are added and the whole mass is next placed in moulds and submitted to the ordinary vulcanizing process, except that it is submitted to that process for a longer period than is usual in the manufacture of ordinary vulcanite. Or a quantity of rags or textile fibres may be commingled with raw india-rubber, together with colouring matter and sulphur after which the mass is vulcanized.

[*Printed*, 4*d*. *No Drawings.*]

A.D. 1875, October 22.—No. 3675.

BARROW, JOHN.—Condensing the vapours evolved during the process of applying india-rubber to fabrics in spreading machines.

A chamber, termed "the evaporating chamber," is formed by placing a loose cover over the steam chest of the spreading machine. With the evaporating chamber are connected other chambers, into which the vapour is caused to flow. Within these chambers the vapour is caused to come in contact with and to be absorbed by an oil or oleaginous absorbent boiling at a higher temperature than that at which the naphtha to be absorbed will boil, which oil when saturated with condensed naphtha is subjected to heat sufficient, without distilling the oil, to distil from it the naphtha, which is condensed and collected, so that it and the oil may be used over again.

This method of dealing with the vapours of naphtha is also applicable for dealing with the vapours of wood naphtha and turpentine.

[*Printed*, 1s. *Drawing.*]

A.D. 1875, November 5.—No. 3862.

JENKS, THOMAS.—(*Provisional protection only.*)—Composition termed "caoutchouc aluta" used for jewellery, buttons, &c., and as a substitute for vulcanite.

Leather is cut up and boiled in water for five hours, then a sufficient quantity of oxalic acid is added to dissolve the leather, and a portion of glue. In another vessel are placed resin, pitch, and Japan wax or beeswax, in suitable proportions, and a portion of copal gum previously dissolved in oil is added. Caoutchouc is dissolved in another vessel with boiled linseed oil under heat. The three solutions are mixed together and a powder formed of plaster of Paris and colored pigments is stirred into the composition to thicken and stiffen it.

[*Printed*, 4d. *No Drawings.*]

A.D. 1875, November 10.—No. 3904.

MORI, FREDRICK.—"Thermo-regulators."

Part of this invention consists "in arranging thermo-
" electric piles inside the case of a vulcanizer for dental
" purposes to generate the electric current by heat instead of
" using a battery to work the thermo-regulator."

[*Printed*, 1s. 2d. *Drawings.*]

A.D. 1875, December 17.—No. 4372.

DUNBAR, HIRAM POND, and LOTHROP, THOMAS CHURCH.—
"Manufacture of articles from vulcanized rubber."

This invention relates to the manufacture of floorcloths and other articles and it consists of a product composed of a foundation of a cheap compound of india-rubber overlaid or inlaid with a series of strips, figures, or characters of a thin and more expensive india-rubber compound, which is capable of receiving any desired color or tint, these strips or figures being in the final stage of the vulcanizing process imbedded in the foundation so that a uniformly even surface exists over the whole.

[*Printed, 6d. Drawing.*]

1876.

A.D. 1876, February 11.—No. 563.

MAGNUS, GUSTAV. — "Manufacture of billiard balls and similar objects."

The object of this invention is to produce a material as a substitute for ivory. It is stated that "the trials heretofore made by others with india-rubber have failed chiefly because they could not vulcanize to a diameter of from about two to three and a half inches without causing the core to crack and the ball becoming porous." Rubber expands considerable in the vulcanizing so that moulds of tin are bulged and even burst, the patentee therefore makes the moulds of cast iron. The inner half spheres of the mould are tinned. The two parts being held together by discs and tie bolts. About ten hours is taken for vulcanizing and a gradually increasing heat is employed. In order to make the balls of the same specific gravity as ivory about 50 per cent. of heavy spar (Schiverspath) is added to the rubber.

[*Printed, 6d. Drawing.*]

A.D. 1876, February 24.—No. 776.

NEWTON, HENRY EDWARD.—(*A communication from Alfred Joseph Macbay.*)—Converting vegetable and animal fibres and fibrous substances of various kinds into substances resembling wood, vulcanite, rubber, gutta percha, or other hard or tough substance, so that the artificial substance produced may be used as a substitute for any of the natural substances.

In carrying out the invention the fibrous substances are consolidated by pressure in moulds or otherwise, and by preference with the addition of resins of various kinds, pitch, tar, gums, size, glue, shellac, rubber, gutter percha, turpentine, petroleum, or any other hydrocarbons or oils and their products, paraffine, wax, tallow, and like substances and their products, farina, starch, or gluten, and the glutinous matter of seeds, grain, pulse, and tubers and their products, lime, chalk, sand, clays, earths, plaster of Paris, Portland and other cements.

[*Printed, 4d. No Drawings.*]

A.D. 1876, April 8.—No. 1502.

MOSELEY, CHARLES. — "Apparatus employed in various " processes where inflammable oils are used."

This invention is particularly applicable to the condensing apparatus described in No. 1637, A.D. 1872, and No. 916, A.D. 1873, but it may be applied to other apparatus for collecting the vapours of naphtha or other solvent used in the manufacture of india-rubber, and to other processes in which inflammable oils are employed. The object of the invention is to confine within certain limits the flames of such vapours or oils when they become ignited by accident. It consists in placing screens of wire gauze or perforated sheet metal in the flues, passages, pipes, or vessels, through which the inflammable vapours or oils circulate, or in which they are contained; these screens do not prevent the passage of the vapours or oils, but in case of fire they intercept the passing of the flames.

[*Printed, 4d. Drawing.*]

A.D. 1876, April 22.—No. 1704.

FIXSEN, BURCHARD.—(*A communication from Ludwig, Danckwerth.*) — "Manufacture of india-rubber and gutta percha " compounds."

The compounds are formed by the combination of ozocerite or ozokerite (also known as fossil resin or fossil wax or earth wax) with india-rubber, or with gutta percha, or with a mixture of india-rubber and gutta percha, or with other materials, which when combined with the ozocerite in suitable proportions will form a substance that may be used in place of ordinary natural or vulcanized india-rubber or gutta percha.

[*Printed*, 4d. *No Drawings.*]

A.D. 1876, May 24.—No. 2186.

WOODWARD, HENRY. — (*A communication from William Henry Lippincott.*)—"Manufacture of balls for billiards or "other similar purposes."

A variety of moulds with suitable vulcanizing apparatus are employed. A central core is first vulcanized, which core is then turned spherical, and afterwards enclosed in another mould of larger size containing rubber sufficient to surround the core and fill the mould, which with its contents is subjected to the same vulcanizing process as the first. This layer is then turned true as before, and in this manner any number of layers may be added until the ball attains the required size.

Any desired color may be obtained by mixing suitable coloring matters with the last layer of india-rubber.

For red and white the following ingredients are found to answer the purpose:—

Red	Para india-rubber	-	8 parts by weight.
	Vermilion	-	6 parts by weight.
White	Para india-rubber	-	8 parts by weight.
	Zinc white	-	5 parts by weight.
	Calcined magnesia	-	1 part by weight.

[*Printed*, 4d. *No Drawings.*]

A.D. 1876, June 3.—No. 2339.

NEWTON, WILLIAM EDWARD.—(*A communication from Walter P. Jenney.*)—The treatment of sludge oil produced in the purification of crude petroleum, asphalte, bitumen, and other substances from which hydrocarbon oils are obtained, and obtaining useful products.

Part of this invention consists in oxidizing sludge oil and producing a resinous substance therefrom.

"It has also been discovered that the resinous substances
"derived from sludge oil by other processes may be com-
"bined with raw or vulcanized india-rubber in all proportions
"from one part of resin to twenty parts of rubber to one
"part of rubber in twenty parts of resin, thereby producing
"a new and useful compound. The compound is made by
"heating in an iron, steel, or other suitable vessel the resin
"derived from sludge oil until it is completely melted, and
"then adding the rubber to it in small pieces, the heat being
"kept sufficiently high to melt both rubber and resin, and
"thoroughly to incorporate them."

The compound may be used as a cement, or for water-proofing, or for making a varnish, or for other purposes.

[*Printed*, 4d. *No Drawings.*]

A.D. 1876, June 16.—N° 2500.

LAKE, WILLIAM ROBERT.—(*A communication from Charles Grasser.*)—"The production of moulds in wax, plaster of
"Paris, and other similar materials and patterns, and
"other articles of india-rubber or other gum capable of
"vulcanization."

"For forming and vulcanizing a pattern or other article
"of soft rubber within a metal mould the raw material is
"applied to the interior of the mould, first in small frag-
"ments so as to fill all the interstices, and then in larger
"pieces or sheets an opening being left to admit to the
"interior water in which the whole is immersed, and which
"receives a heavy pressure to force the rubber against the
"inner surface of the mould. Heat is then applied by steam
"in a surrounding chamber and through the medium of the
"water and the metal mould to the rubber." The mould is
enveloped in an impervious cover connected with the hollow
body within the mould so that the water will pass into the
hollow body to be formed but cannot pass between it and
the mould.

"For producing articles in hard vulcanite by the agency
"of steam, heat, and pressure, the mould is formed of a thin
"body of plaster within a perforated flask or outer mould of
"metal, approximating to the shape of the pattern, so that
"the entire mould may have sufficient strength to resist the

" pressure, and the plaster of which its inner surface is
" formed may not be of sufficient thickness to prevent the
" conduction of the necessary heat for vulcanizing.

" The raw rubber is applied in sheets over an envelope of
" soft vulcanized rubber on a hollow core either porous or
" perforated, which approximates to the shape of the article
" to be formed, the envelope preventing the rupture of the
" raw rubber by the internal steam pressure. The vul-
" canizing heat is produced through the medium of steam
" applied by means of separate chambers to the exterior of
" the mould and to the interior of the material within it, the
" pressure on the interior of the material being in excess of
" that on the exterior of the mould, so as to cause the
" material to be forced in close contact with the inner surface
" of the mould."

The vulcanizing vessel is formed "with an inner chamber
" in which the mould is placed (or any number of them) and
" an outer chamber with which the hollow interior of the
" mould communicates through a hollow screw-plug by
" which the mould is attached to the vulcanizer and by
" suitable ducts.

" In using soft elastic rubber patterns for forming moulds
" of wax, paraffine, or like substance, the said patterns are
" coated with glycerine and a solution of sal ammoniac or
" other suitable salt to prevent adhesion of the wax to the
" rubber."

[*Printed*, 10d. *Drawings*.]

A.D. 1876, June 27.—No. 2652.

LÉVY, DAVID.—Straps or belts for driving machinery.

This invention consists in the combination of one or more
layers of fibrous fabrics united by means of gutta percha.

The layers of fabric start from reels, pass between guide
rollers and are kept apart at this stage by retaining rollers,
after which they join together on their arrival at a draw
plate, the object of which is to distribute the gutta percha,
which is brought between the layers of fabric by "long-
" necked flues" placed between the retaining rollers and
the draw plate. After passing the draw plate the layers of
material pass between two rollers which compress them and

cut off any excess of gutta percha from the edges. Occasionally it is found desirable to pass the belting through a second pair of rollers.

[*Printed, 6d. Drawing.*]

A.D. 1876, July 13.—No. 2866.

DEISS, Augustus, and SCAIFE, Reginald. — "Treating "india-rubber, gutta percha, amber, resin, and other vege- "table gums, and also ceraffine, ozokerite, bitumen, asphalte, "sulphur, and other mineral and animal products in order "to free them from impurities and render them more "valuable."

This invention consists in treating the materials mentioned above by means of solvents, such as bisulphate of carbon, hydrocarbons, essential and other oils, with the assistance of steam or other heat, and a great pressure; also in a filtration and a final regeneration of the solvent used. A strong cast or wrought iron vessel is used. It has a manhole for loading it with the material to be treated and an exit pipe near the bottom to let the solution of the material under treatment run out into a filtering apparatus. This vessel is provided with a steam jacket or other heating appliance for assisting the solvent to act on the material. The solvent is inserted by a force pump or other means into the vessel until the solution is thin enough to pass through a filtering apparatus. The vessel is also supplied with a stirring apparatus.

The next operation is to run off the solution into the filtering apparatus, which consists of a closed iron vessel with a perforated bottom containing the filtering material, such as sawdust, charcoal, bran, moss, or any like substance. The clarified solution is run into an evaporating pan where the gum is freed from the solvent, which passes as vapour into a condenser so as to be collected and re-used.

[*Printed 4d. No Drawings.*]

A.D. 1876, August 31.—No. 3428.

STEWART, Duncan.—Making and repairing balls for golf and other games, "which balls are made of gutta percha."

"The invention consists in dissolving the pure gutta percha "with bisulphate of carbon or other solvent into a soft or "plastic state, and then mixing the same with fine ground cork and metal filings in the proportions suitable for giving the size, elasticity, and weight of ball desired." Sometimes it is found advantageous to add to the mixture a small quantity of fibrous substance in order to give increased cohesion to the mass.

[*Printed*, 4*d*. *No Drawings*.]

A.D. 1876, October 10.—No. 3921.

FORSTER, THOMAS.—"Manufacture of double texture waterproof fabrics."

The patentee says,—"It has been the usual practice hitherto in using the chloride of sulphur combined with bisulphide of carbon as a vulcanizing agent to apply the same only to the rubber surfaces of waterproof goods, on account of the corrosive action of the chloride on the texture.

"According to my invention I apply the above compounds direct to the cloth surfaces of double-texture waterproof fabrics, be they woollen, silk, or cotton fabrics, and after so doing subject the said fabrics to the action of an alkali, by preference ammonia, which by neutralizing the hydrochloric acid (resulting from the decomposition of the chloride of sulphur) prevents its injurious action."

[*Printed*, 2*d*. *No Drawings*.]

A.D. 1876, October 25.—No. 4132.

HEALD, JOHN. — "Machine for grinding and doughing india-rubbers and their compounds for spreading purposes, likewise suitable for paints and other materials."

Three or more grinding rollers are carried in bearings in a suitable frame, the centre or main roller is placed near the middle of the lower part of the frame, and underneath is a receiver. This main roller is made hollow so that steam may be passed through it or hot water for heating purposes or cold for cooling purposes. Above the main roller are two or more smaller rollers driven from the main roller at such speeds that a grinding surface is formed between such rollers and the main roller, all of which lead from front to back of the machine in their grinding action. These rollers are regulated by set screws to or from the main roller. Near the centre of the main roller is fixed a plate or bar in the edge of which is a groove, into which is fitted a piece of elastic material which presses against the main roller and forms the bottom of the hopper on that side of the machine. On the other side of the main roller is a bevelled edge plate which forms a scraping edge to take off the material which passes along with the rollers, this plate forms the bottom of the hopper on the other side of the machine. An agitating roller working in the hopper keeps the material from settling or clogging.

[*Printed*, 6d. *Drawing*.]

A.D. 1876, December 5.—No. 4705.

NEWTON, HENRY EDWARD.—(*A communication from Henri Menier*.)—"Manufacture of telegraphic and other conductors " covered with caoutchouc or other insulating substance."

" The object of the present invention is to cause the " caoutchouc or other insulating substance employed for " covering wires to quickly harden." "To this end the " newly covered wire before vulcanization is conducted " through a vessel or chamber containing a freezing or " refrigerating mixture." "On issuing from the other end " of the freezing or cooling chamber the covered wire can " be immediately coiled up in a suitable vessel or tank, to " facilitate which operation the receiving tank is kept rotating " on its vertical axis by means of suitable gearing."

[*Printed*, 6d. *Drawing*.]

INDEX OF SUBJECT MATTER.

[The numbers refer to the pages on which the Abridgments commence. The names printed in *Italic* are those of the persons by whom the Inventions have been communicated to the Applicants for Letters Patent.]

Ballata :
    Perkins and Tandy, 11.
    Parnacott, 59.

Bands and belts :
    Lake (*Torrey*), 8.
    Poisnel, 13.
    Sterne. 17.
    Rodgers, 18.
    Le Blanc, 22.
    Harris, 29.
    Sutherland, 53.
    Mudford, 69.
    Quin, 71.
    Toussaint. 79.
    Ingram, 89.
    Bousfield (*Scoles and Cowper*), 96.
    Levy, 104.

Cementing, materials for. *See also* Solvents.
    Leather ;
        Toussaint, 1.
        Bugg, 8.
    Metals ;
        Dufilhol, 10.
        Gedge (*Crouzières*), 38.
        Dick, 40.
        Thomson and Connolly, 97.
    Other materials ;
        Toussaint, 1.
        Guenin (*Rigollot*), 2.
        Dufilhol, 10.
        Guenin (*Rigollot*), 47.
        Myerus, 63.
        Dodge, 68.
        Heinzerling and Liepmann, 97.
        Thomson and Connolly, 97.

Cleansing. *See* Preparing, &c.

Coating or covering, compounds and materials for. *See also* Solvents.
    Fabrics and paper ;
        Quin, 4.
        Jeyes, 7.
        Lake (*Torrey*), 8.
        Sintzenich (*Reed*), 9.
        Dodge, 11.
        Macintosh and Boggett, 12.
        Rogers, 16.
        Wadsworth, 18.
        Rostaing, 30.
        Macintosh, 31.
        Wolfgang, 35.
        Johnson (*Murfey*), 50.
        Macintosh, 50.
        Sutherland, 53.
        Walker, 54.
        Walker, 58.
        Macintosh and Boggett, 69.
        Macintosh, 78.
        Greening, 94.
        Newton (*Requa*), 95.
        Heinzerling and Liepmann, 97.
        Forster, 106.
    Leather ;
        Sintzenich (*Reed*), 9.
        Liddell, 29.
        Macintosh, 31.
        Fanshawe and Smith, 44.
        Johnson (*Murfey*), 50.
        Frankenburg, 84.
    Metals ;
        Gray, 3.
        Rogers, 16.
        Turnbull, 27.
        Mac Millan (*Mac Millan*), 28.
        Rostaing, 30.
        Macintosh, 31.
        Wilkinson and Boss, 35.
        Johnson (*Newbrough and Fagan*), 37.
        Gedge (*Crouzières*), 38.
        Dick, 40.

Coating or covering—*cont.*
  Metals—*cont.*
    Lake (*Chapman*), 49.
    Warren, 52.
    Day, 57.
    Chapman, 61.
    Quin, 81.
    Pieri, 87.
    Quin, 90.
    Younghusband, Younghusband, Rockliffe and Rockliffe, 91.
    Greening, 94.
  Other materials;
    Moseley, 2.
    Rogers, 16.
    Macintosh, 31.
    Wolfgang, 35.
    Chapman, 61.
    Heinzerling and Liepmann, 97.
    Younghusband, Younghusband, Rockliffe and Rockliffe, 91.

Colouring. *See* page 116.

Compounds of gutta percha with various ingredients :
  "Acid resin";
    Johnson (*Newbrough*), 46.
  Alkalies;
    Lake (*Day*), 8.
    Gale and Boyden, 63.
  Allamine;
    Lake (*Chapman*), 49.
  Ammonia;
    Fanshawe and Smith, 44.
  Anthracene;
    Perkins and Tandy, 11.
  Arsenic;
    Younghusband, Younghusband, Rockliffe and Rockliffe, 91.
  Ballata;
    Parnacott, 59.
  Balsams;
    Spill, 48.
  Bitumen;
    Gray, 3.
  Black lead. *See* Plumbago.
  Bromine;
    Johnson (*Newbrough and Fagan*), 37.
  Brunswick black;
    Wilkinson and Boss, 35.

Compounds of gutta percha, &c.—*cont.*
  Calcium, chloride of;
    Aspinall, 27.
  Camphor;
    Spill, 48.
  Cane;
    Davis and Struthers, 61.
  Carbon, bi-sulphide of;
    Fanshawe and Smith, 44.
  Catechu;
    Rostaing, 30.
  Chalk. *See* Lime, carbonate of.
  Chloroform;
    Johnson (*Newbrough and Fagan*), 37.
  Clay;
    Johnson (*Newbrough and Fagan*), 37.
    Parnacott, 70.
    Newton (*Macbay*), 100.
  Coal ashes and dust;
    Thomas, 65.
    Parnacott, 70.
  Coorongite;
    Forster and Cow, 34.
  Copper bronze;
    Younghusband, Younghusband, Rockliffe and Rockliffe, 91.
  Cork;
    Johnson (*Hauer and Howell*), 15.
    Stewart, 105.
  Farina. *See also* Starch.
    Newton (*Macbay*), 100.
  Feldspar;
    Lake (*Chapman*), 49.
  Fibres;
    Wadsworth, 18.
    Davis and Struthers, 61.
    Newton (*Macbay*), 100.
  Fire clay;
    Dodge, 68.
  Fuller's earth;
    Sintzenich (*Reed*), 9.
  Glue;
    Gale and Boyden, 63.
    Newton (*Macbay*), 100.
  Gluten;
    Newton (*Macbay*), 100.

Compounds of gutta percha,
&c.—cont.
  Granite;
    Thomas, 65.
  Gum lac. See Shellac.
  Gums;
    Spill, 48.
    Newton (Macbay), 100.
  India-rubber;
    Mayall, 21.
    Rostaing, 30.
    Dick, 40.
    Fanshawe and Smith, 44.
    Thomas, 65.
  Iodine;
    Johnson (Newbrough and Fagan), 37.
  Ironstone, fossil;
    Thomas, 65.
  Kaolin;
    Johnson (Newbrough and Fagan), 37.
  Lead, carbonate of;
    Mayall, 22.
    Gedge (Crouzières), 38.
    Day, 57.
  Lead, oxides of;
    Gedge (Crouzières), 38.
    Day, 57.
  Leather;
    Sintzenich (Reed), 9.
    Gale and Boyden, 63.
  Lime;
    Lake (Chapman), 49.
    Newton (Macbay), 100.
  Lime, carbonate of;
    Mayall, 22.
    Lake (Chapman), 49.
    Newton (Macbay), 100.
  Lime, sulphate of;
    Lake (Chapman), 49.
    Newton (Macbay), 100.
  Litharge. See Lead, oxide of.
  Magnesia;
    Lake (Chapman), 49.
  Magnesium, silicate of;
    Mayall, 21.
    Aspinall, 27.
    Lake (Chapman), 49.
  Metal borings and filings;
    Baker, 85.
    Stewart, 105.

Compounds of gutta percha,
&c.—cont.
  Metallic oxides;
    Fanshawe and Smith, 44.
  Mineral powders;
    Forster and Cow, 34.
  Naphthaline;
    Perkins and Tandy, 11.
  Nitric acid;
    Gale and Boyden, 63.
  Oils, coal;
    Rogers, 16.
  Oils consolidated;
    Parnacott, 59.
  Oils, fatty;
    Spill, 48.
  Oils, mineral;
    Lake (Day), 8.
  Oils, tar and other;
    Dodge, 68.
  Oils, vegetable;
    Lake (Day), 8.
    Rogers, 16.
    Spill, 48.
  Ozokerit;
    Fixsen, 101.
  Paraffin;
    Newton (Macbay), 100.
  Peat;
    Parnacott, 70.
  Petroleum;
    Rogers, 16.
  Pipeclay;
    Mayall, 21.
  Pitch;
    Aspinall, 27.
    Gedge (Crouzières), 38.
    Parnacott, 59.
    Thomas, 65.
    Newton (Macbay), 100.
  Pitch (coal tar);
    Fanshawe and Smith, 44.
  Plaster of Paris. See Lime, sulphate of.
  Plumbago;
    Mayall, 22.
  Portland cement;
    Dodge, 68.
    Newton (Macbay), 100.
  Printers' ink;
    Wilkinson and Boss, 35.

Compounds of gutta percha,
&c.—cont.
- Pumice stone;
  - Lake (*Chapman*), 49.
- Red lead. See Lead, oxides of.
- Resin;
  - Lake (*Day*), 8.
  - Mayall, 21.
  - Turnbull, 27.
  - Aspinall, 27.
  - Mac Millan (*Mac Millan*), 28.
  - Wilkinson and Boss, 35.
  - Gedge (*Crouzières*), 38.
  - Spill, 48.
  - Newton (*Macbay*), 100.
- Road mud;
  - Pernacott, 70.
- Sand;
  - Newton (*Macbay*), 100.
- Sawdust;
  - Dick, 40.
  - Thomas, 65.
  - Parnacott, 70.
- Shellac and gum lac;
  - Jeyes, 7.
  - Dufilhol, 10.
  - Mayall, 21.
  - Dick, 40.
  - Fanshawe and Smith, 44.
  - Lake (*Chapman*), 49.
  - Newton (*Macbay*), 100.
- Silica;
  - Aspinall, 27.
  - Lake (*Chapman*), 49.
- Size;
  - Gale and Boyden, 63.
  - Newton (*Macbay*), 100.
- Slate;
  - Lake (*Chapman*), 49.
- Smudge;
  - Parnacott, 70.
- Soapstone. See Magnesium, silicate of.
- Soda, borate of;
  - Fanshawe and Smith, 44.
- Sodium, chloride of;
  - Parnacott, 70.
- Spirit, coal tar;
  - Fanshawe and Smith, 44.
- Starch;
  - Newton (*Macbay*), 100.
- Stearine;
  - Fanshawe and Smith, 44.

Compounds of gutta percha, &c.—cont.
- Stone ochre;
  - Davis and Struthers, 61.
- Sulphur;
  - Lake (*Day*), 8.
  - Mayall, 21.
  - Mayall, 22.
  - Forster and Cow, 34.
  - Johnson (*Newbrough and Fagan*), 37.
  - Gedge (*Crouzières*), 38.
  - Lake (*Chapman*), 49.
  - Day, 57.
  - Dodge, 68.
- Sulphur, ter-chloride of;
  - Fanshawe and Smith, 44.
- Sulphuric acid;
  - Gale and Boyden, 63.
- Tallow;
  - Newton (*Macbay*), 100.
- Tannin;
  - Rostaing, 30.
- Tar;
  - Gray, 3.
  - Newton (*Macbay*), 100.
- Tar, coal;
  - Jeyes, 7.
  - Wilkinson and Boss, 35.
  - Gedge (*Crouzières*), 38.
  - Gale and Boyden, 63.
- Tar, Stockholm;
  - Pernacott, 59.
- Tungsten oxide;
  - Johnson (*Newbrough and Fagan*), 37.
- Turpentine;
  - Johnson (*Newbrough and Fagan*), 37.
  - Gedge (*Crouzières*), 38.
  - Fanshawe and Smith, 44.
- Varnish;
  - Turnbull, 27.
- Varnish bottoms;
  - Davis and Struthers, 61.
- Wax;
  - Wilkinson and Boss, 35.
  - Fanshawe and Smith, 44.
  - Newton (*Macbay*), 100.
- White lead. See Lead, carbonate of.
- Whiting. See Lime, carbonate of.

Compounds of gutta-percha, &c.—cont.

Wolfram;
   Johnson (*Newbrough and Fagan*), 37.
Zinc;
   Mayall, 21.

Compounds of india-rubber with various ingredients:

"Acid resin;"
   Johnson (*Newbrough*), 46.
Alkalies;
   Lake (*Day*), 8.
   Gale and Boyden, 63.
Allamine;
   Lake (*Chapman*), 49.
Ammonia;
   Thamsen (*Sörensen*), 42.
   Fanshawe and Smith, 44.
Anthracene;
   Perkins and Tandy, 11.
Antimony, sulphide of;
   Queen, 4.
   Loughton and Jackson, 24.
   Lake (*Meyer*), 87.
   Thomson and Conolly, 97.
Asbestos;
   Pigott, 9.
   Sutherland, 53.
   Harris, 70.
   Fish, 92.
Asphalte;
   Quin, 4.
   Day, 24.
   Day, 54.
   Stewart, 49.
   Talling and Seccombe, 88.
   Newton (*Requa*), 95.
Balsams;
   Spill, 48.
Barytes, sulphate of;
   Harris, 70.
Black lead. *See* Plumbago.
Bromine;
   Johnson (*Newbrough and Fagan*), 37.
   Warren, 52.
Calomel. *See* Mercury.
Camphor;
   Spill, 48.
   Day, 54.

Compounds of india-rubber, &c.—cont.

Carbon, bi-sulphide of;
   Fanshawe and Smith, 44.
   Frankenburg, 84.
Carbon, sulphide of;
   Thamsen (*Sörensen*), 42.
Catechu;
   Rostaing, 30.
Chalk. *See* Lime, carbonate of.
Charcoal;
   Forster and Heartfield, 26.
   Macintosh, 78.
Chlorine;
   Warren, 52.
Chloroform;
   Johnson (*Newbrough and Fagan*) 37.
Clay;
   Mayall, 20.
   Johnson (*Newbrough and Fagan*), 37.
   Parnacott, 70.
   Newton (*Macbay*), 100.
Coal ashes and dust;
   Thomas, 65.
   Parnacott, 76.
Collodion;
   Macintosh, 31.
Coorongite;
   Forster and Cow, 34.
Copper, sulphate of;
   Smith and Challenger, 36.
Cork;
   Pigott, 9.
   Johnson (*Hauer and Howell*), 15.
   Wilkinson and Boss, 35.
   Walker, 39.
   Paget (*Lemoine*), 56.
   Tongue (*Montaugè and Brandely*), 93.
Farina. *See also* Starch;
   Newton (*Macbay*), 100.
Feldspar;
   Lake (*Chapman*), 49.
Fibres;
   Moseley, 62.
   Talling and Seccombe, 88.
   Mac Lellan, 98.
Fire clay;
   Dodge, 68.

INDEX OF SUBJECT MATTER. 113

Compounds of india-rubber, &c.—*cont.*
  French Chalk. *See* Magnesium, silicate of.
  Fullers' earth ;
    Sintzenich (*Reed*), 9.
  Glue ;
    Gale and Boyden, 63.
    Newton (*Macbay*), 100.
  Gluten ;
    Newton (*Macbay*), 100.
  Granite ;
    Thomas, 65.
  Gravel ;
    Pieri, 87.
  Gum ;
    Liddell, 29.
    Spill, 48.
    Newton (*Macbay*), 100.
  Gum copal ;
    Jenks, 99,
  Gum lac. *See* Shellac.
  Gutta percha ;
    Stewart, 59.
    Thomas, 65.
    Fanshawe and Smith, 44.
    Rostaing, 30.
    Dick, 40.
    Mayall, 21.
    Mayall, 22.
    Day, 24.
  Hard and soft rubber ;
    Jaques and Banks, 64.
  Heavy spar (Schiverspath) ;
    Magnus, 100.
  Hemp ;
    Tongue (*Montaugè and Brandely*), 93.
  Hydrochloric acid ;
    Day, 24.
  Iodine ;
    Johnson (*Newbrough and Fagan*), 37.
    Warren, 52.
  Ironstone fossil ;
    Thomas, 65.
  Kaolin ;
    Johnson (*Newbrough and Fagan*), 37.
  Lamp black ;
    Mayall, 20.
    Macintosh, 50.

Compounds of india-rubber, &c.—*cont.*
  Lamp black—*cont.*
    Macintosh and Boggett, 69.
    Macintosh, 79.
    Newton (*Requa*), 95.
  Lead, acetate of ;
    Liddell, 29.
  Lead, carbonate of ;
    Mayall, 21.
    Mayall, 22.
    Day, 57.
  Lead, oxides of ;
    Mayall, 20.
    Mayall, 21.
    Day, 24.
    Day, 57.
    Thomson and Connolly, 97.
  Leather ;
    Sintzenich (*Reed*), 9.
    Wilkinson and Boss, 35.
    Smith and Challenger, 36.
    Thamsen (*Sörensen*), 42.
    Walker, 54.
    Stewart, 57.
    Walker, 58.
    Galloway, 58.
    Gale and Boyden, 63.
    Jenks, 99.
  Lime ;
    Lake (*Chapman*), 49.
    Thomson and Watson, 88.
    Newton (*Macbay*), 100.
  Lime, carbonate of ;
    Mayall, 20.
    Mayall, 22.
    Lake (*Chapman*), 49.
    Pieri, 87.
    Newton (*Requa*), 95.
    Newton (*Macbay*), 100.
  Lime, sulphate of ;
    Lake (*Chapman*), 49.
    Jenks, 99.
    Newton (*Macbay*), 100.
  Litharge. *See* Lead, oxides of.
  Magnesia ;
    Quin, 4.
    Mayall, 20.
    Day, 24.
    Lake (*Chapman*), 49.
    Moseley, 62.
    Woodward (*Lippincott*), 102.
  Magnesium, silicate of ;
    Mayall, 21.
    Lake (*Chapman*), 49.
    Warren, 52.
    Sutherland, 53.

Compounds of india-rubber,
&c.—cont.
   Rum;
      Smith and Challenger, M.
   Resin;
      Lake (Day), R.
      Mayall, 21.
      Spill, 6L.
      Myerson, 6L.
      Jenks, M.
      Newton (Mackay), M.
   Rosin, drying oil;
      Newton (Looney), M2.
   Road mud;
      Parnacott, R.
   Sand;
      Newton (Mackay), M.
   Sawdust;
      Fowler, M.
      Hunter and Ransfield, M.
      Dick, 6L.
      Thomas, 6L.
      Parnacott, R.
      Thomas (Mackenzie and Broadley), R.
   Shellac and gum lac;
      Dietzler, M.
      Mayall, 21.
      Dick, 6L.
      Fancherre and Smith, 6L.
      Lake (Chapman), 6L.
      Newton (Mackay), M.
   Silex;
      Lake (Chapman), 6L.
      Sutherland, R.
      Thomson and Connelly, R.
   Size;
      Gale and Baynton, 6L.
      Newton (Mackay), M.
   Slate;
      Lake (Chapman), 6L.
   Sludge oil resin;
      Newton (Looney), M2.
   Starch;
      Parnacott, R.
   Soapstone. See Magnesium, silicate of.
   Soda, bicarbonate of;
      Day, M.
   Soda, borate of;
      Fancherre and Smith, 6L.
   Soda, nitrate of;
      Day, M.

Compounds of india-rubber,
&c.—cont.
   Sodium, chloride of;
      Parnacott, R.
   Soot;
      Michinode, M.
   Spirit, coal tar;
      Fancherre and Smith, 6L.
   Starch. See also Sawdust.
      Newton (Mackay), M.
   Stearic acid;
      Michinode, M.
   Steatite;
      Fancherre and Smith, 6L.
   Steatite. See Magnesium, silicate of.
   Sugar of lead. See Lead, acetate of.
   Sulphur;
      Cain, 6.
      Early, 2.
      Lake (Day), R.
      Mayall, 21.
      Mayall, 22.
      Day, M.
      Palmer and Orr, 21.
      Sellman (Brockbrough and Fagan), R.
      Thomson (Sievier), 6L.
      Lake (Chapman), 6L.
      Sutherland, R.
      Day, A.
      Day, M.
      Galloway, 6L.
      Dutjes, 6L.
      Berlin, R.
      Davies and Miller, M.
      Fancherre, 6L.
      Lake (Myers), 6L.
      Thomson and Watson, R.
      Jeffray and Doucette, 6L.
      Fish, 6L.
      Newton Gillespie, 6L.
      Blue Loftus, 6L.
   Sulphur, re-sulphuride of;
      Fancherre and Smith, 6L.
   Sulphuric acid;
      Day, 21.
      Smith and Challenger, M.
      Gale and Baynton, 6L.
   Talc;
      Figott, 2.
   Tallow;
      Newton (Mackay), M.

H 2

Compounds of india-rubber, &c.—*cont.*
   Tannin;
      Rostaing, 30.
   Tar;
      Newton (*Macbay*), 100.
   Tar, coal;
      Day, 24.
      Day, 54.
      Gale and Boyden, 63.
   Tin, chloride of;
      Day, 24.
   Tungsten oxide;
      Johnson (*Newbrough and Fagan*), 37.
   Turpentine;
      Johnson (*Newbrough and Fagan*), 37.
      Fanshawe and Smith, 44.
   Varnish;
      Mayall, 21.
   Vermillion;
      Rhodes and Miller, 77.
      Woodward (*Lippincott*), 102.
   Water;
      Forster and Heartfield, 26.
      Smith and Challenger, 36.
   Wax;
      Fanshawe and Smith, 44.
      Jenks, 99.
      Newton (*Macbay*), 100.
   Wax, paraffin;
      Coleman, 50.
   White lead. *See* Lead, carbonate of.
   Whiting. *See* Lime, carbonate of.
   Wire gauze;
      Anderson, 56.
      Joehumsen, 60.
      Ingram, 89.
   Wolfram;
      Johnson (*Newbrough and Fagan*), 37.
   Zapotine;
      Conybeare and Naphegyi, 85.
   Zinc;
      Mayall, 21.
   Zinc, oxide of;
      Quin, 4.
      Hooper, 14.

Compounds of india-rubber, &c.—*cont.*
   Zinc oxide of—*cont.*
      Newton (*Requa*), 95.
      Thomson and Connolly, 97.
      Woodward (*Lippincott*), 102.
   Zinc, sulphate of;
      Day, 24.

Colouring india-rubber, gutta percha, &c. *See also* Compounds of gutta percha, and compounds of india-rubber.
   Ford, 49.
   Rhodes and Miller, 77.
   Henderson, 93.
   Woodward (*Lippincott*), 102.

Cutting sheets into strips, threads, &c. *See* Thread, string, &c.

Deodorizing:
   Newton (*Requa*), 95.
   Catlow and Hoyle, 97.

Digesting. *See* Preparing, &c.

Dissolving. *See* Preparing, &c.

Fibres, mixing, with india-rubber, gutta percha, &c.:
   Poisnel, 14.
   Forster, 15.
   Wadsworth, 18.
   Forster and Heartfield, 26.
   Forster and Cow, 32.
   Davis and Struthers, 61.
   Moseley, 62.
   Talling and Seccombe, 88.
   Tongue (*Montaugé and Brandely*), 93.
   Mac Lellan, 98.
   Newton (*Macbay*), 100.

Filtering. *See* Preparing, &c.

Grinding. *See* Preparing, &c.

Hardening india-rubber, gutta percha, &c.:
   Aspinall, 27.
   Chapman, 61.
   Newton (*Menier*), 107.

Masticating. *See* Preparing, &c.

Moulding:
    Halsey, 13.
    Poisnell, 14.
    Taylor, 20.
    Mayall, 22.
    Thompson, 23.
    Forster and Heartfield, 26.
    Phillips, 30.
    Marsh, 30.
    Clark (*Lavater*), 33.
    Phillips, 34.
    Stewart, 46.
    Johnson (*Murfey*), 48.
    Stewart, 51.
    Stewart, 57.
    Jaques and Sterne, 64.
    Wise (*Huebscher*), 66.
    Wilbaux, 66.
    Harris, 67.
    Clark (*Lavater*), 71.
    Venman and Warne, 72.
    Hacking and Hacking, 74.
    Rhodes and Miller, 77.
    Truman, 81.
    Haseltine (*Read*), 83.
    Roberts, 85.
    Harris, 89.
    Magnus, 100.
    Woodward (*Lippincott*), 102.
    Lake (*Grasser*), 103.

Powdering and re-vulcanizing india-rubber:
    Moulton, 16.

Preparing gutta percha (treating the raw material):
    Cleansing;
        Sintzenich (*Reed*), 9.
        Truman, 39.
        Cattell, 73.
        Truman, 81.
        Deiss and Scaife, 105.
    Masticating;
        Truman, 45.
    Straining and Filtering;
        Deiss and Scaife, 105.

Preparing india-rubber (treating the raw material):
    Cleansing;
        Sintzenich (*Reed*), 9.
        Truman, 39.
        Deiss and Scaife, 105.
    Digesting;
        Woodcock, 75.
    Dissolving and reducing;
        Macartney, 45.

Preparing india-rubber, &c.—*cont.*
    Grinding and doughing;
        Heald, 106.
    Heating before masticating or dissolving;
        Hooper, 14.
    Straining and filtering;
        Deiss and Scaife, 105.

Preserving india-rubber, gutta percha, &c., from decay:
    Torrey, 77.
    Turner (*Righter*), 78.

Sheet india-rubber or gutta percha:
    Coating with flock;
        Macintosh and Boggett, 6.
    Coating with pumice stone;
        Macintosh and Boggett, 6.
    Expanding and treating;
        Macintosh and Boggett, 55.
    Making;
        Mayall, 20.
        Mayall, 21.
        Forster and Cow, 32.
        Wilkinson and Boss, 35.
        Smith and Challenger, 36.
        Walker, 39.
        Walker, 54.
        Parnacott, 59.
        Gale and Boyden, 63.
        Thomson and Watson, 88.
        Ingram, 89.
        Young, 94.
        Dunbar and Lothrop, 99.
    Partially cutting to produce ribbed appearance;
        Broadhurst, Swindells, and Kershaw, 41.
    Preparing by puncturing;
        Stocker, 19.
        Hunt (*Haskins*), 25.
        Broadhurst, Swindells, and Kershaw, 41.
        Johnson, (*Murfey*), 49.
    Ribbed appearance;
        Macintosh and Boggett, 6.

Solvents, &c.
    Alcohol used in conjunction with;
        Jeyes, 7.
        Sintzenich (*Reed*), 9.
        Warren, 52.
    Benzine or benzole;
        Sintzenich (*Reed*), 9.
        Forster and Heartfield, 28.
        Johnson (*Smart*), 61.

INDEX OF SUBJECT MATTER.

Solvents, &c.—*cont.*
  Camphine;
    Mayall, 20.
    Mayall, 21
    Mac Cartney, 45.

  Camphor;
    Mac Cartney, 45.

  Carbon, bi-sulphate of;
    Wadsworth, 18.
    Deiss and Scaife, 105.
    Stewart, 105.

  Carbon, bi-sulphuret of;
    Sintzenich (*Reed*), 9.

  Carbon, sulphuret of;
    Guenin (*Rigollot*), 2.
    Tongue (*Montaugé and Brandely*), 93.

  Hydrocarbons generally;
    Newton (*Macbay*), 100.
    Deiss and Scaife, 105.

  Naphtha;
    Guenin (*Rigollot*), 2.
    Quin, 4.
    Wadsworth, 18.
    Mayall, 20.
    Wilkinson and Boss, 35.
    Smith and Challenger, 36.
    Warren, 52.
    Walker, 58.
    Myerns, 65.
    Macintosh and Boggett, 69.
    Frankenburg, 84.

  Oils (coal tar);
    Quin, 4.

  Oils (essential);
    Deiss and Scaife, 105.

  Petroleum spirit;
    Guenin (*Rigollot*), 2.
    Tandy, 5.
    Jeyes, 7.

  Sulphuric ether;
    Johnson (*Smart*), 61.

  Turpentine;
    Gedge (*Crouzières*), 38.
    Thamsen (*Sörensen*), 42.
    Myerns, 65.
    Newton (*Macbay*), 100.

Solvents, recovering:
  Wadsworth, 18.
  Moseley, 67.
  Moseley, 74.
  Barrow, 98.
  Moseley, 101.
  Deiss and Scaife, 105.

Sponge or porous india-rubber or gutta percha:
  Forster and Heartfield, 26.
  Forster and Heartfield, 28.
  Sterne, Jaques, and Fanshawe, 31.

Straining and filtering. *See* **Preparing, &c.**

Substitutes for gutta percha:
  Don and Wright, 65.
  Rolls, 68.
  Conybeare and Naphegyi, 85.
  Lake (*Bell*), 86.
  Lake (*Bell*), 91.
  Newton (*Macbay*), 100.

Substitutes for india-rubber:
  Lake (*Day*), 8.
  Day, 24.
  Day, 54.
  Gale and Boyden, 63.
  Rolls, 68.
  Conybeare and Naphegyi, 85.
  Lake (*Bell*), 86.
  Lake (*Bell*), 91.
  Greening, 94.
  Newton (*Macbay*), 100.

Thread and string of gutta percha, india-rubber, &c.:
  Crossley, 2.
  Hamer, 4.
  Coles, Jaques, and Fanshawe, 16.
  Turner, 36.
  Turner, 37.
  Harris, 76.
  Gilbee (*Boëthius*), 82.

Tubing, hose, &c., apparatus for, and mode of making:
  Quin, 4.
  Luyckx, 5.
  Hamer, 7.
  Lake (*Torrey*), 8.
  Poisnel, 13.
  Mayall, 21.
  Bates, Bates, and Faulknor, 23.
  Forster and Cow, 32.
  Moulton, 42.
  Spill, 48.
  Quin and Eastham, 51.
  Sutherland, 53.
  Harris, 55.
  Lake (*De Wolfe*), 60.
  Quin, 72.
  Harrop, 75.
  Harris, 76.

Tubing, hose, &c.—*cont.*
   Turner (*Righter*), 78.
   Dodge, 78.
   Harris, 80.
   Quin, 81.
   Pieri, 87.
   Quin, 90.

Uniting or joining india-rubber or gutta percha:
   Tandy, 5.
   Gray, 17.
   Forster and Heartfield, 28.
   Myerns, 63.

Vulcanite:
   Colouring;
     Henderson, 93.
     Woodward (*Lippincott*), 102.
   Cutting screws of in lieu of moulding;
     Greenacre, 90.
   Hardening;
     Ryding, 1.
   Preparing;
     Tandy, 5.
     Pigott, 9.
   Shaping and moulding into pens;
     Baker, 62.
   Substitutes for;
     Jenks, 99.
     Conybeare and Naphegyi, 85.
   Uniting broken dough for;
     Tandy, 5.

Vulcanizing, apparatus for and mode of:
   Tandy, 5.
   Gray, 17.
   Gray and Hawkins, 26.
   Gray, 32.
   Jackson, 41.
   Harris, 62.
   Jamieson, 76.
   Young, 94.
   Mori, 99.
   Lake (*Grasser*), 103.

Washers and discs:
   Cutting;
     Grether and Bailey, 10.
     Ingram, 87.
   Embossing;
     Coles, Jaques, and Fanshawe, 15.
   Material for;
     Talling and Seccombe, 88.
     Ingram, 89.
   Moulding;
     Harris, 67.
   Preparing sheet rubber for;
     Stocker, 19.
     Harris, 76.

Waste india-rubber, gutta percha, &c, utilizing:
   Poisnel, 14.
   Turner, 36.
   Turner, 37.
   Mac Cartney, 45.
   Heinzerling and Liepmann, 97.

ERRATA.

Page 10, lines 2 and 3, *for* "bisulpheret" *read* "bisulphuret."

  „ 39, *for* "TRUEMAN" *read* "TRUMAN."

PATENT OFFICE.

All communications relating to Patents, Designs, and Trade Marks, to be addressed to Mr. H. READER LACK, *Comptroller-General of Patents, Designs, and Trade Marks*, at the Patent Office, 25, Southampton Buildings, Chancery Lane, London, W.C.

LIST OF WORKS printed by order of THE PATENT OFFICE, and sold at the Sale Branch, 38, Cursitor Street, Chancery Lane, London, E.C.

I.

1. SPECIFICATIONS of PATENTS for INVENTIONS, DISCLAIMERS, &c., enrolled under the Old Law, from A.D. 1617 to Oct. 1852, comprised in 13,561 Blue Books, or 690 thick vols. imp. 8vo. Total cost price about 600*l*.

2. SPECIFICATIONS of INVENTIONS, DISCLAIMERS, &c., deposited and filed under the Patent Law Amendment Act, 1852, from Oct. 1, 1852, to December 31, 1883, comprised in 125,613 Blue Books, or 3,005 thick vols. imp. 8vo. Total cost price about 3,490*l*.

II.

The prices of the Indexes of Patents, Old and New Law for the years 1617 to 1870, have been reduced to the following uniform rates.

INDEXES to PATENTS of INVENTION under the Old Law, from A.D. 1617 to October 1852:—

CHRONOLOGICAL INDEX. 2 vols. (1554 pages.) Price 10s.; by post, 13s. 2d.

ALPHABETICAL INDEX. 1 vol. (647 pages.) Price 5s.; by post, 6s. 5d.

SUBJECT-MATTER INDEX. 2 vols. (970 pages.) Second Edition. Price 10s.; by post, 12s. 8d.

REFERENCE INDEX of PATENTS, pointing out the Office in which each enrolled Specification may be consulted and the Books in which Specifications, Law Proceedings connected with Inventions, &c. have been noticed. 1 vol. (710 pages.) Second Edition. 1862. Price 5s.; by post, 6s. 5d.

APPENDIX to the REFERENCE INDEX, containing abstracts from such of the early Patents and Signet Bills as describe the nature of the Invention. 1 vol. (91 pages.) Price 1s.; by post, 1s. 6d.

INDEXES of APPLICATIONS for PATENTS and PATENTS GRANTED under the Patent Law Amendment Act, 1852:—

CHRONOLOGICAL INDEXES:—

For 1852 (Oct. 1—Dec. 31) and 1853. (258 pages.) Price 2s.; by post, 3s.

	s. d.	s. d.
[1854, 1855, 1856, 1857, 1858 *out of print*.]		
1859 (196 pages), price	2 0; by post	2 7
1860 (209 „)	„ 2 0 „	2 7
1861 (215 „)	„ 2 0 „	2 7
1862 (237 „)	„ 2 0 „	2 8
1863 (220 „)	„ 2 0 „	2 7
1864 (222 „)	„ 2 0 „	2 7
1865 (230 „)	„ 2 0 „	2 7
1866 (239 „)	„ 2 0 „	2 8
1867 (254 „)	„ 2 0 „	2 8
1868 (274 „)	„ 2 0 „	2 8

ALPHABETICAL INDEXES:—

For 1852 (Oct. 1—Dec. 31) and 1853. (181 pages.) Price 2s. 6d. by post, 3s. 2d.

	s. d.	s. d.
1854 (119 pages), price	2 6; by post	3 1
1855 (129 „)	„ 2 6 „	3 1
1856 (143 „)	„ 2 6 „	3 1
[1857, 1858, 1859, 1860, 1861, 1862 *out of print*.]		
1863 (218 „)	„ 2 6; by post	3 2
1864 (220 „)	„ 2 6 „	3 2

ALPHABETICAL INDEXES—cont.

	s.	d.		s.	d.
1865 (236 pages), price	2	6	,,	3	2
1866 (243 ,,) ,,	2	6	,,	3	2
1867 (258 ,,) ,,	2	6	,,	3	2
1868 (291 ,,) ,,	2	6	,,	3	4
1869 (272 ,,) ,,	2	6	,,	3	3
1870 (242 ,,) ,,	2	6	,,	3	2
1871 (52 ,,) ,,	2	0	,,	2	1½
1872 (61 ,,) ,,	2	0	,,	2	1½
1873 (62 ,,) ,,	2	0	,,	2	2

[1874, 1875 *out of print.*]

| 1876 (135 ,,) ,, | 2 | 0 | ,, | 2 | 3 |

[1877, 1878, 1879, 1880, 1881 *out of print.*]

1882 (183 ,,) ,,	2	0	,,	2	4½
1883 (189 ,,) ,,	2	0	,,	2	4
*1884 { (Part I., Jan. 1 to June 30) }	0	3	,,	0	8
,, { (Part II., July 1 to Sep. 30) }	0	3	,,	0	5

SUBJECT-MATTER INDEXES:—

For 1852 (Oct. 1—Dec. 31). (132 pages.) Price 5*s.*; by post, 5*s.* 7*d.*

	s.	d.		s.	d.
1853 (291 pages), price	5	0 ; by post	5	11
1854 (311 ,,) ,,	5	0	,,	6	0
1855 (311 ,,) ,,	5	0	,,	5	11

[1856, 1857, 1858, 1859, 1860, 1861, 1862, 1863, 1864 *out of print.*]

| 1865 (474 ,,) ,, | 5 | 0 | ,, | 6 | 1 |
| 1866 (465 ,,) ,, | 5 | 0 | ,, | 6 | 0 |

[1867, 1868, 1869, 1870, 1871, 1872, 1873, 1874, 1875 *out of print.*]

| 1876 (143 ,,) ,, | 2 | 0 | ,, | 2 | 3½ |

[*2nd edition.*]

| 1877 (159 ,,) ,, | 2 | 0 | ,, | 2 | 3½ |

[*2nd edition.*]

[1878 *out of print.*]

1879 (187 ,,) ,,	2	0	,,	2	4½
1880 (209 ,,) ,,	2	0	,,	2	5
1881 (238 ,,) ,,	2	0	,,	2	5
1882 (99 ,,) ,,	2	0	,,	2	2½

[*For temporary use.*]

| 1883 (97 ,,) ,, | 2 | 0 | ,, | 2 | 2½ |

[*For temporary use.*]

| *1884 (Jan. 1 to Sep. 30) | 0 | 3 | ,, | 0 | 7 |

---

* See notice on page 18.

III.

'ABRIDGMENTS (in Classes and Chronologically arranged) of SPECIFICATIONS of PATENTED INVENTIONS, from the earliest enrolled to those published under the Act of 1852.

These books are of 12mo. size, and each is limited to inventions of one class only. They are so arranged as to form at once a Chronological, Alphabetical, and Subject-matter Index to the class to which they relate. Inventors are strongly recommended, before applying for Letters Patent, to consult the classes of Abridgments of Specifications which relate to the subjects of their inventions, and by the aid of these works to select the Specifications they may consider it necessary to examine in order to ascertain if their inventions are new. The *preface* of each volume explains (in most cases) the scope of the series of Abridgments which it contains.

The following series of Abridgments (except Nos. 5, 6, 9, 10, 12, 13, 14, 15, 16, 19, 20, 26, 33, 34, 37, 47, 53, 56, 61, 62, 70, 72, 75, 79, 80, 81, 82, 85, 86, 87, 89, 90, 91, 92, 93, 94, 95, 96, 97, and 100) do not extend beyond the end of the year 1866; but it is intended, to continue them to the end of the year 1876. Until that is done the Inventor can continue his search by the aid of the Subject Matter Indexes and the Specifications.

The classes already published are,—

1. DRAINS AND SEWERS; INCLUDING THE MANUFACTURE OF DRAIN TILES AND PIPES, price 1s., by post 1s. 2d.

2. SEWING AND EMBROIDERING (*2nd edition*), price 1s. 6d., by post 1s. 9d.

3. MANURE.—Part I., A.D. 1721-1855, price 4d., by post 5d.—Part II., A.D. 1856-1866, price 1s. 2d., by post 1s. 3½d.

4. PRESERVATION OF FOOD.—Part I., A.D. 1691-1855, price 4d., by post 5d.—Part II., A.D. 1856-1866, price 6d., by post 7d.

5. MARINE PROPULSION (excluding sails).—Parts I., II., & III., A.D. 1618-1857, price 1s. 10d., by post 2s. 1d.—Part IV., A.D. 1857-1866, price 1s. 10d., by post 2s. 2d. *Continued from* A.D. 1866, *in combination with* STEERING AND MANŒUVRING VESSELS [Series No. 75], *under the title of*—
   MARINE PROPULSION (including steering and manœuvring vessels; but excluding sails). Part II., A.D., 1867-1876, price 1s. 6d., by post 1s. 8½d.

6. MANUFACTURE OF IRON AND STEEL.—Part I., A.D. 1620-1866 (*2nd edition*), price 3s. 6d., by post 4s. 0½d.—Part II., A.D. 1867-1876, price 4s. 6d., by post 5s. 2½d.

7. AIDS TO LOCOMOTION, price 6d., by post 7d.

8. STEAM CULTURE, price 8d., by post 9½d.

9. WATCHES, CLOCKS AND OTHER TIMEKEEPERS.—Part I., A.D. 1661-1856, price 8d., by post 9½d.—Part Ia., A.D. 1857-1866, price 8d., by post 9½d.—Part II., A.D. 1867-1876, price 8d., by post 9d.

10. FIRE-ARMS AND OTHER WEAPONS, AMMUNITION, AND ACCOUTREMENTS.—Part I., A.D. 1588-1858, price 1s. 4d., by post 1s. 7½d.—Part Ia., A.D. 1858-1866, price 2s. 2d., by post 2s. 6d. *Continued from* A.D. 1866 *in two Divisions, as follow:*

    FIRE-ARMS, AMMUNITION, &c.:
        DIVISION I., FIRE-ARMS AND SIMILAR WEAPONS.— Part II., A.D. 1867-1876, price 4s. 6d., by post 5s. 4½d.
        DIVISION II., CARTRIDGES, PROJECTILES, AND EXPLOSIVES.— Part II., A.D. 1867-1876, price 2s. 6d., by post 2s. 10½d.

11. MANUFACTURE OF PAPER, PASTEBOARD, AND PAPIER-MÂCHÉ.—Part I., A.D. 1665-1857, price 10d., by post 1s.—Part II., A.D. 1858-1866 (2nd edition), price 1s. 4d., by post 1s. 6½d.

12. CUTTING, FOLDING, AND ORNAMENTING PAPER; (including the general treatment of paper after its manufacture).—Part I. A.D. 1636-1866.— (2nd edition), price 2s., by post 2s. 3d.—Part II. A.D. 1867-1876, price 1s. 6d., by post 1s. 8½d.

13. LETTERPRESS AND SIMILAR PRINTING (excluding electrotelegraphic and photographic printing).—Part I., A.D. 1617-1857, price 2s. 8d., by post 3s. 3d.—Part Ia. A.D. 1858-1866. (2nd edition). price 2s. 6d., by post 2s. 9d.—Part II., A.D. 1867-1876, price 2s. 3d., by post 2s. 7½d.

14. BLEACHING, DYEING, AND PRINTING CALICO AND OTHER FABRICS AND YARNS.—Part I., A.D. 1617-1857, price 3s. 4d., by post 4s. 1d.—Part II. A.D. 1858-1866 (2nd edition), price 3s. 6d., by post 3s. 10d.—Part III. A.D. 1867-1876, price 1s. 6d., by post 1s. 9d.

15. ELECTRICITY AND MAGNETISM, THEIR GENERATION AND APPLICATIONS.— Part I., A.D. 1766-1857, price 3s. 2d., by post 3s. 11d.—Part Ia., A.D. 1858-1866 (2nd edition) price 2s. 8d., by post 3s. 2d. For continuations from A.D. 1867-1876 see series Nos. 92, 93, 94, 95, 96 and 97.

16. PREPARATION OF INDIA-RUBBER AND GUTTA-PERCHA—Part I., A D. 1791-1866 (2nd edition), price 1s. 2d., by post 1s. 4½d.—Part II., A.D. 1867-1876, price 1s., by post 1s. 1½d.

17. PRODUCTION AND APPLICATIONS OF GAS (excepting gas engines).—Part I., A.D. 1681-1858, price 2s. 4d., by post 2s. 11d.—Part II., A.D. 1859-1866 (2nd edition), price 2s. 4d., by post 2s. 8½d.

18. METALS AND ALLOYS (excepting Iron and Steel), Part I., A.D. 1623-1859, price 1s. 10d., by post 2s. 3½d.—Part Ia., A.D. 1860-1866, price 1s. 6d., by post 1s. 8½d.

19. PHOTOGRAPHY.—Part I., A.D. 1839-1859, price 8d., by post 10d.—Part II., A.D. 1860-1866 (2nd edition), price 10d., by post 11½d.—Part III., A.D. 1867-1876, price 9d., by post 10½d.

20. WEAVING.—Part I., A.D. 1620-1859, price 4s., by post 4s. 11½d.—Part Ia., A.D. 1860-1866, price 2s. 8d., by post 3s. 1d.—Part II., A.D. 1867-1876, price 3s. 6d., by post 3s. 11½d.

21. SHIP BUILDING, REPAIRING, SHEATHING, LAUNCHING, &c.—Part I., A.D. 1618-1860, price 2s. 4d., by post 2s. 11d.—Part II., A.D. 1861-1866, price 2s. 6d., by post 2s. 11d.

22. BRICKS AND TILES.—Part I., A.D. 1619-1860, price 1s., by post 1s. 3½d.—Part II. A.D. 1861-1866, price 8d., by post 9½d.

23. PLATING OR COATING METALS WITH METALS.—Part I., A.D. 1637-1860, price 10d., by post 1s. 0½d.—Part II., A.D. 1861-1866 (2nd edition), price 6d. by post 7d.

24. POTTERY.—Part I., A.D. 1626-1861, price 10d., by post 1s.—Part II., A.D. 1862-1866, price 6d., by post 7d.

25. MEDICINE, SURGERY, AND DENTISTRY (2nd edition), price 1s. 10d., by post 2s. 1½d.

26. MUSIC AND MUSICAL INSTRUMENTS, Part I., A.D. 1694-1866 (2nd edition), price 1s. 10d., by post 2s. 1½d.—Part II., A.D. 1867-1876, price 1s. 6d., by post 1s. 8d.

27. OILS, FATS, LUBRICANTS, CANDLES, AND SOAP (2nd edition), price 2s.10d., by post 3s. 4d.

28. SPINNING; INCLUDING THE PREPARATION OF FIBROUS MATERIALS, AND THE DOUBLING OF YARNS AND THREADS.—Part I., A.D. 1624-1863 (out of print).—Part II., A.D. 1864-1866, price 2s. by post 2s. 4d.

29. LACE-MAKING, KNITTING, NETTING, BRAIDING, AND PLAITING (including also the manufacture of fringe and chenille), (2nd edition), price 7s., by post 7s. 7d.

30. PREPARATION AND COMBUSTION OF FUEL (out of print).

31. RAISING, LOWERING, AND WEIGHING (2nd edition), price 3s. 8d., by post 4s. 3½d.

32. HYDRAULICS (2nd edition), price 4s. 8d., by post 5s. 5d.

33. RAILWAYS.—Part I., A.D. 1803-1866 (*2nd edition*). price 2s. 6d., by post 2s. 11d.—Part II., A.D. 1867-1876, price 7s. 6d., by post 8s. 2d.
34. SADDLERY, HARNESS, STABLE FITTINGS, &c.—Part I., A.D. 1625-1866, price 1s., by post 1s. 2d.—Part II., A.D. 1867-1876, price 1s. 2d., by post 1s. 4d.
35. ROADS AND WAYS, price 1s., by post 1s. 2d.
36. BRIDGES, VIADUCTS, AND AQUEDUCTS, price 10d., by post 1s.
37. WRITING INSTRUMENTS AND MATERIALS.—PART I., A.D. 1635-1866, price 1s. 4d., by post 1s. 7d.—PART II., A.D. 1867-1876, price 1s., by post 1s. 1¼d.
38. RAILWAY SIGNALS AND COMMUNICATING APPARATUS (*out of print*).
39. FURNITURE AND UPHOLSTERY price 2s., by post 2s. 4d.
40. ACIDS, ALKALIES, OXIDES, AND SALTS, price 3s. 8d., by post 4s. 3d.
41. AERONAUTICS, price 4d., by post 5d.
42. PREPARATION AND USE OF TOBACCO, price 10d., by post 1s.
43. BOOKS, PORTFOLIOS, CARD-CASES, &c., price 10d., by post, 1s.
44. LAMPS, CANDLESTICKS, CHANDELIERS, AND OTHER ILLUMINATING APPARATUS (excluding inventions for lighting by gas or electricty), price 2s. 6d., by post 2s. 10½d.
45. NEEDLES AND PINS, price 6d., by post 7d.
46. CARRIAGES AND OTHER VEHICLES FOR RAILWAYS, price 5s. 6d., by post 6s. 4d.
47. UMBRELLAS, PARASOLS, AND WALKING STICKS.—Part I., A.D. 1780-1866, price 10d., by post 11¼d.—Part II., A.D. 1867-1876, price 1s., by post 1s. 1¼d.
48. SUGAR, price 1s. 10d., by post 2s. 1¼d.
49. STEAM ENGINE.—Part I. (in 2 vols.), A.D. 1618-1859, price 9s. 4d., by pos 10s. 10½d.—Part II. (in 2 vols.), A.D. 1860-1866, price 4s. 10d. by post 5s. 7d.
50. PAINTS, COLOURS, AND VARNISHES, price 1s. 10d., by post 2s. 1¼d.
51. TOYS, GAMES, AND EXERCISES, price 1s., by post 1s. 2d.
52. VENTILATION, price 1s. 10d., by post 2s. 0½d.
53. FARRIERY; INCLUDING THE MEDICAL AND SURGICAL TREATMENT OF ANIMALS.—Part I. A.D. 1719-1866, price 1s., by post 1s. 1¼d.—Part II. A.D. 1867-1876, price 1s., by post 1s. 1¼d.
54. ARTISTS' INSTRUMENTS AND MATERIALS, price 10d., by post 1s.
55. SKINS, HIDES, AND LEATHER, price 1s. 6d., by post 1s. 8½d.
56. PREPARING AND CUTTING CORK; BOTTLING LIQUIDS; SECURING AND OPENING BOTTLES, &c.—Part I., A.D. 1777-1866, price 1s 6d., by post 1s. 9d.—Part II., A.D. 1867-1876, price 2s. 6d., by post 2s. 8½d.
57. BRUSHING AND SWEEPING, price 1s., by post 1s. 2d.
58. NAILS, RIVETS, BOLTS, SCREWS, NUTS, AND WASHERS, price 1s.,8d., by post 1s. 11½d.
59. HINGES, HINGE JOINTS, AND DOOR SPRINGS, price 8d., by post 9½d.
60. LOCKS, LATCHES, BOLTS, AND SIMILAR FASTENINGS, price 1s. 6d., by post 1s. 9d.
61. COOKING, BREAD-MAKING, AND THE PREPARATION OF CONFECTIONERY.—Part I. A.D. 1634-1866, price 1s. 10d., by post 2s. 1¼d.—Part II. A.D. 1867-1876, price 1s. 6d., by post 1s. 8½d.
62. AIR, GAS, AND OTHER MOTIVE POWER ENGINES.—Part I., A.D. 1635-1866, price 1s. 10d., by post 2s. 1¼d.—Part II., A.D. 1867-1876, price 3s. 6d., by post 4s. 0½d.
63. WATER CLOSETS, EARTH CLOSETS, URINALS, &c., price 10d., by post 1s.
64. SAFES, STRONG ROOMS, TILLS, AND SIMILAR DEPOSITORIES, price 6d., by post 7d.
65. WEARING APPAREL. DIVISION I.—HEAD COVERINGS, price 1s. 4d., post 1s. 6½d.

66. WEARING APPAREL. DIVISION II.—BODY COVERINGS, price 2s. 4d., by post 2s. 8½d.

67. WEARING APPAREL. DIVISION III.—FOOT COVERINGS, price 1s. 10d., by post 2s. 1½d.

68. WEARING APPAREL. DIVISION IV.—DRESS FASTENINGS AND JEWELLERY, price 2s. 10d., by post 3s. 1½d.

69. ANCHORS, price 6d. by post 7d.

70. METALLIC PIPES AND TUBES.—Part I., A.D. 1741-1866, price 1s. 8d., by post 1s. 11d.—Part II., A.D. 1867-1876, price 1s. 3d., by post 1s. 5½d.

71. MINING, QUARRYING, TUNNELLING, AND WELL-SINKING, price 1s. 4d., by post 1s. 6½d.

72. MILKING, CHURNING, AND CHEESE-MAKING.—Part I., A.D. 1777-1866, price 6d., by post 7d.—Part II., A.D. 1867-1876, price 8d., by post 9d.

73. MASTS, SAILS, RIGGING, &c.; INCLUDING APPARATUS FOR RAISING AND LOWERING SHIPS' BOATS, price 1s., by post 1s. 2d.

74. CASKS AND BARRELS, price 8d., by post 9½d.

75. STEERING AND MANŒUVRING VESSELS, Part I., A.D. 1763-1866, price 1s. by post 1s. 2d. *Continued from A.D. 1866, in combination with* MARINE PROPULSION (excluding sails) [Series No. 5], *under the title of*—
MARINE PROPULSION (including steering and manœuvring vessels; but excluding sails), Part II., A.D. 1867-1876, price 1s. 6d., by post 1s. 8½d.

76. OPTICAL, MATHEMATICAL, AND OTHER PHILOSOPHICAL INSTRUMENTS, INCLUDING NAUTICAL, ASTRONOMICAL, AND METEOROLOGICAL INSTRUMENTS, price 2s. 10d. by post 3s. 2d.

77. HARBOURS, DOCKS, CANALS, &c., price 1s. 2d., by post 1s. 4d.

78. GRINDING GRAIN AND DRESSING FLOUR AND MEAL, price 2s. 4d., by post 2s. 6½d.

79. PURIFYING AND FILTERING WATER.—Part I., A.D. 1675-1866, price 1s. 2d., by post 1s. 3½d.—Part II., A.D. 1867-1876, price 6d., by post 7d.

80. ARTIFICIAL LEATHER, FLOORCLOTH, OILCLOTH, OILSKIN, AND OTHER WATERPROOF FABRICS.—Part I., A.D. 1627-1866, price 1s. 10d., by post 2s. 0½d.—Part II., A.D. 1867-1876, price 1s. 6d., by post 1s. 8d.

81. AGRICULTURE. DIVISION I.—FIELD IMPLEMENTS (including methods of tilling and irrigating land).—Part I, A.D. 1618-1866, price 5s. 8d., by post 6s. 2½d.—Part II. A.D. 1867-1876, price 2s., by post 2s. 3½d.

82. AGRICULTURE. DIVISION II.—BARN AND FARMYARD IMPLEMENTS (including the cleansing, drying, and storing of grain).—Part I., A.D. 1636-1866, price 3s., by post 3s. 3½d.—Part II., A.D. 1867-1876, price 1s. 3d., by post, 1s. 5d.

83. AGRICULTURE. DIVISION III.—AGRICULTURAL AND TRACTION ENGINES, price 1s. 6d., by post, 1s. 7½d.

84. TRUNKS, PORTMANTEAUS, BOXES, AND BAGS, price 1s., by post 1s. 1½d.

85. ICE-MAKING MACHINES, ICE SAFES, AND ICE HOUSES (including the use of freezing agents for preserving alimentary substances).—Part I., A.D. 1819-1866, price 6d., by post 7d.—Part II., A.D. 1867-1876, price 1s. 6d., by post 1s. 7½d.

86. UNFERMENTED BEVERAGES, AERATED LIQUIDS, MINERAL WATERS, &c. —Part I., A.D. 1774-1866, price 1s., by post 1s. 1½d.—Part II., A.D. 1867-1876, price 6d., by post 7d.

87. TEA, COFFEE, CHICORY, CHOCOLATE, COCOA, &c.—Part I., A.D. 1704-1866, price 8d., by post 9d.—Part II., A.D. 1867-1876, price 6d., by post 7d.

88. FIRE ENGINES, EXTINGUISHERS, ESCAPES, ALARMS, &c. (including fireproof dresses and fabrics), price 2s., by post 2s. 2½d.

89. WASHING AND WRINGING MACHINES.—Part I., A.D. 1691-1866, price 1s. 6d., by post 1s. 8d.—Part II., A.D. 1867-1876, price 9d., by post 10½d.

90. CHAINS, CHAIN CABLES, &c.—Part I., A.D. 1634-1866, price 9d., by post 10d. Part II., A.D. 1867-1876, price 6d., by post 7d.

91. DRESSING AND FINISHING WOVEN FABRICS, AND MANUFACTURING FELTED FABRICS (including folding, winding, measuring, and packing).—Part I., A.D. 1620-1866, price 3s. 6d., by post 3s. 10½d.—Part II., A.D. 1867-1876, price 1s. 6d., by post 1s. 8½d.

92. ELECTRICITY AND MAGNETISM. DIVISION I.—GENERATION OF ELECTRICITY AND MAGNETISM, A.D. 1766-1866.—Part I., see Series No. 15.;—Part II., A.D. 1867-1876, price 1s., by post 1s. 1½d.

93. ELECTRICITY AND MAGNETISM. DIVISION II.—CONDUCTING AND INSULATING, A.D. 1766-1866.—Part I., see Series, No. 15.—Part II., A.D. 1867-1876, price 1s., by post 1s. 1½d.

94. ELECTRICITY AND MAGNETISM. DIVISION III.—TRANSMITTING AND RECEIVING SIGNALS, CONTROLLING MECHANICAL ACTION AND EXHIBITING ELECTRIC EFFECTS, A.D. 1766-1866.—Part I., see Series No. 15.;—Part II., A.D. 1867-1876, price 2s., by post, 2s. 3d.

95. ELECTRICITY AND MAGNETISM. DIVISION IV.—ELECTRIC LIGHTING, IGNITING, AND HEATING.—Parts I. and II. (in one vol.) A.D. 1869-1876, price 9d., by post 10½d.

96. ELECTRICITY AND MAGNETISM. DIVISION V.—ELECTRO-DEPOSITION AND ELECTROLYSIS.—Parts I. and II. (in one vol.) A.D. 1805-1876, price 1s. 6d., by post 1s. 8½d.

97. ELECTRICITY AND MAGNETISM. DIVISION VI.—ELECTRIC MOTIVE POWER ENGINES AND SIMILAR APPARATUS.—Parts I. and II. (in one vol.) A.D. 1837-1876, price 7d., by post 8d.

98. CARRIAGES AND OTHER VEHICLES FOR COMMON ROADS, price 5s., by post 5s. 8½d.

99. BREWING, WINE-MAKING, AND DISTILLING ALCOHOLIC LIQUIDS, price 3s. 6d., by post 3s. 10d.

100. STARCH, GUM, SIZE, GLUE, AND OTHER STIFFENING AND ADHESIVE MATERIALS.—Parts I. and II. (in one vol.) A.D. 1717-1876, price 2s., by post 2s. 3d.

A Key to the contents of the above volumes of Abridgments will be found on pages 30 to 32.

IV.

OFFICIAL JOURNAL of the PATENT OFFICE, published on the evenings of Tuesday and Friday in each week. Price 2d.; by Post, 3d. Annual Subscription, including postage, 25s. which may be remitted by Post Office Order, made payable at the Post Office, Chancery Lane, to Mr. H. Reader Lack, Comptroller-General of Patents.

Subscriptions to the Official Journal will not be received for a shorter period than three months, such period to commence on either of the following dates:—

| 1st January, | 1st July, or |
| 1st April, | 1st October. |

Annual subscriptions to date from 1st January in each year. All subscriptions must be paid in advance.

CONTENTS OF OFFICIAL JOURNAL.

1. Applications for Patents.
2. Acceptances of Provisional Specifications.
3. Acceptances of Complete Specifications.
4. Patents sealed.
5. Patents on which the annual renewal fee has been paid.
6. Patents which have become void through non-payment of annual renewal fee.
7. Patents on which the 50*l.* renewal fee has been paid.
8. Patents which have become void through non-payment of 50*l.* renewal fee.
9. Patents on which the 100*l.* renewal fee has been paid.
10. Patents which have become void through non-payment of 100*l.* renewal fee.
11. Applications to amend Specifications.
12. Amendments of Specifications.
13. Compulsory licenses.
14. Extensions of Patents.
15. Revocations of Patents.
16. Designs Registered.
17. Trade Marks advertised.
18. Trade Marks registered.
19. Official notices, advertisements, and rules.
20. Weekly price lists of printed Specifications, &c.
21. Occasional supplement of Reports of Patent Law Cases.

V.

1. **PATENTS, DESIGNS, and TRADE MARKS ACT, 1883:**
   Copies of the Act and of the Rules under the Act can be purchased at the Patent Office Sale Branch, 38, Cursitor Street, Chancery Lane.
   Patents, Designs, and Trade Marks Act, 1883. Price 1*s.* 7½*d.*, by post, 1*s.* 9*d.*
   Patents Rules. Price 6*d.*, by post 7*d.*
   Designs Rules. Price 4*d.*, by post 4½*d.*
   Trade Marks Rules. Price 6*d.*, by post 7*d.*

2. **CATALOGUE of the LIBRARY of the PATENT OFFICE** arranged alphabetically, in two volumes.
   Vol. I.—Authors. Price, 31*s.* 6*d.*; by post, 33*s.*
   Vol. II.—Subjects. Price 15*s.* 8*d.*, by post 16*s.* 9*d.*

3. **INDEX to ALL INVENTIONS PATENTED in ENGLAND** from 1617 to 1854 inclusive, arranged under the greatest number of heads, with parallel references to INVENTIONS and DISCOVERIES described in the scientific works of VARIOUS NATIONS, as classified by Professor Schubarth. By B. WOODCROFT, F.R.S. Price 1*s.*; by post, 1*s.* 1*d.*
   The foreign works thus indexed form a portion of the Library of the Patent Office, where they may be consulted.

4. **SUPPLEMENT to the SERIES of LETTERS PATENT and SPECIFICATIONS,** from A.D. 1617 to Oct. 1852; consisting for the most part of Reprints of scarce Pamphlets, descriptive of the early patented Inventions comprised in that Series.

   CONTENTS.

   1. Metallica; or the Treatise of Metallica, briefly comprehending the doctrine of diverse new metallical inventions, &c. By SIMON STURTEVANT. (*Letters Patent*, dated 29*th February* 1611.) Price 1*s.* 4*d.*; by post, 1*s.* 5*d.*

2. A Treatise of Metallica, but not that which was published by Mr. Simon Sturtevant, upon his Patent, &c. By JOHN ROVENZON. (*Letters Patent granted A.D.* 1612.) Price 4d.; by post, 4½d.

3. A Commission directed to Sir Richard Wynne and others to inquire upon oath whether NICHOLAS PAGE or Sir NICHOLAS HALSE was the first inventor of certaine kilnes for the drying of malt, &c. &c. (*Letters Patent, Nos.* 71b *and* 85, *respectively dated* 10*th July* 1634, *and* 23*rd July* 1635.) Price 2d.; by post, 2½d.

4. DUD DUDLEY'S Metallum Martis; or iron made with pit-coale, sea-coale, &c. (*Letters Patent, Nos.* 18 *and* 117, *respectively dated* 22*nd February* 1620, *and* 2*nd May* 1638.) Price 8d.; by post, 8½d.

5. Description of the nature and working of the Patent Waterscoop Wheels invented by WILLIAM WHELER, as compared with the raising wheels now in common use. By J. B. W. Translated from the Dutch by Dr. Tolhausen. (*Letters Patent, No.* 127, *dated* 24*th June* 1642.) Price 2s.; by post, 2s. 1½d.

6. An exact and true definition of the stupendous Water-commanding Engine invented by the Right Honourable (and deservedly to be praised and admired) EDWARD SOMERSET, Lord Marquis of WORCESTER, &c., &c. (*Stat.* 15 *Car. II. c.* 12. *A.D.* 1663.) Price 4d.; by post, 4½d.

7. Navigation improved; or the art of rowing ships of all rates in calms with a more easy, swift, and steady motion than oars can. By THOMAS SAVERY. (*Letters Patent, No.* 347, *dated* 10*th Jan.* 1696.) Price 1s.; by post, 1s. 0½d.

8. The Miner's Friend; or an engine to raise water by fire, described, &c. By THOMAS SAVERY. (*Letters Patent, No.* 356, *dated* 25*th July* 1698, *and Stat.* 10 *&* 11 *Will. III. No.* 61, *A.D.* 1699.) Price 1s.; by post, 1s. 1d.

9. Specimina Ichnographica; or a brief narrative of several new inventions and experiments, particularly the navigating a ship in a calm, &c. By JOHN ALLEN, M.D. (*Letters Patent No.* 513, *dated* 7*th August* 1729.) Price 8d.; by post, 9d.

10. A description and draught of a new-invented Machine for carrying vessels or ships out of or into any harbour, port, or river against wind and tide, or in a calm, &c. By JONATHAN HULLS. (*Letters Patent, No.* 556, *dated* 21*st December* 1736.) Price 8d.; by post, 9d.

11. An historical account of a new method for extracting the foul air out of ships, &c., with the description and draught of the machines by which it is performed, &c. By SAMUEL SUTTON, the Inventor. To which are annexed two relations given thereof to the Royal Society by Dr. Mead and Mr. Watson. (*Letters Patent, No.* 602, *dated* 16*th March* 1744.) Price 1s.; by post, 1s. 1d.

12. The letter of Master WILLIAM DRUMMOND for the construction of machines, weapons, and engines of war for attack or defence by land or sea, &c. Dated the 29th September 1626. (*Scotch Patent, temp. Car. II.*) Price 4d.; by post, 4½d.

13. Contributions to the History of the Steam Engine, being two deeds relating to the erection by Messrs. Boulton and Watt of steam engines on the United Mines at Gwennap, Cornwall, and at Werneth Colliery, near Oldham, Lancashire. From the originals in the Patent Office Library. Price 10d., by post, 10½d.

A FREE LIBRARY and READING ROOMS are open to the Public daily, from 10 till 4 o'clock, in the Patent Office, 25, Southampton Buildings, Chancery Lane. In addition to the printed Specifications, Indexes, Abridgments, and other Patent publications, the Library includes a collection of the Patent Laws and Regulations and Trade Marks Laws and Regulations of Foreign States and of the British Colonies; it also contains the leading British and Foreign Scientific Journals and text-books in the various departments of science and art.

Complete sets of the Patent Office publications (each set including more than 3,960 volumes and costing for printing and paper upwards of £4,150) have been presented to the authorities of the most important towns in the kingdom, on condition that the works shall be rendered daily accessible to the public, for reference or for copying, free of all charge. The following list gives the names of the towns, and shows the place of deposit of each set of the works thus presented:—

Aberdeen (*Mechanics' Institution*).
Belfast (*Queen's College*).
Birmingham (*Central Free Library—Reference Department, Ratcliff Pl.*).
Blackburn (*Free Library and Museum, Library Street*).
Bolton-le-Moors (*Public Library, Exchange Buildings*).
Bradford, Yorkshire (*Public Free Library*).
Brighton (*Free Library, Town Hall*).
Bristol (*Free Library, King Street*).
Burnley (*Office of the Burnley Improvement Commissioners*).
Bury. (*Athenæum*).
Carlisle (*Pub. Free Lib^y, Police Office*).
Cork (*Royal Cork Instⁿ, Nelson Place*).
Crewe (*Railway Station*).
Derby (*Free Library and Museum*).
Dublin (*National Library of Ireland, Kildare St.*).
Dundalk (*Free Library*).
Glasgow (*Stirling's Lib^y, Miller St.*).
Halifax (*Town Hall*).
Huddersfield (*Corporation Offices*).
Hull (*Mechanics' Inst., George St.*).
Ipswich (*Museum Library, Museum Street*).
Keighley (*Mechanics' Inst., North St.*).
Kidderminster (*Public Free Library, Public Buildings, Vicar Street*).
Leamington (*Free Public Library, Bath Street*).
Leeds (*Public Library, Infirmary Buildings*).
Leicester (*Free Library, Wellington Street*).
Liverpool (*Free Public Library, William Brown Street*).
London (*British Museum*).
Macclesfield (*Useful Know. Society*).
Manchester (*Free Reference Library, King Street*).
Newcastle-upon-Tyne (*Public Library, New Bridge Street*).
Newport, Monmouth (*Commercial Room, Town Hall*).
Northampton (*Museum, Guildhall*).
Nottingham (*Free Public Libraries*).
Oldham (*School of Arts and Sciences Lyceum*).
Plymouth (*Free Library*).
Preston, Lancashire (*Dr. Shepherd's Library, Cross St.*).
Reading (*Literary, Scientific, and Mechanics' Institution, London St.*).
Rochdale (*Free Public Library, Town Hall*).
Salford (*Royal Museum and Library, Peel Park*).
Sheffield (*Free Library, Surrey Street*).
Stockport (*Central Free Library*).
Swansea (*Free Library*).
Wigan.
Wolverhampton (*Free Library*).
Wolverton (*Railway Station*).
York (*Lower Council Chamber, Guildhall*).

The Patent Office has also presented complete sets of publications to the following Public Offices, Seats of Learning, Societies, British Colonies, and Foreign States:—

Public Offices, &c.

Admiralty—Chatham Dockyard.
    Sheerness ditto.
    Portsmouth ditto.
    Devonport ditto.
    Pembroke ditto.
Royal Artillery Institution, Woolwich.
War Office, Pall Mall.
    Small Arms Factory, Enfield.

India Office.
Department of Science and Art, South Kensington.
Department of Science and Art, Bethnal Green Museum.
Royal School of Mines, &c., Jermyn Street, Piccadilly.
Museum of Science and Art, Edinburgh.

Seats of Learning and Societies.

Cambridge University.
Trinity College, Dublin.

Queen's College, Galway.
Incorporated Law Society, Chancery Lane, London.

British Colonies.

British Guiana.
Canada—Library of Parliament, Ottawa.
    Bureau of Agriculture, Toronto.
    Board of Arts and Manufactures, Montreal.
Cape of Good Hope.
Ceylon.

India—Bengal.
    Bombay.
    Madras.
Malta.
Mauritius.
New South Wales.
New Zealand.
Queensland.
Sth. Australia—Colonial Institute, Adelaide.

Tasmania.
Trinidad.
Victoria—Parliamentary Library, Melbourne.
    Patent Office, Melbourne.
    Public Library, Melbourne.

Foreign States.

Austria—Polytechnic University, Prague.
    Polytechnic University, Vienna.
Belgium—Ministère de l'Intérieur, Brussels.
    Musée de l'Industrie, Brussels.
France—Bibliothèque Nationale, Paris.
    Conservatoire des Arts et Métiers, Paris.
Germany—Kaiserliches Patentamt, Berlin.
    Alsace—Société Industrielle Mulhouse.
    Bavaria—Königliche Bibliothek, Munich.
    Gotha—Ducal Friedenstein Collection.
    Prussia—Königliche Polytechnische Schule, Aix-la-Chapelle.
    Königliche Bibliothek, Berlin.
    Königliche Polytechnische Schule, Hanover.
    Saxony—Königliche Polytechnische Schule, Dresden.
    Würtemberg—Bibliothek des Musterlagers, Stuttgart.
Italy—Ufficio delle Privative, Rome.
Russia—Bibliothèque Impériale, St. Petersburg.
    Polytechnic School, Riga.
Spain—Madrid.
Sweden—Teknologiska Institutet, Stockholm.
United States—Patent Office, Washington, D.C.
    Astor Library, New York, N.Y.
    State Library, Albany, N.Y.
    Franklin Institute, Philadelphia, Pa.
    Free Public Library, Boston, Mass.
    Public Library, Cincinnati, Ohio.
    Free Public Library, Chicago, Ill.
    Peabody Institute, Baltimore, Md.
    Cornell University, Ithaca, N.Y.
    Mercantile Library, St. Louis, Mo.
    Mechanics' Institute, San Francisco, Cal.

GRANTS of complete series of Abridgments of Specifications have been made to the undermentioned Mechanics' Literary and Scientific Institutions:—

Aberystwith (*Literary and Working Men's Reading Room*).
Alnwick (*Scientific and Mechanical Institution*).
Alton (*Mechanics' Institution*).
Altrincham (*Altrincham and Bowdon Literary Institution*).
Ashburton (*Ashburton Library, East Street*).
Ashby-de-la-Zouch (*Mutual Improvement Society*).
Ashton-under-Lyne, (*Free Library, Town Hall*).
—————— (*Mechanics' Institution*).
Aston, near Birmingham (*Aston Manor Public Library*).
Aylesbury (*Kingsbury Mechanics' Institute*).
Bacup (*Mechanics' Institution*).
Banbury (*Mechanics' Institution*).
Barnstaple (*Literary and Scientific Institution*).
Barrow-in-Furness (*Barrow Working Men's Club and Institute*).
Basingstoke (*Mechanics' Institute and Club*).
Bath (*Athenæum*).
—— (*People's Club and Institute*).
—— (*Royal Literary and Scientific Institution*).
Batley (*Mechanics' Institution*).
Battle (*Young Men's Christian Association*).
Belfast (*Northern Law Club*).
—————— (*People's Literary Institute*).
Berkhampstead, Great (*Mechanics' Institute*).
—————————— (*Working Men's College*).
Birkenhead (*Literary and Scientific Society*).
Birmingham (*Free Library and News Room, Gosta Green*).
—————— (*Graham Street Institution*).
Bodmin (*Literary Institution*).
Bolton (*Mechanics' Institute*).
Bournemouth (*Library and Reading Room*).
Bradford, Yorkshire (*Church Institute*).
—————————— (*Library and Literary Society*).
—————————— (*Mechanics' Institute*).
Braintree (*Braintree and Bocking Literary and Mechanics' Institution*).
Brampton, near Chesterfield (*Local Museum and Literary Institute*).
Breage, Cornwall (*Institution*).
Brigg, Lincolnshire (*Reading Society*).
Bristol (*Athenæum*).
—— (*Institution*).

Bristol (*Law Library Society*).
—— (*Museum and Library, Queen's Road*).
Bromsgrove (*Literary and Mechanics' Institute*).
Burnley (*Literary Institution*).
—————— (*Mechanics' Institution*).
Burslem (*Wedgwood Institute*).
Bury (*Athenæum*).
Bury St. Edmund's (*Athenæum*).
—————————— (*Mechanics' Inst.*).
Calne (*Literary Institution*).
Canterbury (*Westgate Towers*).
Carharrack (*Literary Institute*).
Carmarthen (*Literary and Scientific Institution*).
Cheddar (*Literary Institution*).
Cheltenham (*Permanent Library*).
Chertsey (*Literary and Scientific Institution*).
Chester (*City Library and Reading Room*).
Chesterfield (*Mechanics' Institution*).
Chichester (*Literary Society and Mechanics' Institute*).
Chippenham (*Literary and Scientific Institution*).
Christchurch (*Working Men's Institute*).
Cockermouth (*Mechanics' Institution*).
Coggeshall (*Literary and Mechanics Institution*).
Colchester (*Literary Institution*).
—————— (*Young Men's Christian Association*).
Compstall (*Athenæum*).
Coventry (*Free Library*).
—————— (*Institute*).
—————— (*School of Art*).
Crewe (*Mechanics' Institution*).
Deal (*Deal and Walmer Institute*).
Derby (*Mechanics' Institution*).
Devonport (*Mechanics' Institute*).
Dewsbury (*Mechanics' Institution*).
Diss (*Reading Room and Library*).
Doncaster (*Free Library*).
—————— (*Great Northern Mechanics' Institute*).
—————— (*Young Men's Christian Association*).
Dorchester (*County Museum and Library*).
—————— (*Working Men's Institute*).
Dudley (*Mechanics' Institution*).
Dukinfield (*Village Library and Reading Room*).
Dumbarton (*Philosophical and Literary Society*).
Dumfries (*Mechanics' Institution*).
Dundee (*Young Men's Christian Association and Literary Inst.*)
Dunfermline (*Carnegie Free Library*).

13

Durham (*Mechanics' Institute*).
Eagley, Bolton-le-Moors (*Library and Institute*).
Ealing (*Young Men's Institute*).
East Retford (*Literary and Mutual Improvement Society*).
Ebbw Vale (*Literary and Scientific Institute*).
Eccles, near Manchester (*Provident Industrial Co-operative Society*).
Edinburgh (*Advocates Library*).
—————— (*Association of Science and Art*).
—————— (*Philosophical Institution*).
—————— (*Royal Scottish Society of Arts*).
—————— (*Watt Institution and School of Art*).
—————— (*Working Men's Club*).
Egham (*Literary Institute*).
Egremont (*Mechanics' Institute*).
—————— (*Workmen's Institute*).
Exeter (*Devon and Exeter Albert Memorial Museum, School of Science and Art, and Free Library*).
—————— (*Devon and Exeter Institution*).
Farnham (*Young Men's Association*).
Faversham (*Institute*).
Fowey (*Working Men's Reading Rooms*).
Frome (*Literary and Scientific Institution*).
—————— (*Mechanics' Institution*).
Gainsborough (*Literary, Scientific and Mechanics' Institute*).
Garforth, near Leeds (*Working Men's Club*).
Glasgow (*Athenæum*).
—————— (*Central Working Men's Club and Institute*).
—————— (*City Industrial Museum, Kelvingrove Park*).
—————— (*Institution of Engineers in Scotland*).
—————— (*Mechanics' Institution, Bath Street*).
—————— (*Philosophical Society*).
Godmanchester (*Working Men's Reading Room*).
Gosport (*Gosport and Alverstoke Literary and Scientific Institution*).
Grantham (*Public Literary Institn.*).
Gravesend (*Gravesend and Milton Library and Reading Rooms*).
Greenock (*Library, Watt Monument*).
Guernsey (*Guille Allès Library, Market Place*).
Guildford (*Working Men's Institution*).
Hadleigh (*The Reading Room*).
Halesworth (*Mechanics' Institute*).
Halifax (*Literary and Philosophical Society*).
—————— (*Mechanics' Institute*).
Halstead (*Literary and Mechanics' Institute*).
Handsworth (*Free Public Library*).
Haslingdon (*Institute*).

Hastings (*Literary and Scientific Institute*).
—————— (*Mechanics' Institution*).
Hebden Bridge, near Todmorden (*Mechanics' Institution*).
Helston (*Reading Room and Library*).
Hemel Hempsted (*Mechanics' Inst.*).
Hereford (*Natural History, Philosophical, Antiquarian, and Literary Society*).
Hertford (*Literary and Scientific Institution*).
Heywood (*Public Free Library*).
Hitchin (*Mechanics' Institute*).
Holbeck (*Mechanics' Institution*).
Hollingwood (*Working Men's Club*).
Holt, Norfolk (*Literary Society*).
Holywell Green (*Mechanics' Instit.*)
Horncastle (*Mechanics' Institution*).
Huddersfield (*Mechanics' Institution*).
Hull (*Church Institute*).
—— (*Literary, Scientific, and Mechanics' Institute*).
—— (*Lyceum Library*).
—— (*Royal Institution, Albion Street*).
—— (*Young People's Institute*).
Huntingdon (*Literary and Scientific Institution*).
Inverness (*The Free Library*).
Ipswich (*Working Men's College*).
Kendal (*Christian & Literary Instit.*)
—————— (*Highgate Mechanics' Inst.*).
—————— (*Working Men's Institute*).
Kilmarnock (*Library*).
Kingston - on - Thames (*Workmen's Club and Institute, Fairfield Road*).
Lancaster (*Mechanics' Institute and School of Science*).
Lee, Kent (*Working Men's Instit.*)
Leeds (*Chapeltown Branch Library*).
—— (*Church Institute*).
—— (*Holbeck Branch Library*).
—— (*Hunslet Branch Library*).
—— (*Leeds Library*).
—— (*Mechanics' Institution and Literary Society*).
—— (*Philosophical and Literary Society*).
—— (*Working Men's Institute*).
—— (*Young Men's Christian Association*).
Leek, Staffordshire (*Literary and Mechanics' Institution*).
Leicester (*Law Society*).
Leighton Buzzard (*Working Men's Mutual Improvement Society*).
Leith (*Mechanics' Subscription Library*).
Lewes (*Fitzroy Memorial Library*).
—— (*Mechanics' Institute*).
—— (*School of Science and Art*).
Lincoln (*Mechanics' Institute*).
Liverpool (*Institute*).
—————— (*Medical Institution*).
—————— (*Polytechnic Society*).
Llanelly (*Chamber of Commerce and Reading Room*).
Lockwood (*Mechanics' Institution*).
London (*Bank of England Library and Literary Association*).
—————— (*Beaumont Inst., Mile End*).

London (*Birkbeck Institution, Southampton Buildings, Chancery Lane*).
———— (*Bow and Bromley Institute, Bow Road*).
———— (*Christchurch Working Men's Club, New Street. Lark Hall Lane, Clapham*).
———— (*Free Public Library, Great Smith Street, Westminster*).
———— (*Hackney Working Men's Club*).
———— (*King's College*).
———— (*Literary and Scientific Institution, Walworth*).
———— (*London Association of Foremen Engineers and Draughtsmen*).
———— (*London Institution, Finsbury Circus*).
———— (*London Library, St. James'*).
———— (*Parkes Museum of Hygiene, University College*).
———— (*Royal Architectural Museum and School of Art, Tufton Street, Westminster*).
———— (*Royal Institute of British Architects, Conduit Street, Hanover Square*).
———— (*St. James and Soho Working Men's Club, Rupert Street, Soho*).
———— (*Working Men's Club, Brixton Hill*).
———— (*Working Men's Club and Institute, Battersea*).
———— (*Working Men's Club and Institute Union, Strand*).
———— (*Working Men's College, Great Ormond Street*).
Longwood (*Mechanics' Institution*).
Lowestoft (*Library and Reading Room*).
Lye (*Institution*).
Madeley, Shropshire (*Anstice Memorial, Workmen's Club and Institute*).
Maidstone (*St. Paul's Literary Inst.*).
———— (*Working Men's Club and Institute*).
Manchester (*Ancoats Branch Free Library*).
———— (*Campfield Free Lending Library*).
———— (*Cheetham Branch Library*).
———— (*Chorlton and Ardwick Branch Free Library*).
———— (*Hulme Branch Free Library*).
———— (*Law Library*).
———— (*Mechanics' Institution*).
———— (*Natural History Museum, Peter Street*).
———— (*Owen's College*).
———— (*Portico Library Mosley Street*).
———— (*Rochdale Road Branch Free Library*).
———— (*Royal Exchange Library*).
———— (*Scientific and Mechanical Society*).
———— Working Men's Clubs Association.)

Manningtree (*Manningtree and Mistley Literary and Scientific Institution*).
Mansfield (*Co-operative Industrial Society*).
———— (*Mechanics', Artisans', and Apprentices' Library*).
———— (*Mechanics' Institute*).
Marlborough (*Reading and Mutual Improvement Society*).
———— (*Working Men's Hall*).
Melton Mowbray (*Literary Institute*).
Mere, near Bath (*Literary Association*).
Middlesborough (*Iron and Steel Institute*).
———— (*Mechanics' Institution*).
Middlewich (*Literary and Scientific Institution*).
Mildenhall (*Suffolk Literary Inst.*)
Newark (*Mechanics' Institute*).
Newbury (*Literary and Scientific Institution*).
Newcastle-upon-Tyne (*Mechanics' Institution*).
———— (*Working Men's Club*).
New Mills, near Stockport (*Mechanics' Institute*).
Newport, Isle of Wight (*Young Men's Society and Reading Room*).
Northampton (*Mechanics' Institute*).
North Shields (*Free Library*).
Nottingham (*Mechanics' Institution*).
———— (*Subscription Library, Bromley House*).
Oldham (*Mechanics' Institution, Werneth*).
Old Kilpatrick, near Glasgow (*Public Library*).
Ormskirk (*Public Library*).
Oswestry (*Institute*).
Over, Cheshire (*Working Men's Institute*).
Patricroft (*Mechanics' Institution*).
Pembroke Dock (*Mechanics' Institute*).
Pendleton (*Free Library*).
Penrith (*Free Public Library and Museum*).
Penzance (*Institute*).
———— (*Penzance Library*).
———— (*Working Men's Association*).
Perry Barr, near Birmingham (*Inst.*)
Perth (*Mechanics' Library, High Street*).
Peterborough (*Mechanics' Institution*).
Poole (*Literary and Scientific Institution*).
Port Glasgow (*Public Library*).
Portsea Island (*Young Men's Christian Association*).
Portsmouth (*Public Free Library*).
Preston (*Institution for the Diffusion of Knowledge*).
Redruth (*Redruth Institution*).
Reigate (*Mechanics' Institution*).
Richmond, Surrey (*Free Public Library*).

Rotherham (*Rotherham and Masbro' Literary and Mechanics' Institute*).
Royston (*Institute*).
Rusholme (*Public Hall and Library*).
Ryde, Isle of Wight (*Philosophical and Scientific Society*).
—————— (*Young Men's Christian Association and Literary Institute*).
Saffron Walden (*Literary and Scientific Institution*).
St. Helens (*Public Library*).
St. Just (*Institution*).
St. Leonards (*Mechanics' Institution*).
Salford (*Working Men's College*).
Salisbury (*Literary and Scientific Institution*).
Saltaire (*Literary Institute*).
Scarborough (*Mechanics' and Literary Institute, Vernon Place*).
Selby (*Mechanics' Institute*).
Sevenoaks (*Literary and Scientific Institution*).
Shaftesbury (*Literary Institution*).
Sheerness (*Literary Institute*).
Sheffield (*Branch Free Library*).
—————— (*Brightside Branch Library*).
—————— (*Literary and Philosophical Society, School of Arts*).
Shepton Mallet (*Reading and Mutual Improvement Society*).
Sidmouth (*Mechanics' Hall*).
Skipton, Yorkshire (*Mechanics' Inst.*)
Slough (*Mechanics' Institute*).
Smethwick, Staffordshire (*Library, Reading Room, and Literary Institute*).
Southampton (*Polytechnic Institution*).
—————— (*Workmen's Hall*).
Southend (*Mechanics' Institute*).
South Shields (*Public Free Library*).
Southwell (*Literary Institution*).
Spalding (*Christian Young Men's Association*).
—————— (*Mechanics' Institute*).
Stafford (*Mechanics' Institution*).
Staines (*Mechanics' Institute*).
Stalybridge, Cheshire (*Mechanics' Institution*).
Stamford (*Institution*).
Stockton-on-Tees (*Young Men's Christian Association*).
Stourbridge (*Church of England Association*).
—————— (*Iron Works Reading Room and Library*).
—————— (*Mechanics' Institution*).
—————— (*Working Men's Inst.*)
Stowmarket (*Literary Institution*).
Stratford (*Working Men's Hall*).
Sudbury, Suffolk (*Literary and Mechanics' Institute*).
Swansea (*Royal Institution of South Wales*).
—————— (*South Wales Institute of Engineers*).
—————— (*Working Man's Institute*).

Tavistock (*Mechanics' Institute*).
—————— (*Public Library*).
Thornton, near Bradford (*Mechanics' Institute*).
Truro (*Cornwall County Library*).
—————— (*Institution*).
—————— (*Royal Institution of Cornwall*).
Tunbridge (*Literary and Scientific Institute*).
—————— (*Mechanics' Institute*).
Tunbridge Wells (*Mechanics' Institution*).
—————— (*Society of Literature and Science*).
Turton, near Bolton (*Chapel Town Institute*).
Tynemouth (*Free Public Library*).
Ulverston (*Temperance Hall*).
Uttoxeter (*Mechanics' Literary Institute*).
Uxbridge (*Uxbridge and Hillingdon Reading and Newsroom Institute*).
Wakefield (*Mechanics' Institute*).
Wallingford (*Mechanics' Institute*).
Walsall (*Free Library*).
Walsham-le-Willows, Suffolk (*Inst.*)
Ware (*Institute*).
Warminster (*Athenæum*).
Watford (*Literary Institute*).
—————— (*Public Library*).
Wednesbury (*Free Library*).
Wellingborough (*Working Men's Club*).
Wellington (*Young Men's Christian Association*).
Wells, Somerset (*Young Men's Society*).
West Bromwich (*Free Library*).
Whaleybridge (*Mechanics' Institute*).
Whitby (*Institute*).
—————— (*Museum*).
—————— (*Subscription Library*).
Whitehaven (*Mechanics' Institute*).
Whitstable (*Institute*).
Wilton (*Literary Institute*).
Winchester (*Mechanics' Institution*).
—————— (*Training College*).
Winsford (*Town Hall Reading Room*).
Wirksworth (*Mechanics' Institution*).
Wisbeach (*Mechanics' Institute*).
Witham (*Literary Institution*).
Witney (*Athenæum*).
Wolverhampton (*Law Library*).
—————— (*Library*).
Wolverton (*Institute*).
Woodbridge (*Literary and Mechanics' Institute*).
Worcester (*Public Library and Hastings Museum*).
—————— (*Railway Literary Inst.*)
—————— (*Workman's Hall*).
Workington (*Mechanics' Institute*).
Yarmouth, Great (*Parochial Library and Museum*).
Yeovil (*Mutual Improvement Society*).
York (*Institute of Popular Science, &c.*).
—————— (*North Eastern Railway Library and Reading Room*).

PRESENTATIONS of portions of the Works, published by order of the Patent Office have been made to the following Libraries :—

Armagh (*Town Clerk's Office*).
Aylesbury (*Mechanics' Institution and Literary Society, Kingsbury*).
Boston, Lincolnshire (*Public Offices Market Place*).
Cambridge (*Free Library, Jesus Lane*).
Cardiff (*Free Library and Museum*).
Chester (*Mechanics Institute, St. John Street*).
Coalbrookdale (*Literary and Scientific Institution*).
Coventry (*Watchmakers' Association*).
Dublin (*Dublin Library, D'Olier St.*)
Dundee (*Association of Watchmakers and Jewellers*).
Ennis (*Public Library*).
Gloucester (*Working Men's Institute, Southgate Street*).
Guernsey (*Public Record Office*).
Guildford (*Mechanics' Institute*).
Ipswich (*Mechanics' Institute, Tavern Street*).
Kew (*Library of the Royal Gardens*).
Leominster (*Literary Institute*).
London (*House of Lords*).
——— (*House of Commons*).
——— (*Hon. Soc. of Gray's Inn*).
——— (,, ,, *Inner Temple*).
——— (,, ,, *Lincoln's Inn*).
——— (,, ,, *Middle Temple*).
——— (*Aeronautical Society*).
——— (*British Horological Instit.*)
London (*General Post Office*).
——— (*Guildhall Library*).
——— (*Institute of British Carriage Manufacturers*).
——— (*Inst. of Civil Engineers*).
——— (*Institution of Mechanical Engineers*).
——— (*Metallurgical Department, King's College*).
——— (*Odontological Society*).
——— (*Royal Society*).
——— (*Society of Arts*).
——— (*Society of Telegraph Engineers*).
——— (*United Service Museum*).
Manchester (*Literary and Philosophical Society, George Street*).
——— (*Mechanics' Institution, David Street*).
Newcastle-upon-Tyne (*North of England Institute of Mining Engineers*).
Over Darwen (*Free Public Library*).
Oxford (*Bodleian Library*).
Stretford, near Manchester (*Mechanics' Institute*).
Swindon, New (*Mechanics' Institution*).
Tamworth (*Library and Reading Room, George Street*).
Yarmouth, Norfolk (*Public Library, South Quay*).

British Colonies and Foreign States.

British Columbia—Mechanics' Institute, Victoria.
——— Public Library, New Westminster.
France—Academy of Science, Paris.
Germany—Imperial and Provincial Library of the University, Strasburg.
——— Imperial Statistical Office, Berlin.
——— Polytechnic School, Carlsruhe, Baden.
Italy—Communal Library, Palermo.
——— Royal Institution for the Encouragement of Science, Naples.
Netherlands—Library of the Polytechnic School, Delft.
New Zealand—Athenæum and Mechanics' Institute, Dunedin.
Russia—Imperial Technological Institute, St. Petersburg.
Switzerland—Federal Polytechnic School, Zurich.
Turkey—Literary and Scientific Institute, Smyrna.
United States—American Academy of Arts and Sciences, Boston.
——— American Institute, New York.
United States—American Society of Civil Engineers, New York.
——— City Library Association, Springfield, Massachusetts.
——— Industrial University, Champaign, Illinois.
——— Law Association, Philadelphia.
——— Mercantile Library Association, San Francisco.
——— Mercantile Library Association, Pittsburgh, Pennsylvania.
——— Minnesota Historical Society, Saint Paul, Minnesota.
——— Odd Fellows' Library Association, San Francisco.
——— Patent Office Bar Association, Washington.
——— Public Library, Detroit, Michigan.
——— Rose Polytechnic Institute, Terre Haute, Indiana.
——— Smithsonian Institute, Washington.
——— Wabash College, Crawfordsville, Indiana.
——— Young Men's Christian Assoc., Scranton, Pennsylvania.
Victoria—School of Mines, Ballaarat.

NOTICE RELATIVE TO FULL-SIZE COPIES OF DRAWINGS BELONGING TO THE SPECIFICATIONS OF PATENTS.

Patent Office, 25, Southampton Buildings,
Chancery Lane.

For legal or other purposes the Patent Office will supply, at the undermentioned rates, full-size copies of Drawings belonging to Specifications printed under the new system by the process of Photolithography:

No. of Copies.	Half-sheets Imperial.		Whole sheets Imperial.	
	s.	d.	s.	d.
Single Copies - - - -	25	0	15	0
Not exceeding 6 copies - - -	28	0	18	0
,, 12 - - -	30	0	20	0
,, 25 - - -	32	0	22	0

In cases where from the use of color or other causes a satisfactory Photograph cannot be obtained from the original Drawing, an extra charge will be made to cover the expense of taking a tracing.

There will also be a small additional charge for coloring the copies of colored original Drawings.

Applications stating the number of copies required and accompanied by a remittance sufficient to cover the cost should be addressed to the Comptroller-General.

By Order,
H. READER LACK,
1st January 1884. Comptroller-General of Patents.

ISSUE OF MONTHLY ALPHABETICAL AND SUBJECT MATTER INDEXES OF APPLICATIONS FOR PATENTS.

Patent Office, 25, Southampton Buildings,
Chancery Lane.

In consequence of the very large increase in the number of applicants for Patents, and the inconvenience occasioned to intending Patentees by the long interval which necessarily elapses between the expiration of each year and the publication of the Alphabetical and Subject-matter Indexes for that year, it has been decided to issue for temporary use, until the complete indexes are ready, a monthly index of subjects of invention, compiled from the "titles" only (as the provisional specifications cannot be referred to), each succeeding monthly index, from the second month to the twelfth month of the year, including and superseding the preceding index.

The Alphabetical Index of Names will, as at present, be published in monthly numbers, but divided into two half-yearly parts (*i.e.*, from January to the end of June [Part I.] and from July to the end of December [Part II.]), when both parts will be incorporated to form the complete index for the year.

The Indexes for the year 1884 will be published in parts, and sold either singly or by annual subscriptions at the undermentioned rates:

Months.	Price of Single Copies.		Annual Subscriptions (payable in advance).	
	Alphabetical Index.	Subject matter Index.	Alphabetical Index.	Subject matter Index.
January to June, inclusive [Part I.]	Per Copy, 3d.	Per Copy. 3d.	Per Annum. 3s.*	Per Annum. 3s.*
Monthly, consolidated numbers in continuation	3d.	—		
December (Index for the year)	2s.	2s.		

* If sent by post 2s. extra per annum will be charged.

By Order,
H. READER LACK,
Comptroller-General.

3rd July 1884.

TRADE MARKS JOURNAL.

This Official Paper, issued in pursuance of Rule 26, contains illustrations of all the trade marks applied for under the Trade Marks Registration Acts, as well as the name and calling of each applicant, the description of goods, and the length of time for which such mark has been used, thus affording all persons interested in the use of trade marks authentic information as to the nature of the marks applied for in their respective trades. The Journal is issued in numbers, royal quarto, and is on sale at the cost of 1s. per number, or by subscription 52s. per annum.

THE PATENT MUSEUM

has been transferred to the Department of Science and Art, South Kensington. A complete set of the Patent Office publications can be consulted by the public daily, at the Patent Museum, free of charge.

Abridgments of Specifications.

The following is a KEY to the classes already published. The numbers refer to the list of Abridgments on pages 4, 5, 6, 7, and 8, where the full titles, prices, &c., are given:—

A.

Accordions. *See* Music, &c., 26.
Acetic acid. *See* Acids, 40.
Acids, &c., 40.
Aerated liquids. *See* Unfermented beverages, &c., 86.
Aerating water. *See* Purifying, &c., water, 79.
Aeronautics, 41.
Ageing fabrics. *See* Bleaching, &c., 14.
Agricultural engines. *See* Steam engine, 49.
Agriculture—barn and farmyard implements (including the cleansing, drying, and storing of grain), 82.
Agriculture—field implements and processes, 81.
Agriculture—agricultural and traction engines, 83.
Agriculture, steam. *See* Steam culture, 8.
Air, &c., engines, 62.
Air guns. *See* Fire-arms, 10.
Air pumps of steam engines. *See* Steam engine, 49.
Alarum clocks. *See* Watches, &c., 9.
Alarums, electric. *See* Electricity, 15, 94.
Alarums, fire. *See* Fire engines, &c., 88.
Alarums, gas. *See* Gas, 17.
Albums. *See* Books, 43.
Alcohol distilling. *See* Brewing, &c., 99.
Alkalies. *See* Acids, &c., 40.
Alloys. *See* Metals, &c., 18.
Alum. *See* Acids, &c., 40.
Alumina. *See* Acids, &c., 40.
Aluminium. *See* Metals, &c., 18; Acids, &c., 40.
Amalgamating metals. *See* Metals, &c., 18.
Ambulances. *See* Medicine, &c., 25; Common road carriages, 98.
Ammonia. *See* Acids, &c., 40.
Ammonium. *See* Acids, &c., 40.
Ammunition. *See* Fire-arms, 10.
Anchors, 69.
Anchors for steam ploughing. *See* Agriculture, 81.
Anemometers. *See* Optical, &c., 76.
Aniline. *See* Bleaching, &c., 14.
Animal charcoal. *See* Sugar, 48.
Animals, medical and surgical treatment of. *See* Farriery, &c., 53.
Annealing. *See* Iron, &c., 6; Fuel, &c., 30.
Anthracite furnaces. *See* Fuel, &c., 30.

Antimony. *See* Metals, &c., 18; Acids, &c., 40.
Aqueducts. *See* Bridges, &c., 36.
Arches. *See* Bridges, &c., 36.
Armour plates, rolling. *See* Iron and Steel, 6.
Armour plates, shaping. *See* Shipbuilding, 21.
Arsenic. *See* Metals, &c., 18; Acids, &c., 40.
Arsenic acid and arsenious acid. *See* Acids, 40.
Artificial leather, 80.
Artists' instruments, &c., 54.
Asphalte. *See* Roads, &c., 35.
Astronomical instruments. *See* Optical, &c., 76.
Avellers. *See* Agriculture, 82.
Axles, axletrees, and axleboxes, for common road carriages. *See* Common road carriages, 98.
Axles, axletrees, and axleboxes, for railway carriages, &c. *See* Carriages for railways, 46; Steam engine, 49.

B.

Bagatelle tables. *See* Toys c. 51.
Bags. *See* Trunks, &c., 84.
Bags, paper. *See* Cutting, &c., 12.
Baking-powders. *See* Cooking, 61.
Balances. *See* Raising, &c., 31.
Balancing, &c. millstones. *See* Grinding grain, 78.
Balloons. *See* Aeronautics, 41.
Balloons, toy. *See* Toys 51.
Balls. *See* Toys, 51.
Band boxes. *See* Trunks, &c., 84.
Bands and belts. *See* Wearing apparel, 66.
Barium. *See* Acids, &c., 40.
Barley hummellers. *See* Agriculture, 82.
Barley mills. *See* Grinding grain, 78.
Barometers. *See* Optical, &c., 76.
Barrels, 74.
Barrows. *See* Common road carriages, 98.
Baryta. *See* Acids, &c., 40.
Baskets. *See* Trunks, &c., 84.
Bath chairs. *See* Common road carriages, 98.
Baths for medical use. *See* Medicine, &c., 25.
Bayonets. *See* Fire-arms, 10.
Beacons. *See* Harbours, &c., 77.
Beads. *See* Wearing apparel, 68.
Beds and bedsteads. *See* Furniture, 39.
Beds and bedsteads for invalids. *See* Medicine, &c., 25; Furniture, 39.
Beer engines. *See* Hydraulics, 32.

Beetling. *See* Dressing, &c., 91.
Bellows. *See* Fuel, &c., 30.
Bells, church and musical. *See* Music, &c., 26.
Belts, surgical. *See* Medicine, &c., 25.
Beverages, unfermented, 86.
Bicycles. *See* Common road carriages, 98.
Billiards. *See* Toys, &c., 51.
Bins for corn, &c. *See* Agriculture, 82.
Biscuits. *See* Cooking, 61.
Biscuit ware. *See* Pottery, 24.
Bismuth. *See* Acids, &c., 40.
Bits. *See* Saddlery, 34.
Blacking. *See* Skins, &c., 55; Wearing apparel, 67.
Blast furnaces. *See* Iron and steel, 6.
Blasting. *See* Fire-arms, 10; Mining, &c., 71.
Bleaching, &c., fabrics, 14.
Bleaching fibrous substances. *See* Paper 11; Spinning, 28.
Blinds. *See* Furniture, 39.
Blinds, ventilating. *See* Ventilation, 52.
Blocks. *See* Raising, &c., 31.
Blotters. *See* Writing, 37.
Boas. *See* Wearing apparel, 66.
Boat-building. *See* Ship-building, 21.
Boats, raising and lowering. *See* Raising, &c., 31; Masts, &c., 73.
Bobbin net. *See* Lace-making, 29.
Boiler plates. *See* Iron and steel, 6.
Boiler tubes. *See* Metallic pipes, 70.
Boilers of steam engines. *See* Steam engine, 49.
Bolting, &c., flour. *See* Grinding grain, 78.
Bolts. *See* Locks, &c., 60.
Bolts. *See* Nails, &c., 58.
Bonnet boxes. *See* Trunks, &c., 84.
Bonnets and bonnet boxes. *See* Wearing apparel, 65.
Books, &c., 43.
Boot-cleaning machines. *See* Brushing, 57.
Boot hooks. *See* Wearing apparel, 67.
Boot jacks. *See* Wearing apparel, 67.
Boots. *See* Wearing apparel, 67.
Boracic acid. *See* Acids, 40.
Bottles, caps and capsules for. *See* Preparing and cutting cork, &c., 56.
Bottling. *See* Preparing, &c., cork &c., 56.
Boxes for pens, leads, &c. *See* Writing, 37.
Boxes. *See* Trunks, &c., 84.
Bracelets. *See* Wearing apparel, 68.
Braces. *See* Wearing apparel, 66.
Braid. *See* Lace-making, 29.
Brakes. *See* Carriages for railways, 46; Steam-engine, 49; Mining, 71; Electricity, 15; 94; 97.
Brakes for common road carriages. *See* Common road carriages, 98.
Brass. *See* Metals, &c., 18.
Bread-making. *See* Cooking, &c., 61.
Breakfast powders. *See* Tea, &c., 87.
Breakwaters. *See* Harbours, &c., 77.
Breast pins. *See* Wearing apparel, 68.
Breeches. *See* Wearing apparel, 66.
Brewing, wine-making and distilling alcoholic liquids, 99.

Bricks and tiles, 22.
Bricks, ventilating. *See* Ventilation, 52.
Bridges, &c., 36.
Bridles. *See* Saddlery, 34.
Broadshares. *See* Agriculture, 81.
Bromine. *See* Acids, &c., 40.
Brooches. *See* Wearing apparel, 68.
Bruising mills for beans, grain, gorse, &c. *See* Agriculture, 82.
Brushes for artists. *See* Artists' instruments, 54; Brushing, 57.
Brushing, &c., 57.
Buckles. *See* Wearing apparel, 68.
Buffers. *See* Carriages, &c., for railways, 46.
Bugles. *See* Music, &c., 26.
Bullet-making machines. *See* Fire arms, 10.
Bungs. *See* Preparing and cutting cork, 56.
Buoys. *See* Harbours, &c., 77.
Bustles. *See* Wearing apparel, 66.
Butter and artificial butter. *See* Milking, &c., 72.
Buttons. *See* Wearing apparel, 68.

C.

Cable stoppers. *See* Raising, &c., 31.
Cables, telegraphic. *See* Electricity, 15; 93.
Cabs. *See* Common road carriages, 98.
Caddies. *See* Trunks, &c., 84.
Cadmium. *See* Acids, &c., 40.
Cages, miners' safety. *See* Mining, 71.
Caissons. *See* Harbours, &c., 77.
Cake breakers. *See* Agriculture, 82.
Calcining furnaces. *See* Metals, &c. 18; Fuel, &c., 30.
Calcium. *See* Acids, &c., 40.
Calculating machines. *See* Optical, &c., 76.
Calendering. *See* Dressing and finishing, &c., 91.
Calico, bleaching, dyeing, and printing, 14.
Cameras. *See* Photography, 19; Optical, &c., 76.
Canal navigation. *See* Marine propulsion, 5.
Canals. *See* Harbours, &c., 77.
Candles. *See* Oils, &c., 27.
Candlesticks. *See* Lamps, &c., 44.
Canes, walking sticks, &c. *See* Umbrellas, &c., 47.
Cannon. *See* Fire-arms, 10.
Canvas. *See* Weaving, 20.
Capes. *See* Wearing apparel, 66.
Caps and cap fronts. *See* Wearing apparel, 65.
Caps and capsules for bottles. *See* Preparing and cutting cork, 56.
Capstans. *See* Raising, &c., 31.
Carbon. *See* Acids, &c., 40.
Carbonic acid. *See* Acids, 40.
Cardboard. *See* Paper, 11.
Card cases. *See* Books, &c., 43.
Carding engines. *See* Spinning, 28.

Cards. *See* Cutting, &c. paper, 12; Letterpress printing, &c., 13.
Cards, playing. *See* Toys, &c., 51.
Cargoes, ventilating. *See* Fire engines, &c., 88.
Carpet bags. *See* Trunks, &c., 84.
Carpets. *See* Weaving, 20.
Carriage lamps. *See* Lamps, 44.
Carriages and other vehicles for common roads, 98.
Carriages, &c., for railways, 46.
Carriages for guns. *See* Fire-arms, 10.
Carriages for invalids. *See* Medicine, &c., 25.
Cartridges. *See* Fire-arms, 10.
Cartridges, miner's. *See* Mining, 71.
Carts. *See* Common road carriages, 98.
Cask stands. *See* Casks, 74.
Caskets. *See* Trunks, &c., 84.
Casks, 74.
Casks, cleaning. *See* Brewing, &c., 99.
Castors. *See* Furniture, 39.
Cattle food, medicated. *See* Farriery, &c., 53.
Cattle food, preparing on the farm, not manufacturing for sale. *See* Agriculture, 82.
Cattle medicines. *See* Farriery, &c., 53.
Cement, brush maker's. *See* Brushing, 57.
Centre boards. *See* Steering, 75.
Cesspools. *See* Waterclosets. &c.. 63.
Chaff-cutters. *See* Agriculture, 82.
Chains, chain cables, &c., 90.
Chains, jewellery. *See* Wearing Apparel, 68; Chains, &c., 90.
Chairs. *See* Furniture, 39.
Chairs, invalid. *See* Medicine, 25; Furniture, 39.
Chalybeate waters. *See* Unfermented beverages, &c., 86.
Chamber utensils. *See* Waterclosets, &c., 63.
Chandeliers. *See* Lamps, &c., 44.
Charcoal, animal. *See* Sugar, 48.
Cheese. *See* Milking, &c., 72.
Chemises. *See* Wearing apparel, 66.
Chenille. *See* Lace-making, 29.
Chess. *See* Toys, 51.
Chests. *See* Trunks, &c., 84.
Chicory, manufacturing and preparing for sale. *See* Tea, &c., 87.
Chimes. *See* Music, 26.
Chimneys and chimney tops. *See* Fuel, &c., 30.
Chimneys sweeping. *See* Brushing, 57.
Chinaware. *See* Pottery, 24.
Chlorine. *See* Acids, &c., 40.
Chocolate or cocoa, concentrated extracts of. *See* Tea, &c., 87.
Chocolate or cocoa, manufacturing and preparing for sale. *See* Tea, &c., 87.
Chocolate, preparing as a drink. *See* Unfermented beverages, &c., 86.
Chromium. *See* Acids, &c., 40.
Chromo-lithography. *See* Letterpress and similar printing, 13; Ornamenting paper, &c., 12.
Churning. *See* Milking, &c., 72.
Cigars, cigarettes, and cigar holders. *See* Tobacco, 42.

Cinder sifters. *See* Fuel, &c., 30.
Cisterns. *See* Hydraulics, 32.
Citric acid. *See* Acids, 40.
Clasps and clips. *See* Writing, &c., 37.
Cleaning grain. *See* Agriculture, 82.
Clinometers. *See* Optical, &c., 76.
Clipping and shearing animals. *See* Saddlery, 34; Farriery, &c., 53.
Cloaks. *See* Wearing apparel, 66.
Clocks. *See* Watches, &c., 9.
Clod crushers. *See* Agriculture, 81.
Clogs. *See* Wearing apparel, 67.
Coal scuttles. *See* Fuel, &c., 30.
Coats. *See* Wearing apparel, 66.
Cobalt. *See* Metals, 18; Acids, &c., 40.
Cocks. *See* Hydraulics, 32.
Cocoa or chocolate, concentrated extracts of. *See* Tea, &c., 87.
Cocoa or chocolate, manufacturing and preparing for sale. *See* Tea, &c., 87.
Cocoa, preparing as a drink. *See* Unfermented beverages, &c., 86.
Coffee, concentrated extracts of. *See* Tea, &c., 87.
Coffee, manufacturing and preparing for sale. *See* Tea, &c., 87.
Coffee mills. *See* Tea, &c., 87.
Coffee, preparing as a drink. *See* Unfermented beverages, &c., 86.
Coffer dams. *See* Bridges, 36; Harbours, &c., 77.
Coke ovens. *See* Fuel, &c., 30.
Collars. *See* Wearing apparel, 66.
Collars for horses. *See* Saddlery, 34.
Colours. *See* Paints, 50.
Colours, artists'. *See* Artists instruments, &c., 54.
Combing machines. *See* Spinning, 28.
Commodes. *See* Furniture, 39; Waterclosets, &c., 63.
Compasses, drawing. *See* Optical, &c., 76.
Compasses, magnetic. *See* Optical, &c., 76.
Compasses, mariners'. *See* Optical, &c., 76.
Concertinas. *See* Music, &c., 26.
Condensers of steam engines. *See* Steam engine, 49.
Conductors, electric. *See* Electricity, &c., 15; 93.
Confectionery. *See* Cooking, &c., 61.
Confectionery ices. *See* Ice-making, &c., 85.
Conveying water. *See* Hydraulics, 32.
Cooking, &c., 61.
Copper. *See* Metals, &c., 18.
Copper oxides, &c. *See* Acids, &c., 40.
Copying presses. *See* Writing, &c., 37.
Copying writings. *See* Writing, 37.
Corkcutting, &c., 56.
Corkscrews. *See* Preparing and cutting cork, 56.
Corn, thrashing, cleansing, drying, and storing. *See* Agriculture, 82.
Cornets. *See* Music, 26.
Cots and cradles. *See* Furniture, 39.
Cotton gins. *See* Spinning, 28.

Couches. See Furniture, 39.
Counting number of passengers in common road carriages. See Common road carriages, 98.
Couplings for tubes. See Metallic pipes, &c., 70.
Covers of vehicles. See Common road carriages, 98.
Crab-winches, steam. See Raising, &c., 31; Steam engine, 49.
Cranes. See Raising, &c., 31.
Cranes, hydraulic. See Raising. &c., 31; Hydraulics, 32.
Cranes, steam. See Raising, &c., 31; Steam engine, 49.
Crates. See Trunks, &c., 84.
Cravats. See Wearing apparel, 66.
Crayons. See Artists' instruments, &c., 54.
Crayons and crayon holders. See Writing, &c., 37; Artists' instruments, &c., 54.
Cricket. See Toys, &c., 51.
Crinolines. See Wearing apparel, 66.
Crochet needles and holders. See Needles, 45.
Croquet. See Toys, &c., 51.
Crucibles. See Metals, &c., 18.
Crushing, breaking, &c., ores, &c. See Iron, 6; Metals, &c., 18; Roads, 35.
Crushing grain, &c. See Grinding grain, 78.
Crushing mills for beans, gorse, grain, &c. See Agriculture, 82.
Cultivators. See Agriculture, 81.
Curricle bars. See Common road carriages, 98.
Currycombs. See Saddlery, 34.
Curtains. See Furniture, 39.
Cutting, &c. paper, 12.
Cutting metallic pipes. See Pipes, 70.
Cutting roots, straw &c. See Agriculture, 82.
Cyanogen. See Acids, &c., 40.

D.

Dampers for stamps, envelopes, copying paper &c. See Writing, 37.
Dams. See Harbours, &c., 77.
Dash wheels. See Bleaching, &c., 14.
Decoctions, unconcentrated. See Unfermented beverages, &c., 86.
Decorticating grain and seeds. See Grinding grain, 78.
Dentistry. See Medicine, 25.
Derricks. See Raising, &c., 31.
Derricks, steam. See Raising, &c., 31; Steam engine, 49.
Desks, despatch boxes, and stationery cabinets. See Writing, 37.
Despatch boxes. See Writing, 37; Trunks, &c., 84.
Despatches, mechanism for carrying. See Railways, 33.
Detonating signals. See Railway signals, 38.
Dextrine. See Starch, &c., 100.
Dibbles. See Agriculture, 81.
Dies. See Ornamenting paper, &c., 12.

Diggers and digging machines. See Agriculture, 81.
Distance indicators for common road carriages. See Common road carriages, 98.
Distilling alcoholic liquids. See Brewing, &c., 99.
Diving apparatus. See Raising, &c., 31.
Docks. See Harbours, &c., 77.
Dolls. See Toys, 51.
Door-springs. See Hinges, &c., 59.
Drags. See Common road carriages, 98.
Draining mines. See Mining, 71.
Drain pipes, laying. See Agriculture, 81.
Drain ploughs. See Agriculture, 81.
Drain tiles and pipes. See Drains, &c., 1.
Drains and sewers, 1.
Draughts and draughtboards. See Toys, 51.
Drawers. See Wearing apparel, 66.
Drawing instruments. See Writing, &c., 87; Artists', &c., 54; Optical, mathematical, &c., 76.
Dredgers, steam. See Steam engine, 49; Harbours, &c., 77.
Dredging. See Raising, &c., 31; Harbours, &c., 77.
Dress fastenings. See Wearing apparel, 68.
Dressing and finishing woven fabrics, &c., 91.
Dressing cases. See Trunks, &c., 84.
Dressing composition. See Starch, &c., 100.
Dressing flour and meal. See Grinding grain, 78.
Dressing millstones. See Grinding grain, 78.
Drills, seed and manure. See Agriculture, 81.
Drums. See Music, &c., 26.
Dry docks. See Harbours, &c., 77.
Drying grain, hops, roots, hay, &c. See Agriculture, 82.
Dyeing. See Bleaching, &c., 14.
Dynamometers. See Optical, &c., 76.

E.

Earrings. See Wearing apparel, 68.
Earth closets. See Waterclosets, &c., 63.
Earthenware. See Pottery, 24.
Easels. See Artists' instruments, 54.
Effervescing drinks. See Unfermented beverages, &c., 86.
Elastic bands. See India rubber, 16; Lace-making, 29.
Elastic fabrics. See Weaving, 20; Lace-making, 29.
Electric generators, 92.
Electricity, &c., 15; 92; 93; 94; 95; 96; 97.
Electric lighting, &c., 95.
Electro-deposition, &c., 96.
Electro-etching. See Electro-deposition, &c., 96.
Electrolysis, 96.

Elevators or stackers. *See* Agriculture, 82.
Embankments. *See* Harbours, &c., 77.
Embossing. *See* Ornamenting paper, 12; Letterpress printing, 13; Dressing, &c. fabrics, 91.
Embroidering. *See* Sewing, 2.
Emery cloth, &c. *See* Cutting, &c., paper, 12.
Endless travelling railways. *See* Aids to locomotion, 7; Common road carriages, 98.
Engraving, embossing, and printing rollers. *See* Ornamenting paper, 12; Bleaching, &c. fabrics, 14.
Engravings. *See* Letterpress printing, &c., 13; Artists' instruments, 54.
Envelope-fasteners. *See* Writing, &c., 37.
Envelopes. *See* Cutting, folding, &c. paper, 12.
Epaulets. *See* Wearing apparel, 66.
Erasers. *See* Writing, 37.
Excavating. *See* Raising, &c., 31; Harbours, &c., 77.
Exercises. *See* Toys, &c., 51.
Explosive compounds. *See* Fire-arms, 10; Mining, &c., 71.
Extracts of hops, &c. *See* Brewing, &c., 99.
Extracts, unconcentrated. *See* Unfermented beverages, &c., 86.
Eyelets. *See* Wearing apparel, 68.

F.

Fan blowers. *See* Fuel, &c., 30.
Fans, rotary. *See* Ventilation, 52.
Fares, checking, &c. *See* Common road carriages, 98.
Farriery, &c., 53.
Fats. *See* Oils, &c., 27.
Feeding bottles. *See* Medicine, 25.
Feeding troughs. *See* Agriculture, 82.
Felting. *See* Dressing and finishing; &c., 91.
Fermented beverages, &c. *See* Brewing, &c., 99.
Field implements and processes for agriculture, 81.
Files, binders, clips, and holders for paper. *See* Writing, &c., 37.
Filters, sugar. *See* Sugar, 48.
Filters, water. *See* Purifying, &c. water, 79.
Finings for malt, &c. *See* Brewing, &c., 99.
Finishing fabrics. *See* Dressing, &c. 91.
Fins, steering. *See* Steering, &c., 75.
Fire-arms, 10.
Fire-arms, toy. *See* Toys, 51.
Fire bars. *See* Fuel, &c., 30.
Fire engines, 88.
Fire escapes, 88.
Fire extinguishers, 88.
Fire-grates. *See* Fuel, &c., 30.
Fire-proof depositories. *See* Safes, &c., 64.
Fire-proof dresses and fabrics. *See* Fire engines, &c., 88.
Fireworks. *See* Toys, 51.

Fish joints and plates. *See* Railways, 33.
Fittings for metallic pipes. *See* Pipes, 70.
Flageolets. *See* Music, &c., 26.
Flesh brushes. *See* Brushing, 57.
Floating docks. *See* Harbours, &c., 77.
Floorcloth, 80.
Flues. *See* Fuel, &c., 30.
Fluorine. *See* Acids, &c., 40.
Flutes. *See* Music, &c., 26.
Fog signals. *See* Railway signals, 38.
Folding fabrics. *See* Dressing, &c., 91.
Folding paper. *See* Cutting, &c., 12; Letterpress printing, &c., 13.
Food for cattle, preparing on the farm, not manufacturing for sale. *See* Agriculture, 82.
Food, preservation of, 4.
Footways. *See* Roads, &c., 35.
Fountains. *See* Hydraulics, 32.
Fraud, preventing. *See* Paper, 11 Ornamenting, 12; Printing, 13.
Freezing mixtures and processes. *See* Ice-making, &c., 85.
Frills and frillings. *See* Wearing apparel, 66.
Fringe. *See* Lace, 29; Weaving, 20.
Fruit-cleaning machines. *See* Brushing, 57.
Fruit, machinery for paring, slicing &c. *See* Cooking, &c., 61.
Fuel, 30.
Fulling. *See* Dressing and finishing, &c., 91.
Funeral carriages. *See* Common road carriages, 98.
Funnels. *See* Preparing and cutting cork, &c., 56.
Furnaces. *See* Iron and steel, 6; Metals and alloys, 18; Fuel, &e., 30; Steam-engine, 49.
Furniture, &c., 39.
Furze crushers. *See* Agriculture, 82.
Fusees and fusee cases. *See* Tobacco, 42.
Fuses for firing. *See* Fire-arms, 10; Mining, 71.

G.

Gaiters. *See* Wearing apparel, 66.
Galvanic action. *See* Electro-deposition, &c., 96.
Galvanic batteries. *See* Electricity, 15; 92.
Games. *See* Toys, 51.
Garters. *See* Wearing apparel, 66.
Gas, 17.
Gas engines. *See* Air, &c., engines, 33.
Gas lighting, automatic. *See* Electricity, 94; 95.
Gas meters. *See* Gas, 17.
Gasometers. *See* Gas, 17.
Gas stoves. *See* Gas, 17; Fuel, &c., 30.
Gas tubes. *See* Metallic pipes. 70.
Gates, dock. *See* Harbours, &c., 77.
Gates, lock. *See* Harbours, &c., 77.
Gauges, air. *See* Ventilation, 52.
Gauges, steam. *See* Steam engine, 49.
Gauges, water. *See* Hydraulics, 32; Steam engine, 49.
Gelatine. *See* Starch, &c., 100.

Gig mills. *See* Dressing, &c., 91.
Gilding, &c. paper. *See* Ornamenting, 12.
Girths. *See* Saddlery, 34.
Glass paper, &c., 12.
Globes. *See* Optical, &c., 76.
Globes for lamps. *See* Lamps, 44.
Glove fastenings. *See* Wearing apparel, 68.
Gloves. *See* Wearing apparel, 66.
Gloves of thread. *See* Lace-making, 29.
Glue. *See* Starch, 100.
Gold. *See* Metals,&c., 18; Acids, &c., 40.
Goloshes. *See* Wearing apparel, 67.
Gorse and grain crushers. *See* Agriculture, 82.
Grain, preparing for brewing, &c. *See* Brewing, &c., 99.
Grain, thrashing, cleansing, sorting, measuring, weighing, preserving, storing, &c. *See* Agriculture, 82.
Granaries. *See* Agriculture, 82.
Graphometers. *See* Optical, &c., 76.
Grates. *See* Fuel, &c., 30.
Graving docks. *See* Harbours, &c., 77.
Gridirons for repairing ships. *See* Harbours, &c., 77.
Gridirons. *See* Cooking, &c., 61.
Grinding grain, 78.
Grooming horses by machinery. *See* Brushing, 57.
Grubbers. *See* Agriculture, 81.
Guitars. *See* Music, &c., 26.
Gum. *See* Starch, 100.
Gunboats. *See* Ship-building, 21.
Gunpowder. *See* Fire-arms, 10.
Gutta-percha. *See* India-rubber, 16.
Gutters. *See* Drains, 1; Roads, 35.
Gymnastics. *See* Medicine, &c., 25; Toys, 51.

H.

Habits. *See* Wearing apparel, 66.
Hair-brushing machinery. *See* Brushing, 57.
Hair cloth. *See* Weaving, 20.
Hair pins. *See* Needles, &c., 45.
Hammers, steam. *See* Steam engine, 49.
Hammers, tilt. *See* Iron, &c., 6.
Hammocks. *See* Furniture, 39.
Hand barrows. *See* Common road carriages, 98.
Harbours, &c., 77.
Harmoniums. *See* Music, &c., 26.
Harness. *See* Saddlery, 34.
Harps and harpsichords. *See* Music, &c., 26.
Harrows. *See* Agriculture, 81.
Harvesters. *See* Agriculture, 81.
Hassocks. *See* Furniture, 39.
Hat boxes. *See* Trunks, &c., 84.
Hats, hat bands, and hat boxes. *See* Wearing apparel, 65.
Haymakers. *See* Agriculture, 81.
Hay rakes. *See* Agriculture, 81.
Hay, stacking, packing, and cutting. *See* Agriculture, 82.
Head coverings. *See* Wearing apparel, 65.

Hearses. *See* Common road carriages, 98.
Heating by electricity. *See* Electricity, 95.
Heckling machines. *See* Spinning, 28.
Heliography. *See* Photography, 19.
Helmets. *See* Wearing apparel, 65.
Hides. *See* Skins, 55.
Hinges and hinge joints, 59.
Hoes. *See* Agriculture, 81.
Hoists. *See* Raising, &c., 31.
Hoists, steam. *See* Raising, &c., 31; Steam-engine, 49.
Hooks and eyes. *See* Wearing apparel, 68.
Hop cultivation. *See* Agriculture, 81.
Hops, drying and pocketing. *See* Agriculture, 82; Brewing, &c., 99.
Horns. *See* Music, &c., 26.
Horse clippers. *See* Saddlery, 34; Farriery, 53.
Horse gear. *See* Agriculture, 82.
Horse medicines. *See* Farriery, 53.
Horse shoes and horse shoe nails. *See* Farriery, 53.
Hose pipes. *See* Fire engines, &c., 88.
Hosiery. *See* Wearing apparel, 66.
Hospitals. *See* Medicine, &c., 25.
Hot pressing. *See* Dressing, &c., 91.
House carts. *See* Common road carriages, 98.
Hulling, &c., grain. *See* Grinding grain, 78.
Hummellers. *See* Agriculture, 82.
Hydrants. *See* Hydraulics, 32.
Hydraulics, 32.
Hydrochloric acid. *See* Acids, 40.
Hydrocyanic acid. *See* Acids, 40.
Hydrogen. *See* Acids, &c., 40.
Hydrometers. *See* Brewing, &c., 99.
Hydro-propulsion. *See* Marine propulsion, 5.
Hygrometers. *See* Optical, &c., 76.

I.

Ice creams. *See* Ice-making, &c., 85.
Ice houses, 85.
Ice-making machines, 85.
Ice pails. *See* Ice-making, &c., 85.
Ice safes, 85.
Ice wells. *See* Ice-making, &c., 85.
Igniting by electricity. *See* Electricity, 95.
India-rubber, 16.
India-rubber horse-shoes. *See* Farriery, 53.
Indicators for common road carriages. *See* Common road carriages, 98.
Infusions, unconcentrated. *See* Unfermented beverages, &c., 86.
Ink, printers'. *See* Printing, &c., 13.
Ink (writing, copying, and marking) and inkstands. *See* Writing, &c., 37.
Insulation, electric. *See* Electricity, 15; 93.
Invalid bedsteads. *See* Medicine, &c., 25; Furniture, 39.
Invalid carriages. *See* Common road carriages, 98.

Iodine. *See* Acids, &c., 40.
Iron and steel, 6.
Iron oxides, &c. *See* Acids, &c., 40.
Ironing. *See* Dressing and finishing, &c., 91.
Irrigating and watering land. *See* Agriculture, 81.
Isinglass. *See* Starch, &c., 100.

J.

Jackets. *See* Wearing apparel, 66.
Jacks, hydraulic. *See* Hydraulics, 32.
Jacks, roasting. *See* Cooking, 61.
Jacks, screw. *See* Raising, &c., 31.
Jacquard machines. *See* Weaving, 20; Lace, 29.
Jewellery. *See* Wearing apparel, 68.
Joints and connections. *See* Pipes, 70.

K.

Kaleidoscopes. *See* Optical, &c., 76.
Kamptulicon. *See* Artificial leather, &c., 80.
Keels, sliding. *See* Steering, 75.
Kegs. *See* Casks, 74.
Kettles for the table. *See* Unfermented beverages, &c., 86.
Kilns for drying hops, grain, malt, &c. *See* Agriculture, 82; Brewing, &c., 99.
Kilns. *See* Bricks and tiles, 22; Pottery, 24; Fuel, &c., 30.
Kites. *See* Aeronautics, 41; Toys, 51.
Kneading machines. *See* Cooking, &c. 61.
Knife cleaners. *See* Brushing, 57.
Knitting machines. *See* Lace, 29.
Knobs. *See* Furniture, &c., 39; Locks, 60.

L.

Labels, separating, distributing, damping, and applying. *See* Writing, &c., 37.
Lace-making, knitting, netting, &c., 29.
Lampblack. *See* Paints, 50.
Lamps, &c., 44.
Lamps, cooking. *See* Lamps, 44; Cooking, 61.
Lasts for making boots and shoes. *See* Wearing apparel, 67.
Latches. *See* Locks, &c., 60.
Launching vessels. *See* Ship-building, 21.
Lead. *See* Metals, &c., 18.
Lead for paints. *See* Paints, 50.
Lead, oxides, &c. *See* Acids, &c., 40.
Leather. *See* Skins, &c., 55.
Leather cloth. *See* Artificial leather, 80.
Lee boards. *See* Steering, &c., 75.
Leggings. *See* Wearing apparel, 66.
Lemonade. *See* Unfermented beverages, &c., 86.
Lemon and other fruit squeezers. *See* Unfermented beverages, &c., 86.

Lenses. *See* Optical, &c., 76.
Letterpress printing, 13.
Levels. *See* Optical, &c., 76.
Lifts. *See* Raising, 31.
Lifts, steam. *See* Raising, 31; Steam engine, 49.
Light, electric, &c., 95.
Lighthouse lamps. *See* Lamps, 44.
Lighthouses. *See* Harbours, &c., 77.
Lighting mines. *See* Mining, 71.
Lightning conductors. *See* Electricity, 15; 93.
Limbs, artificial. *See* Medicine, &c., 25.
Lime. *See* Acids, &c. 40.
Lime light. *See* Lamps, &c., 44.
Links. *See* Chains, &c. 90.
Linoleum. *See* Artificial leather, &c., 80.
Liqueurs. *See* Unfermented beverages, &c., 86.
Lithography. *See* Printing, 13; Ornamenting paper, 12.
Loading hay, straw, &c. *See* Agriculture, 81.
Lockets. *See* Wearing apparel, 68.
Locks, &c., 60.
Locks, canal, &c. *See* Harbours, &c., 77.
Locks for guns. *See* Fire-arms, 10.
Locomotion, aids to, 7.
Locomotive steam carriages. *See* Steam engine, 49.
Logs. *See* Optical, &c., 76.
Looking-glasses. *See* Furniture, 39.
Looms. *See* Weaving, 20.
Looped fabrics. *See* Lace-making, &c., 29.
Lowering apparatus. *See* Raising, &c., 31.
Lozenges. *See* Medicine, 25; Cooking, 61.
Lubricants. *See* Oils, &c., 27.

M.

Machine needles. *See* Needles, 45.
Magic lanterns. *See* Toys, 51.
Magnesia. *See* Acids, &c., 40.
Magnesium. *See* Acids, &c., 40.
Magnetism. *See* Electricity, 15; 92; 93; 94; 95; 96; 97.
Malt, drying. *See* Brewing, &c., 99.
Malt, grinding. *See* Brewing, &c., 99.
Malt mills. *See* Grinding grain, 78; Brewing, &c., 99.
Manganese. *See* Acids, &c., 40.
Mangers. *See* Saddlery, &c., 34.
Mangling. *See* Dressing and finishing, &c., 91.
Manifold writers. *See* Writing, 37.
Manœuvring ships and vessels. *See* Steering, &c., 75; Marine propulsion (Part II.), 5.
Mantillas and mantles. *See* Wearing apparel, 66.
Manure, 3.
Manure distributors. *See* Agriculture, 81.

Marine engines. *See* Marine propulsion, 5; Steam engine, 49.
Marine propulsion, 5.
Mariners' compasses. *See* Optical, &c., 76.
Mashing apparatus. *See* Brewing, &c., 99.
Masts, &c., 73.
Mathematical instruments. *See* Artists' instruments, 54; Optical, &c., 76.
Mattresses. *See* Furniture, 39.
Measuring lace. *See* Lace-making, 29.
Measuring woven fabrics. *See* Dressing, &c., 91.
Meat screens. *See* Cooking, 61.
Medicine, &c., 25.
Medicine, and medicated food for animals. *See* Farriery, 53.
Memorandum books. *See* Books. 43.
Mercury. *See* Metals and alloys, 18.
Meridian instruments. *See* Optical, &c., 76.
Metallic pipes and tubes, 70.
Metallic surfaces, protecting. *See* Electro-deposition, &c., 96.
Metals. *See* Metals and alloys, 18; Iron and steel, 6.
Metals, plating. *See* Coating, &c., 23; Electro-deposition, &c., 96.
Metals, separating. *See* Metals, &c., 18.
Meteorological instruments. *See* Optical, &c., 76.
Meters, gas. *See* Gas, 17.
Meters, water. *See* Hydraulics, 32.
Micrometers. *See* Optical, &c., 76.
Microscopes. *See* Optical, &c., 76.
Milking, &c., 72.
Millboard. *See* Paper, 11.
Mills, barley. *See* Grinding grain, 78.
Mills, coffee. *See* Grinding grain, 78.
Mills, flour. *See* Grinding grain, 78.
Mills, malt. *See* Grinding grain, 78; Brewing, &c., 99.
Mills, paint. *See* Paints, 50.
Mills, sugar. *See* Sugar, 48.
Millstones. *See* Grinding grain, 78.
Millstones, balancing. *See* Grinding grain, 78.
Millstones, dressing, &c. *See* Grinding grain, 78.
Mills, water. *See* Hydraulics, 32; Grinding grain, 78.
Mincing machines. *See* Cooking. 61.
Mineral waters. *See* Unfermented beverages, &c., 86.
Miners' lamps. *See* Lamps. 44.
Mines, ventilating. *See* Ventilation 52.
Mining, &c., 71.
Mittens. *See* Wearing apparel, 66.
Mordants. *See* Bleaching, &c., 14.
Motive power. *See* Hydraulics, 32; Steam engine, 49; Air and gas engines, 62.
Moulds, sugar. *See* Sugar, 48.
Mowers. *See* Agriculture, 81.
Muffs. *See* Wearing apparel, 66.
Mules. *See* Spinning, 28.
Muriatic acid. *See* Acids, 40.
Music and musical instruments, 26.
Music stands and stools. *See* Music, &c., 26.

N.

Nails, &c., 58.
Nails, horse-shoe. *See* Farriery, 53. Nails, 58.
Nautical instruments. *See* Optical, &c., 76.
Necklaces and necklets. *See* Wearing apparel, 68.
Neckties. *See* Wearing apparel, 66.
Needle cases. *See* Sewing, 2.
Needles and pins, 45.
Needles for knitting. *See* Lace-making. &c., 29.
Net, bobbin. *See* Lace-making, &c., 29.
Nets, fishing. *See* Lace-making, &c., 29.
Nickel. *See* Metals, &c.; 18; Acids, &c., 40.
Nitre. *See* Acids, &c., 40.
Nitric acid. *See* Acids, 40.
Nitrogen. *See* Acids, &c., 40.
Nosebags. *See* Saddlery, 34.
Nuts. *See* Nails, &c., 58; Railways, 33.

O.

Oars. *See* Marine propulsion, 5.
Oat mills. *See* Agriculture, 82.
Oats, thrashing, cleaning, drying, storing, &c. *See* Agriculture, 82.
Octants. *See* Optical, &c., 76.
Oilcloth, 80.
Oils, &c., 27.
Oilskin, 80.
Optical, &c., instruments, 76.
Ordnance. *See* Fire-arms, 10.
Ores, dressing, disintegrating, reducing, &c. *See* Metals, &c., 18; Iron, &c., 6.
Ores, getting. *See* Mining, &c., 71.
Organs. *See* Music, &c., 26.
Ovens. *See* Fuel, &c., 30.
Ovens, bakers'. *See* Fuel, &c., 30; Cooking, 61.
Overalls. *See* Wearing apparel, 66.
Overcoats. *See* Wearing apparel, 66.
Overshoes. *See* Wearing apparel, 67.
Oxalic acid. *See* Acids, 40.
Oxides. *See* Acids, &c., 40.
Oxygen. *See* Acids, &c., 40.

P.

Packing cases. *See* Trunks, &c., 84.
Packing fabrics. *See* Dressing and finishing, 91.
Packing for pistons of steam engines. *See* Steam engine, 49.
Paddle-wheels. *See* Marine propulsion, 5.
Paints, &c., 50.
Paints for artists. *See* Artists' instruments, &c., 54.
Pantaloons. *See* Wearing apparel, 66.
Paper, cutting, folding, and ornamenting, 12.
Paper-fasteners, and apparatus for classifying and arranging papers. *See* Writing, 37.

Paperhangings. See Ornamenting; paper, 12.
Paper making, 11.
Papier maché. See Paper, 11.
Parachutes. See Aeronautics, 41.
Parasols. See Umbrellas, 47.
Parcels, mechanism for conveying. See Railways, 33.
Passenger register for vehicles. See Common road carriages, 98.
Paste. See Starch, &c., 109.
Pasteboard. See Paper making, 11; Cutting, &c., paper, 12.
Patterns. See Wearing apparel, 67.
Paving. See Roads, 35.
Peat. See Fuel, &c., 39.
Pedometers. See Optical, &c., 76.
Pencil cases and holders. See Writing, &c., 37; Artists' instruments, 54.
Pencil cases, boxes to hold leads for. See Writing, &c., 37.
Pens and penholders. See Writing, &c., 37; Artists' instruments, 54.
Pens, boxes for holding. See Writing, &c., 37.
Pepper, hulling. See Grinding grain, 73.
Perambulators. See Common road carriages, 98.
Percussion caps. See Fire arms, 16.
Perforating paper. See Cutting, &c. paper, 12.
Perpetual motion. See Hydraulics, 32; Air, &c., engines, 62.
Petticoats. See Wearing apparel, 66.
Phenakistoscopes. See Photography, 19; Optical, &c., 76.
Phenic acid. See Acids, 40.
Philosophical instruments. See Optical, &c., 76.
Phosphoric acid. See Acids, 40.
Phosphorus. See Acids, &c. 40.
Photography, 19.
Pianofortes. See Music, &c., 26.
Picture frames. See Furniture, 30.
Piers. See Harbours, &c., 77.
Pile drivers, steam. See Steam engine, 49; Harbours, &c., 77.
Pile fabrics. See Weaving, 20; Lacemaking, 29.
Pile or nap, raising and cutting. See Dressing, &c., 91.
Piles. See Harbours, &c., 77.
Pins. See Needles, &c., 25.
Pipes. See Tobacco, 42.
Pipes, drain. See Drains, &c., 1.
Pipes, metallic, 70.
Pistols. See Fire-arms, 16.
Pistons of steam engines. See Steam engine, 49.
Pit chains. See Mining, &c., 71.
Plaiting. See Lace, &c., 29.
Plating metals. See Electro-deposition, 96.
Playing cards. See Toys, 57.
Ploughs and ploughing machines. See Agriculture, 81.
Plumb levels. See Optical, &c., 76.
Pocket books. See Books, 43.
Porcelain. See Pottery, 34.
Portfolios. See Books, 43.

Portfolios for music. See Music, 26.
Portmanteaus. See Trunks &c., 84.
Potash. See Acids, &c. 40.
Potash water. See Unfermented beverages, &c., 86.
Potassium. See Acids, &c., 40.
Potato diggers. See Agriculture, 82.
Pottery, 34.
Pouches for tobacco. See Tobacco, 42.
Powder flasks. See Fire-arms, 16.
Power looms. See Weaving, 20.
Precious stones, cutting, &c. See Wearing apparel, 68.
Precious stones, setting. See Wearing apparel, 68.
Presses, copying. See Writing, &c.
Presses, hydraulic. See Hydraulics, 32.
Presses, printing, 13.
Pressing fabrics. See Dressing and finishing, 91.
Printing fabrics, yarns, &c. See Bleaching, &c., 14.
Printing, letterpress, &c., 13.
Projectiles. See Fire-arms, 16.
Propellers. See Marine propulsion, 5.
Propulsion, marine, 5.
Prussic acid. See Acids, 40.
Puddling furnaces. See Iron and steel, 6.
Pug mills. See Bricks and tiles, 22.
Pulleys. See Raising, &c., 31.
Pulverizers. See Agriculture, 82.
Pumps. See Hydraulics, 32.
Pumps, steam. See Hydraulics, 32; Steam engine, 49.
Punkas. See Ventilation, 52.
Purifying alcohol. See Brewing, &c., 86.
Purifying and filtering water, 79.
Pyrometers. See Optical, &c., 76.

Q.

Quadrants. See Optical, &c., 76.
Quarrying. See Mining, &c., 71.
Quays. See Harbours, &c., 77.
Quinine. See Acids, &c., 40.

R.

Rafts. See Ship-building, 21.
Rails. See Iron, &c., 6; Railways, 33.
Railway carriages. See Carriages &c. for railways, 46.
Railway signals, &c., 33.
Railways, 33.
Railways, portable endless. See Aids to locomotion, 7; Common road carriages, 98.
Raising, &c., 31.
Raising and lowering ships' boats. See Raising, &c., 32; Masts, &c., 72.
Raising ships for repairing. See Ship-building, &c., 21.
Raising water. See Hydraulics, 32.
Rakes. See Agriculture, 81.
Ranges, cooking. See Fuel, &c., 39; Cooking, 61.
Reaping and mowing machines. See Agriculture, 81.

Reflectors. See Lamps, 44.
Refractory materials. See Metals, &c., 19; Pottery, 24; Bricks, &c., 23.
Refrigerators. See Ice-making, &c., 36; Brewing, &c., 90.
Registering number of passengers in common road carriages. See Common road carriages, 94.
Reservoirs. See Harbours, &c., 77.
Respirators. See Medicine, &c., 36.
Reticules. See Trunks, &c., 34.
Retorts for burning animal charcoal. See Sugar, 89.
Retorts, gas. See Gas, 17.
Reverberatory furnaces. See Iron and steel, 6.
Rice, hulling, &c. See Grinding grain, 79.
Rice, milling, polishing, and otherwise preparing for the market. See Agriculture, 82.
Rick covers. See Artificial leather, &c., 80.
Ricks. See Agriculture, 82.
Riddles for grain, &c. See Agriculture, 82.
Rigging. See Masts, &c., 73.
Rings, finger. See Wearing apparel, 68.
Rinsing. See Washing, &c., 90.
Rivets. See Nails, &c., 56.
Road sweepers. See Brushing, 87.
Roads and ways, 36.
Roasting jacks. See Cooking, 61.
Rockets for pyrotechnic display. See Toys, &c., 51.
Rockets, war. See Fire-arms, 10.
Rocking chairs and horses. See Toys, 51.
Rollers for calico printing. See Bleaching, &c., 14.
Rollers for roads. See Roads, &c., 35.
Rollers, land. See Agriculture, 51.
Roots, cutting, slicing, pulping, washing, drying, and sorting. See Agriculture, 82.
Ropes and bands for mines. See Mining, 71.
Roughing horses. See Farriery, 53.
Rudders. See Steering, 75; Marine propulsion (Part II.), 5.
Ruffles and ruffs. See Wearing apparel, 68.
Rulers. See Writing, 37.
Ruling paper. See Cutting, folding, &c., 12; Artists' instruments, 54.

S.

Sacks. See Weaving, 20.
Saddlery &c., 34.
Safes, &c., 64.
Safety lamps. See Lamps, 44.
Safety pockets. See Wearing apparel, 68.
Safety valves of steam boilers. See Steam engine, 40.
Sails. See Masts, &c., 73.
Salt, common. See Acids, &c., 40.
Saltpetre. See Acids, &c., 40.
Salts. See Acids, &c., 40.

Salt water, obtaining fresh water from. See Purifying &c., water, 79.
Sausage making machines. See Cooking, 61.
Scales. See Raising, &c., 31.
Scarifiers. See Agriculture, 81.
Screening grain, &c. See Agriculture, 82.
Screens. See Furniture, 30.
Screw propellers for carriages and agricultural implements. See Aids to locomotion, 7.
Screw propellers for ships. See Marine propulsion, 5.
Screws. See Nails, &c., 56.
Scythes. See Agriculture, 81.
Sealing wax. See Writing, &c., 37.
Seams and joints. See Pipes, 76.
Sea walls. See Harbours, &c., 77.
Seed sowing. See Agriculture, 81.
Seltzer water. See Unfermented beverages, &c., 96.
Semaphore signals. See Railway signals, 38.
Sewage farming. See Agriculture, 81.
Sewers. See Drains, &c., 1.
Sewers, ventilating. See Ventilation, 82.
Sewing, &c., 2.
Sextants. See Optical, &c., 76.
Shackles. See Chains, &c., 96.
Shades. See Lamps, 44.
Shakos. See Wearing apparel, 66.
Shaving brushes. See Brushing, 87.
Shawl pins. See Wearing apparel, 68.
Shawls. See Wearing apparel, 66.
Shawls, weaving. See Weaving, 20.
Shear legs. See Raising, &c., 31.
Shearing fabrics. See Dressing, &c., 27.
Shearing and clipping animals. See Saddlery, 34; Farriery, &c., 58.
Sheathing metals. See Metals, &c., 18.
Sheep washes, dips, &c. See Farriery, &c., 53.
Ship-building, &c., 21.
Ship lamps and lanterns. See Lamps, 44.
Ships, steering and manoeuvring. See Steering, 75.
Ships, ventilating. See Ventilation, 82.
Shirts. See Wearing apparel, 68.
Shoes. See Wearing apparel, 67.
Sickles and reaping hooks. See Agriculture, 82.
Signal lamps. See Lamps, 44.
Signals. See Electricity, 15; 96; Railway signals, 38.
Silicic acid. See Acids, 40.
Silver. See Metals, &c., 18; Acids, &c., 40.
Singeing fabrics. See Dressing, &c.
Singeing horses. See Saddlery, &c., 34; Farriery, 53.
Siphons. See Hydraulics, 32; Preparing, &c., cork, 54.
Size. See Starch, 100.
Sizing machines. See Weaving, 20.
Skates. See Toys, 51.
Skidding wheels. See Common road carriages, 93.
Skins, &c., 56.
Skirts. See Wearing apparel, 66.

Sleeve links. *See* Wearing apparel, 68.
Slide rules. *See* Optical, &c., 76.
Slippers. *See* Wearing apparel, 67.
Slips. *See* Harbours, &c., 77.
Sluices. *See* Harbours &c. 77.
Smelting furnaces. *See* Iron and steel. 6; Metals. &c., 18.
Smutters. *See* Agriculture, 82.
Snuff and snuff boxes. *See* Tobacco 42.
Soap. *See* Oils, &c., 27.
Socks. *See* Wearing apparel, 66.
Soda. *See* Acids, &c., 40.
Soda water. *See* Unfermented beverages, &c., 86.
Sodium. *See* Acids, &c., 40.
Solitaires. *See* Wearing apparel, 68.
Sounding apparatus. *See* Optical, &c., 76.
Spectacles. *See* Optical, &c., 76.
Spectroscopes. *See* Optical, &c., 76.
Spinning, 28.
Spirit levels. *See* Optical, &c., 76.
Spittoons. *See* Tobacco, &c., 42.
Spontaneous combustion, preventing. *See* Fire engines, &c., 88.
Spring balances. *See* Raising, &c., 31.
Springs for common road carriages. *See* Common road carriages, 98.
Springs for railway carriages. *See* Carriages, &c. for railways, 46.
Spurs. *See* Saddlery, &c., 34.
Stable brushes. *See* Brushing, 57.
Stable fittings. *See* Saddlery, &c., 34.
Stacks and stackers. *See* Agriculture, 82.
Stamping. *See* Cutting, &c. paper, 12; Printing. 13.
Stamps, separating, distributing, damping, and applying. *See* Writing, 37.
Stands for casks. *See* Casks, 74.
Stands for music. *See* Music, &c., 26.
Stannates. *See* Acids, &c., 40.
Starch, 100.
Stationery cases and cabinets. *See* Writing. &c., 37.
Staves, cutting, shaping, &c. *See* Casks, 74.
Stay fastenings. *See* Wearing apparel, 68.
Stays. *See* Wearing apparel, 66.
Steam boilers. *See* Steam engine, 49.
Steam culture, 8.
Steam engine, 49.
Steam gauges. *See* Steam engine, 49.
Steam rams. *See* Ship-building, 21.
Steel. *See* Iron, &c., 6.
Steelyards. *See* Raising, &c., 31.
Steering ships and vessels, 75; (Part II.), 5.
Stencil plates. *See* Printing, 13.
Stereoscopes. *See* Optical, &c., 76.
Stereotype. *See* Letterpress printing, 13.
Stirrups. *See* Saddlery, &c., 34.
Stocking fabrics. *See* Lace-making, 29.
Stocking frames. *See* Lace-making, &c., 29.
Stockings. *See* Wearing apparel, 66.
Stockings, elastic. *See* Medicine, &c., 25.
Stone breakers. *See* Roads, 35.

Stoneware. *See* Pottery, 24.
Stools, music. *See* Music, 26.
Stoppers. *See* Preparing, &c. cork, 56.
Stored goods, ventilating to prevent spontaneous combustion. *See* Fire engines, &c., 88.
Storing grain, &c. *See* Agriculture, 82.
Stoves. *See* Fuel, &c., 30.
Straw elevators. *See* Agriculture, 82.
Straw plait. *See* Lace-making, &c., 29.
Strong rooms. *See* Safes, &c., 64.
Strontia. *See* Acids, &c., 40.
Strontium. *See* Acids, &c., 40.
Studs. *See* Wearing apparel, 68.
Submarine cables. *See* Electricity, &c., 15; 93.
Subsoil ploughs. *See* Agriculture, 81.
Sugar, 48.
Sulphur and sulphuric acid. *See* Acids &c., 40.
Sun dials. *See* Optical, &c., 76; Watches, &c., 9.
Sunshades. *See* Umbrellas, &c., 47.
Surgery for animals. *See* Farriery, &c., 53.
Surgery. *See* Medicine, &c., 25.
Surgical instruments. *See* Medicine, &c., 25.
Surveying instruments. *See* Optical, &c., 76.
Suspension bridges. *See* Bridges, 36.
Sweeping. *See* Brushing, &c., 57.
Sweeping chimneys. *See* Fuel, &c., 30.
Sweeping roads. *See* Roads, &c., 35.
Sweetmeats. *See* Cooking, 61.
Swings. *See* Toys, 51.
Swivel links and swivel hooks. *See* Chains, &c., 90.
Swivels and swivel rings. *See* Wearing apparel, 68.
Syringes. *See* Hydraulics. 32.
Syringes, surgical. *See* Medicine, &c., 25.

T.

Tables. *See* Furniture, 39.
Tags for laces. *See* Wearing apparel, 68.
Tailors' irons. *See* Wearing apparel, 66.
Tannic acid. *See* Acids, 40.
Tanning leather. *See* Skins, 55.
Targets. *See* Fire-arms, 10.
Tarpaulin. *See* Artificial leather, &c., 80.
Tartaric acid. *See* Acids, 40.
Tea, concentrated extracts of. *See* Tea, &c., 87.
Tea, manufacturing and preparing for sale. *See* Tea, &c., 87.
Tea, preparing as a drink. *See* Unfermented beverages, &c., 86.
Teasles. *See* Dressing, &c., 91.
Teeth, artificial. *See* Medicine. &c., 25.
Telegraph poles or posts. *See* Electricity, 15; 93.
Telegraphs, electric. *See* Electricity, 15; 93; 94.
Telescopes. *See* Optical, &c., 76.

Tent covers. *See* Artificial leather, &c., 80.
Tentering. *See* Dressing, &c., 91.
Testing chains. *See* Chains, &c., 90.
Theodolites. *See* Optical, &c., 76.
Thermometers. *See* Optical, &c., 76.
Thimble. *See* Sewing, 2.
Thrashing machines. *See* Agriculture, 82.
Throstles. *See* Spinning, 28.
Tickets. *See* Cutting, &c., paper, 12; Letterpress printing, 13.
Tiles. *See* Drains, &c., 1; Bricks, &c., 22.
Tilling land. *See* Agriculture, 81.
Tills. *See* Safes, &c., 64.
Tin. *See* Metals, &c., 18; Acids, &c., 40.
Tinning. *See* Plating or coating Metals, 23.
Tips, boot and shoe. *See* Wearing apparel, 67.
Tobacco, 42.
Toilet boxes. *See* Trunks, &c., 84.
Tooth brushes. *See* Brushing, 57.
Tops. *See* Toys, 51.
Torpedo boats. *See* Ship-building, 21.
Towing ships and canal boats. *See* Marine propulsion, 5.
Toys, &c., 51.
Tracing cloth and paper. *See* Artists' instruments, &c., 54.
Traction engines. *See* Steam engine, 49; Agriculture, 83.
Traction ropes. *See* Agriculture, 81.
Tramcars. *See* Common road carriages, 98.
Tramways. *See* Railways, 33.
Travelling bags. *See* Trunks, &c., 84.
Trees, boot and shoe. *See* Wearing apparel, 67.
Tricycles. *See* Common road carriages, 98.
Troughs for washing. *See* Washing, &c., 89.
Trouser strap fastenings. *See* Wearing apparel, 68.
Trousers. *See* Wearing apparel, 66.
Trucks. *See* Common road carriages, 98.
Trunks, &c., 84.
Tube brushes. *See* Brushing, 57.
Tubes, metallic. *See* Metallic pipes, 70.
Tubs, washing. *See* Washing machines, &c., 89.
Tungstic acid. *See* Acids, 40.
Tunnelling. *See* Mining, &c., 71.
Turbines. *See* Hydraulics, 32.
Turf cutters. *See* Agriculture, 81.
Turnip cutters. *See* Agriculture, 82.
Turntables. *See* Railways, 33.
Tuyeres. *See* Iron, &c., 6.
Type. *See* Letterpress printing, 13.

U.

Umbrellas, &c., 47.
Unfermented beverages, 86.
Unions for tubes. *See* Metallic pipes, 70.
Upholstery. *See* Furniture, 39.

Urinals. *See* Waterclosets, &c., 63.
Urns for tea, &c. *See* Unfermented beverages, &c., 86.

V.

Vacuum pans for sugar. *See* Sugar, 48.
Valises. *See* Trunks, &c., 84.
Valves, air. *See* Ventilation, 52.
Valves, engine. *See* Steam engine, 49; Air, gas, &c. engines, 62.
Valves, gas. *See* Gas, 17.
Valves, water. *See* Hydraulics, 32.
Valves, watercloset. *See* Waterclosets, 63.
Varnish, boot and shoe. *See* Wearing apparel, 67.
Varnishes. *See* Paints, &c., 50.
Vehicles for common roads. *See* Common road carriages, 98.
Vehicles, ventilating. *See* Ventilation, 52.
Velocipedes, &c. *See* Common road carriages, 98.
Vent pegs and spiles. *See* Preparing and cutting cork, &c., 56.
Ventilating mines. *See* Ventilation, 52; Mining, 71.
Ventilating railway carriages. *See* Carriages, &c. for railways, 46; Ventilation, 52.
Ventilation, 52.
Vermin on animals, destroying. *See* Farriery, 53.
Veterinary art. *See* Farriery, 53.
Viaducts. *See* Bridges, &c., 36.
Vinegar. *See* Acids, &c., 40.
Violins. *See* Music, &c., 26.
Vitriol. *See* Acids, &c., 40.

W.

Wadding. *See* Dressing and finishing, &c., 91.
Wafers. *See* Writing, &c., 37.
Waggon covers. *See* Artificial leather, &c., 80.
Waggons. *See* Common road carriages, 98.
Waggons, railway. *See* Carriages, &c., for railways, 46.
Waistcoats. *See* Wearing apparel, 66.
Walking-sticks. *See* Umbrellas, &c., 47.
Wallets. *See* Trunks, &c., 84.
Wardrobes. *See* Furniture, 39.
Warping land. *See* Agriculture, 81.
Warping machines. *See* Weaving, 20.
Warp machines or frames. *See* Lacemaking, &c., 29.
Washing and sifting ores. *See* Metals, &c., 18.
Washing clothes, &c. *See* Washing machines, &c., 89.
Watches, &c., 9.
Watch protectors. *See* Wearing apparel, 68.
Water aerating. *See* Purifying, &c., water, 79.

Water, chemical treatment of. *See* Purifying, &c., water, 79.
Waterclosets, &c., 63.
Watercourses. *See* Harbours, &c., 77.
Watering land. *See* Agriculture, 81.
Watering roads. *See* Roads, 35.
Water meters. *See* Hydraulics, 32.
Water mills. *See* Hydraulics, 32.
Waterproof fabrics, 80.
Waterproofing leather. *See* Skins, &c., 55.
Waterproofing paper. *See* Cutting, &c., paper, 12.
Water, purifying and filtering, 79.
Water-wheels. *See* Hydraulics, 32.
Wearing apparel,—body coverings, 66.
Wearing apparel,—dress fastenings and jewellery, 68.
Wearing apparel,—foot coverings, 67.
Wearing apparel,—head coverings, 65.
Weaving, 20.
Weighing. *See* Raising, &c., 31.
Well-sinking. *See* Mining, &c., 71.
Wet docks. *See* Harbours, &c., 77.
Wharves. *See* Harbours, &c., 77.
Wheat, thrashing, cleaning, drying, storing, &c. *See* Agriculture, 82.
Wheelbarrows. *See* Common road carriages, 98.
Wheels, railway. *See* Carriages, &c. for railways, 46.
Whips and whip sockets. *See* Saddlery, &c., 34.
Whistles. *See* Railway signals, 38.
Wicks. *See* Lamps, &c., 44.
Winding drums. *See* Raising, &c., 31; Mining, 71; Agriculture, 81.
Winding fabrics. *See* Dressing, &c., 91.

Windlasses. *See* Raising, &c., 31.
Windlasses, steam. *See* Raising, &c., 31; Steam engine, 49.
Windmills. *See* Air. &c., engines, 62.
Windmills used to propel ships. *See* Marine Propulsion 5; Masts, &c., 73.
Window fastenings. *See* Locks, &c., 60.
Wine coolers. *See* Ice-making, &c., 85.
Wine-making. *See* Brewing, &c., 99.
Winnowing machines for grain, &c. *See* Agriculture, 82.
Wire brushes. *See* Brushing, 57.
Wire, telegraphic. *See* Electricity, 15; 93.
Wood paving. *See* Roads, 35.
Work bags and work boxes. *See* Trunks, &c., 84.
Worts, cooling. *See* Brewing, &c., 99.
Wringing. *See* Washing, &c., 89.
Wristbands. *See* Wearing apparel, 66.
Writing instruments, &c., 37.

Y.

Yeast, preparing. *See* Brewing, &c. 99.
Yeast, substitutes for. *See* Cooking, 61.

Z.

Zinc. *See* Metals, &c., 18.
Zinc for paint *See* Paints, 50.
Zinc oxides, &c. *See* Acids, &c., 40.

LONDON: Printed by EYRE AND SPOTTISWOODE,
Printers to the Queen's most Excellent Majesty.
For Her Majesty's Stationery Office.
[4783.—1000.—11/84.]

October, 1884.

www.ingramcontent.com/pod-product-compliance
Lightning Source LLC
Chambersburg PA
CBHW051849300426
44117CB00006B/330